TRANSLATOR AND EDITOR:
Rabbi David Strauss

MANAGING EDITOR:
Baruch Goldberg

EDITOR:
Rabbi Yehezkel Anis

ASSOCIATE EDITOR:
Dr. Jeffrey M. Green

COPY EDITOR:
Alec Israel

BOOK DESIGNER:
Ben Gasner

GRAPHIC ARTIST:
Michael Etkin

TECHNICAL STAFF:
Muriel Stein

Random House Staff

PRODUCTION MANAGER:
Richard Elman

DESIGN DIRECTOR:
Bernard Klein

MANAGING EDITOR:
Amy Edelman

THE TALMUD

THE STEINSALTZ EDITION

VOLUME XV

TRACTATE SANHEDRIN

PART I

Volume XV
Tractate Sanhedrin
Part I

Random House
New York

THE TALMUD

תלמוד בבלי

THE STEINSALTZ EDITION

Commentary by Rabbi Adin Steinsaltz (Even Yisrael)

 Published in the United States by Random House, Inc., New York, and simultaneously in Canada by Random House of Canada Limited, Toronto.

This is an English translation of a work originally published in Hebrew by The Israel Institute for Talmudic Publications, Jerusalem, Israel.

Library of Congress Cataloging-in-Publication Data
(Revised for volume XV)
The Talmud.
English, Hebrew, Aramaic.
Includes bibliographical references.
Contents: v. 1–Tratate Bava metzia–
v. 15 Tratate Sanhedren, pt. 1
Accompanied by a reference guide.
I. Title.
BM499.5.E4 1989 89-842911
ISBN 0-394-57665-9 (guide)
ISBN 0-394-57665-7 (v. 1)
ISBN 0-679-45222-2 (v. 15)

Random House website address: http://www.randomhouse.com/
Printed in the United States of America on acid-free paper

2 4 6 8 9 7 5 3

First Edition

This volume is dedicated to

Ludwig Bravmann and Jack Nash

my seniors and teachers
in charity and doing good in many fields

They personify the principle from Pirkei Avot:
"אמור מעט ועשה הרבה"
"Say little and do much"

Meyer and Pat Berman
Kings Point, New York

The Steinsaltz Talmud in English

The English edition of the Steinsaltz Talmud is a translation and adaptation of the Hebrew edition. It includes most of the additions and improvements that characterize the Hebrew version, but it has been adapted and expanded especially for the English reader. This edition has been designed to meet the needs of advanced students capable of studying from standard Talmud editions, as well as of beginners, who know little or no Hebrew and have had no prior training in studying the Talmud.

The overall structure of the page is similar to that of the traditional pages in the standard printed editions. The text is placed in the center of the page, and alongside it are the main auxiliary commentaries. At the bottom of the page and in the margins are additions and supplements.

The original Hebrew-Aramaic text, which is framed in the center of each page, is exactly the same as that in the traditional Talmud (although material that was removed by non-Jewish censors has been restored on the basis of manuscripts and old printed editions). The main innovation is that this Hebrew-Aramaic text has been completely vocalized and punctuated, and all the terms usually abbreviated have been fully spelled out. In order to retain the connection with the page numbers of the standard editions, these are indicated at the head of every page.

We have placed a *Literal Translation* on the right-hand side of the page, and its punctuation has been introduced into the Talmud text, further helping the student to orientate himself. The *Literal Translation* is intended to help the student to learn the meaning of specific Hebrew and Aramaic words. By comparing the original text with this translation, the reader develops an understanding of the Talmudic text and can follow the words and sentences in the original. Occasionally, however, it has not been possible to present an exact literal translation of the original text, because it is so different in structure from English. Therefore we have added certain auxiliary words, which are indicated in square brackets. In other cases it would make no sense to offer a literal translation of a Talmudic idiom, so we have provided a close English equivalent of the original meaning, while a note, marked "lit.," explaining the literal meaning of the words, appears in parentheses. Our purpose in presenting this literal translation was to give the student an appreciation of the terse and enigmatic nature of the Talmud itself, before the arguments are opened up by interpretation.

Nevertheless, no one can study the Talmud without the assistance of commentaries. The main aid to understanding the Talmud provided by this edition is the *Translation and Commentary,* appearing on the left side of the page. This is Rabbi Adin Steinsaltz's highly regarded Hebrew interpretation of the Talmud, translated into English, adapted and expanded.

This commentary is not merely an explanation of difficult passages. It is an integrated exposition of the entire text. It includes a full translation of the Talmud text, combined with explanatory remarks. Where the translation in the commentary reflects the literal translation, it has been set off in bold type. It has also been given the same reference numbers that are found both in the original text and in the literal translation. Moreover, each section of the commentary begins with a few words of the Hebrew-Aramaic text. These reference numbers and paragraph headings allow the reader to move from one part of the page to another with ease.

There are some slight variations between the literal translation and the words in bold face appearing in the *Translation and Commentary.* These variations are meant to enhance understanding, for a juxtaposition of the literal translation and the sometimes freer translation in the commentary will give the reader a firmer grasp of the meaning.

The expanded *Translation and Commentary* in the left-hand column is intended to provide a conceptual understanding of the arguments of the Talmud, their form, content, context, and significance. The commentary also brings out the logic of the questions asked by the Sages and the assumptions they made.

Rashi's traditional commentary has been included in the right-hand column, under the *Literal Translation.* We have left this commentary in the traditional "Rashi script," but all quotations of the Talmud text appear in standard square type, the abbreviated expressions have all been printed in full, and Rashi's commentary is fully punctuated.

Since the *Translation and Commentary* cannot remain cogent and still encompass all the complex issues that arise in the Talmudic discussion, we have included a number of other features, which are also found in Rabbi Steinsaltz's Hebrew edition.

At the bottom of the page, under the *Translation and Commentary,* is the *Notes* section, containing additional material on issues raised in the text. These notes deepen understanding of the Talmud in various ways. Some provide a deeper and more profound analysis of the issues discussed in the text, with regard to individual points and to the development of the entire discussion. Others explain Halakhic concepts and the terms of Talmudic discourse.

The *Notes* contain brief summaries of the opinions of many of the major commentators on the Talmud, from the period after the completion of the Talmud to the present. Frequently the *Notes* offer interpretations different from that presented in the commentary, illustrating the richness and depth of Rabbinic thought.

The *Halakhah* section appears below the *Notes.* This provides references to the authoritative legal decisions reached over the centuries by the Rabbis in their discussions of the matters dealt with in the Talmud. It explains what reasons led to these Halakhic decisions and the close connection between the Halakhah today and the Talmud and its various interpreters. It should be noted that the summary of the Halakhah presented here is not meant to serve as a reference source for actual religious practice but to introduce the reader to Halakhic conclusions drawn from the Talmudic text.

English commentary and expanded translation of the text, making it readable and comprehensible

Hebrew/Aramaic text of the Talmud, fully vocalized, and punctuated

Literal translation of the Talmud text into English

Marginal notes provide essential background information

Hebrew commentary of Rashi, the classic explanation that accompanies all editions of the Talmud

Numbers link the three main sections of the page and allow readers to refer rapidly from one to the other

Notes highlight points of interest in the text and expand the discussion by quoting other classical commentaries

REALIA

קַלְתָּהּ **Her basket.** The source of this word is the Greek κάλαθος, kalathos, and it means a basket with a narrow base.

Illustration from a Greek drawing depicting such a basket of fruit.

CONCEPTS

פֵּאָה ***Pe'ah*. One of the presents left for the poor** (מַתְּנוֹת עֲנִיִּים). The Torah forbids harvesting "the corners of your field," so that the produce left standing may be harvested and kept by the poor (Leviticus 19:9).

The Torah did not specify a minimum amount of produce to be left as *pe'ah*. But the Sages stipulated that it must be at least one-sixtieth of the crop.

Pe'ah is set aside only from crops that ripen at one time and are harvested at one time. The poor are allowed to use their own initiative to reap the *pe'ah* left in the fields. But the owner of an orchard must see to it that each of the poor gets a fixed share of the *pe'ah* from places that are difficult to reach. The poor come to collect *pe'ah* three times a day. The laws of *pe'ah* are discussed in detail in tractate *Pe'ah*.

TRANSLATION AND COMMENTARY

[1]**and her husband threw her a bill of divorce into her lap or into her basket**, which she was carrying on her head, [2]would you say **here, too,** that **she would not be divorced**? Surely we know that the law is that she *is* divorced in such a case, as the Mishnah (*Gittin* 77a) states explicitly!

אָמַר לֵיהּ [3]Rav Ashi **said** in reply **to** Ravina: The woman's **basket is** considered to be **at rest, and it is she who walks beneath it.** Thus the basket is considered to be a "stationary courtyard," and the woman acquires whatever is thrown into it.

MISHNAH הָיָה רוֹכֵב [4]**If a person was riding on an animal and he saw an ownerless object** lying on the ground, **and he said to another person** standing nearby, **"Give that object to me,"** [5]if **the other person took** the ownerless object **and said, "I have acquired it for myself,"** [6]he has **acquired it** by lifting it up, even though he was not the first to see it, and the rider has no claim to it. [7]But **if, after he gave** the object **to** the rider, the person who picked it up **said, "I acquired** the object **first,"** [8]**he** in fact **said nothing**. His words are of no effect, and the rider may keep it. Since the person walking showed no intention of acquiring the object when he originally picked it up, he is not now believed when he claims that he acquired it first. Indeed, even if we maintain that when a person picks up an ownerless object on behalf of someone else, the latter does *not* acquire it automatically, here, by *giving* the object to the rider, he makes a gift of it to the rider.

GEMARA תְּנַן הָתָם [9]**We have learned elsewhere** in a Mishnah in tractate *Pe'ah* (4:9): **"Someone who gathered *pe'ah*** — produce which by Torah law [Leviticus 23:22] is left unharvested in the corner of a field by the owner of the field, to be gleaned by the poor — **and said, 'Behold, this *pe'ah*** which I have gleaned **is** intended **for so-and-so the poor man,'** [10]**Rabbi Eliezer says:** The person who gathered the *pe'ah* **has acquired it**

בִּרְשׁוּת הָרַבִּים [1]וְזָרַק לָהּ גֵּט לְתוֹךְ חֵיקָהּ אוֹ לְתוֹךְ קַלְתָּהּ — [2]הָכָא נַמִי דְּלָא מְגָרְשָׁה? [3]אֲמַר לֵיהּ: קַלְתָּהּ מֵינָח נַיְיחָא, וְאִיהִי דְּקָא מְסַגְּיָא מִתּוּתָהּ.

משנה [4]הָיָה רוֹכֵב עַל גַּבֵּי בְהֵמָה וְרָאָה אֶת הַמְּצִיאָה, וְאָמַר לַחֲבֵירוֹ "תְּנָה לִי", [5]נְטָלָהּ וְאָמַר, "אֲנִי זָכִיתִי בָּהּ", [6]זָכָה בָּהּ. [7]אִם, מִשֶּׁנְּתָנָהּ לוֹ, אָמַר, "אֲנִי זָכִיתִי בָּהּ תְּחִלָּה", [8]לֹא אָמַר כְּלוּם.

גמרא [9]תְּנַן הָתָם: "מִי שֶׁלִּיקֵּט אֶת הַפֵּאָה וְאָמַר, 'הֲרֵי זוֹ לִפְלוֹנִי עָנִי', [10]רַבִּי אֱלִיעֶזֶר

LITERAL TRANSLATION

in a public thoroughfare [1]and [her husband] threw her a bill of divorce into her lap or into her basket, [2]here, too, would she not be divorced?

[3]He said to him: Her basket is at rest, and it is she who walks beneath it.

MISHNAH [4][If a person] was riding on an animal and he saw a found object, and he said to another person, "Give it to me," [5][and the other person] took it and said, "I have acquired it," [6]he has acquired it. [7]If, after he gave it to him, he said, "I acquired it first," [8]he said nothing.

GEMARA [9]We have learned there: "Someone who gathered *pe'ah* and said, 'Behold this is for so-and-so the poor man,' [10]Rabbi Eliezer says:

RASHI

קלתה — סל שעל ראשה, שנותנת בה כלי מלאכתה וטווי שלה. הכי נמי דלא הוי גיטא — והאנן תנן במסכת גיטין (עז,א): זרק לה גיטה לתוך חיקה או לתוך קלתה — הרי זו מגורשת!

משנה לא אמר כלום — דאפילו אמרינן המגביה מציאה לחבירו לא קנה חבירו, כיון דיהבה ליה — קנייה ממה נפשך. אי קנייה קמא דלא מתכוין להקנות לחבירו — הא יהבה ניהליה במתנה. ואי לא קנייה קמא משום דלא היה מתכוין לקנות — הויא ליה הפקר עד דמטא לידיה דהאי, וקנייה האי כמאי דעקרה מידיה דקמא לשם קנייה.

גמרא מי שליקט את הפאה — אדם בעלמא שאינו בעל שדה. דאי בבעל שדה — לא אמר רבי אליעזר זכה. דליכא למימר "מגו דזכי לנפשיה", דאפילו הוא עני מוזהר הוא שלא ללקט פאה משדה שלו, כדאמר בשחיטת חולין (קלא,ב): "לא תלקט לעני" — להזהיר עני על שלו.

NOTES

מִי שֶׁלִּיקֵּט אֶת הַפֵּאָה **If a person gathered *pe'ah*.** According to *Rashi*, the Mishnah must be referring to someone other than the owner of the field. By Torah law the owner of a field is required to separate part of his field as *pe'ah*, even if he himself is poor, and he may not take the *pe'ah* for himself. Therefore the "since" (מגו) argument

HALAKHAH

קַלְתָּהּ **A woman's basket.** "If a man throws a bill of divorce into a container that his wife is holding, she thereby acquires the bill of divorce and the divorce takes effect." (*Shulḥan Arukh, Even HaEzer* 139:10.)

הַמְלַקֵּט פֵּאָה עֲבוּר אַחֵר **A person who gathered *pe'ah* for someone else.** "If a poor person, who is himself entitled to collect *pe'ah*, gathered *pe'ah* for another poor person, and said, 'This *pe'ah* is for X, the poor person,' he acquires the *pe'ah* on behalf of that other poor person. But if the person who collected the *peah* was wealthy, he does not acquire the *pe'ah* on behalf of the poor person. He must give it instead to the first poor person who appears in the field," following the opinion of the Sages, as explained by Rabbi Yehoshua ben Levi. (*Rambam, Sefer Zeraim, Hilkhot Mattenot Aniyyim* 2:19.)

On the outer margin of the page, factual information clarifying the meaning of the Talmudic discussion is presented. Entries under the heading *Language* explain unusual terms, often borrowed from Greek, Latin, or Persian. *Sages* gives brief biographies of the major figures whose opinions are presented in the Talmud. *Terminology* explains the terms used in the Talmudic discussion. *Concepts* gives information about fundamental Halakhic principles. *Background* provides historical, geographical, and other information needed to understand the text. *Realia* explains the artifacts mentioned in the text. These notes are sometimes accompanied by illustrations.

The best way of studying the Talmud is the way in which the Talmud itself evolved – a combination of frontal teaching and continuous interaction between teacher and pupil, and between pupils themselves.

This edition is meant for a broad spectrum of users, from those who have considerable prior background and who know how to study the Talmud from any standard edition to those who have never studied the Talmud and do not even know Hebrew.

The division of the page into various sections is designed to enable students of every kind to derive the greatest possible benefit from it.

For those who know how to study the Talmud, the book is intended to be a written Gemara lesson, so that, either alone, with partners, or in groups, they can have the sense of studying with a teacher who explains the difficult passages and deepens their understanding both of the development of the dialectic and also of the various approaches that have been taken by the Rabbis over the centuries in interpreting the material. A student of this kind can start with the Hebrew-Aramaic text, examine Rashi's commentary, and pass on from there to the expanded commentary. Afterwards the student can turn to the Notes section. Study of the *Halakhah* section will clarify the conclusions reached in the course of establishing the Halakhah, and the other items in the margins will be helpful whenever the need arises to clarify a concept or a word or to understand the background of the discussion.

For those who do not possess sufficient knowledge to be able to use a standard edition of the Talmud, but who know how to read Hebrew, a different method is proposed. Such students can begin by reading the Hebrew-Aramaic text and comparing it immediately to the *Literal Translation*. They can then move over to the *Translation and Commentary*, which refers both to the original text and to the *Literal Translation*. Such students would also do well to read through the *Notes* and choose those that explain matters at greater length. They will benefit, too, from the terms explained in the side margins.

The beginner who does not know Hebrew well enough to grapple with the original can start with the *Translation and Commentary*. The inclusion of a translation within the commentary permits the student to ignore the *Literal Translation*, since the commentary includes both the Talmudic text and an interpretation of it. The beginner can also benefit from the *Notes*, and it is important for him to go over the marginal notes on the concepts to improve his awareness of the juridical background and the methods of study characteristic of this text.

Apart from its use as study material, this book can also be useful to those well versed in the Talmud, as a source of additional knowledge in various areas, both for understanding the historical and archeological background and also for an explanation of words and concepts. The general reader, too, who might not plan to study the book from beginning to end, can find a great deal of interesting material in it regarding both the spiritual world of Judaism, practical Jewish law, and the life and customs of the Jewish people during the thousand years (500 B.C.E.–500 C.E.) of the Talmudic period.

THE TALMUD
THE STEINSALTZ EDITION

VOLUME XV
TRACTATE SANHEDRIN
PART I

Introduction to Sanhedrin

Introduction to Sanhedrin

Tractate *Sanhedrin* is essentially the "tractate of the Jewish state," not only a tractate concerning judges, as its name would indicate. For tractate *Sanhedrin* contains the model for a Jewish state, and it deals, in its breadth, with all the problems created by a Jewish state. This tractate describes the basic institutions within a state according to Torah law and their reciprocal relations. Moreover, the existence of this tractate cannot be imagined separately from the context of a sovereign Jewish state governed according to the laws of the Torah.

The particular character of the Jewish state is based on independent axioms from which the Halakhot of the state derive in their detail.

The basic idea of Judaism as revealed in its laws, its thought, and its way of life is the overall rule of God, the Creator and Sustainer of the world. Just as He creates and sustains the laws of nature, He also creates human law. The primary source of this entire tractate and of rule of any kind is the will of God. Only by His power do human beings govern, and the various agencies of government receive their authority from Him. A powerful expression of this idea is found in the words of the Prophet Isaiah, "For the Lord is our judge, the Lord is our legislator, the Lord is our king" (Isaiah 33:22). All three of the commonly accepted branches of government are mentioned in this verse, and all of them are linked to God.

At the origin and basis of everything, God is the ultimate legislator, judge, and king. However, divine power and authority have been delegated to human beings to some extent over time, just as they have been given rule over the world and nature to continue the supreme creation.

Strictly speaking, the Jewish state does not have a legislative branch. None of the laws and regulations accepted by the Jewish people beyond the laws of the Torah have the true power of law. They are merely ordinances to regulate matters where Torah law expresses no specific opinion or where it is insufficiently detailed. Or else they are meant to add restrictions, limitations, and amendments to it. The single legislative power is God Himself, or the law of Torah as the revelation of His will. The Torah is the source of the laws of the Jewish state, and all the laws found in it were derived from it and exist according to it. This primary authority therefore persists in its source: the Lord remains the legislator forever.

The judicial branch, by contrast, was entirely given over to the Sages of Israel over the generations — the Sanhedrin. Because of the stability and permanence of Torah law, the judicial branch has great importance; it interprets the laws and relates them to changing conditions of time and place. This authority is given to a complex system of courts, at the head of which stands the Great Sanhedrin, a tribunal consisting of seventy-one members, which takes the place of Moses and the Seventy Elders who were with him. (Numbers 11:16-17. See *Sanhedrin* 17a and elsewhere.)

The executive branch of the Jewish state was in the hands of the king (sometimes known as the Nasi; see Leviticus 4:22; Ezekiel 19:1 and 37:25) and the ministers and officials appointed by him. The king was the head of state, and the commander in chief of the army, and as such responsible for foreign and domestic policy. His position, which was ordinarily though not necessarily inherited, could be compared to that of a president in a modern state. However, when it came to a political decision that affected the entire nation, such as a declaration of war, the king had to receive permission from the Great Sanhedrin, though in most areas the executive branch was entirely independent and not involved with any other branch.

The political structure described in tractate *Sanhedrin* is not a utopian vision unconnected with reality. The tractate does not deal with the "messianic age" or with "the days of David and Solomon." Rather it concerns a period historically close to it. This is particularly evident with regard to the laws governing the king and the High Priest. The king referred to in tractate *Sanhedrin* is not a messianic king or an ideal ruler. He is not from the Davidic line, and in many important matters he does not obey the laws of the Torah as he should (see *Sanhedrin* 19a-b). Clearly the underlying model of the state discussed in the tractate is basically that of the Hasmonean kings or even later monarchs. (For example, the division of function between the king and the High Priest alludes to the time of the Herodian kings.) Indeed, the tractate does not paint an exact picture of the Hasmonean monarchy, since it contains many suggestions for reforms and improvements in the existing situation. However, these changes are realistic, and some of them were actually implemented in the time of the Hasmonean leaders.

When Jewish independence was lost, this tractate gradually lost its practical import as well. Even in Second Temple times the Sanhedrin officially decided to forfeit some of its authority so as not to become an empty symbol of theoretical authority, without executive power. (See the end of tractate *Sotah* and *Sanhedrin* 21a.) The system of laws in *Sanhedrin* became the model for the laws of a state that no longer existed, including laws that were almost impossible to implement under foreign rule or outside the Land of Israel. Nevertheless, many of the laws in this tractate were adapted to the conditions of various periods, and the existing and stable foundation within it has proven useful in every generation. But in principle this tractate applies only to a sovereign Jewish state ruled by Torah law.

The Jewish polity was never limited to the borders of a state as this concept is understood today. The area of authority for the Sanhedrin and Jewish law was not restricted to the political boundaries of the Jewish state but applied wherever Jews were found. To the degree that they enjoyed autonomy that permitted them to apply Jewish law where they lived, there was a small Sanhedrin in every district, and these were subject to the authority of the Great Sanhedrin in Jerusalem. (See tractate *Makkot* 7a.)

Moreover, the law of the Jewish state did not limit itself to preserving public order. Jewish law is simultaneously social, moral, and religious, without distinguishing between a system of rules which organizes relations among people and one which deals with relations between man and God. Even among people, along with the desire to impose order and security in social life, there is also the desire to extirpate sin from society. Sin, of any kind, is regarded as a flaw not only in the soul of the sinner but also in the entire society and the land. (Leviticus 18:25-30, and, more explicitly, Numbers 34:33-34.)

Law and judgment are thus tools not only to organize social affairs but also to impose the divine will on the world, for the construction of a state whose general and detailed laws fulfill that will entirely.

Therefore a Jewish court is different from other courts in the world, both in the aims which it sets for itself and also in the ways of achieving them. "Judgment is of God," as it is written (Deuteronomy 1:17), and the judge who sits in judgment does holy work. (See *Shabbat* 10a and elsewhere.) When the judge sits in judgment, the Torah calls him *"elohim,"* a term usually used for God (Exodus 21:6, 22:8). Hence he is called upon to achieve absolute truth, beyond all human doubt. The function of the court, carried out by "judges and officials" (שׁוֹפְטִים וְשׁוֹטְרִים), is to see to the imposition of divine order and absolute justice to the best of its ability (Deuteronomy 16:19-20). Therefore Jewish law contains special procedures and laws of evidence, all of which serve the end of achieving absolute certainty. In the event of even the slightest doubt, the accused is not found guilty.

Therefore it is not enough for judges to know the law. They must also be ordained (modern ordination being only a pale memory of ancient ordination), meaning that authority is transferred from Moses to the students of his students to the last generation. By virtue of ordination the judges receive not only authority to deliberate but also a kind of divine promise that "God stands in the congregation of God; He judges among the judges" (Psalm 82:1), so that the divine presence will inspire the court. From this authority there follows total obedience to the instructions of the High Court, according to the commandment, "You shall not deviate from the sentence which they shall tell you, to the right or to the left" (Deuteronomy 17:11).

The attempt to achieve absolute justice in judgment, which involves complex laws of evidence and the administrative rules connected with them, could lead to exploitation of this situation by criminals of various types and to the weakening of the foundations of the society and the economy. To prevent lawlessness the courts made wide use of their administrative authority, which derived from the imperative, "and you shall put the evil away from your midst." (Deuteronomy 13:6; 17:7; 19:19; 21:21-22; 24:7.) This authority permitted the court to impose very severe disciplinary measures (confiscation of property, lashes, and even the death penalty) to enforce order in the state and to restrain evildoers of all kinds. (See *Sanhedrin* 81b.) Similarly, they waived some of the most severe demands of judgment in various kinds of monetary disputes to make it possible to maintain orderly economic life. (*Sanhedrin* 46a and elsewhere.) Furthermore, many aspects of practical life were placed in the hands of the executive branch headed by the king.

The king and the entire executive branch were of course required to obey the law of the Torah, because that law stands above everything else, and no one can change it. However, in areas that were not connected to that law, and within the framework of the laws of the country, the king could do what he thought fit. He was entitled to impose taxes, to conscript men for the army or public works (1 Samuel 8:11-12; 1 Kings 5:29-30), and to confiscate property for the public good. Moreover, the king also had a certain judiciary authority, and stood at the head of a system of administrative courts that judged according to the "laws of the kingdom." These courts dealt with the imposition of royal orders and decrees and also were an auxiliary to the chief judiciary system of the Sanhedrin. Administrative courts were needed to impose order when the main courts could not do so for procedural or other reasons, such as the severe laws of evidence.

Given the extent and variety of the subjects discussed in it, tracate *Sanhedrin* is unlike any of the others in the Talmud. Most tractates deal with one or two topics and are based on a few verses from the Torah, from which the relevant Halakhot are derived. However, tractate *Sanhedrin* deals with a great many areas, and its basis in the Torah is essentially an entire book — all of Deuteronomy. Almost all the subjects discussed in Deuteronomy, except matters that are discussed more extensively elsewhere, are clarified in tractate *Sanhedrin*.

Like Deuteronomy itself, the tractate begins with laws of judges and judicial procedures. From there it continues to clarify the bases of civil law and most of criminal law (both affecting relations among people and between people and God), and it concludes with a clarification of the tenets of faith, and, what's more, with Halakhah and Aggadah regarding the coming of the Messiah.

Tractate *Sanhedrin* contains eleven chapters, almost all of which deal with a single detailed subject. Each chapter is known by the first words of the Mishnah passage that begins it.

1. דִּינֵי מָמוֹנוֹת בִּשְׁלֹשָׁה — "Monetary matters are judged by three" — discusses the judicial system from the lowest tribunal to the Great Sanhedrin, and also judges and their mission.

2. כֹּהֵן גָּדוֹל — "The High Priest" — deals with the status of eminent men among the nation: the High Priest and the king.

3. זֶה בּוֹרֵר — "This is the Arbitrator" — includes the structure and procedures of courts.

4. אֶחָד דִּינֵי מָמוֹנוֹת — "Also Monetary Cases" — deals with the special procedures of tribunals of twenty-three.

5. הָיוּ בּוֹדְקִין — "They Would Check" — explains the special means of interrogation of tribunals of twenty-three.

6. נִגְמַר הַדִּין — "The Judgment is Finished" — deals with procedures for execution in general and rules of stoning in particular.

7. אַרְבַּע מִיתוֹת — "Four Deaths" — deals in detail with the forms of capital punishment imposed by courts and with crimes punishable by stoning.

8. בֵּן סוֹרֵר וּמוֹרֶה — "The Rebellious Son" — deals with the laws of the rebellious son, with the right to self-defense, and with the prevention of crime.

9. אֵלּוּ הֵן הַנִּשְׂרָפִין — "These are the Ones who are Burned" — deals with capital punishment by burning, with killing, and with other administrative punishments for improving society.

10. אֵלּוּ הֵן הַנֶּחֱנָקִין — "These are the Ones who are Strangled" — deals with crimes punishable by strangulation, including laws applying to people who challenge the basis of the law.

11. חֵלֶק — "Part" — (number eleven in the Babylonian Talmud, although in the Mishnah and in the Jerusalem Talmud this chapter is the tenth one) — deals with matters of faith and morality and a person's directon in life, as well as hopes and preparation for the coming of the Messiah and the End of Days, when the world will return to full perfection.

Introduction to Chapter One

דִּינֵי מָמוֹנוֹת בִּשְׁלשָׁה

"Moreover you shall provide out of all the people able men, such as fear God, men of truth, hating unjust gain; and place such over them to be rulers of thousands, and rulers of hundreds, and rulers of fifties, and rulers of tens; and let them judge the people at all seasons; and it shall be that every great matter they shall bring to you, but every small matter they shall judge; so shall it be easier for yourself, and they shall bear the burden with you." (Exodus 18:21-22.)

"And the Lord said to Moses: 'Gather to Me seventy men of the elders of Moses whom you know to be the elders of the people, and officers over them; and bring them to the Tent of Meeting, that they may stand there with you. And I will come down and talk with you there: and I will take of the spirit which is upon you, and will put it upon them; and they shall bear the burden of the people with you that you bear it not yourself alone.'" (Numbers 11:16-17.)

"Judges and officers shall you make you in all your gates, which the Lord your God give you throughout your tribes: and they shall judge the people with righteous judgment." (Deuteronomy 16:18.)

"If there arise a matter too hard for you in judgment, between blood and blood, between plea and plea, and between plague and plague, matters of controversy within your gates: then shall you arise and go up to the place which the Lord your God shall choose; and you shall come to the priests the Levites, and to the judge that shall be in those days, and inquire; and they shall tell you the sentence of judgment: and you shall do according to the sentence which they of that place which the Lord shall choose shall tell you." (Deuteronomy 17:8-10.)

Torah law includes all the general rules and details of a Jewish person's life. However, the practical implementation of the Halakhah depends on the Sage and judge. He decides what the practical Halakhah is and how the law is to be interpreted; how it is to be understood in every instance; how to evaluate the facts are they are known; and how to evaluate possible contradictions and errors of fact when they are brought before him.

Essentially the power of the judge or the Sage who teaches Halakhah is as great as the Halakhah itself. The Sage who passes judgment actually embodies the Halakhah in his person, as it is implemented in life. Therefore a central concern is that the judge must truly serve and express the inner will found in the Halakhah.

Moreover, the law of the Torah is not a collection of Halakhot meant simply to organize social life but rather a means of constructing and establishing a particular kind of society. Since the Torah represents a system that strives to achieve absolute truth, the judge must try as much as possible to reach that truth.

The title *"elohim"* given in the Torah to judges endows them with unparalleled power, and also with heavy responsibility, to arrive at true judgment. On the other hand, there are also practical problems of life: disputes between people, violations of the law, and the regulation of relations within society, most of which cannot be resolved by absolute proof. Often the search for such a solution would take considerable time, which in itself would be a miscarriage of justice. Thus the importance attributed to the judge, the Sage, and the teacher of Halakhah in Jewish law is understandable. Indeed the first chapter of tractate *Sanhedrin* deals mainly with questions related to judges: What are the sources of their authority? How do judges deliberate? How are various problems divided among the different courts? What is the area of authority of each court? And what obligations are imposed upon it?

The main concerns of this fundamental chapter are therefore the principles of justice and judgment.

TRANSLATION AND COMMENTARY

MISHNAH By Torah law, courts of justice must be established throughout the Land of Israel. Our Mishnah outlines the authority and the size of the different courts that existed in ancient Israel. There were three types of courts: (1) Courts of three judges, which were authorized to adjudicate civil matters; (2) courts of twenty-three judges, also known as Lesser Sanhedrins, which were entitled to judge most capital cases; and (3) the court of seventy-one judges, known as the Great Sanhedrin, which served as the Supreme Court and Israel's highest legislative and religious body.

דִּינֵי מָמוֹנוֹת בִּשְׁלֹשָׁה [1]Our Mishnah opens with a discussion of the judicial powers of the lowest courts, the courts of three judges. **Monetary cases** are adjudicated **by** a court of **three** judges. [2]Cases of **robbery and** bodily **injury** inflicted by another person are adjudicated **by** a court of **three** judges. [3]Cases involving the payment of **damages and half-damages, double compensation, and fourfold and fivefold compensation** are adjudicated **by** a court of **three** judges.

הָאוֹנֵס, וְהַמְפַתֶּה, וְהַמּוֹצִיא שֵׁם רַע [4]Claims against a **rapist, and a seducer, and the** claim raised **by a slanderer** are judged **by** a court of **three.** [5]**This is the view of Rabbi Meir.** [6]**But the Sages** disagree and **say: The slanderer,** a man who accuses his wife of adultery, is judged **by** a court of **twenty-three,** [7]**because** the judgment **may involve capital punishment.** For if the husband's claim is true, and his wife indeed committed adultery while she was betrothed to him, she is subject to execution, and only a court of twenty-three is authorized to hear capital cases.

מַכּוֹת [8]A case involving the transgression of a negative commandment which is punishable by **lashes** requires a court of **three** judges. [9]**In the name of Rabbi Yishmael it was said:** It requires a court of **twenty-three.**

LITERAL TRANSLATION

MISHNAH [1]Monetary cases (lit., "cases of money") by three. [2]Robberies and [inflicted] injuries by three. [3]Damages and half-damages, double compensation, and fourfold and fivefold compensation by three. [4]The rapist, and the seducer, and the slanderer (lit., "he who brings about a bad name") by three; [5][these are] the words of Rabbi Meir. [6]And the Sages say: The slanderer by twenty-three, [7]because it may involve (lit., "has") capital punishment (lit., "cases").

[8]Lashes by three. [9]In the name of Rabbi Yishmael they said: By twenty-three.

דִּינֵי

[1]מָמוֹנוֹת בִּשְׁלֹשָׁה. [2]גְּזֵילוֹת וַחֲבָלוֹת בִּשְׁלֹשָׁה. [3]נֶזֶק וַחֲצִי נֶזֶק, תַּשְׁלוּמֵי כֶפֶל וְתַשְׁלוּמֵי אַרְבָּעָה וַחֲמִשָּׁה בִּשְׁלֹשָׁה. [4]הָאוֹנֵס, וְהַמְפַתֶּה, וְהַמּוֹצִיא שֵׁם רַע בִּשְׁלֹשָׁה; [5]דִּבְרֵי רַבִּי מֵאִיר. [6]וַחֲכָמִים אוֹמְרִים: מוֹצִיא שֵׁם רַע בְּעֶשְׂרִים וּשְׁלֹשָׁה, [7]מִפְּנֵי שֶׁיֵּשׁ בּוֹ דִּינֵי נְפָשׁוֹת.

[8]מַכּוֹת בִּשְׁלֹשָׁה. [9]מִשּׁוּם רַבִּי יִשְׁמָעֵאל אָמְרוּ: בְּעֶשְׂרִים וּשְׁלֹשָׁה.

RASHI

משנה **דיני ממונות בשלשה** — בגמרא ילפינן להו. **גזילות** — כופר בפקדון, דמשלח בו יד הוי גזלן, וכן החוטף מיד חבירו הוי גזלן, כגכגון "ויגזול את החנית מיד המצרי" (שמואל ב' כג). אבל לוה ולא שילם, לא מיקרי גזלן דמלוה להוצאה ניתנה. **וחבלות** — החובל בחבירו חייב בחמשה דברים, כדאמרינן בבבא קמא (פד,א) "ואיש כי יתן מום בעמיתו" וגו' "כן יעשה לו בממון". ובגמרא פריך: היינו דיני ממונות! **נזק** — דשור המועד או אדם שהזיקו, ובגמרא פריך: היינו חבלות! **תשלומי כפל** — דגניבה שנמצא בידו דכתיב (שמות כב) "אם המצא תמצא בידו" וגו'. **ותשלומי ארבעה וחמשה** — דשור או שה, שטבחו או מכרו. **האונס ומפתה** — נערה בתולה חמשים כסף. **מוציא שם רע** — "לא מצאתי לבתך בתולים" וגו', וענשו אותו מאה כסף" וגו' (דברים כב). **דיני נפשות** — דאם אמת היה שזינתה תחתיו, היא בסקילה. ודיני נפשות בעינן עשרים ושלשה לקמן בפירקין (טו,א). **מכות** — מלקות ארבעים. טעמא דר' ישמעאל ורבנן מפרש בגמרא (י,א) מקראי.

NOTES

The position of tractate *Sanhedrin* in the Talmud. According to *Meiri, Sanhedrin* is the first tractate in the order of *Nezikin*. *Meiri* explains that it was placed before other tractates of the order because the Sages wished to clarify the laws on the composition of the various courts, and on judicial procedure, before proceeding to discuss the various cases. But according to most Rishonim and manuscripts, *Sanhedrin* is the fourth tractate in the order of *Nezikin,* following *Bava Batra.* The last Mishnah in *Bava Batra* concludes with the statement of Rabbi Yishmael: He who wishes to become wise should study monetary cases. Therefore our tractate begins with monetary cases (*Tosafot Rosh*).

HALAKHAH

דִּינֵי מָמוֹנוֹת בִּשְׁלֹשָׁה Monetary cases by three. "Monetary cases, cases of robbery and inflicted injury, cases involving the payment of damages and half-damages, double compensation, and fourfold and fivefold compensation, cases of rape and seduction, and cases involving the punishment of lashes — all require a court of three." (*Rambam, Sefer Shofetim, Hilkhot Sanhedrin* 5:4,8; *Shulḥan Arukh, Ḥoshen Mishpat* 13:1.)

הַמּוֹצִיא שֵׁם רַע The slanderer. "A slanderer is judged by a

BACKGROUND

גְּזֵילוֹת וַחֲבָלוֹת בִּשְׁלֹשָׁה Robberies and inflicted injuries by three. If a person takes an article by force from its rightful owner, or if a bailee takes for himself a deposit which another person entrusted to his safekeeping, he is obliged to return the article to its owner as it was when he took possession of it, and if that is not possible, he must reimburse the owner for the article's value at the time of the robbery or expropriation. If a person inflicts bodily harm on another, he must indemnify the injured party for the damage caused him (i.e., the decrease in that person's value), and compensate him for his pain and suffering, medical expenses, loss of earnings, and humiliation. These cases require a court of three judges.

נֶזֶק וַחֲצִי נֶזֶק...בִּשְׁלֹשָׁה Damages and half-damages...by three. If a person damaged somebody else's property, or if his animal caused damage during the course of its normal activities, e.g., while walking or eating, or if the animal caused the damage while behaving abnormally, e.g., goring or kicking, and the animal had already three times caused damage in that manner, the owner must reimburse the injured party in full for the damage done to his property. If the damage caused by the animal resulted from abnormal and unexpected behavior, and the animal did not have a history of behaving that way, the owner of the animal is liable for only one-half of the damage (Exodus 21:35). If a person stole property, he must repay twice the value of the stolen article, i.e., he must restore the principal to its owner — the article itself or, when the article is unavailable, its value — and he must make an additional payment equal to the value of the article (Exodus 22:3). If someone stole a sheep and then sold it or slaughtered it, he must repay its owner four times the value of the sheep. If the stolen animal is an ox, he must repay its owner five times the animal's worth (Exodus 21:37). These cases are adjudicated by a court of three.

הָאוֹנֵס, וְהַמְפַתֶּה, וְהַמּוֹצִיא שֵׁם רַע בִּשְׁלֹשָׁה The rapist, the seducer and the slanderer by three. If a man

TRANSLATION AND COMMENTARY

עִיבּוּר הַחֹדֶשׁ [1]**The addition of an extra day to a month** was done **by** a court of **three** judges.

עִיבּוּר הַשָּׁנָה [2]**The addition of an extra month to a year** was done **by** a court of **three** judges. [3]**This is the view of Rabbi Meir.** [4]**Rabban Shimon ben Gamliel** disagrees and **says:** The deliberations **started with three judges.** If two of the judges thought an additional month was necessary, two more judges joined the deliberations, [5]so that there were **five** judges **discussing** the matter. If three of the judges thought there was good reason to add an extra month, two more judges were asked to participate in the deliberations, bringing the total to seven. [6]These **seven** judges **made the final decision.** [7]But even Rabban Shimon ben Gamliel agrees that **if the final decision** to add an extra month to the year **was made by** a court of **three** judges, **the intercalation** of the year **is** valid.

סְמִיכַת זְקֵנִים [8]If the Sanhedrin issued an erroneous Halakhic ruling, and a majority of the people acted in accordance with that ruling, and afterwards the error came to light, a bull must be sacrificed as a communal sin-offering, and members of the Sanhedrin must press their hands down on the head of the animal (Leviticus 4:13-21). This rite of **the elders pressing their hands** down on the head of the sacrifice had to be performed by three members of the Sanhedrin.

וַעֲרִיפַת עֶגְלָה [9]When a murder victim is found outside a town and it is not known who killed him, the following procedure takes place (Deuteronomy 21:1-9): Judges from the Sanhedrin come to the site and take measurements to determine which town is closest to the corpse. Elders of that town must then bring a heifer that has never been used for any work and break its neck in a riverbed that is not tilled. The elders wash their hands and make a statement absolving themselves from guilt. The measurement of the distance between the corpse and the closest town that precedes the **breaking** of **the neck of the heifer** has to be done **by three** judges selected from the Sanhedrin. [10]**This is the view of Rabbi Shimon.** [11]**Rabbi Yehudah** disagrees and **says:** It has to be performed **by five** members of the Sanhedrin.

הַחֲלִיצָה [12]A man whose brother died without children is obliged by Torah law to marry his deceased brother's widow, or perform the *halitzah* ceremony which releases the woman from the levirate tie and allows her to marry someone else (Deuteronomy 25:7-10). ***Halitzah*** must be performed before a court of **three** judges. [13]A girl under the age of twelve can be married off by her father. If, however, her father is no longer alive, then according to Torah law she cannot be married while still a minor. Nevertheless, the

[1]עִיבּוּר הַחֹדֶשׁ בִּשְׁלֹשָׁה.
[2]עִיבּוּר הַשָּׁנָה בִּשְׁלֹשָׁה; [3]דִּבְרֵי
רַבִּי מֵאִיר. [4]רַבָּן שִׁמְעוֹן בֶּן
גַּמְלִיאֵל אוֹמֵר: בִּשְׁלֹשָׁה
מַתְחִילִין, [5]וּבַחֲמִשָּׁה נוֹשְׂאִין
וְנוֹתְנִין, [6]וְגוֹמְרִין בְּשִׁבְעָה. [7]וְאִם
גָּמְרוּ בִּשְׁלֹשָׁה, מְעוּבֶּרֶת.
[8]סְמִיכַת זְקֵנִים [9]וַעֲרִיפַת עֶגְלָה
בִּשְׁלֹשָׁה; [10]דִּבְרֵי רַבִּי שִׁמְעוֹן.
[11]רַבִּי יְהוּדָה אוֹמֵר: בַּחֲמִשָּׁה.
[12]הַחֲלִיצָה [13]וְהַמֵּיאוּנִין בִּשְׁלֹשָׁה.

LITERAL TRANSLATION

[1]Intercalation of the month by three.

[2]The intercalation of the year by three; [3][these are] the words of Rabbi Meir. [4]Rabban Shimon ben Gamliel says: With three they begin, [5]and with five they discuss, [6]and with seven they decide (lit., "finish"). [7]And if they decide with three, it is intercalated.

[8]The placing of the elders' [hands] [9]and breaking the neck of the heifer by three; [10][these are] the words of Rabbi Shimon. [11]Rabbi Yehudah says: By five.

[12]*Halitzah* [13]and refusals by three

RASHI

עיבור החדש — בגמרא מפרש. **עיבור השנה** — שהיו בית דין יושבין ורואין אם צריכין לעבר מפני האביב והתקופה, כדאמרינן בגמרא, מילתיה דר' שמעון מיפרשא בגמרא בברייתא (י,ב). **סמיכת זקנים** — על ראש פר העלם דבר של צבור. **חליצה בשלשה** — ביבמות יליף לה בפרק "מצות חליצה" (קא,א). **מיאונין** — יתומה קטנה שהשיאוה אמה ואחיה לדעתה, יוצאה בלא גט במיאון, כל זמן שלא גדלה תחתיו. ובשלשה בעינן, דכל דתקון רבנן כעין דאורייתא תקון. ומיאונין דרבנן, דמדאורייתא אפילו מיאון לא בעיא, דאין קדושי קטנה כלום אלא אם כן קדשה אביה, דכתיב (דברים כב) "את בתי נתתי לאיש הזה".

NOTES

מֵיאוּנִין בִּשְׁלֹשָׁה **Refusals by three.** A number of Aharonim question why the Mishnah does not mention that bills of divorce require a court of three. According to some, it was not necessary for the Mishnah to mention bills of divorce,

HALAKHAH

court of twenty-three," following the Sages. (*Rambam, Sefer Shofetim, Hilkhot Sanhedrin* 5:3.)

עִיבּוּר הַשָּׁנָה **Intercalation of the year.** "The intercalation of the year requires seven judges," following Rabban Shimon ben Gamliel. (*Rambam, Sefer Shofetim, Hilkhot Sanhedrin* 5:7.)

עֲרִיפַת עֶגְלָה **The breaking of the neck of the heifer.** "The breaking of the neck of the heifer requires a court of five," following Rabbi Yehudah. (*Rambam, Sefer Shofetim, Hilkhot Sanhedrin* 5:5.)

raped an unmarried girl who was aged between twelve and twelve-and-a-half, or if he persuaded the girl to have sexual relations with him, he must pay damages according to the laws of personal injury, as well as a fine equivalent to "the virgin's dowry," i.e., fifty shekels (Exodus 22:16; Deuteronomy 22:29). If a man falsely claimed that his wife was not a virgin when she married him, and he brought false witnesses to testify that she had committed adultery while betrothed to him, he is punished by flogging, and must pay his wife's father a fine of one hundred shekels (Deuteronomy 22:13-19). Judgment concerning the fines in these three cases is passed by a court of three judges.

BACKGROUND

עִיבּוּר הַחֹדֶשׁ בִּשְׁלֹשָׁה **The intercalation of the new month by three.** See p.10b.

עִיבּוּר הַשָּׁנָה **The intercalation of an extra month.** See p.10b.

סְמִיכַת זְקֵנִים **The placing of the elders' hands.** In the Talmud this term can have different meanings: (1) The rite of the elders pressing their hands down on the head of the bull brought as a communal sin-offering, and (2) the ordination of Sages.

CONCEPTS

חֲלִיצָה ***Halitzah.*** Lit., "removal." The ceremony that frees the widow of a man who died without children from the obligation to marry one of her deceased husband's brothers and allows her to remarry (see Deuteronomy 25:7-10). The term *halitzah* is derived from the central element of this ceremony, which involves the removal by the widow of a special sandal from the foot of one of her deceased husband's brothers. *Halitzah* must be performed before a court of three judges. The laws governing this ceremony are discussed in detail in tractate *Yevamot.*

LITERAL TRANSLATION

[1]Fourth-year produce, [2]and second tithe whose value is not known, [3]by three.

[4]Consecrated property by three.

[5]Valuations — movable goods by three. [6]Rabbi Yehudah says: One of them [must be] a priest. [7]And landed property — nine and a priest. [8]And a person likewise.

[9]Capital cases by twenty-three.

[1]נֶטַע רְבָעִי, [2]וּמַעֲשֵׂר שֵׁנִי שֶׁאֵין דָּמָיו יְדוּעִין, [3]בִּשְׁלֹשָׁה.
[4]הַהֶקְדֵּשׁוֹת בִּשְׁלֹשָׁה.
[5]הָעֲרָכִין הַמִּטַּלְטְלִים בִּשְׁלֹשָׁה.
[6]רַבִּי יְהוּדָה אוֹמֵר: אֶחָד מֵהֶן כֹּהֵן. [7]וְהַקַּרְקָעוֹת — תִּשְׁעָה וְכֹהֵן. [8]וְאָדָם כַּיּוֹצֵא בָּהֶן.
[9]דִּינֵי נְפָשׁוֹת בְּעֶשְׂרִים וּשְׁלֹשָׁה.

RASHI

נטע רבעי – אם בא לחללו על המעות, וכן מעשר שני. **שאין דמיהן ידועין** – כגון פירות והרקיבו, שאין להם שער בשוק. **וההקדשות** – הבא לפדותן צריך שלשה לשומן. **הערכין המטלטלין** – בגמרא מפרש (יד,ב). **אחד מהם כהן** – דכתיב כהן בפרשה "כערכך הכהן" וגו' (ויקרא כז). **והקרקעות** – של הקדש צריך תשע והעשירי כהן, לשומן אם בא לפדותן, בגמרא (טו,א) מפרש ויליף להו מקראי. **ואדם** – הבא לפדות עצמו מיד הקדש צריך עשרה לשומו, ובגמרא (שם) פריך: אדם מי קדיש?! **דיני נפשות** – בעשרים ושלשה, לקמן יליף לה במתניתין.

TRANSLATION AND COMMENTARY

Sages decreed that her mother or brothers may marry her off with her consent. The girl may terminate this marriage before she reaches the age of twelve by formally indicating "refusal," i.e., by declaring that she does not want the marriage. The marriage is nullified retroactively, and so a bill of divorce is not necessary. The **refusal** ceremony (*"me'un"*) must be performed before a court of **three** judges.

נֶטַע רְבָעִי [1]If a person wishes to redeem his **fourth-year produce, he** must redeem it in accordance with the assessment of three experts at appraising the costs of growing and harvesting the produce, for with respect to fourth-year produce, those costs may be deducted from the redemption money. [2]Similarly, if someone wishes to redeem his **second tithe,** and **the** precise **value** of the produce **is not known** (if, for example, the second tithe produce has begun to rot, so that it has no fixed market value), [3]he must redeem it in accordance **with** the assessment of **three** judges.

הַהֶקְדֵּשׁוֹת [4]If a person wishes to redeem **property** which has been **consecrated** to the Temple, an assessment of the property's value must be made **by three** judges.

הָעֲרָכִין הַמִּטַּלְטְלִים [5]If a person made a vow of **valuation,** using the expression, "I promise to pay the value [עֵרֶךְ] of such-and-such," or "I promise to pay my value," but he does not have any money, and he wishes to pay with **movable goods,** the movable property must be assessed **by three** judges. [6]**Rabbi Yehudah says: One of** the three appraisers must be **a priest,** as the verse states (Leviticus 27:12): "As the priest values it." [7]**And** if the person wishes to pay his vow of valuation with **landed property,** or if he consecrated landed property to the Temple and now wishes to redeem it, the land must be assessed by ten judges — one of whom must be **a priest.** [8]And the assessment of the value of **a person is likewise** done by ten people, one of whom must be a priest.

דִּינֵי נְפָשׁוֹת [9]The Mishnah now lists those cases that fall under the category of **capital cases** and are

CONCEPTS

נֶטַע רְבָעִי **Fourth-year produce.** Fruit growing on a tree during the first three years after it was planted is called *orlah*, and may not be eaten (nor may any other benefit be derived from it). The fruit that grows during the fourth year must be taken to Jerusalem and eaten there. If it cannot be taken to Jerusalem, it is redeemed and the redemption money is taken to Jerusalem, where it is spent on food and drink. A similar law applies to second tithe, the tithe set aside during the first, second, fourth, and fifth years of the Sabbatical cycle after the priestly dues have been given to the priests, and the first tithe has been given to the Levites. Second-tithe produce must either be taken to Jerusalem to be eaten there by its owner, or it must be redeemed, and the redemption money is then taken to Jerusalem and spent on food.

BACKGROUND

שֶׁאֵין דָּמָיו יְדוּעִין **Whose value is not known.** The value of ordinary fruits does not usually have to be assessed by a court, for it is determined in the marketplace. However, fruit sometimes spoils, necessitating a special evaluation of its price.

הַקַּרְקָעוֹת **Landed property.** Land is regarded as a secure and durable asset. Hence there are many differences in the Halakhah between the sale and appraisal of land and that of movable goods. Another restriction regarding the sale of land is that one is only authorized to do so at the age of twenty.

NOTES

for it follows logically that if refusals (which only terminate a marriage that is Rabbinic in nature) require three judges, then all the more so do bills of divorce (which dissolve a Torah-based marriage) require a court of three. Others argue just the opposite, that refusals require three judges, but bills of divorce do not, and in fact nowhere in the Talmud is such a requirement mentioned. According to the first group, refusals were modeled on bills of divorce, for both put an end to a state of marriage. According to the second group, refusals were modeled on *ḥalitzah*, for in both cases one party refuses to marry or remain married to the other (see *Maharam Shiff, Rashash, Ḥamra Veḥaye, Rabbi Isaac Ḥaver*).

HALAKHAH

דִּינִים הַנִּידוֹנִים בִּשְׁלֹשָׁה **Cases judged by three.** "The intercalation of the month, the placing of the hands of the elders on the head of a sacrifice, *ḥalitzah*, refusals, the assessment of fourth-year produce and second tithe whose value is not known, the assessment of consecrated property, and the assessment of movable goods for the payment of vows of valuation — all require a court of three." (*Rambam, Sefer Shofetim, Hilkhot Sanhedrin* 5:6; 4:3; *Sefer Zeraim, Hilkhot Ma'aser Sheni* 9:6; *Sefer Hafla'ah, Hilkhot Arkhin* 8:2; *Sefer Korbanot, Hilkhot Ma'asei HaKorbanot* 3:10; *Shulḥan Arukh, Even HaEzer* 169:1.)

הַהֶקְדֵּשׁוֹת **Consecrated property.** "The assessment of land which had been consecrated to the Temple, as well as the assessment of a person whose value had been consecrated to the Temple, must be made by ten people — one of whom must be a priest." (*Rambam, Sefer Hafla'ah, Hilkhot Arakhin* 8:2.)

דִּינֵי נְפָשׁוֹת **Capital cases.** "Capital cases must be judged by a court of twenty-three judges. Cases involving the execution of animals — e.g., the case of an ox that gored a person, or an animal that copulated with a person — require a court of twenty-three judges." (*Rambam, Sefer Shofetim, Hilkhot Sanhedrin* 5:2.)

[1]הָרוֹבֵעַ וְהַנִּרְבָּע בְּעֶשְׂרִים וּשְׁלֹשָׁה, [2]שֶׁנֶּאֱמַר: "וְהָרַגְתָּ אֶת הָאִשָּׁה וְאֶת הַבְּהֵמָה". [3]וְאוֹמֵר: "וְאֶת הַבְּהֵמָה תַּהֲרֹגוּ".
[4]שׁוֹר הַנִּסְקָל בְּעֶשְׂרִים וּשְׁלֹשָׁה, [5]שֶׁנֶּאֱמַר: "הַשּׁוֹר יִסָּקֵל וְגַם בְּעָלָיו יוּמָת". [6]כְּמִיתַת בְּעָלִים כָּךְ מִיתַת הַשּׁוֹר.
[7]הַזְּאֵב וְהָאֲרִי הַדּוֹב וְהַנָּמֵר וְהַבַּרְדְּלָס וְהַנָּחָשׁ — [8]מִיתָתָן בְּעֶשְׂרִים וּשְׁלֹשָׁה. [9]רַבִּי אֱלִיעֶזֶר אוֹמֵר: כָּל הַקּוֹדֵם לְהוֹרְגָן זָכָה. [10]רַבִּי עֲקִיבָא אוֹמֵר: מִיתָתָן בְּעֶשְׂרִים וּשְׁלֹשָׁה.
[11]אֵין דָּנִין לֹא אֶת הַשֵּׁבֶט, [12]וְלֹא אֶת נְבִיא הַשֶּׁקֶר, [13]וְלֹא אֶת כֹּהֵן גָּדוֹל, [14]אֶלָּא עַל פִּי בֵּית דִּין שֶׁל שִׁבְעִים וְאֶחָד.
[15]וְאֵין מוֹצִיאִין לְמִלְחֶמֶת הָרְשׁוּת אֶלָּא עַל פִּי בֵּית דִּין

LITERAL TRANSLATION

[1]The animal that copulated with a woman and the animal with whom a man copulated by twenty-three, [2]as it is said: "And you shall kill the woman and the beast." [3]And it says: "And the beast you shall kill."

[4]The ox to be stoned by twenty-three, [5]as it is said: "The ox shall be stoned, and its owner also shall be put to death." [6]Like the death of the owner so the death of the ox.

[7]The wolf, and the lion, and the bear, and the leopard, and the hyena, and the snake — [8]their death is by twenty-three. [9]Rabbi Eliezer says: Whoever is first to kill them merits. [10]Rabbi Akiva says: Their death is by twenty-three.

[11]A tribe, [12]or a false prophet, [13]or a High Priest may not be tried [14]except by a court of seventy-one.

[15][The people] may not be sent (lit., "brought out") to an optional war except by a court

RASHI

הרובע והנרבע — שור שרבע אשה, ובהמה שנרבעת לאיש, נידונית הבהמה ליסקל. **בעשרים ושלשה** — כאדם הרובע, דאיתקוש להדדי, והרגת את האשה ואת הבהמה בהמה — היינו רובע, ואיתקוש בהמה לאשה, מה אשה בעשרים ושלשה אף בהמה בעשרים ושלשה. **ואומר "ואת הבהמה תהרוגו"** — בנרבע כתיב. **שור הנסקל** — שנגח אדם ומת. **כמיתת בעלים** — אם היה נידון בחיוב מיתת בית דין דבעי עשרים ושלשה, כך מיתת השור. דהי "בעליו יומת" קרא יתרא להך דרשא, ולא דנתחייב קטלא, כדמפרש טעמא בגמרא (שם). **הזאב והארי כו'** — שהמיתו אדם, ונידונין בסקילה כשור, דאמרינן בבבא קמא, אחד שור ואחד כו', ב"שור שנגח את הפרה" (נד,ב). **ברדלס** — חיה היא. **ואין דנין לא את השבט** — רובו של שבט שעבדו עבודה זרה במזיד. **נביא השקר** — בחנק, בגמרא (טז,א) בעי: מנלן דבעי שבעים ואחד? **במלחמת הרשות** — כל מלחמה קרי רשות לבד ממלחמת יהושע, שהיתה לכבוש את ארץ ישראל.

TRANSLATION AND COMMENTARY

adjudicated **by** a court of **twenty-three** judges. [1]**The animal that copulated with a woman and the animal with whom a man copulated** are sentenced to stoning **by** a court of **twenty-three** judges, [2]**as it is said** (Leviticus 20:16): **"And** if a woman approach any beast, and lie down before it, **you shall kill the woman and the beast."** [3]**And** another verse **says** (Leviticus 20:15): **"And** if a man lie with a beast, he shall surely be put to death; **and the beast you shall kill."** Just as the man or woman is judged by a court of twenty-three, so too must the animal be judged by a court of twenty-three.

שׁוֹר הַנִּסְקָל [4]**An ox which** gored a person and killed him **must be stoned** to death. The verdict of death by stoning must be delivered **by** a court of **twenty-three** judges, [5]**as it is said** (Exodus 21:29): "But if the ox was wont to gore with his horn in time past, and his owner had been warned, yet he had not kept him in, but it killed a man or a woman, **the ox shall be stoned, and its owner also shall be put to death."** [6]The laws that apply to **the execution of the owner** apply **also to the execution of the ox.**

הַזְּאֵב וְהָאֲרִי [7]Even though the verse speaks only of an ox which gored a person and killed him, the same law applies to any other dangerous animal. Thus, if **a wolf, or a lion, or a bear, or a leopard, or a hyena, or a snake** killed a person, [8]the verdict of **execution must be** delivered **by** a court of **twenty-three** judges. [9]**Rabbi Eliezer says: Whoever is first to** go and **kill** a dangerous creature deserves **merit,** for by killing it he prevents it from striking again. [10]**Rabbi Akiva says:** If one of these creatures killed a person, the verdict of **execution must be** delivered **by** a court of **twenty-three.**

אֵין דָּנִין לֹא אֶת הַשֵּׁבֶט [11]The Mishnah now lists cases and issues which require the Great Sanhedrin. If **an** entire **tribe** of Israel or the majority thereof committed idolatry, the trial can only be by a court of seventy-one judges. [12]**A false prophet** is liable to death, and can only be tried by a court of seventy-one judges. [13]If **a High Priest** is charged with a capital offense, [14]he too **can only be tried by a court of seventy-one** judges.

וְאֵין מוֹצִיאִין [15]A Jewish King **cannot send** the nation to fight **an optional war** — one waged to enlarge the boundaries of the Land of Israel or to subjugate the neighboring nations — without the permission of

HALAKHAH

בֵּית דִּין שֶׁל שִׁבְעִים וְאֶחָד A court of seventy-one judges. "An entire tribe of Israel which violated the prohibition against idolatry, a false prophet, and a High Priest who is accused of committing a capital offense, can only be tried

BACKGROUND

הָרוֹבֵעַ וְהַנִּרְבָּע An animal which copulated with a woman.... The Torah states that if a person copulated with an animal, the person and the animal have to be killed (Leviticus 20:15-16). Although permission from a court is not needed to kill the animal, the Sages ruled on the basis of Scripture that whenever an animal is executed by court order, this must be done following the procedures of capital trials for humans — by a court of twenty-three. Some Sages maintain that, even regarding the details, the trial must follow the procedures applied to trials of humans.

אֶלָּא עַל פִּי בֵּית דִּין שֶׁל שִׁבְעִים וְאֶחָד Except by a court of seventy-one. A court of seventy-one is the highest authority among the Jewish people, standing in place of Moses. The judgments it delivers are known as הַדָּבָר הַגָּדוֹל ("the great matter"), issues affecting the whole Jewish nation or its leaders.

LANGUAGE

בַּרְדְּלָס Leopard. This word is derived from the Greek πάρδαλις, *pardalis*, meaning a leopard or cheetah and, by extension, spotted creatures and objects of various types.

REALIA

בַּרְדְּלָס Leopard. In the Talmud this word does not refer to a single kind of animal, but to at least three. One kind is a small animal similar to a mongoose (see below, *Rashi* and *Tosafot*, 15b). Another type is the hyena, and some authorities believe that this is the animal referred to here. Others maintain that the animal referred to here is the cheetah, a spotted member of the cat family, *Acinonyx jubatus,* which is found in Asia and Africa. This animal reaches a length of 180 cm. (including the tail), is yellowish brown, and is spotted with dark patches.
Since the cheetah is the fastest of all land animals and is easily tamed, it is used in many places for hunting other animals, mainly deer. Although cheetahs usually do not attack human beings, they are large and dangerous enough to injure and even kill.

שֶׁל שִׁבְעִים וְאֶחָד.
[1]אֵין מוֹסִיפִין עַל הָעִיר וְעַל הָעֲזָרוֹת אֶלָּא עַל פִּי בֵּית דִּין שֶׁל שִׁבְעִים וְאֶחָד.
[2]אֵין עוֹשִׂין סַנְהֶדְרִיוֹת לַשְּׁבָטִים אֶלָּא עַל פִּי בֵּית דִּין שֶׁל שִׁבְעִים וְאֶחָד.
[3]אֵין עוֹשִׂין עִיר הַנִּדַּחַת אֶלָּא עַל פִּי בֵּית דִּין שֶׁל שִׁבְעִים וְאֶחָד.
[4]אֵין עוֹשִׂין עִיר הַנִּדַּחַת בַּסְּפָר, [5]וְלֹא שָׁלֹשׁ. [6]אֲבָל עוֹשִׂין אַחַת אוֹ שְׁתַּיִם.
[7]סַנְהֶדְרִין גְּדוֹלָה הָיְתָה שֶׁל שִׁבְעִים וְאֶחָד, וּקְטַנָּה שֶׁל עֶשְׂרִים וּשְׁלֹשָׁה. [8]מִנַּיִן לַגְּדוֹלָה שֶׁהִיא שֶׁל שִׁבְעִים וְאֶחָד? [9]שֶׁנֶּאֱמַר: "אֶסְפָה לִּי שִׁבְעִים

LITERAL TRANSLATION

of seventy-one.

[1][Additions] may not be made to the city and to the [Temple] Courtyards except by a court of seventy-one.

[2][Lesser] Sanhedrins may not be established for the tribes except by a court of seventy-one.

[3][A city] may not be condemned (lit., "made") an idolatrous city (lit., "a city that was led astray") except by a court of seventy-one. [4]An idolatrous city on the border may not be condemned, [5]nor three. [6]But one or two.

[7]The Great Sanhedrin had seventy-one [members], and a Lesser [Sanhedrin] had twenty-three. [8]From where [do we know] that the Great [Sanhedrin] had seventy-one? [9]As it is said: "Gather to me seventy

TRANSLATION AND COMMENTARY

the court of seventy-one judges.

אֵין מוֹסִיפִין [1]The sanctity of Jerusalem is greater than the sanctity of the rest of the Land of Israel, and the sanctity of the Temple is greater than the sanctity of the rest of Jerusalem. The limits of **the city** of Jerusalem **and the** Temple **Courtyards can only be expanded with** the permission of **the court of seventy-one** judges.

אֵין עוֹשִׂין [2]**Courts** of twenty-three judges **can only be established for the tribes** of Israel **by the court of seventy-one** judges.

אֵין עוֹשִׂין [3]A city whose entire population or the majority thereof committed idolatry is called an idolatrous city and is governed by the following Biblical passage (Deuteronomy 13:16-17): "You shall surely smite the inhabitants of that city with the edge of the sword destroying it utterly, and all that is in it." **An idolatrous city can only be condemned by the court of seventy-one** judges. [4]**An idolatrous city cannot be condemned** for destruction if it is situated **on the border** of Israel. Rather, its guilty inhabitants are judged as individuals, and the city itself is spared, in order not to impair the defense of the country's borders. [5]**Three** cities which are situated close to each other **cannot** be condemned as idolatrous cities. [6]**But one or two** cities, even if they are close to each other, **can be condemned**.

סַנְהֶדְרִין גְּדוֹלָה [7]The Mishnah now cites a disagreement about the number of members of the Great Sanhedrin. **The Great Sanhedrin had seventy-one members, and a Lesser Sanhedrin had twenty-three.** [8]**From where do we know that the Great Sanhedrin had seventy-one?** [9]**As it is said** (Numbers 11:16): **"Gather**

RASHI

על העיר – ירושלים. **סנהדריות** – שהיו מושיבים סנהדרי קטנה של עשרים ושלשה בכל עיר ועיר, כדכתיב (דברים טז) "תתן לך בכל שעריך" וצריכין בית דין הגדול שבלשכת הגזית לצאת ולהושיבם וכו׳, יליף בגמרא (טז,ב). **בספר** – כרך המבדיל בין ישראל לנכרים, ובלעז *מרק״א, ובגמרא (שם) מפרש טעמא.

LANGUAGE

סַנְהֶדְרִין Sanhedrin. The source of this word is the Greek συνέδιον, *synhedion,* which means a council, especially a council of notables, judges, or governors. *Bertinoro* interprets the word as an abbreviation of שׂוֹנְא הַדְרַת פָּנִים — "contempt for pretension and favoritism" — one of the virtues of the Sanhedrin.

LANGUAGE (RASHI)

מרק״א* From the Old French, *marche,* which means a border area.

NOTES

אֵין מוֹסִיפִין עַל הָעִיר Additions may not be made to the city. We learned elsewhere in the Mishnah (*Shevuot* 14a) that the city of Jerusalem and the Temple Courtyards can only be expanded with the permission of the king, a Prophet, the *urim vetumim*, and the Great Sanhedrin. *Tosafot* (*Shevuot* 15a) note that there is no disagreement between the two Mishnahs. Our Mishnah does not mention that the king, a Prophet, and the *urim vetumim* are also required, for it does not mean to teach us all the laws regarding the expansion of Jerusalem and the Temple Courtyards, but rather wishes only to list the judicial and administrative functions of the Great Sanhedrin.

קְטַנָּה שֶׁל עֶשְׂרִים וּשְׁלֹשָׁה A Lesser Sanhedrin had twenty-three. *Sifrei* learns in a slightly different manner that a Lesser Sanhedrin requires twenty-three judges. "The congregation shall judge" teaches ten, and "the congregation shall deliver" teaches another ten. An analogy is then drawn between the witnesses and the judges. Just as two witnesses are required to convict a person of a capital offense, so too is a majority of two judges required to hand

HALAKHAH

by a court of seventy-one judges. An idolatrous city can only be condemned by a court of seventy-one judges." (*Rambam, Sefer Shofetim, Hilkhot Sanhedrin* 5:1.)

עִיר הַנִּדַּחַת בַּסְּפָר An idolatrous city on the border. "An idolatrous city cannot be condemned for destruction if it sits on the border of the Land of Israel. The same court cannot condemn as idolatrous any three cities which are situated close to each other. But it can condemn three cities which are at a distance from each other." (*Rambam, Sefer Mada, Hilkhot Avodah Zarah* 4:4.)

סַנְהֶדְרִין גְּדוֹלָה The Great Sanhedrin. "The Great Sanhedrin had seventy-one members and a Lesser Sanhedrin had twenty-three." (*Rambam, Sefer Shofetim, Hilkhot Sanhedrin* 1:3.)

איש מִזִּקְנֵי יִשְׂרָאֵל״, [1] וּמֹשֶׁה עַל גַּבֵּיהֶן. [2] רַבִּי יְהוּדָה אוֹמֵר: שִׁבְעִים.

[3] וּמִנַּיִן לִקְטַנָּה שֶׁהִיא שֶׁל עֶשְׂרִים וּשְׁלֹשָׁה? [4] שֶׁנֶּאֱמַר: ״וְשָׁפְטוּ הָעֵדָה...וְהִצִּילוּ הָעֵדָה״. [5] עֵדָה שׁוֹפֶטֶת [6] וְעֵדָה מַצֶּלֶת, [7] הֲרֵי כָּאן עֶשְׂרִים. [8] וּמִנַּיִן לָעֵדָה שֶׁהִיא עֲשָׂרָה? [9] שֶׁנֶּאֱמַר: ״עַד מָתַי לָעֵדָה הָרָעָה הַזֹּאת״? [10] יָצְאוּ יְהוֹשֻׁעַ וְכָלֵב. [11] וּמִנַּיִן לְהָבִיא עוֹד שְׁלֹשָׁה? [12] מִמַּשְׁמַע שֶׁנֶּאֱמַר: ״לֹא תִהְיֶה אַחֲרֵי רַבִּים לְרָעֹת״, [13] שׁוֹמֵעַ אֲנִי שֶׁאֶהְיֶה עִמָּהֶם לְטוֹבָה. [14] אִם כֵּן, לָמָּה נֶאֱמַר: ״אַחֲרֵי רַבִּים לְהַטֹּת?״ [15] לֹא כְּהַטָּיָיתְךָ לְטוֹבָה הַטָּיָיתְךָ

LITERAL TRANSLATION

men from the elders of Israel," [1] and Moses was over them. [Here are seventy-one.] [2] Rabbi Yehudah says: Seventy.

[3] And from where [do we know] that a Lesser [Sanhedrin] had twenty-three? [4] As it is said: "And the congregation shall judge...and the congregation shall deliver." [5] A congregation to judge [6] and a congregation to deliver, [7] here are twenty. [8] And from where [do we know] that a congregation is ten? [9] As it is said: "How long shall I bear with this evil congregation?" [10] Joshua and Caleb are excluded. [11] And from where [do we know] to bring another three? [12] By inference from what is said: "You shall not follow after the many to do evil," [13] I infer that I must be with them to do good. [14] If so, why is it stated: "After the many to incline"? [15] Your inclination for good shall not be like your inclination

TRANSLATION AND COMMENTARY

to Me seventy men from the elders of Israel, whom you know to be the elders of the people, and officers over them; and bring them to the Tent of Meeting, that they may stand there with you." [1] **And Moses stood at the head** of the seventy, as it is said (Numbers 11:17): "And they shall bear with you the burden of the people that you not bear it yourself alone." Together there are seventy-one. [2] **Rabbi Yehudah says:** The Great Sanhedrin had only **seventy** members.

וּמִנַּיִן לִקְטַנָּה [3] **And from where do we know that a Lesser Sanhedrin had twenty-three?** [4] **As it is said** in the verses that deal with a murderer (Numbers 35:24-25): **"And the congregation shall judge** between the slayer and the avenger of blood according to these judgments. [5] **And the congregation shall deliver** the slayer out of the hand of the avenger of blood." Thus, we see that in order to try capital cases, we need a court with enough members to be considered **a congregation** ("a group of ten," as will be discussed below) **which judges,** i.e., finds the defendant guilty, [6] **and a congregation which delivers,** i.e., finds him innocent. [7] We **now have twenty.** [8] **And from where do we know that** the term **"a congregation" refers to ten?** [9] **As it is said** regarding the spies whom Moses sent to scout the Land of Israel (Numbers 14:27): **"How long shall I bear with this evil congregation?"** Even though there were twelve spies, the term "congregation" refers to a group of ten, [10] for we **exclude Joshua and Caleb** who did not join the others as they spread the evil report about the land. [11] **And from where do we know** that we have to **add another three** so that the Lesser Sanhedrin will have twenty-three members? From the verse (Exodus 23:2): "You shall not follow the many to do evil...after the many to incline." [12] **By inference from what is said** in the first part of the verse: **"You shall not follow after the many to do evil,"** from which I learn that we do not sentence a man to death on account of there being more judges who find him guilty than there are who find him innocent, [13] **I infer that I must be with** the majority **to do good** and follow the majority of judges in favor of acquittal. [14] **If so, why does** the end of the verse **state: "After the many to incline"?** This teaches that we are to follow the majority opinion. [15] Hence, the verse must mean that **your inclination for good,** to acquit, **shall**

RASHI

עדה שופטת — עשרה מחייבין. **ועדה מצלת** — עשרה מזכין, אשמעינן קרא דצריך עשרים, שאם יחלקו, יהיו עשרה מחייבין ועשרה מזכין. **לעדה הרעה** — במרגלים כתיב. **לרעות** — אם הרוב מחייבין, לא תלך אחריהם להרוג. **שומע אני** — דלטובה, לזכות, הלך אחריהן, שאפילו מיעוט המזכים, ורבים המחייבין, כתיב: "לא תהיה אחרי רבים לרעות", אם כן למה נאמר: "אחרי רבים להטות"? משום זכות לא איצטריך ליה, אלא — אפילו לחייב הלך אחריהן! **לא בהטייתך** — אחרי רבים לזכות, אני אומר לך לנטות אחרי רבים לחובה, אלא — לזכות על פי אחד, אפילו אין יתירין מזכין על המחייבין אלא אחד — זכה. אבל לחובה, עד שיהו מחייבין עודפין על המזכין שנים. והכי קאמר: "לא תהיה אחרי רבים לרעות" על פי אחד, אבל אחרי רבים — בשנים אפילו לרעות,

NOTES

down the conviction. And since a court cannot be composed of an even number of judges (twenty-two), we must add another judge, bringing the total to twenty-three. The Geonim note that the name of God is mentioned twenty-three times in the first chapter of Genesis before the creation of man, teaching us that a human life can only be taken by a court of twenty-three.

BACKGROUND

רַבִּי יְהוּדָה אוֹמֵר: שִׁבְעִים **Rabbi Yehudah says: Seventy.** Rabbi Yehudah maintained that seventy men were appointed to serve on the Supreme Court that would be the highest authority among the Jewish people, whereas Moses was an even higher authority, because he received the law from the mouth of the Holy One, blessed be He, and he cannot be regarded as a judge in that court.

SAGES

רַבִּי יְהוּדָה **Rabbi Yehudah (bar Il'ai).** When the Mishnah mentions Rabbi Yehudah without a patronymic, it is referring to Rabbi Yehudah son of Rabbi Il'ai, one of the greatest Tannaim of the fourth generation. He was one of the last five of Rabbi Akiva's disciples, and his father, Rabbi Il'ai, had been a disciple of Rabbi Eliezer. Rabbi Yehudah received Rabbi Eliezer's teachings from his father. In his youth he studied with Rabbi Tarfon, and he transmits teachings in his name as well as in the names of the other Sages of Yavneh: Rabbi Eliezer, Rabbi Yehoshua, Rabban Gamliel, Rabbi Elazar ben Azaryah, Rabbi Yishmael, and Rabbi Yose HaGelili. But Rabbi Yehudah's main teacher was Rabbi Akiva, according to whose teachings he laid the foundations for the Halakhic exegesis of Leviticus in a work known as the *Sifra* (or *Torat Kohanim*). According to tradition, an unattributed statement in the *Sifra* is the teaching of Rabbi Yehudah. He was ordained by Rabbi Yehudah ben Bava and is frequently quoted in Aggadic exegesis together with Rabbi Neḥemyah. In differences of opinion between Rabbi Yehudah and Rabbi Meir, or between Rabbi Yehudah and Rabbi Shimon, the Halakhah follows Rabbi Yehudah. Among his disciples were Rabbi Elazar son of Rabbi Shimon, Rabbi Yishmael son of Rabbi Yose, and Rabbi Yehudah HaNasi. His son, Rabbi Yose son of Rabbi Yehudah, was also a famous Sage.

HALAKHAH

הַטָּיָיתְךָ לְטוֹבָה וְלְרָעָה **Your inclination for good and for evil.** "The defendant in a capital case can be acquitted by a

לְרָעָה. [1]הַטָּיָיתְךָ לְטוֹבָה עַל פִּי אֶחָד, [2]הַטָּיָיתְךָ לְרָעָה עַל פִּי שְׁנַיִם [2B] [3]וְאֵין בֵּית דִּין שָׁקוּל, [4]מוֹסִיפִין עֲלֵיהֶם עוֹד אֶחָד, [5]הֲרֵי כָּאן עֶשְׂרִים וּשְׁלֹשָׁה. [6]וְכַמָּה יְהֵא בָּעִיר וּתְהֵא רְאוּיָה לְסַנְהֶדְרִין? [7]מֵאָה וְעֶשְׂרִים. [8]רַבִּי נְחֶמְיָה אוֹמֵר: מָאתַיִם וּשְׁלֹשִׁים, [9]כְּנֶגֶד שָׂרֵי עֲשָׂרוֹת.

גמרא [10]אַטּוּ גְּזֵילוֹת וַחֲבָלוֹת לָאו דִּינֵי מָמוֹנוֹת נִינְהוּ? [11]אָמַר רַבִּי אַבָּהוּ: [12]מָה ״הֵן קָתָנֵי״. [13]מָה הֵן דִּינֵי מָמוֹנוֹת? [14]גְּזֵילוֹת וַחֲבָלוֹת. [15]אֲבָל הוֹדָאוֹת וְהַלְוָאוֹת לֹא.

LITERAL TRANSLATION

for evil. [1]Your inclination for good based on one. [2]Your inclination for evil based on two. [2B] [3]And a court cannot be [of] even [numbers], [4]we add to them one more. [5]Thus there are twenty-three.

[6]And how many must there be in the town so that it be fit to have a Sanhedrin? [7]One hundred and twenty. [8]Rabbi Neḥemyah says: [9]Two hundred and thirty, corresponding to the officers of tens.

GEMARA [10]Are robberies and injuries not monetary cases? [11]Rabbi Abbahu said: [12]It teaches "what are they." [13]What are monetary cases? [14]Robberies and injuries. [15]But admissions and loans not.

TRANSLATION AND COMMENTARY

not be like your inclination for evil, to convict. [1]Rather, **your inclination for good**, to acquit, **can be based on a** bare majority of **one** vote. [2]And **your inclination for evil,** to convict, **must be based on a** clear majority of **two.** Thus, a Lesser Sanhedrin must have twenty-two members, for if there is a "congregation which delivers" (ten judges who find the defendant innocent), the defendant cannot be convicted unless there are another twelve judges who find him guilty, making for a majority of two in favor of conviction. [2B] [3]**But** since **a court cannot be** composed **of** an **even** number of judges, to avoid a tie [4]**we** must **add another** judge to the twenty-two. [5]Thus a Lesser Sanhedrin comprises **twenty-three** judges.

וְכַמָּה יְהֵא בָּעִיר [6]**How many** inhabitants **must there be in a town so that it be fit to have** a Lesser **Sanhedrin** established there? [7]**One hundred and twenty**. [8]**Rabbi Neḥemyah** disagrees and **says:** There must be at least **two hundred and thirty**, so that each member of the Sanhedrin may be considered as having authority over ten people, [9]**corresponding to the officers of ten** (see Exodus 18:21), which is the smallest number of people that have officers appointed over them.

GEMARA אַטּוּ גְּזֵילוֹת וַחֲבָלוֹת [10]We learned in the Mishnah: "Monetary cases are adjudicated by a court of three judges. Cases of robbery and inflicted injury are adjudicated by a court of three judges." The Gemara asks: **Are not** cases of **robbery and** inflicted **injury** subsumed under the category of **monetary cases?** Why did the Mishnah list them separately?

אָמַר רַבִּי אַבָּהוּ [11]**Rabbi Abbahu said:** The second clause of the Mishnah was not intended to convey anything new, [12]but rather to explain **what** cases the first clause **is** referring to. The first clause of the Mishnah teaches that monetary cases are adjudicated by three judges. [13]The second clause then explains: **What are the monetary cases** referred to in the first clause? [14]Cases of **robbery and** inflicted **injury.** [15]**But** cases of **admission** — when the plaintiff brings witnesses who testify that the defendant admitted before them that he owes the plaintiff money — **and** cases of **loan** — when the plaintiff brings witnesses who testify that they saw the defendant borrowing money from the plaintiff — are **not** governed by the same rule.

RASHI

הלכך על כרחך עשרים ושנים בעינן, דבציר מעשרה מזכין ליכא למימר, דהא כתיב "והצילו העדה", ותו לא משכחת חובה בציר משנים עשר. **ואין בית דין שקול** — אין עושין בית דין זוגות, שאם יחלקו לחצאין הוי להו פלגא ופלגא, ולא משכחת לה הטייתך לטובה על פי עד אחד, הלכך מוסיפין עליהן עוד אחד. ובגמרא (יז,א) פריך: כיון דאין בית דין שקול ומצרכת עשרים ושלשה, הטייה לרעה על פי שנים לא משכחת לה! **מאה ועשרים** — בגמרא (שם) מפרש כנגד מי. **מאתים ושלשים** — דהיינו עשרים ושלשה עשיריות, שיהא כל אחד מבית דין שר של עשרה, דבציר מעשרה לא אשכחן שררה.

גמרא מה הן קתני — האי גזילות וחבלות, פירושא דדיני ממונות הוא דלא תימא כל דיני ממונות במשמע, ולמעוטי הלואות והודאות שהן באין על גמילות חסדים, ואיכא נעילת דלת בפני לוין, כדאמרינן לקמן, הלכך מעטינהו. ולקמן מפרש ממאי מעטינהו. **הודאות והלואות** — שניהן על עסקי מלוה הן, הודאות — שבא לדון בעדי הודאה, שמביא עדים שאומרים: בפנינו הודה לו. הלואות — שבא לדון בעדי הלואה, שמעידין: בפנינו הלוהו, והלה כופר בשתיהן. וכי האי לישנא טובא איכא בהך מכילתא. הודאה אחר הודאה הלואה אחר הלואה — מצטרפין בפרק שלישי (סנהדרין ל,א) גבי עדים זוממין. ואית דמפרשי: הודאות — שמודה במקצת, הלוואות — שכופר הכל. וראשון עיקר, דמכדי שניהן על עסקי מלוה הם כדאוקימנא טעמא לקמן משום נעילת דלת בפני לוין. מאי שנא דהא קרי הלוואה, והא לא קרי הלוואה, הודאות וכפירות איבעי ליה למיתני! תנא גזילות וחבלות — לפרושא.

HALAKHAH

majority of one, but he can only be convicted by a majority of two." (*Rambam, Sefer Shofetim, Hilkhot Sanhedrin* 8:1.)

וְכַמָּה יְהֵא בָּעִיר And how many must there be in the town. "A Lesser Sanhedrin of twenty-three judges must be established in every city in the Land of Israel which has a hundred and twenty inhabitants or more." (*Rambam, Sefer Shofetim, Hilkhot Sanhedrin* 1:3.)

BACKGROUND

תְּהֵא רְאוּיָה לְסַנְהֶדְרִין So that it be fit to have a Sanhedrin. Although the judges in a court received no salary, and the presence of a court in a city was no burden on the people of that city, nevertheless it did not seem worthy to the Sages that an important court such as a Sanhedrin (of twenty-three judges) should sit in a small town, even if there were worthy Sages there. Hence they determined that a city must be of a certain size for a Sanhedrin to sit there. Naturally this does not require that a Sanhedrin must function in every settlement of that size.

אַטּוּ גְּזֵילוֹת וַחֲבָלוֹת? Are not robberies and inflicted injuries...? The question the Sages are considering is the syntactical meaning of the first sentence. Is it a specific Halakhah (as in the opinion of Rav Abbahu), so that "money judgments" means specifically disputes over money? Or is it a general introductory sentence, meaning any judgment entailing a monetary obligation upon one of the parties, following which the details are presented?

SAGES

רַבִּי נְחֶמְיָה Rabbi Neḥemyah. A Tanna of the fifth generation, Rabbi Neḥemyah was one of Rabbi Akiva's youngest disciples, and he continued to teach the Torah during the era of religious persecution. According to one tradition, he was a descendant of the Biblical leader, Nehemiah the son of Ḥachaliah. His Halakhic teachings are found in various places in the Mishnah, and it seems that he was particularly well versed in Aggadah. In the Talmud, and even more in the Midrashim, many disagreements are found between Rabbi Neḥemyah and his colleague Rabbi Yehudah, and many of his interpretations of Biblical verses are preserved. According to the Jerusalem Talmud, he was a potter, and it is known that he lived very frugally.

רַבִּי אַבָּהוּ Rabbi Abbahu. A Palestinian Amora of the third generation, Rabbi Abbahu was the most important of Rabbi Yoḥanan's disciples. He was the head of a yeshivah and a judge in Caesarea, as well as the representative of the Jewish people to the Romans. He also transmitted teachings in the name of Resh Lakish, Rabbi Elazar, Rabbi Yose bar Ḥanina, and others. Rabbi Zera was a student and colleague of his. His other colleagues were Rabbi Ḥiyya bar Abba, and Rabbi Ammi and Rabbi Assi, the heads of the Tiberias Yeshivah. Among his students were Rabbi Yonah, Rabbi Yose, and Rabbi Yirmeyah. Sages gathered around him, and they became known as the "Rabbis of Caesarea." He was prolific in Aggadah and was an excellent preacher. He spoke Greek well, and taught that language to his daughter. His father-in-law was Rabbi Taḥlifa of Caesarea, and his sons were the Sages Ḥanina, Avimi, and Zera.

[1]וּצְרִיכָא, [2]דְּאִי תָּנָא דִּינֵי מָמוֹנוֹת, [3]הֲוָה אָמִינָא דַּאֲפִילּוּ הוֹדָאוֹת וְהַלְוָאוֹת. [4]תְּנָא גְּזֵילוֹת וַחֲבָלוֹת. [5]וְאִי תָּנָא גְּזֵילוֹת וַחֲבָלוֹת, וְלָא קָתָנֵי דִּינֵי מָמוֹנוֹת, [6]הֲוָה אָמִינָא: הוּא הַדִּין דַּאֲפִילּוּ הוֹדָאוֹת וְהַלְוָאוֹת. [7]וְהַאי דְּקָתָנֵי גְּזֵילוֹת וַחֲבָלוֹת [8]מִשּׁוּם דְּעִיקַּר שְׁלֹשָׁה דִּכְתִיבִי, [9]בִּגְזֵילוֹת וַחֲבָלוֹת כְּתִיבִי. [10]גְּזֵילוֹת, [11]דִּכְתִיב: "וְנִקְרַב בַּעַל הַבַּיִת אֶל הָאֱלֹהִים", [12]חֲבָלוֹת, [13]מַה לִּי חָבַל בְּגוּפוֹ, מַה לִּי חָבַל בְּמָמוֹנוֹ. [14]תָּנָא: מָה הֵן דִּינֵי מָמוֹנוֹת? [15]גְּזֵילוֹת וַחֲבָלוֹת. [16]אֲבָל הוֹדָאוֹת וְהַלְוָאוֹת לֹא. [17]וּלְמַאי? [18]אִילֵימָא דְּלָא בָּעֵינַן

LITERAL TRANSLATION

[1]And it was necessary. [2]For had it taught monetary cases, [3]I might have said even admissions and loans. [4]It taught robberies and injuries. [5]And had it taught robberies and injuries, and it did not teach monetary cases, [6]I might have said the same law [applies] even to admissions and loans. [7]And that which it taught [about] robberies and injuries is [8]because the source of three that is written, [9]regarding robberies and injuries is written. [10]Robberies, [11]for it is written: "And the master of the house shall be brought to the judges." [12]Injuries, [13]what is it to me if he injured his body, what is it to me if he injured his property? [14]It taught: What are monetary cases? [15]Robberies and injuries. [16]But admissions and loans not. [17]And for what? [18]If you say that we do not need

TRANSLATION AND COMMENTARY

וּצְרִיכָא [1]The Gemara now explains why the Mishnah was so formulated. **It was necessary** for the Mishnah to teach the law first in general terms and then to add a clarification. [2]**For had** the Mishnah taught that only **monetary cases** are adjudicated by three judges, [3]**I might have said** that this regulation applies **even** to cases of **admission and loan.** [4]**Therefore,** the Mishnah **taught** in the second clause that cases of **robbery and** inflicted **injury** are adjudicated by three judges, implying that cases of admission and loan are not governed by the same rule. [5]**And had** the Mishnah **taught** that only cases of **robbery and** inflicted **injury** are adjudicated by three judges, **without** first **teaching** that three judges are required in **monetary cases,** [6]**I might have said that the law applies** not only to cases of robbery and inflicted injury, but **even to** cases of **admission and loan.** [7]**And** I would have said that the Mishnah only **taught** the law with respect to cases of **robbery and** inflicted **injury,** [8]**because the** Biblical **source that three** judges are required in monetary cases [9]**is found** in the passage dealing with **robbery and** inflicted **injury.** [10]The Gemara explains: Three judges are required to adjudicate cases of **robbery,** [11]**for the verses** relating to an unpaid bailee who was accused by the depositor of having taken for himself the article that had been entrusted to his safekeeping **state** (Exodus 22:7-8): **"And the master of the house shall be brought to the judges";** "The cause of both parties shall come before the judges"; "Whom the judges shall condemn." The mention of "judges" three times teaches that a case of robbery must be adjudicated by a court of three judges (see below, p.3b). [12]And it follows logically that the same law applies to cases of inflicted **injury,** [13]for **what difference** does it make **whether** someone **injured** another person's **body, or injured** another person's **property?** If three judges are required in cases of robbery, the same number of judges should be required in cases of inflicted injury. [14]**Therefore,** the Mishnah **taught:** Monetary cases are adjudicated by three judges. And then it added the clarification: **What are the monetary cases** referred to here? [15]Cases of **robbery and** inflicted **injury.** [16]**But** cases of **admission and loan** are **not** governed by the same law.

וּלְמַאי [17]The Gemara asks: **And regarding which** aspect of the law are cases of admission and loan treated differently from cases of robbery and inflicted injury? [18]**If you say that** in cases of admission and loan, a

RASHI

"ונקרב בעל הבית אל האלהים" — מדכתב בפרשה "אלהים" שלשה זימני, נפקא לן דבעינן שלשה, והאי קרא כתיב בשומר חנם, וזה טוענו ששלח יד בפקדונו, דהיינו גזילות. **מה לי חבל בממונו** — ממשמע שנאמר שלשה בחובל בממונו, אף חובל בגופו בכלל, הלכך בהא נמי כתיב ביה. **ואי לא תנא דיני ממונות, הוה אמינא הנך** — משום דבגווייהו כתב נקט להו, ולעולם הוא הדין לדיני מלוה, להכי תנא: דיני ממונות, ותנא: ומה הן דיני ממונות? גזילות וחבלות, למעוטי הודאות והלואות, דאם כן דכולן במשמע, כיון דתנא דיני ממונות ניסתוק! **ולמאי** — הלכתא שייריהו חוץ לדיני מלוה, למעוטינהו מאי? **דברי הכל** — לקמן (ו,א) קאי, דפליגי בפשרה, ואשמעינן רבי אבהו דבדין כולהו מודו דבעינן שלשה.

NOTES

הָאֱלֹהִים The judges. In Biblical Hebrew, the word *elohim* almost always — over two thousand times — refers to the God of Israel. The word is sometimes used in reference to powerful people, judges in particular. In Psalms 82:1, both meanings of the word are found in the same verse: "God [אֱלֹהִים] stands in the congregation of God; he judges among judges [אֱלֹהִים]." Regarding the Biblical passage pertaining to an unpaid bailee, it is clear from the context that the term refers to judges.

שְׁלשָׁה — [1]וְהָאָמַר רַבִּי אַבָּהוּ: [2]שְׁנַיִם שֶׁדָּנוּ דִּינֵי מָמוֹנוֹת, [3]לְדִבְרֵי הַכֹּל אֵין דִּינֵיהֶם דִּין! [4]אֶלָּא דְּלָא בָּעֵינַן מוּמְחִין. [5]מַאי קָסָבַר? [6]אִי קָסָבַר עֵירוּב פָּרָשִׁיּוֹת כָּתוּב כָּאן, [7]לִיבָּעֵי נַמִי מוּמְחִין. [8]וְאִי קָסָבַר אֵין עֵירוּב פָּרָשִׁיּוֹת כָּתוּב כָּאן, [9]שְׁלשָׁה לָמָּה לִי?

LITERAL TRANSLATION

three — [1]but surely Rabbi Abbahu said: [2]Two who adjudicate monetary cases, [3]according to everyone their decision is not a decision!

[4]Rather, that we do not need experts.

[5]What does he maintain? [6]If he maintains a mixture of passages is written here, [7]let him also require experts. [8]And if he maintains that a mixture of passages is not written here, [9]why do I need three?

TRANSLATION AND COMMENTARY

court of **three** judges **is not required,** there is a difficulty, [1]**for surely Rabbi Abbahu** himself **said** differently. [2]For Rabbi Abbahu said: If **two** judges **adjudicated monetary cases** of any kind — even a case of admission or loan, [3]**all agree that their decision is not a** binding **decision**, for a court cannot consist of fewer than three judges.

אֶלָּא [4]**Rather,** it must be that cases of admission and loan are treated differently from cases of robbery and inflicted injury, in that cases of robbery and inflicted injury must be adjudicated by expert, ordained judges, whereas cases of admission and loan **do not require a court** consisting of **expert,** ordained **judges,** but may be adjudicated by three laymen.

מַאי קָסָבַר [5]The Gemara wishes to clarify the Mishnah's position. **What does** the Tanna of our Mishnah **maintain?** As noted, the triple mention of the word "judges" in the Biblical passage dealing with an unpaid bailee who was suspected of misappropriating a deposit teaches us that three judges are required in cases of robbery and inflicted injury. The term אֱלֹהִים which is used in that very passage for "judges" — a term which denotes authority and office — teaches that the judges before whom such cases are to be brought must be ordained. Now, elsewhere (*Bava Kamma* 97a), the Amoraim disagree about whether the Biblical section referring to an unpaid bailee (Exodus 22:6-8) deals exclusively with that subject, or whether mixed into that passage is a clause which really belongs in the section dealing with loans (Exodus 22:24-26). What is the position of the Tanna of our Mishnah who says that three judges are required in cases of loan and admission, but they need not be authorized? [6]**If he maintains that this is a mixture of Biblical passages,** as some Sages maintain (*Bava Kamma* 97a) that a clause which really belongs in the passage dealing with loans (Exodus 22:24-26), is mixed in the Biblical passage referring to an unpaid bailee (Exodus 22:6-8) [7]**he should also require expert,** ordained **judges** to adjudicate cases regarding loans, for according to this position the term אֱלֹהִים — the source for ordained judges — is found in a section that not only deals with an unpaid bailee, but also with loans. [8]**And if he maintains that there is here no mixture of Biblical passages,** but rather that the passage dealing with an unpaid bailee refers exclusively to that subject, [9]**why does he require three** judges in cases of loan and admission, for the source requiring three judges is found in a section that deals only with an unpaid bailee, and not with loans?!

RASHI

מומחין — סמוכין, ונטלו רשות מנשיא לדון כדאמרינן לקמן בפירקין (ה,א). **ומאי קסבר** — תנא דידן דמעטינהו? **אי קסבר עירוב פרשיות כתיב כאן** — דאיכא למאן דאמר ב״הגוזל עצים״ (בבא קמא קז,א) שהפרשיות הכתובות ב״אלה המשפטים״ מעורבבות הן, שיש מקרא כתוב בפרשה זו שאינו יכול לעמוד בה, אלא מפרשה אחרת הוא, כגון ״אשר יאמר כי הוא זה״ (שמות כב) דילפינן מיניה: מודה במקצת הטענה — ישבע כו׳, שכתב בשומר חנם, לאו אשומר חנם קאי, דשומרין אף על פי שלא הודו במקצת חייבין לישבע. דהודאה מקצת הטענה אפרשת ד״אם כסף תלוה״ קאי (שם), דהתם הוא דבעינן הודאה במקצת, ואי לא מודה כלום, חזקה — אם טענת התובע אמת, לא היה יכול זה להעיז פניו נגדו ולומר: לא הלויתני, הלכך אפילו שבועה לא בעי, אבל בפיקדון דליכא גמילות חסדים מעיז פניו וכופר הכל, ובעי שבועה. והאי תנא דמתניתין אי סבירא ליה נמי דהאי ״אשר יאמר כי הוא זה״ בהלואה משתעי, הרי נאמר אלהים בהאי קרא, דמשמע מומחין לשון שררה ורבנות כדמתרגמינן ״ראה נתתיך אלהים לפרעה״ (שם ז) לשון רבנות וליבעי מומחין. **ואי קסבר** — דהאי קרא לאו בהלואה משתעי. **שלשה מנלן?** — בהלואה, הא מתלתא אלהים נפקא לן לקמן (ג,ב), ואלהים בהלואה לא כתיב.

BACKGROUND

מוּמְחִין **Expert.** Here the term refers to someone who is authorized to do something for which he is clearly qualified. According to the Halakhah, an expert judge must have been ordained by other ordained rabbis who gave him the title of "Rabbi." Hence he has the authorization and endorsement of the highest Jewish authority that he is permitted to serve as a judge in money matters.

NOTES

עֵירוּב פָּרָשִׁיּוֹת **A mixture of passages.** This expression is interpreted in several ways. The Geonim gave it quite a broad meaning. In their opinion, anywhere in the Torah where rulings are derived from each other is an example of a "mixture of passages." Similarly, when two rulings can be derived from a single verse, this too is a "mixture of passages." Further, when a single verse teaches laws of various types, this is a "mixture of passages" as well. One

HALAKHAH

שְׁנַיִם שֶׁדָּנוּ **Two who judged.** "If two judges adjudicated a monetary case, their decision is not binding, unless the two litigants had previously agreed to accept the decision," following Rabbi Abbahu against Shmuel. (*Shulḥan Arukh, Ḥoshen Mishpat* 3:1-2.)

דְּלָא בָּעֵינַן מוּמְחִין **That we do not need expert, ordained judges.** "A court adjudicating monetary cases must have at least three members. The court is valid even if none of its three members is an expert, ordained judge, provided that at least one of them is somewhat familiar with the law." (*Rema,* following *Tur* in the name of *Rosh,* based on the Gemara below, p.3a.) (*Shulḥan Arukh, Ḥoshen Mishpat* 3:1.)

SAGES

רַבִּי חֲנִינָא Rabbi Ḥanina. When the name of the Amora Rabbi Ḥanina is used without a patronymic in the Talmud, the reference is to Rabbi Ḥanina bar Ḥama, a first-generation Amora from Eretz Israel. Rabbi Ḥanina originally came from Babylonia, although he immigrated to Eretz Israel at a relatively early age, and studied there with Rabbi Yehudah HaNasi, who was very fond of him, and indeed remarked that Rabbi Ḥanina was "not a human being, but an angel." Rabbi Ḥanina also studied with Rabbi Yehudah HaNasi's most distinguished students, in particular with Rabbi Ḥiyya. On his deathbed, Rabbi Yehudah HaNasi designated Rabbi Ḥanina as the head of his yeshivah, although the latter, in his great modesty, refused to accept the position as long as his older colleague, Rabbi Efes, was still alive.

Rabbi Ḥanina lived in Sepphoris, where he earned a living as a dealer in honey, from which he became wealthy and established a large academy. He was renowned for his acuity, as well as for his righteousness and piety.

Numerous Halakhic and Aggadic teachings of Rabbi Ḥanina appear in the Babylonian and the Jerusalem Talmud. He lived to a great age, and had many students over an extended period, among them Rabbi Yehoshua ben Levi, a student-colleague of his, and Rabbi Yoḥanan, who studied with him for many years.

His son was the Amora Rabbi Ḥama the son of Rabbi Ḥanina.

BACKGROUND

בְּדְרִישָׁה וּבַחֲקִירָה Inquiry and investigation. These are the obligations imposed upon judges according to the Torah (Deuteronomy 13:15) which says that the witnesses must be questioned thoroughly ("then shalt thou inquire, and make search, and ask diligently..."). In the following chapters of the tractate this form of examination is described, and it is explained that if witnesses cannot indicate precisely the place and the time of the event, or if

TRANSLATION AND COMMENTARY

לְעוֹלָם [1]The Gemara explains: **In fact,** the Tanna of our Mishnah **maintains that there is here a mixture of Biblical passages.** [2]**And by right he should require expert,** ordained, **judges,** not only in cases of robbery and inflicted injury, but **also** in cases of loans and admissions. [3]**And the reason that expert,** ordained, **judges are not required** in cases of loans **is** the same as that **cited** in **Rabbi Ḥanina's ruling.** [4]**For Rabbi Ḥanina said:** A court is obliged to subject the evidence of witnesses to searching scrutiny. [5]**By Torah law inquiry** (*derishah* — examination of the substance of the witnesses' testimony) **and investigation** (*ḥakirah* — examination of the witnesses' statements with respect to the time and place at which the event about which they are testifying occurred) **are required in both monetary and capital cases,** [3A] [6]**as it is said** (Leviticus 24:22): **"You shall have one manner of law,"** equating monetary and capital cases. And since the Torah explicitly states that inquiry and investigation are required in capital cases, this should apply to monetary cases as well. [7]**What,** then, **is the reason** the Sages **said** that in **monetary cases inquiry and investigation are not required?** [8]**So as not to bolt the door before borrowers.** Potential lenders might not lend money for fear that they will not be able to recover what is owed to them. A borrower might deny having taken the loan, and the testimony of witnesses who were present when the loan was transacted might be disqualified because of inconsistencies found in their testimony during inquiry and investigation. Similarly, argues the Gemara, the Sages dispensed with the Torah requirement that disputes involving loans must be adjudicated by courts consisting of expert, ordained, judges, and recognized courts composed of laymen. The Sages were concerned that potential lenders would not lend money for fear that they would not be able to find ordained judges to hear their case if a borrower failed to repay them.

[1]לְעוֹלָם קָסָבַר עֵירוּב פָּרָשִׁיּוֹת כָּתוּב כָּאן. [2]וּבְדִין הוּא דְּלִיבְעֵי נַמִי מוּמְחִין. [3]וְהַאי דְּלָא בָּעֵינַן מוּמְחִין מִשּׁוּם דְּרַבִּי חֲנִינָא. [4]דְּאָמַר רַבִּי חֲנִינָא: [5]דְּבַר תּוֹרָה, אֶחָד דִּינֵי מָמוֹנוֹת וְאֶחָד דִּינֵי נְפָשׁוֹת בִּדְרִישָׁה וּבַחֲקִירָה, [3A] [6]שֶׁנֶּאֱמַר: "מִשְׁפַּט אֶחָד יִהְיֶה לָכֶם". [7]וּמַה טַּעַם אָמְרוּ דִּינֵי מָמוֹנוֹת לָא בָּעֵינַן דְּרִישָׁה וַחֲקִירָה? [8]כְּדֵי שֶׁלֹּא תִּנְעוֹל דֶּלֶת בִּפְנֵי לוֹוִין.

LITERAL TRANSLATION

[1]In fact he maintains a mixture of passages is written here. [2]And by right he requires also experts. [3]And that we do not require experts is because of Rabbi Ḥanina['s ruling]. [4]For Rabbi Ḥanina said: [5][By] Torah law, both monetary cases and capital cases require inquiry and investigation, [3A] [6]as it is said: "You shall have one manner of law." [7]And what is the reason they said [that] monetary cases do not require inquiry and investigation? [8]So as not to bolt the door in the face of borrowers.

RASHI

משום דרבי חנינא — ותקנתא דרבנן הוא. **בדרישה וחקירה** — צריך לבדוק את העדים באיזה יום באיזו שעה הלוהו. **שנאמר משפט אחד יהיה לכם** — ממונות כנפשות. וכיון דכתיב דרישה וחקירה בדיני נפשות, דכתיב (דברים יג) "ודרשת" "וחקרת", הוא הדין לדיני ממונות. **שלא תנעול דלת** — שימנעו מלהלוות, שמא יכפור, והעדים יטעו, ולא תהא עדותן מכוונת — ויפסיד. והכא נמי, שמא לא ימצא מומחין לכופו לדין.

NOTES

of these interpretations is exemplified by the interpretation found also in *Tosafot* (*Bava Kamma* 107a), which maintains that the expression means that what was said in the verse, "and both of them shall come before the judges," refers to different details, regarding both a partial admission and a counter-claim (see *Ran*). And *Rabbenu Ḥananel* says the meaning is that the passages found in the Torah portion of *Mishpatim* (the section in the book of Exodus where these laws appear) is a "mixture of passages." That is, the passages are mixed up so that the laws appearing in one passage apply to the other passages as well.

מִשְׁפַּט אֶחָד יִהְיֶה לָכֶם You shall have one manner of law. *Ramah* notes that the proof text (Leviticus 24:22), "You shall have one manner of law," refers to what was written in the previous verse (21): "And he that kills a beast, he shall make restitution for it; and he that kills a man, he shall be put to death." The second verse draws an analogy between the cases discussed in the first verse — monetary cases (the killing of a beast) and capital cases (the killing of a man).

The Rishonim ask: Inquiry and investigation are also mentioned in the Biblical passage dealing with false, conspiring witnesses (Deuteronomy 19:18), the laws regarding which are applied not only in capital cases, but also in monetary cases! So why does Rabbi Ḥanina derive from the verse, "You shall have one manner of law," that monetary cases also require inquiry and investigation? *Rosh* answers that if we only had the passage pertaining to false, conspiring witnesses, we might have thought that inquiry and investigation are only required when a second set of witnesses comes to invalidate the testimony of the first set, calling into question the truth of the first witnesses' testimony. But otherwise, the witnesses' testimony does not have to be scrutinized. Thus, the verse, "You shall have one manner of law," comes and teaches that inquiry and investigation are required in all cases.

כְּדֵי שֶׁלֹּא תִּנְעוֹל דֶּלֶת In order not to bolt the door. As a

HALAKHAH

בְּדְרִישָׁה וּבַחֲקִירָה Inquiry and investigation. "In monetary cases, except in cases of inflicted injury, the evidence of the witnesses need not be subjected to inquiry and investigation. If, however, the court suspects that the witnesses

[1] אֶלָּא מֵעַתָּה טָעוּ לֹא יְשַׁלְּמוּ! [2] כָּל שֶׁכֵּן אַתָּה נוֹעֵל דֶּלֶת בִּפְנֵי לוֹוִין.
[3] אִי הָכִי, תַּרְתֵּי קָתָנֵי: דִּינֵי מָמוֹנוֹת בִּשְׁלֹשָׁה הֶדְיוֹטוֹת. [4] גְּזֵילוֹת וַחֲבָלוֹת בִּשְׁלֹשָׁה מוּמְחִין. [5] וְעוֹד: ״שְׁלֹשָׁה״ ״שְׁלֹשָׁה״ לָמָּה לִי?

LITERAL TRANSLATION

[1] But now [if] they erred they should not pay! [2] All the more so you bolt the door in the face of borrowers.

[3] If so, it teaches two [laws]: Monetary cases by three ordinary persons. [4] Robberies and inflicted injuries by three experts. [5] And furthermore, "three" "three" why do I need [them]?

TRANSLATION AND COMMENTARY

אֶלָּא מֵעַתָּה [1] The Gemara states: **Now** that you said that the Sages enacted that a court of laymen is competent to adjudicate monetary cases (except cases of robbery and inflicted injury), **if** laymen **erred** and issued an erroneous ruling, **they should not** be liable to **pay** for the damage they caused! However, the Mishnah (*Bekhorot* 28b) states that only ordained judges are exempt from paying for the damage that they caused.

כָּל [2] The Gemara responds: **All the more so would the door be bolted before borrowers,** since potential lenders would fear that the judges might erroneously exempt their debtors from obligation, causing them to suffer a loss which they cannot recover from the judges who erred in their judgment.

אִי הָכִי [3] The Gemara now questions Rabbi Abbahu's interpretation of the Mishnah. **If** indeed it is **so**, that cases of loans and admissions must be adjudicated by three judges who need not be ordained, and only cases of robbery and inflicted injury must be brought before ordained judges, why did Rabbi Abbahu interpret the second clause of the Mishnah — "robbery and inflicted injury are adjudicated by three" — as teaching the terms of reference of the first clause of the Mishnah — "monetary cases are adjudicated by three"? He should have explained the Mishnah in a simpler manner, saying that the Mishnah **teaches** us **two** separate **laws,** dividing them into two clauses to tell us that they are not entirely identical in their requirements. The first clause teaches that **monetary cases** (loans and admissions) are adjudicated **by** a court of **three laymen.** [4] And the second clause teaches that cases of **robbery and inflicted injury** are adjudicated **by** a court of **three ordained judges.** The Gemara now raises a second objection against Rabbi Abbahu's interpretation of the Mishnah: [5] **And furthermore,** if indeed the second clause of the Mishnah teaches the terms of reference of the first clause, **why did** the Mishnah state the word **"three" twice?** The Mishnah should have read: Monetary cases, including cases of robbery and inflicted injury, are adjudicated by three judges. The Mishnah's use of the word "three" at the end of each clause implies that it is teaching two separate laws!

RASHI

אלא מעתה טעו — הדיוטות בדיני ממונות לא ישלמו, דכיון דברשות רבנן קא נחתי הוו להו כמומחין, וכל המומחה לבית דין אם טעה — פטור מלשלם, כדלקמן ב״אחד דיני ממונות״ (לג,א), הא שאינו מומחה — חייב. **כל שכן שאתה נועל דלת** — דסבר: דלמא טעו בי דינא, ופטרי ליה, ומפסידנא. **אי הכי** — דבהודאות והלואות שלשה בעינן למה ליה לרבי אבהו לאוקומה למתניתין ב״מה הן קתני״? **תרתי קתני** — מלי למימר: דיני ממונות — דהיינו הודאות והלואות — בשלשה כל דהו, וגזילות וחבלות — בשלשה מומחין, ומשום דחלוקין בדיניהן לא כללינהו בחד כללא. **ועוד** — אי חדא קתני, למה לי למיתני תרי

their testimony contains a contradiction, even in a small detail, it is unacceptable. Careful examination is likely to disqualify many witnesses and thus to end trials for technical reasons.

LANGUAGE

הֶדְיוֹט **Layman.** From the Greek ἰδιώτης, *idiotes*, meaning "common man," "layman," or "ordinary person." All these meanings are found in Rabbinic literature, although the word הֶדְיוֹט is used primarily to distinguish between common people and those in high office.

NOTES

general rule, the Rabbis may enact that a positive precept prescribed by Torah law need not be fulfilled in some cases by invoking the principle: שֵׁב וְלֹא תַעֲשֶׂה — "sit and do not do." Thus, the Rabbis are authorized to relax the rules pertaining to witnesses in monetary cases, and say that inquiry and investigation are not required. However, the Rabbis' authority to uproot a Torah law by means of a positive act (קוּם עֲשֵׂה — "get up and do") is far more limited. How then could the Rabbis dispense with the Torah requirement that monetary cases must be adjudicated by courts consisting of three expert, ordained, judges, and empower three ordinary laymen to serve as judges? The Rabbinic enactment was apparently based on the rule הֶפְקֵר בֵּית דִּין הֶפְקֵר — "property declared ownerless by the court is ownerless." According to this rule, the Rabbis are authorized to divest a person of ownership of property, and transfer it to another person. This authority allows the Rabbis almost a free hand in the various fields of civil law (*Sanhedrei Ketanah*).

טָעוּ לֹא יְשַׁלְּמוּ **If they erred they should not pay.** Our commentary follows *Rashi,* who understands that the Gemara is arguing that since the Rabbis enacted that laymen are competent to adjudicate monetary cases, laymen should also be exempt from paying for the damage caused by their errors in judgment, like expert, ordained judges. *Tosafot* argues that since the Rabbis enacted that laymen may adjudicate monetary cases, in order to prevent potential lenders from bolting the door before borrowers, they should have exempted those laymen from liability for their erroneous judgments, so as not to discourage them from participating in the judicial process, which would defeat the purpose of their enactment. Elsewhere in the tractate (*Sanhedrin* 32b), *Rashi* offers a third explanation: The Gemara argues that since the Rabbis enacted that inquiry and investigation of the witnesses are not required in monetary cases, lay judges who err in their decision should be exempt from liability, for they can argue that had they examined the witnesses as required by Torah law, the matter would have been clarified and they would not have issued their erroneous judgment.

״שְׁלֹשָׁה״ ״שְׁלֹשָׁה״ לָמָּה לִי? **"Three" "three" — why do I need them?** *Tosafot* note that sometimes the Gemara asks

HALAKHAH

are lying, it must investigate their testimony so that the truth is revealed." (*Shulḥan Arukh, Ḥoshen Mishpat* 30:1.)

LITERAL TRANSLATION

[1] Rather, Rava said: It teaches two [laws] [2] on account of Rabbi Ḥanina.

[3] Rav Aḥa the son of Rav Ika said: [4] According to Torah law one is also qualified, [5] for it is stated: "In righteousness shall you judge your neighbor."

[6] But on account of those who sit at [street] corners.

[7] But even with three, might they not all be [people] who sit at [street] corners.

[8] It is impossible that there is not among them one who is learned.

[1] אֶלָּא, אָמַר רָבָא: תַּרְתֵּי קָתָנֵי,
[2] מִשּׁוּם דְּרַבִּי חֲנִינָא.
[3] רַב אַחָא בְּרֵיהּ דְּרַב אִיקָא אָמַר: [4] מִדְּאוֹרַיְיתָא חַד נַמִי כָּשֵׁר, [5] שֶׁנֶּאֱמַר: "בְּצֶדֶק תִּשְׁפֹּט עֲמִיתֶךָ".
[6] אֶלָּא מִשּׁוּם יוֹשְׁבֵי קְרָנוֹת.
[7] אַטּוּ בִּתְלָתָא, מִי לָא הָווּ יוֹשְׁבֵי קְרָנוֹת?
[8] אִי אֶפְשָׁר דְּלֵית בְּהוּ חַד דְּגָמֵיר.

TRANSLATION AND COMMENTARY

אֶלָּא [1] **Rather, Rava said:** Indeed, the Mishnah **teaches** us **two** separate **laws.** The first clause teaches that monetary cases concerning loans and admissions are adjudicated by a court of three laymen. And the second clause teaches that cases of robbery and inflicted injury are adjudicated by a court of three ordained judges. The reason for this is that the Rabbis enacted that monetary cases (to the exclusion of cases of robbery and inflicted injury) may be heard before three laymen, [2] **on account** of the argument put forward by **Rabbi Ḥanina** that certain Torah requirements must be relaxed to ensure that the door is not bolted before borrowers.

רַב אַחָא בְּרֵיהּ דְּרַב אִיקָא [3] The Gemara now presents a different interpretation of the Mishnah. **Rav Aḥa the son of Rav Ika said:** As was argued above by Rava, the Mishnah teaches us two separate things — that monetary cases concerning loans and admissions are adjudicated by a court of three laymen, and that cases of robbery and inflicted injury are adjudicated by a court of three ordained judges. But whereas, according to Rava, the Rabbis relaxed the requirements set by the Torah, and allowed laymen to judge monetary cases, according to Rav Aḥa the son of Rav Ika, the Rabbis imposed more stringent requirements than did the Torah. [4] For, **by Torah law,** three judges are required in cases of robbery and inflicted injury, but **even a single** judge **is fit** to adjudicate cases of loans and admissions, [5] **as it says** (Leviticus 19:15): **"In righteousness shall you judge your neighbor,"** the singular form of the verb "you shall judge" (תִּשְׁפֹּט) teaching that certain cases may be heard by a court of one.

אֶלָּא [6] **But** the Rabbis enacted that three judges are required even in cases of loans and admissions, **on account of** the idle **people who sit at street corners** and are ignorant of the law. The Rabbis were concerned that, when the courts are busy, people might present their claims before those who sit idly at street corners with nothing to do, they being the only ones available to hear the case.

אַטּוּ בִּתְלָתָא [7] The Gemara objects: Even if there are **three** judges, **can** it **not be** that all three are ignorant **people who sit at street corners?**

אִי אֶפְשָׁר [8] The Gemara answers: **It is impossible that there is not among them one who is knowledgeable** about the laws of loans and admissions.

RASHI

זמני "שלשה"? הכי איבעי למיתני: דיני ממונות, שהן גזילות וחבלות – בשלשה. **תרתי קתני** – דודאי שלשה בעינן, דעירוב פרשיות כתיב כאן, ומיהו בהדיוטות סגי משום דרבי חנינא. והכי קאמר: דיני ממונות, דהיינו הודאות והלואות – בשלשה הדיוטות, וגזילות וחבלות – בשלשה מומחין. **מדאורייתא חד נמי כשר** – בהודאה והלואה, דכתיב "תשפוט" לשון יחיד, ואין עירוב פרשיות כאן, ומתניתין ודאי תרתי קתני, כדאמרן. ומיהו שלשה בהודאות והלואות, לאו מדאורייתא – אלא מדרבנן. **גזירה משום יושבי קרנות** – תגרין, שאין בקיאין בטיב דינין, ויזכה את החייב ויחייב את הזכאי. **דגמיר** – ששמע מחכמים ומדיינין הלכות דין מלוה.

NOTES

a question of this sort — why did the Tannaitic source use a certain word twice in two consecutive clauses? — while other times it does not raise the question. It has been suggested that there is special reason to raise the question here, for we see that, later in the Mishnah, several different cases are included in a single clause, with the requirement for three judges being mentioned only once, as in "damages and half-damages, double compensation, and fourfold and fivefold compensation by three." This being the case, if the second clause of the Mishnah comes merely to teach the terms of reference of the first clause, and not to teach a new regulation, the Mishnah should surely not have mentioned the word "three" in both clauses (*Rabbi Yosef Rafael*).

חַד נַמִי כָּשֵׁר **One is also qualified.** According to Rav Aḥa the son of Rav Ika, by Torah law a single judge is fit to adjudicate monetary cases. *Ramah* notes that the same verse, "In righteousness shall you judge your neighbor," which teaches us that one judge suffices, also teaches that while the judge need not be an authorized expert (מוּמְחֶה), he must be knowledgeable concerning the law, for if not the judgment cannot be issued "in righteousness."

אִי אֶפְשָׁר דְּלֵית בְּהוּ חַד דְּגָמֵיר **It is impossible that there is not among them one who is knowledgeable.** Presumably, the litigants would prefer that the case be heard by a qualified judge, but the Rabbis were concerned that the litigants might mistakenly choose an idle person who is available to hear the case but totally ignorant of the law. Thus, they enacted that three judges are required, for it is highly unlikely that the parties would thrice make the same mistake (*Rabbi Yoel ben Moshe*).

SAGES

רָבָא **Rava.** A great Babylonian Amora of the fourth generation, Rava was a colleague of Abaye. His father, Rav Yosef bar Ḥama, was also a famous Sage. Rava's outstanding teacher was Rav Naḥman bar Ya'akov, and Rava was also a student of Rav Ḥisda, with whom he studied together with his colleague Rami bar Ḥama. Rav Ḥisda's daughter married Rami bar Ḥama, and when Rami bar Ḥama died she married Rava. Rava also studied with Rav Yosef. He founded a yeshivah in Meḥoza. In all the many Halakhic controversies between him and Abaye the Halakhah follows him, except for six cases (יע״ל קג״ם — see *Bava Metzia,* Part II, p.26). After Abaye's death, Rava was appointed head of the Pumbedita Yeshivah, which he transferred to his home city of Meḥoza. Among his students were Rav Pappa and Rav Huna the son of Rav Yehoshua. A great number of Sages transmit teachings in his name: Rav Zevid, Mar the son of Rav Yosef, Rav Mesharshiya, Rav Pappi, Ravina, and others. After his death the yeshivah of Meḥoza split in two, and Rav Naḥman bar Yitzḥak took his place as the head of the Pumbedita Yeshivah, while Rav Pappa established a yeshivah of his own in Neresh.

רַב אַחָא בְּרֵיהּ דְּרַב אִיקָא **Rav Aḥa the son of Rav Ika.** A fifth-generation Babylonian Amora, Rav Aḥa the son of Rav Ika was the nephew of Rav Aḥa bar Ya'akov (both Sages apparently lived in the same city, Papunya). Rav Aḥa the son of Rav Ika studied with many fourth- and fifth-generation Amoraim, and engaged in Halakhic discussions with Rav Pappa, and later with Rav Ashi. His teachings — some of which were transmitted by his student, Rav Huna bar Manoaḥ — are cited in various places in the Talmud.

BACKGROUND

יוֹשְׁבֵי קְרָנוֹת **Those who sit at street corners.** Most commentators explain יוֹשְׁבֵי קְרָנוֹת to mean "people who do not attend the Bet HaMidrash but rather spend their time in idle chatter on

[1]אֶלָּא מֵעַתָּה טָעוּ לֹא יְשַׁלְּמוּ! [2]כָּל שֶׁכֵּן דִּנְפִישִׁי יוֹשְׁבֵי קְרָנוֹת. [3]מַאי אִיכָּא בֵּין רָבָא לְרַב אַחָא בְּרֵיהּ דְּרַב אִיקָא? [4]אִיכָּא בֵּינַיְיהוּ דְּאָמַר שְׁמוּאֵל: [5]שְׁנַיִם שֶׁדָּנוּ — דִּינֵיהֶן דִּין, [6]אֶלָּא שֶׁנִּקְרְאוּ בֵּית דִּין חָצוּף. [7]לְרָבָא לֵית לֵיהּ דִּשְׁמוּאֵל. [8]לְרַב אַחָא בְּרֵיהּ דְּרַב אִיקָא אִית לֵיהּ דִּשְׁמוּאֵל. [9]"נֶזֶק וַחֲצִי נֶזֶק וכו'". [10]נֶזֶק הַיְינוּ חֲבָלוֹת! [11]מִשּׁוּם דְּקָא בָּעֵי לְמִיתְנָא חֲצִי נֶזֶק, [12]תָּנֵי נַמִי נֶזֶק שָׁלֵם. [13]חֲצִי נֶזֶק נַמִי הַיְינוּ חֲבָלוֹת!

LITERAL TRANSLATION

[1]But now if they erred they should not pay! [2]All the more so will there be more [of those] who sit at [street] corners. [3]What is [the difference] between Rava and Rav Aḥa the son of Rav Ika? [4]There is [a difference] between them [regarding] what Shmuel said: [5]Two who judged — their decision is a decision, [6]but they are called an impudent court. [7]Rava does not agree with (lit., "have") Shmuel. [8]Rav Aḥa the son of Rav Ika agrees with Shmuel. [9]"Damages and half-damages, etc." [10]Damages is the same as inflicted injuries! [11]Since he wished to teach half-damages, [12]he taught also full damages. [13]Half-damages is also the same as inflicted injuries!

TRANSLATION AND COMMENTARY

אֶלָּא מֵעַתָּה [1]The Gemara continues: **Now** that you say that laymen can serve as judges, and not only by Rabbinic enactment, but even according to Torah law, **if** laymen **err** in their judgment **they should not** be liable to **pay** for the damage which that decision might cause!

כָּל שֶׁכֵּן [2]The Gemara addresses this point: Had the Sages also exempted laymen judges who err in their judgment from liability for the damage which they cause, then **all the more so would** idle **people who sit at street corners** participate in the judicial process, for they would know that they could not be held liable for erroneous rulings.

מַאי אִיכָּא [3]The Gemara continues: Both Rava and Rav Aḥa the son of Rav Ika agree that cases of loans and admissions are judged by a court of three laymen, and that cases of robbery and inflicted injury require three ordained judges. **What,** then, **is the** practical **difference between** the position of **Rava and** the position of **Rav Aḥa the son of Rav Ika?**

אִיכָּא בֵּינַיְיהוּ [4]The Gemara answers: **There is a difference between** the two positions **with respect to what Shmuel said,** for he said: [5]If **two judged** a monetary case, **their judgment is binding** on the litigants, [6]**but** these two judges **are called an impudent court,** for the case should have been heard by a court of three. [7]**Rava does not agree with Shmuel,** for Rava maintains that three judges are required by Torah law, and therefore a judgment by two is invalid. [8]And **Rav Aḥa the son of Rav Ika agrees with Shmuel** that a judgment reached by two judges is valid, for he maintains that, by Torah law, only one judge is needed, and the Rabbinic enactment requiring three judges does not invalidate a decision handed down by two.

נֶזֶק וַחֲצִי נֶזֶק [9]The Gemara now examines the next clause of the Mishnah: "Cases involving the payment of **damages and half-damages** are adjudicated by a court of three." The Gemara expresses its astonishment at the repetition of something which appears to have been mentioned earlier in the Mishnah: [10]Surely **damages is** one of the payments included in cases of **inflicted injury** already mentioned in the second clause of the Mishnah!

מִשּׁוּם [11]The Gemara accounts for the apparent superfluity. **Since** the Tanna of the Mishnah **wished to teach** that cases involving the payment of **half-damages** are adjudicated by three judges, and that we would not have known from the earlier clause pertaining to cases of inflicted injury, [12]**he also taught** that cases involving the payment of **full damages** are adjudicated by a court of three.

חֲצִי נֶזֶק [13]The Gemara is not satisfied with this answer. But surely **half-damages is also** subsumed under the category of **inflicted injury,** for if as the result of an animal's abnormal and unexpected behavior, it causes someone bodily injury, the animal's owner is liable for half of the damage. Why, then, did the

RASHI

טעו לא ישלמו — דהא ברשות נחתי אפילו מדאורייתא. **כל שכן דנפישי יושבי קרנות** — דלא איכפת להו למיגמר. **לרבא** — דאמר: מדאורייתא תלתא בעינן, לית ליה דשמואל דאמר: דיניהן דין. **בית דין חצוף** — שעברו על תקנת חכמים. **היינו נזק היינו חבלות** — מאי קרי "נזק" ומאי קרי "חבלות"? הא נזק אחד מחמשה דברים של חבלות הוא, וליתני: "חבלות", ולא בעי "נזק". **חצי נזק נמי היינו חבלות** — דשור תם שחבל, אינו משלם אלא חצי נזק, וכיון דתנא "חבלות", אף חצי נזק במשמע.

HALAKHAH

חֲצִי נֶזֶק **Half-damages.** "Since the payment of half the value of the damage resulting from an animal's unexpected behavior is regarded as a fine, a case involving such a payment can only be adjudicated by a court of three expert, ordained, judges." (*Shulḥan Arukh, Ḥoshen Mishpat* 1:1.)

street corners (*Arukh*). Others explain this term as referring to merchants who have stores on street corners.

SAGES

שְׁמוּאֵל **Shmuel.** One of the greatest Babylonian Amoraim of the first generation, Shmuel was Rav's colleague. His father, Abba bar Abba, was a Sage of the city of Neharde'a. In addition to his prominence as a Torah scholar, Shmuel became a great expert in medicine and astronomy, and was especially famous as an eye doctor. Because of his knowledge of astronomy he was known as שְׁמוּאֵל יַרְחִינָאָה — "Shmuel the expert in months." And because of his profound knowledge in civil matters, the Halakhah follows him in that area. Among his students were Rav Naḥman, who succeeded to his position as head of the yeshivah in Neharde'a, and Rav Yehudah (bar Yeḥezkel), who founded the Pumbedita Yeshivah.

BACKGROUND

בֵּית דִּין חָצוּף **An impudent court.** The main idea in support of Shmuel's approach regarding two judges is that once two judges have reached a certain decision, there would seem to be no need for a third. For even if the third judge disagrees with the other two, they nonetheless constitute a majority. However, Shmuel agrees that this is an "impudent" court, because it began with an even number of judges, which is against the opinion of the Sages. Over the generations, until the end of the Geonic period, the Sages were divided as to whether to accept Shmuel's view, until they finally decided against it, entirely rejecting the idea of a two-member panel of judges.

נֶזֶק הַיְינוּ חֲבָלוֹת **Damages is the same as inflicted injuries.** The term חֲבָלוֹת — "inflicted injuries" — as normally understood, does not include all the sense of the broader term, "damages." For the latter term also covers damage by fire and other kinds of damage. Nevertheless, it has already been explained that the principle invoked here is that there is

[1]תָּנָא מָמוֹנָא, וְקָתָנֵי קְנָסָא. [2]הָנִיחָא לְמַאן דְּאָמַר: פַּלְגָא נִיזְקָא קְנָסָא. [3]אֶלָּא לְמַאן דְּאָמַר פַּלְגָא נִיזְקָא מָמוֹנָא, [4]מַאי אִיכָּא לְמֵימַר? [5]אֶלָּא: אַיְּידֵי דְּקָא בָּעֵי לְמִיתְנָא תַּשְׁלוּמֵי כֶּפֶל וְתַשְׁלוּמֵי אַרְבָּעָה וַחֲמִשָּׁה, [6]דְּמָמוֹן [3B] שֶׁאֵינוֹ מִשְׁתַּלֵּם בְּרֹאשׁ הוּא, [7]תְּנָא נַמִי חֲצִי נֶזֶק, [8]דְּמָמוֹן שֶׁאֵינוֹ מִשְׁתַּלֵּם בְּרֹאשׁ הוּא. [9]וְאַיְּידֵי דְּקָא בָּעֵי לְמִיתְנָא חֲצִי נֶזֶק, [10]תְּנָא נַמִי נֶזֶק.

[11]שְׁלֹשָׁה, מְנָלַן? [12]דְּתָנוּ רַבָּנַן: [13]״׳וְנִקְרַב בַּעַל הַבַּיִת אֶל הָאֱלֹהִים׳ — הֲרֵי כָּאן אֶחָד.

LITERAL TRANSLATION

[1][The Tanna] taught compensation (lit., "money"), and he taught a fine.

[2]This is well according to the one who says [that] half-damages is a fine. [3]But according to the one who says [that] half-damages is compensation, [4]what is there to say?

[5]Rather, since he wished to teach double compensation, and fourfold and fivefold compensation, [6]which is compensation [3B] that is not payment for the principal, [7]he taught also half-damages, [8]which is compensation that is not payment for the principal. [9]And since he wished to teach half-damages, [10]he taught also damages.

[11]Three, from where do we [derive]? [12]As our Rabbis taught: [13]"'And the master of the house shall be brought to the judges' — here is one.

TRANSLATION AND COMMENTARY

Mishnah have to teach us again that cases involving the payment of half-damages are adjudicated by three judges?

תָּנָא מָמוֹנָא [1]The Gemara answers: **The Tanna** first **taught** that three judges are required in cases of inflicted injury, where the subject of the suit is **compensation, and** then **he taught** that three judges are required in a case involving the payment of half-damages, which is not compensation for the damage suffered, but **a fine** imposed by the Torah.

הָנִיחָא לְמַאן דְּאָמַר [2]The Gemara objects: **This** explanation **is well according to the** Amora **who says** that the **half-damages** liability **is** indeed **a fine.** [3]**But according to the** Amora **who says** that the **half-damages** liability **is** also **a compensatory payment,** [4]**what is there to say?**

אֶלָּא [5]The Gemara presents an alternative explanation of the Mishnah. Indeed, the Mishnah did not have to teach us that cases involving the payment of damages or half-damages are adjudicated by a court of three judges, for that follows from what was taught earlier in the Mishnah, that cases of inflicted injury are adjudicated by a court of three. **But since** the Tanna of the Mishnah **wished to teach** in the next clause that three judges are required in cases involving the payment of **double compensation, and of fourfold and fivefold compensation,** [6]those **being payments** [3B] **that are not for the exact amount** of the damage caused, but rather in excess of that amount, [7]**he taught also** that three judges are required in cases involving the payment of **half-damages,** [8]**which is** also **a payment that is not for the exact amount** of the damage caused, but rather for less than that amount. [9]**And since** the Tanna **wished to teach** that cases involving the payment of **half-damages** are adjudicated by three judges, [10]**he taught also** that three judges are required in cases involving the payment of full **damages.**

שְׁלֹשָׁה מְנָלַן [11]The Gemara inquires into the Biblical source of the ruling that monetary cases are adjudicated by a court of three judges: **From where do we derive** that **three** judges are required in monetary cases? The Gemara answers that the source of this law is discussed in the following Baraita: [12]**Our Rabbis taught:** "Regarding an unpaid bailee who claims that an article which had been entrusted to his safekeeping was stolen, the Torah states (Exodus 22:7): [13]**'And the master of the house shall be brought to the judges' —**

RASHI

חבלות ממונא הוא דאפחתיה לדמים — אלי נזק קנסא הוא, דסתם שוורים אינס נוגחים, ולא היה לבעלים לשמרו כל זמן שלא הועד, ולא בעי לשלומי מידי, אלא קנסא הוא דקנסיה רחמנא כדי שירבה בשמירת שוורים. **פלגא נזקא ממונא** — בפרק "ארבעה אבות" (בבא קמא טו,א) פליגי בה, דקסבר: סתם שוורים נגחנים הס, ומדינא כולהו בעי לשלומי, דהוה ליה למינטריה, ורחמנא הוא דחס עליה.

NOTES

הָנִיחָא לְמַאן דְּאָמַר This is well according to the one who says. In tractate *Bava Kamma* (15a), the Amoraim disagree about the nature of the half-damages liability. One Amora maintains it is a compensatory payment similar to the full damages liability. He maintains that, in general, animals are prone to gore and to kick, and so a person must take care to prevent his animal from causing damage through such behavior; and failure to do so is regarded as negligence. But the Torah took into consideration the fact that a particular animal had not yet demonstrated a propensity for goring or kicking, and so it limited the owner's liability to half the value of the damage that it caused. The other Amora disagrees and says that the half-damages liability is a fine, since in general animals are not prone to gore or

no difference between robbery and inflicted injury, and anyone who illegally causes financial loss to his fellow may be sued before a court of three members.

[1]׳עַד הָאֱלֹהִים יָבֹא דְּבַר שְׁנֵיהֶם׳ — הֲרֵי כָּאן שְׁנַיִם. [2]׳אֲשֶׁר יַרְשִׁיעֻן אֱלֹהִים׳ — הֲרֵי כָּאן שְׁלֹשָׁה. [3]דִּבְרֵי רַבִּי יֹאשִׁיָּה. [4]רַבִּי יוֹנָתָן אוֹמֵר: רִאשׁוֹן תְּחִילָּה נֶאֱמַר, [5]וְאֵין דּוֹרְשִׁין תְּחִילּוֹת. [6]אֶלָּא: ׳עַד הָאֱלֹהִים יָבֹא דְּבַר שְׁנֵיהֶם׳ — הֲרֵי כָּאן אֶחָד. [7]׳אֲשֶׁר יַרְשִׁיעֻן אֱלֹהִים׳ — הֲרֵי כָּאן שְׁנַיִם. [8]וְאֵין בֵּית דִּין שָׁקוּל, מוֹסִיפִין עֲלֵיהֶן עוֹד אֶחָד. [9]הֲרֵי כָּאן שְׁלֹשָׁה״.

[10]נֵימָא בְּדוֹרְשִׁין תְּחִילּוֹת קָמִיפַּלְגִי, [11]דְּמָר סָבַר דּוֹרְשִׁין תְּחִילּוֹת, [12]וּמָר סָבַר אֵין דּוֹרְשִׁין תְּחִילּוֹת.

LITERAL TRANSLATION

[1]'The cause of both parties shall come before the judges' — here is two. [2]'Whom the judges shall condemn' — here is three. [3][These are] the words of Rabbi Yoshiyah. [4]Rabbi Yonatan says: The first one was stated at the beginning, [5]and we do not interpret beginnings. [6]Rather, 'The cause of both parties shall come before the judges' — here is one. [7]'Whom the judges shall condemn' — here is two. [8]And a court may not be even [numbered], [so] we add to them one more. [9]Here are three."

[10]Shall we say [that] they disagree about intrepreting beginnings, [11]for the one master maintains we interpret beginnings, [12]and the other master maintains we do not interpret beginnings?

RASHI

אין דורשין תחלות – למניין, דלגופיה אתא, דלבעי מומחין, ד״אלהים״ לשון גדולה ורבנות. **ואין בית דין שקול** – אין עושין בית דין זוגות, דצריך לקיים בו ״אחרי רבים להטות״, ואם יתחלקו לחצאין, אין כאן רבים.

TRANSLATION AND COMMENTARY

here is the source for one judge. [1]And the next verse states (Exodus 22:8): **'The cause of both parties shall come before the judges' — here is** the source for a **second** judge. [2]And that same verse continues: **'Whom the judges shall condemn' — here is** the source for a **third** judge. [3]**This is the view of Rabbi Yoshiyah,** who understands that the triple mention of the word "judges" teaches that a court of three judges is required. [4]**Rabbi Yonatan** disagrees and **says: The first** instance of the word "judges" **is the first occurrence** of that word in our passage, [5]**and we may not interpret the first occurrence** of a word in a passage. When a key word appears more than once in the Torah's discussion of a certain law, an exegetical inference may be drawn from the repetition, but an exegetical inference may not be drawn from the first occurrence of the word in the passage, since it is not superfluous, and it is needed to teach the law itself. In our case, the first instance of the word "judges" teaches that the matter must be brought before a court, and so nothing may be inferred from that word regarding the number of judges required. [6]**Rather,** the requirement of three judges is derived as follows: The verse states: **'The cause of both parties shall come before the judges' — here is** the source for **one** judge. [7]And that same verse continues: **'Whom the judges shall condemn...' — here** is the source for a **second** judge. [8]**And** since **a court may not comprise** an **even number** of judges, to avoid a tie, **we** must **add to these** two **one more** judge. [9]Hence, a court **must comprise three** judges."

נֵימָא בְּדוֹרְשִׁין תְּחִילּוֹת [10]The Gemara wishes to understand the disagreement between Rabbi Yoshiyah and Rabbi Yonatan: **Shall we say that** the two Tannaim **disagree about** whether or not **we may interpret the first occurrence** of a word in a passage, [11]**for one master** — Rabbi Yoshiyah — **maintains that we** may in fact **interpret the first occurrence** of a word in a passage, and so the first instance of the word "judges" can be joined to the other two, [12]**and the other master** — Rabbi Yonatan — **maintains that we may not interpret the first occurrence** of a word in a passage?

BACKGROUND

דּוֹרְשִׁין תְּחִילּוֹת We interpret beginnings. On this and the following pages several interpretations are offered in which proof for various numbers connected with the Halakhah is adduced from the number of times a subject or a word appears in the Torah. This method does not always provide conclusive proof, but it alludes to matters that can be learned from the use of language and the repeated reference to topics. The main lesson is learned here from the repeated use of a word when a pronoun could have been used to prevent its repetition. Each such use of the word is regarded as superfluous, and thus something can be adduced from it. However, there is a difference of opinion as to whether every appearance of the word counts, or whether one skips the first appearance, which is needed to define the topic.

NOTES

to kick. If an animal caused damage by kicking or goring, this is regarded as an inevitable accident, and so by right the animal's owner should be totally exempt from liability. But the Torah imposed a fine upon the owner, making him liable for half the damage, in order to encourage him to take greater care of his animal. There are a number of practical differences between these two viewpoints.

נֵימָא בְּדוֹרְשִׁין תְּחִילּוֹת קָמִיפַּלְגִי? Shall we say that they disagree about interpreting beginnings? Why should we not say that Rabbi Yoshiyah and Rabbi Yonatan disagree about whether we may interpret the first occurrence of a word in a passage? Rabbi Yonatan explains that his position is based on the principle that we do not interpret the first occurrence of a word in a passage, and we see elsewhere (*Sukkah* 6b) that the matter is under dispute among the Tannaim. *Rashash* answers that we find in the Mekhilta that Rabbi Yoshiyah himself maintains that we do not interpret the first occurrence of a word in a passage. Thus, it is preferable to say that here Rabbi Yoshiyah disagrees with Rabbi Yonatan about another matter, and so we can avoid saying that Rabbi Yoshiyah's two statements contradict each other.

TRANSLATION AND COMMENTARY

לָא [1]The Gemara rejects this suggestion: **No, all** the Tannaim — both Rabbi Yoshiyah and Rabbi Yonatan — **agree that,** as a rule, **we may not interpret the first occurrence** of a word in a passage. [2]But **Rabbi Yoshiyah can say to you** that here it is different. [3]For **if** the first instance of the word teaches us only that the matter must be brought before a court, **the verse should have read: [4]"And the master of the house shall be brought to the judge,"** using the usual word for judge, שׁוֹפֵט. [5]**What is** the reason why the verse used the unusual word for **judge,** אֱלֹהִים? [6]**Conclude from this** that the unusual word was chosen **for** the exegetical inference that may be drawn from it regarding **the number** of judges comprising a court.

וְרַבִּי יוֹנָתָן [7]The Gemara asks: **And** how does **Rabbi Yonatan** counter this argument? [8]The Gemara explains: Rabbi Yonatan can say that the verse **uses common speech, as people** are accustomed to **say:** [9]**He who has a case which needs to be judged, let him come before a judge,** meaning a qualified judge, and not a layman. Just as ordinary usage distinguishes between a qualified judge and a layman, so, too, does the verse make this distinction, using the word אֱלֹהִים and not שׁוֹפֵט in order to teach us that the court should be made up of authorized judges, and not laymen. Nothing, therefore, may be inferred from the word with respect to the number of judges required.

וְרַבִּי יֹאשִׁיָּה [10]The Gemara examines Rabbi Yoshiyah's position. Rabbi Yoshiyah derives the law that monetary cases are adjudicated by a court of three from the triple mention of the word "judges." By implication, had the word "judges" been mentioned only twice, we would have thought that two judges suffice. Hence, it follows that, according to Rabbi Yoshiyah, a court may be made up of an even number of judges. But is it really true that **Rabbi Yoshiyah does not accept** the principle that **a court** must comprise an **uneven number** of judges? [11]**But surely it was taught** in a Baraita: **"Rabbi Eliezer the son of Rabbi Yose the Galilean says:** [12]**Why does the verse state** [Exodus 23:2]: **'To incline after the many to incline'?** [13]From here we may understand that **the Torah said: Establish for yourself a court of** an **uneven number** of judges, so that there will always be a majority opinion." Does Rabbi Yoshiyah disagree with Rabbi Eliezer the son of Rabbi Yose the Galilean and his interpretation of the verse?

סָבַר לַהּ כְּרַבִּי יְהוּדָה [14]The Gemara answers: In fact Rabbi Yoshiyah **agrees with Rabbi Yehudah, who said** that the Great Sanhedrin had **seventy** members. [15]**As we have learned** in our Mishnah: **"The Great Sanhedrin had seventy-one members.** [16]**Rabbi Yehudah says:** The Great Sanhedrin had only **seventy."** We see that, according to Rabbi Yehudah, a court need not have an odd number of judges, and Rabbi Yoshiyah agrees with that view.

[1]לָא, דְּכוּלֵּי עָלְמָא אֵין דּוֹרְשִׁין תְּחִילּוֹת. [2]אָמַר לָךְ רַבִּי יֹאשִׁיָּה: [3]אִם כֵּן, נֵימָא קְרָא: [4]"וְנִקְרַב בַּעַל הַבַּיִת אֶל הַשּׁוֹפֵט", [5]מַאי "אֶל הָאֱלֹהִים"? [6]שְׁמַע מִינָּהּ לַמִּנְיָינָא.

[7]וְרַבִּי יוֹנָתָן? [8]לִישָּׁנָא דְּעָלְמָא נָקַט, כִּדְאָמְרִי אֱינָשֵׁי: [9]מַאן דְּאִית לֵיהּ דִּינָא, לִיקְרַב לְגַבֵּי דַּיָּינָא.

[10]וְרַבִּי יֹאשִׁיָּה לֵית לֵיהּ בֵּית דִּין נוֹטֶה? [11]וְהָתַנְיָא: "רַבִּי אֱלִיעֶזֶר בְּנוֹ שֶׁל רַבִּי יוֹסֵי הַגְּלִילִי אוֹמֵר: [12]מַה תַּלְמוּד לוֹמַר: 'לִנְטֹת אַחֲרֵי רַבִּים לְהַטֹּת'. [13]הַתּוֹרָה אָמְרָה: עֲשֵׂה לְךָ בֵּית דִּין נוֹטֶה".

[14]סָבַר לַהּ כְּרַבִּי יְהוּדָה, דְּאָמַר: שִׁבְעִים. [15]דִּתְנַן: "סַנְהֶדְרִי גְּדוֹלָה הָיְתָה שֶׁל שִׁבְעִים וְאֶחָד. [16]רַבִּי יְהוּדָה אוֹמֵר: שִׁבְעִים".

LITERAL TRANSLATION

[1]No, everybody (lit., "the entire world") [maintain that] we do not interpret beginnings. [2]Rabbi Yoshiyah can say to you: [3]If so, let the verse say: [4]"And the master of the house shall be brought to the judge [שׁוֹפֵט]." [5]What is אֶל הָאֱלֹהִים? [6]Conclude from this [that it is] for the number.

[7]And Rabbi Yonatan? [8]It used common speech, as people say: [9]He who has a lawsuit, let him come before a judge.

[10]And does Rabbi Yoshiyah not [require] a court of an uneven number (lit., "a court which leans")? [11]But surely it was taught: "Rabbi Eliezer the son of Rabbi Yose the Galilean says: [12]Why does the verse state: 'To incline after the many to incline'? [13]The Torah said: Make for yourself a court of an uneven number."

[14]He agrees with Rabbi Yehudah, who said: Seventy. [15]As we have learned: "The Great Sanhedrin consisted of seventy-one. [16]Rabbi Yehudah says: Seventy."

RASHI

אם כן – דלא למידרשיה אתא, לכתוב "אל השופט". **לגבי דיינא** – אצל דיין הרגיל, ולא אצל הדיוט. **ורבי יאשיה** – דבעי קרא לאתויי שלישי, מי לית ליה בית דין נוטה, שצריך שלא יהא בית דין שקול, כדי שיתקיים בו הטייה אחרי רבים, ולדידיה ארבעה או ששה כשרין. דאי בעי בית דין נוטה, קרא לאיתויי שלישי למה ליה? **והתניא כו'** – והא קרא דריש. **סבר לה** – רבי יאשיה כרבי יהודה, דאמר: סנהדרי גדולה – שבעים, דהוו להו זוגות, וקרא מוקי לה לקמן לדרשה אחריתי.

SAGES

רַבִּי יֹאשִׁיָּה Rabbi Yoshiyah. Also known as Rabbi Yoshiyah Rabbah (the Great), to distinguish him from the Amora of the same name. Rabbi Yoshiyah was a Tanna who belonged to the generation that lived prior to the completion of the Mishnah. He came from the city of Hutzal in Babylonia and immigrated to Eretz Israel to study with Rabbi Yishmael. He and his colleague, Rabbi Yonatan, were Rabbi Yishmael's closest disciples. He generally appears in the Talmud in association with Rabbi Yonatan, with whom he disagrees about certain basic issues of Halakhic exegesis. He seems to have returned to Babylonia to study with Rabbi Yehudah ben Betera. Rabbi Aḥai, Rabbi Yoshiyah's son, was also an important Sage, and also lived in Hutzal.

רַבִּי יוֹנָתָן Rabbi Yonatan. A Tanna who was a member of the generation that lived prior to the completion of the Mishnah, Rabbi Yonatan was a disciple of Rabbi Yishmael and a colleague of Rabbi Yoshiyah, with whom he differed on many issues of Halakhic exegesis. It is likely that he emigrated from Eretz Israel to Babylonia, and this may be the reason why his name does not appear in the Mishnah.

BACKGROUND

בֵּית דִּין נוֹטֶה A court of an uneven number (lit., "a court which leans [to the majority]"). In fact, even when there is an even number of judges, it is unlikely that their opinions will be evenly divided. Moreover, an odd-numbered panel of judges might also reach a tie vote, if one of the judges abstains because he is unable to reach a decision. The question was whether the Torah requires that every judicial panel must be set up from the start so that there can always be a majority, or whether that is not really necessary.

TRANSLATION AND COMMENTARY

אֵימַר דִּשְׁמַעַתְּ לֵיהּ [1]The Gemara asks: **Granted that you heard Rabbi Yehudah** express his opinion **regarding the Great Sanhedrin, for there are verses** from which he learned that the Sanhedrin was made up of seventy members (see below, 17a). [2]But **did you hear** him express his opinion **regarding other courts** that they may consist of an even number of judges? [3]**And if you argue** that, according to Rabbi Yehudah, **there is** in fact **no difference** between the various courts, [4]**surely we have learned** otherwise in our Mishnah: "The rite of **the elders pressing their hands** down on the head of the communal sin-offering sacrificed because of an unwitting transgression committed by the community has to be performed by three judges. **And** measuring the distance between a corpse found along a roadside and the nearest town (this precedes the **breaking** of **the neck of the heifer**) has to be performed **by three** judges. [5]**This is the view of Rabbi Shimon.** [6]**Rabbi Yehudah says:** Each of these ceremonies requires **five** judges." [7]**And** in explaining this matter **we asked: What is Rabbi Yehudah's reason** for five judges being required for these two ceremonies? For the verse regarding the communal sin-offering states (Leviticus 4:15): "And the elders of the congregation shall place their hands on the head of the bullock before the Lord." [8]And Rabbi Yehudah expounded the verse as follows: **"And they shall place their hands** on the head of the bullock" — the plural form of the verb "they shall place" teaches that **two** judges are required. [9]**"The elders of the congregation"** — the plural form of the word "elders" teaches that **two** more judges are required, bringing the total to four. [10]**And** since **a court may not be** made up **of** an **even number** of judges, [11]**we** must **add** yet **another** judge to the four, so that **there are five.** Thus, we see that Rabbi Yehudah himself accepts the principle that a court must comprise an odd number of judges.

דְּרַבִּי יֹאשִׁיָּה עֲדִיפָא [12]The Gemara answers: **Rabbi Yoshiyah's** position is **more** radical **than** that of **Rabbi Yehudah.** [13]**For** it is only **regarding the Great Sanhedrin** that **Rabbi Yehudah does not accept** the principle that a court must comprise an odd number of judges. [14]**But regarding other courts,** Rabbi Yehudah **accepts** that principle. [15]**However, Rabbi Yoshiyah does not accept** the principle that a court must be made up of an odd number of judges, **even regarding the rest of the courts.** Thus, according to Rabbi Yoshiyah, the Torah had to mention the word "judges" three times in order to teach us that monetary cases are adjudicated by a court of three.

LITERAL TRANSLATION

[1]Say that you heard Rabbi Yehudah regarding the Great Sanhedrin about which verses are written. [2]Regarding other courts did you hear? [3]And if you say there is no difference, [4]surely we have learned: "Placing of the elders' [hands] and breaking the neck of the heifer by three. [5][These are] the words of Rabbi Shimon. [6]Rabbi Yehudah says: By five." [7]And we said: What is the reason of Rabbi Yehudah? [8]"And they shall place [their hands]" — two. [9]"The elders [of the congregation]" — two. [10]And a court may not be [of] even [numbers], [so] we add to them one more. [11]Here are five.

[12]Rabbi Yoshiyah['s opinion] is more than that of Rabbi Yehudah. [13]For Rabbi Yehudah regarding the Great Sanhedrin does not hold (lit., "have") [the requirement of an uneven number]. [14]But regarding other courts he has. [15]And Rabbi Yoshiyah regarding other courts also does not have.

[1]אֵימַר דִּשְׁמַעַתְּ לֵיהּ לְרַבִּי יְהוּדָה בְּסַנְהֶדְרִי גְּדוֹלָה דִּכְתִיבִי קְרָאֵי. [2]בִּשְׁאָר בֵּי דִּינָא מִי שְׁמַעַתְּ לֵיהּ? [3]וְכִי תֵּימָא לָא שְׁנָא, [4]וְהָתְנַן: "סְמִיכַת זְקֵנִים וַעֲרִיפַת עֶגְלָה בִּשְׁלֹשָׁה. [5]דִּבְרֵי רַבִּי שִׁמְעוֹן. [6]רַבִּי יְהוּדָה אוֹמֵר: בַּחֲמִשָּׁה". [7]וְאָמְרִינַן: מַאי טַעֲמָא דְּרַבִּי יְהוּדָה? [8]"וְסָמְכוּ" — שְׁנַיִם. [9]"זִקְנֵי" — שְׁנַיִם. [10]וְאֵין בֵּית דִּין שָׁקוּל, מוֹסִיפִין עֲלֵיהֶן עוֹד אֶחָד. [11]הֲרֵי כָּאן חֲמִשָּׁה!

[12]דְּרַבִּי יֹאשִׁיָּה עֲדִיפָא מִדְּרַבִּי יְהוּדָה. [13]דְּאִילּוּ רַבִּי יְהוּדָה בְּסַנְהֶדְרִי גְּדוֹלָה הוּא דְּלֵית לֵיהּ. [14]הָא בִּשְׁאָר בֵּי דִּינָא אִית לֵיהּ, [15]וְרַבִּי יֹאשִׁיָּה בִּשְׁאָר בֵּי דִּינָא נַמִי לֵית לֵיהּ.

RASHI

דכתיבי קראי — לקמן (יז,א) בשילהי פירקין. **סמיכת זקנים** — על ראש פר העדה. **ואין בית דין שקול** — וסתם "זקנים" בית דינא משמע. **עדיפא מדרבי יהודה** — כלומר, רבי יאשיה חיזק את דבריו יותר מדרבי יהודה.

NOTES

בְּסַנְהֶדְרִי גְּדוֹלָה דִּכְתִיבִי קְרָאֵי **Regarding the Great Sanhedrin about which verses are written.** The question was raised: Even though the Torah states that the Great Sanhedrin has seventy members, why not say that since a court cannot have an even number of judges, another judge must be added, bringing the total to seventy-one? *Ran* answers that this principle can only be invoked in a case where the Torah does not state explicitly the number of judges comprising the court, as with a court of three or twenty-three. But regarding the Great Sanhedrin, the Torah states explicitly that it is composed of seventy members, and so we cannot add to that number. *Tosefot Yom Tov*

SAGES

רַבִּי שִׁמְעוֹן **Rabbi Shimon.** Where the name Rabbi Shimon occurs without a patronymic in Tannaitic literature, it usually refers to Rabbi Shimon bar Yoḥai, one of the greatest Tannaim of the generation preceding the completion of the Mishnah. Rabbi Shimon was a close disciple of Rabbi Akiva, and regarded himself as following in his teacher's path. Rabbi Akiva thought very highly of his disciple, saying of him, "It is sufficient for you that I and your Creator know your power." Rabbi Shimon was a master of both Halakhah and Aggadah, and his teachings are quoted frequently throughout the Talmud. Although the Halakhah does not always follow his rulings (especially against Rabbi Yose and Rabbi Yehudah), nevertheless in many important areas of Halakhah his opinion prevails. Rabbi Shimon used a particular method of Halakhic exegesis called "seeking the reason for the verse" — drawing Halakhic conclusions from the Bible on the basis of the spirit and intent of particular passages.

Rabbi Shimon was sent to Rome as an emissary of the Jews, though he was deeply hostile to the Romans. Because he did not conceal his feelings about them, he was sentenced to death and forced to remain in hiding for many years.

His character was ascetic, and he tended to be stringent in his rulings. He was famous in his generation as a righteous man and as a miracle worker, and there are many stories about the wonders he performed.

Sifrei — a collection of Halakhic Midrashim on Numbers and Deuteronomy — was produced in his academy. He is also the central figure in the principal book of Kabbalah, the Zohar, and was regarded with extraordinary veneration in his own time and in following generations. Among his major students was Rabbi Yehudah HaNasi, the editor of the Mishnah. Rabbi Elazar the son of Rabbi Shimon was also a famous Sage.

[1]וְאֶלָּא ״הַאי לִנְטֹת״ — מַאי עָבֵיד לֵיהּ?
[2]מוֹקִים לָהּ בְּדִינֵי נְפָשׁוֹת.
[3]אֲבָל בְּדִינֵי מָמוֹנוֹת לֹא? [4]אֶלָּא הָא דִּתְנַן: [5]״שְׁנַיִם אוֹמְרִים: זַכַּאי, וְאֶחָד אוֹמֵר: חַיָּיב — זַכַּאי. [6]שְׁנַיִם אוֹמְרִים חַיָּיב, וְאֶחָד אוֹמֵר זַכַּאי — חַיָּיב״ — [7]נֵימָא דְּלָא כְּרַבִּי יֹאשִׁיָּה!
[8]אֲפִילּוּ תֵּימָא רַבִּי יֹאשִׁיָּה. [9]מַיְיתֵי לָהּ בְּקַל וָחוֹמֶר מִדִּינֵי נְפָשׁוֹת. [10]וּמָה דִּינֵי נְפָשׁוֹת דַּחֲמִירִי [11]אָמַר רַחֲמָנָא:

TRANSLATION AND COMMENTARY

וְאֶלָּא הַאי ״לִנְטֹת״ [1]The Gemara asks: **But what does** Rabbi Yoshiyah **do with** the verse, **"To incline after the many to incline,"** from which Rabbi Eliezer the son of Rabbi Yose the Galilean derived that a court must comprise an odd number of judges?

מוֹקִים לָהּ [2]The Gemara answers: Rabbi Yoshiyah **applies** the verse **to capital cases.** As we learned in our Mishnah, this part of the verse teaches that while condemnation in capital cases must be reached by at least a majority of two, a decision of acquittal may be reached by a majority of one. Thus, a court which hears a capital case (a Lesser Sanhedrin) must have an odd number of judges, for if the court is even-numbered, there cannot be a majority of less than two.

אֲבָל בְּדִינֵי מָמוֹנוֹת לֹא [3]The Gemara asks: **But** is it really true that regarding **monetary cases** Rabbi Yoshiyah does **not** accept the principle that the court must comprise an odd number of judges? [4]If so, then a difficulty arises from **that which we learned** in a Mishnah found later in the tractate (*Sanhedrin* 29a): [5]**"If two** of the three judges **say** that the defendant is **free of liability, and one** judge **says** that he is **liable,** a ruling is issued that the defendant **is free of liability.** [6]**If two** of the judges **say** that the defendant is **liable, and one** judge **says** that he is **free of liability,** a ruling is issued that the defendant **is liable."** Now, this Mishnah's rulings are based on the assumption that we follow the opinion of the majority of the members of the court. [7]**Shall we say that** this Mishnah **is not in accordance with** the view of **Rabbi Yoshiyah?** Does Rabbi Yoshiyah maintain that the decision must be unanimous?

אֲפִילּוּ תֵּימָא [8]The Gemara answers: **You can even say** that the Mishnah was taught in accordance with the opinion of **Rabbi Yoshiyah.** He agrees that if the opinions are divided, we follow the majority. [9]**He learns** that we follow the majority opinion **by means of an *a fortiori* inference** drawn **from** the rule governing **capital cases.** [10]For **if regarding capital cases,** which are more **severe,** [11]**the Torah said:**

LITERAL TRANSLATION

[1]But this "To incline" — what does he do with it?
[2]He applies it to capital cases.
[3]But monetary cases not? [4]But that which we have learned: [5]"[If] two say: Free of liability, and one says: liable, he is free of liability. [6][If] two say: Liable, and one says: Free of liability, he is liable" — [7]shall we say that it is not in accordance with Rabbi Yoshiyah?
[8]You can even say Rabbi Yoshiyah. [9]He brings it with an *a fortiori* inference from capital cases. [10]If [regarding] capital cases which are severe [11]the Torah (lit., "the Merciful") said:

RASHI

אלא האי לנטות מאי עביד ליה — בשלמא לרבי יהודה — מוקי לה בשאר בית דין. **בדיני נפשות** — שתתקיים בו הטייתך לטובה על פי אחד, כדאמרה במתניתין, ואי הוי זוגות, ליכא הטייה בפחות משנים. **לימא דלא כרבי יאשיה** — דאי כרבי יאשיה, כיון דשלישי מקראי יליף להו, ולאו משום נוטה, צריך שתהא דעת שלשתן שוה. **אפילו תימא רבי יאשיה** — מודה דהיכא דחלוקין, אזלינן בתר רובא.

NOTES

suggests that this is precisely what the Gemara meant when it said: Say that you heard Rabbi Yehudah regarding the Great Sanhedrin (where seventy) is written in the verse. Since the Torah states explicitly that the Great Sanhedrin is composed of seventy judges, it must mean that we should not invoke the rule that a court may not be made up of an even number of judges.

שְׁנַיִם אוֹמְרִים: זַכַּאי If two say: Free of liability. The Rishonim ask: What is the Gemara's question? Perhaps, indeed, Rabbi Yoshiyah maintains that a court can only render an opinion if the decision of its members is unanimous. Now the Mishnah rules that if two of the judges say the defendant is free of liability, and one judge says he is liable, the defendant is found free of liability. The reason for this ruling might not be because we follow the majority opinion, but rather because the defendant cannot be judged liable unless all of the judges agree with that verdict. *Rabbenu Zerahyah HaLevi* answers that the Gemara asks only on the basis of the second case, in which two of the judges say the defendant is liable, and one judge says he is free of liability. Since the Mishnah rules that in such a case the defendant is judged liable, it follows that we follow the majority opinion. *Ran* argues that the Gemara also considers the first case of the Mishnah, where a ruling is issued that the defendant is free of liability. That case also proves that we follow the majority opinion, for were that not so, no ruling would be issued, and the defendant would still be able to be found liable in a different court.

קַל וָחוֹמֶר מִדִּינֵי נְפָשׁוֹת An *a fortiori* inference from capital cases. The Rishonim ask: Why do we not restrict the use of this *a fortiori* inference by invoking the principle of *dayo*, literally, "it is sufficient"? As a general rule, we draw the inference that if the law is lenient in a more serious case, then it will certainly be lenient in a less serious one, and the leniency in the serious case is the maximum leniency with respect to this law. Thus, it should follow that

TRANSLATION AND COMMENTARY

If the opinions are divided, **follow** the opinion of **the majority,** [1]then **all the more so** should we say that the verdict follows the opinion of the majority in **monetary cases**.

תָּנוּ רַבָּנַן [2]**Our Rabbis taught** a related Baraita, which states: **"Monetary cases** are adjudicated **by** a court of **three** judges. [3]**Rabbi** Yehudah HaNasi **says:** Monetary cases are adjudicated **by** a court of **five** judges, **so that** if the opinions are divided, **the** majority **verdict can be reached** by **three** of the judges."

אַטּוּ בִּתְלָתָא [4]The Gemara asks: And **if** a court is divided, and it is composed of only **three** judges, [5]**can the verdict not be reached** by **two** of the judges who constitute a majority of that court? Why are five judges needed to reach a majority verdict?

הָכִי קָאָמַר [6]The Gemara answers: Rabbi Yehudah HaNasi meant to **say as follows:** Monetary cases are adjudicated by a court of five judges, **because** the opinions might be divided and **the verdict** must be reached based on the opinions **of three** judges. [7]The Gemara notes: **From here** we see that Rabbi Yehudah HaNasi **maintains that** when the Torah **spoke about three** judges, **it was referring to the verdict.**

מְגַדֵּף בָּהּ רַבִּי אַבָּהוּ [8]**Rabbi Abbahu ridiculed** this suggestion: **Now,** if you say that when the Torah specified a certain number of judges, it was referring to the number of judges whose views form the majority opinion on which the court's verdict must be based, it follows that **the Great Sanhedrin should need one hundred and forty-one** judges, [9]**so that the verdict can be delivered on the basis of** the views of **seventy-one** of its members. [10]**And,** similarly, **a Lesser Sanhedrin should need forty-five** judges,

זִיל בָּתַר רוּבָּא, [1]דִּינֵי מָמוֹנוֹת לֹא כָּל שֶׁכֵּן?
[2]תָּנוּ רַבָּנַן: "דִּינֵי מָמוֹנוֹת בִּשְׁלֹשָׁה. [3]רַבִּי אוֹמֵר: בַּחֲמִשָּׁה, כְּדֵי שֶׁיִּגָּמֵר הַדִּין בִּשְׁלֹשָׁה".
[4]אַטּוּ בִּתְלָתָא, [5]מִי לֹא גָּמַר דִּינָא בִּתְרֵי?
[6]הָכִי קָאָמַר: מִפְּנֵי שֶׁגְּמַר דִּין בִּשְׁלֹשָׁה. [7]אַלְמָא קָסָבַר: תְּלָתָא כִּי כְּתִיבִי בִּגְמַר דִּינָא כְּתִיבִי.
[8]מְגַדֵּף בָּהּ רַבִּי אַבָּהוּ: אֶלָּא מֵעַתָּה תְּהֵא סַנְהֶדְרִי גְּדוֹלָה צְרִיכָה מֵאָה וְאַרְבָּעִים וְאֶחָד [9]כְּדֵי שֶׁיִּגָּמֵר הַדִּין בְּשִׁבְעִים וְאֶחָד. [10]וּתְהֵא סַנְהֶדְרִי קְטַנָּה צְרִיכָה אַרְבָּעִים וַחֲמִשָּׁה

LITERAL TRANSLATION

Follow the majority, [1]monetary cases all the more so.

[2]Our Rabbis taught: "Monetary cases by three. [3]Rabbi says: By five, so that the verdict can be reached [lit., 'judgment be concluded'] by three."

[4]If with three, [5]can it conclude the judgment by two?

[6]Thus he said: Because the conclusion of the judgment is with three. [7]Hence he maintains [that] the three that was written was written with respect to the conclusion of the judgment.

[8]Rabbi Abbahu ridiculed it: Now the Great Sanhedrin should require one hundred and forty-one [9]so that the judgment will conclude with seventy-one. [10]And the Lesser Sanhedrin should require forty-five

RASHI

כדי שיגמר הדין — אם יחלקו, שיהא שלשה רוב ונלך אחריהם. **אטו** — כי הוו תלתא, מעיקרא מי לא גמיר דינא בתרי? **מפני גמר דין** — שצריך שלשה בגמר דין. **אלא מעתה** — דקראי בגמר דין קיימי. **תהא סנהדרי גדולה כו'** — אלא מאי טעמא לא אמרת הכי.

TERMINOLOGY

מְגַדֵּף בָּהּ רַבִּי פְּלוֹנִי **Rabbi X ridiculed it,** i.e., strongly disapproved ot it. An expression used by the Gemara to introduce a strong objection and refutation of an argument previously mentioned.
Rav Sherira Gaon (cited by *Arukh)* explains the word מְגַדֵּף to mean that Rabbi Abbahu displayed astonishment with his hands, moving them in the same manner as someone who scrapes out (גרף = גדף) a dish. Others understand the term to denote intense disapproval and even ridicule.

NOTES

just as the defendant in a capital case can only be convicted if there is majority of two judges who find him guilty, so too the defendant in a monetary case should only be found liable if there is a majority of two! But the Mishnah says that the defendant can be found liable by a majority of one! The Rishonim respond that the Gemara argues that Rabbi Yoshiyah learns that we follow the majority opinion in monetary cases by means of an *a fortiori* inference drawn from the same rule that governs capital cases. But the distinction between the majority needed for an "evil" ruling or a conviction, and the majority needed for a "good" ruling or an acquittal, which applies in capital cases, cannot be extended to monetary cases. For in civil cases there is no "evil" ruling and no "good" ruling, since a ruling which is good for one of the litigants is bad for the other. Thus, once we say that we follow the majority opinion in civil cases, we must follow a majority of one in all situations, whether the defendant is found liable or not (*Remah, Meiri, Ran*).

תְּהֵא סַנְהֶדְרִי קְטַנָּה צְרִיכָה אַרְבָּעִים וַחֲמִשָּׁה **The Lesser Sanhedrin should have forty-five.** The Rishonim remark that Rabbi Abbahu's objection regarding a Lesser Sanhedrin is imprecise. First, because the verses "The congregation shall judge" and "The congregation shall deliver" can certainly not both be referring to the number of judges who must agree about the verdict. And second, even if both verses teach us about the number of judges required for the conclusion of the judgment, only thirty-nine judges are necessary — twenty in favor of acquittal and nineteen in favor of conviction, or twenty-one in favor of conviction and eighteen in favor of acquittal — and not forty-five judges as stated in the Gemara (see *Tosafot* and *Ran*).

[1]כְּדֵי שֶׁיִּגָּמֵר הַדִּין בִּשְׁלֹשָׁה וְעֶשְׂרִים! [2]אֶלָּא: ״אֶסְפָה לִּי שִׁבְעִים אִישׁ״ אָמַר רַחֲמָנָא, מִשְּׁעַת אֲסִיפָה שִׁבְעִים. [3]״וְשָׁפְטוּ הָעֵדָה... וְהִצִּילוּ הָעֵדָה״ — [4]נַמִי, מִשְּׁעַת שְׁפִיטַת הָעֵדָה. [5]הָכִי נַמִי: ״וְנִקְרַב בַּעַל הַבַּיִת אֶל הָאֱלֹהִים״ — [6]מִשְּׁעַת קְרִיבָה שְׁלֹשָׁה.

[7]אֶלָּא, הַיְינוּ טַעֲמָא דְּרַבִּי: [8]״אֲשֶׁר יַרְשִׁיעֻן אֱלֹהִים״ — תְּרֵי. [9]נֶאֱמַר ״אֱלֹהִים״ לְמַטָּה, [10]וְנֶאֱמַר ״אֱלֹהִים״ לְמַעְלָה. [11]מַה לְּמַטָּה שְׁנַיִם, [12]אַף לְמַעְלָה שְׁנַיִם. [13]וְאֵין בֵּית דִּין שָׁקוּל, [14]מוֹסִיפִין עֲלֵיהֶם עוֹד אֶחָד. [15]הֲרֵי כָּאן חֲמִשָּׁה [4A] [16]וְרַבָּנַן: [17]״יַרְשִׁיעֻן״ כְּתִיב.

LITERAL TRANSLATION

[1]so that the judgment will conclude with twenty-three. [2]Rather, the Torah said: "Gather to me seventy men" — from the time of gathering seventy. [3]"And the congregation shall judge...and the congregation shall deliver" — [4]also from the time of the congregation's judgment. [5]So too: "And the master of the house shall be brought to the judges" — [6]from the time of being brought [to the judges] three.

[7]Rather, this is the reason of Rabbi: [8]"Whom the judges shall condemn" — two. [9]"Judges" was stated below, [10]and "judges" was stated above. [11]Just as below two, [12]so too above two. [13]And a court may not be [of] even [numbers], [14][so] we add to them one more. [15]Here are five. [4A] [16]And the Rabbis: [17]It is written: "He shall condemn [יַרְשִׁיעֻן]."

TRANSLATION AND COMMENTARY

[1]**so that the verdict can be delivered on the basis of** the views of **twenty-three** of its members. Why, then, don't you come to this conclusion? [2]**Because the Torah said** (Numbers 11:16): **"Gather to me seventy men** from the elders of Israel," implying that **from the time of gathering,** when the Great Sanhedrin convenes, it should comprise **seventy** judges. And similarly, when the Torah taught the number of judges comprising a Lesser Sanhedrin which hears capital cases, it said (Numbers 35:24-25): [3]**"And the congregation shall judge** between the slayer and the avenger of blood according to these judgments. **And the congregation shall deliver** the slayer out of the hand of the avenger of blood" — [4]implying **also** that it is **from the time of the congregation's judgment,** when the court convenes to judge a case, that twenty-three judges are required. [5]**So too,** then, when the Torah taught the number of judges comprising a court whose jurisdiction is limited to civil matters, it said (Exodus 22:7): **"And the master of the house shall be brought to the judges"** — [6]implying that it is **from the time** that the parties **are brought** before the court, and not from the time that the verdict is delivered, that **three** judges are required. Thus, it cannot be that Rabbi Yehudah HaNasi maintains that when the Torah spoke about three judges it was referring to the number of judges who must agree on the verdict.

אֶלָּא [7]Hence Rabbi Yehudah HaNasi's position must be understood differently: **Rather, this is Rabbi** Yehudah HaNasi's **reasoning:** The number of judges required to adjudicate monetary cases is derived from the passage regarding an unpaid bailee who claims that an article which had been entrusted into his safekeeping was stolen (Exodus 28:7-8). An exegetical inference may not be drawn from the first mention of the word "judges" found in that section (verse 7), as explained above. But the next verse (8) states: "The cause of both parties shall come before the judges; and whom the judges shall condemn, he shall pay double to his neighbor." [8]The second clause, **"whom the judges shall condemn** [יַרְשִׁיעֻן]**,"** uses the plural form of the verb "condemn," implying that **two** judges are required. [9]And since the word **"judges" was stated below** in the second clause, [10]and the same word **"judges" was stated above** in the first clause, an analogy may be drawn between the two. [11]**Just as below** in the second clause, the word "judges" means **two,** [12]**so too above** in the first clause, the word "judges" means **two.** Hence, four judges are required. [13]**And** since **a court may not be** composed **of** an **even number** of judges, to avoid a tie, [14]**we** must **add to these** four **one more** judge. [15]Hence, a court **must be** composed of **five** judges. [4A] [16]**And the Rabbis** who maintain that monetary cases are adjudicated by a court of three judges counter Rabbi Yehudah HaNasi's argument: [17]The word upon which Rabbi Yehudah HaNasi bases his entire inference, "יַרְשִׁיעֻן," **is spelled** defectively without a ו. While the word is pronounced as if it were spelled with a ו (יַרְשִׁיעוּן — the plural form of the verb), the meaning of the word for Halakhic purposes is established

RASHI

דאספה לי כו׳ — רבי אבהו קאמר לה לכולה מילתא, ובלשון קושיא. **ושפטו העדה** — וילפינן מיניה במתניתין עשרים ושלשה לסנהדרי קטנה. **ונקרב בעל הבית אל האלהים** — דילפינן מיניה, משעת קריבה קאמר. **ירשיעון** — לשון רבים. **למטה** — ״ירשיעון אלהים״. **למעלה** — ״עד האלהים יבא״. והאוא ד״ונקרב״ לא קחשיב, דקסבר אין דורשין תחילות. **ושפטו העדה** — וילפינן מיניה במתניתין עשרים ושלשה לסנהדרי קטנה. **ונקרב בעל הבית אל האלהים** — דילפינן מיניה, משעת קריבה קאמר. **ירשיעון** — לשון רבים. **למטה** — ״ירשיעון אלהים״. **למעלה** — ״עד האלהים יבא״. והאוא ד״ונקרב״ לא קחשיב, דקסבר אין דורשין תחילות.

TRANSLATION AND COMMENTARY

according to its consonantal text, the actual letters of the word. Since the spelling of the word יַרְשִׁיעֻן suggests the singular form of the verb, **"he shall condemn,"** the clause, "whom the judges shall condemn," serves as a source for only one judge, and thus the entire passage teaches us that only three judges are required.

אָמַר רַבִּי יִצְחָק בַּר יוֹסֵי [1]The Gemara now cites the following statement which supports this interpretation of Rabbi Yehudah HaNasi's position. **Rabbi Yitzḥak bar Yose said in the name of Rabbi Yoḥanan: Rabbi** Yehudah HaNasi, **Rabbi Yehudah ben Ro'etz, Bet Shammai, Rabbi Shimon, and Rabbi Akiva all maintain** the same principle: [2]**The vocalized text of the Torah,** and not its consonantal text, **is authoritative.**

רַבִּי [3]The Gemara now presents the matter in detail: We see that **Rabbi** Yehudah HaNasi maintains that the vocalized text of the Torah is authoritative from **that which was said** above.

וְרַבִּי יְהוּדָה בֶּן רוֹעֵץ [4]As for the opinion of **Rabbi Yehudah ben Ro'etz** that the vocalized text of the Torah is authoritative, **it was taught** in the following Baraita: "The Torah describes various regulations governing a woman who gave birth: 'If a woman has conceived seed, and born a male child, then she shall be unclean seven days....And she shall then continue in her blood of her purifying for thirty-three days....But if she bear a female child, then she shall be unclean two weeks [שְׁבֻעַיִם], as in her menstruation; and she shall continue in her blood of her purifying for sixty-six days' [Leviticus 12:2,4-5]. [5]**The disciples asked Rabbi Yehudah ben Ro'etz**: How do we know that a woman who gave birth to a girl is ritually impure for only two weeks? Why should we read the word שבעים as *shevu'ayim*, 'two weeks'? Since the Biblical text is not vocalized, and the spelling of the word is defective, [6]**we can read** it as שִׁבְעִים, *shiv'im*, **'seventy.'** [7]Thus, **we might have thought that a woman who gave birth to a girl is ritually impure for seventy days!** [8]Rabbi Yehudah ben Ro'etz **said** to the disciples: It can be demonstrated that the word should be read as 'two weeks,' and not as 'seventy.' For the Torah **declared** a woman first **ritually impure and** then **ritually pure in the case** where she gave birth to **a boy.** [9]**And** the Torah also **declared** a woman first **ritually impure and** then **ritually pure** when she gave birth to **a girl.**

[1]אָמַר רַבִּי יִצְחָק בַּר יוֹסֵי אָמַר רַבִּי יוֹחָנָן: רַבִּי, וְרַבִּי יְהוּדָה בֶּן רוֹעֵץ, וּבֵית שַׁמַּאי, וְרַבִּי שִׁמְעוֹן, וְרַבִּי עֲקִיבָא, כּוּלְּהוּ סְבִירָא לְהוּ: [2]יֵשׁ אֵם לַמִּקְרָא.
[3]רַבִּי — הָא דַּאֲמָרַן.
[4]וְרַבִּי יְהוּדָה בֶּן רוֹעֵץ, דְּתַנְיָא: [5]״שָׁאֲלוּ תַּלְמִידִים אֶת רַבִּי יְהוּדָה בֶּן רוֹעֵץ: [6]אֶקְרָא אֲנִי: ׳שִׁבְעִים׳. [7]יָכוֹל תְּהֵא יוֹלֶדֶת נְקֵבָה טְמֵאָה שִׁבְעִים. [8]אָמַר לָהֶן: טִימֵּא וְטִיהֵר בַּזָּכָר, [9]וְטִימֵּא וְטִיהֵר בַּנְּקֵבָה.

LITERAL TRANSLATION

[1]Rabbi Yitzḥak bar Yose said in the name of Rabbi Yoḥanan: Rabbi, and Rabbi Yehudah ben Ro'etz, and Bet Shammai, and Rabbi Shimon, and Rabbi Akiva all maintain: [2]The vocalized text [of the Torah] is authoritative (lit., "the reading has a mother").

[3]Rabbi — that which we said.

[4]And Rabbi Yehudah ben Ro'etz, as it was taught: [5]"The disciples asked Rabbi Yehudah ben Ro'etz: [6]I can read: 'Seventy [שִׁבְעִים].' [7]I might have thought that a woman who gave birth to a girl is ritually impure for seventy [days]. [8]He said: It declared ritually impure and it declared ritually pure regarding a boy, [9]and it declared ritually impure and it declared ritually pure regarding a girl.

RASHI

יש אם למקרא — בתר קרייה אזלינן, דהיא עיקר. **הא דאמרן** — "ירשיעון" קרינן. **אקרא אני** — יכולני לקרות "וטמאה שבעים כנדתה" (ויקרא יב) דהא לא כתיב "שבועיים" מלא. **טמא בזכר** — שבעת ימים. **וטיהר** — שלשים ושלשת ימים. **וטימא בנקבה** — לשבועיים. **וטיהר** — ששים יום וששת ימים.

NOTES

יֵשׁ אֵם לַמִּקְרָא **The vocalized text of the Torah is authoritative.** *Remah* explains why the consonantal text of the Torah, and not the vocalized text, is called the *masoret*, lit., "the handed down tradition." The term *masoret* refers to that which is known to only a small number of people, that knowledge being carefully handed down from one generation to the next. The vocalized text of the Torah is widely known, for most people know how the text should be read. But the consonantal text is known to only a limited number of people, the scribes who note the precise spelling — whether plene or defective — of each and every word of the Torah.

טִימֵּא וְטִיהֵר **It declared ritually impure and it declared ritually pure.** Elsewhere (*Zevaḥim* 38a), the Gemara proves that the word שבעים must be read as *shevu'ayim*, "two weeks," and not as *shiv'im*, "seventy," from the next word in the verse: כְּנִדָּתָהּ — "as in her menstruation." That word teaches that a woman who gave birth to a girl is ritually impure for the same number of days as a woman who gave birth to a boy, seven days, plus the number of days that a woman is ritually impure when she menstruates, another seven days, for a total of fourteen days or two weeks.

BACKGROUND

יֵשׁ אֵם לַמִּקְרָא **The vocalized text of the Torah is authoritative.** Although ancient Hebrew writing did not have vowel signs, certain letters — א, ה, ו, and י — were used as vowels to indicate the vocalization. The consonantal text of Scripture as handed down in the tradition sometimes includes these letters (known as *matres lectionis*), in which case the spelling of the word is plene; but sometimes these letters are omitted, in which case the spelling of the word is defective. When the *mater lectionis* is missing, the word can often be read in two ways, one vocalization of the word usually representing the singular form of the word, and another the plural. Occasionally, the different vocalizations represent entirely different words. The Sages disagree about the interpretation of words with defective spelling. According to some, the consonantal text of the Torah, the actual spelling of the words, is authoritative, and so a word whose defective spelling represents a singular form should be interpreted for Halakhic purposes as a singular form. According to others, the vocalized text of the Torah, the accepted pronunciation of the words, is authoritative, and so a word which is plural according to the traditional Masoretic vocalization should be interpreted for Halakhic purposes as a plural form, even if its spelling is defective. The five Tannaim mentioned here all agree that it is the vocalized text of the Torah, and not the consonantal text, which is authoritative, as will be demonstrated in the Gemara.

SAGES

רַבִּי יְהוּדָה בֶּן רוֹעֵץ **Rabbi Yehudah ben Ro'etz.** This Tanna is mentioned only here, and it is not known what generation he belonged to or where he lived.

רַבִּי **Rabbi.** This is the epithet of Rabbi Yehudah HaNasi, who compiled and edited the Mishnah. Rabbi Yehudah HaNasi was the son of Rabban Shimon Ben Gamaliel II, and he studied Torah with his father and also with the

TRANSLATION AND COMMENTARY

[1]**Just as** the Torah **declared** a woman **ritually pure** when she gives birth to **a boy** for thirty-three days, when the woman gives birth to **a girl,** it declared her ritually pure for **twice** that time, sixty-six days. [2]**So too** it stands to reason that in contrast to the seven days for which the Torah **declared** a woman **ritually impure** when she gave birth to **a boy,** [3]when the woman gave birth to **a girl,** it declared her ritually impure for **twice** that period of time, two weeks. Thus, it follows by logical argument that the word שבעים must be read as *shevu'ayim*, 'two weeks,' and not as *shiv'im*, 'seventy.' [4]**After** the disciples **left** the Academy, Rabbi Yehudah ben Ro'etz **went out and searched for them** in order to call them back and correct what he had said. [5]When he found them, **he said: You do not need this** proof. For according to the accepted tradition regarding the pronunciation of the Biblical text, [6]**we read** the word שבעים as *shevu'ayim*, **'two weeks,'** [7]**and** we maintain that **the vocalized text of the Torah is authoritative.** The word should be interpreted for Halakhic purposes according to its traditional pronunciation."

בֵּית שַׁמַּאי [8]As for **Bet Shammai**'s opinion that the vocalized text of the Torah is authoritative, **we have learned** in a Mishnah (*Zevaḥim* 36b): "The sprinkling of sacrificial blood on the altar is the essential element necessary for a sacrifice to bring about atonement. The blood of burnt-offerings, guilt-offerings, and peace-offerings is sprinkled on two opposite corners of the altar so that it will run down on each of the four sides. The blood of sin-offerings is sprinkled on each of the four corners of the altar. This is the prescribed procedure for sprinkling sacrificial blood on the altar. The Tannaim disagree whether atonement was achieved if a smaller number of sprinklings was performed. [9]**Bet Shammai say:** Regarding **all** sacrifices whose blood **is sprinkled on the outer altar,** [10]if the priest **presented** the sacrificial blood **with** only **one sprinkling** instead of the required two, **he achieved atonement** for the owner of the sacrifice, [11]**as it is said** [Deuteronomy 12:27]: **'And the blood of your sacrifices shall be poured out** upon the altar of the Lord,' implying that a single sprinkling of the blood suffices. [12]But regarding **a sin-offering,** which initially requires four separate sprinklings, the atonement is achieved only if the priest presented the sacrificial blood **with** at least **two sprinklings.** [13]**Bet Hillel** disagree and **say: Even** in the case of **a sin-offering,** [14]if the priest **presented** the sacrificial blood **with** only **one sprinkling, he achieved atonement** for the owner of the sacrifice." [15]**And Rav Huna asked:**

[1]מַה כְּשֶׁטִּיהֵר בַּזָּכָר, בַּנְּקֵבָה כִּפְלַיִם, [2]אַף כְּשֶׁטִּימֵּא בַּזָּכָר, [3]בַּנְּקֵבָה כִּפְלַיִם. [4]לְאַחַר שֶׁיָּצְאוּ, יָצָא וּמְחַזִּיר אַחֲרֵיהֶם. [5]אָמַר לָהֶן: אִי אַתֶּם זְקוּקִים לְכָךְ. [6]'שְׁבוּעַיִם' קָרֵינַן, [7]וְיֵשׁ אֵם לַמִּקְרָא".

[8]בֵּית שַׁמַּאי, דִּתְנַן: [9]"בֵּית שַׁמַּאי אוֹמְרִים: כָּל הַנִּיתָּנִין עַל מִזְבֵּחַ הַחִיצוֹן, [10]שֶׁנְּתָנָן בְּמַתָּנָה אַחַת, כִּיפֵּר, [11]שֶׁנֶּאֱמַר: 'וְדַם זְבָחֶיךָ יִשָּׁפֵךְ'. [12]וּבְחַטָּאת שְׁתֵּי מַתָּנוֹת. [13]וּבֵית הִלֵּל אוֹמְרִים: אַף בְּחַטָּאת, [14]שֶׁנְּתָנָן בְּמַתָּנָה אַחַת, כִּיפֵּר". [15]וְאָמַר רַב הוּנָא:

LITERAL TRANSLATION

[1]Just as what it declared ritually pure regarding a boy, regarding a girl it is double, [2]so too what it declared ritually impure regarding a boy, [3]regarding a girl it is double. [4]After they went out, he went out and searched for them. [5]He said to them: You do not need this. [6]We read: 'Two weeks [שְׁבֻעַיִם],' [7]and the vocalized text [of the Torah] is authoritative."

[8]Bet Shammai, as we have learned: [9]"Bet Shammai say: All that are sprinkled on the outer altar, [10]if he sprinkled with one sprinkling, he atoned, [11]as it is said: 'And the blood of your sacrifices shall be poured out.' [12]And a sin-offering [with] two sprinklings. [13]And Bet Hillel say: Even a sin-offering, [14]if he sprinkled with one sprinkling, he atoned." [15]And Rav Huna said:

RASHI

כפלים – וטומאה דיולדת זכר – שבעה, הלכך דנקבה – שבועיים. **כל הניתנין** – עולה ושלמים ואשם, הטעונין שתי מתנות שהן ארבע, שנתנם במתנה אחת. **כיפר** – דכתיב "ודם זבחיך ישפך", שפיכה אחת במשמע.

NOTES

"וְדַם זְבָחֶיךָ יִשָּׁפֵךְ" **"And the blood of your sacrifices shall be poured out."** The end of the verse, "and you shall eat the meat," implies that the verse refers to those sacrifices of which certain portions are eaten. How, then, do we know that one sprinkling of blood suffices for burnt-offerings, offerings that are totally consumed on the altar? *Ran* explains that when the burnt-offering is consumed by the fire, it is regarded as being "eaten" by the altar.

HALAKHAH

כָּל הַנִּיתָּנִין **All that are sprinkled.** "Regarding all those sacrifices the blood of which is sprinkled on the outer altar, including the sin-offering, if the priest presented the sacrificial blood with only one sprinkling, he has effected atonement," following Bet Hillel. (*Rambam, Sefer Avodah, Hilkhot Pesulei HaMukdashin* 2:1.)

students of Rabbi Akiva. After rising to the presidency of the Sanhedrin he was acknowledged as the greatest Sage of his generation, and all his contemporaries accepted his authority. Since Rabbi Yehudah HaNasi was also very wealthy and enjoyed friendly relations with the Roman Emperor, he exploited the propitious moment, which he feared would not be prolonged, in order to compile and edit an agreed upon and accepted version of the Mishnah, which would contain most of the Halakhic decisions of the Oral Torah. Rabbi relied to a great extent upon an early compilation of Mishnayot by Rabbi Meir, but he added the opinions of other Sages and also issued many new Halakhic decisions in his House of Study. Although his own teachings do not often appear in the Mishnah, his method is evident in that he cited many teachings without mentioning their authors in order to show that they represented the main approach. Rabbi Yehudah HaNasi was famous for his great righteousness and even during his lifetime he was called, "Our Holy Rabbi." Although he possessed great wealth, he himself did not take pleasure in it. Because of Rabbi's status as the leader of the Jews and as the chief Sage of his generation (the Sages said that from the time of Moses there had been none like him, combining Torah with greatness, making him the greatest man of his generation in every sense), the Mishnah became the chief Halakhic foundation for the study of the Oral Law in all the following generations.

Rabbi had two sons, Rabban Gamliel, who succeeded him as Nasi, and Rabbi Shimon, who is usually referred to as Rabbi Shimon son of Rabbi. Rabbi Shimon the son of Menasya, his younger contemporary, said that all the virtues attributed to the great Sages of the generation were found in Rabbi and his sons.

SAGES

בֵּית שַׁמַּאי וּבֵית הִלֵּל **Bet Shammai and Bet Hillel.** These two "houses" were schools founded by the disciples of the last pair of Sages, Shammai and Hillel. Although

מַאי טַעֲמָא דְּבֵית שַׁמַּאי? "קַרְנֹת", "קַרְנֹת", "קַרְנֹת" — [1]הֲרֵי כָּאן שֵׁשׁ. [2]אַרְבַּע לְמִצְוָה, [3]וּשְׁתַּיִם לְעַכֵּב. [4]וּבֵית הִלֵּל אוֹמְרִים: "קְרָנוֹת", "קַרְנֹת", "קַרְנֹת" — [5]הֲרֵי כָּאן אַרְבַּע. [6]שָׁלֹשׁ לְמִצְוָה, [7]וְאַחַת לְעַכֵּב. [8]וְאֵימָא כּוּלְּהוּ לְמִצְוָה! [9]כַּפָּרָה בִּכְדִי לָא אַשְׁכַּחַן. [10]רַבִּי שִׁמְעוֹן, דְּתַנְיָא:

LITERAL TRANSLATION

What is the reason of Bet Shammai? "Corners," "corners," "corners" — [1]thus here are six. [2]Four for the prescribed manner (lit., "for the commandment"), [3]two being indispensable. [4]And Bet Hillel say: "Corners [קְרָנוֹת]," "corner [קַרְנֹת]," "corner [קַרְנֹת]" — [5]thus here are four. [6]Three for the prescribed manner, [7]one being indispensable.

[8]But say all are the prescribed manner!

[9]Atonement without anything we do not find.

[10]Rabbi Shimon, as it was taught:

RASHI

קרנות קרנת קרנת — (ויקרא ד) בחטאת של מזבח החיצון כתיב, בשעיר דנשיא כתיב "קרנת" חסר, ובכשבה דיחיד כתיב (שם) "קרנות" מלא, ובשעיר דיחיד כתיב (שם) "קרנת" חסר. אבל הנך דפר כהן משיח, והעלם דבר, במזבח הפנימי כתיב (שם). והתם כולהו מודו דמתנה אחת מעכבת בהן. ובית שמאי אזלי בתר קרייה. **ואימא** — לבית הלל כולהו למצוה, דהא כולהו צריכי למכתב למצוה, ועיכוב דחדא מנא להו? אימא אף על פי שלא נתן כלום — כיפר. **בבדי** — בלא כלום.

TRANSLATION AND COMMENTARY

What is Bet Shammai's reason for saying this? He answered: Because the verses dealing with the sprinkling of the blood of a sin-offering mention the word "corners" (קַרְנֹת) three times (Leviticus 4:25, 30,34). Bet Shammai maintain that the vocalized text of the Torah is authoritative, and so the word "corners" (קַרְנֹת) is interpreted as a plural form, implying two sprinklings. [1]Since the word "corners" is mentioned three times, we have **here** reference to **six** sprinklings. [2]**Four** of those six sprinklings are mentioned in order to teach that **initially** the blood should be presented upon the altar with four sprinklings. [3]The remaining **two** are mentioned in order to teach that two of the sprinklings are **indispensable** for atonement. Thus, if the priest failed to present the sacrificial blood with at least two sprinklings, he did not achieve atonement. [4]**And Bet Hillel say:** The consonantal text of the Torah as handed down in the tradition is authoritative. Since the first instance of the word **"corners"** is spelled plene (קרנות), implying two sprinklings, and then the second instance of the word **"corner"** is spelled in a defective manner (קַרְנֹת), implying one sprinkling, and the third instance of the word **"corner"** is also spelled in a defective manner (קַרְנֹת), implying once again a single sprinkling, [5]we have **here** reference to **four** sprinklings. [6]**Three** of those four sprinklings were mentioned to teach that **initially** the blood should be sprinkled upon the altar three times (in addition to the requisite one). [7]And **one** of the four sprinklings was mentioned in order to teach that one of the sprinklings **is indispensable** for atonement.

וְאֵימָא כּוּלְּהוּ [8]The Gemara asks: **But** according to Bet Hillel, who maintain that the Torah refers only to four sprinklings of the blood of a sin-offering, you should **say** that **all** four of those sprinklings were mentioned in order to teach **the prescribed manner** in which the sacrificial blood should be presented upon the altar, but all of them are dispensable for atonement!

כַּפָּרָה [9]The Gemara rejects that idea: **We do not find** even a single case where **atonement** is achieved **without any** sprinkling of blood at all. Thus, at least one sprinkling of the blood of the sin-offering must be indispensable for atonement.

רַבִּי שִׁמְעוֹן [10]Returning to the list of Sages who hold that the vocalized text of the Torah is authoritative, the Gemara says: **Rabbi Shimon** also maintains that the vocalized text of the Torah is authoritative, **as it was taught** in a Baraita which deals with the minimum number of walls required for a sukkah, the temporary structure in which a Jew is commanded to dwell for seven days during the Sukkot Festival.

NOTES

קַרְנֹת, קַרְנֹת Corner, corner. All agree here that one does base an interpretation upon the first mention of a subject or word. For when one does not know something (like the number of walls required for a sukkah or the number of judges required to try a case), it must be derived both from the matter itself and from the number of times it is mentioned. However, here, since the corners of the altar have a specific number, everything is derived from the number of times they are mentioned (*Rabbenu Yonah*).

וְאֵימָא כּוּלְּהוּ לְמִצְוָה But say all of them are prescribed. The Gemara suggests that perhaps the four sprinklings were mentioned in order to teach that initially the blood should be sprinkled upon the altar four times, with none of the sprinklings being indispensable for atonement. However, it could not have advanced the converse argument that the four sprinklings were mentioned in order to teach that four sprinklings are indispensable for atonement. For we can only infer that a certain regulation is indispensable if special emphasis is placed upon it by Scripture, e.g., if the Torah refers to it as a statute, or says "thus is the law" (*Remah*).

they themselves disagreed only regarding a few matters, their disciples founded schools that differed both in Halakhic decisions and in world outlook.

The differences between the two schools cannot be defined simply, though in general the House of Shammai tended to be stricter in matters of Halakhah, and the House of Hillel tended to be more lenient. The House of Shammai usually strove to exhaust the logical consequences of an issue, whereas the House of Hillel tended to make allowances for existing reality and its problems.

Although there were many differences of opinion between the two schools, and some of them touched upon very grave matters, personal relations between the Sages of both schools were generally friendly and marked by mutual respect. Although the majority of Sages followed the House of Hillel, the House of Shammai was considered more sharp-witted. Hence, for more than a century, until after the destruction of the Temple, the controversies between them remained unresolved. Ultimately it was agreed that the Halakhah would follow the House of Hillel, and today's Halakhic tradition derives from it.

BACKGROUND

זְרִיקַת דָּם Sprinkling of sacrificial blood. The sprinkling of sacrificial blood on the altar is one of the four essential actions in the offering of every animal sacrifice in the Temple. The presentation of the blood on the altar is the essential element necessary for a sacrifice to bring about atonement. The blood of burnt-offerings, guilt-offerings, and peace-offerings is sprinkled on two opposite corners of the altar so that it will run down on each of the four sides. The blood of sin-offerings is sprinkled on each of the four corners of the altar. This is the prescribed procedure for sprinkling sacrificial blood on the altar. The Tannaim disagreed about whether or not atonement was achieved if a smaller number of sprinklings were performed.

כַּפָּרָה בִּכְדִי Atonement without anything. The essential element of atonement

[1]״שְׁתַּיִם כְּהִלְכָתָן, [2]וּשְׁלִישִׁית אֲפִילּוּ טֶפַח. [3]רַבִּי שִׁמְעוֹן אוֹמֵר: שָׁלֹשׁ כְּהִלְכָתָן, [4]וּרְבִיעִית אֲפִילּוּ טֶפַח״. [5]בְּמַאי קָמִיפַּלְגִי? [6]רַבָּנַן סָבְרִי: יֵשׁ אֵם לַמָּסוֹרֶת. [7]וְרַבִּי שִׁמְעוֹן סָבַר: יֵשׁ אֵם לַמִּקְרָא. [8]רַבָּנַן סָבְרִי: יֵשׁ אֵם לַמָּסוֹרֶת. [9]״בַּסֻּכֹּת״, ״בַּסֻּכֹּת״, ״בַּסֻּכּוֹת״ — [10]הֲרֵי כָּאן אַרְבַּע. [11]דַּל חַד קְרָא לְגוּפֵיהּ, [12]פָּשׁוּ לְהוּ תְּלָת. [13]אֲתַאי הִלְכְתָא גְּרַעֲתָא לַשְּׁלִישִׁית וְאוֹקִימְתָּא אַטֶּפַח. [14]וְרַבִּי שִׁמְעוֹן סָבַר: ״בַּסֻּכֹּת״, ״בַּסֻּכֹּת״, ״בַּסֻּכּוֹת״ — [15]הֲרֵי כָּאן שֵׁשׁ. [16]דַּל חַד קְרָא לְגוּפֵיהּ, [17]פָּשׁוּ לְהוּ אַרְבַּע. [18]אֲתַאי הִלְכְתָא גְּרַעֲתָא לָרְבִיעִית, וְאוֹקְמֵיהּ אַטֶּפַח.

LITERAL TRANSLATION

[1]"Two in the proper way, [2]and a third even a handbreadth. [3]Rabbi Shimon says: Three in the proper way, [4]and a fourth even a handbreadth." [5]About what do they disagree? [6]The Rabbis maintain: The consonantal text [of the Torah] is authoritative. [7]And Rabbi Shimon maintains: The vocalized text [of the Torah] is authoritative. [8]The Rabbis maintain: The consonantal text [of the Torah] is authoritative. [9]"In booths [בַּסֻּכֹּת]," "in booths [בַּסֻּכֹּת]," "in booths [בַּסֻּכּוֹת]" — [10]thus here are four. [11]Remove one verse for the thing itself, [12][and] three are left. [13]The Halakhah came [and] reduced the third and set it at a handbreadth. [14]And Rabbi Shimon maintains: "In booths", "in booths," "in booths" — [15]thus here are six. [16]Remove one verse for the thing itself, [17][and] four are left. [18]The Halakhah came [and] reduced the fourth and set it at a handbreadth.

TRANSLATION AND COMMENTARY

[1]The Rabbis (the anonymous first Tanna of the Mishnah) maintain that "a sukkah must have **two** walls **of proper dimensions** (a minimum length of seven handbreadths, and a minimum height of ten handbreadths), [2]**and a third** wall that may **even** be only **a handbreadth** in width. [3]**Rabbi Shimon** disagrees and **says:** A sukkah must have **three** walls **of proper dimensions,** [4]**and a fourth** wall that may **even** be only **a handbreadth** in width." [5]**About what do** these Tannaim **disagree?** [6]**The Rabbis maintain** that it is **the consonantal text of the Torah** that **is authoritative.** [7]**And Rabbi Shimon maintains** that it is **the vocalized text of the Torah** that **is authoritative.** [8]**The Rabbis maintain** that **the consonantal text of the Torah is authoritative.** [9]The Torah states (Leviticus 23:42-43): "You shall dwell **in booths** [בַּסֻּכֹּת] for seven days; all that are home born in Israel shall dwell **in booths** [בַּסֻּכֹּת]. That your generations may know that I made the children of Israel dwell **in booths** [בַּסֻּכּוֹת], when I brought them out of the land of Egypt; I am the Lord your God." The first two times that the word "booths" is mentioned, the spelling of the word is defective, and so it is interpreted for Halakhic purposes as a singular form. Thus, each of those instances teaches one booth. The third time that the word is mentioned, it is spelled plene, and so it is interpreted as a plural form, teaching another two booths. [10]Hence, we have **here** reference to **four** booths. [11]**Subtract** the reference to a single booth in **the first verse, for** it comes to teach us **the thing itself,** that a Jew is obligated to dwell in a booth for the seven days of the Sukkot Festival. [12]You **are then left** with references to **three** booths, those references alluding to the number of walls that a sukkah requires. It is known that a Halakhah was handed down to Moses at Sinai that one of the walls of the sukkah need not be complete. [13]**That Halakhah comes and reduces the third** wall of the sukkah **and sets it at a handbreadth.** Hence, the Rabbis maintain that a sukkah must have two complete walls and a third wall the width of only a handbreadth. [14]**And Rabbi Shimon maintains** that the vocalized text of the Torah is authoritative. The Torah states: **"In booths," "in booths," "in booths"** — each of which is plural according to the traditional Masoretic vocalization, and therefore interpreted as a plural form for Halakhic purposes. [15]Hence, we have **here** reference to **six** booths, each instance of the word "booths" implying two booths. [16]**Subtract** the reference to two booths in **the first verse, for** that verse comes to teach us **the thing itself,** that a Jew is obligated to dwell in a booth for the seven days of the Sukkot Festival. [17]You **are then left** with references to **four** booths, those references alluding to the number of walls that a sukkah requires. [18]**The Halakhah** which was handed to Moses at Sinai **comes and reduces the fourth** wall of the sukkah **and**

RASHI

שתים — דפנות של סוכה. **כהלכתן** — שלימות. **אפילו טפח** — ברום עשרה טפחים. **למסורת** — שנמסרה כתיבתו לכתבו חסירה. **אתאי הלכתא** — דאמרינן התם: מחיצות הלכה למשה מסיני, ומוקמינן לה לגרוע לדופן אחת.

in any sacrifice is the sprinkling of blood on the altar. If all the rituals, including the sprinkling, have been performed properly, then the owner of the offering attains atonement. Although sacrifice also includes the offering of all or part of the animal's meat on the altar, or the eating of some of the meat by the priests, these features do not affect atonement, and there is no atonement without sprinkling of blood.

BACKGROUND

דְּפָנוֹת הַסּוּכָּה The walls of the sukkah. The Torah does not specify exactly how a sukkah must be built, and most of the Halakhot regarding this matter are traditions in the Oral Law. The Sages deduced from these verses that a rectangular sukkah must have complete walls, extending the entire length of the sukkah, but they disagreed as to whether two complete walls are sufficient, and the third wall can be a symbolic handbreadth in width, or whether there must be three complete walls, plus a symbolic handbreadth for the fourth one.

LANGUAGE

״קְרָנֹת״, ״בַּסֻּכֹּת״ "Corners," "in booths." The Sages, who understand defective plural spellings where the "vav" is missing, as in קְרָנֹת and סֻכֹּת as singular forms, rely on the use of the letter "tav" as a feminine singular ending, like the Arabic ة (*ta marbuta*), which is a similar ending in place of the "heh" that ordinarily indicates the feminine singular.

HALAKHAH

שְׁתַּיִם כְּהִלְכָתָן וּשְׁלִישִׁית אֲפִילּוּ טֶפַח Two in the proper way, and a third even a handbreadth. "A sukkah must have two complete walls (at least seven handbreadths wide) and a third wall that may be only a handbreadth in width," following the Sages, against Rabbi Shimon. (*Shulhan Arukh, Orah Hayyim* 630:2.)

LITERAL TRANSLATION

[1] Rabbi Akiva, as it was taught: [2] "Rabbi Akiva says: From where [do we derive] that a *revi'it* of blood which issued from two corpses causes ritual impurity in a tent? [3] For it is said: 'And he shall not go in unto any dead bodies [נַפְשֹׁת מֵת].' [4] Two bodies and one measure." [5] And the Rabbis: It is written: "Body [נַפְשֹׁת]."

[6] Rav Aḥa bar Ya'akov strongly objected to this: [7] Is there anyone who does not maintain [that] the vocalized text [of the Torah] is authoritative? [8] But surely it was taught: "'In its mother's milk [חָלָב].' [9] I might have thought: [In its mother's] fat [חֵלֶב]. [4B] [10] [But] you say: The vocalized text [of the Torah] is authoritative."

[1] רַבִּי עֲקִיבָא, דְּתַנְיָא: [2] "רַבִּי עֲקִיבָא אוֹמֵר: מִנַּיִין לָרְבִיעִית דָּם שֶׁיָּצְאָה מִשְּׁנֵי מֵתִים שֶׁמְּטַמֵּא בְּאֹהֶל? [3] שֶׁנֶּאֱמַר: 'עַל כָּל נַפְשֹׁת מֵת לֹא יָבֹא'. [4] שְׁתֵּי נְפָשׁוֹת וְשִׁיעוּר אֶחָד".

[5] וְרַבָּנַן: "נַפְשֹׁת" כְּתִיב.

[6] מַתְקִיף לָהּ רַב אַחָא בַּר יַעֲקֹב: [7] מִי אִיכָּא דְּלֵית לֵיהּ יֵשׁ אֵם לַמִּקְרָא? [8] וְהָתַנְיָא "בַּחֲלֵב אִמּוֹ" [9] יָכוֹל בְּחֵלֶב [4B] [10] אָמַרְתָּ: יֵשׁ אֵם לַמִּקְרָא".

RASHI

נפשות – היינו דם דאיקרי נפש. **רביעית** – היא שיעור חיותו של אדם, ובלאו הכי לא איקרי מת עד שיהא בו שיעור מיתה. **שתי נפשות** – משמע משני בני אדם, וכתב: "מת", כדי מיתה – היינו רביעית. ורבנן פליגי עליה ואמרי: עד שיהא השיעור מאדם אחד, ד"נפשת" חסר כתיב. **בחלב אמו** – יכול בחֵלֶב אמו אבל בחָלָב מותר לבשל. **נפשות** – היינו דם דאיקרי נפש. **רביעית** – היא שיעור חיותו של אדם, ובלאו הכי לא איקרי מת עד שיהא בו שיעור מיתה. **שתי נפשות** – משמע משני בני אדם, וכתב: "מת", כדי מיתה – היינו רביעית. ורבנן פליגי עליה ואמרי: עד שיהא השיעור מאדם אחד, ד"נפשת" חסר כתיב. **בחלב אמו** – יכול בחֵלֶב אמו אבל בחָלָב מותר לבשל. **אמרת יש אם למקרא** – וליכא מאן דפליג, דאי פליגי, בשר בחלב מנא לן דאסור?

TRANSLATION AND COMMENTARY

sets it at a handbreadth. Hence, Rabbi Shimon maintains that a sukkah must have three complete walls and a fourth wall that need be only a handbreadth wide.

רַבִּי עֲקִיבָא [1] **Rabbi Akiva** is also of the opinion that the vocalized text of the Torah is authoritative, **as it was taught** in a Baraita dealing with the ritual impurity caused by blood which issued from a corpse. A *revi'it* of the blood of a dead person conveys ritual impurity in the same way as the corpse itself by contact, by being carried, and by "tent impurity" — where the blood overshadows a person or an object, or a person or an object overshadows the blood, or something a handbreadth wide overshadows both the blood and the person or the object. [2] The Baraita states: **"Rabbi Akiva says: From where do we derive** the ruling **that a *revi'it* of blood which issued from two corpses** can also **cause ritual impurity in a tent?** [3] **For it is said** [Leviticus 21:11]: **'And he** [a priest] **shall not go in to any dead bodies** [נַפְשֹׁת מֵת].' The word נַפְשֹׁת translated here as 'bodies' refers to the blood that sustains life in the body. Since the vocalized text of the Torah is authoritative, the word נַפְשֹׁת, which is plural according to the traditional Masoretic vocalization, is interpreted as a plural form for Halakhic purposes. [4] Thus, we may infer that blood coming from **two bodies,** even if it is of only **one measure,** a single *revi'it*, imparts ritual impurity." [5] **And the Rabbis** who disagree with Rabbi Akiva maintain that it is the consonantal text of the Torah that is authoritative. The word upon which Rabbi Akiva bases his exegesis **is spelled** נפשת without a ו. Since the defective spelling represents the singular form of the word, the verse can only teach us that ritual impurity is imparted from a *revi'it* of blood which issued from a single corpse.

מַתְקִיף לָהּ [6] **Rav Aḥa bar Ya'akov strongly objected to** Rabbi Yoḥanan's argument that these cases can be explained as reflecting a disagreement about the authority of the vocalized text of the Torah. [7] **Is there anyone who does not maintain that the vocalized text of the Torah is authoritative?** [8] **But surely it was taught** in a Baraita as follows: "The verse states [Exodus 23:19]: 'You shall not cook a kid **in its mother's milk.'** But since the Biblical text is not vocalized, [9] **we might have thought** that we should not read 'in its mother's milk [בַּחֲלֵב, *baḥalev*],' but rather: **In its mother's fat** [בְּחֵלֶב, *beḥelev*]. According to this reading, only cooking meat in fat would be forbidden. [4B] [10] **But you** will **say** in response: It is **the vocalized text of the Torah** that **is authoritative,** and according to the accepted pronunciation the word is read *'baḥalev.'* Thus, the Torah

SAGES

רַבִּי עֲקִיבָא Rabbi Akiva. The greatest of the Tannaim, Rabbi Akiva (ben Yosef) belonged to the fourth generation. He began his Torah education when already an adult, and studied under Rabbi Eliezer and Rabbi Yehoshua for many years. Numerous stories are told in Rabbinic literature of his devotion to Torah study, of the loyalty of his wife, and of the financial difficulties they had to overcome.

Rabbi Akiva was responsible for the first systematic arrangement and division of the Oral Law. This work was continued by his disciple Rabbi Meir, and formed the basis of the Mishnah as finally edited by Rabbi Yehudah HaNasi. Rabbi Akiva was also the founder of a new school of Biblical interpretation, according to which almost all the regulations of the Oral Law are found to have their basis in the text of the Bible. Rabbi Akiva was active in the period between the destruction of the Second Temple and the Bar Kokhba revolt, in the preparations for which he took an active part. He died as a martyr at the hands of the Romans.

NOTES

יָכוֹל בְּחֵלֶב I might have thought: In its mother's fat. Our commentary follows *Rashi,* who understands that the Baraita explains why we do not say that the word should be read as *beḥelev* (בְּחֵלֶב), rather than *baḥalev* (בַּחֲלֵב), so

HALAKHAH

שְׁתֵּי נְפָשׁוֹת וְשִׁיעוּר אֶחָד Two bodies and one measure. "A *revi'it* of blood which did not issue from a single body, but rather from two corpses, does not impart ritual impurity," following the Sages against Rabbi Akiva. (*Rambam, Sefer Taharah, Hilkhot Tum'at Met* 4:1.)

[1]אֶלָּא, דְּכוּלֵּי עָלְמָא יֵשׁ אֵם לַמִּקְרָא. [2]וְרַבִּי וְרַבָּנַן בְּהָא קָמִיפַּלְגִי: [3]רַבִּי סָבַר: "יַרְשִׁיעֻן אֱלֹהִים" — אַחֲרִינֵי.

[4]וְרַבָּנַן סָבְרִי: "יַרְשִׁיעֻן" — [5]דְּהָאֵיךְ וְהַאי.

[6]וְרַבִּי יְהוּדָה בֶּן רוֹעֵץ — [7]לָא פְּלִיגִי רַבָּנַן עֲלֵיהּ.

[8]בֵּית הִלֵּל, דְּתַנְיָא: "'וְכִפֶּר', 'וְכִפֶּר', 'וְכִפֶּר' — [9]מִפְּנֵי הַדִּין. [10]וַהֲלֹא דִּין הוּא: נֶאֱמַר דָּמִים לְמַטָּה, [11]וְנֶאֱמַר דָּמִים לְמַעְלָה.

LITERAL TRANSLATION

[1]Rather, all Sages (lit., "the entire world") agree that the vocalized text [of the Torah] is authoritative. [2]And Rabbi and the Sages disagree about this: [3]Rabbi maintains: "They shall condemn" — other [judges]. [4]And the Sages maintain: [5]"They shall condemn" — that one and this one.

[6]And Rabbi Yehudah ben Ro'etz — [7]the Sages do not disagree with him.

[8]Bet Hillel, as it was taught: "'And he shall make atonement,' 'And he shall make atonement,' 'And he shall make atonement' — [9]on account of a logical argument [against it]. [10]For is this not an argument: Blood is stated below, [11]and blood is stated above.

TRANSLATION AND COMMENTARY

forbids the cooking of meat in milk." Now, all must agree with this Baraita that the vocalized text of the Torah is authoritative.

אֶלָּא [1]The Gemara now rejects all that has been said up to this point. **Rather, all** the Tannaim **agree that the vocalized text of the Torah is authoritative,** so that we interpret the words of the Torah the way they are pronounced, and the Tannaitic disputes above may be explained in another way. [2]**And Rabbi** Yehudah HaNasi **and the Sages** who disagree about the number of judges needed for the adjudication of monetary cases **disagree about the following:** [3]**Rabbi** Yehudah HaNasi **maintains:** When the Torah stated (Exodus 22:8): "Whom the judges **shall condemn,"** it was referring to **another** set of **judges** in addition to the judges mentioned in the previous verse (22:7): "The cause of both parties shall come before the judges." Just as the second verse refers to two judges, because according to the accepted pronunciation of the word יַרְשִׁיעֻן ("they shall condemn") the verb is plural, so too does the first verse refer to two judges. Hence, we have four judges. Since a court may not be composed of an even number of judges, we must add another judge, bringing the total to five. [4]**And the Sages** who disagree with Rabbi Yehudah HaNasi **maintain:** Indeed, the word יַרְשִׁיעֻן is a plural form implying two judges, for all agree that the vocalized text of the Torah is authoritative. But when the Torah stated: [5]"And the judges **shall condemn,"** it did not mean to add to the judges mentioned in the previous verse, for **those** judges **and these** judges are the very same. Thus, the verses refer to two judges, and since a court may not be composed of an even number of judges, we must add a third judge.

וְרַבִּי יְהוּדָה בֶּן רוֹעֵץ [6]**And** as for the position of **Rabbi Yehudah ben Ro'etz,** it would be wrong to infer from the Baraita that he alone maintains that the vocalized text of the Torah is authoritative, [7]for **the** other **Sages do not disagree with him.**

בֵּית הִלֵּל [8]**And** as for **Bet Hillel,** the reason why they say that even a single sprinkling of the blood of the sin-offering achieves atonement is the following, **as it was taught** in a Baraita: "In Leviticus 4:26 the verse states: **'And he shall make atonement'**; in Leviticus 4:31 the verse also states: **'And he shall make atonement'**; and in Leviticus 4:35 the verse again states, **'And he shall make atonement.'** Why does the Torah repeat this phrase three times regarding sin-offerings offered on the outer altar? [9]**On account of a logical argument** which could have led us to the erroneous conclusion that if the priest omitted even one of the sprinklings, there would be no atonement. The Gemara now presents the argument. [10]**For is this not a** valid **argument: Blood is mentioned below** with respect to a bird sacrificed as a sin-offering [Leviticus 5:9], [11]**and blood is mentioned above** with respect to an animal sacrificed as a sin-offering [Leviticus 4:25,30,34], and so an analogy may be

RASHI

ירשיעון אלהים אחריני — לבד מ"אלהים" האמור למעלה בעינא תרתי, ולמעלה דומיא דלמטה — הרי ארבע. **דהיאך והאי** — "ירשיעון אלהים" האמור למעלה, ו"אלהים" האמור כאן, ולעולם לשון רבים משמע. **וכפר וכפר וכפר** — בשעיר נשיא, ובשעירה דיחיד, ובכבשה דיחיד כתיב (ויקרא ד). **ומשמע** — דסגי בכפרה אחת, כדמפרש. **מפני הדין** — הוצרכו ליכתב כולן, דאי לא הוו כתיבי הוו מייתנא מדינא — דכולהו מתנות מעכבי. שיכול לא גרסינן. **והלא דין הוא** — דלא ליעכבו, למה לי לרבויי דבכפרה אחת סגי? **נאמרו דמים** — בפרשה למטה גבי חטאת העוף דשמיעת הקול, דכתיב (ויקרא ה) "והזה מדם החטאת על קיר המזבח". **ונאמרו דמים למעלה** — בחטאת בהמה.

NOTES

that cooking meat in fat would be forbidden, while cooking meat in milk would be permitted. *Ran* argues that this creates a difficulty, for even if we assume that the consonantal text is authoritative, neither form is defective in spelling, so why should the reading *beḥelev* be given priority over the reading *baḥalev*? Thus, the Baraita intends to explain why we do not read the word both ways, so that cooking meat in either milk or fat would be forbidden.

מַה דָּמִים הָאֲמוּרִים לְמַטָּה,[1] שֶׁנְּתָנָן בְּמַתָּנָה אַחַת, כִּיפֵּר,[2] אַף דָּמִים הָאֲמוּרִים לְמַעְלָה,[3] שֶׁנְּתָנָן בְּמַתָּנָה אַחַת, כִּיפֵּר.[4] אוֹ כַּלֵּךְ לְדֶרֶךְ זוֹ: נֶאֱמַר דָּמִים[5] בַּחוּץ, וְנֶאֱמַר דָּמִים בִּפְנִים.[6] מַה דָּמִים הָאֲמוּרִים בִּפְנִים,[7] חִיסֵּר אַחַת מִמַּתָּנוֹת לֹא[8] עָשָׂה, וְלֹא כְּלוּם, אַף דָּמִים[9] הָאֲמוּרִים בַּחוּץ, חִיסֵּר אַחַת[10] מִמַּתָּנוֹת, לֹא עָשָׂה כְּלוּם. נִרְאֶה לְמִי דּוֹמֶה.[11] דָּנִין חוּץ[12] מֵחוּץ, וְאֵין דָּנִין חוּץ מִפְּנִים.[13] אוֹ כַּלֵּךְ לְדֶרֶךְ זוֹ:[14] דָּנִין[15] חַטָּאת וְאַרְבַּע קְרָנוֹת מֵחַטָּאת וְאַרְבַּע קְרָנוֹת, וְאַל יוֹכִיחַ זֶה[16] שֶׁאֵין חַטָּאת וְאַרְבַּע קְרָנוֹת.

LITERAL TRANSLATION

[1]Just as [regarding] the blood stated below, [2]if he sprinkled it with one sprinkling, he atoned, [3]so too [regarding] the blood stated above, [4]if he sprinkled it with one sprinkling, he atoned. [5]Or go this way: Blood is stated outside, [6]and blood is stated inside. [7]Just as [regarding] the blood that is stated inside, [8][if] he omitted one of the sprinklings, he did not do anything, [9]so too [regarding] the blood that is stated outside, [10][if] he omitted one of the sprinklings, he did not do anything. [11]Let us see to which it is similar. [12]We infer outside from outside, [13]and we do not infer outside from inside. [14]Or go this way: [15]We infer a sin-offering and four corners from a sin-offering and four corners, [16]and do not prove from something that is not a sin-offering and four corners.

TRANSLATION AND COMMENTARY

drawn between them.' [1]**Just as regarding the blood** that is **mentioned below** with respect to a bird sacrificed as a sin-offering, [2]**if** the priest **presented it** upon the altar **with** only **one sprinkling, he achieved atonement** for the owner of the sacrifice — for a bird-offering even initially requires only one sprinkling — [3]let us say that **so too regarding the blood** that is **mentioned above** with respect to an animal sacrificed as a sin-offering, [4]**if** the priest **presented it** upon the altar **with** only **one sprinkling, he achieved atonement.** [5]**Or,** alternatively, you may **go this way: Blood is mentioned** with respect to the ordinary sin-offerings whose blood is sprinkled **outside** of the Sanctuary on the outer altar in the Temple Courtyard, [6]**and blood is mentioned** with respect to those sin-offerings whose blood is sprinkled **inside** the Sanctuary on the golden altar [Leviticus 4:7,18], and so an analogy may be drawn between the two sets of sacrifices. [7]**Just as regarding the blood that is mentioned** with respect to the sin-offerings whose blood is sprinkled **inside** the Sanctuary, [8]**if** the priest **omitted** even **one of the sprinklings, he did not accomplish anything** and there is no atonement [as we learned elsewhere in the Mishnah; *Zevaḥim* 36b], [9]let us say that **so too regarding the blood that is mentioned** with respect to the ordinary sin-offerings whose blood is sprinkled **outside** of the Sanctuary, [10]**if** the priest **omitted** even **one of the sprinklings, he did not accomplish anything,** and there is no atonement. Since the analogy can be drawn either way, [11]**let us see to which** case **is** more **similar to** animal sin-offerings sacrificed on the outer altar. [12]It can be argued that **we** should **infer** the law regarding an animal sin-offering sacrificed on the **outer** altar **from** a bird sin-offering sacrificed on the **outer** altar, [13]**rather than inferring** the law regarding a sin-offering sacrificed on the **outer** altar **from** the law regarding a sin-offering sacrificed on the golden altar **inside** the Sanctuary. [14]**Or,** alternatively, you may **go this way:** [15]**We** should **infer** the law regarding **a sin-offering,** the blood of which must be sprinkled on the **four corners** of the altar, from another **sin-offering,** the blood of which must be sprinkled on the **four corners** of the golden altar, [16]**and** we should **not prove** anything **from** a sacrifice **which is not a sin-offering,** and the blood of which does not have to be sprinkled on the **four corners** of the altar. According to this argument, if a priest presented the sacrificial blood of an ordinary sin-offering with only one sprinkling, there is atonement. Since the argument can go

RASHI

שנתנו במתנה אחת כיפר — דהא לא כתיב "קרנות". לשון אחר, נאמרו דמים למטה — למטה מחוט הסיקרא, בעולה ושלמים ואשם, ונאמר דמים למעלה — למעלה מחוט הסיקרא, דהיינו חטאת בהמה דכתיבי בה "קרנות" (ויקרא ד), מה דמים האמורים למטה שנתנן במתנה אחת כיפר, דהא אפילו בית שמאי מודו בשאר קרבנות דכתיב (דברים יב) "ודם זבחיך ישפך". לשון אחר, למטה — בפרשה תחתונה "דויקרא" באשמות כתיבי. לשון אמצעי עיקר. **בפנים** — חטאות הפנימיות, דפר כהן משיח, והעלם דבר, הטעונין שבע הזיות על הפרוכת ועל מזבח הזהב. ותנן בהו: מתנה אחת מהן מעכבת, ב"איזהו מקומן" (זבחים מז, א), ונפקא לן מקראי ב"הקומץ" רבה (מנחות כז,א): "ועשה... כאשר עשה" מה תלמוד לומר? לכפול בהזאות, מלמד שאם חסר אחת מכל המתנות — לא עשה כלום. **דנין חטאת** — ונאמרו בה "קרנות", מחטאות הפנימיות שהן חטאות ונאמרו בה (ויקרא ד): "קרנות המזבח" קטורת הסמים. **ואל יוביח זה** — דם האשם שאינו חטאות ולא נאמרו בה "קרנות" אלא "סביב". וללישנא דחטאת העוף נמי אינו חטאת וארבע קרנות, כלומר אף על פי שמן חטאות, לא נאמרו בו "קרנות" וכולן שמעתיה ודחטאת העוף לא סלקא לו.

LANGUAGE

כַּלֵּךְ Go. This word is found in Rabbinical Hebrew and in Halakhic Midrashim, where it is often written, אוֹ לְכָה לְךָ — "or go away" — or, הוֹלְכָה לְךָ. The word כַּלֵּךְ itself can be interpreted in several ways. *Ḥokhmat Manoaḥ* maintains that it is an abbreviation of לְכָה לְךָ, and *Rabbi Ya'akov Emden* argues that it is an abbreviation of כַּלֵּה וָלֵךְ — "finish and go."

TRANSLATION AND COMMENTARY

either way, [1] **the verses** come to our assistance and **state** [Leviticus 4:26,31,35]: **'And he shall make atonement,' 'And he shall make atonement,' 'And he shall make atonement.'** [2] The Torah states three times that the priest attains atonement for the owner of the sacrifice **on account of the logical argument** that could have been made and that would have led us to an erroneous conclusion. The words, 'he shall make atonement,' imply that there is atonement in any case, even if the priest did not perform the sacrificial service in the prescribed manner. [3] Thus, the Torah states: **'And he shall make atonement,'** teaching that while ideally there should be four sprinklings of blood, there is atonement **even if** the priest **only presented three sprinklings** of blood. [4] The Torah then states again: **'And he shall make atonement,'** teaching that there is atonement **even if** the priest **only presented two sprinklings** of blood. [5] And the Torah then states yet another time: **'And he shall make atonement,'** teaching that the priest brings the owner of the sacrifice atonement in any case, **even if he only presented one sprinkling** of blood." Thus, we see that Bet Hillel do not base their position that atonement is achieved with a single presentation of sacrificial blood on the principle that the consonantal text of the Torah is authoritative, but rather on their exposition of the verses.

[1] תַּלְמוּד לוֹמַר: ׳וְכִפֶּר׳, ׳וְכִפֶּר׳, ׳וְכִפֶּר׳ [2] מִפְּנֵי הַדִּין. [3] ׳כִּיפֵּר׳ — אַף עַל פִּי שֶׁלֹּא נָתַן אֶלָּא שְׁלֹשָׁה. [4] ׳כִּיפֵּר׳ — אַף עַל פִּי שֶׁלֹּא נָתַן אֶלָּא שְׁתַּיִם. [5] ׳כִּיפֵּר׳ — אַף עַל פִּי שֶׁלֹּא נָתַן אֶלָּא אַחַת״.

[6] וְרַבִּי שִׁמְעוֹן וְרַבָּנַן בְּהָא פְּלִיגִי: [7] רַבִּי שִׁמְעוֹן סָבַר: סְכָכָא לָא בָּעֵי קְרָא. [8] וְרַבָּנַן סָבְרִי: סְכָכָא בָּעֵי קְרָא.

[9] וְרַבִּי עֲקִיבָא וְרַבָּנַן בְּהָא פְּלִיגִי: [10] רַבִּי עֲקִיבָא סָבַר: ״נַפְשֹׁת״ תַּרְתֵּי מַשְׁמַע. [11] וְרַבָּנַן סָבְרִי: ״נַפְשֹׁת״ דְּעָלְמָא מַשְׁמַע.

LITERAL TRANSLATION

[1] The verse states: 'And he shall make atonement,' 'And he shall make atonement,' 'And he shall make atonement' [2] on account of [that] logical argument. [3] 'And he shall make atonement' — even if he only sprinkled three [sprinklings]. [4] 'And he shall make atonement' — even if he only sprinkled two [sprinklings]. [5] 'And he shall make atonement' — even if he only sprinkled one [sprinkling]."

[6] And Rabbi Shimon and the Sages disagree about this: [7] Rabbi Shimon maintains: The covering does not require a verse. [8] And the Sages maintain: The covering requires a verse.

[9] And Rabbi Akiva and the Sages disagree about this: [10] Rabbi Akiva maintains: "Bodies [נַפְשֹׁת]" implies two. [11] And the Sages maintain: It means "bodies" in general.

RASHI

ור׳ שמעון ורבנן – כולהו יש אם למקרא סבירא להו, וכי מדלית חד "בסוכות" לגופיה, פשו להו ארבעה. אבל רבנן סברי: סככה בעי קרא, פשו להו שלש דפנות, וגרעתא הלכתא לשלישית. ור׳ שמעון סבר: סככה לא בעי קרא, דמקרא דמדלינן לגופיה נפקא. דהא בלא סככה לא מיקריה סוכה. **נפשות דעלמא** – ולעולם חדא משמע, אלא הכי קאמר: על אחת מכל נפשות מת שבעולם לא יבא. בפרשת "שמע" ובפרשת כי "יביאך" כתיב "לטטפת" חסר וי״ו, אבל בפרשת "והיה אם שמוע" כתיב "לטוטפות" מלא, הרי כאן ארבע בתים לתפילין של ראש, אבל של יד אינה אלא אחת.

וְרַבִּי שִׁמְעוֹן וְרַבָּנַן [6] As for **Rabbi Shimon and the Sages** who disagree about the number of walls required for a sukkah, both agree that the vocalized text of the Torah is authoritative, and so the triple mention of the word "booths" implies six booths. And they also agree that we do not count the reference to two booths in the first verse, because that verse comes to teach us the basic law that a Jew is obligated to dwell in a temporary booth during the Sukkot Festival, so we are left with references to four booths. What they **disagree about** is the basis for the law that the sukkah must be roofed with branches. [7] **Rabbi Shimon maintains:** The law **that the sukkah must be covered does not require a** special **verse,** for that is implicit in the name given to the temporary booth, sukkhah, which means a covered booth. Thus, we have references to four booths, and since the Halakhah reduces one wall of the sukkah to a handbreadth, a sukkah requires three complete walls and one wall a handbreadth in width. [8] **And the Sages maintain:** The law **that the sukkah must be covered requires a** special **verse.** Thus, one of the references to booths must be used to teach us the matter of the covering, and so we are left with references to three booths. But since the Halakhah reduces one wall of the sukkah, a sukkah requires only two complete walls and one wall a handbreadth in width.

וְרַבִּי עֲקִיבָא וְרַבָּנַן [9] As for **Rabbi Akiva and the Sages** who disagree about whether a *revi'it* of blood which issues from two corpses imparts ritual impurity in a tent, they both agree that the vocalized text of the Torah is authoritative, and so the word נַפְשֹׁת should be interpreted as a plural form. But they **disagree about** the following: [10] **Rabbi Akiva maintains:** The word **"bodies** [נַפְשֹׁת]**"** implies two, and therefore a *revi'it* of blood, even if it issues from two different bodies, imparts ritual impurity. [11] **And the Sages maintain:** The verse speaks about **"bodies" in general,** not about a *revi'it* of blood which issued from two separate bodies.

[1]וְדכוּלֵּי עָלְמָא יֵשׁ אֵם לַמִּקְרָא? [2]וְהָתַנְיָא: [3]״׳לְטוֹטָפֹת׳, ׳לְטֹטָפֹת׳, ׳לְטוֹטָפֹת׳ — [4]הֲרֵי כָּאן אַרְבַּע. [5]דִּבְרֵי רַבִּי יִשְׁמָעֵאל. [6]רַבִּי עֲקִיבָא אוֹמֵר: אֵינוֹ צָרִיךְ. [7]טַט בְּכַתְפֵּי שְׁתַּיִם. [8]פַּת בְּאַפְרִיקִי שְׁתַּיִם״.

[9]אֶלָּא, לְעוֹלָם פְּלִיגִי. [10]וְהָנֵי מִילֵּי כִּי פְּלִיגִי — הֵיכָא דְּשָׁנֵי קְרָא מִמָּסוֹרֶת. [11]אֲבָל הַאי ״חֲלֵב״ וְ״חֵלֶב״ דְּכִי הֲדָדֵי נִינְהוּ — [12]יֵשׁ אֵם לַמִּקְרָא.

[13]וַהֲרֵי ״יִרְאֶה״ ״יֵרָאֶה״ דְּכִי הֲדָדֵי נִינְהוּ, [14]וּפְלִיגִי! [15]דְּתַנְיָא: ״יוֹחָנָן בֶּן דַּהֲבַאי אוֹמֵר מִשּׁוּם

LITERAL TRANSLATION

[1]But do all agree that the vocalized text [of the Torah] is authoritative? [2]But surely it was taught: [3]"'As frontlets [לְטוֹטָפֹת],' 'as frontlets [לְטֹטָפֹת],' 'as frontlets [לְטוֹטָפֹת]' — [4]here are four. [5][These are] the words of Rabbi Yishmael. [6]Rabbi Akiva says: This is not necessary. [7]*Tat* [טַט] in Katfi [means] two. [8]*Pat* [פַּת] in Afriki means two."

[9]Rather, in fact, they disagree. [10]And in which cases (lit., "these things") do they disagree — where the vocalized text differs from the consonantal text. [11]But this *ḥalev* ("milk") and *ḥelev* ("fat") are the same — [12][all agree that] the vocalized text [of the Torah] is authoritative.

[13]But surely *yir'eh* [and] *yera'eh* are the same, [14]and they disagree! [15]For it was taught: "Yoḥanan ben Dahavai says in the name of

TRANSLATION AND COMMENTARY

וְדכוּלֵּי עָלְמָא [1]The Gemara asks: **But** is it really true that **all** Tannaim **agree that the vocalized text of the Torah is authoritative?** [2]**But surely it was taught** otherwise in a Baraita: [3]"Regarding tefillin the Torah states [Exodus 13:16]: 'And **for frontlets** [לְטוֹטָפֹת] between your eyes.' And it states [Deuteronomy 6:9]: 'And they will be **as frontlets** [לְטֹטָפֹת] between your eyes.' And it states [Deuteronomy 11:18]: 'And they will be **as frontlets** [לְטוֹטָפֹת] between your eyes.' In two instances the word *totafot* is spelled in a defective manner, and so it is taken as a singular form, implying a single *totefet*, or compartment of the tefillin box worn on the head. In the third instance the word is spelled plene, and so it is taken as a plural form, implying two compartments. [4]Thus, we have **here** references to **four** separate compartments which together form the cube of the tefillin worn on the head. [5]**This is the position of Rabbi Yishmael.** [6]**Rabbi Akiva says: This** method of interpretation **is not necessary**, for the word *totafot* itself implies four. How so? [7]The word ***tat*** [טַט] in the language spoken in **Katfi means two,** [8]and also the word ***pat*** [פַּת] in the language spoken in **Afriki means two.** Thus, it is from the word *totafot* itself that we learn that there are four separate compartments in the tefillin box worn on the head." The Baraita shows that, according to Rabbi Yishmael, the consonantal text of the Torah is authoritative. Thus, it cannot be unanimously maintained among the Tannaim that the vocalized text of the Torah is authoritative.

אֶלָּא [9]The Gemara now suggests a modified version of the position that it had earlier rejected: **Rather,** we must conclude that the Tannaim do **in fact disagree** about whether the vocalized or the consonantal text of the Torah is authoritative. As for the objection raised earlier — that if the consonantal text of the Torah is authoritative, how do we know that it is forbidden to eat meat cooked in milk? — we can say as follows: [10]What we said above, **concerning the Tannaim disagreeing** about whether the vocalized or the consonantal text of the Torah is authoritative, applies only **when the vocalized text differs from the consonantal text,** i.e., if a letter is missing from a word, but it is pronounced as if that letter were there. For example, where a word which is plural according to the traditional Masoretic vocalization is spelled in a defective manner as if it were a singular form. [11]**But here** the word ***ḥalev*** ("milk") **and** the word ***ḥelev*** ("fat") **are** both spelled in **the same** manner, חלב. [12]In such a case, **all agree that the vocalized text of the Torah is authoritative,** and we interpret the word the way it is pronounced, *ḥalev*. Thus, the Torah forbids the cooking of meat in milk, and not the cooking of meat in fat.

אֶלָּא [13]The Gemara raises an objection: **But surely** the word ***yir'eh*** **and** the word ***yera'eh*** **are** both spelled in **the same** manner, יראה, [14]**and** nevertheless the Tannaim **disagree** about the interpretation of a word with those letters. [15]**For it was taught** in a Baraita: **"Yoḥanan ben Dahavai says in the name of**

RASHI

כתפי – שם מקום, כשרוצים לומר שתים, אומר: טט. **ואפריקי** – נמי מקום וקורין לשתים – פת. **דשני קרא ממסורת** – באותיות הקריה יתירות על המסורת, כמו ״לטוטפות״ ״בסוכות״ ״קרנות״, דאיכא למימר: מדשני – ודאי תרווייהו דרשינן. **אבל חלב וחלב דכי הדדי נינהו** – כולי עלמא מודו דיש אם למקרא.

LANGUAGE

טַט, פַּת ***Tat, Pat.*** Many scholars have tried to identify the places named here and the foreign words that are cited. Some believe that "Katfei" is a version of "Coptic," and that in that language *"aft"* means "two." Others maintain that "Afriki" here does not refer to Africa but to Phrygia in Asia Minor, and that *"pat"* is related to the Gothic *"bathos"* (which has related roots in Indo-European languages), meaning "the two of them." In any event, these words and places have not yet been adequately identified.

BACKGROUND

דְּשָׁנֵי קְרָא מִמָּסוֹרֶת Where the vocalized text differs from the consonantal text. In many places in the Torah, an oral tradition (קְרִי) exists regarding the pronunciation of certain words. Occasionally the word cannot be read at all as written in the Masoretic text (כְּתִיב), so the oral tradition is clearly the only way of reading it. However, sometimes the word can also be read as written, and in such cases it may be said that the Torah itself offers different ways of understanding it. (See *Radak,* who considers both the written and the oral form whenever they differ.) Hence controversy may arise regarding which of the readings determines the Halakhah. But if the tradition records no difference regarding the written form of a word, clearly one must follow the accepted tradition and not invent a new way of reading.

SAGES

יוֹחָנָן בֶּן דַּהֲבַאי Yoḥanan ben Dahavai. This Sage is mentioned only in the Baraita. He apparently belonged to the generation prior to the one that completed the Mishnah, and he learned Torah from the Sages of Yavneh. Only a few of his Aggadic and Halakhic teachings have been preserved.

HALAKHAH

לְטוֹטָפֹת As frontlets. "The cube of the tefillin worn on the head is made from one piece of leather formed into four separate subcompartments, and the cube of the tefillin worn on the arm is formed of a single compartment." (*Shulḥan Arukh, Oraḥ Ḥayyim* 32:38.)

רַבִּי יְהוּדָה בֶּן תֵּימָא: [1]הַסּוּמָא בְּאַחַת מֵעֵינָיו פָּטוּר מִן הָרְאִיָּה, [2]שֶׁנֶּאֱמַר: ״יִרְאֶה״, ״יֵרָאֶה״. [3]כְּדֶרֶךְ שֶׁבָּא לִרְאוֹת, כָּךְ בָּא לֵירָאוֹת. [4]מַה לִּרְאוֹת בִּשְׁתֵּי עֵינָיו, [5]אַף לֵירָאוֹת בִּשְׁתֵּי עֵינָיו!״

[6]אֶלָּא, אָמַר רַב אַחָא בְּרֵיהּ דְּרַב אִיקָא: [7]אָמַר קְרָא: ״לֹא תְבַשֵּׁל גְּדִי״ — [8]דֶּרֶךְ בִּישּׁוּל אָסְרָה תּוֹרָה.

LITERAL TRANSLATION

Rabbi Yehudah ben Tema: [1]Someone who is blind in one eye is exempt from appearing [in the Temple], [2]as it is said: *'Yir'eh,' 'yera'eh.'* [3]In the way that He comes to see, so He comes to be seen. [4]Just as to see with two eyes, [5]so too to be seen with two eyes!"

[6]Rather, Rav Aḥa the son of Rav Ika said: [7]The verse says: "You shall not cook a kid" — [8]the Torah forbade in the manner of cooking.

TRANSLATION AND COMMENTARY

Rabbi Yehudah ben Tema: [1]**Someone who is blind,** even **in** only **one eye, is exempt from** the obligation of every Jewish male **to appear in the Temple** on each of the three Pilgrim Festivals. [2]The blind man's exemption is derived from the verse **which states** [Deuteronomy 16:16]: 'Three times a year shall all your males appear [יֵרָאֶה] before the Lord your God in the place which he shall choose.' Now, according to its spelling, the word יראה can be read as *yir'eh,* 'he shall see,' but according to the accepted tradition, it is pronounced *yera'eh,* 'he shall be seen,' or 'he shall appear' (as it was translated above). For Halakhic purposes the verse is interpreted in both ways: All your males shall see the Lord, and all your males shall appear before and be seen by the Lord. Thus, an analogy may be drawn between the manner in which you see the Lord, and the manner in which the Lord sees you. [3]**In the same way that He sees** you, **so** too **is He seen** by you. [4]**Just as** He, figuratively speaking, **sees** you **with two eyes,** meaning with total vision, [5]**so too** does He come **to be seen** by you **with two eyes!** Thus, a person who is blind in one eye is exempt from the obligation to appear in the Temple." Hence, according to Yoḥanan ben Dahavai, even when two different words are spelled alike, we do not interpret a word with that spelling only according to its accepted pronunciation, but also according to its other possible pronunciation. Why, then, do we not say that the Torah forbids not only the cooking of meat in milk, but also the cooking of meat in fat, for the word חלב can mean either one?

אֶלָּא [6]The Gemara concludes: **Rather, Rav Aḥa the son of Rav Ika said:** The Tannaim do in fact disagree about whether the vocalized text of the Torah or its consonantal text is authoritative, even when the vocalized text does not differ from the consonantal text. However, with respect to prohibiting the mixing of meat and milk, all agree that the Torah forbids the cooking of meat in milk. [7]For **the verse says** (Exodus 23:19): **"You shall not cook a kid"** — [8]**the Torah forbade** something which falls under **the category of cooking.** Preparing food in milk is called cooking; preparing food in fat is called frying. Since the Torah talks about a prohibition involving cooking, we must interpret the word חלב as "milk," and not as "fat."

RASHI

יראה כל זכורך כתיב — וקרינא יֵרָאֶה תרווייהו דרשינן: ״יֵרָאֶה כל זכורך״ — שיראו פני השכינה. יֵרָאֶה — משמע שיתראו לפניו שהוא בא לראותו, היקיש ראייתך לראיתו, כדרך שהקדוש ברוך הוא בא לראותך, כך בא ליראות לו, מה הוא רואה אותך כשהוא שלם שנאמר (דברים יא): ״עיני ה׳ אלהיך בה מראשית״, אף אתה רואה אותו בשתי עיניך. אלמא, אף על גב דכי הדדי נינהו — דרשינן מסורת. וגבי ״חלב אמו״ מאן לימא דלא לידרש ״חלב אמו״ בתר מסורת. **דרך בישול** — חָלָב גלול כמים, ואיכא בישול. אבל חֵלֶב אינו בישול אלא טגון.

NOTES

לִרְאוֹת לֵירָאוֹת **To see, to be seen.** Our commentary follows *Rashi* (here and in *Ḥagigah* 2a), according to the reading and interpretation of *Maharshal.* According to *Rashi,* Yoḥanan ben Dahavai argued as follows: In the same manner that He (God), sees you, so too is He seen by you. Just as He, figuratively speaking, sees you with two eyes (with perfect vision), so too is He seen by you with two eyes. Thus, a person who is blind, even in only one eye, is exempt from the obligation to appear in the Temple. *Tosafot* and others raised a number of objections against *Rashi.* First, the subject of the comparison cannot be God. God does not come to the Temple, for He is already there. And second, the comparison should start with the way that the word is actually read, *yera'eh* — "he shall be seen" — and proceed to the other way that the word can possibly be read, *yir'eh* — "he shall see" — and not the other way around.

Rabbenu Tam, Remah, Ran and others suggest a different interpretation: In the same manner that someone who is under obligation to appear in the Temple is seen, so too does he see. Just as he is seen by One with two eyes (God who has perfect vision), so too does he see with two eyes. But a person who is blind, even in only one eye, is exempt from this obligation.

דֶּרֶךְ בִּישּׁוּל אָסְרָה תּוֹרָה **The Torah forbade the manner of cooking.** Our commentary follows *Rashi,* who explains that the Torah forbade something which falls under the category

HALAKHAH

הַסּוּמָא בְּאַחַת מֵעֵינָיו **Someone who is blind in one eye.** "A person who is blind even in only one eye, is exempt from the obligation to appear in the Temple on the three Pilgrim Festivals," following Yoḥanan ben Dahavai. (*Rambam, Sefer Korbanot, Hilkhot Ḥagigah* 2:1.)

SAGES

רַבִּי יְהוּדָה בֶּן תֵּימָא **Rabbi Yehudah ben Tema.** He was a Tanna, but it is not known in which generation he lived. We possess little information about his life, but his teachings are preserved in both the Aggadah and the Halakhah. He was probably one of the Sages present in Kerem BeYavneh after the destruction of the Second Temple.

רַב אַחָא בְּרֵיהּ דְּרַב אִיקָא **Rav Aḥa the son of Rav Ika.** A fifth-generation Babylonian Amora, Rav Aḥa the son of Rav Ika was the nephew of Rav Aḥa bar Ya'akov (both Sages apparently lived in the same city, Papunya). Rav Aḥa the son of Rav Ika studied with many fourth- and fifth-generation Amoraim, and engaged in Halakhic discussions with Rav Pappa, and later with Rav Ashi. His teachings — some of which were transmitted by his student, Rav Huna bar Manoaḥ — are cited in various places in the Talmud.

TRANSLATION AND COMMENTARY

תָּנוּ רַבָּנַן [1]The Gemara now returns to the main topic under discussion: **Our Rabbis taught** the following Baraita: **"Monetary cases** are adjudicated **by** a court of **three** judges. [5A] [2]**And if** a person **was** publicly **recognized** as an **expert** in the law, [3]**he may judge** monetary matters **even singly."**

אָמַר רַב נַחְמָן [4]The Gemara elaborates what is meant by a recognized expert. **Rav Naḥman said: Someone like me** comes under the category of a recognized expert and **may** therefore **judge monetary cases singly.** [5]**And similarly, Rabbi Ḥiyya said: Someone like me** is considered a recognized expert and **may** therefore **judge monetary cases singly.**

אִיבַּעְיָא לְהוּ [6]The following **problem arose in discussion** among the Sages: What precisely did these Sages mean when they said that "someone like me" is a recognized expert? [7]**Did they mean** to say: **Someone like me, for I** have **learned** the corpus of civil law from my teachers, [8]**and** I am able to **exercise my** power of **reasoning,** and understand the rationale of the law, and draw valid Halakhic conclusions, [9]**and** I have also **received authorization** to serve as a judge from the Nasi (the president of the Sanhedrin) or the Exilarch (the lay head of the Jewish community in Babylonia). For in addition to being great Talmudic scholars, both Rav Naḥman and Rabbi Ḥiyya received authorization to serve as judges. [10]**But** if **someone who did not receive** such **authorization** from the Nasi or the Exilarch judged a monetary case singly, [11]**his judgment is not valid.** [12]**Or perhaps** they meant to say: **Even** if a person **did not receive authorization** to serve as a judge from the Nasi or the Exilarch, if he learned the law and understands its intricacies, he is regarded as a recognized expert, [13]so that **his decision is valid,** even if it is issued singly?

[1]תָּנוּ רַבָּנַן: ״דִּינֵי מָמוֹנוֹת
בִּשְׁלֹשָׁה. [5A] [2]וְאִם הָיָה
מוּמְחֶה לָרַבִּים, [3]דָּן אֲפִילּוּ
יְחִידִי״.
[4]אָמַר רַב נַחְמָן: כְּגוֹן אֲנָא דָּן
דִּינֵי מָמוֹנוֹת בִּיחִידִי. [5]וְכֵן אָמַר
רַבִּי חִיָּיא: כְּגוֹן אֲנָא דָּן דִּינֵי
מָמוֹנוֹת בִּיחִידִי.
[6]אִיבַּעְיָא לְהוּ: [7]כְּגוֹן אֲנָא,
דִּגְמִירְנָא, [8]וּסְבִירְנָא, [9]וּנְקִיטְנָא
רְשׁוּתָא? [10]אֲבָל לָא נָקֵיט
רְשׁוּתָא — [11]דִּינֵיהּ לָא דִּינָא.
[12]אוֹ דִּילְמָא: אַף עַל גַּב דְּלָא
נָקֵיט רְשׁוּתָא, [13]דִּינֵיהּ דִּינָא?

LITERAL TRANSLATION

[1]Our Rabbis taught: "Monetary cases by three. [5A] [2]And if he was a recognized [lit., 'for many, public'] expert, [3]he may judge even singly."

[4]Rav Naḥman said: [Someone] like me may judge monetary cases singly. [5]And similarly, Rabbi Ḥiyya said: [Someone] like me may judge monetary cases singly.

[6]It was asked of them: [7][Did they mean someone] like me, that has learned, [8]and can reason, [9]and has received authorization? [10]But someone who has not received authorization, [11]his judgment is not a judgment. [12]Or perhaps: Even though he has not received authorization, [13]his decision is a decision?

RASHI

דן אפילו ביחיד — דכתיב (ויקרא יט): ״בצדק תשפוט״. וקסבר: אין כאן עירוב פרשיות. **דגמירנא** — שמועות דינין מרבותי. **וסבירנא** — יודע אני להוסיף וליישב טעמים מדעתי. **ונקיטנא רשותא** — מריש גלותא, דיינא דיני ממונות ביחידי. **דיניה לאו דינא** — והדר דינא לגמרי.

NOTES

of cooking. Thus, it cannot mean that cooking meat in fat is forbidden, for that is not cooking, but rather frying. Others explain the Gemara as follows: The Torah forbade the eating of something which is forbidden only on account of the way it was cooked. Thus, it cannot mean that cooking meat in fat is forbidden, for *ḥelev* — non-kosher animal fat — is in and of itself forbidden to be eaten, regardless of whether or how it is cooked (see *Tosafot, Rabbenu Yonah, Ran,* and *Rosh*).

מוּמְחֶה לָרַבִּים **A recognized expert.** *Rav Sherira Gaon* explains that the term *mumḥeh* as it is used here means "tested" or "proven." The expression *mumḥeh lerabbim* refers to someone who is thoroughly fluent in the Mishnah and Gemara, has sound Halakhic judgment, is often asked about Halakhic matters, and never makes a mistake. Thus, his expertise is recognized by all.

יָחִיד מוּמְחֶה **A single, expert judge.** Some commentators suggest that an expert judge may judge alone, because even in the case of three judges the verdict is rendered by the decisive vote of one judge. Consequently a single judge, whose ability to weigh all facets of a case are well known, takes the place of three judges (*Geonim, Rabbi Yehudah Almandri*).

מוּמְחֶה לָרַבִּים דָּן אֲפִילּוּ יְחִידִי **A recognized expert may judge even singly.** *Ran* summarizes the matter of a *mumḥeh* as follows: There are three types of "expert" judges: (1) A judge who was formally ordained by his teachers; (2) a publicly recognized expert on the law who

HALAKHAH

מוּמְחֶה לָרַבִּים **A recognized expert.** "A person who is publicly recognized as an expert in the law, someone known to have thorough familiarity with the law and sound judgment in its application, may judge monetary cases even singly. *Rema* notes that today nobody is recognized as an expert in the law having the authority to coerce a person to appear before him in judgment." (*Shulḥan Arukh, Ḥoshen Mishpat* 3:2.)

BACKGROUND

מוּמְחֶה **Expert judge.** This word is derived from a special meaning of the root מחה, which is unlike its meaning in other derivatives. The meaning here is something that has been examined and verified, something that has been shown to be true. Related meanings are found in ancient inscriptions.

TERMINOLOGY

אִיבַּעְיָא לְהוּ **It was asked of them,** i.e., they (the scholars in the Academy) asked. This expression usually introduces a problem raised anonymously in the Gemara.

SAGES

רַב נַחְמָן **Rav Naḥman.** This is Rav Naḥman bar Ya'akov, a Babylonian Amora of the second and third generations. Rav Naḥman's father was a scribe at the court associated with the Amora Shmuel. Rav Naḥman studied with Shmuel, whose rulings he frequently cites, and with Rabbah bar Avuha, one of Rav's disciples and a member of the Exilarch's family (according to some opinions he was himself the Exilarch).

Rav Naḥman married Rabbah bar Avuha's daughter, Yalta, a learned and strong-willed woman. By his marriage Rav Naḥman became connected with the House of the Exilarch, and after some time he was appointed judge of the House of the Exilarch in Neharde'a. Because of his status in the House of the Exilarch, and because of his profound knowledge of monetary law, Rav Naḥman was considered the greatest authority in this field.

Rav Naḥman discusses Halakhic problems with a great many Sages, in particular Rav Huna, Rav Yehudah, Rav Sheshet, and Rav Ḥisda.

Although Rav Naḥman did not serve as an official head of a yeshivah, many members of his generation studied with him; the great Amora Rava was his outstanding disciple.

Rav Naḥman seems to have been wealthy all his life, and was regarded as the greatest Sage of his generation and the authoritative teacher of Torah in his city. Several of Rav Naḥman's sons were scholars.

רַבִּי חִיָּיא **Rabbi Ḥiyya.** Originating from the town of Kafri

TRANSLATION AND COMMENTARY

תָּא שְׁמַע [1]The Gemara suggests a resolution to this problem: **Come and hear** the following illustrative story, **for Mar Zutra the son of Rav Naḥman,** who had not been authorized by the Exilarch to serve as a judge, **issued a** certain **judgment** singly **and erred** in his decision. [2]**He came** for advice **before Rav Yosef**, who **said to him:** [3]**If** the two litigants **agreed to have you judge them, you need not compensate** the injured party, since their acceptance of you as a judge exempts you from all liability. [4]**But if** they did **not** accept you, and you coerced them to appear before you, **go pay** the injured party. [5]**Infer from this** that even **if someone did not receive authorization** from the Exilarch, if he was publicly recognized as an expert in the law, [6]**his decision is valid,** even if it was issued singly. The Gemara affirms that its conclusion is correct: Indeed, [7]it may be **inferred from this** that someone who is recognized as an expert in the law may judge monetary cases singly, even if he did not receive the Exilarch's authorization.

אָמַר רַב [8]**Rav said:** If **someone wishes to judge** monetary cases, [9]**and to be exempt** from all liability **should he err** in his decision, [10]**he should receive authorization** to serve as a judge **from the House of the Exilarch.** [11]**And similarly Shmuel said:** In order to exempt himself from all liability, [12]a person who wishes to judge monetary cases **should receive authorization** to serve as a judge **from the House of the Exilarch.**

[1]תָּא שְׁמַע: דְּמָר זוּטְרָא בְּרֵיהּ דְּרַב נַחְמָן דָּן דִּינָא וְטָעָה. [2]אֲתָא לְקַמֵּיהּ דְּרַב יוֹסֵף, אֲמַר לוֹ: [3]אִם קִיבְּלוּךְ עֲלַיְיהוּ, לֹא תְּשַׁלֵּם, [4]וְאִי לֹא, זִיל שַׁלֵּים. [5]שְׁמַע מִינָּהּ: כִּי לָא נָקֵיט רְשׁוּתָא, [6]דִּינֵיהּ דִּינָא. [7]שְׁמַע מִינָּהּ.

[8]אָמַר רַב: הַאי מַאן דְּבָעֵי לְמֵידַן דִּינָא, [9]וְאִי טָעָה מִיבָּעֵי לְמִיפַּטְרָא, [10]לִישְׁקוֹל רְשׁוּתָא מִבֵּי רֵישׁ גָּלוּתָא. [11]וְכֵן אָמַר שְׁמוּאֵל: [12]לִשְׁקוֹל רְשׁוּתָא מִבֵּי רֵישׁ גָּלוּתָא.

LITERAL TRANSLATION

[1]Come [and] hear, for Mar Zutra the son of Rav Naḥman issued a ruling and erred. [2]He came before Rav Yosef, [who] said to him: [3]If they accepted you upon themselves, you do not pay. [4]And if not, go pay. [5]Infer from this: If he has not received authorization, [6]his judgment is a judgment. [7]Infer from this.

[8]Rav said: Someone who wishes to judge a case, [9]and wishes to be exempt if he errs, [10]let him receive authorization from the House of the Exilarch (lit., "the head of the Exile"). [11]And similarly Shmuel said: [12]Let him receive authorization from the House of the Exilarch.

RASHI

דן דינא – ביחידי. **אי קבלוך עלייהו** – לגמרי, ליכא אחריך אם לדין אם לטעות, ולא יתבעוך – לא תשלם. **ואי לא זיל שלים** – ואי לא קבלו טעותך עליהם, דאמרו לך: דיינת לן דין תורה – זיל שלים, ומיהו מיהדר דינא – לא. אלמא גמיר וסביר, וכי לא נקיט רשותא דיניה דינא ולא מהדר. **לישקול רשותא** – דכיון דברשות נחת – לא משלם.

NOTES

did not receive ordination; and (3) a publicly recognized expert in the law who also received authorization to serve as a judge from the Nasi or the Exilarch. Someone who is recognized as an expert in the law may judge cases even singly, and even if he was not authorized by the Exilarch or Nasi to do so; but if he errs in his judgment, he is liable for any damage which results from his decision. However, if he received authorization, not only may he judge cases even singly, but he is also exempt from all liability for his errors in judgment. An ordained judge may judge even singly, and is exempt from all liability, even if he was not authorized by the Exilarch or the Nasi to serve as a judge, for his ordination stands in place of authorization.

HALAKHAH

דָּן דִּינָא וְטָעָה He issued a judgment and erred. "If a person was publicly recognized as an expert in the law, and he received authorization from the Exilarch or the Nasi of Eretz Israel to serve as a judge, or he was accepted by the two litigants to act in that capacity, and he issued a judgment based on an error of discretion, the judgment is subject to revision. If the judgment cannot be revised, the judge is exempt from liability for the damage he caused. But if had not been authorized to serve as a judge, and had not been accepted by the two litigants to act in that capacity, he must compensate the injured party for the damage his erroneous judgment caused him." (*Shulḥan Arukh, Ḥoshen Mishpat* 25:2.)

לִישְׁקוֹל רְשׁוּתָא Let him receive authorization. "The Exilarchs in Babylonia have the authority of kings. Any person qualified to serve as a judge and authorized by the Exilarch to function in that capacity is authorized to be a judge anywhere in the world and coerce litigants to appear before him. Any person qualified to serve as a judge and authorized to serve in that capacity by the Nasi of Eretz Israel is authorized to work as a judge and to coerce litigants to appear before him anywhere in Eretz Israel, as well as in the towns that are situated along its borders. But his authority to coerce the parties to appear before him does not extend outside of Eretz Israel, unless he was authorized by the Exilarch as well." (*Rambam, Sefer Shofetim, Hilkhot Sanhedrin* 4:13,14.)

in Babylonia, Rabbi Ḥiyya was one of the last of the Tannaim, and a student and colleague of Rabbi Yehudah HaNasi. Rabbi Ḥiyya came from a distinguished family which was descended from King David and produced many Sages. While he still lived in Babylonia he was already considered a great Torah scholar, and when he left Babylonia with members of his family to settle in Eretz Israel, there were those who said, in exaggeration, that the Torah would have been forgotten in Eretz Israel had he not arrived from Babylonia to reestablish it. Upon his arrival in Eretz Israel, he became the student and colleague of Rabbi Yehudah HaNasi. He also became a close friend of Rabbi Yehudah HaNasi and in particular of his son, Rabbi Shimon, who was Rabbi Ḥiyya's business partner. Rabbi Ḥiyya was one of the greatest Sages of his generation. Not only was he a great Torah scholar, but he was also very pious, as is related in many places in the Talmud. His great achievement was the editing of collections of Baraitot, as a kind of supplement to the Mishnah edited by Rabbi Yehudah HaNasi. These collections, which he seems to have edited in collaboration with his colleague and student, Rabbi Oshaya, were considered extremely reliable, so much so that it was said that any Baraitot not reported by them were not worthy of being cited in the House of Study.

It seems that, upon his arrival in Eretz Israel, he received some financial support from the House of the Nasi, but he mainly earned his living from international trade on a large scale, especially in silk. He had twin daughters, Pazi and Tavi, from whom important families of Sages were descended. He also had twin sons, Yehudah (Rabbi Yannai's son-in-law) and Ḥizkiyah, who were important scholars in the transitional generation between the Tannaim and the Amoraim. They apparently took their father's place at the head of his yeshivah in Tiberias, where he lived. All of Rabbi Yehudah HaNasi's students were Rabbi Ḥiyya's colleagues, and he was also on close terms with

TRANSLATION AND COMMENTARY

פְּשִׁיטָא [1]The Gemara now clarifies the geographical limits of the jurisdiction of the Exilarch and of the Nasi: **It is obvious that** if the Exilarch **here,** in Babylonia, authorized a person **to** serve as a judge **here**, in Babylonia, [2]**or** if the Nasi **there,** in Eretz Israel, authorized a person **to** serve as a judge **there,** in Eretz Israel, the authorization **is valid.** [3]**And** it is obvious that if the Exilarch **here**, in Babylonia, authorized a person **to** serve as a judge **there**, in Eretz Israel, the authorization **is also valid.** The Exilarch's authority is greater than that of the Nasi, [4]**for** the Exilarch **here**, in Babylonia, **is** referred to by his **scepter,** that symbol of royal authority and political power with which he is invested, [5]**and** the Nasi **there**, in Eretz Israel, **is** referred to as **a lawgiver,** the head of an academy with far less political authority. [6]**As it was taught** in a Baraita, which expounds the verse, "The scepter shall not depart from Yehudah, nor the lawgiver from between his feet" (Genesis 49:10): [7]**"'The scepter shall not depart from Judah' —** [8]**this** is an allusion to **the Exilarchs in Babylonia who** are descendants of Judah and **rule over Israel with a scepter.** The Exilarchs in Babylonia are invested with the authority of a king, both by virtue of their Davidic ancestry and by virtue of the powers granted them by the non-Jewish authorities. [9]**'Nor the lawgiver from between his feet' — this** is an allusion to other leaders of Israel who can trace their lineage back to Judah, [10]**the descendants of Hillel** the Elder **who** fill the position of Nasi of Eretz Israel and **teach Torah in public."** Since the Exilarch's authority exceeds that of the Nasi, the judicial authorization conferred by the Exilarch in Babylonia is valid in Eretz Israel. [11]But **what is the law** if the Nasi **there**, in Eretz Israel, authorized a person **to serve as a judge here,** in Babylonia? Is the Nasi's authorization valid?

תָּא שְׁמַע [12]The Gemara answers: **Come and hear** the following story: [13]**Rabbah bar Ḥanah,** who had left Eretz Israel for Babylonia, **issued a** certain **judgment** while he was in Babylonia **and erred** in his decision. [14]Upon his return to Eretz Israel, Rabbah bar Ḥanah **came before Rabbi Ḥiyya,** whom he wished to consult. [15]Rabbi Ḥiyya **said to him: If** the two litigants **accepted you** as a judge, **you need not pay** the injured party. [16]**But if** they did **not** accept you as a judge, but rather you ordered the two litigants to appear before you, **go and pay** for the damage you caused. [17]**But surely** before he left for Babylonia **Rabbah bar Ḥanah had received authorization** to serve as a judge from the Nasi in Eretz Israel (as will be explained below)!

[1]פְּשִׁיטָא, מֵהָכָא לְהָכָא [2]וּמֵהָתָם לְהָתָם, מְהַנֵּי. [3]וּמֵהָכָא לְהָתָם, נַמִּי מְהַנֵּי, [4]דְּהָכָא "שֵׁבֶט" [5]וְהָתָם "מְחוֹקֵק", [6]כִּדְתַנְיָא: [7]"'לֹא יָסוּר שֵׁבֶט מִיהוּדָה' — [8]אֵלּוּ רָאשֵׁי גָלֻיּוֹת שֶׁבְּבָבֶל, שֶׁרוֹדִין אֶת יִשְׂרָאֵל בְּשֵׁבֶט. [9]'וּמְחֹקֵק מִבֵּין רַגְלָיו' — [10]אֵלּוּ בְּנֵי בָנָיו שֶׁל הִלֵּל, שֶׁמְּלַמְּדִין תּוֹרָה בָּרַבִּים. [11]מֵהָתָם לְהָכָא, מַאי? [12]תָּא שְׁמַע: [13]דְּרַבָּה בַּר חָנָה דָּן דִּינָא וְטָעָה. [14]אֲתָא לְקַמֵּיהּ דְּרַבִּי חִיָּיא. [15]אֲמַר לֵיהּ: אִי קִיבְּלוּךְ עֲלַיְיהוּ, לָא תְּשַׁלֵּם, [16]וְאִי לָא, זִיל שַׁלֵּים. [17]וְהָא רַבָּה בַּר חָנָה רְשׁוּתָא

LITERAL TRANSLATION

[1]It is obvious, from here to here, [2]and from there to there, it is effective. [3]And from here to there, it is also effective, [4]for here is a scepter [5]and there is a lawgiver, [6]as it was taught: [7]"'The scepter shall not depart from Judah' — [8]these are the Exilarchs in Babylonia who rule over Israel with a scepter. [9]'Nor the lawgiver from between his feet' — [10]these are the descendants [lit., 'sons of the sons'] of Hillel who teach Torah in public." [11]From there to here, what [is the law]?

[12]Come [and] hear, [13]for Rabbah bar Ḥanah judged a case and erred. [14]He came before Rabbi Ḥiyya, [15][who] said to him: If they accepted you upon themselves, you do not pay. [16]And if not, go pay. [17]But surely Rabbah bar Ḥanah received authorization!

RASHI

מהכא להכא — מריש גלותא לבבל, למידן דינא בבבל. **ומהתם להתם** — מנשיא דארץ ישראל, לדון בארץ ישראל. **שבט** — לשון שררה, ויש להן רשות להפקיר, דהפקר בית דין הפקר דכתיב (עזרא י): "וכל אשר לא יבא וגו'" ביבמות ב"האשה רבה" (פט,ב). **מחוקק** — שררה מועטת. **שרודים את העם** — שיש להם כח ורשות מאת מלכי פרס. **בני בניו של הלל** — הלל נשיא היה, כדאמר בפסחים ב"אלו דברים" (סו,א): הושיבוהו בראש ומינוהו נשיא עליהם. **דן דינא** — בבבל, וטעה. **אתא** — לארץ ישראל לקמיה דר' חייא.

NOTES

שֵׁבֶט **Scepter.** The Exilarch represents the status of a king, since he is a descendant of the House of David and appointed by the Persian King (*Ran*).

וּמְחֹקֵק מִבֵּין רַגְלָיו **A lawgiver from between his feet.** *Tosafot* and others (following the Jerusalem Talmud) explain that the difference in authority between the Exilarch and the Nasi stems from the fact that the Exilarchs descend from David through an entirely male line, whereas the Nasis trace their lineage to David through his female descendants (their male ancestry connects them to the tribe of Benjamin).

the Tanna Rabbi Shimon ben Ḥalafta. Rabbi Yehudah HaNasi's younger students (Rabbi Ḥanina, Rabbi Oshaya, Rabbi Yannai, and others) all studied under Rabbi Ḥiyya as well, and to some degree were considered his disciples. Rabbi Ḥiyya's nephews, Rabbah bar Ḥana, and, above all, the great Amora Rav, were his outstanding disciples. He also appears as one of the central figures in the Zohar. Rabbi Ḥiyya was buried in Tiberias, and his two sons were later buried at his side.

SAGES

מָר זוּטְרָא בְּרֵיהּ דְּרַב נַחְמָן **Mar Zutra the son of Rav Naḥman.** A Babylonian Amora of the third and fourth generations, Mar Zutra was a close disciple of his father, Rav Naḥman, and a colleague of Rava and Abaye, with whom he engaged in Halakhic discussions. Mar Zutra's teachings are mentioned in various parts of the Babylonian Talmud. Little is known of his private life. He seems to have been a wealthy man, and, being the son of Rav Naḥman, he was also related to the family of the Exilarch. He apparently served as a judge from an early age.

רַב **Rav.** This is Rav Abba bar Aivo, the greatest of the first generation of Babylonian Amoraim. Rav was born in Babylonia to a prominent family which had produced many Sages and was descended from King David. He immigrated to Eretz Israel with the family of his uncle, Rabbi Ḥiyya, and studied Torah there, mainly from Rabbi Yehudah HaNasi. Rav was appointed to Rabbi Yehudah's court and remained in Eretz Israel for some time before returning to Babylonia, where he settled. Though there had been Torah centers in Babylonia before his time (in Hutzal and in Neharde'a), Rav founded the great yeshivah in Sura, raising the level of Torah study in Babylonia to that of Eretz Israel. After some time he was acknowledged as the outstanding Torah Sage in Eretz Israel as well. Since Rav discussed Halakhic questions with the last of the Tannaim, a principle was stated in the Talmud according to which Rav's authority

הֲוָה נָקֵיט! [1]שְׁמַע מִינָּהּ: מֵהָתָם לְהָכָא, לָא מְהַנֵּי. [2]שְׁמַע מִינָּהּ.
[3]וְלָא מְהַנֵּי? [4]וְהָא רַבָּה בַּר רַב הוּנָא כִּי הֲוָה מִינְצֵי בַּהֲדֵי דְּבֵי רֵישׁ גָּלוּתָא אֲמַר: [5]לָאו מִינַּיְיכוּ נְקִיטְנָא רְשׁוּתָא. [6]נְקִיטְנָא רְשׁוּתָא מֵאַבָּא מָרִי, [7]וְאַבָּא מָרִי מֵרַב, [8]וְרַב מֵרַבִּי חִיָּיא, [9]וְרַבִּי חִיָּיא מֵרַבִּי!
[10]בְּמִילְּתָא דְעָלְמָא הוּא דְּאוֹקִים לְהוּ.
[11]וְכִי מֵאַחַר דְּלָא מְהַנֵּי, [12]רַבָּה בַּר חָנָה רְשׁוּתָא דְּנָקַט לָמָּה לִי?
[13]לָעֲיָירוֹת הָעוֹמְדִים עַל הַגְּבוּלִין.
[14]מַאי רְשׁוּתָא?
[15]כִּי הֲוָה נָחֵית רַבָּה בַּר חָנָה לְבָבֶל, [16]אָמַר לֵיהּ רַבִּי חִיָּיא לְרַבִּי: [17]בֶּן אָחִי יוֹרֵד לְבָבֶל, [18]יוֹרֶה? [19]יוֹרֶה. [20]יָדִין? [21]יָדִין. [22]יַתִּיר בְּכוֹרוֹת?

LITERAL TRANSLATION

[1]Infer from this: From there to here, it is not effective. [2]Infer from this.

[3]Is it not effective? [4]But surely Rabbah bar Rav Huna when he was quarreling with the Exilarch said: [5]Not from you did I receive authorization. [6]I received authorization from my father, my master. [7]And my father, my master, from Rav. [8]And Rav from Rabbi Ḥiyya. [9]And Rabbi Ḥiyya from Rabbi.

[10]With mere words he put them [off].

[11]If it is not effective, [12]why did Rabbah bar Ḥanah receive authorization?

[13]For the towns that stand on the border.

[14]What is authorization?

[15]When Rabbah bar Ḥanah went down to Babylonia, [16]Rabbi Ḥiyya said to Rabbi: [17]"My brother's son is going down to Babylonia, [18]may he rule [on matters of ritual law]?" [19]"He may rule." [20]"May he judge?" [21]"He may judge." [22]"May he permit firstborns?"

TRANSLATION AND COMMENTARY

[1]**Infer from this** that if the Nasi living **there,** in Eretz Israel, authorized a person **to** serve as a judge **here,** in Babylonia, the authorization **is not valid.** The Gemara confirms this conclusion: [2]Indeed, it may be **inferred from this** that the Nasi's authorization is not valid in Babylonia.

וְלָא מְהַנֵּי [3]The Gemara questions this conclusion: But **is it** really true that the Nasi's authorization is **not valid** in Babylonia? [4]**Surely** the following story indicates otherwise! Once, **when Rabbah bar Rav Huna was quarreling with** members of the House of the Exilarch in Babylonia, he **said** to them: [5]It was **not from you** that **I received** my **authorization** to serve as a judge, and therefore I need not submit to you. [6]Rather **I received** my **authorization from my father and teacher.** [7]**And my father and teacher** received his authorization **from Rav.** [8]**And Rav** received his authorization **from Rabbi Ḥiyya.** [9]**And Rabbi Ḥiyya** received his authorization **from Rabbi** Yehudah HaNasi, the president of the Sanhedrin in Eretz Israel. Hence the Nasi's authorization is indeed valid even in Babylonia!

בְּמִילְּתָא דְעָלְמָא הוּא [10]The Gemara rejects this argument: You cannot bring proof from this story, for Rabbah bar Rav Huna knew that the authorization he had received from Rabbi Yehudah HaNasi was not valid in Babylonia, and it was **merely with words** that **he was putting off** the members of the House of the Exilarch.

וְכִי מֵאַחַר [11]The Gemara asks: **If** the Nasi's authorization **has no validity** in Babylonia, [12]**why did Rabbah bar Ḥanah** bother to **receive authorization** before he left Eretz Israel for Babylonia?

לָעֲיָירוֹת [13]The Gemara explains: The authorization that Rabbah bar Ḥanah received was valid **in the towns situated along the borders** of Babylonia, where the people tended to submit to the authorities in Eretz Israel.

מַאי רְשׁוּתָא [14]The Gemara asks: **What** precisely **is** the **authorization** under discussion here? The Gemara answers this question by relating the following story: [15]**When Rabbah bar Ḥanah** was about to leave Eretz Israel and **go to Babylonia,** [16]**Rabbi Ḥiyya said to Rabbi** Yehudah HaNasi: [17]**My brother's son,** Rabbah bar Ḥanah, **is going to Babylonia.** [18]Do you authorize **him** to **issue rulings** as to whether particular activities or things are permitted or forbidden? [19]Rabbi Yehudah HaNasi answered: **"He may issue rulings** on such matters." [20]Rabbi Ḥiyya then asked: "Do you authorize him to **judge** monetary cases?" [21]Rabbi Yehudah answered: **"He may judge** monetary cases." Rabbi Ḥiyya then asked if his nephew's authority could be expanded even further: [22]"Do you authorize Rabbah bar Ḥanah to **permit firstborn** animals to be slaughtered?"

RASHI

שמע מינה מהתם להכא לא מהני – דהא רבה בר חנה רשותא הוה נקיט מרבי, דנשיא דארץ ישראל היה, כדאמרן לקמן בשמעתין: בן אחי יורד לבבל וכו׳. **לא מינייכו נקיטנא רשותא** – ואיני כפוף לכם. **על הגבולין** – הנמשכות אחר ארץ ישראל. **מאי רשותא** – דרבה בר חנה. **יורה** – איסור והיתר, אמר להם רבי: יורה, ולקמן פריך: אי גמיר, למה ליה רשותא בהוראה? **ידין** – ברשות, ויפטר מלשלם. **יתיר בבכורות** – יראה במומין, ואם קבוע הוא יתירנו לשוחטו. דביומיה דרבי אין לבכור תקנה עד שיפול בו מום, דאחר חורבן היה.

is equal to that of the Tannaim; a Baraita cannot be used to challenge his teachings, since he too is a Tanna. Indeed, according to a Geonic tradition, when "Rav [or Rabbi] Abba" is quoted in a Baraita, the reference is to Rav. Three passages in the Talmud refer to Rabbi Abba, the Tanna.

Rav's closest friend and his opponent in Halakhic discussions was Shmuel, and their controversies are recorded throughout the Talmud. In matters of ritual law the Halakhah follows Rav, and in civil matters it follows Shmuel.

Rav lived to a ripe old age and had many disciples. In fact, all the Sages of the following generation were his students, and teachings cited in his name comprise a significant part of the Babylonian Talmud. The most famous of his students were Rav Huna, Rav Yehudah, Rav Ḥisda and Rav Hamnuna. Rav had at least two sons, Aivo and Ḥiyya. Ḥiyya bar Rav was a Sage, and Rav's grandson, Shimi bar Ḥiyya, was also an important Sage, who had the opportunity of studying with his grandfather. Rav married into the family of the Exilarch and Rabbana Neḥemyah and Rabbana Ukva, Sages descended from the Exilarch, were Rav's grandsons by his daughter.

BACKGROUND

רֵישׁ גָּלוּתָא Exilarch. The Exilarch in Babylonia was a direct descendant of the House of David, from the line of Johoiachin, King of Judea. The Parthian and Sassanian rulers all accorded the Exilarch rule over the autonomous Jewish community within their realm in Babylonia, as did the Muslims who followed them.

The Exilarch was third in rank beneath the king, following the vizier, and he conducted himself like a great minister of the kingdom. The Exilarch's regime was thus quite real, and he had the authority to appoint judges and to impose their decisions through the power of the monarchy.

נָשִׂיא President of the Sanhedrin. Initially the position

TRANSLATION AND COMMENTARY

(The male firstborn of cattle, sheep, or goats belonging to a Jew must be given to a priest and offered on the altar in the Temple, and the meat may be eaten only by the priests and their families. However, if a firstborn animal has a physical blemish which disqualifies it from being offered as a sacrifice, it can be slaughtered and eaten like any other nonsacred kosher animal. If a firstborn animal has a blemish, the animal must be brought to a Sage who is authorized to determine whether the blemish is a permanent one disqualifying the animal from being offered as a sacrifice.) [1]Rabbi Yehudah HaNasi answered: "**He may permit** firstborn animals to be slaughtered."

כִּי הֲוָה נָחֵית [2]The Gemara continues with a similar story about Rav: **When Rav** was about to leave Eretz Israel and **go to Babylonia,** [3]**Rabbi Ḥiyya said to Rabbi** Yehudah HaNasi: **"My sister's son,** Rav, **is going to Babylonia.** [4]Do you authorize **him** to **issue rulings** regarding whether particular activities or things are permitted or forbidden?" [5]Rabbi Yehudah HaNasi answered: **"He may issue rulings** on such matters." [6]Rabbi Ḥiyya then asked: "Do you authorize Rav to **judge** monetary cases?" [7]Rabbi Yehudah HaNasi answered: **"He may judge** monetary cases." [8]Rabbi Ḥiyya then asked him about a third area: "Do you authorize Rav to **permit firstborn** animals who acquired a physical blemish to be slaughtered?" [9]This time Rabbi Yehudah HaNasi withheld his permission, and answered: "Rav **may not permit** firstborn animals to be slaughtered."

מַאי שְׁנָא [10]The stories recorded here describing the authorizations conferred upon Rabbah bar Ḥanah and Rav pose a number of questions: **What was the difference** between Rabbah bar Ḥanah and Rav **that** Rabbi Ḥiyya **referred to the one Sage,** Rabbah bar Ḥanah, as **"my brother's son,"** [11]**and the other Sage,** Rav, **he referred to** as **"my sister's son"?** [12]**And should you suggest that that is the way it was,** that Rabbah bar Ḥanah was his brother's son, and Rav was his sister's son, [13]**surely a Sage said: Aivo** (the father of Rav), **Ḥanah** (the father of Rabbah bar Ḥanah), **Shela, Marta, and Rabbi Ḥiyya** [14]**were all the sons of Abba bar Aḥa Karsala from Kafrei!** Thus, both Rav and Rabbah bar Ḥanah were sons of Rabbi Ḥiyya's brothers. Why, then, did Rabbi Ḥiyya refer to Rav as his sister's son?

רַב [15]The Gemara explains: **Rav was the son of** Rabbi Ḥiyya's **brother** and **also the son of his sister.** (Rav's father was Rabbi Ḥiyya's paternal half-brother, and his mother was Rabbi Ḥiyya's maternal half-sister. Thus, the marriage was permitted, for Rav's father and mother had no parents in common.) [16]**Rabbah bar Ḥanah was the son of** Rabbi Ḥiyya's **brother,** [17]but **not the son of his sister.** Rabbi Ḥiyya referred to Rav as his sister's son in order to emphasize that he was related to him not only through his brother, but also through his sister.

[1]יַתִּיר.

[2]כִּי הֲוָה נָחֵית רַב לְבָבֶל, [3]אָמַר לֵיהּ רַבִּי חִיָּיא לְרַבִּי: בֶּן אֲחוֹתִי יוֹרֵד לְבָבֶל, [4]יוֹרֶה? [5]יוֹרֶה. [6]יָדִין? [7]יָדִין. [8]יַתִּיר בְּכוֹרוֹת? [9]אַל יַתִּיר.

[10]מַאי שְׁנָא לְמָר דְּקָא קָרֵי בֶּן אָחִי, [11]וּמַאי שְׁנָא לְמָר דְּקָא קָרֵי בֶּן אֲחוֹתִי? [12]וְכִי תֵּימָא הָכִי הֲוָה מַעֲשֶׂה, [13]וְהָאָמַר מָר: אַיְבוּ, וְחָנָה, וְשֵׁילָא, וּמָרְתָא, וְרַבִּי חִיָּיא — [14]כּוּלְּהוּ בְּנֵי אַבָּא בַּר אַחָא כַּרְסַלָּא מִכַּפְּרֵי הָווּ!

[15]רַב, בַּר אֲחוּהּ דַּהֲוָה בַּר אַחְתֵּיהּ. [16]רַבָּה בַּר חָנָה בַּר אֲחוּהּ [17]דְּלָאו בַּר אַחְתֵּיהּ.

LITERAL TRANSLATION

[1]"He may permit."

[2]When Rav went down to Babylonia, [3]Rabbi Ḥiyya said to Rabbi: "My sister's son is going down to Babylonia, [4]may he decide [on matters of ritual law]?" [5]"He may decide." [6]"May he judge?" [7]"He may judge." [8]"May he permit firstborns?" [9]"He may not permit."

[10]What is the difference that this Sage he called "my brother's son," [11]and what is the difference that this Sage he called "my sister's son"? [12]And if you say that this was the case, [13]but surely the master said: Aivo, and Ḥanah, and Shela, and Marta, and Rabbi Ḥiyya — [14]all of them were the sons of Abba bar Aḥa Karsala from Kafrei!

[15]Rav was the son of his brother who was [also] the son of his sister. [16]Rabbah bar Ḥanah was the son of his brother [17]who was not the son of his sister.

RASHI

אל יתיר — לקמן מפרש טעמא. איבו — אבוה דרב הוה, כדאמרינן ב"אור לארבעה עשר" (פסחים ד,א): אמר ליה אייבו קייס כו'. וחנה — אבוה דרבה. מכפרי — מקום.

NOTES

חָנָה, שֵׁילָא, וּמָרְתָא **Ḥana, and Shela, and Marta.** *Rav Hai Gaon* notes that these are women's names, and because they were women of distinction, their sons were called by their name and not their father's.

of president of the Sanhedrin in Eretz Israel had only Halakhic significance. However, with the decline of the Hasmonean kingdom, the president of the Sanhedrin came to wield the sole authority that did not derive from the Romans or from Herod. During the Great Rebellion, the president grew even stronger (Rabban Shimon ben Gamliel was a leader of the rebellion), though the power of the presidency mainly increased afterwards. When Rabban Yoḥanan ben Zakkai reestablished the Sanhedrin in Yavneh, the presidency became the highest Jewish institution that was recognized by everyone (in the absence of all other independent rule). Since the presidency had been occupied by members of the family of Hillel for a hundred years during Temple times, it became a hereditary position, like a monarchy. Moreover, since the family of Hillel was related, though not directly, to the House of David, it also enjoyed a degree of regal splendor. Although the actual power of the presidents was acknowledged by the authorities, they were given no executive powers (except for a few presidents). Therefore the Nasi in Eretz Israel did not rule through the power of coercion but rather mainly through the people's willingness to accept some sort of Jewish rule.

BACKGROUND

מִשְׁפַּחַת רַב The family of Rav.

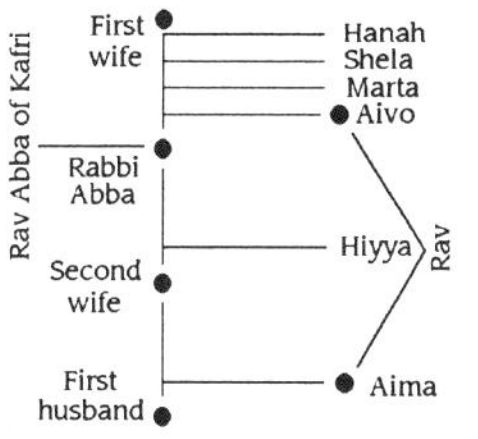

This diagram shows the unique relationship between Rabbi Ḥiyya and Rav. Rabbi Abba married a woman who bore him Ḥanah (the father of Rabbah bar Ḥanah), Shela, Marta, and Aivo (the father of Rav). Rabbi Abba also married another woman, who brought with her a daughter from a previous marriage (Aima). Rabbi Ḥiyya was born of Rabbi Abba's second marriage. Later Aivo

TRANSLATION AND COMMENTARY

אִי בָּעֵית, אֵימָא [1]The Gemara now suggests: **And if you wish,** you can **say** that there was another reason why Rabbi Ḥiyya referred to Rav as his sister's son: [5B] [2]Rabbi Ḥiyya referred to his nephew Rav as his sister's son **on account of his wisdom,** [3]**for the verse states:** (Proverbs 7:4): **"Say to wisdom: You are my sister."** By calling him "my sister's son," Rabbi Ḥiyya hinted at Rav's wisdom.

יַתִּיר בְּכוֹרוֹת [4]It was related, above, that when Rabbi Ḥiyya asked Rabbi Yehudah HaNasi, "Do you authorize Rav to **permit** the slaughter of **firstborn** animals that have acquired a physical blemish?", [5]Rabbi Yehudah HaNasi answered: "Rav **may not permit** the slaughter of firstborn animals." [6]The Gemara asks: **What is the reason** that Rabbi Yehudah HaNasi withheld permission? [7]**If you say** that Rabbi Yehudah HaNasi withheld the authorization **because** Rav **was not wise** enough for the task, this could not be so, [8]for **surely we said** above **that** Rav **was very wise!** [9]The Gemara now suggests a second explanation: **Rather,** perhaps you can say that Rabbi Yehudah HaNasi withheld the authorization **because** Rav **was not an expert on defects,** and therefore was unable to distinguish between permanent defects which disqualify an animal for sacrifice, and passing defects which do not. [10]**But** this, too, is impossible, for **surely Rav said** about himself: **Eighteen months I spent with a herdsman** observing the animals and their physical blemishes in order **to learn which defect is permanent and which defect is passing.** Hence Rabbi Yehudah HaNasi could not have disqualified Rav because of his lack of knowledge.

אֶלָּא [11]**Rather,** explains the Gemara, Rabbi Yehudah did not authorize Rav to permit the slaughter of firstborn animals with certain defects because he wished **to bestow** a special **honor upon Rabbah bar Ḥanah,** so that the Babylonian community would treat him with the proper respect. There was no concern that people would treat Rav badly, for his wisdom and personality commanded the respect that was his due.

וְאִיבָּעֵית אֵימָא [12]The Gemara offers another explanation: **And if you wish,** you can **say** that Rabbi Yehudah HaNasi withheld the authorization [13]**for this very reason, that Rav was a great expert on defects.** [14]Because he was such an expert, **he would permit** the slaughter of firstborn animals with **defects that** most **people do not recognize** as permanent. [15]**And** afterwards people **would** mistakenly **say** about some other defect: **"Rav** once **permitted** the slaughter of a firstborn animal that had **a defect** just **like this,"** when in fact the animal permitted by Rav had a slightly different defect. [16]Thus, people **would** erroneously **come to permit** firstborn animals to be slaughtered because of **passing defects.**

LITERAL TRANSLATION

[1]And if you wish, say: [5B] [2]On account of his wisdom, [3]for it is written: "Say to wisdom: You are my sister."

[4]"May he permit firstborns?" [5]"He may not permit."

[6]What is the reason? [7]If you say because he was not wise, [8]surely we said that he was very wise! [9]Rather, because he was not an expert on defects. [10]But surely Rav said: Eighteen months I spent (lit., "grew up") with a herdsman to learn which is a permanent defect and which is a passing defect! [11]Rather, to bestow honor upon Rabbah bar Ḥanah.

[12]And if you wish, say: [13]Because of this itself that Rav was a great expert on defects, [14]and he would permit defects that people do not know [about], [15]and they would say: "[A defect] like this Rav permitted," [16]and they would come to permit a passing defect.

[1]וְאִי בָּעֵית, אֵימָא: [5B] [2]עַל שֵׁם חָכְמָתוֹ [3]דִּכְתִיב ״אֱמֹר לַחָכְמָה אֲחֹתִי אָתְּ״.

[4]״יַתִּיר בְּכוֹרוֹת״? [5]אַל יַתִּיר״.

[6]מַאי טַעֲמָא? [7]אִילֵימָא מִשּׁוּם דְּלָא חַכִּים, [8]הָא קָא אָמְרִינַן דְּחַכִּים טוּבָא! [9]אֶלָּא, מִשּׁוּם דְּלָא בְּקִיעַ בְּמוּמֵי. [10]וְהָאֲמַר רַב: שְׁמוֹנָה עָשָׂר חֳדָשִׁים גָּדַלְתִּי אֵצֶל רוֹעֵה בְּהֵמָה לֵידַע אֵיזֶה מוּם קָבוּעַ וְאֵיזֶה מוּם עוֹבֵר!

[11]אֶלָּא, לַחֲלֹק לוֹ כָּבוֹד לְרַבָּה בַּר חָנָה.

[12]וְאִיבָּעֵית אֵימָא: [13]מִשּׁוּם הָא גּוּפֵיהּ, דְּרַב בְּקִיעַ בְּמוּמֵי טְפֵי, [14]וְשָׁרֵי מוּמֵי דְּלָא יָדְעִי אֱינָשֵׁי, [15]וְאָמְרִי: ״כִּי הַאי גַּוְונָא שְׁרָא רַב״, [16]וְאָתוּ לְמִשְׁרֵי מוּם עוֹבֵר.

RASHI

על שם חכמתו — שהיה רב חכם ביותר, קרי ליה ״בן אחותו״. **הא קאמר דחכים טובא** — דהא תרצת דעל שם חכמתו קריה ״בן אחותו״. **לחלק כבוד לרבה** — כדי שינהגו בו בני בבל כבוד, שבק ליה האי חשיבותא, דאילו לרב הוו נהגי ביה יקר בלאו הכי. **אי בעית אימא** — הא דקאמר ״אל יתיר״. **משום היא גופא** — משום הא מילתא דקאמר: שמונה עשר חדשים גדלתי וכו׳. **דלא ידעי אינשי** — אינו ניכר לרבים שהוא מום.

HALAKHAH

בְּקִיעַ בְּמוּמֵי **He was an expert on defects.** "According to some authorities, a Sage may not issue authorization if it would appear to the less educated public that he permitted something that is actually forbidden (as we see that Rav was denied permission to authorize the slaughter of firstborn animals on account of that concern). *Shakh* notes that this applies only if the Sage issues the authorization without any explanation. But if he explains his reasoning

(Rav Ḥiyya's half-brother) married Aima, his step-sister (who was also Rabbi Ḥiyya's half-sister on his mother's side), and they gave birth to Rav. Hence Rav was Rabbi Ḥiyya's nephew both ways, since his father was Rabbi Ḥiyya's half-brother, and his mother was Rabbi Ḥiyya's half-sister.

SAGES

רַבָּה בַּר חָנָה **Rabbah bar Ḥanah.** His full name was "Rav Abba bar Ḥanah," as he is called in the Jerusalem Talmud. Born in Babylonia, he immigrated to Eretz Israel and was an Amora of the first generation.

According to the Gemara he was Rav's cousin, and he was apparently older, though in time he sat before Rav as a student-colleague. Rabbah bar Ḥanah was a student of the generation of Rabbi Ḥiyya and of Rabbi Yehudah HaNasi, and he was regarded as one of the prominent Sages of the generation following Rabbi's death.

From what is said here and from other sources it appears that Rabbah bar Ḥanah finally returned to Babylonia, living there for many years until he died. In Babylonia he is recorded in discussion with Shmuel and his students.

BACKGROUND

יַתִּיר בְּכוֹרוֹת **May he permit firstborns?** The Torah rules (Exodus 13 and elsewhere) that the male firstborn of kosher animals are consecrated to God. When the Temple stood, firstborn animals were sacrificed, and their meat was eaten by the priests. However, when a firstborn animal acquired a blemish making it unfit for sacrifice, it became the priest's property, to be slaughtered and eaten wherever he wished. The sanctity of the firstborn does not depend on the Temple and it exists to this day. However, since they cannot be sacrificed, firstborn animals are permitted to graze until they acquire a blemish. An expert can determine whether the blemish is transitory, one that will heal, or permanent. In antiquity there were experts who examined the blemishes of firstborn animals, and these had to master both the

TRANSLATION AND COMMENTARY

יוֹרֶה [1]In the stories about Rabbah bar Ḥanah and Rav, it was mentioned that Rabbi Ḥiyya asked Rabbi Yehudah HaNasi: "Do you authorize **him** to **issue rulings** regarding whether particular activities or things are permitted or forbidden?" [2]Rabbi Yehudah HaNasi answered: **"He may issue rulings** on such matters." [3]The Gemara asks: **If** the Sage **learned** the laws pertaining to these subjects and mastered them, [4]**why does he need to receive authorization** to issue rulings about them?

מִשּׁוּם [5]The Gemara explains: Authorization is required **because of a** certain **incident that occurred.** [6]**For it was taught** in a Baraita: **"Once Rabbi** Yehudah HaNasi **went to a certain place, and saw people kneading their dough in a state of ritual impurity.** [7]**He said to them: Why are you kneading your dough in a state of ritual impurity?** [8]**They said to him:** We have taken precautions to prevent ritual impurity. For **a certain scholar** once **came here,** [9]**and ruled for us that marsh water does not make food susceptible** to contract **ritual impurity.** We knead our dough in marsh water, and thus we can use kneading troughs that are ritually impure." Food or produce contracts ritual impurity if it has been severed from the ground and has come into contact with a liquid. Seven liquids make foodstuffs susceptible to ritual impurity: water, wine, honey, olive oil, milk, dew, and blood. The people thought that they could prevent the contamination of their bread by kneading its dough with marsh water, for they understood from the visiting scholar that marsh water does not make foodstuffs susceptible to ritual impurity. [10]The truth of the matter was, however, that the scholar had **taught them** that **"the liquid of eggs** [מֵי בֵיצִים — *'mei betzim'*]" does not render foodstuffs liable to contract ritual impurity, [11]**but** the people **thought that he had said "marsh water** [מֵי בְּצָעִים — *'mei betza'im'*]." In the Hebrew there is a difference of only one letter between these words, and the

[1]״יוֹרֶה״? [2]״יוֹרֶה״. [3]אִי גָּמֵיר, [4]רְשׁוּתָא לָמָּה לִי לְמִישְׁקַל? [5]מִשּׁוּם מַעֲשֶׂה שֶׁהָיָה. [6]דְּתַנְיָא: ״פַּעַם אַחַת הָלַךְ רַבִּי לְמָקוֹם אֶחָד, וְרָאָה בְּנֵי אָדָם שֶׁמְּגַבְּלִין עִיסּוֹתֵיהֶם בְּטוּמְאָה. [7]אָמַר לָהֶם: מִפְּנֵי מָה אַתֶּם מְגַבְּלִין עִיסּוֹתֵיכֶם בְּטוּמְאָה? [8]אָמְרוּ לוֹ: תַּלְמִיד אֶחָד בָּא לְכָאן, [9]וְהוֹרָה לָנוּ מֵי בְצָעִים אֵין מַכְשִׁירִין. [10]וְהוּא ״מֵי בֵיצִים״ דְּרַשׁ לְהוּ, [11]וְאִינְהוּ סָבוּר: ״מֵי בְצָעִים״ קָאָמַר.

LITERAL TRANSLATION

[1]"May he issue rulings?" [2]"He may issue rulings." [3]If he learned, [4]why does he need to receive authorization?

[5]Because of an incident that occurred. [6]For it was taught: "Once Rabbi went to a certain place, and saw people kneading their dough in [a state of] ritual impurity. [7]He said to them: Why are you kneading your dough in [a state of] ritual impurity? [8]They said to him: A certain scholar [lit., 'disciple'] came here, [9]and ruled for us that marsh water does not make [food] susceptible [to contract ritual impurity]." [10]And he taught them, "the liquid of eggs [מֵי בֵיצִים]," [11][but] they thought [that] he said "marsh water [מֵי בְּצָעִים]."

RASHI

בטומאה — לא הוו מקפידין לטהר כליהם. **מי בצעים** — אגם, *מריש״ק בלעז. **אין מכשירין** — וממימי בצעים אנו לשין, הלכך לא מקבלה עיסה טומאה. **מי ביצים** — הלש עיסה בביצים של תרנגולת ואווז.

NOTES

רְשׁוּתָא לָמָּה לִי לְמִישְׁקַל? **Why does he need to receive authorization?** The Rishonim ask: The Gemara below (6a) cites a Mishnah which teaches that if a judge issued an erroneous decision and declared as ritually impure that which was in fact ritually pure, the judge must pay for the damage caused by his ruling. *Tosafot* argue that the authorization given to Rav to adjudicate monetary cases suffices to exempt him from all liability, even for damage resulting from erroneous decisions regarding ritual matters.

Others maintain that Rabbi Ḥiyya's request for permission to authorize Rav to rule on ritual matters implies that such authorization was necessary, even in cases where an erroneous decision would not have caused a financial loss (*Ri*). *Rabbi David Bonfil* argues that an expert on the law who did not receive authorization from the Exilarch or the Nasi to serve as a judge is liable for the damage resulting from his erroneous decisions in matters of monetary law but bears no liability for the damage resulting from a mistaken ruling regarding a ritual matter.

מְגַבְּלִין עִיסּוֹתֵיכֶם בְּטוּמְאָה **They were kneading their dough in a state of ritual impurity.** It has been asked: Since there is no prohibition against eating ordinary food that is ritually impure, why was Rabbi Yehudah HaNasi concerned about it? Some answer that Rabbi Yehudah HaNasi apparently maintained that it is forbidden to cause foodstuffs in Eretz Israel to contract ritual impurity (*Margaliyot HaYam*).

Others suggest that dough should certainly be prepared in such a manner that it remains ritually pure, for *ḥallah* must be separated from it, and *ḥallah* which is ritually impure is not fit to be given to a priest (*Geonim*).

מֵי בֵיצִים **The liquid of eggs.** The Jerusalem Talmud records a slightly different version of this story, according to which

HALAKHAH

or cites a supporting text, issuing such authorization is permitted." (*Shulḥan Arukh, Yoreh De'ah* 242:10.)

מֵי בֵיצִים **The liquid of eggs.** "There are seven liquids which render foodstuffs liable to contract ritual impurity:

Halakhah and veterinary medicine.

LANGUAGE (RASHI)

מריש״ק* From the Old French *mares,* meaning "a marsh," or "a pond."

TRANSLATION AND COMMENTARY

people misunderstood what the scholar had said. [1]**And** those people **also erred about** the following Mishnah (*Parah* 8:10): [2]**"The water of the Kramiyon** River **and the water of the Piga** River **are unfit** to be used in the purification offering of the Red Heifer, **because that** water **is** regarded as **marsh water."** [3]**And** the people living in that place **thought** to themselves: [4]**Since** marsh water **is unfit to be used for the purifying water,** [5]it is reasonable to assume that **it can also not render food ritually susceptible** to contract **ritual impurity.** [6]**But** the truth of the matter is that **this is not so,** for **there, regarding purifying water,** [7]**we need** fresh **running water** from a spring, as the verse states (Numbers 19:17): "And running water shall be put thereto in a vessel," and marsh water is not running water. [8]But **here any water renders food susceptible** to contract **ritual impurity,** even standing water, and so marsh water should also make food susceptible to ritual impurity. This mistake regarding marsh water occurred because a scholar did not take care to explain his teachings clearly so that they would be properly understood.

[1]וְטָעוּ נַמִי בְּהָא: [2]"מֵי קְרָמְיוֹן וּמֵי פִיגָה פְּסוּלִין, מִפְּנֵי שֶׁהֵן מֵי בְצָעִים". [3]וְאִינְהוּ סָבוּר: [4]מִדִּלְגַבֵּי חַטָּאת פְּסִילִי, [5]אַכְשׁוּרֵי נַמִי לָא מַכְשְׁרִי. [6]וְלֹא הִיא. הָתָם, לְעִנְיַן חַטָּאת, [7]בָּעֵינַן מַיִם חַיִּים. [8]הָכָא אַכְשׁוּרֵי כָּל דְּהוּ מַכְשְׁרִי. [9]תָּנָא: "בְּאוֹתָהּ שָׁעָה גָּזְרוּ: [10]תַּלְמִיד אַל יוֹרֶה אֶלָּא אִם כֵּן נוֹטֵל רְשׁוּת מֵרַבּוֹ". [11]תַּנְחוּם בְּרֵיהּ דְּרַבִּי אַמִי אִיקְלַע לְחַתָר, [12]דְּרַשׁ לְהוּ:

LITERAL TRANSLATION

[1]And they also erred about this: [2]"The water of the Kramiyon and the water of the Piga are unfit, because they are marsh water." [3]And they thought: [4]Since they are unfit [to be used] for purifying [water], [5]they also do not make [food] susceptible [to ritual impurity]. [6]But it is not so. There, regarding purifying [water], [7]we need running (lit., "living") water. [8]Here any [water] makes [food] susceptible to ritual impurity.

[9][A Sage] taught: "At that time they decreed: [10]A scholar may not issue a ruling unless he receives authorization from his master."

[11]Tanḥum the son of Rabbi Ammi happened to come to Ḥatar, [12][where] he taught them:

RASHI

קרמיון ופיגה — נהרות של אגמים. **פסולין** — למי חטאת, מפני שהן מי בצעים ואנו "מים חיים אל כלי" בעינן. **נוטל רשות מרבו** — וכי יהיב ליה רבו רשותא מידק דייק ביה שיהא לשונו פתוח, ולא יטעו השומעין את דבריו. **לחתר** — מקום.

תָּנָא [9]The Gemara now records a second Baraita which relates to this incident: **A Sage taught: "At that time** the Rabbis **decreed:** [10]A Torah **scholar may not issue a ruling unless he** first **receives authorization from his master** to issue such rulings. The Rabbis presumed that a master scholar would not confer authorization upon his disciple unless he knew that the disciple was aware of the consequences of being misunderstood and could express himself with great care and precision."

תַּנְחוּם בְּרֵיהּ דְּרַבִּי אַמִי [11]The Gemara continues with another anecdote dealing with a ruling issued by a Torah scholar: **Tanḥum the son of Rabbi Ammi happened to come to** a certain place called **Ḥatar,** [12]**where he taught:**

BACKGROUND

קְרָמְיוֹן וּפִיגָה Kramiyon and Piga. These are apparently the names of two rivers in Eretz Israel. Piga is another name for the Yarkon, which was swampy at that time, and a city named Figi stood near its source. Kramiyon is apparently the Na'aman River, near Akko, and to this day its water flows into marshes. It was known by its Latin name, Candavion. However, some scholars believe that Kramiyon and Piga are Amana and Papar, rivers of Damascus that also flow into marshes.

מֵי חַטָּאת Purifying water. Water mixed with the ashes of the Red Heifer was used to purify people and objects that had contracted ritual impurity by contact with a dead body. Fresh, running water from a spring that is fit to drink was placed in a container, and a small amount of ashes from the Red Heifer was added. The resulting mixture, called *mei ḥatat* ("purifying water"), was sprinkled on the people or objects to be purified. Now, as the Mishnah states, marsh water is not fit to be used in the purification offering.

חַתָר Ḥatar. Some authorities maintain that this is the name of a place near Tyre where the surf undermines (לַחְתּוֹר) and erodes the sandstone. Others believe that Ḥatar is the abbreviation of חַד־אֲתַר, meaning "somewhere," and not the name of any specific place.

NOTES

the scholar spoke about *mei betzim*, "the liquid of eggs," and that is what the people heard. But while the scholar was referring to the white of the egg, the people understood from him that the water in which eggs were boiled cannot make food susceptible to ritual impurity.

מֵי קְרָמְיוֹן וּמֵי פִיגָה The water of the Kramiyon and the Piga. The Rishonim formulate a question: Elsewhere, the Gemara refers to the Kramiyon and the Piga as rivers, and so apparently they are bodies of flowing water. Why, then, are they regarded as marsh water with respect to the purification offering? *Tosafot* explain that the Kramiyon and Piga rivers do indeed fall into the category of running water. But the considerable quantity of foreign matter that is deposited in their waters makes the water unfit to be used for the purification ceremony. For the verse states that "the running water shall be put thereto in a vessel," and the foreign matter is seen as intervening between the water and the vessel. Elsewhere (*Bava Batra* 74b), *Tosafot* explain that while the Kramiyon and the Piga are indeed flowing rivers, their waters are unfit for the purification offering because there are places where they mix with marsh water. *Ran* writes that the Kramiyon and Piga rivers themselves are fit for the purification offering, for they are flowing water. The Mishnah which states that the water of those rivers is unfit to be used in the purification offering refers to the ponds into which those rivers flow.

לְחַתָר To Hatar. Some explain that Hatar is not a place-name, but rather an abbreviated form of the words חַד־אֲתַר, "a certain place." (*Margaliyot HaYam*.)

HALAKHAH

Water, dew, olive oil, wine, milk, blood, and honey. Other liquids, including the liquid of eggs, do not render foodstuffs liable to contract ritual impurity." (*Rambam, Sefer Taharah, Hilkhot Tum'at Okhlim* 1:2.)

בָּעֵינַן מַיִם חַיִּים We need running water. "The water that must be mixed with the ashes of the Red Heifer to make purifying water must come from a spring or a running river. Naturally flowing water which was mixed with standing water is not fit to be used to make purifying water." (*Rambam, Sefer Taharah, Hilkhot Parah Adamah* 6:1,10,13.)

מוּתָּר לְלַתּוֹת חִיטִּין בַּפֶּסַח. [1]אָמְרוּ לוֹ: לָאו רַבִּי מָנִי דְּמִן צוֹר אִיכָּא הָכָא? [2]וְתַנְיָא: "תַּלְמִיד אַל יוֹרֶה הֲלָכָה בִּמְקוֹם רַבּוֹ, [3]אֶלָּא אִם כֵּן הָיָה רָחוֹק מִמֶּנּוּ שָׁלֹשׁ פַּרְסָאוֹת [4]כְּנֶגֶד מַחֲנֵה יִשְׂרָאֵל". [5]אֲמַר לְהוּ: לָאו אַדַּעְתַּאי.

[6]רַבִּי חִיָּיא חַזְיֵיה לְהַהוּא גַּבְרָא דַּהֲוָה קָאֵי בְּבֵית הַקְּבָרוֹת, [7]אֲמַר לֵיהּ: "לָאו בֶּן אִישׁ פְּלוֹנִי כֹּהֵן אַתָּה"? [8]אֲמַר לֵיהּ: "אִין", [9]אֲבוּהּ דְּהַהוּא גַּבְרָא גְּבַהּ עֵינַיִם הֲוָה. [10]נָתַן עֵינָיו בִּגְרוּשָׁה וְחִילְּלוֹ.

LITERAL TRANSLATION

It is permitted to moisten wheat on Passover. [1]They said to him: Is not Rabbi Mani from Tyre here? [2]And [surely] it was taught: "A scholar may not issue a Halakhic ruling in his master's vicinity, [3]unless he was at a distance from him of three Persian miles [4]corresponding to the Camp of Israel." [5]He said to them: It was not on my mind.

[6]Rabbi Ḥiyya saw a certain man who was standing in a graveyard, [7][and] said to him: "Are you not the son of So-and-so the priest?" [8]He said to him: "Yes, [9][but] that man's father was a man of raised eyes. [10]He set his eyes on a divorcee and caused him to lose [(lit., 'profaned') his priestly status]."

TRANSLATION AND COMMENTARY

It is permissible to moisten wheat on Passover before it is ground in order to make grinding easier, and there is no concern that the wheat will become leavened during that brief moment. [1]People **said to him: Is not** your teacher **Rabbi Mani from Tyre here** in the area? [2]**And** surely **it was taught** in a Baraita: **"A** Torah **scholar may not issue a Halakhic ruling in his master's vicinity,** [3]**unless he was at a distance from him of three Persian miles,** [4]a distance which **corresponds to the** length of **the Camp of Israel** during the period of their wandering through the desert. For the verse states [Exodus 33:7]: 'And everyone who sought the Lord went out to the Tent of the Meeting which was outside of the camp.' Whoever was in doubt about a point of law crossed the Israelite encampment — a distance of three Persian miles — and went out to consult with Moses, even though there must have been people along the way who were fit to rule on the matter." [5]Tanḥum **said to them: I was not aware** that my teacher Rabbi Mani was in the vicinity.

רַבִּי חִיָּיא [6]The Gemara relates yet another anecdote: **Rabbi Ḥiyya saw a certain man standing in a graveyard,** [7]**and said to him: "Are you not the son of So-and-so the priest?** Why, then, are you standing in a graveyard, when a priest is forbidden to contract ritual impurity through proximity with a corpse or a grave?" [8]The man **said to** Rabbi Ḥiyya: **"Yes,** I am the son of a priest, [9]**but my father was a man of raised eyes,** lusting after that which was forbidden to him. **He set his eyes on a divorcee,** who is forbidden to a priest, and married her, and I was born from the union. [10]Thus, my father **caused me to lose my priestly status,** for a son born to a priest and a woman whom the priest is forbidden to marry is unfit for the priesthood."

RASHI

מותר ללתות – לשרות מעט במים ולכותשן במכתשת, ולא חיישינן לחימוץ הואיל וכותשן מיד. **כנגד מחנה ישראל** – דכל מאן דבעי מילתא אזיל לגבי משה דכתיב (שמות לג): "והיה כל מבקש ה' וגו'", אף על גב שהמחנה שלש פרסאות ואתו לגבי משה רבותא דמשה שאני. מחנה ישראל שלש פרסאות דכתיב (במדבר לג): "ויחנו על הירדן מבית הישימות עד אבל השטים" ואמר רבה בר בר חנה: לדידי חזי לי ההוא אתרא, והוה תלתא פרסי בעירובין (נה,ב) וביומא (עה,ב). **רבי חייא חזייה כו'** – לא איתפרש לן מאי בעיא הכא, ונראה בעיני דהא אתא לאשמעינן, אף על גב דרבי חייא תלמידו דרבי הוה, ובמקומו דרבי הוה, לא חלק לו כבוד לרבי מלהפריש זה מן האיסור. דלענין אפרושי מאיסורא אין כאן מורה הלכה לפני רבו, כדאמרינן פרק "הדר עם הנכרי" (עירובין סג) ובמסכת שביעית ירושלמי בפרק "שלש ארצות" מצאתי בההוא עובדא דההוא דקאי בבית הקברות, דלא גרסינן ביה רבי חייא, אלא רבי הוה, ושני דברים הללו ראה רבי בעכו: דמי בילים אין מכשירין, והאי. ולא גרסינן דהוה קאי בבית הקברות אלא בעכו, שבה ארץ ישראל ויש בה ארץ העמים, וראה אותן העומדים בגבול ארץ ישראל שהיו מגבלין עיסותיהן בטומאה, ותמה, עד שאמרו לו: תלמיד אחד בא לכאן כו'. וחזר וראה אותו כהן עומד בקצת העיר שחוץ לגבול ארץ ישראל, אמר לו: והרי הוא זה ארץ העמים שגזרו עליה טומאה כבית הקברות?! ואמר ליה: לאו בן איש כהן פלוני אתה? כו', ולכך נשנו מעשים הללו זה אצל זה. **גבה עינים** – הלך אחר עיניו. **נתן עיניו בגרושה** – ונשאה, וממנה נולדתי והריני חלל.

SAGES

רַבִּי מָנִי דְּמִן צוֹר **Rabbi Mani from Tyre.** Some authorities believe that this is Rav Mani the son of Rabbi Yonah and one of the greatest Amoraim in Eretz Israel during the fourth generation. According to the story related in the Jerusalem Talmud, Rabbi Mani was living in the city of Sepphoris at that time.

HALAKHAH

מוּתָּר לְלַתּוֹת חִיטִּין בַּפֶּסַח **It is permissible to moisten wheat on Passover.** "While according to Talmudic law it is permissible to moisten wheat on Passover before grinding, the Geonim decreed that it is forbidden, for we are no longer familiar with the process by which the wheat can be moistened without becoming leavened." (*Shulḥan Arukh, Oraḥ Ḥayyim* 453:5.)

תַּלְמִיד אַל יוֹרֶה הֲלָכָה בִּמְקוֹם רַבּוֹ **A disciple may not issue a Halakhic ruling in his master's vicinity.** "A Torah scholar may not issue a Halakhic ruling in his master's proximity, and if he does issue such a ruling, he is considered as being liable for the death penalty." (*Shulḥan Arukh, Yoreh De'ah* 242:4.)

נָתַן עֵינָיו בִּגְרוּשָׁה וְחִילְּלוֹ **He set his eyes on a divorcee and caused him to lose his priestly status.** "A son born to a priest and a woman whom the priest is forbidden to marry is unfit for the priesthood, and is therefore permitted to contract ritual impurity resulting from proximity to a corpse or a grave." (*Shulḥan Arukh, Yoreh De'ah* 373:2.)

TRANSLATION AND COMMENTARY

פְּשִׁיטָא [1]The Gemara now returns to the matter of the authorization conferred upon a scholar by the Nasi or Exilarch: The law **is clear with respect to partial authorization,** [2]for **surely it was said** above that such authorization **is valid.** We saw that Rabbi Yehudah HaNasi authorized Rav to judge some cases, but withheld his authorization to permit first-born animals for slaughter. [3]But **what is the law** with respect to authorization to which **a condition** had been attached, such as when authorization was conferred for a limited period of time?

תָּא שְׁמַע [4]The Gemara answers: **Come and hear** an answer to this question from the following story, [5]**for Rabbi Yoḥanan said to Rav Shemen** when he was about to leave Eretz Israel and go to Babylonia: [6]**"You have our authorization** to rule on Halakhic matters from now on and **until you return to us."** Thus, we see that authorization may be conferred upon a scholar with a condition attached, such as a limitation on the period during which that authorization is valid.

גּוּפָא [7]The Gemara now proceeds to analyze at length the position of Shmuel cited above (3a): **Returning to our subject,** we see that **Shmuel said:** [8]If **two** laymen **judged** a monetary case, **their judgement is binding** on the litigants, [9]**but** the two judges **are called an impudent court,** for the case should have been heard by a court of three. [10]**Rav Naḥman sat** in the Academy **and recited this tradition** before his disciples. [11]**Rava raised an objection to Rav Naḥman** from a Mishnah (*Sanhedrin* 29a): [12]**"Even if two** of the judges **found the defendant free of liability or two** of the judges **found him liable, and** the third judge **said: 'I do not know,'** [13]**they add** two more **judges,** and the enlarged court reconsiders the case. Since the third judge was unable to decide on the matter, he is viewed as having been absent from the deliberations." [14]Now, **if it** — Shmuel's statement — **is** true, then even if the third judge is regarded as absent, [15]the two judges who agreed on the verdict **should be considered like two** judges **who judged** a monetary case, and so it should not be necessary to add any more judges!

[1]פְּשִׁיטָא, לְפַלְגָא — [2]הָא קָאָמַר דִּמְהַנֵּי. [3]עַל תְּנַאי מַאי? [4]תָּא שְׁמַע: [5]דַּאֲמַר לֵיהּ רַבִּי יוֹחָנָן לְרַב שֶׁמֶן: [6]"הֲרֵי אַתָּה בִּרְשׁוּתֵנוּ, עַד שֶׁתָּבֹא אֶצְלֵנוּ". [7]גּוּפָא, אָמַר שְׁמוּאֵל: [8]שְׁנַיִם שֶׁדָּנוּ — [9]דִּינֵיהֶם דִּין, אֶלָּא שֶׁנִּקְרָא בֵּית דִּין חָצוּף. [10]יְתֵיב רַב נַחְמָן וְקָאָמַר לְהָא שְׁמַעְתָּא. [11]אֵיתִיבֵיהּ רָבָא לְרַב נַחְמָן: [12]"אֲפִילּוּ שְׁנַיִם מְזַכִּין אוֹ שְׁנַיִם מְחַיְּיבִין, וְאֶחָד אוֹמֵר: 'אֵינִי יוֹדֵעַ', [13]יוֹסִיפוּ הַדַּיָּינִין". [14]וְאִי אִיתָא, [15]לֶהֱווּ כִּשְׁנַיִם שֶׁדָּנוּ!

LITERAL TRANSLATION

[1]It is clear that [regarding] partial [authorization] — [2]surely we said that is effective. [3]On condition, what [is the law]?

[4]Come [and] hear: [5]For Rabbi Yoḥanan said to Rav Shemen: [6]"You have our authorization until you come [back] to us."

[7][Returning to] the statement quoted above (lit., "the thing itself"), Shmuel said: [8]Two who judged — [9]their judgment is a judgment, but they are called an impudent court. [10]Rav Naḥman sat and repeated this, teaching. [11]Rava raised an objection to Rav Naḥman: [12]"Even if two find [the defendant] free of liability or two find [him] liable, and one says: 'I do not know,' [13]they add judges." [14]And if it is, [15]let them be like two who judged!

RASHI

לפלגא — כגון רב, דיהיבי להו רשותא למידן ולא להתיר בכורות. **על תנאי** — כגון עד שנה או עד שנתים ולא יותר. **מאי** — מהני בתוך הזמן או לא. **לרב שמן** — כשהיה פורש ממנו וירד לבבל. **ברשותינו** — רשות נתונה לך לדון. **אפילו שנים מזכין כו'** — משנה היא [ב"זה בורר"] (סנהדרין כט,א). **יוסיפו הדיינין** — דהוה ליה כמאן דלא הוה התם ואישתכח דתרי הוא דהוי, ואנן בעינן מעיקרא תלתא, דאי נמי גמר דינא בתרי דהוי רובא שפיר דמי.

SAGES

רַב שֶׁמֶן **Rav Shemen.** He was apparently Rav Shemen bar Abba, see below, 14a.

רַבִּי יוֹחָנָן **Rabbi Yoḥanan.** This is Rabbi Yoḥanan bar Nappaḥa, one of the greatest Amoraim, whose teachings are of primary importance both in the Babylonian and in the Jerusalem Talmud. He lived in Tiberias and lived to a great age. Almost nothing is known of his family origins. He became an orphan at an early age and, although his family apparently owned considerable property, he spent most of his wealth in pursuit of constant Torah studies, so that he actually became poor. He was just old enough to study under Rabbi Yehudah HaNasi, the editor of the Mishnah. But most of his Torah knowledge was gained from Rabbi Yehudah HaNasi's students, from Ḥizkiyah ben Ḥiyya, Rabbi Oshaya, Rabbi Ḥanina and Rabbi Yannai, who greatly praised him. In time he became the head of a yeshivah in Tiberias, which marked the beginning of a period when his fame and influence constantly increased. For a long time Rabbi Yoḥanan was the leading Rabbinic scholar of the entire Jewish world, not only in Eretz Israel but also in Babylonia, whose Sages respected him greatly. Many of them came to Eretz Israel and became his outstanding students. He was a master of both Halakhah and Aggadah. His teachings in both areas are found in many places, and serve as a basis for both of the Talmuds. In recognition of his intellectual and spiritual greatness, the Halakhah is decided according to his opinion in almost every case, even when Rav or Shmuel, the great Amoraim of Babylonia (whom he himself regarded as his superiors), disagree with him. Only when he disagrees with his teachers in Eretz Israel (such as Rabbi Yannai and Rabbi Yehoshua ben Levi) does the Halakhah not follow his opinion.

Rabbi Yoḥanan was renowned for being handsome, and much was said in praise of his good looks. By nature he was excitable, so that occasionally he was too severe with his friends and students,

NOTES

בֵּית דִּין חָצוּף **An impudent court.** Our commentary follows *Rashi* and others who understand that, according to Shmuel, a judgment issued by a two-man court is valid, but the court is called impertinent, for its members disregarded the Rabbinic enactment that a monetary case must be heard by a court comprising three judges. *Ran* and *Meiri* propose an alternative explanation according to which a two-man court is called an "exposed" court, for it can only render a decision if the two judges agree on the verdict, and so when the court renders a decision, the opinion of each judge is laid bare to all. But a three-man court can issue a ruling based on the majority opinion, and so the opinion of each of its members is not automatically revealed.

HALAKHAH

לְפַלְגָא **Partial authorization.** "The Nasi or the Exilarch may authorize a scholar to rule on certain matters, but not on others (provided that the scholar is fit to rule on all matters; *Jerusalem Talmud*). For example, he may authorize him to rule in monetary cases but not on the permissibility of particular activities or things, and vice versa. So, too, may authorization be conferred upon a scholar for a limited period of time." (*Rambam, Sefer Shofetim, Hilkhot Sanhedrin* 4:8,9.)

TRANSLATION AND COMMENTARY

שָׁאנֵי הָתָם [1]Rav Naḥman answered: **It is different there,** in the case of the Mishnah, [2]**because from the outset** the judges **sat** to hear the case **bearing in mind** that it would be decided by a court of **three.** [3]But **here,** in the case discussed by Shmuel, the judges **did not sit** to hear the case **bearing in mind** that it would be decided by a court of **three.**

אֵיתִיבֵיהּ [4]**An objection was raised** against Shmuel from a Baraita which stated: [5]**"Rabban Shimon ben Gamliel says: Judgment** requires a court of **three** judges. [6]But **a compromise** can be arbitrated by a court of **two.** [7]**The power of compromise is greater than the power of judgment.** [8]**For if two** judge a case, each of **the litigants can retract** and demand that the case be heard by a court of three. [9]**But if two arbitrated a compromise** and the compromise decision has already been executed, [10]**the litigants cannot retract** and say that they want the compromise to be arbitrated by a court of three." This Baraita poses a difficulty for Shmuel, for he maintains that if two judges have rendered a judgment, the decision is binding on both parties.

וְכִי תֵּימָא [6A] [11]The Gemara now suggests a resolution of this difficulty: **You might say that,** indeed, according to Rabban Shimon ben Gamliel, the judgment of a monetary case requires a court of three, and that if a case was adjudicated by two, the decision is not binding on the two litigants. **But the Rabbis disagree with Rabban Shimon ben Gamliel** and say that if two judges rendered a decision, it is binding. And Shmuel follows the opinion of the Rabbis. **But this** resolution does not stand, [12]for **surely Rabbi Abbahu said:** If **two** judges **adjudicated** a monetary case, [13]**all agree that their decision is not binding.** Thus, Rabban Shimon ben Gamliel's ruling is not in dispute, and the difficulty that it poses for Shmuel stands.

גַּבְרָא אַגַּבְרָא [14]The Gemara refutes this objection: **Are you casting** the position of **one** Amora, Rabbi Abbahu, **against** that of **another,** Shmuel? The objection raised here against Shmuel is not from the Baraita itself, but from Rabbi Abbahu's interpretation of that Baraita. According to Rabbi Abbahu, all agree that a decision rendered by two judges is not valid. Shmuel disagrees and says that this is the position of Rabban Shimon ben Gamliel, but the other Rabbis maintain that such a decision is binding.

[1]שָׁאנֵי הָתָם [2]דְּמֵעִיקָּרָא אַדַּעְתָּא דִּתְלָתָא יְתִיבִי. [3]הָכָא לָאו אַדַּעְתָּא דִּתְלָתָא יְתִיבִי.

[4]אֵיתִיבֵיהּ: [5]"רַבָּן שִׁמְעוֹן בֶּן גַּמְלִיאֵל אוֹמֵר: הַדִּין בִּשְׁלֹשָׁה, [6]וּפְשָׁרָה בִּשְׁנַיִם. [7]וְיָפֶה כֹּחַ פְּשָׁרָה מִכֹּחַ הַדִּין. [8]שֶׁשְּׁנַיִם שֶׁדָּנוּ, בַּעֲלֵי דִינִין יְכוֹלִין לַחֲזוֹר בָּהֶן, [9]וּשְׁנַיִם שֶׁעָשׂוּ פְּשָׁרָה — [10]אֵין בַּעֲלֵי דִינִין יְכוֹלִין לַחֲזוֹר בָּהֶן.

[6A] [11]וְכִי תֵּימָא פְּלִיגִי רַבָּנַן עֲלֵיהּ דְּרַבָּן שִׁמְעוֹן בֶּן גַּמְלִיאֵל, [12]וְהָאָמַר רַבִּי אַבָּהוּ: שְׁנַיִם שֶׁדָּנוּ, [13]לְדִבְרֵי הַכֹּל, אֵין דִּינֵיהֶם דִּין!

[14]גַּבְרָא אַגַּבְרָא קָא רָמֵית?

LITERAL TRANSLATION

[1]It is different there [2]because from the outset they sat with three in mind. [3]Here they did not sit with three in mind.

[4]They raised an objection: [5]"Rabban Shimon ben Gamliel says: Judgment with three, [6]and compromise with two. [7]And the power of compromise is greater than the power of judgment. [8]For [if] two judged, the litigants can retract, [9]but [if] two arbitrated a compromise, [10]the litigants cannot retract."

[6A] [11]And if you say that the Rabbis disagree with Rabban Shimon ben Gamliel, [12]but surely Rabbi Abbahu said: Two who judged, [13]according to all, their judgment is not a judgment.

[14]Are you casting one man against another?

RASHI

לפלגא — כגון רב, דיהיבי להו רשותא למידן ולא להתיר בכורות. **על תנאי** — כגון עד שנה או עד שנתים ולא יותר. **מאי** — מהני בתוך הזמן או לא. **לרב שמן** — כשהיה פורש ממנו וירד לבבל. **ברשותינו** — רשות נתונה לך לדון. **אפילו שנים מזכין כו'** — משנה היא [ב"זה בורר"] (סנהדרין כט,א). **יוסיפו הדיינין** — דהוה ליה כמאן דלא הוה התם ואישתכח דתרי הוא דהוי, ואנן בעינן מעיקרא תלתא, דאי נמי גמר דינא בתרי דהוי רובא שפיר דמי. **שנים שעשו פשרה אין בעלי דינין יכולין לחזור בהן** — שהרי נתרצו, ועל פיהן עשו. **גברא אגברא** — ר' אבהו אדשמואל, שמואל סבר: פליגי רבנן עליה דרבן שמעון בן גמליאל.

but immediately afterwards he was stricken with remorse. We know that his life was full of suffering. Ten of his sons died in his lifetime. There is a Geonic tradition that one of his sons, Rabbi Matena, an Amora of Babylonia, did not predecease him. The death of Rabbi Yoḥanan's student, friend and brother-in-law, Resh Lakish, for which he considered himself responsible, hastened his own death.

Rabbi Yoḥanan had many students. In fact, all the Amoraim of Eretz Israel in succeeding generations were his students and benefited from his teachings — so much so that he is said to be the author of the Jerusalem Talmud. His greatest students were his brother-in-law Resh Lakish, Rabbi Elazar, Rabbi Ḥiyya bar Abba, Rabbi Abbahu, Rabbi Yose bar Ḥanina, Rabbi Ammi, and Rabbi Assi.

TERMINOLOGY

גַּבְרָא אַגַּבְרָא קָא רָמֵית? Are you casting one man against another? Sometimes, after an objection has been raised to the view of one Amora based on the statement of another Amora, the Talmud asks this question, meaning: "Why do you raise an objection to Rabbi A's viewpoint from a statement by Rabbi B? Surely both have the same authority and are entitled to differ!"

NOTES

גַּבְרָא אַגַּבְרָא קָא רָמֵית? Are you casting one man against another? This expression and similar ones derive from the difference of authority between a Tanna and an Amora. An Amora is subservient to the words of Tannaim, and if it is found that a Tanna contradicts him, his ruling is nullified. However, in the case of contradictory Amoraic rulings, one cannot be used to challenge another, and they are usually regarded as equal in authority. Here, however, it is proved that the challenge to Shmuel does not derive from the rulings of the Tannaim but rather from an interpretation by an Amora, Rabbi Abbahu, of those rulings, and that Shmuel has a right to contest it.

SAGES

רַבִּי אַבָּא **Rabbi Abba.** An Amora of the third generation, Rabbi Abba was born in Babylonia. He was a disciple of Rav Huna and Rav Yehudah. He immigrated to Eretz Israel like his colleague Rabbi Zera, and probably settled in Tiberias.

TRANSLATION AND COMMENTARY

גּוּפָא [1]**Returning to the statement quoted above:** [2]**Rabbi Abbahu said:** If **two** judges **adjudicated a monetary case,** [3]**all agree that their decision is not binding.** [4]**Rabbi Abba raised an objection against Rabbi Abbahu** from a Mishnah in *Bekhorot* (28b) which states: [5]**"If** a single judge **issued an** erroneous **ruling, and freed the liable party from liability, or imposed liability upon a party who was not** actually **liable,** [6]**or declared as impure** produce or the like which was in fact **ritually pure, or declared as pure** that which was in fact **ritually impure** — [7]in each of these cases **that which was done was done** and the ruling stands, **and** the judge **must pay from his own pocket** for the damage that was caused by his ruling." This Mishnah cannot refer to a single judge who was recognized as an expert in the law, for the next clause of the Mishnah teaches that if the judge was a recognized as an expert, he is exempt from paying for the damage he caused, implying that the first clause deals with ordinary laymen. Moreover, the Mishnah states that what was done was done. The single judge's decision is binding. Now, this Mishnah poses no problem according to Shmuel, who only spoke about a ruling rendered by two judges. For he could agree that a ruling issued by a single judge is valid, but he spoke about a ruling rendered by two judges in order to teach they are called an impudent court. According to Rabbi Abbahu, however, there is a difficulty, for he maintains that a decision rendered by a court consisting of fewer than three members is not binding!

הָכָא בְּמַאי עָסְקִינַן [8]The Gemara answers: There would be no inconsistency if Rabbi Abbahu was referring to a case where two judges coerced the litigants to appear before them. But **here,** in the Mishnah, **we are dealing with** a case [9]**where** the two litigants **accepted upon themselves** the decision of a single judge. In such a case, even Rabbi Abbahu agrees that the ruling issued by the single judge is valid and binding on both parties.

[1]גּוּפָא: [2]אָמַר רַבִּי אַבָּהוּ: שְׁנַיִם שֶׁדָּנוּ דִּינֵי מָמוֹנוֹת, [3]לְדִבְרֵי הַכֹּל אֵין דִּינֵיהֶם דִּין. [4]אֵיתִיבֵיהּ רַבִּי אַבָּא לְרַבִּי אַבָּהוּ: [5]״דָּן אֶת הַדִּין, וְזִיכָּה אֶת הַחַיָּיב וְחִיֵּיב אֶת הַזַּכַּאי, [6]טִימֵּא אֶת הַטָּהוֹר טִיהֵר אֶת הַטָּמֵא — [7]מַה שֶׁעָשָׂה עָשׂוּי, וּמְשַׁלֵּם מִבֵּיתוֹ״. [8]הָכָא בְּמַאי עָסְקִינַן [9]דְּקִיבְּלוּהוּ עֲלַיְיהוּ.

LITERAL TRANSLATION

[1][Returning] to the statement quoted above (lit., "the thing itself"): [2]Rabbi Abbahu said: Two who judged monetary cases, [3]according to all, their judgment is not a judgment. [4]Rabbi Abba raised an objection against Rabbi Abbahu: [5]"If someone adjudicated a case [lit., 'judged a judgment'], and freed the liable party from liability, or imposed liability upon the party who was not liable, [6][or] declared the ritually pure impure [or] the ritually impure pure — [7]what was done was done, and he pays from his own pocket [lit., 'his house']."

[8]What we are dealing with here is [9]when they accepted him upon themselves.

RASHI

דן את הדין — במומחה ליכא למימר, מדקתני סיפא "אם היה מומחה לבית דין". **דן את הדין** — יחידי משמע. **ומשלם מביתו** — בפירקין דלקמן (לג,א) מוקי לה שנשא ונתן ביד, מדקתני: מה שעשה עשוי. אלמא דיניה דינא, דאי לא דינא — ליהדר.

NOTES

מַה שֶּׁעָשָׂה עָשׂוּי, וּמְשַׁלֵּם מִבֵּיתוֹ **What was done was done, and he pays from his pocket.** As the Gemara explained, we are speaking here of an error in discretion. Thus the judge should be able to say, "Bring me proof that I erred, and I will pay." And it must be said that this indeed is the case. *Riva* explains that, there is no way to prove the judge's error; however, the judge, because of his fear of Heaven, discovers the error and sees it as his duty to pay. The Jerusalem Talmud says that, though his judgment stands, he pays, because he acted arrogantly and judged as a single judge, against the advice of the Sages.

HALAKHAH

דָּן אֶת הַדִּין, וְזִיכָּה אֶת הַחַיָּיב **If someone rendered a judgment, and freed the liable party from liability.** "If a person was publicly recognized as an expert in the law, but was not authorized to serve as a judge, nor had been accepted by the litigants to serve in that capacity, or if he was not publicly recognized as an expert in the law, but had been accepted as a judge by the parties, and issued a ruling based on an error in discretion, the following distinction applies: If the judge himself gave money to one of the parties which rightfully belonged to the other party, the judgment is not subject to revision, and the judge must compensate the injured party for the damage that was done him. But if the judge did not hand over the money himself, the judgment may be revised, and only if there is irrecoverable damage must the judge offer compensation. *Rema* notes that, according to some authorities (*Rosh, Tur*), even if the judge did not hand over the money himself, the judgment is not subject to revision, but rather the judge must pay the injured party for the damage that he caused him." (*Shulḥan Arukh, Ḥoshen Mishpat* 25:3.)

TRANSLATION AND COMMENTARY

אִי הָכִי [1]The Gemara asks: **If so, why does the** judge have to **pay from his** own **pocket** if he issued an erroneous decision? Surely the litigants agreed to accept the judge's decision, whatever it might be!

דַּאֲמָרוּ לֵיה [2]The Gemara answers: The judge is liable for any damage caused by his erroneous decisions, **because** the litigant injured by the judge's error can **say to him:** "When we accepted you as a judge we meant that you should **judge us according to Torah law.**" Therefore if he erred and did not judge according to Torah law, he must pay.

אֲמַר לֵיה [3]The Gemara now wishes to clarify the type of error for which the judge is liable: **Rav Safra said to Rabbi Abba:** [4]**With what** type of **error** is the Mishnah in *Bekhorot* dealing? [5]**If you say that** it is dealing with **an erroneous ruling about a Mishnaic law,** when a judge ruled against a clear and undisputed Halakhah stated explicitly in the Mishnah or some other authoritative source, there is a difficulty. [6]**For surely Rav Sheshet said in the name of Rabbi Ammi:** [7]If a judge **issued an erroneous ruling about an** undisputed **Mishnaic law,** the ruling **is subject to revision.** The judge need not offer any compensation, for the case is retried. [8]**Rather,** the Mishnah must be dealing with a case where the judge **erred in his discretion.**

הֵיכִי דָּמֵי [9]The Gemara clarifies the matter further: **How do we visualize the case of an error in the weighing of opinion?** If a judge issued a ruling regarding a matter about which the law is in dispute, then how can it be said that the ruling was issued in error? Who says that the alternative way of deciding the matter is any more correct than the way the judge already decided? [10]**Rav Pappa said: We are dealing with a case where two Tannaim or two Amoraim disagreed with each other,** [11]**and it was not stated** explicitly anywhere **that the law was in accordance with the one master or the other master,** [12]but **it was commonly accepted** among the judges to rule **in accordance with one of** the two views,

LITERAL TRANSLATION

[1]If so, why does he pay from his pocket?
[2]Because they said to him: "Judge us according to Torah law."
[3]Rav Safra said to Rabbi Abba: [4]About what did he err? [5]If you say that he erred regarding a Mishnaic law, [6]but surely Rav Sheshet said in the name of Rabbi Ammi: [7]If someone erred regarding a Mishnaic law, he can retract! [8]Rather, where he erred in the weighing of opinion.
[9]How do we visualize (lit., "how is it like") the case of [an error in] the weighing of opinion? [10]Rav Pappa said: If two Tannaim or two Amoraim disagreed with each other, [11]and it was not stated [that] the law was in accordance with the one master or the other master, [12]and the general practice was in accordance with one of them,

---

אִי הָכִי, אַמַּאי מְשַׁלֵּם מִבֵּיתוֹ? [2]דַּאֲמָרוּ לֵיהּ: "דַּיְּינַתְּ לָן דִּין תּוֹרָה". [3]אָמַר לֵיהּ רַב סָפְרָא לְרַבִּי אַבָּא: [4]דִּטְעָה בְּמַאי? [5]אִילֵימָא דִּטְעָה בִּדְבַר מִשְׁנָה, [6]וְהָאָמַר רַב שֵׁשֶׁת אָמַר רַבִּי אַמִּי: [7]טָעָה בִּדְבַר מִשְׁנָה, חוֹזֵר! [8]אֶלָּא דִּטְעָה בְּשִׁיקּוּל הַדַּעַת. [9]הֵיכִי דָּמֵי בְּשִׁיקּוּל הַדַּעַת? [10]אָמַר רַב פַּפָּא: כְּגוֹן תְּרֵי תַנָּאֵי וּתְרֵי אָמוֹרָאֵי דְּפָלִיגִי אַהֲדָדֵי, [11]וְלָא אִיתְּמַר הִלְכְתָא לָא כְּמָר וְלָא כְּמָר, [12]וְסוּגְיִין דְּעָלְמָא אַלִּיבָּא דְּחַד מִינַּיְיהוּ,

RASHI

דִּין תּוֹרָה — וְכֵיוָן דְּטָעָה לָאו דִּין תּוֹרָה דָּן. **בִּדְבַר מִשְׁנָה** — שֶׁמִּשְׁנָה מְפוֹרֶשֶׁת שֶׁטָּעָה בָּהּ. **חוֹזֵר** — מַחֲזִיר אֶת הַדִּין וְאֵינוֹ מְשַׁלֵּם מִבֵּיתוֹ, דְּכֵיוָן דִּדְבַר מְפוֹרָשׁ הוּא, אֵין דִּינוֹ דִּין. **וְסוּגְיָא דְעָלְמָא** — הִילּוּךְ דִּינָא כְּחַד מִינַּיְיהוּ, וְאָזַל אִיהוּ וַעֲבַד כְּאִידַךְ. **הִלְכַּךְ** — דַּיְּינֵיהּ לָא הֲדַר, וְכֵיוָן דְּלָא אִיתְּמַר הִלְכְתָא לָא כְּמַר וְלָא כְּמַר, הַאי בַּעַל דִּין דְּנִיקַּט לָא בַּעֵי לִשַׁלּוּמֵי, דְּאָמַר לֵיהּ: פַּסְקַתְּ לִי לְדִינַאי. וּמִיהוּ, אִיהוּ בַּעֵי שַׁלּוּמֵי, כֵּיוָן דְּסוּגְיִין דְּעָלְמָא כְּאִידַךְ.

NOTES

סוּגְיָא דְּעָלְמָא **The general trend of practice.** That is to say, most of those who deal with this Halakhah tend to accept this approach, but it is not yet a full Halakhic ruling (*Geonim*).

HALAKHAH

טָעָה בִּדְבַר מִשְׁנָה **He erred about a Mishnaic law.** "If a judge issued an erroneous decision, ruling against a clear and undisputed law stated clearly in the Mishnah, the Gemara, or the accepted codes (such as the undisputed rulings found in *Shulḥan Arukh;* see *Pitḥei Teshuvah*), the decision is subject to revision." (*Shulḥan Arukh, Ḥoshen Mishpat* 25:1.)

טָעָה בְּשִׁיקּוּל הַדַּעַת **He erred in his discretion.** "An error in discretion occurs when there are conflicting views among the Tannaim or the Amoraim, and the law has not been formally decided, yet a judge rules in accordance with one opinion, not realizing that the other opinion has been accepted in practice throughout the world (or throughout the country; *Shakh*)." (*Shulḥan Arukh, Ḥoshen Mishpat* 25:2.)

SAGES

רַב סָפְרָא **Rav Safra.** A Babylonian Amora of the third and fourth generations. He is found in Halakhic discussions as a student and a colleague of the greatest Sages of the third generation, such as Rabbah and Rav Yosef. He remained active during the generation of their students, Abaye and Rava. Rav Safra was apparently a merchant, and frequently visited Eretz Israel, where he held discussions with Sages such as Rabbi Abba and Rabbi Abbahu. He was an expert in Halakhah, and is not quoted so frequently in Aggadic passages. Rav Safra was famous for his personal qualities, in particular his punctiliousness in avoiding the slightest deviation from the truth. Since Rav Safra traveled widely, he did not have his own yeshivah, and was not often found in the House of Study.

רַב שֵׁשֶׁת **Rav Sheshet.** He was a famous Babylonian Amora of the second and third generations, a colleague of Rav Naḥman and of Rav Ḥisda. He was outstanding in his knowledge of Mishnayot and Baraitot, which he acquired through exceptional diligence. In his controversies with Rav Naḥman, the Geonim decided the Halakhah according to Rav Sheshet in all matters of ritual law. Rav Sheshet was blind. Many of the Amoraim of the third and fourth generations, including Rava, were his students.

רַב פַּפָּא **Rav Pappa.** One of the leading Babylonian Amoraim of the fifth generation, Rav Pappa was a student of Abaye and of Rava, and a colleague of Rav Huna the son of Rav Yehoshua. After Rava's death, Rava's yeshivah divided — part went to Pumbedita with Rav Naḥman bar Yitzḥak, and the other part went to Neresh with Rav Pappa. Rav Pappa's yeshivah was famous and had many students. Among his disciples were Rav Ashi and Ravina. Rav Pappa served as head of his yeshivah for nineteen years.

BACKGROUND

טָעָה בִּדְבַר מִשְׁנָה **If someone erred regarding a Mishnaic law.** When a judge errs in a matter of Mishnah (as interpreted in the Gemara and by the Rabbis, this term includes any clear and simple Halakhic ruling), his ruling is not regarded as an error in the judicial process but as a miscarriage of justice, as if no trial at all had been held. If the judge caused damage by his error, he can be sued only according to the laws of damages.

LITERAL TRANSLATION

[1]and he went and acted in accordance with the other — [2]this is [an error in] the weighing of opinion.

[3]Shall we say this is a Tannaitic dispute (lit., "like the Tannaim")? [4]"Compromise by three. [5][These are] the words of Rabbi Meir. [6]And the Sages say: Compromise by a single [judge]."

[7]They thought [that] according to everybody we compare compromise to judgment. [8]Do they not argue about this? [9]That the one master maintains: A judgment is by three. [10]And the other master maintains: A judgment is by two?

[1]וַאֲזַל אִיהוּ וַעֲבַד כְּאִידָךְ — [2]הַיְינוּ שִׁיקּוּל הַדַּעַת.

[3]לֵימָא כְּתַנָּאֵי? [4]"בִּיצּוּעַ בִּשְׁלֹשָׁה. [5]דִּבְרֵי רַבִּי מֵאִיר. [6]וַחֲכָמִים אוֹמְרִים: פְּשָׁרָה בְּיָחִיד".

[7]סַבְרוּהָ: לְכוּלֵּי עָלְמָא מַקְשִׁינַן פְּשָׁרָה לְדִין. [8]מַאי לָאו בְּהָא קָמִיפַּלְגִי? [9]דְּמָר סָבַר: דִּין בִּשְׁלֹשָׁה. [10]וּמָר סָבַר: דִּין בִּשְׁנַיִם?

RASHI

לימא כתנאי — הא דאמרינן דשמואל ור' אבהו פליגי. **ביצוע** — פשרה. **סברוה** — רבנן אמוראי, בני הישיבה, ובעו למימר מהכא דבדשמואל ור' אבהו פליגי. **דכולי עלמא** — רבנן ור' מאיר.

TRANSLATION AND COMMENTARY

[1]and this judge **went and acted in accordance with the other** view, and afterwards he found out that his decision was contrary to the commonly accepted view, [2]**this is an error in the weighing of opinion,** regarding which we say that the ruling stands, and the judge must compensate the party who suffered a loss as a result of his erroneous decision. The ruling stands because it does reflect an authoritative opinion. But the judge must compensate the party who was damaged by the ruling, for he ruled against the opinion commonly accepted by the judicial authorities.

לֵימָא כְּתַנָּאֵי [3]Returning to the dispute between Shmuel and Rabbi Abbahu, the Gemara suggests: **Shall we say** that **this** disagreement between Shmuel and Rabbi Abbahu about the validity of a ruling issued by a court of two **is** actually the subject of **an** earlier **Tannaitic dispute?** [4]For it was taught in a Baraita: **"A compromise** which is based on the exercise of the judges' discretion (as opposed to a judgment which is rendered according to the laws governing the matter in dispute) requires a court consisting of **three judges.** [5]**This is the view of Rabbi Meir.** [6]**But the Sages disagree** and **say: A compromise** may be effected by a court consisting of even **a single judge."**

סַבְרוּהָ [7]The Amoraim who suggested that the disagreement between Shmuel and Rabbi Abbahu corresponds to the earlier dispute between the Tannaim **assumed that according to all** the Tannaim — both Rabbi Meir and the Sages — **we may draw a comparison between compromise and judgment** which is rendered according to the laws governing the matter in dispute, for the verse states (II Samuel 8:15): "And David executed judgment and charity to all his people," and as will be explained below, justice which involves both judgment and charity can only be found in compromise. And since the Torah describes compromise as a judgment, it follows that an analogy may be drawn between the two. [8]**Do** Rabbi Meir and the Sages, then, **not argue about the** following matter? [9]**The one master** — Rabbi Meir — **maintains: A judgment** rendered according to the laws governing the matter in dispute requires a court of **three** judges. Since judgment and compromise are comparable, a compromise which is based on the exercise of the judges' discretion can also only be effected by a court of three judges. [10]**And the other master** — the Sages — **maintains: A judgment** can be issued by a court of **two** or even one judge. And since the laws pertaining to judgment may be applied to compromise, a compromise may also be effected by a court of two or even one judge. Thus, Rabbi Abbahu follows the view of Rabbi Meir, and Shmuel follows that of the Rabbis!

NOTES

בִּיצּוּעַ וּפְשָׁרָה **Compromise.** There is a change in terminology here. Rabbi Meir uses the word בִּיצּוּעַ and the Sages use פְּשָׁרָה. This difference in terminology appears to be connected to the different attitudes toward the essence of compromise. Some interpret compromise as taking property illicitly from one party to the dispute, a form of robbery. For that reason they derive the term בִּיצּוּעַ from the word בצע, coveted property. According to this view one should not effect a compromise but rather insist on a true judicial ruling (*Remah*). Others derive the term בִּיצּוּעַ from a different root, meaning to divide something into two equal parts, and for this discretion is needed. However, פְּשָׁרָה means to find some level of compromise between the two parties (*Riva*). Others argue that בִּיצּוּעַ means a breaking, and therefore one must be cautious regarding it, whereas פְּשָׁרָה means to make water lukewarm (פּוֹשְׁרִים) by mixing hot and cold (*Rosh*).

HALAKHAH

פְּשָׁרָה בְּיָחִיד **Compromise by a single judge.** "If the parties agree, a comprise can be effected by even a single judge," following the Sages against Rabbi Meir. (*Shulḥan Arukh, Ḥoshen Mishpat* 12:7.)

[1]לֹא, דְּכוּלֵּי עָלְמָא דִּין בִּשְׁלֹשָׁה. [2]וְהָכָא בְּהָא קָמִיפַּלְגִי, [3]דְּמָר סָבַר: מַקְשִׁינַן פְּשָׁרָה לְדִין, [4]וּמָר סָבַר: לָא מַקְשִׁינַן פְּשָׁרָה לְדִין.

[5]לֵימָא תְּלָתָא תַּנָּאֵי בִּפְשָׁרָה, [6]דְּמָר סָבַר: בִּשְׁלֹשָׁה; [7]וּמָר סָבַר: בִּשְׁנַיִם; [8]וּמָר סָבַר בְּיָחִיד?

[9]אָמַר רַב אַחָא בְּרֵיהּ דְּרַב אִיקָא, [10]וְאִיתֵימָא רַבִּי יֵימָר בַּר שֶׁלֶמְיָא: [11]מַאן דַּאֲמַר תְּרֵי, [12]אֲפִילּוּ חַד נַמִי, [13]וְהַאי דְּקָאָמַר תְּרֵי, [14]כִּי הֵיכִי דְּלֶיהֱווּ עֲלֵיהּ סָהֲדֵי.

[15]אָמַר רַב אַשִׁי: שְׁמַע מִינָּהּ פְּשָׁרָה אֵינָהּ צְרִיכָה קִנְיָן. [16]דְּאִי סָלְקָא דַּעְתָּךְ צְרִיכָה קִנְיָן,

LITERAL TRANSLATION

[1]No, according to everybody a judgment is by three. [2]And here they argue about this, [3]that the one master maintains: We compare compromise to judgment, [4]and the other master maintains: We do not compare compromise to judgment.

[5]Shall we say [that there are] three Tannaim regarding compromise, [6]that the one master maintains: By three; [7]and the other master maintains: By two; [8]and the other master maintains: By a single [judge]?

[9]Rav Aḥa the son of Rav Ika said, [10]and some say [it was] Rabbi Yema bar Shelemya: [11]The one who said two, [12]even one also. [13]And [the reason] that he said two, [14]in order that they be witnesses to it.

[15]Rav Ashi said: Infer from this [that a] compromise does not require an act of acquisition. [16]For if you think [that] it requires an act of acquisition,

TRANSLATION AND COMMENTARY

לֹא [1]The Gemara rejects this suggestion and explains that Rabbi Meir and the Sages disagree about a different issue. **No, according to all** the Tannaim — both Rabbi Meir and the Sages — **a judgment** requires a court of **three** judges. [2]**And here** the Tannaim **argue about** the following matter: [3]**The one master** — Rabbi Meir — **maintains: We** may indeed **draw a comparison between compromise and judgment,** and since a judgment requires a court of three, so too can a compromise be effected only by a court of three. [4]**And the other master** — the Sages — **maintains: We may not compare compromise to judgment.** Even though a judgment requires three judges, a compromise can be effected by two judges or even by one judge.

לֵימָא [5]The Gemara now examines how many different views there are regarding the number of judges required to effect a compromise: The Baraita recorded only two positions on the matter, but perhaps **we should say that there are** actually **three** different **Tannaitic** views **regarding** the number of judges required for a **compromise?** [6]**The one master** — Rabbi Meir — **maintains** that a compromise can only be effected by **three** judges; **the other master** — Rabban Shimon ben Gamliel, whose view is recorded in the Baraita which was cited earlier in the Gemara — [7]**maintains** that a compromise can even be effected by **two;** [8]**and the third master** — the Sages — **maintains** that a compromise requires only **one** judge.

אָמַר [9]The Gemara rejects this suggestion: **Rav Aḥa the son of Rav Ika said,** [10]**and there are some who say** that **it was Rabbi Yema bar Shelemya** who put forward this argument: [11]Rabban Shimon ben Gamliel, **who said** that only **two** judges are required for a compromise, actually maintains [12]that **even a single judge** is sufficient. Once we say that three judges are not required, because judgment and compromise are not comparable, there is no advantage to two judges over a single judge. [13]**And** Rabban Shimon ben Gamliel **said** that a compromise should be effected by **two** judges, not because he maintains that a compromise effected by a single judge is invalid, [14]but rather **so that there will be witnesses to** the compromise, and neither party will be able to deny the terms of the decision.

אָמַר רַב אַשִׁי [15]**Rav Ashi said: Infer from** Rabbi Meir's position that **compromise** requires a court of three, but **does not require an act of acquisition,** a formal procedure rendering the parties' acceptance of the compromise as legally binding. [16]**For if you think** that **compromise requires an act of acquisition** in order to

BACKGROUND

פְּשָׁרָה וְקִנְיָן Compromise and an act of acquisition. Since a compromise is not a legal ruling, it does not carry the authority of a court, which can obligate the parties to implement its decision. In order for a compromise to be enforceable, the parties must agree in advance to accept it. If they do not accept it, the compromise decision is regarded as only a recommendation, which either party may or may not accept.

RASHI

מקשינן פשרה לדין — דכתיב (שמואל ב ח): "משפט וצדקה" ואמרינן לקמן דזהו ביצוע, אלמא דאיתקוש למשפט. **תלתא תנאי** — פליגי בפשרה, ר' מאיר סבר בשלשה, רבן שמעון בן גמליאל סבר לעיל (ה,ב) בשנים, ורבנן דפליגי אדר' מאיר סברי ביחיד. **מאן דאמר תרי אפילו בחד** — מכשר דכיון דלא מקשינן ליה לדין, מה לי תרי מה לי חד.

NOTES

מַאן דַּאֲמַר תְּרֵי, אֲפִילּוּ בְּחַד The one who said two, even one also. The reason for this is that judgment is a kind of battle. When each side has an opposing opinion, there must be three judges to decide. But with compromise, since

HALAKHAH

פְּשָׁרָה צְרִיכָה קִנְיָן Compromise requires an act of acquisition. "Even if the litigants consented to the court effecting a compromise, they may reject the compromise as long as an act of acquisition [*kinyan*] had not been performed by

לְמַאן דְּאָמַר צְרִיכָה, [1]תְּלָתָא לָמָּה לִי? [2]תִּסְגֵּי בִּתְרֵי, וְלִיקְנֵי מִינֵּיהּ!

[3]וְהִלְכְתָא: פְּשָׁרָה צְרִיכָה קִנְיָן.

[4]תָּנוּ רַבָּנַן: כְּשֵׁם שֶׁהַדִּין בִּשְׁלֹשָׁה, [5]כָּךְ בִּיצּוּעַ בִּשְׁלֹשָׁה. [6B] [6]נִגְמַר הַדִּין, [7]אִי אַתָּה רַשַּׁאי לִבְצוֹעַ.

[8]סרמ״ש בנק״ש סִימָן.

[9]״רַבִּי אֱלִיעֶזֶר בְּנוֹ שֶׁל רַבִּי יוֹסֵי הַגְּלִילִי אוֹמֵר: [10]אָסוּר לִבְצוֹעַ, [11]וְכָל הַבּוֹצֵעַ הֲרֵי זֶה חוֹטֵא, [12]וְכָל הַמְבָרֵךְ אֶת הַבּוֹצֵעַ הֲרֵי זֶה מְנָאֵץ, [13]וְעַל זֶה נֶאֱמַר: ׳בֹּצֵעַ בֵּרֵךְ נִאֵץ ה׳״, [14]אֶלָּא,

LITERAL TRANSLATION

according to the one who says it requires [an act of acquisition], [1]why do I need three? [2]Two should suffice, and let him perform an act of acquisition! [3]And the law is: Compromise requires an act of acquisition.

[4]Our Rabbis taught: "Just as judgment is by three, [5]so too is a compromise by three. [6B] [6][If] the judgment was concluded, [7]you are not permitted to arbitrate a compromise."

[8]Mnemonic: SRM"SH BNK"SH (סרמ״ש בנק״ש).

[9]"Rabbi Eliezer the son of Rabbi Yose the Galilean says: [10]It is forbidden to arbitrate a compromise, [11]and whoever arbitrates a compromise is a sinner. [12]And whoever praises one who arbitrates a compromise blasphemes. [13]And about this it is said: "He who praises one who arbitrates a compromise blasphemes God." [14]Rather,

TRANSLATION AND COMMENTARY

render the parties' acceptance of the compromise as legally binding, [1]**why do I need** a court of **three** judges to effect the compromise? [2]A court of **two** judges or even a single judge **should suffice** to effect a compromise, provided that the parties **perform a valid act of acquisition** to ratify their acceptance of the compromise decision!

וְהִלְכְתָא [3]The Gemara concludes its discussion with a ruling on the matter: **The law is** that **compromise does** in part **require a valid act of acquisition** to render the decision legally binding, even if the decision was reached by a court of three judges. Thus the parties may retract from the compromise as long a valid mode of acquisition has not been performed by them.

תָּנוּ רַבָּנַן [4]The Gemara continues with another Baraita pertaining to compromise: **Our Rabbis taught: "Just as a judgment** rendered according to the laws governing a matter in dispute requires a court of **three** judges, [5]**so too does a compromise** require **three judges.** [6B] [6]**If the judgment has** already **been concluded,** [7]**the** court **is no longer permitted to arbitrate a compromise."**

סרמ״ש בנק״ש סִימָן [8]The Gemara now presents several different opinions regarding the desirability of compromise. **A mnemonic device** which can help the student remember the names of the eight authorities whose views are recorded here **is SRM"SH BNK"SH** (סרמ״ש בנק״ש), each letter representing a different Sage: Rabbi Eliezer the son of Rabbi Yose the Galilean, Rabbi Eliezer, Rabbi Meir, Rabbi Yehoshua ben Korḥah, Rabbi Yehudah HaNasi, Rabbi Shimon ben Menasya, Resh Lakish, and once again Rabbi Yehoshua ben Korḥah.

רַבִּי אֱלִיעֶזֶר [9]It was taught in a Baraita: **"Rabbi Eliezer the son of Rabbi Yose the Galilean says:** Once a case has been brought to court, [10]it **is forbidden to arbitrate a compromise.** Not only is compromise forbidden, [11]but **whoever arbitrates a compromise is** regarded as **a sinner,** for compromise necessarily involves a deviation from Torah law to the disadvantage of one of the litigants. [12]**And whoever praises one who arbitrates a compromise blasphemes** God. [13]**And about** such a person **the verse states** [Psalms 10:3]: **'He who praises an arbitrator blasphemes God.'** Rabbi Eliezer the son of Rabbi Yose the Galilean explains the verse condemning as a blasphemer someone who commends [בֵּרֵךְ] a judge who effects a compromise [בּוֹצֵעַ]. [14]**Rather** than

RASHI

תיסגי בתרי וליקני מיניה — דכיון דקנו מיניה למה לי בית דין? לא תהא אלא מתנה בעלמא ומדעתו, והיא מתקיימת אלא להכי בעינן תלתא, לייפות כח בית דין, דאף על גב דלא קנו מיניה לא ניהדרו. **והלכתא פשרה צריכה קנין** — ואפילו נעשית בשלשה. **מאן דאמר תרי אפילו בחד** — מכשר דכיון דלא מקשינן ליה לדין, מה לי תרי מה לי חד. **תיסגי בתרי וליקני מיניה** — דכיון דקנו מיניה למה לי בית דין? לא תהא אלא מתנה בעלמא ומדעתו, והיא מתקיימת אלא להכי בעינן תלתא, לייפות כח בית דין, דאף על גב דלא קנו מיניה לא ניהדרו. **והלכתא פשרה צריכה קנין** — ואפילו נעשית בשלשה. **נגמר הדין** — שאמרו: איש פלוני אתה זכאי, איש פלוני אתה חייב. **אסור לבצוע** — משבאו לדין אסור לדיינים לבצוע. **המברך** — המשבח.

NOTES

everyone intends to compromise, there is no dispute among the judges, and they agree to a single opinion. Hence even one judge is sufficient.

HALAKHAH

them, for a compromise requires an act of acquisition even if it is effected by a court of three." (According to some authorities, only a compromise effected by a court of two requires an act of acquisition, but not a compromise effected by a court of three; see *Pitḥei Teshuvah*.) (*Shulḥan Arukh, Ḥoshen Mishpat* 12:7.)

TRANSLATION AND COMMENTARY

compromise, **'let the law cut through the mountain.'** Let even the most difficult case be decided according to the strict letter of the law, [1]**as it is said** [Deuteronomy 1:17]: 'Do not be afraid of any man, **for the judgment is God's.'** [2]**And similarly Moses,** who was the first to judge Israel according to Torah law, **would say: 'Let the law cut through the mountain.'** [3]**But** his brother **Aaron,** who was not a judge, **loved peace and pursued peace, and caused peace to reign between a man and his fellow.** [4]**As the verse** which is understood as referring to Aaron **states** [Malakhi 2:6]: **'The Torah of truth was in his mouth, and iniquity was not to be found on his lips; he walked with me in peace and uprightness, and turned many away from iniquity.'"**

רַבִּי אֱלִיעֶזֶר אוֹמֵר [5]The Baraita continues with two other explanations of the verse (Psalms 10:3): **"Rabbi Eliezer says: If someone stole a *se'ah* of wheat, and ground it** into flour, **and baked it** into bread, **and,** when he was preparing the dough, **separated *ḥallah* from it** [the portion of dough which by Torah law must be given to the priests; Numbers. 15:20], [6]**how can he recite the blessing** that is ordinarily recited prior to the separation of *ḥallah?* [7]Someone who recites a blessing over stolen property **does not bless** God, **but instead blasphemes** Him. [8]**About** such a person **the verse states: 'He who steals** [בֹּצֵעַ] **and recites a blessing** [בֵּרֵךְ] over the stolen goods **blasphemes God** [נִאֵץ ה'].'"

יִקּוֹב הַדִּין אֶת הָהָר, [1]שֶׁנֶּאֱמַר: 'כִּי הַמִּשְׁפָּט לֵאלֹהִים הוּא'. [2]וְכֵן מֹשֶׁה הָיָה אוֹמֵר: "יִקּוֹב הַדִּין אֶת הָהָר". [3]אֲבָל אַהֲרֹן אוֹהֵב שָׁלוֹם וְרוֹדֵף שָׁלוֹם, וּמֵשִׂים שָׁלוֹם בֵּין אָדָם לַחֲבֵירוֹ, [4]שֶׁנֶּאֱמַר: 'תּוֹרַת אֱמֶת הָיְתָה בְּפִיהוּ וְעַוְלָה לֹא נִמְצָא בִשְׂפָתָיו; בְּשָׁלוֹם וּבְמִישׁוֹר הָלַךְ אִתִּי וְרַבִּים הֵשִׁיב מֵעָוֹן'". [5]"רַבִּי אֱלִיעֶזֶר אוֹמֵר: הֲרֵי שֶׁגָּזַל סְאָה שֶׁל חִטִּים וּטְחָנָהּ וַאֲפָאָהּ וְהִפְרִישׁ מִמֶּנָּה חַלָּה, [6]כֵּיצַד מְבָרֵךְ? [7]אֵין זֶה מְבָרֵךְ, אֶלָּא מְנָאֵץ. [8]וְעַל זֶה נֶאֱמַר: 'וּבֹצֵעַ בֵּרֵךְ נִאֵץ ה'".

LITERAL TRANSLATION

let the law cut through the mountain, [1]as it is said: "For the judgment is God's." [2]And similarly Moses would say: "Let the law cut through the mountain." [3]But Aaron loved peace and pursued peace, and caused peace to reign between a man and his fellow, [4]as it is said: "The Torah of truth was in his mouth, and iniquity was not to be found on his lips; he walked with Me in peace and uprightness, and turned many away from iniquity.'"

[5]"Rabbi Eliezer says: [If] someone stole a *se'ah* of wheat, and ground it, and baked it, and separated from it *ḥallah*, [6]how can he recite a blessing? [7]He does not recite a blessing, but rather he blasphemes. [8]And about this it is said: 'He who steals [and] recites a blessing blasphemes God.'"

RASHI

אבל אהרן אוהב שלום ורודף שלום — וכיון שהיה שומע מחלוקת ביניהם, קודם שיבואו לפניו לדין היה רודף אחריהן, ומטיל שלום ביניהן. **תורת אמת וגו'** — משתעי באהרן "כי שפתי כהן ישמרו דעת וגו'" (מלאכי ב). **הרי שגזל כו'** — ו"בוצע" לשון גזילה דכתיב (משלי א): "כן ארחות כל בוצע בצע את נפש בעליו יקח".

BACKGROUND

מֹשֶׁה וְאַהֲרֹן Moses and Aaron. The distinction between Moses and Aaron here is not connected to an assumption about the different characters of the two brothers, but to the change that occurred in their relationship by virtue of their status. Moses was, on the one hand, the supreme judge of the Jewish people (see Exodus 18), and also the one who transmitted divine law to the people. Hence he was required to adhere strictly to the demands of the law. Aaron, however, had no judicial position in his capacity as High Priest, and, being close to the people all his life, he was capable of serving as an intermediary between people and of effecting compromises.

הֲרֵי שֶׁגָּזַל סְאָה וכו' If someone stole a *se'ah* of wheat etc. These words do not pertain only to this and similar instances belonging to the Halakhic category of "a commandment performed in sin" (מִצְוָה הַבָּאָה בַּעֲבֵירָה). They are of general application, meaning that a person should not think that, by being scrupulous regarding commandments between man and God, he may atone for sins committed against his fellow man, and, more extensively, that a person cannot observe a certain commandment and regard it as atonement for his sins.

NOTES

יִקּוֹב הַדִּין אֶת הָהָר 'Let the law cut through the mountain.' *Arukh* understands that the word יִקּוֹב is used here in the sense of "hole." If a judge concludes that the law requires that a hole be bored through a mountain, he must indeed cut through the mountain despite the difficulty. But יִקּוֹב can also mean "to interpret," or "to clarify," meaning that even if the matter is as difficult for the judge to clarify as climbing a mountain, he must still interpret it.

גָּזַל סְאָה שֶׁל חִטִּים If someone stole a *se'ah* of wheat. *Halakhot Gedolot* explains that Rabbi Eliezer also explains the word *botze'a* to mean "compromise," for someone who recites a blessing when he separates *ḥallah* from dough which was prepared from stolen wheat compromises with God's commandments, accepting the commandment to separate *ḥallah,* while disregarding the prohibtion against robbery.

HALAKHAH

גָּזַל סְאָה שֶׁל חִטִּים If someone stole a *se'ah* of wheat. "If someone eats something that is forbidden to him (even if it is forbidden only by Rabbinic decree), he may not be invited by the other participants in the meal to join together to say Grace after Meals, nor is he permitted to recite a benediction before or after eating. According to some authorities (*Rabbenu Manoaḥ*), if someone stole wheat and ground it into flour and then baked it into bread, he may recite a benediction over the bread, for he acquired the wheat through the physical change, and the bread is now his (though he has to compensate the person from whom he stole the grain). Others (*Bet Yosef, Rosh* according to *Rashi* and *Rambam*) maintain that he may not recite a benediction over the bread, even though it belongs to him, for God's Name may not be recited over stolen property." (*Shulḥan Arukh, Oraḥ Ḥayyim* 196:1.)

[1]"רַבִּי מֵאִיר אוֹמֵר: לֹא נֶאֱמַר בּוֹצֵעַ אֶלָּא כְּנֶגֶד יְהוּדָה, [2]שֶׁנֶּאֱמַר: 'וַיֹּאמֶר יְהוּדָה אֶל אֶחָיו מַה בֶּצַע כִּי נַהֲרֹג אֶת אָחִינוּ'? [3]וְכָל הַמְבָרֵךְ אֶת יְהוּדָה, הֲרֵי זֶה מְנָאֵץ, [4]וְעַל זֶה נֶאֱמַר: 'וּבֹצֵעַ בֵּרֵךְ נִאֵץ ה'"'.

[5]"רַבִּי יְהוֹשֻׁעַ בֶּן קָרְחָה אוֹמֵר: מִצְוָה לִבְצוֹעַ, [6]שֶׁנֶּאֱמַר: "אֱמֶת וּמִשְׁפַּט שָׁלוֹם שִׁפְטוּ בְּשַׁעֲרֵיכֶם". [7]וַהֲלֹא בְּמָקוֹם שֶׁיֵּשׁ מִשְׁפָּט אֵין שָׁלוֹם, [8]וּבְמָקוֹם שֶׁיֵּשׁ שָׁלוֹם אֵין מִשְׁפָּט. [9]אֶלָּא, אֵיזֶהוּ מִשְׁפָּט שֶׁיֵּשׁ בּוֹ שָׁלוֹם? [10]הֱוֵי אוֹמֵר: זֶה בִּיצּוּעַ. [11]וְכֵן בְּדָוִד הוּא אוֹמֵר: 'וַיְהִי דָוִד עוֹשֶׂה מִשְׁפָּט וּצְדָקָה'. [12]וַהֲלֹא כָּל מָקוֹם שֶׁיֵּשׁ מִשְׁפָּט אֵין צְדָקָה, [13]וּצְדָקָה אֵין מִשְׁפָּט, [14]אֶלָּא, אֵיזֶהוּ מִשְׁפָּט שֶׁיֵּשׁ בּוֹ צְדָקָה? [15]הֱוֵי אוֹמֵר: זֶה בִּיצּוּעַ".

LITERAL TRANSLATION

[1]"Rabbi Meir says: [The word] *botze'a* [בוצע] was stated only in reference to Judah, [2]as it is said: 'What profit [בֶּצַע] is it if we slay our brother?' [3]And whoever praises Judah blasphemes, [4]and about this it is said: 'He who praises the one who spoke about profit blasphemes God.'"

[5]"Rabbi Yehoshua ben Korḥah says: It is a meritorious deed to arbitrate a compromise, [6]as it is said: 'Execute truth and the judgment of peace in your gates.' [7]But surely where there is judgment there is no peace, [8]and where there is peace there is no judgment. [9]Rather, which is a judgment that contains peace? [10]Say: This is a compromise. [11]And similarly, regarding David, it states: 'And David executed judgment and charity [to all his people].' [12]But surely wherever there is judgment there is no charity, [13]and [where there is] charity there is no judgment. [14]Rather, which is a judgment which contains charity? [15]Say: This is a compromise."

TRANSLATION AND COMMENTARY

רַבִּי מֵאִיר אוֹמֵר [1]**"Rabbi Meir says: The word** *botze'a* [בּוֹצֵעַ] was used here **in reference to** the unbefitting behaviour of **Judah** who proposed selling Joseph to the Ishmaelites. [2]**For the verse states** [Genesis 37:26]: **'And Judah said to his brothers: "What profit** [בֶּצַע] is it if we slay our brother, and conceal his blood?"' [3]**And whoever praises Judah** for the way he acted, arguing that his was the only way to save Joseph's life, **blasphemes** God. [4]**About** such a person **the verse states: 'He who praises** [בֵּרֵךְ] **the one who spoke about profit** [בֹּצֵעַ] **blasphemes God** ['נִאֵץ ה].'"

רַבִּי יְהוֹשֻׁעַ בֶּן קָרְחָה [5]The Baraita now presents the opposite view regarding the desirability of compromise: **"Rabbi Yehoshua ben Korḥah says: It is a mitzvah** — a meritorious deed — for a court **to effect a compromise,** [6]**as the verse states** [Zechariah 8:16]: **'Execute truth and the judgment of peace in your gates.'** [7]This verse poses a difficulty, for **surely where there is judgment** and adherence to the letter of the law, **there is no peace** between the two litigants. [8]**And where** the litigation ends with **peace** reigning between the two parties, **there is no** true **judgment,** for to arrive at absolute justice, we must strictly follow the letter of the law, which is usually only in one party's favor. [9]**How, then, can** there **be a judgment which attains peace?** [10]You must **say** that **this** verse refers to **compromise.** [11]**And similarly, regarding** King **David, the verse states** [II Samuel 8:15]: **'And David executed judgment and charity to all his people.'** [12]**But surely where there is judgment** and a strict adherence to the letter of the law, **there is no charity** or consideration given to the financial circumstances of the two parties. [13]**And where there is charity, there is no judgment,** for the law is one and the same for rich and poor. [14]**How, then, can** there **be a judgment which involves charity?** [15]You must **say** that **this** verse refers to **compromise."**

RASHI

כנגד יהודה — שהיה לו לומר: נחזירנו לאבינו, אחרי שהיו דבריו נשמעין לאחיו.

NOTES

כְּנֶגֶד יְהוּדָה **In reference to Judah.** *Ramah* understands that, according to Rabbi Meir as well, the word *botze'a* means compromise. By suggesting that Joseph be sold to the Ishmaelites, Judah effected a compromise with his brothers, for he saved Joseph from certain death in the pit, but did not insist on returning him to their father.

Yefeh Mar'eh adds that one might have argued that, since the sale of Joseph to the Ishmaelites eventually led to the rescue of the House of Jacob during the years of famine, Judah did indeed act in a praiseworthy manner. Thus, it was necessary for Scripture to teach that Judah acted wrongly, and that praising Judah's conduct is blasphemy.

וַיְהִי דָוִד עֹשֶׂה מִשְׁפָּט וּצְדָקָה **And David executed judgment and charity.** It has been asked: According to Rabbi Yehudah HaNasi, what was special about David? Surely it is every judge's responsibility to judge fairly, and remove illicit possessions! Some suggest that after David issued a ruling, he did not hand the matter over for execution to an

HALAKHAH

מִצְוָה לִבְצוֹעַ **It is a meritorious deed to compromise.** "It is a mitzvah for the judge to ask the parties at the outset whether they want their dispute resolved according to the law or by means of a compromise," following Rabbi Yehoshua ben Korḥah. (*Shulḥan Arukh, Ḥoshen Mishpat* 12:2.)

SAGES

רַבִּי יְהוֹשֻׁעַ בֶּן קָרְחָה **Rabbi Yehoshua ben Korḥah.** Little is known about the life of Rabbi Yehoshua ben Korḥah. Judging by the names of the Sages with whom he discusses, it seems that he was one of the students of Rabbi Akiba. Some commentators maintain that "Korḥah" is an epithet of Rabbi Akiba himself, so that Rabbi Yehoshua would be his son, who is mentioned in several places. However, this is difficult to accept both in itself and because of the order of generations. As noted in tractate *Megillah* (8a), Rabbi Yehoshua ben Korḥah lived a long time. Thus he was probably born soon after the destruction of the Temple, but was active mainly after the murder of Rabbi Akiba. Rabbi Yehoshua ben Korḥah's Halakhic and Aggadic teachings are found in the Mishnah and in Baraitot, and from them we see that he had a witty way of speaking and employed his polemical skills in arguments with heretics and non-Jews.

רַבִּי מֵאִיר **Rabbi Meir.** He was one of the greatest Tannaim of the generation before the completion of the Mishnah. We do not have definite information about Rabbi Meir's parentage, though it is said that he came from a family of converts descended from the imperial family in Rome.

While he was still a young man, his extraordinary sharpness of mind in Torah studies was noted, and he studied with two of the greatest scholars of the generation, Rabbi Yishmael and Rabbi Akiva. He was also the only student who continued to draw upon traditions taught by Elisha ben Avuyah, despite the latter's apostasy. Rabbi Meir was one of the closest disciples of Rabbi Akiva, who ordained him at a very early age. He was ordained again later by Rabbi Yehudah ben Bava.

Rabbi Meir was officially appointed as "Hakham," the third in rank below the Nasi, or president, of the Sanhedrin. The discussions between him and his colleagues, Rabbi Yehudah, Rabbi Yose, Rabbi Shimon, and Rabbi Elazar, are among the most important elements of the Mishnah.

[1]אֲתַאן לְתַנָּא קַמָּא: [2]"דָּן אֶת הַדִּין, זִיכָּה אֶת הַזַּכַּאי וְחִיֵּיב אֶת הַחַיָּיב, [3]וְרָאָה שֶׁנִּתְחַיֵּיב עָנִי מָמוֹן וְשִׁלֵּם לוֹ מִתּוֹךְ בֵּיתוֹ, [4]זֶה מִשְׁפָּט וּצְדָקָה. [5]מִשְׁפָּט לָזֶה, וּצְדָקָה לָזֶה. [6]מִשְׁפָּט לָזֶה — שֶׁהֶחֱזִיר לוֹ מָמוֹן, [7]וּצְדָקָה לָזֶה — שֶׁשִּׁילֵּם לוֹ מִתּוֹךְ בֵּיתוֹ. [8]וְכֵן בְּדָוִד הוּא אוֹמֵר: 'וַיְהִי דָּוִד עֹשֶׂה מִשְׁפָּט וּצְדָקָה לְכָל עַמּוֹ'. [9]מִשְׁפָּט לָזֶה — שֶׁהֶחֱזִיר לוֹ אֶת מָמוֹנוֹ, [10]וּצְדָקָה לָזֶה — שֶׁשִּׁילֵּם לוֹ מִתּוֹךְ בֵּיתוֹ.

[11]קַשְׁיָא לֵיהּ לְרַבִּי: [12]הַאי "לְכָל עַמּוֹ" — [13]"לָעֲנִיִּים" מִיבָּעֵי לֵיהּ!

[14]אֶלָּא: "רַבִּי אוֹמֵר: אַף עַל פִּי שֶׁלֹּא שִׁילֵּם מִתּוֹךְ בֵּיתוֹ,

LITERAL TRANSLATION

[1]We have come to the first Tanna: [2]"If someone judged a judgment, [and] freed from liability the party who was not liable, and imposed liability upon the party who was liable, [3]and he saw that a poor man had been obligated [to pay] money, and he paid him from his [own] pocket [lit., 'his house'], [4]this is judgment and charity. [5]Judgment to this one, and charity to that one. [6]Judgment to this one that he returned money to him, [7]and charity to that one that he paid him from his [own] pocket. [8]And similarly regarding David it states: 'And David executed judgment and charity to all his people.' Judgment to this one, and charity to that one. [9]Judgment to this one that he returned his money to him, [10]and charity to that one that he paid him out of his [own] pocket."

[11]Rabbi had a difficulty: [12]This "to all his people" — [13]it should have [said] "to the poor"!

[14]Rather: "Rabbi says: Even though he did not pay from his [own] pocket,

TRANSLATION AND COMMENTARY

אֲתַאן לְתַנָּא קַמָּא [1]The Baraita now records a position which **brings us back to** the opinion of **the first Tanna** of the Baraita, Rabbi Eliezer the son of Rabbi Yose the Galilean, according to whom compromise is neither a mitzvah nor prohibited, but merely permissible, unless a verdict has been delivered: [2]**"If a judge issued a ruling, and freed from liability the party whom** he found **was not liable, and imposed liability upon the party whom** he decided **was liable,** [3]**and** then the judge **saw that** it was **a poor man** whom he **had obligated to pay money, and** he **paid** the poor man's adversary **out of his** own **pocket,** [4]**this** exemplifies the joining of **judgment and charity.** [5]For the judge executed **judgment for this one** — the poor man's adversary — **and** he performed **charity for that one** — the poor man himself. [6]The judge executed **judgment for this one** — the poor man's adversary — **for he restored his money,** [7]**and** he performed **charity for that one** — the poor man — **for he paid** the sum on his behalf **out of his** own **pocket.** [8]**And similarly regarding** King **David the verse states: 'And David executed judgment and charity to all his people.'** How so? King David executed judgment for the one, and charity for the other. [9]He executed **judgment for the one** in whose favor he ruled, for **he returned money to him** which was rightfully **his,** [10]**and** he performed **charity for the one** whom he found liable, for if that person was a poor man, David **paid** his adversary the amount of the award **out of his** own **pocket."** According to this explanation, there is no Scriptural proof that it is a mitzvah to effect a compromise, for when David executed judgment and charity, he issued his rulings according to the strict letter of the law, and only afterwards did he charitably come to the rescue of the poor and pay their debts.

קַשְׁיָא לֵיהּ לְרַבִּי [11]**Rabbi** Yehudah HaNasi **had a difficulty** with this second explanation of the verse regarding King David. [12]According to **this** explanation, the expression **"to all his people"** is imprecise, for if the verse meant that David would pay the debts of the poor out of his own pocket, [13]it **should have stated:** "And David executed judgment and charity **to the poor"!**

אֶלָּא [14]**Rather, Rabbi** Yehudah HaNasi explains the verse as follows, and **says: Even if** the judge **did not**

RASHI

אתאן לתנא קמא – תנא קמא דאמר: אסור לבצוע, דריש ליה להאי "משפט וצדקה" שהיה דוד דן את הדין, וחייב את החייב, וראה שהיה עני מחויב ממון, והיה משלם לבעל דינו מתוך ביתו.

Rabbi Meir's greatest achievement was apparently a continuation of the (oral) editing and organization of the Halakhah according to the Oral Law. Rabbi Yehudah HaNasi followed Rabbi Meir in this task, and for that reason we have the principle that all anonymous Mishnayot are to be attributed to Rabbi Meir (סְתָם מִשְׁנָה רַבִּי מֵאִיר). Because he was involved in the effort to force the resignation of Rabban Shimon ben Gamliel, the head of the Sanhedrin, Rabbi Meir was punished by him, and for a long period his teachings were not cited in his name, being instead introduced by the expression "others say" (אֲחֵרִים אוֹמְרִים).

His private life was full of suffering. His two sons died during his lifetime, though he is known to have left a daughter. His wife, Beruria, famous for her wisdom and piety, died in tragic circumstances. Ultimately he had to go into exile in Asia Minor, where he died. In his will he requested that his body be taken to Eretz Israel, and that it be buried temporarily near the sea, whose waves reach Eretz Israel.

During his lifetime, Rabbi Meir was famous not only for his extraordinary sharpness of mind, which exceeded that of everyone in his generation, but also for his virtuous qualities. He was peace-loving and modest. He was known as an outstanding preacher, and it is said that his death marked the end of "the tellers of parables." Some of his animal fables were retold over many generations. He was also known as a miracle-worker; charity boxes in his name, "Rabbi Meir the Miracle-Worker" (רַבִּי מֵאִיר בַּעַל הַנֵּס), were a primary source of contributions to Eretz Israel for many years.

NOTES

officer of the court, but rather he himself saw that the property was returned to its rightful owner (*Yedei Moshe*). Others argue that the verse teaches that David always issued just rulings and never erred in matters of Halakhah, and so even the party who lost the case left the court with the feeling that he had been treated charitably (see *Maharsha, Iyyun Ya'akov*).

שֶׁשִּׁילֵּם לוֹ מִתּוֹךְ בֵּיתוֹ That he paid him out of his own pocket. Some suggest that David would offer the money to the poor litigant even before he delivered his verdict, so that the litigant would not be distressed when he heard the decision, wondering where he would find the money he was required to pay (*Ḥamra Veḥaye*).

TRANSLATION AND COMMENTARY

pay the debts of the poor man **out of his** own **pocket, this judgment which involves charity.** [1]For if a judge issued a just ruling, he executed **judgment for one** party, **and charity for the other.** [2]He executed **judgment for one** party, for he **returned money to him** which was his according to the law. [3]**And** he performed **charity for the other** party, **for he removed a stolen article,** money that did not belong to him, **from his possession.**

רַבִּי שִׁמְעוֹן בֶּן מְנַסְיָא [4]The Baraita continues its discussion of compromise: **"Rabbi Shimon ben Menasya says:** [5]**If two** people **have come before you for a judgment, before you have heard their arguments,** [6]**or after you have heard their arguments** but you still **do not know which way the judgment leans,** [7]**you may say to them: Go out and** seek a **compromise.** [8]But **after you have heard their arguments,** and you already **know which way the judgment inclines** and how you will decide the case, [9]**you may no** longer **say to them: Go out and** seek a **compromise,** [10]**for the verse states** [Proverbs 17:14]: **'The beginning of strife is like letting water out; therefore leave off contention, before it breaks out.'** If you wish to neutralize a quarrel, you should do so at the beginning of the strife, before hearing and weighing the litigants' claims. [11]**Before the dispute has been laid bare, you may abandon it** and advise the litigants to seek a compromise. [12]But **once the dispute has been laid bare, you may not abandon it** and suggest to the parties that a compromise be effected."

וְרֵישׁ לָקִישׁ אָמַר [13]The Gemara now notes that Resh Lakish made a similar distinction, for **Resh Lakish said: If two** people **have come** before you **for a judgment,** [14]and **one is soft,** not aggressive or violent, while the other is **tough** — [15]**before you have heard** each of **their arguments, or after you have heard their**

[1]זֶהוּ מִשְׁפָּט וּצְדָקָה. מִשְׁפָּט לָזֶה, וּצְדָקָה לָזֶה. [2]מִשְׁפָּט לָזֶה — שֶׁהֶחֱזִיר לוֹ מָמוֹנוֹ, [3]וּצְדָקָה לָזֶה — שֶׁהוֹצִיא גְּזֵילָה מִתַּחַת יָדוֹ".

[4]"רַבִּי שִׁמְעוֹן בֶּן מְנַסְיָא אוֹמֵר: [5]שְׁנַיִם שֶׁבָּאוּ לְפָנֶיךָ לְדִין, עַד שֶׁלֹּא תִּשְׁמַע דִּבְרֵיהֶן, [6]אוֹ מִשֶּׁתִּשְׁמַע דִּבְרֵיהֶן וְאִי אַתָּה יוֹדֵעַ לְהֵיכָן דִּין נוֹטֶה, [7]אַתָּה רַשַּׁאי לוֹמַר לָהֶן: צְאוּ וּבִצְעוּ. [8]מִשֶּׁתִּשְׁמַע דִּבְרֵיהֶן וְאַתָּה יוֹדֵעַ לְהֵיכָן הַדִּין נוֹטֶה — [9]אִי אַתָּה רַשַּׁאי לוֹמַר לָהֶן: צְאוּ וּבִצְעוּ, [10]שֶׁנֶּאֱמַר 'פּוֹטֵר מַיִם רֵאשִׁית מָדוֹן; וְלִפְנֵי הִתְגַּלַּע הָרִיב נְטוֹשׁ'. [11]קוֹדֶם שֶׁנִּתְגַּלַּע הָרִיב, אַתָּה יָכוֹל לְנָטְשׁוֹ. [12]מִשֶּׁנִּתְגַּלַּע הָרִיב אִי אַתָּה יָכוֹל לְנָטְשׁוֹ".

[13]וְרֵישׁ לָקִישׁ אָמַר: שְׁנַיִם שֶׁבָּאוּ לְדִין, [14]אֶחָד רַךְ וְאֶחָד קָשֶׁה, [15]עַד שֶׁלֹּא תִּשְׁמַע

LITERAL TRANSLATION

this is judgment and charity. [1]Judgment to this one, and charity to that one. [2]Judgment to this one to whom he returned his money, [3]and charity to the one from whose possession he removed a stolen article."

[4]"Rabbi Shimon ben Menasya says: [5][If] two have come before you for a judgment, before you have heard their arguments, [6]or after you have heard their arguments but you do not know which way the judgment leans, [7]you are permitted to say to them: Go out and compromise. [8]After you have heard their arguments and you know which way the judgment leans, [9]you are not permitted to say to them: Go out and compromise, [10]for it is said: 'The beginning of strife is like letting water out; therefore leave off contention, before it breaks out.' [11]Before the dispute has been laid bare, you may abandon it. [12]Once the dispute has been laid bare, you may not abandon it."

[13]And Resh Lakish said: [If] two have come for a judgment, [14]one soft and one tough, [15]before you have heard

RASHI

פוטר מים ראשית מדון — אם באת לפטור ולהשליך המריבה המשולה כמים כדלקמן, ולשום שלום ביניהן. **ראשית מדון** — קודם שתשא ותתן בדין פטור אותה. **נטשהו** — ורדוף אחר השלום. **קשה** — בעל מריבה מטריח דיינין.

SAGES

רַבִּי שִׁמְעוֹן בֶּן מְנַסְיָא Rabbi Shimon ben Menasya. A fifth-generation Tanna. His father's name, Menasya, is apparently an Aramaic or Hellenized form of the Hebrew מְנַשֶּׁה, Menasheh. Rabbi Shimon ben Menasya was an outstanding disciple of Rabbi Meir, although he also studied with other Tannaim, such as Rabbi Shimon bar Yoḥai. A colleague of Rabbi Yehudah HaNasi, Rabbi Shimon ben Menasya nevertheless took issue with him on a number of occasions, although he greatly respected him.

Some authorities maintain that Rabbi Shimon ben Menasya was a member of the "holy congregation of Jerusalem" (קְהָלָא קַדִּישָׁא דְּבִירוּשָׁלַיִם), a select group of men who engaged in Torah study and prayer, attempting to remain in Jerusalem after the Jews were expelled from the city.

רֵישׁ לָקִישׁ Resh Lakish. Rabbi Shimon ben Lakish, commonly known as Resh Lakish, was one of the greatest of the Palestinian Amoraim. He was a student, colleague, and brother-in-law of Rabbi Yoḥanan.

As a youth, Resh Lakish studied Torah and showed great talent. However, apparently constrained by dire poverty, he sold himself as a gladiator in the Roman arena. Many stories are told of his exceptional courage and physical strength. In time, following a meeting with Rabbi Yoḥanan, he returned to the world of Torah, beginning as Rabbi Yoḥanan's student and then becoming his colleague and marrying his sister.

Rabbi Yoḥanan and Resh Lakish had many Halakhic differences of opinion. However, in great measure Resh Lakish's intention was not to disagree with Rabbi Yoḥanan, but rather to clarify and elucidate matters by means of dialectical argument. Rabbi Yoḥanan regarded him with great respect, and used to say, "My equal disagrees with me."

Resh Lakish was famous for his piety and rigor, and it was said that one could lend money without witnesses to a person with whom Resh Lakish spoke in public, for he

NOTES

"פּוֹטֵר מַיִם רֵאשִׁית מָדוֹן" **"The beginning of strife is like letting water out."** It appears that one must interpret the words, פּוֹטֵר מַיִם רֵאשִׁית מָדוֹן — "The beginning of strife is like letting water out" — to mean that the judge does not enter the judgment at all but merely proposes a compromise, while וְלִפְנֵי הִתְגַּלַּע הָרִיב נְטוֹשׁ — "therefore leave off contention, before it breaks out" — means that after the trial has begun, though judgment has not yet been reached, abandon the dispute and come to a compromise (*Arukh*).

HALAKHAH

שְׁנַיִם שֶׁבָּאוּ לְדִין **If two have come for a judgment.** "If two people have come before a judge, one gentle and the other tough, the judge can refuse to hear their case. However, he can only do so before hearing their arguments, or even after hearing them, as long as he has not decided in whose favor he will rule. But if he has heard their arguments and decided in whose favor he will decide, he can no longer tell them that he will not adjudicate the case. On the other hand, if he has been appointed as a judge for the community, he must attend to every case." (*Shulḥan Arukh, Ḥoshen Mishpat* 12:1.)

דִּבְרֵיהֶם, אוֹ מִשֶּׁתִּשְׁמַע דִּבְרֵיהֶן וְאֵין אַתָּה יוֹדֵעַ לְהֵיכָן דִּין נוֹטֶה — [1]אַתָּה רַשַּׁאי לוֹמַר לָהֶם: אֵין אֲנִי נִזְקָק לָכֶם, [2]שֶׁמָּא נִתְחַיֵּיב חָזָק וְנִמְצָא חָזָק רוֹדְפוֹ. [3]מִשֶּׁתִּשְׁמַע דִּבְרֵיהֶן וְאַתָּה יוֹדֵעַ לְהֵיכָן הַדִּין נוֹטֶה, [4]אִי אַתָּה יָכוֹל לוֹמַר לָהֶן אֵינִי נִזְקָק לָכֶם, [5]שֶׁנֶּאֱמַר ״לֹא תָגוּרוּ מִפְּנֵי אִישׁ״.

[6]״רַבִּי יְהוֹשֻׁעַ בֶּן קָרְחָה אוֹמֵר: מִנַּיִין לְתַלְמִיד שֶׁיּוֹשֵׁב לִפְנֵי רַבּוֹ וְרָאָה זְכוּת לֶעָנִי וְחוֹבָה לֶעָשִׁיר, [7]מִנַּיִין שֶׁלֹּא יִשְׁתּוֹק? [8]שֶׁנֶּאֱמַר: ׳לֹא תָגוּרוּ מִפְּנֵי אִישׁ׳״.

[9]״רַבִּי חָנִין אוֹמֵר: לֹא תַּכְנִיס דְּבָרֶיךָ מִפְּנֵי אִישׁ״.

[10]״וִידוּ עֵדִים יוֹדְעִים אֶת מִי הֵן מְעִידִין, [11]וְלִפְנֵי מִי הֵן מְעִידִין,

LITERAL TRANSLATION

their arguments, or after you have heard their arguments but you do not know which way the judgment leans, [1]you are permitted to say to them: I am not bound to you, [2]lest the strong one be found liable, and the strong one will harass (lit., "pursue") him. [3]After you have heard their argument and you know which way the judgment leans, [4]you may not say to them: I am not bound to you, [5]as it is said: "Do not be afraid of any man." [6]"Rabbi Yehoshua ben Korḥah says: From where [do we derive] that a disciple who is sitting before his master and sees an argument that is favorable to the poor man and unfavorable to the wealthy man, [7]from where [do we know] that he should not remain silent? [8]For it is stated: 'Do not be afraid of any man.'" [9]"Rabbi Ḥanin says: Do not hold back your arguments because of any man." [10]"And the witnesses must know against whom they are testifying, [11]and before whom they are testifying,

TRANSLATION AND COMMENTARY

arguments, but still **do not know which way the judgment leans,** [1]**you may say to them:** Go and present your claims before another judge, for **I am not bound** to hear **your** case. A judge might prefer not to adjudicate such a case, [2]for **perhaps he will find the stronger** party **liable, and that stronger party will** then **pursue** and harass **him** until he revises his decision. [3]But **after you have heard** the two litigants' **arguments, and you know which way the judgment leans** and that the stronger party will be found liable, [4]**you may not say to them:** Go to another court, for **I am not bound** to hear **your** case, [5]**as it is said** (Deuteronomy 1:17): **"Do not be afraid of any man."**

רַבִּי יְהוֹשֻׁעַ בֶּן קָרְחָה [6]It was taught in a Baraita: **"Rabbi Yehoshua ben Korḥah says: From where do we know that** if **a disciple is sitting before his master,** and a case comes before the master for adjudication, **and** the disciple **sees an argument that is favorable to** one of the litigants who is **a poor man and unfavorable to** the other litigant who is **a wealthy man,** and this argument had escaped the master's attention, [7]**from where do we know that** the disciple **should not remain silent,** but should voice his opinion, so that justice will be done? [8]**As it is said: 'Do not be afraid of any man.'"**

רַבִּי חָנִין [9]**"Rabbi Ḥanin says:** The verse should be understood as follows: **Do not hold back your** arguments and leave them hidden inside you **because of any man** — not out of respect for your master, nor out of fear of one of the litigants."

וִידוּ עֵדִים [10]The Baraita continues: **"And** before they testify, **the witnesses must understand against whom they are testifying** (for if they lie they do not testify only against one of the parties to the dispute, but also, as it were, against God Himself), [11]**and before whom they are testifying** (not only before the earthly

RASHI

הכי גרסינן: **שמא יתחייב חזק ונמצא רודפו** — רודף את הדיין להפך את הדין. **שיושב לפני רבו** — ובא דין לפני רבו ולא לפניו, וראה התלמיד זכות לעני וחובה לעשיר, ורבו טועה בדין, מניין שלא יחלוק כבוד לרבו וישתוק — תלמוד לומר כו׳. ולקמן (ז,א) מפרש מאי משמע ד״לא תגורו״ לשון כינוס הוא. **את מי הן מעידין** — כאילו הן מעידין בהקדוש ברוך הוא, כדאמר לקמן (ח,א) שמטריחין אותו להחזיר ממון לבעליו.

spoke only to people of unblemished character. When he died, he left a son who was notable for his talents and genius.

NOTES

וְנִמְצָא חָזָק רוֹדְפוֹ **And the strong one will harass.** A number of Rishonim had the following reading: "Lest the *soft* one [the weak litigant] be found liable, and the strong one will harass him." Thus, Resh Lakish was referring to a judge who was afraid that he might find the weak party liable, and the strong party would then harass the weaker one, and violently extort money owed to him. (*Halakhot Gedolot, Ran, Meiri.*)

HALAKHAH

מִנַּיִין לְתַלְמִיד שֶׁיּוֹשֵׁב לִפְנֵי רַבּוֹ...? **From where do we derive that a disciple who is sitting before his master...?** "If a judge was about to rule in favor of one of the litigants, and his disciple, who was sitting before him, saw an argument that was favorable to the other litigant, the disciple must put that argument before his master, and if he remains silent, he is in violation of the commandment, 'Keep far from a false matter.'" (*Shulḥan Arukh, Ḥoshen Mishpat* 9:7.)

TRANSLATION AND COMMENTARY

judges, but before God), [1]**and who will punish them in the future** if they testify falsely, [2]**as it is said** [Deuteronomy 19:17]: **'And both the men, between whom is the controversy, shall stand before the Lord,** before the priests and the judges, who shall be in those days.' As the Gemara explains elsewhere (*Shevuot* 30a), "the men" who are mentioned here are the witnesses, and the verse teaches that the witnesses are seen as standing before the Lord. [3]**And before** they hear a case, **the judges must understand whom they are judging** (for not only do they judge the litigants who come before them, but also, as it were, God Himself), [4]**and before whom they are judging** (before God), **and who will punish them in the future** if they do not judge righteously, [5]**as it is said** [Psalms 82:1]: **'God stands in the congregation of God.'** [6]**And similarly regarding Jehoshafat the verse states** [II Chronicles 19:6]: **'And he said to the judges: See what you are doing, for it is not before man that you judge, but before the Lord.'** [7]**Lest the judge say** to himself: If so, **why should I** accept **this trouble** as a judge? I will be liable for punishment should I err in my judgment. [8]**The** very same **verse concludes: 'Who is with you in the judgment.'** A judge must decide in accordance with what is 'with him,' the way his heart tells him to decide. [9]**A judge has nothing but what his eyes see,** and his heart understands. If a judge considers the case to the best of his ability, he need not be concerned that he will be liable for punishment if he makes an erroneous decision."

הֵיכִי דָּמֵי [10]The Baraita cited above taught that once a decision has been reached, the court is no longer permitted to effect a compromise. The Gemara asks: **What** precisely **is** meant here by **the conclusion of the judgment?**

[1]וּמִי עָתִיד לִיפָּרַע מֵהֶן, [2]שֶׁנֶּאֱמַר: ׳וְעָמְדוּ שְׁנֵי הָאֲנָשִׁים אֲשֶׁר לָהֶם הָרִיב לִפְנֵי ה׳׳. [3]וִיהוּ הַדַּיָּינִין יוֹדְעִין אֶת מִי הֵן דָּנִין, [4]וְלִפְנֵי מִי הֵן דָּנִין, וּמִי עָתִיד לִיפָּרַע מֵהֶן, [5]שֶׁנֶּאֱמַר: ׳אֱלֹהִים נִצָּב בַּעֲדַת אֵל׳. [6]וְכֵן בִּיהוֹשָׁפָט הוּא אוֹמֵר: ׳וַיֹּאמֶר אֶל הַשֹּׁפְטִים: רְאוּ מָה אַתֶּם עֹשִׂים, כִּי לֹא לְאָדָם תִּשְׁפְּטוּ, כִּי אִם לה׳׳, [7]שֶׁמָּא יֹאמַר הַדַּיָּין מַה לִּי בְּצַעַר הַזֶּה? [8]תַּלְמוּד לוֹמַר: ׳עִמָּכֶם בִּדְבַר מִשְׁפָּט׳. [9]אֵין לוֹ לַדַּיָּין אֶלָּא מַה שֶּׁעֵינָיו רוֹאוֹת״.

[10]הֵיכִי דָּמֵי גְּמָר דִּין?

LITERAL TRANSLATION

[1]and who will punish them in the future, [2]as it is said: 'And both the men, between whom is the controversy, shall stand before the Lord.' [3]And the judges must know whom they are judging, [4]and before whom they are judging, and who will exact punishment from them in the future, [5]as it is said: 'God stands in the congregation of God.' [6]And similarly regarding Jehoshaphat it says: 'And he said to the judges: See what you are doing, for it is not before man that you judge, but before the Lord.' [7]Lest the judge say: Why should I be in this trouble? [8]The verse states: 'Who is with you in the judgment.' [9]The judge only has what his eyes see."

[10]How do we visualize (lit., "how is it like") the conclusion of the judgment?

RASHI

ועמדו שני האנשים אשר להן הריב — ואוקמינן במסכת שבועות (ל, א): בעדים הכתוב מדבר. **מה לי לצער הזה** — שאם אטעה — איענש. **תלמוד לומר** — ביהושפט "עמכם בדבר משפט" לפי מה שעם לבבכם, שלבבכם נוטה בדבר, כלומר בטענותיהם — "עמכם במשפט" לפי אותן דברים תשפוטו ולא תיענשו. **דאין לו לדיין** — לירא ולמנוע עצמו מן הדין. **אלא לפי מה שעיניו רואות** — לידון, ויתכוין להוציאו לצדקו ולאמיתו, ושוב לא יענש. **היכי דמי גמר דין** — דאמרינן לעיל: שוב אין אתה רשאי לבצוע.

NOTES

אֶת מִי הֵן מְעִידִין...וְאֶת מִי הֵן דָּנִין **Against whom they are testifying...and whom they are judging.** Not only do the witnesses testify against one of the parties to the dispute, but also, as it were, against God Himself. Similarly, the judges try not only the litigants, but also, as it were, God Himself. According to the Jerusalem Talmud, as well as our Gemara (below, 8a), God is involved in judgment in the sense that if money ends up in the wrong hands because of the judicial proceedings, God Himself must return it to its rightful owner (see *Rashi, Remah* and others).

HALAKHAH

לִפְנֵי מִי הֵן דָּנִין **Before whom they are judging.** "During the court proceedings, a judge must sit in fear and trepidation, in solemnity and covered by his tallit (it is not the current custom for a judge to don his tallit, but rather he puts on the outer garment that he wears to synagogue; *Shelah*), for when he sits in judgment he stands before God." (*Shulḥan Arukh, Ḥoshen Mishpat* 8:2.)

אֶלָּא מַה שֶּׁעֵינָיו רוֹאוֹת **What his eyes see.** "A judge need not be concerned that he will be punished if he delivers an erroneous decision, for a judge depends solely on what his eyes see." (*Shulḥan Arukh, Ḥoshen Mishpat* 8:2 [*Rema*].)

הֵיכִי דָּמֵי גְּמַר דִּין **How do we visualize the conclusion of the judgment.** "Even if the judge has heard the arguments of the two parties, and he already knows in whose favor

TRANSLATION AND COMMENTARY

אָמַר רַב יְהוּדָה [1]**Rav Yehudah said in the name of Rav:** The judgment is considered concluded when the judges declare their verdict, stating: [2]**So-and-so, you are liable;** [3]**So-and-so, you are free of liability.**

אָמַר רַב [4]The Gemara now records a ruling on the desirability of compromise. **Rav said: The law is in accordance with** the view of **Rabbi Yehoshua ben Korḥah**, that it is a mitzvah for a court to effect a compromise.

אִינִי [5]The Gemara raises an objection: **Is it** really **so, that** Rav rules that compromise is a mitzvah? [6]**But surely Rav Huna, who was a disciple of Rav,** accepted his master's rulings, [7]**and whenever** two people **came before Rav Huna** to have him adjudicate a dispute, **he would ask them:** [8]**Do you want me** to adjudicate the case and render **a judgment, or do you want a compromise?** Now, if Rav ruled that compromise is a mitzvah, why did his pupil Rav Huna offer the litigants a choice between judgment and compromise?

מַאי מִצְוָה [9]The Gemara responds by first asking another question: **What did Rabbi Yehoshua ben Korḥah mean** when he **said that** compromise **is a mitzvah?** [7A] [10]He meant that **it is a mitzvah** (a meritorious act) for the judge **to ask** the two parties: **Do you want a judgment, or do you want a compromise?**

הַיְינוּ תַּנָּא קַמָּא [11]The Gemara objects: If this is what Rabbi Yehoshua ben Korḥah meant, then **his** position **is the** same as that of **the** anonymous **first Tanna** of the Baraita, who said that if the judgment has already been concluded, the court is no longer permitted to effect a compromise, implying that before the verdict is delivered, compromise is a permissible option.

אִיכָּא בֵּינַיְיהוּ [12]The Gemara explains: **There is** a practical difference **between** them **with respect to** whether or not it is **a mitzvah** for the judge to propose a compromise. [13]**Rabbi Yehoshua ben Korḥah maintains** that **it is a mitzvah,** [14]**and the** anonymous **first Tanna maintains** that it is only **a** permissible **option.**

[1]אָמַר רַב יְהוּדָה אָמַר רַב: [2]אִישׁ פְּלוֹנִי, אַתָּה חַיָּיב; [3]אִישׁ פְּלוֹנִי, אַתָּה זַכַּאי.

[4]אָמַר רַב: הֲלָכָה כְּרַבִּי יְהוֹשֻׁעַ בֶּן קָרְחָה.

[5]אִינִי? [6]וְהָא רַב הוּנָא תַּלְמִידֵיהּ דְּרַב הֲוָה, [7]כִּי הֲוָה אָתוּ לְקַמֵּיהּ דְּרַב הוּנָא, אֲמַר לְהוּ: [8]אִי דִּינָא בָּעֵיתוּ אִי פְּשָׁרָה בָּעֵיתוּ?

[9]מַאי מִצְוָה נַמִי דְּקָאָמַר רַבִּי יְהוֹשֻׁעַ בֶּן קָרְחָה? [7A] [10]מִצְוָה לְמֵימְרָא לְהוּ: אִי דִּינָא בָּעֵיתוּ, אִי פְּשָׁרָה בָּעֵיתוּ.

[11]הַיְינוּ תַּנָּא קַמָּא!

[12]אִיכָּא בֵּינַיְיהוּ מִצְוָה. [13]רַבִּי יְהוֹשֻׁעַ בֶּן קָרְחָה סָבַר: מִצְוָה. [14]תַּנָּא קַמָּא סָבַר: רְשׁוּת.

LITERAL TRANSLATION

[1]Rav Yehudah said in the name of Rav: [2]So-and-so, you are liable; [3]So-and-so, you are free of liability.

[4]Rav said: The law is in accordance with Rabbi Yehoshua ben Korḥah.

[5]Is it so? [6]But surely Rav Huna was a disciple of Rav, [7]and when they came before Rav Huna, he would say to them: [8]Do you wish a judgment, [or] do you wish a compromise?

[9]What is the meritorious deed about which Rabbi Yehoshua ben Korḥah spoke? [7A] [10]It is a mitzvah to say to them: Do you wish a judgment, [or] do you wish a compromise?

[11]This is the first Tanna!

[12]There is between them a mitzvah. [13]Rabbi Yehoshua ben Korḥah maintains: It is a mitzvah. [14]The first Tanna maintains: It is optional.

RASHI

מצוה למימר להו – ברישא: אי דינא בעיתו אי פשרה בעיתו, דפתחינן להו בפשרה. **היינו תנא קמא** – דאמר: נגמר הדין – אי אתה רשאי לבלוע, הא מקודם גמר דין – רשאי לבלוע, והכי נמי רשות הוא. **איכא בינייהו מצוה** – להזכיר פשרה, לתנא קמא – ליכא מצוה.

NOTES

Remah had the following reading "אֶת מַה הֵם מְעִידִים" "וְאֶת מַה הֵם דָּנִים" — "about what are they testifying" and "about what are they judging." That which appears on the surface to be a monetary dispute is, in a certain sense, a capital case, for Scripture views the unjust removal of money from a person's possession as the taking of his life (see Proverbs 22:22-23).

HALAKHAH

he will rule, it remains a mitzvah for him to effect a compromise. But if the judgment has already been concluded and the judge has issued his verdict, holding one party liable and the other free of liability, a compromise may no longer be effected, following the first Tanna of the Baraita who does not appear to disagree with Rabbi Yehoshua ben Korḥah. According to *Baḥ* (following *Tosafot*), a compromise can no longer be effected once the judge has decided in whose favor he will rule. A compromise can still be effected even after the verdict has been delivered, if that verdict requires one of the parties to swear an oath. Even if the judgment has already been concluded, a person other than the judge can still effect a compromise outside of the courtroom." (*Shulḥan Arukh, Ḥoshen Mishpat* 12:2.)

LITERAL TRANSLATION

[1]This is Rabbi Shimon ben Menasya! [2]There is between them: [3]After you have heard their arguments, and you know which way the judgment leans, [4]you are not permitted to say to them: Go out and compromise.

[5]And it disagrees with Rabbi Tanḥum bar Ḥanilai. [6]For Rabbi Tanḥum bar Ḥanilai said: This verse was not quoted except in reference to the incident of the [golden] calf, [7]for it is said: "And Aaron saw, and built an altar before it." [8]What did he see? [9]Rabbi Binyamin bar Yefet said in the name of Rabbi Elazar: He saw Ḥur slaughtered before him. [10]He said: If I do not listen to them, [11]now they will do to me as they did to Ḥur, [12]and [the verse] will be fulfilled through me: "Shall the priest and the prophet be slain in the sanctuary of the Lord," [13]and there will never be a remedy for them.

[1]הַיְינוּ דְּרַבִּי שִׁמְעוֹן בֶּן מְנַסְיָא! [2]אִיכָּא בֵּינַיְיהוּ: [3]מִשֶּׁתִּשְׁמַע דִּבְרֵיהֶן, וְאַתָּה יוֹדֵעַ לְהֵיכָן הַדִּין נוֹטֶה, [4]אִי אַתָּה רַשַּׁאי לוֹמַר לָהֶן צְאוּ וּבִצְעוּ.

[5]וּפְלִיגָא דְּרַבִּי תַּנְחוּם בַּר חֲנִילָאי. [6]דְּאָמַר רַבִּי תַּנְחוּם בַּר חֲנִילָאי: לֹא נֶאֱמַר מִקְרָא זֶה אֶלָּא כְּנֶגֶד מַעֲשֵׂה הָעֵגֶל, [7]שֶׁנֶּאֱמַר: "וַיַּרְא אַהֲרֹן וַיִּבֶן מִזְבֵּחַ לְפָנָיו". [8]מָה רָאָה? [9]אָמַר רַבִּי בִּנְיָמִין בַּר יֶפֶת אָמַר רַבִּי אֶלְעָזָר: רָאָה חוּר שֶׁזָּבוּחַ לְפָנָיו. [10]אָמַר: אִי לָא שָׁמַעְנָא לְהוּ [11]הָשְׁתָּא עָבְדוּ לִי כִּדְעָבְדוּ בְּחוּר, [12]וּמִיקַּיֵּים בִּי: "אִם יֵהָרֵג בְּמִקְדַּשׁ ה׳ כֹּהֵן וְנָבִיא", [13]וְלָא הָוְיָא לְהוּ תַּקַּנְתָּא לְעוֹלָם.

TRANSLATION AND COMMENTARY

הַיְינוּ [1]The Gemara raises another objection: If the first Tanna maintains that suggesting compromise is just a permissible option, then his position **is the same as** that of **Rabbi Shimon ben Menasya!**

אִיכָּא בֵּינַיְיהוּ [2]The Gemara answers: **There is** a practical difference **between** them. According to Rabbi Shimon, [3]**after** the judge **has heard** both parties' **arguments and** he **knows which way the judgment leans,** [4]he **may no longer say to them: Go out and** seek a **compromise.** But the anonymous first Tanna maintains that, until the verdict is actually delivered, the judge may advise the parties to seek a compromise.

וּפְלִיגָא [5]The Gemara now returns to discuss the verse בוצע ברך נאץ ה׳. The Tannaim who suggested different explanations of the verse all **disagree with Rabbi Tanḥum bar Ḥanilai,** [6]**for Rabbi Tanḥum bar Ḥanilai** understood the verse differently and **said: This verse was stated in reference to the incident of the golden calf** that Aaron made, compromising with the demand of the Israelites that he provide them with a god to lead them, [7]**as it is said** (Exodus 32:5): **"And Aaron saw, and built an altar before it."** [8]**What did** Aaron **see?** [9]**Rabbi Binyamin bar Yefet said in the name of Rabbi Elazar: He saw** his nephew **Ḥur,** who had tried to dissuade the people from sin, **slaughtered before him.** [10]When Aaron saw what the people had done to Ḥur, **he said** to himself: **If I do not listen to them** and do as they wish, [11]**they will now do to me as they did to Ḥur.** I too will be put to death, [12]and **through my** death **will be fulfilled the verse** (Lamentations 2:20), **"Shall the priest and the prophet be slain in the sanctuary of the Lord."** [13]And if the people commit that crime, **there will be no remedy** or pardon **for them.**

SAGES

רַבִּי תַּנְחוּם בַּר חֲנִילַאי **Rabbi Tanḥum bar Ḥanilai.** A Palestinian Amora of the second and third generations, Rabbi Tanḥum was a student of Rabbi Yehoshua ben Levi, from whom he seems to have learned mostly Aggadah. Rabbi Tanḥum's own teachings are mainly Aggadic. They were transmitted by the Sages of Eretz Israel in the following generation.

BACKGROUND

רָאָה חוּר שֶׁזָּבוּחַ לְפָנָיו **He saw Ḥur slaughtered before him.** The Bible does not mention the killing of Ḥur, and the Sages knew of it from the Oral Tradition. However, the Bible (Exodus 24:14) mentions that Ḥur was appointed by Moses to share in the leadership of the people with Aaron. However, after Moses descended from Mount Sinai, Ḥur was no longer mentioned. According to Rabbinic tradition, Ḥur was the son of Miriam, Moses' sister. Ḥur's grandson, Betzalel, was the chief architect of the Tabernacle.

RASHI

איכא בינייהו משתשמע דבריהם — לתנא קמא אפילו שמע דבריהם — רשאי לבצוע עד שיגמר הדין ויאמר: זה זכאי וזה חייב. לר׳ שמעון בן מנסיא משתשמע את דבריהם וידעת להיכן נוטה, אף על גב דלא נגמר — אין רשאי לבצוע. **מקרא זה** — "ובוצע ברך". **אלא כנגד מעשה העגל** — שעשה אהרן פשרה בינו לבין עצמו, והורה היתר לעצמו לעשות להם את העגל. **ויבן מזבח** — הבין מהזבוח לפניו שהרגו את חור על שלא עשה להם. **אהרן** — כהן ונביא היה. **ולא הויא להו תקנתא** — דהא סופן לעשות כן, בזכריה בן יהוידע, ויחרב בית המקדש על כך.

NOTES

"אִם יֵהָרֵג בְּמִקְדַּשׁ ה׳?" **"Shall the priest and the prophet be slain in the sanctuary of the Lord?"** It should not be considered surprising that Aaron was guided in his behavior by a verse in Lamentations which was not written until many years later, for as *Tosafot* note elsewhere (*Gittin* 68a), the contents of certain verses found in the later books of the Bible were known many generations earlier. The Gemara expresses the idea that was known to Aaron using the verse found in Lamentations.

כֹּהֵן וְנָבִיא **Priest and prophet.** A number of commentators ask: How would Aaron's death have been a fulfillment of the prophecy that a priest and a Prophet shall be slain in the Sanctuary? At that point Aaron had not yet been given the priesthood, and a Sanctuary had not yet been erected! *Maharsha* suggests that Aaron was a firstborn, and at that time the sacrificial service could be conducted by a firstborn on any altar, and so the death of Aaron would have been considered like the death of a priest in the Temple. Others suggest that the prophecy relates to the assassination of different leaders of Israel: If three different leaders are put to death, thought Aaron, there would be no remedy for the people of Israel. Aaron saw that Ḥur the Prophet had already been killed, and that Zechariah the priest would be put to death in the future, and so he feared that if he too were killed, there would be no pardon for that crime (*Imrei Tzvi*).

לָא הָוְיָא לְהוּ תַּקַּנְתָּא לְעוֹלָם **There will never be a remedy for them.** *Maharsha* explains that the Torah commands that the priest and the Prophet be obeyed, and it imposes capital punishment on anyone who disobeys them. Thus, the

TRANSLATION AND COMMENTARY

[1]Thus, **it is better that they make the calf, for it is possible that there will be a remedy for them through repentance.** According to Rabbi Tanḥum bar Ḥanilai, it was in reference to Aaron's behavior during this incident that the Psalmist said: "He who praises one who arbitrates a compromise blasphemes God."

וְהָנֵי תַּנָּאֵי [2]The Gemara asks: **The Tannaim** who do not agree with Rabbi Shimon ben Menasya, that a judge may advise the litigants to seek a compromise before deciding in whose favor to rule, [3]**how do they interpret** the verse: **"The beginning of strife is like letting water out;** therefore leave off contention, before it breaks out"? Rabbi Shimon ben Menasya interpreted this verse as dealing with compromise, [4]but the other Tannaim can interpret it **as did Rav Hamnuna,** [5]**for Rav Hamnuna said: The beginning of a person's** final **judgment concerns** his study of the **words of Torah.** When a person dies and is brought before his Maker for judgment, the first question is whether he devoted himself properly to Torah study. [6]This is learned **from the verse that states: "The beginning of strife is like letting water out."** Rav Hamnuna explains the word פּוֹטֵר in the sense of freeing from obligation, and the word מָדוֹן is derived from the root דין and denotes judgment. Thus the verse teaches that the first matter considered when a person stands before the Heavenly Judge is whether he exempted himself from the obligation to study Torah, which is likened to water, as it is said (Isaiah 55:1): "Ho, every one that thirsts, come to the water."

אָמַר רַב הוּנָא [7]**Rav Huna said: Strife is likened to a channel made by a** sudden **rush of water.** [8]**If it** is allowed to **widen, it will** continue to **widen,** and it will be impossible to close. Similarly, if two people begin to quarrel, and no steps are taken immediately to settle their differences, the discord cannot be contained. This is the meaning of the verse, "The letting out of water [פּוֹטֵר מַיִם] *is* the beginning of strife [רֵאשִׁית מָדוֹן]."

אַבַּיֵי קַשִּׁישָׁא [9]**Abaye the Elder said:** Strife **is likened to a plank on a wooden bridge.** When the plank is

[1]מוּטָּב דְּלִיעֶבְדוּ לָעֵגֶל, אֶפְשָׁר הָוְיָא לְהוּ תַּקַּנְתָּא בִּתְשׁוּבָה.
[2]וְהָנֵי תַּנָּאֵי: [3]"פּוֹטֵר מַיִם רֵאשִׁית מָדוֹן", מַאי דָּרְשֵׁי בֵּיהּ?
[4]כִּדְרַב הַמְנוּנָא, [5]דַּאֲמַר רַב הַמְנוּנָא: אֵין תְּחִילַּת דִּינוֹ שֶׁל אָדָם נִידּוֹן אֶלָּא עַל דִּבְרֵי תוֹרָה, [6]שֶׁנֶּאֱמַר "פּוֹטֵר מַיִם רֵאשִׁית מָדוֹן".
[7]אָמַר רַב הוּנָא: הַאי תִּיגְרָא דָּמְיָא לְצִינּוֹרָא דְּבִידְקָא דְּמַיָּא; [8]כֵּיוָן דְּרָווּח רָוַוח.
[9]אַבַּיֵי קַשִּׁישָׁא אָמַר: דָּמֵי

LITERAL TRANSLATION

[1]It is better that they make the calf, [for] it is possible that they will have a remedy through repentance.

[2]And how do these Tannaim interpret: [3]"The beginning of strife is like letting water out"? [4]In accordance with Rav Hamnuna, [5]for Rav Hamnuna said: The beginning of a person's judgment does not concern anything except the study (lit., "words of") Torah, [6]as it is said: "The beginning of strife is like letting water out."

[7]Rav Huna said: Strife is likened to a channel made by a rush of water; [8]once it widens it widens.

[9]Abaye the Elder said: It is likened

RASHI

והני תנאי — דלית להו "משתמע דבריהם — אי אתה רשאי לבצוע". האי "פוטר מים" מאי דרשי ביה? **תחילת דינו** — לעתיד לבא. **על דברי תורה** — שלא עסק בתורה. **פוטר מים** — שפוטר התורה מעליו, הוא ראשית מדונו, תורה נמשלה למים דכתיב (ישעיה נה): "הוי כל צמא לכו למים". **לצינורא דבידקא** — כשהנהר גדל פעמים שהוא יוצא לשדות שעל אגפיו כעין ניגרים וצינורות קטנים, ואם אינו סותמו מיד, הולך ומרחיב ושוב אינו יכול לסותמו. והיינו דקאמר קרא "פוטר מים ראשית מדון", כלומר ראשית מדון ומריבה דומה לפוטר מים. **פוטר** — פותח, כמו "פטר רחם" (שמות יג).

SAGES

רַב הַמְנוּנָא Rav Hamnuna. A Babylonian Amora of the second generation, Rav Hamnuna was a student of Rav. Another Amora of the same name lived in the next generation and was a student of Rav Ḥisda.

The Rav Hamnuna referred to here was one of the students of Rav who remained in his House of Study and continued the tradition of "the School of Rav," so that it is said that the expression "the School of Rav" (בֵּי רַב) refers to Rav Hamnuna.

רַב הוּנָא Rav Huna. One of the greatest Babylonian Amoraim of the second generation, Rav Huna was most closely associated with his teacher, Rav. Rav Huna was of aristocratic descent, and belonged to the House of the Exilarchs. For many years, however, he lived in great poverty. Later he became wealthy and lived in comfort, distributing his money for the public good.

Rav Huna was the greatest of Rav's students, so much so that Shmuel, Rav's colleague, used to treat him with honor and direct questions to him. After Rav's death Rav Huna became the head of the yeshivah of Sura and occupied that position for about forty years. His eminence in Torah and his loftiness of character helped make the Sura Yeshivah the preeminent center for many centuries. Because of Rav Huna's great knowledge of Torah, the Halakhah is almost always decided according to his view against all his colleagues and the other members of his generation (except in monetary matters, where Rav Naḥman's views are followed).

Rav Huna had many students, some of whom received their Torah knowledge directly from him; moreover, Rav's younger students continued to study with Rav Huna, his disciple. Rav Huna's son, Rabbah bar Rav Huna, was one of the greatest Sages of the next generation.

NOTES

killing of someone who is both a priest and a Prophet is a heinous crime for which atonement cannot be achieved through repentance alone. *Rabbi Tzvi Ḥayyot* suggests that the passage be understood in light of *Rambam's* statement (*Hilkhot Rotze'aḥ* 4:9): "Even though there are certain sins which are even more serious than murder, there is no sin which is as destructive to civilized living as is murder, not even idolatry, and certainly not forbidden sexual relationships or the desecration of the Sabbath. Someone who is guilty of murder is regarded as absolutely wicked, and all the good deeds that he has performed throughout his life do not outweigh this one sin, and will not save him from punishment." Thus, Aaron preferred that the people practice idolatry, which can be remedied through repentance, rather than commit murder, for which there is no remedy.

HALAKHAH

אֵין תְּחִילַּת דִּינוֹ שֶׁל אָדָם The beginning of a person's judgment. "A person is judged first in reference to his devotion to Torah study, and only afterwards in reference to the rest of his deeds." (*Shulḥan Arukh, Yoreh De'ah* 246:19.)

לְגוּדָא דְּגַמְלָא, [1]כֵּיוָן דְּקָם — קָם.

[2]שמע״י ושת״י שב״ע זמירו״ת הו״א סִימָן.

[3]הַהוּא דַּהֲוָה קָאָמַר וְאָזֵיל: טוּבֵיהּ דְּשָׁמַע וַאֲדִישׁ, [4]חָלְפוּהּ בִּישְׁתֵּיהּ מְאָה. [5]אֲמַר לֵיהּ שְׁמוּאֵל לְרַב יְהוּדָה: קְרָא כְּתִיב: [6]״פּוֹטֵר מַיִם רֵאשִׁית מָדוֹן״ — [7]רֵישׁ מְאָה דִּינֵי.

[8]הַהוּא דַּהֲוָה קָאָמַר וְאָזֵיל: אַתַּרְתֵּי תְּלָת גַּנָּבָא לָא מִיקְטַל. [9]אֲמַר לֵיהּ שְׁמוּאֵל לְרַב יְהוּדָה: קְרָא כְּתִיב: [10]״כֹּה אָמַר ה׳ עַל שְׁלֹשָׁה פִּשְׁעֵי יִשְׂרָאֵל וְעַל אַרְבָּעָה לֹא אֲשִׁיבֶנּוּ״.

[11]הַהוּא דַּהֲוָה קָאָמַר וְאָזֵיל: שַׁב בֵּירֵי לְשַׁלְמָנָא, [12]וַחֲדָא לַעֲבֵיד בִּישׁ. [13]אֲמַר לֵיהּ שְׁמוּאֵל לְרַב יְהוּדָה: קְרָא כְּתִיב: [14]״כִּי שֶׁבַע יִפּוֹל צַדִּיק וְקָם וְרָשָׁע יִפּוֹל בְּאֶחָת״.

LITERAL TRANSLATION

to a plank of a wooden bridge, [1]once it is established it is established.

[2]The sign is "Hear, two, seven, songs, another [שמע״י ושת״י שבע זמירו״ת הו״א]."

[3]A certain person would say: Good for one to hear and to be silent (lit., "indifferent"), [4][for] a hundred evils will pass him. [5]Shmuel said to Rav Yehudah: It is written in a verse: [6]"The beginning of strife is like letting water out" — [7]the beginning of a hundred judgments.

[8]A certain person would say: For two or three [thefts] a thief is not executed. [9]Shmuel said to Rav Yehudah: It is written in a verse: [10]"Thus says the Lord: For three transgressions of Israel, but for the fourth I will not turn away."

[11]A certain person would say: Seven pits for a righteous man, [12]and one for an evildoer. [13]Shmuel said to Rav Yehudah: It is written in a verse: [14]"For a righteous man falls seven times, and yet rises up again; but the wicked stumble into mischief."

TRANSLATION AND COMMENTARY

first set in place, the bridge is unsteady. [1]But **as** people step on it, **it becomes fixed** solidly, and soon **it becomes permanently fixed.** The same may be said about strife. The longer people continue to quarrel, the more irreversible the contention becomes.

שמע״י [2]The Gemara continues this discussion with a popular saying relating to the verse, "Letting out water," and mentions several other popular adages that are also adaptations of ideas from the Bible. **A mnemonic device** which can help the student remember the various adages is **"Hear, two, seven, songs, another,"** each word representing a different saying.

ההוא [3]It was related that **a certain person would always say: It is good for someone to hear** insults against himself **and remain silent** and not respond, **for** if he is able to restrain himself, [4]**a hundred evils** which would have afflicted him had he entered into the conflict **will pass** by him. [5]**Shmuel said to Rav Yehudah:** The idea expressed in that saying **is written in a verse:** [6]**"The beginning of strife is like letting water out."** The words רֵאשִׁית מָדוֹן (translated above as "the beginning of strife") should be understood as רֵישׁ מְאָה דִּינֵי — [7]**the beginning of a hundred judgments.** One who enters into an unnecessary conflict opens himself up to a hundred judgments, and one who avoids strife saves himself from that fate.

ההוא [8]It was related that **a certain person would always say: For only two or three thefts a thief is not executed.** [9]**Shmuel said to Rav Yehudah:** This idea **is** found already **in the verse** (Amos 2:6): [10]**"Thus says the Lord: For three transgressions of Israel,** I will turn away his punishment, **but for the fourth I will not turn away."**

ההוא [11]It was further related that **a certain man would always say: Seven pits** may be dug **for a righteous man,** and he will be not fall into any one of them, [12]while at the same time **a single** pit may lie open before **an evildoer,** and he will fall right in. [13]**Shmuel said to Rav Yehudah:** This notion **is written in the verse** (Proverbs 24:16): [14]**"For a righteous man falls seven times, and yet rises up again, but the wicked stumble into mischief"** and do not escape.

RASHI

לגודא דגמלא — דפין של גשר בתחילה כשדורסין עליהם — מנענעות, וסוף — מתחזקות ונקבעות במקומן. והכי נמי כשאדם מרבה בקטטה — מתחזקת ובאה, ולא מקרא נפקא. **טוביה דשמע ואדיש** — אשריו ששומע חרפתו ושותק ומרגיל בכך. ואדיש — כמו: דדש — דש (גיטין נו,ב). **חלפוה בישתיה מאה** — הלכו להם בשתיקתו מאה רעות שהיו באות עליו על ידי התגר. **פוטר מים** — המתחיל (מדון) ופותח בקטטה, הוא תחילת מאה דיני. **מדון** — נוטריקון מאה דני. לישנא אחרינא: ״מדון״ בגימטריא מאה. **אתרי תלת גנבי לא מיקטיל** — כלומר אם עובר אדם עבירה פעמים ושלש ולא באה עליו פורענות, אל יתמה, דאתרי תלת — גנבא לא מיקטיל, וסופו ללקות באחרונה. **שב בירי לשלמנא** — שבע בורות כרויות לרגלי איש שלום, ומכולם ינצל. **וחד בירא לעביד ביש** — לעושה רשעה. **יפול** — בתקלה ראשונה הבאה לו.

HALAKHAH

עַל שְׁלֹשָׁה פִּשְׁעֵי יִשְׂרָאֵל **For three transgressions of Israel.** "When the Heavenly Court judges a person, it disregards his first two sins, and considers his wrongdoings from his third sin onwards. This applies to an individual; but in the

TRANSLATION AND COMMENTARY

הַהוּא [1]A story is told about **a certain person who would always say:** Even if **someone leaves the court having had his cloak removed** — the court having ordered him to hand over the garment in payment of a debt — [2]**he should** happily **sing a song, and go on his way.** Surely the judges decided the case in a just manner, and so he did not really lose anything. [3]**Shmuel said to Rav Yehudah:** This idea **is already found in the verse** with which Jethro concludes his proposal for a judicial system to be established for the Israelites (Exodus 18:23): [4]**"And all this people shall go to their place in peace."** All the people, even those against whom the judges ruled, shall go home from the court in peace, all of them knowing that justice was done.

הַהוּא [5]The Gemara now relates that **a certain person would always say:** If a woman **slumbers, the basket** of palm fronds **upon** her head **drops** and her handiwork, which she keeps inside, is ruined. [6]**Shmuel said to Rav Yehudah:** The idea expressed here, that laziness leads to ruin, **is** already **found in the verse** (Ecclesiastes 10:18): [7]**"By much slothfulness the beams collapse, and** through idleness of the hands the house leaks."

הַהוּא [8]A story is told about **a certain person who would always say: The man in whom I** had always **put my trust** betrayed me and **raised his fist and stood against me.** [9]**Shmuel said to Rav Yehudah:** This notion **is** also **found in the verse** (Psalms 41:10): [10]**"Even my own familiar friend, in whom I trusted,** who did eat of my bread, has lifted up his heel against me."

הַהוּא [11]There was yet **another person who would say: When the love** between my wife and me **was strong,**

[1]הַהוּא דַּהֲוָה קָאָמַר וְאָזֵיל: דְּאָזֵיל מִבֵּי דִינָא שְׁקַל גְּלִימָא — [2]לִיזְמַר זֶמֶר, וְלֵיזִיל בְּאוֹרְחָא. [3]אֲמַר לֵיהּ שְׁמוּאֵל לְרַב יְהוּדָה: קְרָא כְּתִיב: [4]״וְגַם כָּל הָעָם הַזֶּה עַל מְקֹמוֹ יָבֹא בְשָׁלוֹם״.

[5]הַהוּא דַּהֲוָה קָאָמַר וְאָזֵיל: הִיא נָיְימָא, וְדִיקוּלָא שָׁפֵיל. [6]אֲמַר לֵיהּ שְׁמוּאֵל לְרַב יְהוּדָה: קְרָא כְּתִיב: [7]״בַּעֲצַלְתַּיִם יִמַּךְ הַמְּקָרֶה וגו׳״.

[8]הַהוּא דַּהֲוָה קָאָמַר וְאָזֵיל: גַּבְרָא דִּרְחִיצְנָא עֲלֵיהּ אַדְיֵיהּ לִגְזִיזֵיהּ וְקָם. [9]אֲמַר לֵיהּ שְׁמוּאֵל לְרַב יְהוּדָה: קְרָא כְּתִיב: [10]״גַּם אִישׁ שְׁלוֹמִי אֲשֶׁר בָּטַחְתִּי בוֹ וגו׳״.

[11]הַהוּא דַּהֲוָה קָאָמַר וְאָזֵיל: כִּי רְחִימְתִּין הֲוָה עַזִּיזָא,

LITERAL TRANSLATION

[1]A certain person would say: Someone who leaves the court having had his cloak removed [from him] — [2]let him sing a song, and go on his way. [3]Shmuel said to Rav Yehudah: It is written in a verse: [4]"And all this people shall go to their place in peace."

[5]A certain person would say: She slumbers, and the basket drops. [6]Shmuel said to Rav Yehudah: It is written in a verse: [7]"By slothfulness the beams collapse, etc."

[8]A certain person would say: The man in whom I trusted raised his fist and stood [against me]. [9]Shmuel said to Rav Yehudah: It is written in a verse: [10]"Even my own familiar friend, in whom I trusted, etc."

[11]A certain person would say: When our love was strong,

RASHI

דמבי דינא שקלוה גלימיה — מי שנטלו בית דין טליתו לפורעה לאחר. **ליזמר וליזיל** — הואיל ודין אמת דנו, לא הפסיד כלום, אלא גזילה הוציאו מידו. **כל העם הזה** — ביתרו כתיב, ומשמע לא שנא זכאי ולא שנא חייב, כולן במשמע. **היא ניימא ודיקולא שפיל** — כשהאשה מנמנמת הסל שעל ראשה שהיא נותנת בו פלכה ומלאכת ידיה בו — שפיל, כלומר מתוך שהיא עצלה אין מלאכתה ניכרת, וכולן משלות הן. **אדייה לגזיזיה וקם** — הרים אגרופו עלי ועמד לנגדי. **רחימתין הוה עזיזא** — כשאהבתינו היתה עזה ביני לאשתי.

REALIA

דִּיקוּלָא Basket.

A Roman picture of a non-Jewish woman during the Talmudic period bearing a basket on her head. These baskets were woven of palm fronds (דֶּקֶל), which is what gave them their name.

LANGUAGE

גְּזִיזֵיהּ Fist. Some authorities believe that it is derived from the Greek γαισος, *gaisos*, meaning "a spear."

NOTES

הִיא נָיְימָא, וְדִיקוּלָא שָׁפֵיל She slumbers, and the basket drops. This parable, which expresses the idea that laziness leads to ruin, is explained in various ways. *Arukh* explains the matter as follows: A lazy woman falls asleep alongside the river, her basket lying at her side, and the river sweeps the basket away while she sleeps and is unaware of what is happening. *Remah* offers the following explanation: While a lazy man sleeps, his palm tree (דֶּקֶל) withers because nobody tends to it.

אַדְיֵיהּ לִגְזִיזֵיהּ He raised his fists. This parable about betrayal is also explained in several ways. *Arukh* explains the saying as follows: The man whom I had always trusted betrayed me and raised a *weapon* against me. *Ramah* writes: This man in whom I had always trusted picked up his *load and* left. He saw that I was in need, and he set down the load that he was carrying in order to help me. But he gave up in the middle, picked up his load, and left me stranded.

HALAKHAH

case of a community, the third sin is disregarded as well." (*Rambam's* ruling follows *Rif's* reading in *Yoma;* but according to the standard text, the third sin of an individual is also disregarded.) (*Rambam, Sefer Mada, Hilkhot Teshuvah* 3:5.)

LANGUAGE

סַפְסֵירָא Sword. The word derives from the Persian *shavshir,* meaning "sword."

[1]אַפּוּתְיָא דְסַפְסֵירָא שְׁכִיבַן. [2]הָשְׁתָּא דְּלָא עַזִּיזָא רְחִימְתִּין, פּוּרְיָא בַּר שִׁיתִּין גַּרְמִידֵי לָא סָגֵּי לָן. [3]אֲמַר רַב הוּנָא: קְרָאֵי כְּתִיבִי, [4]מֵעִיקָּרָא כְּתִיב: "וְנוֹעַדְתִּי לְךָ שָׁם וְדִבַּרְתִּי אִתְּךָ מֵעַל הַכַּפֹּרֶת", [5]וְתַנְיָא: אָרוֹן תִּשְׁעָה וְכַפּוֹרֶת טֶפַח — הֲרֵי כָּאן עֲשָׂרָה, [6]וּכְתִיב: "וְהַבַּיִת אֲשֶׁר בָּנָה הַמֶּלֶךְ שְׁלֹמֹה לַה׳ שִׁשִּׁים אַמָּה אָרְכּוֹ וְעֶשְׂרִים רָחְבּוֹ וּשְׁלֹשִׁים אַמָּה קוֹמָתוֹ". [7]וּלְבַסּוֹף כְּתִיב: "כֹּה אָמַר ה׳ הַשָּׁמַיִם כִּסְאִי וְהָאָרֶץ הֲדֹם רַגְלָי; [8]אֵיזֶה בַיִת אֲשֶׁר תִּבְנוּ לִי וגו׳".

[9]מַאי מַשְׁמַע דְּהַאי "לֹא תָגוּרוּ" לִישָּׁנָא דְּכַנּוֹשֵׁי הוּא? [10]אֲמַר רַב נַחְמָן, אֲמַר קְרָא: [11]"וְיַיִן לֹא תִשְׁתֶּה וְלֹא תֶאֱגֹר". [12]רַב אַחָא בַּר יַעֲקֹב אָמַר מֵהָכָא: "תָּכִין בַּקַּיִץ לַחְמָהּ, אָגְרָה בַקָּצִיר מַאֲכָלָהּ". [13]רַב אַחָא בְּרֵיהּ דְּרַב אִיקָא אָמַר מֵהָכָא: "אֹגֵר בַּקַּיִץ בֵּן מַשְׂכִּיל.

LITERAL TRANSLATION

[1]we could lie on the width of a sword. [2]Now when our love is not strong, a sixty-cubit bed does not suffice for us. [3]Rav Huna said: It is written in the verses. [4]At first it is written: "And there I will meet with you, and I will speak with you from above the covering." [5]And it was taught: "The ark is nine [handbreadths], and the covering [one] handbreadth — here are ten." [6]And it is written: "And the house which King Solomon built for the Lord, its length was sixty cubits, and its breadth was twenty cubits, and its height was thirty cubits." [7]And at the end it is written: "The heaven is My throne, and the earth is My footstool; [8]where is the house that you would build for Me?"

[9]From where [may we] infer that this "Do not be afraid" is a term of gathering in? [10]Rav Naḥman said: The verse says: [11]"You shall not drink of wine, nor shall you gather [the grapes]." [12]Rav Aḥa bar Ya'akov said: From here: "Provides her bread in the summer, and gathers her food in the harvest." [13]Rav Aḥa the son of Rav Ika said: From here: "He that gathers in the summer is a wise son."

TRANSLATION AND COMMENTARY

[1]**we could lie** together **on the width of a sword.** [2]**But now that our love is not strong,** even **a sixty cubit bed is not large enough for us.** [3]**Rav Huna said:** The idea expressed in this saying **is already found in Scripture.** [4]**First, the verse** regarding the Holy Ark **states** (Exodus 25:22): **"And there I will meet with you, and I will speak with you from above the covering** of the ark of testimony." [5]**And it was taught** in a Baraita: **"The ark** itself **was nine handbreadths** high, **and the covering** that lay upon it was **another handbreadth** thick, so that together the ark and its covering **were ten** handbreadths high." When the Tabernacle was first erected and the love between God and Israel was strong, the Divine Presence dwelled on the small covering of the Ark of the Covenant. [6]**And** later **the verse** that records the dimensions of Solomon's Temple **states** (I Kings 6:2): **"And the house which King Solomon built for the Lord, its length was sixty cubits, and its breadth was twenty cubits, and its height was thirty cubits."** [7]**And** even **later** in Scripture, **the verse states** (Isaiah 66:1): **"The heaven is My throne, and the earth is My footstool;** [8]**where is the house that you would build for Me,** and where is the place of My rest?" After the people of Israel sinned, the Divine Presence could not confine itself to the Temple, even though it was so big.

מַאי מַשְׁמַע [9]The Gemara now explains Rabbi Ḥanin's statement, in the Baraita cited above, that the verse, "Do not be afraid of any man [לֹא תָגוּרוּ מִפְּנֵי אִישׁ]", should be understood to mean that you must not veil your arguments and hold them inside you because of any man. **From where may we infer that** the expression לֹא תָגוּרוּ, which would ordinarily be understood as **"do not be afraid," is** to be taken here as **a term** denoting **gathering in and** hiding away? [10]**Rav Naḥman said:** From **the verse** that **says** (Deuteronomy 28:39): [11]**"You shall not drink of wine, nor shall you gather** [תֶאֱגֹר] **the grapes."** [12]**Rav Aḥa bar Ya'akov said: From here** (Proverbs 6:8): **"Provides her bread in the summer, and gathers** [אָגְרָה] **her food in the harvest."** [13]**Rav Aḥa the son of Rav Ika said: From here** (Proverbs 10:5): **"He that gathers** [אֹגֵר] **in the summer is a wise son."**

RASHI

אפותיא דספסירא שכיבן — על רוחב הסייף היינו שוכבים שנינו. **לא סגי לן** — לא די לנו. **הרי כאן עשרה** — גובה מן הקרקע הרי שהקדוש ברוך הוא משרה שכינתו בעשרה טפחים סמוך לקרקע. ועוד: באורך הכפורת באמתה וחצי. **ולבסוף** — בבית המקדש היה גבוה שלשים אמה, ואורכו ששים. וכשחטאו נאמר להם "איזה בית אשר תבנו לי" שתוכל שכינתי להיות מצומצמת בתוכו.

NOTES

לִישָּׁנָא דְּ"כַנּוֹשֵׁי" הוּא A term of "gathering in." It has been suggested that the Gemara cites three different verses which demonstrate that the expression לֹא תָגוּרוּ can be taken as a term denoting "gathering in," because it wishes to teach that a judge must not fear any man, not even if that person is full of good qualities ("wine"), or if he is financially dependent upon him ("provides...bread"), or if he is a Torah scholar ("a wise son"). (*HaBoneh.*)

LITERAL TRANSLATION

[1]The sign is "truth, money, see [אמ"ת ממו"ן ירא"ה]." [2]Rabbi Shmuel bar Naḥmani said in the name of Rabbi Yonatan: Any judge who judges an [absolute] true judgment (lit., "a true judgment to its truth") causes the Divine Presence to dwell in Israel, [3]as it is said: "God stands in the congregation of God; He judges among judges." [4]And any judge who does not judge an absolute true judgment causes the Divine Presence to depart [from the midst of] Israel, [5]as it is said: "For the violence done to the poor, for the sighing of the needy, now will I arise, says the Lord, etc."

[6]And Rabbi Shmuel bar Nahman said in the name of Rabbi Yonatan: Any judge who takes from this one and gives to that one unjustly — [7]the Holy One, blessed be He, takes from him his soul, [8]as it is stated: "Do not rob the poor, because he is poor; nor oppress the afflicted in the gate. For the Lord will plead their cause, and rob the life of those who rob them."

[9]And Rabbi Shmuel bar Naḥmani said in the name of Rabbi Yonatan: [10]A judge should always view himself as if a sword is lying between his thighs,

[1]אמ"ת ממו"ן ירא"ה סִימָן. [2]אָמַר רַבִּי שְׁמוּאֵל בַּר נַחְמָנִי אָמַר רַבִּי יוֹנָתָן: כָּל דַּיָּין שֶׁדָּן דִּין אֱמֶת לַאֲמִיתּוֹ מַשְׁרֶה שְׁכִינָה בְּיִשְׂרָאֵל, [3]שֶׁנֶּאֱמַר "אֱלֹהִים נִצָּב בַּעֲדַת אֵל בְּקֶרֶב אֱלֹהִים יִשְׁפֹּט". [4]וְכָל דַּיָּין שֶׁאֵינוֹ דָּן דִּין אֱמֶת לַאֲמִיתּוֹ — גּוֹרֵם לַשְּׁכִינָה שֶׁתִּסְתַּלֵּק מִיִּשְׂרָאֵל, [5]שֶׁנֶּאֱמַר: "מִשֹּׁד עֲנִיִּים מֵאַנְקַת אֶבְיוֹנִים עַתָּה אָקוּם יֹאמַר ה׳ וגו׳".

[6]וְאָמַר רַבִּי שְׁמוּאֵל בַּר נַחְמָן אָמַר רַבִּי יוֹנָתָן: כָּל דַּיָּין שֶׁנּוֹטֵל מִזֶּה וְנוֹתֵן לָזֶה שֶׁלֹּא כַּדִּין — [7]הַקָּדוֹשׁ בָּרוּךְ הוּא נוֹטֵל מִמֶּנּוּ נַפְשׁוֹ, [8]שֶׁנֶּאֱמַר "אַל תִּגְזָל דָּל כִּי דַל הוּא וְאַל תְּדַכֵּא עָנִי בַשָּׁעַר. כִּי ה׳ יָרִיב רִיבָם, וְקָבַע אֶת קֹבְעֵיהֶם נָפֶשׁ".

[9]וְאָמַר רַבִּי שְׁמוּאֵל בַּר נַחְמָנִי אָמַר רַבִּי יוֹנָתָן: [10]לְעוֹלָם יִרְאֶה דַּיָּין עַצְמוֹ כְּאִילּוּ חֶרֶב מוּנַּחַת לוֹ בֵּין יַרְכוֹתָיו,

TRANSLATION AND COMMENTARY

אמ"ת [1]The Gemara continues with a series of Amoraic statements regarding judicial conduct and responsibility: **A mnemonic device** which can help the student remember the various statements is **"truth, money, see,"** each word alluding to a different statement.

וְאָמַר [2]**Rabbi Shmuel bar Naḥmani said in the name of Rabbi Yonatan: Any judge who delivers an absolutely true judgment causes the Divine Presence to dwell in Israel,** [3]**as it is said** (Psalms 82:1): **"God stands in the congregation of God; He judges among judges."** When the judges adjudicate the cases brought before them as if God Himself were judging the cases along with them, i.e., when the judges adjudicate the cases according to His laws, God stands in the midst of His congregation. [4]**And any judge who does not deliver an absolutely true judgment causes the Divine Presence to depart** from the midst of **Israel,** [5]**as it is said** (Psalms 12:6): **"For the violence done to the poor, for the sighing of the needy, now will I arise, says the Lord."**

וְאָמַר [6]**And Rabbi Shmuel bar Naḥman said in the name of Rabbi Yonatan: Any judge who unjustly takes** money **from one** litigant **and gives** it **to another** because he delivered a faulty decision — [7]**the Holy One, blessed be He, takes from** that judge **his soul,** [8]**as it is said** (Proverbs 22:22-23): **"Do not rob the poor, because he is poor; nor oppress the afflicted in the gate. For the Lord will plead their cause, and rob the life of those who rob them."**

וְאָמַר [9]**And Rabbi Shmuel bar Naḥmani said in the name of Rabbi Yonatan:** [10]**A judge should always** *see* **himself as if** there were **a sword between his thighs,** ready to cut him if he turns in any way from the right

SAGES

רַבִּי שְׁמוּאֵל בַּר נַחְמָנִי **Rabbi Shmuel bar Naḥmani.** A Palestinian Amora of the second and third generations, Rabbi Shmuel bar Naḥmani was an important teacher of Aggadah. He was a disciple of Rabbi Yonatan and transmitted many teachings in his name. He also studied with Rabbi Yehoshua ben Levi. He lived in Lydda in central Palestine.

RASHI

עתה אקום — אסתלק משער בית דין.

NOTES

דִּין אֱמֶת לַאֲמִיתּוֹ **An absolutely true judgment.** Elsewhere (*Bava Batra* 8b), *Tosafot* explains that this refers to a judge who uses his discretion to disregard the testimony of witnesses who he suspects are lying, even if he has no formal evidence to confirm his suspicions.

HALAKHAH

כָּל דַּיָּין שֶׁדָּן דִּין אֱמֶת לַאֲמִיתּוֹ **Any judge who judges an absolutely true judgment.** "While the court is in session, a judge must sit in fear and trepidation, for he stands before God when he administers justice. Any judge who does not deliver an absolutely true judgment causes the Divine Presence to depart from the midst of Israel. If a judge takes money from its rightful owner and gives it to another person, God will take that judge's soul. Any judge who renders an absolutely true judgment is regarded as having established order throughout the world and causes the Divine Presence to dwell in Israel." (*Shulḥan Arukh, Ḥoshen Mishpat* 8:2.)

SAGES

רַבִּי יֹאשִׁיָּה Rabbi Yoshiyah. This appears to be the Amora Rabbi Yoshaya, who lived in Eretz Israel at the time of the third and fourth generations of Amoraim there. Rabbi Yoshiyah was a student of Rabbi Yoḥanan's, and he lived a long life, becoming one of the oldest Sages in the following generation. His teachings are found mainly in the Jerusalem Talmud, but he is also mentioned in the Babylonian Talmud on various subjects.

רַבִּי חִיָּיא בַּר אַבָּא Rabbi (Rav) Ḥiyya bar Abba. An Amora of the third generation, Rabbi Ḥiyya bar Abba was born in Babylonia and immigrated to Eretz Israel in his youth. He was young enough to study under members of the first generation of Amoraim in Eretz Israel — Rabbi Ḥanina and Rabbi Yehoshua ben Levi. However, he was mainly a student of Rabbi Yoḥanan, and Rabbi Zera says of him that he was precise in reporting his master's teachings. After Rabbi Yoḥanan's death, he studied with Rabbi Elazar. Among his colleagues were Rabbi Abbahu, Rabbi Ammi, and Rabbi Assi. His sons also became Sages, the most prominent being Rabbi Abba.

[1] וְגֵיהִנָּם פְּתוּחָה לוֹ מִתַּחְתָּיו, [7B] [2] שֶׁנֶּאֱמַר: ״הִנֵּה מִטָּתוֹ שֶׁלִּשְׁלֹמֹה שִׁשִּׁים גִּבֹּרִים סָבִיב לָהּ מִגִּבֹּרֵי יִשְׂרָאֵל כֻּלָּם אֲחֻזֵי חֶרֶב מְלֻמְּדֵי מִלְחָמָה אִישׁ חַרְבּוֹ עַל יְרֵכוֹ מִפַּחַד בַּלֵּילוֹת״ — [3] מִפַּחְדָּהּ שֶׁל גֵּיהִנָּם שֶׁדּוֹמֶה לַלַּיְלָה.

[4] דְּרַשׁ רַבִּי יֹאשִׁיָּה וְאִיתֵּימָא רַב נַחְמָן בַּר יִצְחָק: [5] מַאי דִּכְתִיב: ״בֵּית דָּוִד כֹּה אָמַר ה׳ דִּינוּ לַבֹּקֶר מִשְׁפָּט וְהַצִּילוּ גָזוּל מִיַּד עוֹשֵׁק״, [6] וְכִי בַּבֹּקֶר דָּנִין וְכָל הַיּוֹם אֵין דָּנִין? [7] אֶלָּא: אִם בָּרוּר לְךָ הַדָּבָר כַּבֹּקֶר — אָמְרֵהוּ, [8] וְאִם לָאו — אַל תֹּאמְרֵהוּ.

[9] רַבִּי חִיָּיא בַּר אַבָּא אָמַר רַבִּי יוֹנָתָן מֵהָכָא: [10] ״אֱמֹר לַחָכְמָה אֲחֹתִי אָתְּ״. [11] אִם בָּרוּר לְךָ הַדָּבָר כַּאֲחוֹתְךָ שֶׁהִיא אֲסוּרָה לְךָ, אוֹמְרֵהוּ; [12] וְאִם לָאו, אַל תֹּאמְרֵהוּ.

LITERAL TRANSLATION

[1] and *Gehinnom* is open for him below him, [7B] [2] as it is said: "Behold, it is his litter, that of Solomon! Sixty valiant men are round about it, of the mighty men of Israel. All girt with swords, and expert in war; every man has his sword upon his thigh because of the fear by night" — [3] because of the dread of *Gehinnom* which is similar to night.

[4] Rabbi Yoshiyah expounded (and there are some who say [that it was] Rav Naḥman bar Yitzḥak): [5] What is that which is written: "O house of David, thus says the Lord: Execute judgment in the morning, and deliver him that is robbed out of the hand of the oppressor"? [6] Do we judge in the morning, and the entire day we do not judge? [7] Rather, if the matter is as clear to you as the morning, say it; [8] and if not, do not say it.

[9] Rabbi Ḥiyya bar Abba said in the name of Rabbi Yonatan: From here: [10] "Say to wisdom: You are my sister." [11] If the matter is as clear to you as it is that your sister is forbidden to you, say it; [12] and if not, do not say it.

TRANSLATION AND COMMENTARY

path, [1] **and** as if *Gehinnom* were lying **open below him,** ready to swallow him up should he render a false judgment, [7B] [2] **as it is said** (Song of Songs 3:3-8): **"Behold, it is his litter, that of Solomon! Sixty valiant men are round about it, of the mighty men of Israel. All girt with swords, and expert in war; every man has his sword upon his thigh because of the fear by night."** This verse is read to mean that sixty valiant Torah scholars surrounded Solomon while he sat in judgment. Each of the scholars was an expert in war — the war of Torah. And each man viewed himself as if a sword were lying between his thighs, [3] **because of the dread of** being sent to *Gehinnom*, **which is likened unto night.**

דְּרַשׁ רַבִּי יֹאשִׁיָּה [4] **Rabbi Yoshiyah expounded (and there are some who say that it was Rav Naḥman bar Yitzḥak who said this):** [5] **What is** the meaning of **that which is written** (Jeremiah 21:12): **"O house of David, thus says the Lord: Execute judgment in the morning, and deliver him that is robbed out of the hand of the oppressor?"** Why does the verse mention the morning? [6] **Do we judge** only **in the morning, and not during the** rest of the **day?** [7] **Rather,** the verse means to teach that **if the matter is as clear to you as the morning,** then **announce** your decision. [8] **But if** the matter is **not** yet absolutely clear to you, then **do not announce** your decision.

רַבִּי חִיָּיא בַּר אַבָּא [9] **Rabbi Ḥiyya bar Abba said in the name of Rabbi Yonatan: This** manner of judicial conduct is learned **from here** (Proverbs 7:4): [10] **"Say to wisdom: You are my sister."** [11] **If the matter** under consideration **is as clear to you as it is that your sister is forbidden to you,** then **announce** your decision. [12] **But if** the matter is **not** yet clear to you, then **do not announce** your decision.

RASHI

מטתו שלשלמה — שכנו של מקום. **ששים גבורים** — תלמידי חכמים, וששים לאו דוקא. **מלומדי מלחמה** — מלחמתה של תורה. **אם ברור לך** — הדין כבקר שהוא מאיר. **אומרהו** — והכי משמע ״דינו לבקר הוציאו לאור משפט״.

NOTES

אִם בָּרוּר לְךָ הַדָּבָר כַּבֹּקֶר If the matter is as clear to you as the morning. Some explain the Midrash as follows: If it is as clear to a judge that his decision is correct as it is clear to him that the morning marks the beginning of a new day, then he should go ahead and announce his decision. But if he is not yet certain about the correctness of his ruling, he should consider the matter further (*Rabbenu Ḥananel, Remah*).

אִם בָּרוּר לְךָ הַדָּבָר כַּאֲחוֹתְךָ If the matter is as clear to you as your sister. *Rabbenu Ḥananel* explains: If it is as clear to a judge that his ruling is correct as it is clear to him that a certain woman is his sister, who is forbidden to him, then he should issue the ruling; but if not, he should give the matter further consideration.

HALAKHAH

אִם בָּרוּר לְךָ הַדָּבָר כַּבֹּקֶר If the matter is as clear to you as the morning. "A judge must be careful in judgment, and not issue a ruling unless he has thoroughly investigated the matter, so that his decision is as clear to him as the sun." (*Shulḥan Arukh, Ḥoshen Mishpat* 10:1.)

[1]אָמַר רַבִּי יְהוֹשֻׁעַ בֶּן לֵוִי: עֲשָׂרָה שֶׁיּוֹשְׁבִין בַּדִּין — [2]קוֹלָר תָּלוּי בְּצַוַּאר כּוּלָּן.

[3]פְּשִׁיטָא!

[4]לֹא צְרִיכָא אֶלָּא לְתַלְמִיד הַיּוֹשֵׁב לִפְנֵי רַבּוֹ.

[5]רַב הוּנָא כִּי הֲוָה אָתֵי דִּינָא לְקַמֵּיהּ, מִיכְנִיף וּמַיְיתִי עֲשָׂרָה רַבָּנַן מִבֵּי רַב. [6]אָמַר: כִּי הֵיכִי דְּלִימְטְיָין שִׁיבָּא מִכְּשׁוּרָא.

[7]רַב אַשִׁי, כִּי הֲוָה אָתֵי טְרֵיפְתָּא לְקַמֵּיהּ [8]מִכְנִיף וּמַיְיתִי לְהוּ לְכוּלְּהוּ טַבָּחֵי דְּמָתָא מְחַסְיָא, [9]אֲמַר: כִּי הֵיכִי דְּלִימְטְיָין שִׁיבָּא מִכְּשׁוּרָא.

[10]כִּי אֲתָא רַב דִּימִי, אֲמַר: דְּרַשׁ רַב נַחְמָן בַּר כֹּהֵן: [11]מַאי דִּכְתִיב: "מֶלֶךְ בְּמִשְׁפָּט יַעֲמִיד אָרֶץ וְאִישׁ תְּרוּמוֹת יֶהֶרְסֶנָּה", [12]אִם דַּיָּין דּוֹמֶה לְמֶלֶךְ, שֶׁאֵינוֹ צָרִיךְ לִכְלוּם, [13]יַעֲמִיד אָרֶץ; [14]וְאִם דּוֹמֶה לְכֹהֵן שֶׁמְּחַזֵּר בְּבֵית הַגְּרָנוֹת, [15]יֶהֶרְסֶנָּה.

LITERAL TRANSLATION

[1]Rabbi Yehoshua ben Levi said: Ten who sit for judgment — [2]the chain hangs on the neck of all of them.

[3]It is obvious!

[4]No, it is necessary [in reference] to a disciple who sits before his master.

[5]Rav Huna, when a judgment would come before him, would assemble and bring ten Rabbis from the Academy. [6]He would say: In order that [only] a chip of the beam will reach us.

[7]Rav Ashi, when a *trefah* [animal] would be brought before him, [8]would gather and bring all of the slaughterers of Mata Meḥasya. [9]He would say: In order that [only] a chip of the beam will reach us.

[10]When Rav Dimi came, he said: Rav Naḥman bar Kohen expounded: [11]What is that which is written: "The king by justice establishes the land; but he who exacts gifts destroys it"? [12]If a judge is similar to a king who does not need anything, [13]he will establish the land; [14]and if he is similar to a priest who goes around the granary, [15]he will destroy it.

TRANSLATION AND COMMENTARY

אָמַר רַבִּי יְהוֹשֻׁעַ בֶּן לֵוִי [1]**Rabbi Yehoshua ben Levi said:** If **ten** scholars **convened for judgment,** [2]**the chain hangs on the necks of all of them;** if one of them was aware that his colleagues were issuing an erroneous decision, and he said nothing, he too is liable for punishment for the faulty judgment.

פְּשִׁיטָא [3]**This is obvious,** for by remaining silent he expressed his agreement with the decision!

לֹא צְרִיכָא [4]The Gemara answers: **No, it is necessary** to say this **regarding a disciple who was sitting before his master.** Although the disciple is not included among the judges, if he sees that his master is in error, he should correct him, and if he fails to do so, he too is responsible for the erroneous decision.

רַב הוּנָא [5]It was related that **when a case came before Rav for judgment, he would assemble and bring** another **ten Rabbis from the Academy** to join him in the courtroom. Explaining his behaviour, [6]Rav **would say:** I do this **so that only a chip of the beam**, a small portion of the responsibility, **will fall upon me.**

רַב אַשִׁי [7]It was further related that **when** a Halakhic question regarding the permissibility of **an animal with a fatal organic disease was brought before Rav Ashi,** [8]**he would assemble and bring together all the slaughterers of** the city of **Mata Meḥasya** — who were familiar with the intricacies of the laws regarding such an animal — to participate in the decision. [9]Rav Ashi **would** explain his behaviour, **saying:** I do this **in order that only a chip of the beam**, a small part of the responsibility, **will fall upon me.**

כִּי אֲתָא [10]The Gemara continues: **When Rav Dimi came** to Babylonia from Eretz Israel, **he reported** that **Rav Naḥman bar Kohen had expounded** as follows: [11]**What is** the meaning of **that which is written** (Proverbs 29:4): **"The king by justice establishes the land; but he who exacts gifts destroys it"?** [12]**If a judge is like a king who does not need anything,** and is not dependent on others, [13]**he will establish** justice throughout **the land.** [14]**But if** a judge is dependent upon other people — either financially or with respect to his mastery of the law — so that he **is like a priest who must go around the granary** to collect the priestly gifts, [15]**he will destroy** the judicial process.

RASHI

קולר תלוי — עונשה של הטייה. **לתלמיד היושב לפני רבו** — ובא דין לפני רבו, והוא לא נזקק לדבר, נענש אם שתק והוא מבין ברבו שטועה. **דנמטיין שיבא מכשורא** — שיגיענו נסורת קטנה מן הקורה, כלומר, שאם נטעה — ישתלש העונש בין כולנו ויקלו מעלי. **שיבא** — נסורת, כמו (הושע ח): "כי שבבים יהיה עגל שומרון" ומתרגמינן: לניסרי לווחין. **טבחי** — בקיאין בטריפות. **אם דומה הדיין למלך** — שבקי בטיב דינין, ומלא חכמה כמלך זה שהוא עשיר. **שמחזר על הגרנות** — לשאול תרומותיו, ואף זה צריך לחזור לשאול בית דין.

HALAKHAH

מַיְיתִי עֲשָׂרָה רַבָּנַן מִבֵּי רַב **He would bring ten Rabbis from the Academy.** "A court comprising three members is considered to be a full court, but it is praiseworthy for the court to be composed of a larger number of judges." (*Shulḥan Arukh, Ḥoshen Mishpat* 3:4.)

LANGUAGE

קוֹלָר **Collar.**

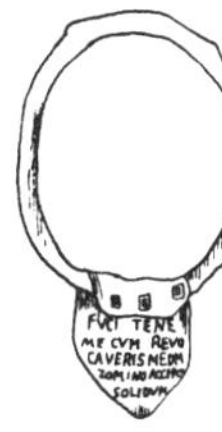

A prisoner's chain from the Talmudic period.

This word derives from the Latin *"collare,"* meaning a chain which used to be placed on the necks of animals or prisoners.

SAGES

רַב דִּימִי **Rav Dimi.** An Amora of the third and fourth generations, Rav Dimi lived both in Babylonia and in Eretz Israel. He seems to have been a Babylonian who moved to Eretz Israel in his youth. He returned to Babylonia several times, taking with him the teachings of Eretz Israel. Rav Dimi was responsible for the transmission of these teachings, and in the Jerusalem Talmud he is called Rav Avdimi (or Avduma) Naḥota. He was one of the Sages who were given the title רַבָּנַן נְחוּתֵי — "the emigrant Rabbis" — because they carried the teachings of Eretz Israel to Babylonia, mainly the teachings of Rabbi Yoḥanan, Resh Lakish, and Rabbi Elazar. Others who shared in this task were Rabbah bar Bar Ḥanah and Ulla, and later Ravin, Rav Shmuel bar Yehudah, and others. The Talmud reports dozens of Halakhic decisions that Rav Dimi took from one Torah center to the other, and he debated with the greatest Sages of his generation about them. At the end of his life he seems to have returned to Babylonia, where he died.

רַב נַחְמָן בַּר כֹּהֵן **Rav Naḥman bar Cohen.** A Palestinian Amora of the fourth generation. A few of his teachings are found in the Babylonian and Jerusalem Talmuds.

BACKGROUND

כֹּהֵן שֶׁמְּחַזֵּר בְּבֵית הַגְּרָנוֹת **A priest who goes around the granary.** While the donation of terumah to a priest

[1]דְּבֵי נְשִׂיאָה אוֹקְמוּ דַּיָּינָא דְּלָא הֲוָה גְּמִיר. [2]אֲמַר לֵיהּ לִיהוּדָה בַּר נַחְמָנִי מְתוּרְגְּמָנֵיהּ דְּרֵישׁ לָקִישׁ: [3]״קוּם עֲלֵיהּ בָּאָמוֹרָא״. [4]קָם, גָּחֵין עֲלֵיהּ, [5]וְלָא אֲמַר לֵיהּ וְלָא מִידֵּי. [6]פָּתַח וְאָמַר: [7]״׳הוֹי אוֹמֵר לָעֵץ הָקִיצָה עוּרִי לְאֶבֶן דּוּמָם הוּא יוֹרֶה? הִנֵּה, הוּא תָּפוּשׂ זָהָב וָכֶסֶף, וְכָל רוּחַ אֵין בְּקִרְבּוֹ׳. [8]וְעָתִיד, הַקָּדוֹשׁ בָּרוּךְ הוּא, לִיפָּרַע מִמַּעֲמִידִין, [9]שֶׁנֶּאֱמַר ׳וַה׳ בְּהֵיכַל קָדְשׁוֹ; הַס מִפָּנָיו כָּל הָאָרֶץ׳״.

[10]אָמַר רֵישׁ לָקִישׁ: כָּל הַמַּעֲמִיד דַּיָּין עַל הַצִּיבּוּר שֶׁאֵינוֹ הָגוּן כְּאִילּוּ נוֹטֵעַ אֲשֵׁירָה בְּיִשְׂרָאֵל, [11]שֶׁנֶּאֱמַר: ״שֹׁפְטִים וְשֹׁטְרִים תִּתֶּן לְךָ״, [12]וּסְמִיךְ לֵיהּ: ״לֹא תִטַּע לְךָ אֲשֵׁרָה כָּל עֵץ״.

LITERAL TRANSLATION

[1][Members] of the House of the Nasi appointed a judge who had not learned. [2]He said to Yehudah bar Naḥmani, Resh Lakish's interpreter: [3]"Stand by him as an interpreter." [4]He stood up, [and] bent down next to him, [5]but he did not say anything to him. [6]He began (lit., "opened") and said: [7]"'Woe to him that says to the wood, Awake; to the dumb stone, Arise, can it teach? Behold, it is overlaid with gold and silver, and there is no breath at all in it.' [8]In the future, the Holy One, blessed be He, will punish those who appoint [unfit judges], [9]as it is said: 'But the Lord is in his holy Temple; let all the earth keep silence before him.'"

[10]Resh Lakish said: Whoever appoints a judge over a community who is not fit is considered as if he planted an asherah in Israel, [11]as it is stated: "Judges and officers shall you make yourself," [12]and following it: "You shall not plant for yourself an asherah of any tree."

TRANSLATION AND COMMENTARY

דְּבֵי נְשִׂיאָה [1]It once happened that **members of the House of the Nasi** of Eretz Israel **appointed a judge who was not a learned** scholar. [2]**They told Yehudah bar Naḥmani,** who ordinarily served as **Resh Lakish's interpreter,** standing by his side during his lectures and conveying his words to the audience: [3]**"Stand by the** newly appointed judge, and serve **as his interpreter** while he delivers his sermon." [4]Yehudah bar Naḥmani **stood** by the judge's side, **and bent down next to him** to hear what the judge was saying so that he could convey his message to the audience, [5]**but** the judge **did not say anything to him,** for he was not a learned man. [6]Yehudah bar Naḥmani began to speak on his own **and said:** "There is a verse which states [Habakkuk 2:19]: [7]**'Woe to him that says to the wood, Awake; to the dumb stone, Arise, can it teach? Behold, it is overlaid with gold and silver, and there is no breath at all in it.'** [8]And he added: **"In the future, the Holy One, blessed be He, will punish those who appoint unfit judges** over Israel, [9]**as the very next verse states** [2:20]: **'But the Lord is in his holy Temple; let all the earth keep silence before him.'"**

אָמַר רֵישׁ לָקִישׁ [10]**Resh Lakish said: Whoever appoints an unfit judge over a community** [11]**is considered as if he planted an asherah** (a tree worshipped as part of idolatrous rites) **in Israel,** [12]**as the verse states** (Deuteronomy 16:18): **"Judges and officers shall you make yourself** in all your gates," **and** immediately **following** the passage teaching the regulations concerning the appointment of judges, the verse states (16:21): **"You shall not plant thee an asherah of any tree."** An unqualified judge will cause the Divine Presence to depart from the midst of Israel, as will the idolatrous worship of a tree.

RASHI

קום עליה באמורא — להשמיע דרשה לציבור מה שילחוש לך. **וה׳ בהיכל קדשו** — סמוך להאי קרא ד״הוי אומר לעץ הקיצה עורה לאבן וגו׳״ ״הוא יורה הנה הוא תפוש וגו׳״ כתב ״הס מפניו כל הארץ״ — יכלה על עון הזה את כל הארץ. **כל עץ** — משמע דיין, דכתיב (דברים כ): ״כי האדם עץ השדה״ ומוקמינן ליה בתלמיד.

was an obligation from the Torah, a landowner could decide to which priest he wished to give the donation. Therefore a priest who wished to receive terumah had to go from threshing floor to threshing floor and ask the owners to give him his share. Understandably, this practice created a relationship of dependence upon the donor.

SAGES

יְהוּדָה בַּר נַחְמָנִי **Rabbi Yehudah bar Naḥmani.** Sometimes referred to as Bar Naḥman or Bar Neḥemyah, Rabbi Yehudah bar Naḥmani was a Palestinian Amora of the second and third generations, and one of the greatest preachers of his time. In addition to his position as the interpreter of Resh Lakish, he and his colleague Rabbi Levi used to preach homiletical sermons to the public, in preparation for the main sermon given by Rabbi Yoḥanan. In the Talmud and the Midrashim, Aggadic teachings are presented in his name, and he also frequently quotes his teacher, Resh Lakish.

NOTES

דַּיָּין עַל הַצִּיבּוּר שֶׁאֵינוֹ הָגוּן **A judge who is not fit.** Here the Gemara says that whoever appoints an unfit judge is considered as if he had planted a tree used for idolatrous purposes, and it cites as proof the verse (Deuteronomy 16:21) dealing with such a tree that immediately follows the section referring to the appointment of judges. But *Rambam* (*Hilkhot Sanhedrin* 3:8) writes that whoever appoints an unfit judge is considered as if he had set up a pillar for forbidden sacrificial service, and he cites the very next verse (Deuteronomy 16:22): "You shall not set up a pillar which the Lord your God hates." *Maharik* (Responsa, No. 117) explains that both verses allude to the appointment of unfit judges, since they are inserted between the Biblical section dealing with the appointment of judges and additional sections dealing with judicial proceedings. The first verse teaches that a person who is unfit to serve as a judge because of his venal character may not be appointed to the position, even if he is an expert in the law. Such a

HALAKHAH

דַּיָּין עַל הַצִּיבּוּר שֶׁאֵינוֹ הָגוּן **A judge who is not fit.** "If someone appoints as a judge a person who is not fit for the position or familiar with the Torah's wisdom, he violates a negative Biblical prohibition. If a judge was appointed on account of his money, it is forbidden to appear before him for a judgment, and it is even a mitzvah to treat him with contempt." (*Shulḥan Arukh, Ḥoshen Mishpat* 8:1.)

TRANSLATION AND COMMENTARY

אָמַר רַב אַשִׁי [1]**Rav Ashi added:** If someone appointed an unfit judge in a place **where there are** true **Torah scholars, he is considered as if he planted** a tree devoted to idolatry right **next to the altar,** [2]**as it is said:** "You shall not plant thee an asherah of any tree **near the altar of the Lord your God."**

כְּתִיב [3]The Gemara continues with a related Midrashic reading: **The verse states** (Exodus 20:23): **"You shall not make with Me gods of silver, neither shall you make for yourselves gods of gold."** [4]It may be asked: The verse teaches that **gods of silver and gold may not be made.** [5]**But does** this mean that gods **of wood are permitted?** Surely all idols are absolutely forbidden! [6]Rather, **Rav Ashi said:** The verse means to condemn **a judge** — as we saw above (2b), the word *eloha* can mean "judge" — **who came** to his position **because of the silver or gold** that he paid the authorities in order to receive his appointment.

רַב [7]It was related that **whenever Rav came to court** to adjudicate a case, **he would say** of himself **as follows:** [8]**"Of his own free will, he goes out to death,** for he will be liable to pay with his life if he issues an erroneous ruling. When he sits on the judicial bench, [9]**he does not do** anything which will him help meet **the needs of his household, and empty-handed he will return to his house,** for a judge is not paid for his services. [10]**Oh, that his return** home **should be like his departure,** free of liability for erroneous decisions."

כִּי הָוֵי [11]The Gemara now relates that **whenever** Rav **saw a group of scribes following after him** in his honor, **he would** cite to himself the verses that **say** (Job 20:6-7): [12]**"Though his excellency mount up to the heavens,** and his head reach the clouds; [13]**Yet he shall perish for ever like his own dung;** They who have seen him shall say, 'Where is he?'" Rav would remind himself of his mortality, in order to stop himself from succumbing to pride.

LITERAL TRANSLATION

[1]Rav Ashi said: And where there are Torah scholars he is considered as if he planted next to the altar, [2]as it is stated: "Beside the altar of the Lord your God."

[3]It is written: "You shall not make with Me gods of silver, [neither shall you make for yourselves] gods of gold." [4]Gods of silver and gods of gold may not be made. [5]But of wood are permitted? [6]Rav Ashi said: A judge who comes for silver, and a judge who comes for gold.

[7]When he came to court, Rav would say as follows: [8]"Of his own free will he goes out to death, [9]and he does not do for the needs of his household, and empty-handed he returns to his house, [10]and if only the return were like the departure."

[11]When he would see a group of scribes [following] after him, he would say: [12]"Though his excellency mount up to the heavens, etc.; [13]Yet he shall perish for ever like his own dung, etc."

[1]אָמַר רַב אַשִׁי: וּבִמְקוֹם שֶׁיֵּשׁ תַּלְמִידֵי חֲכָמִים כְּאִילּוּ נְטָעוֹ אֵצֶל מִזְבֵּחַ, [2]שֶׁנֶּאֱמַר "אֵצֶל מִזְבַּח ה׳ אֱלֹהֶיךָ".

[3]כְּתִיב: "לֹא תַעֲשׂוּן אִתִּי אֱלֹהֵי כֶסֶף וֵאלֹהֵי זָהָב". [4]אֱלֹהֵי כֶסֶף וֵאלֹהֵי זָהָב הוּא דְּלָא עָבְדִי. [5]הָא דְּעֵץ שָׁרֵי? [6]אָמַר רַב אַשִׁי: אֱלוֹהַּ הַבָּא בִּשְׁבִיל כֶּסֶף, וֶאֱלוֹהַּ הַבָּא בִּשְׁבִיל זָהָב.

[7]רַב כִּי הֲוָה אָתֵי לְבֵי דִינָא אָמַר הָכִי: [8]"בִּרְעוּת נַפְשֵׁיהּ לְקַטְלָא נָפֵיק, [9]וּצְבִי בֵּיתֵיהּ לֵית הוּא עָבֵיד, וְרֵיקָן לְבֵיתֵיהּ עָיֵיל, [10]וּלְוַאי שֶׁתְּהֵא בִּיאָה כִּיצִיאָה".

[11]כִּי הָוֵי חָזֵי אַמְבּוּהָא דְּסָפְרֵי אַבַּתְרֵיהּ, אָמַר: [12]"אִם יַעֲלֶה לַשָּׁמַיִם שִׂיאוֹ" [וגו׳]; [13]"כְּגֶלְלוֹ לָנֶצַח יֹאבֵד וגו׳".

RASHI

אצל מזבח — ותלמידי חכמים מכפרין ומגינין כמזבח. **אלוה הבא בשביל כסף** — דיין שהעמידוהו על ידי שנתן ממון למלך על כך. **לדינא** — לדון. **לקטלא** — לישא עליו חטא, ועל עצמו היה אומר. **וצבי ביתיה לית הוא עביד** — צרכי ביתו אינו עושה כאן. **וריקן לביתיה עייל** — שאינו משתכר כאן כלום. **ולואי שתהא ביאה** — שאחזור לביתי כיציאה שיצאתי מביתי בלא חטא, שלא אטעה ואענש. **אמבוהא** — סיעת אנשים. **אם יעלה לשמים וגו׳** — כדי שלא תזוח דעתו עליו היה אומר כך. **בגללו** — גלל רעי.

BACKGROUND

וּצְבִי בֵּיתֵיהּ For his house's needs. By law, a judge receives no fee or salary for sitting in judgment, and only in certain cases is a judge permitted to receive compensation for interrupting his ordinary work. Hence a judge earns nothing by serving the public as a volunteer.

LANGUAGE

אַמְבּוּהָא A group. This word derives from the Persian *anbûh*, meaning a multitude of people.

NOTES

person is likened to a live tree, for he has a fertile mind which can bear fruit in the form of a correct understanding of the law, but nevertheless may deliberately pervert justice. The second verse teaches that a person who is unfit to serve as a judge because of his lack of legal knowledge may not be appointed to a judicial post, even if he has a flawless character and is unquestionably honest, for such a person, who may be likened to an inanimate stone pillar, does not have the legal expertise to fill the role properly.

[1]מָר זוּטְרָא חֲסִידָא, כִּי הָווּ מְכַתְּפִי לֵיהּ בְּשַׁבְּתָא דְּרִיגְלָא, [2]אָמַר הָכִי: ״כִּי לֹא לְעוֹלָם חֹסֶן; וְאִם נֵזֶר לְדוֹר וָדוֹר״.
[3]דְּרַשׁ בַּר קַפָּרָא: מְנָא הָא מִילְּתָא דְּאָמְרוּ רַבָּנַן, ״הֱווּ מְתוּנִין בַּדִּין״? [4]דִּכְתִיב: ״לֹא תַעֲלֶה בְמַעֲלֹת״, [5]וּסְמִיךְ לֵיהּ: ״וְאֵלֶּה הַמִּשְׁפָּטִים״.
[6]אָמַר רַבִּי אֱלִיעֶזֶר: מִנַּיִין לַדַּיָּין שֶׁלֹּא יִפְסַע עַל רָאשֵׁי עַם קוֹדֶשׁ? [7]שֶׁנֶּאֱמַר: ״לֹא תַעֲלֶה בְמַעֲלֹת״, [8]וּסְמִיךְ לֵיהּ: ״וְאֵלֶּה הַמִּשְׁפָּטִים״.
[9]״אֲשֶׁר תָּשִׂים״? [10]״אֲשֶׁר תְּלַמְּדֵם״ מִיבָּעֵי לֵיהּ!
[11]אָמַר רַבִּי יִרְמְיָה וְאִיתֵימָא רַבִּי חִיָּיא בַּר אַבָּא: [12]אֵלּוּ כְּלֵי הַדַּיָּינִין.
[13]רַב הוּנָא, כִּי הֲוָה נָפֵק לְדִינָא אָמַר הָכִי: [14]אַפִּיקוּ לִי מָאנֵי חֲנוּתַאי: מַקֵּל וּרְצוּעָה, וְשׁוֹפָרָא וְסַנְדְּלָא.

LITERAL TRANSLATION

[1]Mar Zutra Ḥasida, when they would carry him on their shoulders on the Sabbath of the Festival, [2]would say as follows: "For riches are not forever; and does the crown endure unto all generations?"

[3]Bar Kappara expounded: From where [do we derive] this matter which the Rabbis said, "Be careful in judgment"? [4]For it is written: "Do not go up by steps," [5]and following it: "And these are the judgments."

[6]Rabbi Eliezer said: From where [do we derive] that a judge should not stride over the heads of the holy people? [7]For it is stated: "Do not go up by steps," [8]and following it: "And these are the judgments." [9]"Which you shall set." [10]It should have said: "Which you shall teach them"!

[11]Rabbi Yirmiyah said (and some say [it was] Rabbi Ḥiyya bar Abba): [12]These are the tools of the judges.

[13]Rav Huna, when he would go out for a judgment, would say as follows: [14]Take out for me the tools of my trade: A stick, a strap, a horn, and a sandal.

TRANSLATION AND COMMENTARY

מָר זוּטְרָא חֲסִידָא [1]A similar story is told about **Mar Zutra Ḥasida** whose attendants **carried him on their shoulders on the Sabbath of the Festival** in order to bring him to the public lecture. To remain humble in spite of this honor, [2]**he would** cite to himself the verse that **says** (Proverbs 27:24): **"For riches are not forever; and does the crown endure unto all generations?"**

דְּרַשׁ בַּר קַפָּרָא [3]**Bar Kappara expounded: From where do we derive this matter which the Rabbis said** elsewhere in the Mishnah (*Avot* 1:1): **"Be careful in judgment** and thoroughly examine all aspects of the case before you render a decision"? [4]**For the verse says** (Exodus 20:23): **"Do not go up by steps** to my altar," [5]**and** the verse that immediately **follows it** says (Exodus 21:1): **"And these are the judgments."** The prohibition against "going up by steps" is taken here as a prohibition against acting with haste. The proximity of the two verses teaches that this prohibition against acting with haste should be applied to the matter of judgments.

אָמַר רַבִּי אֱלִיעֶזֶר [6]**Rabbi Eliezer said: From where do we derive** the idea **that a judge should not** behave arrogantly and **stride over the heads of the holy people?** [7]**For the verse says** (Exodus 20:23): **"Do not go up by steps** to my altar," [8]**and** the verse that immediately **follows it** says: **"And these are the judgments."**

אֲשֶׁר תָּשִׂים [9]Having mentioned the first half of the verse (Exodus 21:1): "And these are the judgments," the Gemara now explains the second half of the verse, which reads: **"Which you shall set** before them." The Gemara states: At first glance, the expression used here seems inappropriate, [10]for the verse **should have said:** "And these are the judgments **which you shall teach them,"** for the judgments must be taught to the people, and not set before them!

אָמַר רַבִּי יִרְמְיָה [11]**Rabbi Yirmiyah said (and some say** that **it was Rabbi Ḥiyya bar Abba** who said this): [12]**These are the judges' tools which** a judge must set before himself when he hears a case (as will be explained immediately).

רַב הוּנָא [13]The Gemara continues: **When he went out to adjudicate** a case, **Rav Huna would say as follows:** [14]**Take out for me the tools of my trade: A stick and a strap** with which to administer lashes, **a horn** with which to announce an excommunication, **and a sandal** with which to perform the *ḥalitzah* ceremony.

RASHI

מכתפי להו — נושאין אותן על הכתף, שהיו זקינים ואינם יכולין לרוץ, ומטריחין את הציבור לעמוד בפניהם, לפיכך היו עבדיהם נושאין אותם מהר. **בשבתא דרגלא** — שבת שדורשין בו בהלכות הרגל, והיינו שלשים יום קודם הרגל. **מתונים** — רגילין בהמתנה, כדי לעיין בה יפה קודם שתחתכוהו. **במעלות** — בחזקה ובמרוצה. **על ראשי עם קדש** — שכשהיה המתורגמן דורש היו הציבור יושבין לארץ, והמפסיע ביניהן לילך ולישב במקומו נראה כמפסיע על ראשן. **וסמיך ליה ואלה המשפטים** — כלומר אף לשופטים אני מזהיר. **כלי הדיינים** — דשייכא בהו שימה, דבר המטלטל. **רצועה** — למלקות. **מקל** — למכת מרדות עד שיחזור בו. **שופר** — לשמתא ונידוי. **סנדל** — לחליצה.

NOTES

מַקֵּל וּרְצוּעָה **A stick and a strap.** *Rashi* and others explain that the strap was used for lashes administered by Torah law, whereas the stick was used for lashes administered only by Rabbinic decree. Others explain that the strap was

BACKGROUND

שַׁבְּתָא דְּרִיגְלָא **On the Sabbath of the Festival.** Ordinarily the Sages would lecture only before students in the yeshivah, and even in the annual study sessions, only learned students of Torah would gather. However, the Sabbath during the intermediate days of a holiday were different, because then the entire community would gather to hear sermons given by the greatest Sages of the yeshivot, or by the Exilarch. There was therefore an enormous audience on these special Sabbaths, and of course the density of the crowd was considerable.

שֶׁלֹּא יִפְסַע עַל רָאשֵׁי עַם קוֹדֶשׁ **Should not stride over the heads of the holy people.** This description is based on the order of seating in Mishnaic and Talmudic times. The head of the yeshivah or the Sage giving the sermon would sit facing the audience. Everyone would sit in rows before him on the ground. The places in these rows were reserved, with the most distinguished people sitting closest to the speaker. If an important Sage came to the assembly late, and everyone was already seated, he would have to step over the heads of the seated in order to reach his place.

SAGES

מָר זוּטְרָא חֲסִידָא **Mar Zutra the Ḥasida.** This Sage is mentioned several times in the Talmud, but no Torah teachings are presented in his name. However, his good deeds are recounted, with praise for his humility and scrupulousness regarding other people's money and honor. Since he has the title "Master," he must have belonged to the House of the Exilarch, and it also appears from what is told of him that he was borne on a litter when he went to hear the holiday sermon of the Exilarch or one of his household. Some people believe that he himself was the Exilarch.

בַּר קַפָּרָא **Bar Kappara.** A Sage from Eretz Israel during the transitional generation between the Tannaim and the Amoraim. Bar Kappara's given name is not known (some say that it was

TRANSLATION AND COMMENTARY

וָאֲצַוֶּה אֶת שֹׁפְטֵיכֶם בָּעֵת הַהִיא [1]The Gemara now explains each phrase of another verse which deals with judges: The verse states (Deuteronomy 1:16): **"And I commanded your judges at that time,** saying: Hear the causes between your brethren, and judge righteously between every man and his brother, and his stranger." [2]**Rabbi Yoḥanan said:** The word "command" is used by Scripture whenever it calls for zealous activity. [3]Here the verse means that the judges are commanded to **be quick regarding the stick and the strap,** to instill the people with awe for the court.

שָׁמֹעַ בֵּין אֲחֵיכֶם וּשְׁפַטְתֶּם [4]The verse continues: **"Hear the causes between your brethren, and judge."** [5]**Rabbi Ḥanina said:** The phrase, "between your brethren," serves as **a warning to the court that it should not hear the arguments of one litigant before his fellow litigant arrives.** [6]The same verse also serves as **a warning to the litigant that he should not present his arguments to the judge before his fellow litigant arrives,** [7]for the verse can **also be read** as follows: **"Sound the causes between your brethren."**

רַב כָּהֲנָא [8]**Rav Kahana said:** These two prohibitions may be derived **from here** (Exodus 23:1): [9]The verse states: **"You shall not accept an evil report,"** but the word תִשָּׂא, *tisa,* can also be read as if it were vocalized תַשִּׂיא, *tasi,* so that the verse means: [10]**"You shall not bear a false report."** Thus, the verse forbids a judge from hearing the arguments of one litigant if the other litigant is not present, and it also forbids the one litigant from presenting his case before the judge if his fellow litigant is not there.

[1]״וָאֲצַוֶּה אֶת שֹׁפְטֵיכֶם בָּעֵת הַהִיא״. [2]אָמַר רַבִּי יוֹחָנָן: [3]כְּנֶגֶד מַקֵּל וּרְצוּעָה תְּהֵא זָרִיז.
[4]״שָׁמֹעַ בֵּין אֲחֵיכֶם וּשְׁפַטְתֶּם״. [5]אָמַר רַבִּי חֲנִינָא: אַזְהָרָה לְבֵית דִּין שֶׁלֹּא יִשְׁמַע דִּבְרֵי בַּעַל דִּין קוֹדֶם שֶׁיָּבֹא בַּעַל דִּין חֲבֵירוֹ, [6]וְאַזְהָרָה לְבַעַל דִּין שֶׁלֹּא יַטְעִים דְּבָרָיו לַדַּיָּין קוֹדֶם שֶׁיָּבֹא בַּעַל דִּין חֲבֵירוֹ. [7]קְרִי בֵּיהּ נַמִי: ״שַׁמַּע בֵּין אֲחֵיכֶם״.
[8]רַב כָּהֲנָא אָמַר מֵהָכָא: [9]מִ״לֹּא תִשָּׂא״ — [10]״לֹא תַשִּׂיא״.

LITERAL TRANSLATION

[1]"And I commanded your judges at that time." [2]Rabbi Yoḥanan said: [3]Regarding the stick and the strap be quick.

[4]"Hear the causes between your brethren, and judge." [5]Rabbi Ḥanina said: [This is] a warning to the court that it should not hear the arguments of [one] litigant before his fellow litigant arrives, [6]and a warning to a litigant that he should not present his arguments to the judge before his fellow litigant arrives. [7]Read in it also: "Sound [the causes] between your brethren."

[8]Rav Kahana said: From here: [9]"You shall not accept [an evil report]" — [10]"you shall not bear [a false report]."

RASHI

ואצוה — כל צואה לשון זירוז הוא דתניא (קדושין כט,ב): כל מקום שנאמר "צו" אינו אלא לשון זירוז, ועל מה זירז? — על המקל ועל הרצועה, שיהו מטילין אימה על הציבור לשם שמים. **שמוע בין אחיכם** — כשיהיו שניהם יחד שמעו דבריהם, ולא תשמעו דברי זה בלא זה, שמסדר דברי שקר כדברי אמת, לפי שאין מכחישו, ומכיון שלב הדיין נוטה לו לזכות, שוב אין לבו מהפך בזכות השני כל כך. **שמע** — דצריך בין אחיכם, כשתהיו שניכם יחד משמע. **לא תשא** — לא תקבל שמע שוא, אזהרה לדיין. וקרי ביה נמי "לא תשיא" — אזהרה לבעל דין.

Shimon), and he may have been the son of Rabbi Elazar HaKappar. Bar Kappara was one of the important disciples of Rabbi Yehudah HaNasi, and, as a colleague of Rabbi Ḥiyya, he edited a special collection of Baraitot taken from the Talmud and known as תָּנֵי בַּר קַפָּרָא. His Halakhot are found in many places in the Talmud. He was one of the great preachers of his generation, and several Aggadot from his sermons are found in both the Babylonian and Jerusalem Talmuds. Bar Kappara was famous for his sharp and agile mind, and some of his sayings on various subjects are also preserved by the Talmud. He seems to have been considered a master of Scripture in his generation, so that even Rabbi Yehudah HaNasi asked him the meaning of various Biblical verses. Bar Kappara revered his teacher, and he was the main eulogist at his funeral.
Almost all the Sages of the first generation of Amoraim were his disciples (including his nephew, Rabbi Yehudah ben Pada), and they transmit many Halakhic teachings in his name. It seems that in his later years he lived in Galilee, and was buried in the town of Parod.

NOTES

used for the administration of lashes, whereas the stick was used to threaten those who do not accept the judge's decision (*Ri Almandri*).

כְּנֶגֶד מַקֵּל וּרְצוּעָה תְּהֵא זָרִיז Regarding the stick and the strap be quick. Our commentary follows *Rashi* and others who explain that Rabbi Yoḥanan understands the verse as calling upon the judge to be zealous and use his stick and his strap whenever necessary. *Rosh* understands the matter in just the opposite manner and maintains that the verse teaches that the judge must refrain from using the stick and the strap to instill fear in the public, and must patiently bear with the people. *Rabbi David Bonfil* suggests that the verse teaches that the judge must be particularly zealous with respect to prohibitions punishable by lashes, to avoid becoming liable to the very same punishment that he ordinarily metes out to others.

שֶׁלֹּא יִשְׁמַע דִּבְרֵי בַּעַל דִּין That it should not hear the arguments of one litigant. Elsewhere (*Shevuot* 31a), the Gemara derives these two prohibitions from a different verse (Exodus 23:7): "Keep yourself far from a false matter." Hearing the arguments of one litigant when his fellow litigant is not there is forbidden, because it invites falsehood. The litigant presenting his case can say what he wants when there is nobody there to contradict him.

HALAKHAH

שֶׁלֹּא יִשְׁמַע דִּבְרֵי בַּעַל דִּין That he should not hear the arguments of one litigant. "A judge is forbidden to hear the arguments of one litigant if the other litigant is not present. A litigant is also forbidden to present his case if his fellow litigant is not there." (*Shulḥan Arukh, Ḥoshen Mishpat* 17:5.)

[1]״וּשְׁפַטְתֶּם צֶדֶק״. [2]אָמַר רֵישׁ לָקִישׁ: צַדֵּק אֶת הַדִּין וְאַחַר כָּךְ חָתְכֵהוּ,
[3]״בֵּין אִישׁ וּבֵין אָחִיו וּבֵין גֵּרוֹ״. [4]אָמַר רַב יְהוּדָה: אֲפִילּוּ בֵּין בַּיִת לַעֲלִיָּיה.
[5]״וּבֵין גֵּרוֹ״. [6]אָמַר רַב יְהוּדָה: אֲפִילּוּ בֵּין תַּנּוּר לְכִירַיִם.
[7]״לֹא תַכִּירוּ פָנִים בַּמִּשְׁפָּט״. [8]רַבִּי יְהוּדָה אוֹמֵר: לֹא תַכִּירֵהוּ. [9]רַבִּי אֶלְעָזָר אוֹמֵר: לֹא תְנַכְּרֵהוּ.

LITERAL TRANSLATION

[1]"And judge righteously." [2]Resh Lakish said: Justify the judgment and afterwards decide.

[3]"Between a man and his brother, and his stranger." [4]Rav Yehudah said: Even between a house and the upper story.

[5]"And his stranger." [6]Rav Yehudah said: Even between a fixed stove and a portable stove.

[7]"Do not recognize persons in judgment." [8]Rabbi Yehudah says: Do not favor him. [9]Rabbi Eliezer says: Do not treat him as a stranger.

TRANSLATION AND COMMENTARY

וּשְׁפַטְתֶּם צֶדֶק [1]The Gemara now continues its interpretation of the verse cited above: "And I commanded your judges at that time, saying: Hear the causes between your brethren, **and judge righteously** between every man and his brother, and his stranger." [2]**Resh Lakish said:** The phrase, "And judge righteously," teaches that a judge must first be able to **justify the judgment** to himself, and be absolutely certain, **and** only **afterwards** should he **announce his decision.**

בֵּין אִישׁ וּבֵין אָחִיו וּבֵין גֵּרוֹ [3]The verse continues: **"Between a man and his brother, and his stranger."** [4]**Rav Yehudah said:** We learn from here that **even** if the dispute **between** the two litigants concerns only a small amount of money, for instance if two brothers disagree over how to divide an estate that they have inherited, who is to receive the main floor of **the house and** who is to receive **the upper story, the** judge must give the case as careful consideration as if it were a dispute involving a great deal of money.

וּבֵין גֵּרוֹ [5]The verse concludes: **"And his stranger."** [6]**Rav Yehudah said:** The word גֵּרוֹ, translated here as "his stranger," can also be understood to mean "household." **Even** if the dispute **between** the two brothers relates to such matters as the question of who is to receive **the fixed stove and** who is to receive **the portable stove,** the judge must treat the matter as if it were a major case.

לֹא תַכִּירוּ פָנִים בַּמִּשְׁפָּט [7]The Gemara now proceeds to the next verse which, also deals with judges and judicial conduct. The verse states (Deuteronomy 1:17): **"Do not recognize persons in judgment, but** hear the small as well as the great; do not be afraid of the face of any man, for the judgment is God's. And the cause that is too hard for you, bring it to me, and I will hear it." [8]**Rabbi Yehudah says:** The phrase, "do not recognize persons in judgment," admonishes the judge that if one of the litigants is a personal friend, **he should not show him favor** during the hearing. [9]**Rabbi Eliezer says:** The phrase teaches that if one of the litigants is a personal enemy, the judge **should not** display his animosity toward the litigant but **treat him as a stranger.** A judge may not display his feelings toward either party.

RASHI

בין איש ובין אחיו – שנפלה להם בית בירושה, אל תאמר: טול אתה בית ואחיך עליה, – ומה בכך? הרי לכל אחד יש לו דירה! אלא העלה אותן בדמים, והשוה חלוקתן על ידי מעות. **בין גרו** – לשון מגור, תשמישי דירה, אל תאמר יטול זה תנור וזה כירה, שהרי תנור עודף על הכירה וצריך להוסיף דמים. **לא תכירהו** – אם הוא אוהבך. **לא תנכרהו** – אם הוא שונאך לא תעשה לו כנכרי לחייבו.

NOTES

צַדֵּק אֶת הַדִּין **Justify the judgment.** Our commentary follows *Rambam* (*Hilkhot Sanhedrin* 21:9), who writes that the judge must first justify his decision in his heart, and only afterwards should he announce his ruling. Similarly, *Rashash* writes: If a judge has a Halakhic question regarding a certain accepted ruling, he should not decide a case brought before him on the basis of that ruling, but rather he should first resolve his difficulty, and only then should he decide on the matter brought before him for adjudication. *Maharsha* understands this regulation in an entirely different manner: At the outset, the judge should seek a judgment which involves charity (צְדַק אֶת הַדִּין), meaning that he should propose a compromise. But if the parties do not want to compromise, and the judge has heard all their arguments and knows in whose favor he plans to rule, he must decide the case strictly according to the laws governing the dispute.

בֵּין בַּיִת לַעֲלִיָּיה **Between a house and the upper story.** Some say the verse teaches that a judge must be thoroughly familiar with the law, so that he knows the difference in value between the main floor of a house and its upper story, and that he knows how close to a wall

HALAKHAH

אֲפִילּוּ בֵּין בַּיִת לַעֲלִיָּיה **Even between a house and the upper story.** "A judge must relate to a case involving a perutah in the same manner as he relates to a case involving a hundred maneh." (*Shulḥan Arukh, Ḥoshen Mishpat* 10:4.)

TRANSLATION AND COMMENTARY

אוֹשְׁפִּיזְכָנֵיהּ דְּרַב [1]It was related that **Rav's innkeeper** once **came before him for a judgment.** [2]Rav **said to him: "Are you not my innkeeper?"** [3]The innkeeper **answered: "Yes,** indeed I am." [4]The innkeeper then **said to** Rav: **"I have a** case which requires **adjudication,** and I want you to be the judge." [5]Rav **answered:** [8A] **"I am disqualified** from rendering **judgment** in **your** case, because of our relationship outside the courtroom." [6]**Rav said to Rav Kahana: "Go and adjudicate** the case." [7]When Rav Kahana **saw that** the innkeeper **was** acting in an **arrogant** manner, thinking that he would receive special treatment because of his connection to Rav, [8]**he said to him: "If you obey, obey.** [9]**And if not, I will take Rav out of your ears,"** meaning that he would punish the innkeeper until he had forgotten that he ever knew Rav.

כַּקָּטֹן כַּגָּדֹל תִּשְׁמָעוּן [10]The verse cited above (Deuteronomy 1:17) continues: **"Hear the small as well as the great."** [11]**Resh Lakish said:** This clause admonishes the judge **that a case involving a perutah should be as dear to him as a case involving a hundred maneh.**

[1]אוֹשְׁפִּיזְכָנֵיהּ דְּרַב אֲתָא לְקַמֵּיהּ לְדִינָא. [2]אֲמַר לוֹ: "לָאו אוֹשְׁפִּיזְכָנִי אַתְּ"? [3]אֲמַר לוֹ: "אִין". [4]אֲמַר לֵיהּ: "דִּינָא אִית לִי". [5]אֲמַר לֵיהּ: [8A] פְּסִילְנָא לָךְ לְדִינָא. [6]אֲמַר לֵיהּ רַב לְרַב כָּהֲנָא: "פּוּק דַּיְינֵיהּ". [7]חַזְיֵיהּ דַּהֲוָה קָא גָּאֵיס בֵּיהּ, [8]אֲמַר לֵיהּ: "אִי צָיְיתַתְּ, צָיְיתַתְּ. [9]וְאִי לָא, מַפִּיקְנָא לָךְ רַב מֵאוּנָךְ". [10]"כַּקָּטֹן כַּגָּדֹל תִּשְׁמָעוּן". [11]אָמַר רֵישׁ לָקִישׁ: שֶׁיְּהֵא חָבִיב עָלֶיךָ דִּין שֶׁל פְּרוּטָה, כְּדִין שֶׁל מֵאָה מָנֶה.

LITERAL TRANSLATION

[1]Rav's innkeeper came before him for a judgment. [2]He said to him: "Are you not my innkeeper?" [3]He said to him: "Yes." [4]He said to him: "I have a judgment." [5]He said to him: [8A] "I am disqualified [from rendering] judgment to you." [6]Rav said to Rav Kahana: "Go out [and] judge him." [7]He saw that he was arrogant [to him], [8][and] said to him: "If you obey, obey. [9]And if not, I will take Rav out of your ears." [10]"Hear the small as well as the great." [11]Resh Lakish said: That a judgment regarding a perutah should be as dear to you as a judgment regarding a hundred maneh.

RASHI

אמר ליה — ההוא גברא לרב. **ולאו אושפיזכני את** — כלומר אין אתה זכור שעשיתי עמך חסד? **אמר ליה** — רב: אין. **אמר ליה ההוא גברא דינא אית לי** — ורוצה אני שתהא דיין. **פסילנא לך** — שהזכרתני טובתך. **חזייה** — רב כהנא לההוא גברא. **דהוה גאיס ביה** — ברב, סומך ובוטח עליו ומדבר גבוהות. **מפיקנא לך רב מאונך** — אודיעך שאין רב יכול לסייעך, דמשמתינא לך.

LANGUAGE

אוֹשְׁפִּיזְכָנֵיהּ Innkeeper. The source of this word is the Middle Persian *aspanj,* meaning "an inn," and the word means "an innkeeper," "a host."

BACKGROUND

גָּאֵיס בֵּיהּ He was arrogant. According to *Rashi,* this means that he depended upon him, believing that Rav sided with him. Accordingly, the word גִּיס means "side." However, the word גָּאֵיס could be related to גַּסּוּת, meaning coarseness or arrogance, for it was clear from his words that he was contemptuous of Rav Kahana. Thus, the word could mean, "his heart was coarse toward," "he behaved coarsely toward" — i.e., that he felt he was closely associated to him and therefore had no shame.

REALIA

פְּרוּטָה וּמֵאָה מָנֶה A perutah and a hundred maneh. The perutah was the smallest coin in circulation among the Jews in antiquity. A dinar was worth one hundred and ninety-two perutot. A maneh was worth one hundred dinarim. Therefore one hundred manehs are worth approximately two million perutot.

Perutah

Maneh

NOTES

a person is permitted to place his stove (*Rabbenu Ḥananel, Arukh*). *Maharsha* explains that the verse admonishes the judge to judge righteously between "a man," i.e., someone of more advanced age, "and his brother," a younger sibling. He may not rule that when their father's estate is divided between them, the older son with the larger family should receive the main floor of the house and the larger — fixed — stove, and the younger brother with the smaller family should receive the upper story and the smaller — portable — stove. Instead, all the property must be assessed in value and divided equally between the two. Others suggest that the verse teaches that even when the dispute revolves around the question of who is to receive the main floor of the house and who the upper story, the judge must listen carefully to the arguments put forward by each of the parties, and not say that the issues are clear to him even without hearing the parties out (*Iyyun Ya'akov*).

מַפִּיקְנָא לָךְ רַב מֵאוּנָךְ I will take Rav out of your ears. Here and elsewhere *Rashi* and *Tosafot* explain this phrase as a threat of excommunication. The word אוּנָךְ can be understood as "your ears" — Rav Kahana threatened the innkeeper that he would take Rav out of his ears, meaning that he would excommunicate him, which would terminate all communication between him and Rav. Alternatively, the word אוּנָךְ can be understood as "your power" (see *Baḥ*'s emendation of *Rashi*) — Rav Kahana

HALAKHAH

פְּסִילְנָא לָךְ לְדִינָא I am disqualified with respect to you for judgment. "If the plaintiff sent the judge a gift before the judge summoned the defendant to appear before him, the defendant cannot disqualify the judge from hearing the case. As an act of piety, however, the judge may step down from the case, if he thinks that the gift has made him partial to one of the litigants." (*Shulḥan Arukh, Ḥoshen Mishpat* 9:2.)

פּוּק דַּיְינֵיהּ Go out and judge him. "Even if the members of a court are disqualified from adjudicating a certain case because of their personal feelings toward one of the litigants, they may appoint other judges to hear the case in their place" (*Rema,* following *Maharik*). (*Shulḥan Arukh, Ḥoshen Mishpat* 7:7.)

פְּרוּטָה וּמֵאָה מָנֶה A perutah and a hundred maneh. "A judge must give precedence to the case that was brought before him first (even if that case involves only a meager sum, and a case which was brought before him later involves a much larger sum)." (*Shulḥan Arukh, Ḥoshen Mishpat* 15:1.)

SAGES

רַבִּי חָמָא בְּרַבִּי חֲנִינָא Rabbi Ḥama the son of Rabbi Ḥanina. A Palestinian Amora of the second generation, Rabbi Ḥama was the son of Rabbi Ḥanina bar Ḥama. Like his father, he lived in Tzipori. He was a colleague of Rabbi Yoḥanan and Resh Lakish, and was famous for his Aggadic teachings, which are transmitted by Rabbi Levi and Rabbi Shmuel bar Natan.

רַב נַחְמָן בַּר יִצְחָק Rav Naḥman bar Yitzḥak. One of the leading Babylonian Amoraim of the fourth generation. Rav Naḥman bar Yitzḥak was born in Sura. His mother was the sister of Rav Aḥa bar Yosef. His principal teacher was Rav Naḥman bar Ya'akov, but he also studied under Rav Ḥisda. After the death of Rava, Rav Naḥman bar Yitzḥak was appointed head of the Pumbedita Yeshivah.

TRANSLATION AND COMMENTARY

לְמַאי הִלְכְתָא [1]The Gemara asks: **Regarding which law** was this said? [2]**If you say** that the verse teaches that a judge must **consider** a minor case **and issue a ruling about it** just as scrupulously as he would deal with a major case, [3]**this is obvious,** for an unjust ruling regarding a perutah is also a perversion of justice! [4]**Rather,** the verse comes to teach that if a case involving a perutah comes before a judge for adjudication, and then a second case involving a hundred maneh comes before him, the judge must **give** the first case **precedence** over the second, regardless of the sums involved.

לֹא תָגוּרוּ מִפְּנֵי אִישׁ [5]The verse continues: **"Do not be afraid of any man."** [6]**Rabbi Ḥanan said:** This part of the verse is directed at the judges, issuing a clear instruction: **Do not withhold your arguments** and leave them hidden inside you **because of any man.**

כִּי הַמִּשְׁפָּט לֵאלֹהִים הוּא [7]The same verse continues: **"For the judgment is God's."** [8]**Rabbi Ḥama the son of Rabbi Ḥanina said: The Holy One, blessed be He, said:** [9]**It is not enough that the wicked take money from** its rightful owner **and illegally give it to someone else.** [10]**But they** even **trouble Me to return the money** in question **to its rightful owner.** This is the meaning of the verse: "For the judgment is God's." If a judge issues an improper ruling, it is as though he has exacted money from God Himself. And God must now return the money to its rightful owner.

וְהַדָּבָר אֲשֶׁר יִקְשֶׁה מִכֶּם [11]The next part of the verse states: **"And the cause that is too hard for you,** bring it to me, and I will hear it." [12]**Rabbi Ḥanina said (and some say** that it was **Rabbi Yoshiyah** who said this): **For this** arrogant remark **Moses** our master **was punished.** He received his punishment when the daughters of Zelophehad asked him about their right to an inheritance, and he was unable to rule on the matter, for he had not been taught the law, [13]**as it is said** (Numbers 27:5): **"And Moses brought their cause before the Lord."**

מַתְקִיף לָהּ [14]Rav Naḥman bar Yitzḥak strongly objected to this assessment of Moses' remark: **Does the verse state: "And I will let you hear,"** meaning that I will always have ready answers? [15]Rather, **the verse states: "And I will hear it"!** You will bring me your questions, [16]and **if I** have **learned** the matter, I will share with you what **I learned.** [17]**And if** I do **not** know the answer, **I will go and learn the** answer from God! Thus, there was no arrogance here on Moses' part.

[1]לְמַאי הִלְכְתָא? [2]אִילֵימָא לְעִיּוּנֵי בֵּיהּ וּמִיפְסְקֵיהּ, [3]פְּשִׁיטָא! [4]אֶלָּא, לְאַקְדּוּמֵיהּ.

[5]״לֹא תָגוּרוּ מִפְּנֵי אִישׁ״. [6]אָמַר רַבִּי חָנָן: אַל תַּכְנִיס דְּבָרֶיךָ מִפְּנֵי אִישׁ.

[7]״כִּי הַמִּשְׁפָּט לֵאלֹהִים הוּא״. [8]אָמַר רַבִּי חָמָא בְּרַבִּי חֲנִינָא: אָמַר הַקָּדוֹשׁ בָּרוּךְ הוּא: [9]לֹא דַּיָּין לָרְשָׁעִים שֶׁנּוֹטְלִין מִזֶּה מָמוֹן וְנוֹתְנִים לָזֶה שֶׁלֹּא כַּדִּין, [10]אֶלָּא שֶׁמַּטְרִיחִין אוֹתִי לְהַחֲזִיר מָמוֹן לִבְעָלָיו.

[11]״וְהַדָּבָר אֲשֶׁר יִקְשֶׁה מִכֶּם״. [12]אָמַר רַבִּי חֲנִינָא וְאִיתֵימָא רַבִּי יֹאשִׁיָּה: עַל דָּבָר זֶה נֶעֱנַשׁ מֹשֶׁה, [13]שֶׁנֶּאֱמַר: ״וַיַּקְרֵב מֹשֶׁה אֶת מִשְׁפָּטָן לִפְנֵי ה׳״.

[14]מַתְקִיף לָהּ רַב נַחְמָן בַּר יִצְחָק: [15]מִי כְּתִיב ״וְאַשְׁמִיעֲכֶם״? [16]״וּשְׁמַעְתִּיו״ כְּתִיב: אִי גְּמִירְנָא, גְּמִירְנָא. [17]וְאִי לָא, אָזְלִינָא וְגָמֵירְנָא!

LITERAL TRANSLATION

[1]For which law? [2]If you say to consider it and rule about it, [3]this is obvious. [4]Rather, to give it precedence.

[5]"Do not be afraid of any man." [6]Rabbi Ḥanan said: Do not withhold your arguments because of any man.

[7]"For the judgment is God's." [8]Rabbi Ḥama the son of Rabbi Ḥanina said: The Holy One, blessed be He, said: [9]It is not enough that the wicked take money from this one and give it to that one unlawfully, [10]but they trouble Me to return the money to its owner.

[11]"And the cause that is too hard for you." [12]Rabbi Ḥanina said and some say Rabbi Yoshiyah: For this Moses was punished, [13]as it is said: "And Moses brought their cause before the Lord."

[14]Rav Naḥman bar Yitzḥak strongly objected: [15]Is it written: "And I will let you hear"? [16]It is written: "And I will hear it"! If I learned, I learned. [17]And if not, I will go and learn!

RASHI

אילימא לעיוני ביה ומיפסקיה — לאמיתו. **לאקדומיה** — אם בא לפניך דין של פרוטה, וחזר ובא דין אחר של מנה, הקודם לפניך — הקדם לחתוך.

"כי המשפט לאלהים הוא" — כאילו אתה דן ומוציא ממון מיד הקדוש ברוך הוא, שהרי עליו להחזיר ממון לבעליו. **על דבר זה** — שנטל שררה לעצמו, לומר "תקריבון אלי" (דברים א). שהיה לו לומר: תקריבון לפני השכינה. **נענש משה** — שלא זכה, שלא נאמר לו פרשת נחלות, עד שבא מעשה לפניו ולא ידע מה להשיב.

NOTES

warned the innkeeper that he would excommunicate him and thus remove Rav as the source of his power.

TRANSLATION AND COMMENTARY

אֶלָּא כִּדְתַנְיָא [1]**Rather,** Moses had not been taught the law that was to be applied in the case of the daughters of Zelophehad for a different reason, **as it was taught** in a Baraita: "Do not think that had the daughters of Zelophehad not asked to receive their father's inheritance in Eretz Israel, and had the gatherer of sticks not violated the Sabbath prohibitions [see Numbers 15:32-36], these laws would not have been included in the Torah. [2]For **it had been intended that the passage concerning inheritance should be written** in the Torah **through Moses our master,** [3]and it was only because **the daughters of Zelophehad were found meritorious** that the section **was written through them.** [4]**And** similarly, **it had been intended that the passage concerning the gatherer** of sticks **should be written** in the Torah **through Moses our master,** [5]and it was only because **the gatherer** of sticks **was found guilty** that the section **was written through him.** [6]This comes **to teach you that a bad thing** is brought about **through one who is guilty, and a good thing** is brought about **through a meritorious person."**

כְּתִיב [7]The Gemara presents another comment about these verses dealing with judges and judicial conduct: **The verse states** (Deuteronomy 1:16): **"And I commanded your judges at that time"** — teaching that Moses admonished the judges that it was their responsibility to impose the Torah's judicial system upon the community. [8]**And** two verses later (1:18) **it states: "And I commanded you at that time** all the things which you should do" — teaching that Moses directed his remarks at the community at large. [9]**Rabbi Elazar said in the name of Rabbi Simlai:** The two verses complement each other. **This** second verse **is a warning to the community that the fear of the judge should be upon them,** meaning that the people must accept the judge's authority. [10]**And** the first verse is **a warning to the judge that he should bear with the community** and accept all the trouble that the people cause him. [11]The Gemara asks: **How much** trouble must the judge accept? [12]**Rabbi Ḥanan said (and some say** that it was **Rabbi Shabbetai** who said this): A judge must emulate Moses, who bore with the people of Israel [13]**"as a nursing father carries the sucking child"** (Numbers 11:12).

LITERAL TRANSLATION

[1]Rather, as it was taught: [2]"It had been intended that the passage concerning inheritance should be written through Moses our master, [3]but the daughters of Zelophehad merited [it] and it was written through them. [4]It had been intended that the passage concerning the gatherer should be written through Moses our master, [5]but the gatherer was guilty and it was written through him. [6]To teach you that a bad thing is brought about through one who is guilty, and a good thing through one who is meritorious."

[7]It is written: "And I commanded your judges at that time." [8]And it is written: "And I commanded you at that time." [9]Rabbi Elazar said in the name of Rabbi Simlai: [This is] a warning to the community that the fear of the judge should be upon them, [10]and a warning to the judge that he should bear [with] the community. [11]How much? [12]Rabbi Ḥanan said and some say Rabbi Shabbetai: [13]"As a nursing father carries the sucking child."

אֶלָּא כִּדְתַנְיָא: [2]"רְאוּיָה פָּרְשַׁת נְחָלוֹת שֶׁתִּיכָּתֵב עַל יְדֵי מֹשֶׁה רַבֵּינוּ, [3]אֶלָּא שֶׁזָּכוּ בְּנוֹת צְלָפְחָד וְנִכְתַּב עַל יָדָן. [4]רְאוּיָה הָיְתָה פָּרְשַׁת מְקוֹשֵׁשׁ שֶׁתִּיכָּתֵב עַל יְדֵי מֹשֶׁה רַבֵּינוּ, [5]אֶלָּא שֶׁנִּתְחַיֵּיב מְקוֹשֵׁשׁ וְנִכְתְּבָה עַל יָדוֹ. [6]לְלַמֶּדְךָ שֶׁמְּגַלְגְּלִין חוֹבָה עַל יְדֵי חַיָּיב, וּזְכוּת עַל יְדֵי זַכַּאי".

[7]כְּתִיב: "וָאֲצַוֶּה אֶת שֹׁפְטֵיכֶם בָּעֵת הַהִיא", [8]וּכְתִיב: "וָאֲצַוֶּה אֶתְכֶם בָּעֵת הַהִיא". [9]אָמַר רַבִּי אֶלְעָזָר אָמַר רַבִּי שִׂמְלַאי: אַזְהָרָה לַצִּיבּוּר שֶׁתְּהֵא אֵימַת דַּיָּין עֲלֵיהֶן. [10]וְאַזְהָרָה לַדַּיָּין שֶׁיִּסְבּוֹל אֶת הַצִּיבּוּר. [11]עַד כַּמָּה? [12]אָמַר רַבִּי חָנָן וְאִיתֵימָא רַבִּי שַׁבְּתַאי: [13]"כַּאֲשֶׁר יִשָּׂא הָאֹמֵן אֶת הַיֹּנֵק".

RASHI

כתיב "ואצוה את שופטיכם" — משמע, את חכמיהם הזהיר להדריך ציבור במשפט והחקים על כרחם. וכתיב ואצוה אתכם — דלציבור עצמם הזהיר, ומה הוצרך להזהירן?

SAGES

רַבִּי אֶלְעָזָר (בֶּן פְּדָת) **Rabbi Elazar (ben Pedat).** One of the greatest Palestinian Amoraim, he came originally from Babylonia and studied there with Rav and Shmuel. But it seems that he immigrated to Eretz Israel as a young man, married, and became the main disciple of Rabbi Yoḥanan. The spiritual affinity between Rabbi Elazar and Rabbi Yoḥanan was so great that occasionally an objection is raised to an argument presented in the name of one of them because it conflicts with the other's teachings, since they are assumed to have adopted the same approach to Halakhah. Rabbi Elazar venerated his teacher, and Rabbi Yoḥanan said of him: "Have you seen the son of Pedat, who sits and expounds the Torah like Moses from the very mouth of the Almighty?" Rabbi Elazar was a priest. He was very poor most of his life, and his material situation apparently did not improve until his later years, when he was one of the leaders of the nation.

NOTES

שֶׁתְּהֵא אֵימַת דַּיָּין עֲלֵיהֶן **That the fear of the judge should be upon them.** The Gemara does not ask here to what extent the community must fear the judges, as it asks to what extent the judges must bear with the community. But elsewhere it is explained that "the fear of one's master should be equal to the fear of Heaven," implying that the judges' authority must be accepted unequivocally (*Iyyun Ya'akov*).

הָאֹמֵן אֶת הַיֹּנֵק **As a nursing father carries the sucking child.** *Sifrei* (to Deuteronomy 1:1) takes this verse quite

HALAKHAH

דַּיָּין וְצִיבּוּר **A judge and the community.** "A judge must bear with his community and all the trouble that they cause him, and the community is obligated to treat its judges with respect and fear." (*Shulḥan Arukh, Ḥoshen Mishpat* 8:4.)

TRANSLATION AND COMMENTARY

כְּתִיב [1]Having reconciled the discrepancy between these two verses, the Gemara now resolves a similar discrepancy found elsewhere in Scripture. One **verse states** (Deuteronomy 31:7): "And Moses called to Joshua, and said to him in the sight of all Israel: Be strong and courageous, **for you shall go** with this people to the land which the Lord has sworn to their fathers to give them." [2]**And** later in the chapter another **verse states** (31:23): "And God commanded Joshua the son of Nun, and said: Be strong and courageous, **for you shall bring** the children of Israel into the land of which I swore to them." [3]**Rabbi Yoḥanan said** that the difference between the verses can be explained as follows: **Moses said to Joshua:** "For you shall go with this people" — without imposing absolute authority over them, for the people shall enter into the land under the leadership provided by [4]**you and** the rest of **the elders of the generation.** [5]But **the Holy One, blessed be He, said to** Joshua: "For you shall bring the children of Israel." [6]**Take a stick and strike their heads** if necessary, for you are given absolute authority to bring the people into the Promised Land. [7]**There can be** only **one leader for the generation, and there cannot be two leaders for the generation,** for ultimate authority must reside in the hands of one person.

תָּנָא [8]The Gemara now resumes its clarification of our Mishnah: **A Tanna taught** a Baraita which states: **"A summons requires three."** [9]The Gemara asks: **What is meant** here **by a summons?** [10]**You might say** that the Baraita **refers to the summons to say grace** — when three or more men have eaten together, the Grace after Meals is preceded by *zimmun,* "a summons," by which the participants in the meal are asked to join together to say grace. But this is problematic, [11]**for surely it was taught** in a more detailed Baraita: **"A summons and the summons to say grace** require **three,"** implying that a summons and the summons to say grace are two different things! [12]However, **you might say** that this second Baraita **explains itself,** and that this is the way the Baraita should be understood: [13]**What is meant by a summons? The summons to say grace.** [14]But this too is problematic, **for surely it was taught in** yet another Baraita: **"A summons with three; the summons to say grace with three."** The placement of word "three" at the end of each clause implies that the Baraita is indeed teaching two separate regulations. [15]**Rather** ask, **what is meant** here **by a summons? A summons for**

[1]כְּתִיב: "כִּי אַתָּה תָּבוֹא. [2]וּכְתִיב: "כִּי אַתָּה תָּבִיא". [3]אֲמַר רַבִּי יוֹחָנָן: אָמַר לוֹ מֹשֶׁה לִיהוֹשֻׁעַ: [4]אַתָּה וְהַזְּקֵנִים שֶׁבְּדוֹר עִמָּהֶם. [5]אָמַר לוֹ הַקָּדוֹשׁ בָּרוּךְ הוּא: [6]טוֹל מַקֵּל, וְהַךְ עַל קָדְקֳדָם. [7]דַּבָּר אֶחָד לַדּוֹר, וְאֵין שְׁנֵי דַּבָּרִין לַדּוֹר. [8]תָּנָא: "זִימּוּן בִּשְׁלֹשָׁה". [9]מַאי זִימּוּן? [10]אִילֵימָא בִּרְכַּת זִימּוּן — [11]וְהָתַנְיָא: "זִימּוּן וּבִרְכַּת זִימּוּן בִּשְׁלֹשָׁה"! [12]וְכִי תֵּימָא: פָּרוֹשֵׁי קָמְפָרֵשׁ: [13]מַאי זִימּוּן? בִּרְכַּת זִימּוּן — [14]וְהָתַנְיָא: "זִימּוּן בִּשְׁלֹשָׁה, בִּרְכַּת זִימּוּן בִּשְׁלֹשָׁה"! [15]אֶלָּא: מַאי זִימּוּן?

LITERAL TRANSLATION

[1]It is written: "For you shall go." [2]And it is written: "For you shall bring." [3]Rabbi Yoḥanan said: Moses said to Joshua: [4]You and the elders of the generation among them. [5]The Holy One, blessed be He, said: [6]Take a stick and strike their heads. [7]There is one leader for the generation, and there are not two leaders for the generation.

[8][A Tanna] taught: "A summons [*zimmun*] with three." [9]What is a summons? [10]If you say [it refers to] the summons to say grace — [11]but surely it was taught: "A summons and the summons to say grace with three!" [12]And if you say: It explains: [13]What is [meant by] a summons? The summons to say grace — [14]but surely it was taught: "A summons with three; the summons to say grace with three!" [15]Rather, what is a summons?

RASHI

"כי אתה תבוא את העם" — משמע, גם אתה כאחד מהן. **כי אתה תביא** — משמע (לשון) שררה נוהג עליהן. **משה אמר לו זקנים שבדור עמהם** — על פיהם עשה מעשה, ולא תשתרר עליהם. דההוא קרא ד"כי אתה תבוא" — משה אמרו, כדכתיב ביה "אל הארץ אשר נשבע ה׳ וגו׳", ובמקרא ד"כי אתה תביא" כתיב "אל הארץ אשר נשבעתי לאבותיכם וגו׳" — אלמא דהקדוש ברוך הוא בעצמו אמרו. **דבר אחד** — מנהיג אחד.

BACKGROUND

דַּבָּר אֶחָד לַדּוֹר There is one leader for the generation. The idea is found frequently in the teaching of the Sages, that wherever leadership is required (unlike judgment, which demands scrutiny and good sense), one does not appoint two people to positions of equal status, for this causes disagreement and inefficiency. This opinion alludes to the system of government practiced in several states in ancient times, such as Rome, where there were two consuls.

NOTES

literally, for it understands that Moses later rebuked the people of Israel for what they had done in the desert, for they had brought their sucking infants to Moses and thrown them into his lap, demanding that he provide them with maintenance.

HALAKHAH

זִימּוּן בִּשְׁלֹשָׁה A summons with three. "If three people ate a meal together, the Grace after Meals must be preceded by a special blessing known as *zimmun.*" (*Shulḥan Arukh, Oraḥ Ḥayyim* 192:1.)

אַזְמוֹנֵי לְדִין. [1]כִּי הָא דַּאֲמַר רָבָא: הָנֵי בֵּי תְּלָתָא דַּיָּינֵי דְּיָתְבִי, [2]וְאָזֵיל שְׁלִיחָא דְּבֵי דִינָא וַאֲמַר מִפּוּמָּא דְּחַד, [3]לֹא אֲמַר כְּלוּם, [4]עַד דַּאֲמַר מִשְּׁמֵיהּ דְּכוּלְּהוּ. [5]הָנֵי מִילֵּי בְּלֹא יוֹמָא דְּדִינָא. [6]אֲבָל בְּיוֹמָא דְּדִינָא, לֵית לָן בָּהּ.

[7]"תַּשְׁלוּמֵי כֶּפֶל כו'". [8]שָׁלַח לֵיהּ רַב נַחְמָן בַּר רַב חִסְדָּא לְרַב נַחְמָן בַּר יַעֲקֹב: [9]יְלַמְּדֵנוּ רַבֵּינוּ: דִּינֵי קְנָסוֹת בְּכַמָּה? [10]מַאי קָמִיבַּעְיָא לֵיהּ? [11]הָא אֲנַן תְּנַן "בִּשְׁלֹשָׁה"!

[12]אֶלָּא, יָחִיד מוּמְחֶה קָמִיבַּעְיָא לֵיהּ, [13]דָּאֵין דִּינֵי קְנָסוֹת אוֹ לֹא?

LITERAL TRANSLATION

A summons to judgment. [1]As Rava said: [If] three judges convened, [2]and an officer of the court went and said in the name of one [of them], [3]he did not say anything, [4]unless he said in the name of all of them. [5]This applies (lit., "these words") when it is not a court day. [6]But on a court day, it does not matter (lit., "we have nothing in it").

[7]"Double compensation, etc." [8]Rav Naḥman bar Rav Ḥisda sent to Rav Naḥman bar Ya'akov: [9]Let our master teach us: Cases concerning fines with how many?

[10]What did he ask him? [11]Surely we learned: "By three"!

[12]Rather, he asked about a single expert judge, [13]does he adjudicate cases concerning fines or not?

TRANSLATION AND COMMENTARY

judgment. A subpoena delivered by an officer of the court must be issued in the name of three judges. [1]**As Rava said: If three judges convened, and an officer of the court went** to summon the litigant to appear before the judges, [2]**and he delivered** the summons **in the name of** only **one of** the judges, [3]**the summons is not valid.** Punitive measures may not be taken against a litigant who failed to appear on the specified date, [4]**unless** the court officer **delivered** the summons **in the name of all three of** the judges. [5]The Gemara notes: **This** only **applies if** the defendant was summoned to appear on a day that was **not** a fixed **court day.** [6]**But** if the defendant was summoned to appear **on a fixed court day, it does not matter** whether the summons was delivered in the name of three judges or only one. In any event it is clear that the litigant is being summoned to appear before a court of three.

תַּשְׁלוּמֵי כֶּפֶל [7]We learned in our Mishnah: "Cases involving the payment of **double compensation,** and fourfold and fivefold compensation are adjudicated by a court of three judges." [8]**Rav Naḥman bar Rav Ḥisda sent** the following question **to Rav Naḥman bar Ya'akov:** [9]**Let our master teach us: How many judges** are required to adjudicate **cases involving fines?** Is the number of judges required different from the number required in cases of ordinary compensation?

מַאי קָמִיבַּעְיָא לֵיהּ [10]The Gemara is astonished by this question: **What** was Rav Naḥman bar Rav Ḥisda **asking?** [11]**Surely we learned** in our Mishnah: "Cases involving the payment of double compensation, and fourfold and fivefold compensation, which are fines, are adjudicated **by** a court of **three** judges"!

אֶלָּא [12]The Gemara now explains the question: **It appears that,** Rav Naḥman bar Rav Ḥisda must have been **asking about a single judge** who was publicly recognized as an **expert** in the law, [13]**whether or not he may adjudicate cases involving fines.** Do we say that just as he may adjudicate cases involving ordinary monetary compensation (see above, 5a), so too may he adjudicate cases involving fines? Or perhaps the requirements regarding fines are stricter, and three judges are required!

RASHI

יומא דדינא – שני וחמישי תקנת עזרא היא, בבא קמא (פב,ב). **אזמוני לדינא** – בית דין ששולחין שלוחם לבעל דין, שצועקים עליו לבא ולדון לפניהם, צריך השליח להזמינו בשם שלשתן. **ואמר משמיה דחד** – פלוני דיין מזמינך – לא אמר כלום. ואי לא אזיל – לא משמתינן ליה. **דיני קנסות** – זה שמשלם יותר מדינו.

SAGES

רַב נַחְמָן בַּר יַעֲקֹב Rav Naḥman bar Ya'akov. This is the great Sage who is usually called simply Rav Naḥman. Here his father's name is indicated to distinguish between him and Rav Naḥman bar Rav Ḥisda.

HALAKHAH

אָזֵיל שְׁלִיחָא דְּבֵי דִינָא An agent of the court went. "If the defendant was summoned to appear in court, and that summons was delivered in the name of only a single judge, the defendant is not liable for excommunication if he failed to honor the summons and appear in court. He is only liable for excommunication if the summons was delivered to him in the name of three judges. This ruling applies only if the defendant was summoned to appear in court on a day that was not a fixed court day. But if he was summoned to appear on a fixed court day and did not come, he is liable for excommunication even if the summons was delivered to him in the name of only a single judge." (*Shulḥan Arukh, Ḥoshen Mishpat* 11:2.)

דִּינֵי קְנָסוֹת Cases concerning fines. "Cases involving fines can only be adjudicated by a court of three authorized judges who were formally ordained in Eretz Israel." (*Rambam, Sefer Shofetim, Hilkhot Sanhedrin* 5:8.)

SAGES

אֲבוּהּ דַּאֲבוּךְ The father of your father. It appears that the expression that should have been used here is אֲבוּךְ דְּאִמָּךְ — "your mother's father," i.e., Rav Ḥanan bar Rabbah (Abba), one of Rav's great students, who transmitted many teachings in his name. Rav Ḥanan bar Rabbah was the father-in-law of Rav Ḥisda, one of Rav's youngest students, and also transmitted to him teachings in the name of Rav.

TRANSLATION AND COMMENTARY

אֲמַר לֵיהּ [1]Rav Naḥman bar Ya'akov **said to** Rav Naḥman bar Rav Ḥisda: **We** have **already learned** the answer to your question in our Mishnah, which stated: [2]"Cases involving the payment of **double compensation, and fourfold and fivefold compensation, are** adjudicated **by** a court of **three** judges." The Gemara explains how this statement answers Rav Naḥman's question: [3]Now, **what** does the Mishnah mean here when it speaks of **three** judges? [4]**You might say** that the Mishnah means to teach that **three laymen** sit as judges in such cases. But this is problematic, [5]for **surely your grandfather said in the name of Rav:** [6]**Even ten** people, **if they are** only **laymen, are disqualified** from serving as judges **in cases involving fines.** [7]**Rather,** the Mishnah must be referring to **expert judges,** [8]**and yet** the Tanna **said** that **three** judges are required, implying that no single judge can adjudicate cases involving fines.

וַחֲכָמִים אוֹמְרִים [9]The Gemara now discusses the next clause of our Mishnah, where Rabbi Meir and the Sages disagree about the number of judges required to adjudicate a case involving a slanderer, i.e., a husband who claims that his wife was not a virgin at the time of marriage. According to Rabbi Meir, the case may be heard by a court of three judges. **The Sages** disagree and **say** that the case of **a slanderer** must be judged **by** a court of **twenty-three** judges. Now, if the husband can produce witnesses who can testify that his wife committed adultery during the period of her betrothal, even Rabbi Meir would agree that a court of twenty-three judges is required, for if the woman is found guilty, she will be liable to death by stoning, and capital cases must be heard by a court of twenty-three judges. Rather, we must be dealing with a husband who claims that his wife was not a virgin when they engaged in their first act of sexual intercourse, and so he should be entitled to divorce her without paying her her ketubah. The husband is believed when he puts forward such a claim and the wife cannot prove otherwise. Rabbi Meir maintains that the case can be heard by three judges, just like any other monetary matter. But the Sages say that the case must be tried by a court of twenty-three, because, as they explain, it may be a capital case. The Gemara assumes initially that the Sages meant that the case must be heard by a court of twenty-three, because there is a case involving a slanderer which can lead to a capital sentence, where the husband has witnesses that his wife committed adultery during the period of their betrothal. [10]Thus, the Gemara asks: **What does it matter that** there is a case involving a slanderer which can **lead to a capital sentence?** In the case under discussion, the husband does not have witnesses to testify to his wife's adultery, and so three judges should suffice to adjudicate his financial claim against his wife, that he should be allowed to divorce her without paying her her ketubah!

[1]אֲמַר לֵיהּ: תְּנִיתוּהָ: [2]"תַּשְׁלוּמֵי כֶפֶל וְתַשְׁלוּמֵי אַרְבָּעָה וַחֲמִשָּׁה בִּשְׁלֹשָׁה". [3]מַאי שְׁלֹשָׁה? [4]אִילֵימָא שְׁלֹשָׁה הֶדְיוֹטוֹת — [5]הָאֲמַר אֲבוּהּ דַּאֲבוּךְ מִשְּׁמֵיהּ דְּרַב: [6]אֲפִילּוּ עֲשָׂרָה, וְהֵן הֶדְיוֹטוֹת, פְּסוּלִין לְדִינֵי קְנָסוֹת. [7]אֶלָּא, מוּמְחִין, [8]וְקָאָמַר שְׁלֹשָׁה.

[9]"וַחֲכָמִים אוֹמְרִים: מוֹצִיא שֵׁם רַע בְּעֶשְׂרִים וּשְׁלֹשָׁה". [10]וְכִי יֵשׁ בּוֹ דִּינֵי נְפָשׁוֹת, מַאי הָוֵי?

LITERAL TRANSLATION

[1]He said to him: We [already] learned: [2]"Double compensation, and fourfold and fivefold compensation by three." [3]What is three? [4]If you say three laymen (lit., "commoners") — [5]surely the father of your father said in the name of Rav: [6]Even ten, if they are laymen, are disqualified [to judge] cases concerning fines. [7]Rather, expert judges, [8]and he said three.

[9]"And the Sages say: The slanderer by twenty-three." [10]And if it has a capital case, what of it?

RASHI

המוציא שם רע — "לא מצאתי לבתך בתולים" ובא להפסידה כתובתה ולא להרגה, שאינו מביא עדים שזינתה תחתיו. דאי אנפשות קאתי — לא אמר רבי מאיר בשלשה. **וחכמים אומרים כו'** — מפני שיש בו דיני נפשות קסלקא דעתך דהכי קאמרי, משום דאיכא מוציא שם רע דשייך ביה דיני נפשות. וכגון שמביא עדים. ובגמרא פרכינן: וכי יש בו דיני נפשות מאי הוי? השתא מיהא לאו דיני נפשות הוא, דליכא עדים!

NOTES

מוֹצִיא שֵׁם רַע The slanderer. Two lines of interpretation run through the entire passage concerning the slanderer. Our commentary follows *Rashi, Ran, Meiri* and others who understand that the slanderer in question is a husband who claims that his wife was not a virgin when they engaged in their first act of sexual intercourse, and so she must forfeit her ketubah settlement. *Rabbenu Tam, Rabbenu Ḥananel, Rabbenu Yonah, Ramah,* and others understand

HALAKHAH

מוֹצִיא שֵׁם רַע The slanderer. "The case of a slanderer must be adjudicated from the outset by a court of twenty-three, for if the husband's claim proves to be true, his wife is liable to capital punishment," following the Sages. (*Rambam, Sefer Shofetim, Hilkhot Sanhedrin* 5:3.)

[1]אָמַר עוּלָּא: בְּחוֹשְׁשִׁין לְלַעַז קָמִיפַּלְגִי. [2]רַבִּי מֵאִיר סָבַר: אֵין חוֹשְׁשִׁין לְלַעַז. [3]וְרַבָּנַן סָבְרִי: חוֹשְׁשִׁין לְלַעַז.

[4]רָבָא אָמַר: כּוּלֵּי עָלְמָא לְלַעַז לָא חָיְישִׁינַן. [5]וְהָכָא בְּחוֹשְׁשִׁין לִכְבוֹדָן שֶׁל רִאשׁוֹנִים קָמִיפַּלְגִי, [6]וְהָכָא בְּמַאי עָסְקִינַן? [7]כְּגוֹן דְּאִיכְּנִיף בֵּי עֶשְׂרִין וּתְלָתָא לְמֵידַן דִּינֵי נְפָשׁוֹת, [8]וְאִיבַּדּוּר, [9]וַאֲמַר לְהוּ: דַּיְּינוּ לִי מִיהָא דִּינֵי מָמוֹנוֹת.

LITERAL TRANSLATION

[1]Ulla said: They disagree about [whether] we are concerned about gossip. [2]Rabbi Meir maintains: We are not concerned about gossip. [3]And the Rabbis maintain: We are concerned about gossip.

[4]Rava said: All agree that we are not concerned about gossip. [5]And here they disagree about [whether] we are concerned about the honor of the first ones. [6]And here what are we dealing with? [7]Such as when twenty-three gathered to judge a capital case, [8]and they dispersed, [9]and he said to them: Judge me nevertheless regarding the monetary matter.

TRANSLATION AND COMMENTARY

אָמַר עוּלָּא [1]**Ulla said:** Rabbi Meir and the Sages **disagree about whether** or not **we are concerned about gossip,** and the question is as follows: When the court convenes to consider the husband's financial claim against his wife, that she must forfeit her ketubah settlement because she was not a virgin at the time of marriage, the matter will become the subject of public gossip, and, as a result, witnesses — who are currently unknown to the husband — might come forward and testify that the woman did indeed commit adultery while she was betrothed, making her liable to capital punishment. [2]**Rabbi Meir maintains** that **we are not concerned about** such **gossip.** [3]**And the Rabbis** disagree **and say** that **we are** indeed **concerned about gossip.** Hence the suit concerning the woman's ketubah must be brought before a court of twenty-three.

רָבָא אָמַר [4]**Rava said:** The dispute between Rabbi Meir and the Sages can be understood in a different manner. **All** — both Rabbi Meir and the Sages — **agree that we are not concerned** about **gossip.** [5]**Here** Rabbi Meir and the Sages **disagree about whether** or not **we are concerned about the honor of the first** set of judges who convened to adjudicate the case. [6]**What case are we dealing with?** [7]**Where the** husband said that he would bring witnesses to testify that his wife committed adultery while she was betrothed to him, and so **twenty-three** judges **gathered to adjudicate** what they thought would be **a capital case.** But the husband was unable to produce the witnesses, [8]**and** so the judges **dispersed,** for they were no longer needed. [9]The husband then **said to** some of the judges who remained: **"Adjudicate for me at least the monetary matter** regarding my wife's ketubah. Even though I cannot prove that my wife was guilty of adultery, I should be able to cause her to forfeit her ketubah settlement on the basis of my claim that I did not find her to be a virgin." The Sages say that in such a case we are concerned about the honor of the twenty-three judges who had gathered at the beginning to adjudicate what was thought to be a capital case. All twenty-three judges must be called back to adjudicate the monetary matter regarding the woman's ketubah. Concluding the case with only three judges might be regarded as insulting to the original twenty-three judges. Rabbi Meir disagrees and says we are not concerned that this would be considered an insult to the twenty-three judges. The matter can be decided by three judges, like any other monetary dispute.

RASHI

ורבי מאיר סבר אין חוששין ללעז — אין חוששין שמא כשיבואו לבית דין ויצא הקול, ישמעו עדים ויבואו ויעידו שזינתה תחתיו ועכשיו אין הבעל יודע בהן ותבעי עשרים ושלשה — דשמא יבא לידי דיני נפשות. **ורבנן סברי** — חוששין. **דכולי עלמא לא חיישינן ללעז** — ואם תחילת תביעתו של בעל לא בא לידון על פי עדים, אלא על ידי עצמו ולהפסידה כתובתה, מודו רבנן דבשלשה. **והכא כגון דאיכניף עשרים ושלשה** — שאמר הבעל להביא עדים שזינתה תחתיו ולא מצא. **ואיבדור** — הדיינין והלכו להם. **ואמר** — הואיל ואין לי עדים, דנו לי מיהת בשלשה דיני ממונות להפסידה כתובתה על ידי עצמו, דקיימא לן (כתובות י,א): חכמים תיקנו להם לבנות ישראל לבתולה — מאתים, ולאלמנה — מנה, והם האמינוהו להפסידה על פיו. חזקה אין אדם טורח בסעודה ומפסידה. רבי מאיר סבר, בשלשה. דאין חוששין לכבוד הראשונים, ודנין אפילו בשלשה. ורבנן סברי, חוששין לכבוד הראשונים ובעי כולהו.

SAGES

עוּלָּא **Ulla.** A Palestinian Amora of the second and third generations. Ulla was the most important of those scholars who transmitted information and Halakhic rulings from Eretz Israel to the Diaspora. He would likewise transmit the Halakhic teachings of the Babylonian scholars to their counterparts in Eretz Israel. His full name seems to have been Ulla the son of Yishmael. Ulla was one of the disciples of Rabbi Yoḥanan, and was also responsible for conveying to Babylonia the Torah rulings laid down in Eretz Israel.

It seems that Ulla made frequent journeys, and would travel from place to place teaching Torah. (For this reason Yalta, the wife of Rav Naḥman, described him as a "peddler" [*Berakhot* 51b].) In the eyes of the Babylonian scholars, Ulla was particularly important, and the scholars of the second generation of Amoraim there treated him with great respect. Thus Rav Ḥisda referred to him as "our teacher who comes from Eretz Israel," and Rav Yehudah sent his son to learn Halakhic practice from Ulla's conduct.

In the Jerusalem Talmud, in which he is generally referred to as Rabbi Ulla the son of Yishmael (or "Ulla, the traveler down to Babylonia"), Torah rulings are recorded in his name. Many scholars of the next generation were his pupils.

Of his private life we know nothing. It is possible that the Amora Rabbah the son of Ulla was his son.

We know that Ulla died in Babylonia on one of his journeys, and that he was brought back to Eretz Israel to be buried.

NOTES

that we are dealing here with the girl's father, who demands that the husband pay him the fifty-shekel fine for slandering his daughter and falsely claiming that she was not a virgin.

חוֹשְׁשִׁין לְלַעַז **We are concerned about gossip.** Following his own opinion, that we are dealing here with the claim for the fine brought by the girl's father against her husband, *Rabbenu Ḥananel* explains the question regarding gossip as follows: If the matter of the husband's fine is heard by a court of three and the husband's claim proves to be true, the case might once again become a capital case which must be heard by a court of twenty-three. Thus people might begin to gossip and say that the original three judges were not fit to judge! *Ramah* writes that the issue is as follows: If the matter of the husband's fine is heard by a court of three, his claim might prove to be true, and the case might become a capital case which must be heard by a Lesser Sanhedrin. Thus, people might begin to gossip and say that the original court of three judged a capital case.

[8B] [1]מֵיתִיבִי: [2]״וַחֲכָמִים אוֹמְרִים: תְּבָעוֹ מָמוֹן בִּשְׁלֹשָׁה. [3]תְּבָעוֹ נְפָשׁוֹת, בְּעֶשְׂרִים וּשְׁלֹשָׁה״. [4]בִּשְׁלָמָא לְרָבָא, תְּבָעוֹ מָמוֹן תְּחִלָּה, בִּשְׁלֹשָׁה. [5]תְּבָעוֹ נְפָשׁוֹת תְּחִלָּה [6]אֲפִילּוּ מָמוֹן בְּעֶשְׂרִים וּשְׁלֹשָׁה. [7]אֶלָּא לְעוּלָּא קַשְׁיָא!

[8]אָמַר רָבָא: אֲנִי וַאֲרִי שֶׁבַּחֲבוּרָה תַּרְגֵּימְנָא, [9]וּמַנּוּ — רַב חִיָּיא בַּר אָבִין: [10]הָכָא בְּמַאי עָסְקִינַן? [11]שֶׁהֵבִיא הַבַּעַל

LITERAL TRANSLATION

[8B] [1]They raised an objection: [2]"And the Sages say: If he demanded of him money, by three. [3]If he demanded capital punishment, by twenty-three." [4]Granted according to Rava, if he demanded of him money at first, by three. [5]If he demanded capital punishment at first, [6]even money is by twenty-three. [7]But according to Ulla, it is difficult!

[8]Rava said: I and the lion of the group explained, [9]and who is he — Rav Ḥiyya bar Avin: [10]What we are dealing with here? [11]If the husband brought

TRANSLATION AND COMMENTARY

מֵיתִיבִי [8B] [1]**An objection was raised** against Ulla's explanation from a Baraita which states: [2]**"And the Sages say: If** the husband **had a monetary claim** against his wife, the case may be heard **by** a court of **three** judges. [3]But **if** the husband's **claim involved capital punishment,** the case must be heard **by** a court of **twenty-three** judges." [4]The Gemara now continues: **Granted, according to Rava,** we can explain the Baraita as follows: **If** the husband claimed that his wife was not a virgin at the time of marriage, but he did not say that he had witnesses who could testify that his wife had committed adultery during the period of her betrothal to him, it follows that **from the start he had** only **a monetary claim** against her. He only wished to divorce her without paying her her ketubah, and such a case could be adjudicated **by** a court of **three** judges. [5]But **if** the husband claimed that he had witnesses to his wife's adultery, so that **from the very beginning** his **claim involved capital punishment,** and twenty-three judges gathered to hear the case, [6]then **even** if the husband was unable to produce witnesses, so that he had only a **monetary claim** against his wife (that she should forfeit her ketubah because she was not a virgin at the time of her marriage), the case would still have to be adjudicated by those **twenty-three** judges. For to decide the case with three judges would be disrespectful of those who had gathered earlier to adjudicate what they thought would be a capital case. [7]**But according to Ulla, there is a problem here.** For, according to Ulla, the Sages were concerned that if a court convened to consider the husband's monetary claim against his wife, the matter would become the subject of gossip, and witnesses might come forward and testify that she had committed adultery while she was betrothed to her husband. Thus, the Sages required twenty-three judges, not only when the husband said that he had witnesses to his wife's adultery, but even in the case where he only came with a monetary claim against her for not being a virgin. In what sort of case, then, did the Sages say that only three judges are required?

אָמַר רָבָא [8]The Gemara answers: **Rava said: I and the lion of the group** of scholars **explained** this Baraita even according to Ulla. (The Gemara adds parenthetically: [9]**And who is** this lion of the group of scholars? It is **Rav Ḥiyya bar Avin.**) [10]**Here** in the Baraita **we are dealing with** a case [11]**where the husband** first

RASHI

וחכמים אומרים תבעו ממון כו׳ — ברייתא היא. **תבעו ממון תחילה** — דלא בא לידון בעדים אלא על פיו, ולהפסידה כתובתה, מודינן דבשלשה. **תבעו נפשות תחילה** — דאמר להביא עדים. **אפילו ממון** — כגון אם לא מצא עדים, ואמר: דונו לי מיהא להפסידה כתובה, אף על פי כן בעינן עשרים ושלשה משום כבוד ראשונים. **אלא לעולא** — דאמר: רבנן ללעז חיישי שמא ישמעו עדים ויבואו, תבעו ממון בשלשה היכי משכחת לה לעולם עשרים ושלשה לרבנן בעינן, משום דחוששין ללעז!

BACKGROUND

אֲרִי שֶׁבַּחֲבוּרָה The lion of the group. This expression is a rhetorical one meaning a great person, the most important Sage. It seems that, especially in Eretz Israel, the term חֲבוּרָה — "group" — was quite well defined and referred to a group of Sages who sat together regularly in the House of Study. They served as a kind of permanent staff, unlike many other Sages who were only occasionally in contact with one another, when they met at general assemblies (יַרְחֵי כַּלָּה) for the purpose of studying Torah, and similar events.

SAGES

רַב חִיָּיא בַּר אָבִין Rav Ḥiyya bar Avin. He was an Amora in Babylonia during the third and fourth generations, and he studied with the Sages of the second and third generations of Amoraim: Rav Huna, Rav Ḥisda, and Rav Sheshet. It appears that he eventually moved to Eretz Israel and studied with the disciples of Rabbi Yoḥanan. In the Jerusalem Talmud he is called Ḥiyya bar Nun. He later returned to Babylonia in the time of Abaye and Rava, and by then he was then regarded as one of the greatest Sages of that generation.

NOTES

תְּבָעוֹ מָמוֹן If he sued him for money. There are certain difficulties according to *Rashi,* who understands that the husband claims that his wife was not a virgin, and so he should be entitled to divorce her without paying her her ketubah. However, if this is correct, the Baraita should not read: תְּבָעוֹ — "if he demanded of him," but rather: תְּבָעָה — "if he demanded of her," for the husband makes the claim against his wife. Moreover, the term תְּבִיעָה — "demand, claim," is inappropriate here, for the husband does not claim anything from his wife. Rather, he comes to free himself of the claim that his wife has against him. *Ran* explains that the expression, תְּבָעוֹ מָמוֹן, can be understood to mean: "If he demands it, i.e., money." Thus the term "demand" is appropriate, for the husband demands that the court destroy the woman's ketubah deed, so that she can no longer present him with a claim for the sum recorded therein.

אֲרִי שֶׁבַּחֲבוּרָה The lion in the group. In several places, Rava describes Rav Ḥiyya bar Avin as the "lion of the group," leading some to suggest that this expression may not be just an ordinary term of praise. The term might allude to a specific role which Rav Ḥiyya bar Avin filled, as the head of the assembly of scholars who convened biannually during the months of Elul and Adar. Thus, Rav Ḥiyya bar Avin might have been considered "the lion of the group," the leading member of those who participated in that assembly.

עֵדִים שֶׁזִּינְּתָה, [1]וְהֵבִיא הָאָב עֵדִים וְהֵזִימּוּם לְעֵדֵי הַבַּעַל. [2]בָּא לִגְבּוֹת מָמוֹן מִבַּעַל, בִּשְׁלֹשָׁה, [3]וּבִמְקוֹם נְפָשׁוֹת, בְּעֶשְׂרִים וּשְׁלֹשָׁה.
[4]אַבַּיֵי אָמַר: [5]דְּכוּלֵּי עָלְמָא חָיְישִׁינַן לְלַעַז, [6]וּמִשּׁוּם כְּבוֹדָן שֶׁל רִאשׁוֹנִים. [7]הָכָא בְּמַאי עָסְקִינַן — [8]כְּגוֹן דְּאַתְרוּ בָּהּ

LITERAL TRANSLATION

witnesses that she committed adultery, [1]and the father brought witnesses and they refuted the husband's witnesses. [2][If] he came to collect money from the husband, by three. [3]And where there is capital punishment, by twenty-three.

[4]Abaye said: [5]All agree that we are concerned about gossip [6]and the honor of the first ones. [7]What are we dealing with here? [8]Such as if they warned her

TRANSLATION AND COMMENTARY

brought a set of **witnesses** who testified **that** his wife had **committed adultery** during the period of her betrothal, so that she is liable to death by stoning, [1]**and** then his wife's **father brought** a second set of **witnesses, who refuted** the testimony of **the husband's witnesses** by testifying that they had been elsewhere when the incident about which they had testified had supposedly occurred. In such a case, if the testimony of the second pair of witnesses is accepted, that of the first pair is rejected. Furthermore, they are liable to the penalty that they had sought to inflict on the defendant by their testimony. Once it is established that the husband brought false witnesses, his claim that his wife was not a virgin is disbelieved. The husband is forbidden to divorce his wife, and he must pay her father a fine of one hundred shekels. The monetary claim the Baraita refers to is the claim that the father can now make against the husband. According to this, the meaning of the Baraita is as follows: [2]If the woman's father **came to collect** this **money from the husband,** the case is adjudicated **by** a court of **three** judges. Even Ulla agrees that in such a case there is no concern that, as a result of the first hearing, other witnesses might still come forward and testify that the woman had committed adultery, for the husband's case was based on the testimony of false witnesses. [3]**But wherever there is** a possibility that the hearing might lead to a sentence of **death,** for instance if the husband came to court claiming that his wife should forfeit her ketubah payment because she was not a virgin at the time of their marriage, the case must be heard **by** a court of **twenty-three** judges.

אַבַּיֵי אָמַר [4]**Abaye** offered another interpretation of the dispute between Rabbi Meir and the Sages, and **said:** The disagreement between Rabbi Meir and the Sages should be understood as follows: [5]**All** — both Rabbi Meir and the Sages — **agree** that if the husband brought a monetary claim against his wife, that she must forfeit her ketubah payment because she was not a virgin when she married, the case must be heard by a court of twenty-three judges, for **we are concerned** that the **gossip** generated by the hearing might cause witnesses to come forward and testify about the woman's adultery, turning the matter into a capital case. [6]**And** both Rabbi Meir and the Sages also agree that if the hearing started with twenty-three judges, it must conclude with the same number of judges, even if it was reduced from a capital offense to a monetary claim, for we are concerned about **the honor of the first** set of judges who convened to adjudicate the case. [7]**Here**, in the Mishnah, **we are dealing with a** case **where** the husband brought witnesses at the very outset to testify about his wife's adultery, [8]and they testified before a court of three judges that **they had warned** the woman immediately prior to her transgression that adultery was against the law, and that if she violated the prohibition, she would be liable

RASHI

והזימום — דתו ליכא למיחש ללעז, דאיגלי מילתא דאהני סהדי סמיך, והני סהדי שקרי נינהו, ואפילו להפסידה כתובתה לא מיהמני, דהשתא בתר סהדי שקרי קא מהדר ושקורי קמשקר, ובעי למיתב מאה סלע לאב, ולו תהיה לאשה. ותבעו ממון דקאמרי רבנן, אתביעת מאה סלע שהאב תובע קאי, והכי קאמר: בא האב לגבות ממון מבעל שנמצא כבר שקרן — בשלשה, דהזמנה אחריתי היא, ואפילו כבוד ראשונים ליכא למימר הכא, דדינא אחרינא הוא, דמעיקרא — בעל הוה תובע, והשתא — אב קא תבע. **ובמקום דאיכא דיני נפשות** — כלומר וכל היכא דאיכא למיחש לנפשות, כגון בתחילת הדין אפילו אין לו עדים, יש לחוש שמא ישמעו ויבואו עדים — עשרים ושלשה בעי, ואית דמפרשי: כל תביעת ממון דהא שמעתתא — אמאה כסף דאב תבע לבעל, ואי אפשר לומר כן, דהא לא מחייב בעל מאה סלעים אלא אם כן הביא עדים והוזמו, דכל זמן שלא הביא עדים נאמן אף להפסידה כתובה כדפרישית לעיל, ואי בשהוזמו עדיו איירי מתניתין, תו ליכא למימר חוששין ללעז ועוד: מדגרסינן בתירוצא דרב חייא בר אבין, בא לגבות ממון מבעל, דפריש דר׳ חייא להאי תבעו ממון — אמאה סלע, מכלל דעד השתא הוה שמעינן תבעו ממון — אבעל, ואיהו תבע להפסיד כתובה. **אביי אמר** — אי בשלא הביא עדים דכולי עלמא חוששין ללעז ובעינן עשרים ושלשה, דילמא שמעי סהדי ואתו, ומדבעינן עשרים ושלשה ברישא, אפילו ממון בעשרים ושלשה, דחוששין לכבודן של ראשונים, והכא בפלוגתא דמתניתין כגון שהביא עדים בתחילת הזמנתו לדין, דתו ליכא למיחש סהדי אחריני, והני אמרי באפי תלתא דהתרו בה מיתה סתם, ולא הזכירו לה סקילה כדין נערה המאורסה, רבי מאיר סבר: תו ליכא הכא דיני נפשות, ובהני שלשה סגי למידן דיני ממונות דכתובה, דכי נמי יוזמו — ישלם מאה כסף, ורבנן סברי: כיון דאתרו בה מיתה, דיני נפשות איכא ומיקטלא, והאי תנא הוא וכו׳, וברייתא דקתני לרבנן תבעו ממון — בשלשה, כדתרצה רב חייא בר אבין.

סְתָם. [1]וְהַאי תַּנָּא הוּא, [2]דְּתַנְיָא: ״וּשְׁאָר כָּל חַיָּיבֵי מִיתוֹת שֶׁבַּתּוֹרָה אֵין מְמִיתִין אוֹתָם אֶלָּא בְּעֵדָה, וְעֵדִים, וְהַתְרָאָה, [3]וְעַד שֶׁיּוֹדִיעוּהוּ שֶׁהוּא חַיָּיב מִיתָה בְּבֵית דִּין. [4]רַבִּי יְהוּדָה אוֹמֵר: עַד שֶׁיּוֹדִיעוּהוּ בְּאֵיזֶה מִיתָה הוּא נֶהֱרָג״.

[5]רַב פַּפָּא אָמַר: [6]הָכָא בְּאִשָּׁה חֲבֵירָה עָסְקִינַן. [7]וְקָמִיפַּלְגִי בִּפְלוּגְתָּא דְּרַבִּי יוֹסֵי בַּר יְהוּדָה וְרַבָּנַן. [8]דְּתַנְיָא: ״רַבִּי יוֹסֵי בַּר יְהוּדָה אוֹמֵר: [9]חָבֵר אֵין צָרִיךְ

LITERAL TRANSLATION

without specifying. [1]And it is this Tanna, [2]for it was taught: "And the rest of those who are liable to capital punishment in the Torah we do not execute them without a congregation, and witnesses, and a warning, [3]and unless they inform him that he is liable to execution by the court. [4]Rabbi Yehudah says: Unless they inform him by which [form of] execution he will be executed."

[5]Rav Pappa said: [6]Here we are dealing with a scholarly woman. [7]And they argue about the [matter in] dispute between Rabbi Yose bar Yehudah and the Sages. [8]For it was taught: "Rabbi Yose bar Yehudah says: [9]A scholar does not need

TRANSLATION AND COMMENTARY

to the death penalty, but they **did not specify** the method of execution to which she would be liable — death by stoning. According to Rabbi Meir, the case may continue to be heard by a court of three judges, for it is no longer a capital case, while according to the Sages twenty-three judges must decide the case, for the woman is liable to the death penalty. [1]And they disagree about the matter that was in dispute between **the following Tannaim,** [2]**for it was taught** in a Baraita: **"And** as for **the rest of those who are liable to capital punishment by Torah law, the death sentence may not be imposed unless** the defendant has been judged by a court consisting of **a congregation** of twenty-three judges, and unless testimony to the offense was submitted by two qualified **witnesses,** [3]and unless **a warning** was given to the defendant immediately prior to his transgression that the act he was about to commit was unlawful, **and unless the** witnesses **informed** the defendant at that time **that he would be liable to execution by the court.** [4]**Rabbi Yehudah says:** The death sentence may not be imposed **unless the** witnesses **had** also **informed** the defendant prior to his transgression **by which form of execution he would be executed** in the event that he was found guilty — stoning, burning, slaying or strangling." Rabbi Meir agrees with Rabbi Yehudah. The death sentence cannot be imposed unless the woman was specifically warned that she would be executed by stoning. Thus, only three judges are required to adjudicate the matter of the woman's ketubah payment. And the Sages agree with the anonymous first Tanna of the Baraita that a person can be put to death for a capital offense even if he had not been informed prior to his transgression exactly how he would be executed. Thus, the woman's case must be heard by a court of twenty-three judges.

רַב פַּפָּא אָמַר [5]**Rav Pappa said:** The disagreement between Rabbi Meir and the Sages can be understood in a slightly different manner. [6]**Here,** in the Mishnah, **we are dealing with** witnesses who testified before a court of three judges that they did not warn the wife against violating the prohibition because she was **a scholarly woman** who was thoroughly familiar with the law. Rabbi Meir and the Sages disagree about whether the case as it stands is a capital case. [7]**They argue about** the same **matter** that is **in dispute between Rabbi Yose bar Yehudah and the Sages,** [8]**for it was taught** in a Baraita: **"Rabbi Yose bar Yehudah says:** [9]**A scholar need not** receive **a warning** prior to his violation of a prohibition in order to be liable to punishment,

RASHI

ושאר כל חייבי מיתות כו׳ — גבי מסית קאי, דרחמנא אמר (דברים יג): ״לא תחמול ולא תכסה״ ונהרג בלי התראה על ידי הכמנת עדים. **עדה** — עשרים ושלשה. **ועד שיודיעוהו** — עדיו בשעת התראה שהוא חייב מיתה בבית דין אם יעבור עבירה זו, ומיהו אף על גב דלא מזכרי ליה איזו מיתה, התראה היא — ומחייב, כרבנן. **רב פפא** — כדאביי נמי סבירא ליה דחוששין ללעז ולכבודן של ראשונים, והכא דאמר רבי מאיר בשלשה, כגון שהביא עדים עמו בתחלת הזמנתו לדין, ואמרו שלא התרו בה לפי שהאשה חבירה היא ולא הוצרכנו להתרות בה, רבי מאיר סבר, אף על גב דחבירה היא לא מיקטלא, הלכך לא צריכין לאיכנופי תו עשרים ושלשה, אלא שלשה לדון דיני ממונות דכתובה, ורבנן סברי: כרבי יוסי ברבי יהודה.

SAGES

רַבִּי יוֹסֵי בַּר יְהוּדָה **Rabbi Yose bar Yehudah.** He was a Tanna of the last generation and is generally called Rabbi Yose the son of Rabbi Yehudah. He was the son of the Tanna Rabbi Yehudah bar Il'ai and apparently studied mainly with his father. Rabbi Yose the son of Rabbi Yehudah was a colleague of Rabbi Yehudah HaNasi's, and we find discussions between them on many subjects. His teachings are cited in the Mishnah and in Baraitot.

CONCEPTS

הַתְרָאָה **Warning.** In Torah law, corporal punishment and especially the death sentence cannot be imposed unless guilt has been proven beyond all doubt. The testimony of two witnesses is not sufficient to establish this. The transgressor has to have been warned, the principle being, "We do not punish unless we have warned." One must inform the transgressor that he is about to commit a transgression, and the witnesses must hear the warning. The gravity of the offense must also be explained. Otherwise it cannot be ascertained that the transgressor committed his crime intentionally and in full knowledge of the gravity of what he was about to commit.

חָבֵר **An associate, a colleague.** In the Talmudic period, this referred to a person who became a member of a group dedicated to the precise observance of mitzvot. A person who wished to enter such a society had formally to accept its practices in the presence of three other members. The main stress of these groups was the strict observance of the laws of terumah and tithes and careful adherence to ritual purity, so much so that they would eat even nonsacred food (*hullin*) in a state of ritual purity. In practice, all Torah scholars were *haverim*. However, many of the common people and even some Samaritans were included in this category. Acceptance as a *haver* removed an individual from the category of a "common, uneducated person" (*am ha'aretz*), and his statements regarding tithes and ritual purity were

HALAKHAH

שְׁאָר כָּל חַיָּיבֵי מִיתוֹת **The rest of those who are liable for capital punishment.** "The case of a person suspected of incitement to idolatry is not judged in the same manner as other capital cases. The court may intentionally hide witnesses in order to apprehend the offender, who — unlike all other offenders who are liable to be sentenced to death — does not have to receive a warning prior to his violation of the prohibition." (*Rambam, Sefer Shofetim, Hilkhot Sanhedrin* 11:5.)

חָבֵר אֵין צָרִיךְ הַתְרָאָה **A scholar does not need a warning.** "A scholar, as much as an ignorant person, needs to receive a warning prior to his violation of a prohibition in order to be liable for punishment," following the Sages against Rabbi Yose bar Yehudah. (*Rambam, Sefer Shofetim, Hilkhot Sanhedrin* 12:2.)

הַתְרָאָה, [1]לְפִי שֶׁלֹּא נִיתְּנָה הַתְרָאָה אֶלָּא לְהַבְחִין בֵּין שׁוֹגֵג לְמֵזִיד״.

[2]רַב אַשִׁי אָמַר: [3]כְּגוֹן [9A] דְּאַתְרוּ בֵּיהּ מַלְקוֹת, [4]וְלָא אַתְרוּ בֵּיהּ קְטָלָא. [5]וְקָמִיפַּלְגִי בִּפְלוּגְתָּא דְּרַבִּי יִשְׁמָעֵאל וְרַבָּנַן, [6]דִּתְנַן: מַכּוֹת בִּשְׁלֹשָׁה. [7]מִשּׁוּם רַבִּי יִשְׁמָעֵאל אָמְרוּ: בְּעֶשְׂרִים וּשְׁלֹשָׁה.

LITERAL TRANSLATION

a warning, [1]for a warning was only given to distinguish between the unintentional and the intentional [offender]."

[2]Rav Ashi said: [3]Where [9A] they warned her for lashes, [4]but they did not warn her for execution. [5]And they disagree about the [matter in] dispute between Rabbi Yishmael and the Sages. [6]For we have learned: "Lashes by three. [7]In the name of Rabbi Yishmael they said: By twenty-three."

TRANSLATION AND COMMENTARY

[1]**for** the obligation of **warning** the offender **was only imposed in order to** enable the court to **distinguish between the unintentional** offender who is ignorant of the law, **and the intentional offender.** Halakhah recognizes ignorance of the law as a valid defense, and so unless a person is warned immediately prior to his transgression that he is about to violate a prohibition, he can later claim that he had acted under the mistaken belief that his behavior was permitted. But a Torah scholar cannot present such a claim, for surely he is familiar with the law, and so he is subject to punishment even if he had not been warned prior to his transgression." The Sages of our Mishnah agree with Rabbi Yose bar Yehudah that a scholar is subject to punishment even if he or she did not receive any warning. Thus, if witnesses told the court that they saw a scholarly woman committing adultery, but they did not warn her that adultery was against the law, the death sentence can still be imposed, and so a court of twenty-three judges is required to hear the case. And Rabbi Meir agrees with the Sages who disagree with Rabbi Yose bar Yehudah and say that a warning is required in all cases, even where the defendant is a scholarly person. Thus, if the witnesses say that they did not warn the scholarly woman against committing adultery, she is not liable to any punishment, and so only three judges are needed to adjudicate the matter of her ketubah payment.

רַב אַשִׁי אָמַר [2]**Rav Ashi said:** The disagreement between Rabbi Meir and the Sages can be understood in yet another manner. [3]Here, in the Mishnah, we are dealing with a case **where** [9A] the husband brought witnesses to his wife's adultery who testified that **they had warned her** that if she committed the transgression, she was liable **to be lashed,** [4]**but they did not warn her** that she was liable **to be executed.** All Tannaim agree that the case as it stands is not a capital case, for a defendant cannot be executed unless he or she has been warned prior to committing the transgression that the offense is punishable by death. And all also agree that if a person violated a prohibition which, if all the necessary conditions were fulfilled, was punishable by death, but the person had only been warned that he or she would be liable to lashes, the punishment is indeed lashes. Thus, if the woman is found guilty of adultery, she will be liable to lashes. [5]**And** Rabbi Meir and the Sages **disagree about** how many judges are required to adjudicate a case involving the punishment of lashes — **a matter** which **is in dispute between Rabbi Yishmael and the Sages.** [6]**For we have learned** in our Mishnah: "A case involving the punishment of **lashes** requires a court of **three** judges. [7]**It was said in the name of Rabbi Yishmael:** A case involving lashes must be judged **by** a court of **twenty-three** judges." Rabbi Meir agrees with the Sages of our Mishnah who say that a case which might lead to lashes

RASHI

אלא להבחין — שלא יוכל לומר: סבור הייתי שמותר. **דאתרו ביה מלקות ולא אתרו בה קטלא** — דהא ודאי לא מיקטלא, אלא לוקה, דאין לך מיתת בית דין שלא נאמר בה לאו, וקסבר: לאו שניתן לאזהרת מיתת בית דין, לוקין עליו כי אתרו בה מלקות ולא קטלא. **משום רבי ישמעאל אמרו בעשרים ושלשה** — טעמא מפרש לקמן (י,א).

accepted as true and acted upon. In later generations, the term *ḥaver* took on a more restricted meaning and was used to refer only to important scholars.

BACKGROUND

שׁוֹגֵג Intentional offender. The Halakhah recognizes ignorance of the law as a valid defense. And so, unless a person is warned immediately prior to his transgression that he is about to violate a prohibition, he can later claim that he had acted under the mistaken belief that his behavior was permitted. But a Torah scholar cannot present such an argument, for surely he is familiar with the law, and is therefore subject to punishment even if had not been warned prior to his transgression.

NOTES

לֹא נִיתְּנָה הַתְרָאָה **A warning was only given.** As it is explained in the Gemara, the obligation to warn the offender that he is violating the law was imposed in order to enable the court to distinguish between the unintentional and the intentional offender. Unless he was warned immediately prior to his offense, the transgressor can later claim that he had not known that his action was forbidden. There are two types of ignorance which can exempt a person from punishment: (1) Ignorance of the law — for example, if he did not know that a certain activity was forbidden on the Sabbath. (2) Ignorance of fact — for example, if he did not know that the day was the Sabbath. When Rabbi Yose bar Yehudah said that a Torah scholar is liable to punishment, even if he was not warned before he sinned, he was referring to the first type of ignorance. A Torah scholar cannot later claim that he did not know that the act he performed was forbidden, for surely he was thoroughly familiar with the law. But Rabbi Yose bar Yehudah agrees that even a Torah scholar can claim ignorance of the second type, and so he is only liable to punishment if he was warned about the facts of the case prior to his transgression (*Remah*).

פְּלוּגְתָּא דְּרַבִּי יִשְׁמָעֵאל וְרַבָּנַן **The matter in dispute between Rabbi Yishmael and the Sages.** It may be objected:

TRANSLATION AND COMMENTARY

can be adjudicated by a court of three. And the Sages agree with Rabbi Yishmael that such a case must be heard by a court of twenty-three judges.

רָבִינָא אָמַר [1]The Gemara presents another explanation of the disagreement between Rabbi Meir and the Sages. **Ravina said:** Here, in the Mishnah, we are dealing with a case **where** the husband brought three witnesses to testify that his wife had committed adultery during the period of her betrothal, [2]and **one of the** three **witnesses was found to be** closely **related** to the accused or to one of the other witnesses, **or** for some reason was **disqualified** from giving testimony. [3]**And** Rabbi Meir and the Sages **disagree about** whether the case as it stands is a capital case. Can the woman be convicted on the basis of the testimony of the remaining two witnesses whose eligibility to give testimony had not been challenged? They argue about **the** same **matter** which is **in dispute between Rabbi Yose and the Sages,** [4]who disagreed regarding the opinion **of Rabbi Akiva.** [5]**For we have learned** elsewhere in the Mishnah (*Makkot* 5b and 6b): "The verse states [Deuteronomy 17:6]: 'At the mouth of two witnesses, or three witnesses shall he that is worthy of death be put to death.' If the accused can be convicted and executed on the basis of the testimony of two witnesses, why did the verse mention a third witness? [6]**Rabbi Akiva says:** Scripture **only came** and mentioned **the third witness** in order **to** teach that the Torah **is stringent with him and** that [7]**the law** regarding perjury **applies to him** just **as it** applies **to the** other two witnesses. You might think that since the defendant could have been convicted on the basis of the testimony of the first two witnesses, and

[1]רָבִינָא אָמַר: [2]כְּגוֹן שֶׁנִּמְצָא אֶחָד מִן הָעֵדִים קָרוֹב אוֹ פָּסוּל. [3]וְקָמִיפַּלְגִי בִּפְלוּגְתָּא דְּרַבִּי יוֹסֵי וְרַבִּי, [4]אַלִּיבָּא דְּרַבִּי עֲקִיבָא. [5]דִּתְנַן, [6]״רַבִּי עֲקִיבָא אוֹמֵר: לֹא בָּא שְׁלִישִׁי אֶלָּא לְהַחְמִיר עָלָיו, [7]לַעֲשׂוֹת דִּינוֹ כַּיּוֹצֵא בְּאֵלּוּ.

LITERAL TRANSLATION

[1]Ravina said: [2]Where one of the witnesses was found to be a relative or disqualified. [3]And they disagree about the [matter in] dispute between Rabbi Yose and the Sages, [4]according to Rabbi Akiva. [5]For we have learned: [6]"Rabbi Akiva says: The third one only came to be stringent with him, [7][and] to make his law like theirs.

RASHI

אחד מן העדים — והיו שם שלשה או ארבעה, שיכולה עדות להתקיים בשאר. **הא דרבי עקיבא** — במסכת מכות. **לא בא שלישי כו׳** — דממשמע שנאמר (דברים יט): ״על פי שנים עדים״ (יקום) כל שכן שלשה למה נאמר ״או...שלשה עדים״ — אלא להחמיר עליו, ליתן חומר בעדי שקר שלישי זה אף על פי שלא היה זה נידון על פיו למיתה שהרי בשנים שהעידו תחלה נמי היה נידון, אפילו הכי עשה הכתוב את דינו כיוצא באלו, שאם הוזמו — יהרג אף השלישי מפני שנטפל לעוברי עבירה.

BACKGROUND

נִמְצָא אֶחָד מֵהֶן קָרוֹב אוֹ פָּסוּל One of them was found to be a relative or disqualified. The basic problem here is that, since the witnesses testify as a group (for the testimony of a single witness has no legal weight), the entire group must be treated as a single entity, though there is no actual need for all of their testimony. Therefore, when a significant flaw is found in one of the witnesses, not only is his testimony rejected, but so is that of the entire group. Moreover, since all the witnesses are regarded as a single entity, they can be punished if one of them proves to be a perjurer.

SAGES

רַבִּי יוֹסֵי Rabbi Yose. This is Rabbi Yose ben Ḥalafta, one of the greatest Tannaim. He was one of the generation that lived before the completion of the Mishnah, and the imprint of his teachings is evident throughout Tannaitic literature.

His father, known as Abba Ḥalafta, was also considered one of the Sages of his generation, and his family, according to one tradition, was descended from Jehonadab the son of Rachab (see II Kings 10:15 ff.).

In addition to studying with his father, Rabbi Yose was an outstanding student of Rabbi Akiva. Rabbi Yose and his contemporaries, the other students of Rabbi Akiva (Rabbi Meir, Rabbi Yehudah, and Rabbi Shimon bar Yoḥai), formed the center of Talmudic scholarship of that entire generation. In his Halakhic method, as in his way of life, Rabbi Yose was moderate; he refrained from taking an extreme position on Halakhic issues. Because of his moderation and the logic of his teachings, the Halakhah follows him in every instance, against all his colleagues. A well-known principle in the Halakhah is that "Rabbi Yose's views are based on sound reasoning" (רַבִּי יוֹסֵי נִימוּקוֹ עִמּוֹ), and therefore the Halakhah is always in accordance with his view.

Just as Rabbi Yose was a great master of the Halakhah, so too was he famous for his

NOTES

Surely we learned in the Mishnah that the Sages require a court of twenty-three in the case of a slanderer, because "it can develop into a case of capital punishment." How, then, can it be suggested that Rabbi Meir and the Sages disagree over how many judges are required in a case involving lashes? *Remah* explains that, when the Sages said that the case of a slanderer must be heard by a court of twenty-three judges, because "it can develop into a case of capital punishment," they meant that twenty-three judges are required in that case because it can involve lashes. They referred to lashes as a case involving capital punishment, for they agreed with Rabbi Yishmael that lashes stand in the place of execution (as is explained by Rava, below, p. 10a).

לֹא בָּא שְׁלִישִׁי אֶלָּא לְהַחְמִיר עָלָיו The third one only came to be more stringent with him. In the Mishnah of tractate *Makkot* (5b), Rabbi Akiva's position appears after that of Rabbi Shimon, who said that the verse, "At the mouth of two witnesses, or three witnesses shall he that is worthy of death be put to death," teaches that, just as in the case of two witnesses, no one is punished as a false, conspiring witness unless both witnesses are found guilty of perjury, so too in the case of three witnesses, no one is liable for punishment unless all three witnesses are found to have testified falsely. The Rishonim disagree about Rabbi Akiva's position on this matter. According to *Rashi* and others, Rabbi Akiva agrees with Rabbi Shimon that none of the three witnesses can be punished for perjury unless all three are found guilty of the crime. Rabbi Akiva merely means to say that the verse does not come to tell us that, for we would have known that even without the verse. Others argue that Rabbi Akiva disagrees with Rabbi Shimon, arguing that the verse does not come to teach us the lenient approach that none of the witnesses is liable for punishment unless all three are found to have testified falsely, but rather the stringent ruling, that if all three are

HALAKHAH

נִמְצָא אֶחָד מֵהֶן קָרוֹב אוֹ פָּסוּל One of the witnesses was found to be a relative or disqualified. "If there were many witnesses to a certain event, and one of them was found to be related to the accused or otherwise disqualified from serving as a witness, the testimony of all the witnesses is invalid. This applies only if all the witnesses intended to testify, but if they did not all intend to testify, the testimony of the competent witnesses remains valid. In such a case, the witnesses are asked whether they intended from the outset to testify in court or merely to see what was happening. If all those who say that they intended from the outset to testify are competent to serve as witnesses, their testimony is valid. These regulations apply both in monetary cases and in capital cases." (*Shulḥan Arukh, Ḥoshen Mishpat* 36:1.)

"And similarly, if a deed was signed by many people, and

[1]אִם כֵּן עָנַשׁ הַכָּתוּב אֶת הַנִּיטְפָּל לְעוֹבְרֵי עֲבֵירָה כָּעוֹבְרֵי עֲבֵירָה. [2]עַל אַחַת כַּמָּה וְכַמָּה שֶׁיְּשַׁלֵּם שָׂכָר אֶת הַנִּיטְפָּל לְעוֹשֵׂה מִצְוָה כְּעוֹשֵׂה מִצְוָה. [3]וּמָה שְׁנַיִם, נִמְצָא אֶחָד מֵהֶן קָרוֹב אוֹ פָּסוּל, [4]עֵדוּתָן בְּטֵלָה, [5]אַף שְׁלֹשָׁה, נִמְצָא אֶחָד מֵהֶן קָרוֹב אוֹ פָּסוּל, [6]עֵדוּתָן בְּטֵלָה. [7]וּמִנַּיִין שֶׁאֲפִילּוּ מֵאָה? [8]תַּלְמוּד לוֹמַר: עֵדִים״.

[9]אָמַר רַבִּי יוֹסֵי: בַּמֶּה דְּבָרִים אֲמוּרִים? [10]בְּדִינֵי נְפָשׁוֹת.

LITERAL TRANSLATION

[1]If so Scripture punished the accessory to those who violate a prohibition like those who violate a prohibition. [2]All the more so will He reward the accessory to one who fulfills a commandment like one who fulfills a commandment. [3]And just as with two, if one of them was found to be related or disqualified, [4]their testimony is invalid, [5]so too with three, if one of them was found to be a relative or disqualified, [6]their testimony is invalid. [7]And from where [do we derive] that even a hundred? [8]The verse states: 'Witnesses.'"

[9]Rabbi Yose says: In what [case] are these things said? [10]In capital cases.

TRANSLATION AND COMMENTARY

so the testimony of the third witness was unncessary, the third witness should not be liable to the same punishment as the first two, if three of them were guilty of perjury. Rabbi Akiva translated this rule into a general principle: [1]**It being so,** that the third witness is also liable to the punishments reserved for false, conspiring witnesses, it may be inferred that **Scripture punishes the accessory to those who violate a prohibition** just **as** it punishes **the** principal **violators of the prohibition,** for the third witness is treated as an accessory to the main offenders — the first two witnesses whose testimony would have sufficed to convict the defendant. [2]**All the more so,** then, **will** God **reward the accessory to one who fulfills a commandment**, as He rewards **one who himself fulfills a commandment,** for the measure of God's goodness is greater than the measure of His retribution, as the verse teaches [Exodus 20:5]: 'For I the Lord your God am a jealous God, punishing the iniquity of the fathers upon the children unto the third and fourth generation of those that hate me; but showing mercy to thousands of generations of those that love me and keep my commandments.' Another regulation may be inferred from Scripture's mention of the third witness: [3]**Just** as with **two witnesses, if one of** the two **was found to be** closely **related to** the accused **or** otherwise **disqualifed** from giving testimony, [4]**their testimony is invalid,** for there is now only one qualified witness, and there must always be at least two witnesses, [5]**so too** with **three** witnesses, **if one of** the three **was found to be** closely **related** to the accused or to one of the other witnesses **or** otherwise **disqualified from** giving testimony, [6]**their testimony is invalid,** even though there are still two other competent witnesses, for the ineligibility of any one witness invalidates the evidence of the whole group of witnesses. [7]**And from where do we derive that** if there were **even a hundred witnesses** who came as a group to testify against the accused, and one of them was found to be ineligible, all of their testimony is invalid? [8]From **the verse that states:** 'At the mouth of two witnesses, or three **witnesses'** — the word 'witnesses' teaching that the same law applies no matter how many witnesses there are."

אָמַר רַבִּי יוֹסֵי [9]The later Tannaim disagree about the scope of Rabbi Akiva's ruling: **Rabbi Yose says: In which cases does this rule apply,** that the ineligibility of one witness invalidates the entire group of witnesses? [10]Only **in capital cases,** for the verse states (Numbers 35:25): "And the congregation shall deliver the slayer," teaching that in capital cases we must seek out ways to invalidate the testimony given against the accused

RASHI

קל וחומר שישלם שכר וכו׳ — דקיימא לן מדה טובה מרובה ממדת פורענות, הלכך קל וחומר הוא. **במה דברים אמורים** — דעדותן בטלה. **בדיני נפשות** — דרחמנא אמר (במדבר לה) "והצילו העדה" דמהדרינן בתר זכותא לבטל העדות, ולא יהרג לא הוא ולא הס.

piety. The Talmud tells many stories about his modesty, his humility, and his sanctity. It is related that Elijah the Prophet would reveal himself to him every day, and several conversations between him and Elijah are recorded in the Talmud. Rabbi Yose was apparently the main editor of a series of Baraitot on the history of the Jewish people known as *Seder Olam*. For many years he lived in Tzipori (Sepphoris) in Galilee, and earned his living as a leather worker.

Many of the Sages of the following generation, including Rabbi Yehudah HaNasi, the editor of the Mishnah, were his students. But the students to whom he was closest were his five sons, all of whom were Sages in their generation. The most famous of them were Rabbi Eliezer ben Rabbi Yose, one of the great masters of Aggadah, and Rabbi Yishmael ben Rabbi Yose.

BACKGROUND

בְּדִינֵי נְפָשׁוֹת Capital cases. The reason for the difference is that, in capital cases, the court is especially obliged to look for some way of finding the accused innocent. Therefore, although the flaw found in a single witness belonging to a group may be merely technical, it is sufficient to disqualify the testimony of the entire group. However, in monetary matters, where either side could be innocent or guilty, and one party's exoneration is the other party's liability, there is no imperative to take such a technical flaw into account.

NOTES

found guilty of perjury, all three are liable for punishment. But if only two of the witnesses are found guilty of perjury, they are indeed liable to punishment, even if the testimony of the third witness has not been refuted (*Ritva, Ran*). According to a third opinion (*Rabbi Yitzḥak Ibn Giyyat*), Rabbi Akiva goes even further and says that if two of the witnesses are found guilty of perjury, then all three witnesses are liable to the death penalty, even if it has not been proven that the third witness testified falsely.

HALAKHAH

one of them was found to be related to one of the parties or otherwise disqualified from serving as a witness — if it is clear that they all signed as witnessess, the deed is void, but if not, the validity of the document is established through the signatures of those who are qualified to serve as witnesses." (*Shulḥan Arukh, Ḥoshen Mishpat* 45:12.)

TRANSLATION AND COMMENTARY

so that we might acquit him. [1]**But in monetary cases, the testimony is established by the other members** of the group of witnesses whose eligibility to give testimony was not challenged. [2]**Rabbi** Yehudah HaNasi disagrees and **says: Both** in **monetary cases and** in **capital cases,** if one member of a group of witnesses was disqualified from giving testimony, the evidence given by the whole group of witnesses is invalid. But Rabbi Yehudah HaNasi qualifies this ruling: [3]**And when** do we say that in capital cases the ineligibility of any one witness invalidates the evidence of the whole group of witnesses? [4]**If** the witness who was later disqualified was the one who **had warned** the offender against violating the prohibition prior to his transgression. By issuing the warning, the ineligible witness indicated that he intended to testify, and so the testimony of the entire group of witnesses is invalid. [5]**But if** the ineligible witness **did not warn** the offender against committing the transgression, [9B] the testimony of the other eligible witnesses is not invalidated, even though the disqualified person also happened to witness the transgression. [6]This must be so, otherwise **what should two brothers and a third person** who was not related to them **do if** together **they saw someone kill another person?** A person is disqualified to serve as a witness not only if he is related to the accused, but also if he is related to one of the other witnesses. But rather, it must be that a relative who witnessed a transgression, but had no intention of testifying against the offender, does not invalidate the testimony of the rest of the witnesses. Now, as for the disagreement in our Mishnah between Rabbi Meir and the Sages, we are dealing with a case where the husband brought three witnesses to testify that his wife had committed adultery during the period of her betrothal, and one of the three was disqualified. However, he had not joined with the others in warning the woman against committing the transgression. Rabbi Meir agrees with Rabbi Yose that in capital cases it makes no difference whether the relative witnessed the transgression silently or vocally warned the offender not to commit the crime. Thus, the case at hand is no longer a capital case, and the matter of the woman's ketubah can be adjudicated by a court of three. And the Sages agree with Rabbi Yehudah HaNasi that if the relative did not warn the offender against violating the prohibition, he does not invalidate the testimony of the other witnesses. Thus, the case at hand remains a capital case, and a court of twenty-three judges is required.

[1]אֲבָל בְּדִינֵי מָמוֹנוֹת, תִּתְקַיֵּים עֵדוּת בַּשְּׁאָר. [2]רַבִּי אוֹמֵר: אֶחָד דִּינֵי מָמוֹנוֹת וְאֶחָד דִּינֵי נְפָשׁוֹת. [3]וְאֵימָתַי? [4]בִּזְמַן שֶׁהִתְרוּ בָּהֶן. [5]אֲבָל בִּזְמַן שֶׁלֹּא הִתְרוּ בָּהֶן [9B] [6]מָה יַעֲשׂוּ שְׁנֵי אַחִים וְאֶחָד שֶׁרָאוּ בְּאֶחָד שֶׁהָרַג אֶת הַנֶּפֶשׁ?

LITERAL TRANSLATION

[1]But in monetary cases, the testimony is established by the others. [2]Rabbi says: Both monetary cases and capital cases. [3]And when? [4]When they warned them. [5]But when they did not warn them [9B] [6]what should two brothers and one [other witness] do if they saw [some]one killing the person?

RASHI

רבי אומר אחד דיני ממונות ואחד דיני נפשות – שוין בכך דעדותן בטלה. **ואימתי** – בדיני נפשות עדותן בטלה. **בזמן שהתרו** – הקרוב או הפסול בעוברי עבירה שגילו דעתם שאף הם נעשים עדים, והרי הכתוב הקיש שלשה לבטל העדות אם יש קרוב או פסול, אבל לא התרו הקרוב והפסול בעוברי עבירה אלא שתקו, והכשרים התרו בהן, אין אלו נעשים עדים ותתקיים העדות בשאר. **דאם כן מה יעשו שני אחין ואחד** – כשר עמהם. **שראו באחד שהרג את הנפש** – ופלוגתא דרבי מאיר ורבנן נמי כגון שנמצא אחד מן השלשה קרוב או פסול וראה ושתק ולא התרה, רבי מאיר סבר לה כרבי יוסי דאמר: בדיני נפשות לא שנא התרה ולא שנא שתק – עדותן בטלה, ורבנן סברי כרבי, דהיכא דשתק – תתקיים העדות בשאר, ומיקטלא.

NOTES

בִּזְמַן שֶׁהִתְרוּ בָּהֶן When they warned them. The Rishonim disagree about the nature of this warning. Our commentary follows *Rashi* and others, who understand that it is the warning given by the witnesses to the offender. If the witness who was later found to be related to the accused had warned the offender against violating the prohibition prior to his transgression, the testimony of the entire group of witnesses is invalid, for by issuing the warning he indicated that he intended to testify against the offender together with the others who witnessed the transgression. But if that witness had not warned the offender against committing the transgression, the testimony of the other witnesses is not invalidated just because the relative happened to have witnessed the offense. According to others (*Tosafot, Geonim*), we are dealing here with the interrogation of the witnesses conducted by the court. The court asks the witnesses whether at the time that they witnessed the offense, they intended to come to court and testify about the matter, or they simply meant to see what was happening. If the relative says that he intended from the outset to serve as a witness, the testimony of the entire group is invalid. But if he says that he did not intend to serve as a witness, the testimony of the other witnesses remains valid. Some distinguish between monetary cases and capital cases, arguing that in capital cases the testimony of the entire group is invalidated if the relative

TRANSLATION AND COMMENTARY

וְאִיבָּעֵית אֵימָא [1]The Gemara continues: **And if you wish,** you can **say** that the disagreement between Rabbi Meir and the Sages can be explained differently: [2]Here, in the Mishnah, **other** people who were at the scene of the transgression **warned** the woman against committing adultery, [3]**but the witnesses** who saw the act and came to court to testify against the woman **did not issue any** such **warning.** [4]**And they disagree about the** same **matter** that is **in dispute between Rabbi Yose and the Sages,** [5]**for we have learned** elsewhere in the Mishnah (*Makkot* 6b): "If two people witnessed a capital offense from a window, and two other people witnessed the same offense from another window, and one person who stood between them warned the offender not to commit the transgression, and the warning was heard by the witnesses, the law is as follows: If at least one of those standing at one window could see at least one of those standing at the other window, they are all treated as a single group of witnesses. Otherwise they are treated as two separate groups of witnesses. (If they are all treated as a single group of witnesses, then nobody can be punished as a false conspiring witness unless all of them were found to be false, conspiring witnesses. Conversely, if they are all treated as a single group of witnesses, then even if only one of them is disqualified from testimony, all of their testimony is invalid.) As we have learned: [6]**"Rabbi Yose says:** The warning issued by the person who is not a witness does not suffice. The accused can **never be sentenced to execution unless the two witnesses** who testified against him in court **warned him with their own mouths** against committing the offense, [7]**as it is said** [Deuteronomy 17:6]: **'At the mouth of two witnesses,** or three witnesses, shall he that is worthy of death be put to death.'" Rabbi Meir agrees with Rabbi Yose. Thus, the case at hand is not a capital case, and the matter of the woman's ketubah can be adjudicated by a court of three. The Sages follow the Rabbis who disagree with Rabbi Yose and say that the warning need not be issued by the witnesses. Thus, the case at hand is indeed a capital case, and must be heard by a court of twenty-three judges.

וְאִיבָּעֵית אֵימָא [8]The Gemara now suggests another explanation of the disagreement between Rabbi Meir and the Sages: **And if you wish,** you can **say** that the disagreement should be understood as follows: [9]Here, in the Mishnah, the witnesses **contradicted themselves in the course of the** cross-**examination** about incidental circumstances which do not touch directly on substantial issues (such as the color of the clothing worn by the accused), [10]**but they did not contradict themselves in the course of the investigation** conducted by the judges with respect to the time and the place at which the event to which they testified occurred, or with respect to the basic facts of the case. As was explained earlier in the tractate (above, p. 2b), a court is obliged to subject the evidence of witnesses to searching scrutiny in order to make sure that they are telling the truth. Three kinds of examination are necessary: (1) *Derishah* or inquiry — an examination of the substance of the witnesses' testimony: Who committed the offense? What did he do? Was he warned prior to the commission of the offense? (2) *Ḥakirah* or investigation — an examination of the witnesses' statements with respect to the time and the place at which the offense was committed. (3) *Bedikah* or examination — a cross-examination concerning the incidental circumstances related to the witnesses' basic testimony. If

[1]וְאִיבָּעֵית אֵימָא: [2]כְּגוֹן שֶׁהִתְרוּ בָּהּ אֲחֵרִים, [3]וְלֹא הִתְרוּ בָּהּ עֵדִים. [4]וְקָמִיפַּלְגִי בִּפְלוּגְתָּא דְּרַבִּי יוֹסֵי וְרַבָּנַן. [5]דִּתְנַן: "רַבִּי יוֹסֵי אוֹמֵר: [6]לְעוֹלָם אֵינוֹ נֶהֱרָג עַד שֶׁיְּהוּ פִּי שְׁנֵי עֵדָיו מַתְרִין בּוֹ, [7]שֶׁנֶּאֱמַר: 'עַל פִּי שְׁנַיִם עֵדִים'".

[8]וְאִיבָּעֵית אֵימָא: [9]כְּגוֹן דְּאִיתְכַּחוּשׁ בִּבְדִיקוֹת, [10]וְלֹא אִיתְכַּחוּשׁ בַּחֲקִירוֹת.

LITERAL TRANSLATION

[1]And if you wish, say: [2]Where others warned her, [3]but the witnesses did not warn her. [4]And they disagree about the [matter in] dispute between Rabbi Yose and the Sages. [5]For we have learned: "Rabbi Yose says: [6]He is never executed unless the mouths of his two witnesses warned him, [7]as it is said: 'At the mouth of two witnesses.'"

[8]And if you wish, say: [9]Where they contradicted themselves during the examinations, [10]but they did not contradict themselves during the investigations.

RASHI

בבדיקות — זה אומר: כליו של בועל שחורים, וזה אומר: לבנים. **חקירות** — איזה יום ואיזו שעה, וכיוצא בהם, שהעדים באים על ידיהם לידי הזמה. ורבי מאיר סבר: הכחשת בדיקות שמה הכחשה, ולא מיקטלא, ורבנן סברי: כיון דבחקירה נמצאו מכוונים, הכחשה דבדיקות לאו הכחשה היא, דלא רמו סהדי אדעתיהו למיבדק כולי האי.

BACKGROUND

דְּאִיתְכַּחוּשׁ בִּבְדִיקוֹת Where they contradicted themselves during the examinations. This topic is discussed at length below (pp. 40a ff.). It is evident that a contradiction in the essentials of testimony disqualifies that testimony, but the question is whether a contradiction in other details is sufficient to prove that one of the witnesses is lying. See below (p. 41a), where a distinction is drawn between details that are irrelevant to the subject and those which prove that the witnesses did not clearly see the act itself.

NOTES

warned the offender against committing the transgression, while in monetary cases (where no warning was issued to the defendant) the entire group's testimony is invalidated if the relative says that he intended to serve as a witness (see *Meiri*).

1 וְקָמִיפַּלְגִי בִּפְלוּגְתָּא דְּבֶן זַכַּאי וְרַבָּנַן. 2 דִּתְנַן: "מַעֲשֶׂה וּבָדַק בֶּן זַכַּאי בְּעוּקְצֵי תְּאֵנִים".
3 אָמַר רַב יוֹסֵף: הֵבִיא הַבַּעַל עֵדִים שֶׁזִּינְּתָה, 4 וְהֵבִיא הָאָב עֵדִים וֶהֱזִימּוּם לְעֵדֵי הַבַּעַל, 5 עֵדֵי הַבַּעַל נֶהֱרָגִין, 6 וְאֵין מְשַׁלְּמִין מָמוֹן. 7 חָזַר וְהֵבִיא

LITERAL TRANSLATION

[1]And they disagree about the [matter in] dispute between Ben Zakkai and the Sages. [2]For we have learned: "It once happened that Ben Zakkai examined [them] regarding stems of figs."

[3]Rav Yosef said: [If] the husband brought witnesses that she committed adultery, [4]and the father brought witnesses, and they refuted the husband's witnesses, [5]the husband's witnesses are executed, [6]but they do not pay money. [7][If] the husband brought

TRANSLATION AND COMMENTARY

the two witnesses contradict each other on matters which are essential to the issue, during the inquiry or the investigation, all agree that their testimony is invalid. But the Tannaim disagree about the law in the case where the witnesses contradict each other with respect to the incidental details. [1]Rabbi Meir and the Sages **argue about the** same **matter**, which **is in dispute between Ben Zakkai and the Sages**, [2]**for we have learned** elsewhere in the Mishnah (*Sanhedrin* 40a): **"It once happened that Ben Zakkai examined** the witnesses **with** respect to **the stems of figs** that they had mentioned in their testimony. The witnesses testified that an offense had been committed under a fig tree, and Ben Zakkai interrogated them about the shape and the length of the stems of the figs. There were certain inconsistencies in their answers, and Ben Zakkai invalidated their testimony." Rabbi Meir agrees with Ben Zakkai that even a contradiction concerning incidental detail can invalidate the witnesses' testimony. Thus, the case in the Mishnah is not a capital case, and the matter of the woman's ketubah can be adjudicated by a court of three. The Sages follow the Rabbis who disagree with Ben Zakkai and say that the witnesses' testimony is not invalidated by a contradiction which arises under cross-examination regarding incidental details. Thus, the case in the Mishnah is indeed a capital case which can only be adjudicated by a court of twenty-three judges.

אָמַר רַב יוֹסֵף [3]The Gemara now returns to the case of a slanderer: **Rav Yosef said: If the husband brought** a set of **witnesses** who testified **that his** wife **had committed adultery** during the period of her betrothal, [4]**and the** woman's **father** then **brought** a second set of **witnesses** who **refuted the husband's witnesses** by testifying that the first pair of witnesses could not have witnessed the event about which they testified, for they were elsewhere (together with the father's witnesses) at the time that the event supposedly took place, [5]**the husband's witnesses are** subject to the penalty they sought to inflict by their testimony on the woman. Since their testimony would have resulted in having the woman put to death, they are now **liable to the death sentence.** [6]**But** they **do not** have to **pay** the woman **the value** of her ketubah, even though their testimony would also have resulted in its forfeiture, for there is a general rule that if a person committed an act entailing two penalties, the more severe penalty is imposed upon him, and he is exempt from the monetary compensation. [7]But **if,** after his first set of witnesses were refuted, **the husband brought another** set of

RASHI

בעוקצי תאנים — שאמרו העדים: תחת תאנה נעשה מעשה, אמר לו: תאנה זו עוקציה דקין או עוקציה גסין? עוקצין — זנבות תאנים, כמו (סוכה לד,ב): ניטל עוקצו. **עדי הבעל נהרגין** — שבאו להורגה. **ואין משלמין ממון** — אף על פי שהיו מפסידין אותה כתובה, אין משלמין טובת הנאת כתובתה כדין שאר זוממי כתובה, במסכת מכות (ג,ב), דכיון דבשבילה הן נהרגין אין משלמין לה ממון, דמתחייב בנפשו — פטור מן התשלומין, דכתיב (שמות כא): לא יהיה אסון ענוש יענש, ואי משום מאה סלע דהוו בעו לאפסודיה לאב והוה ליה מיתה לזה — לאשה, ותשלומין לזה — לאב לאו עלייהו רמו לשלומי אלא על הבעל, שהרי על ידן הבעל בא לשלם לאב, דכל זמן שלא הביא הבעל עדים שזינתה תחתיו אינו מתחייב לשלם מאה סלע על ידי עצמו, כדאמרינן בכתובות (מו,א) דלא קרינא ביה ואם אמת היה וגו׳, דבלאו עדים לא מיקטלא, הלכך איהו נמי לא מיחייב אלא אם כן הביא עדים שזינתה והוזמו.

SAGES

רַב יוֹסֵף **Rav Yosef.** The son of Ḥiyya, Rav Yosef was one of the greatest Amoraim in Babylonia during the third generation. He was a disciple of Rav Yehudah and a colleague of Rabbah, and was head of the Pumbedita Yeshivah for two-and-a-half years. He was known as "Sinai" because of his expert knowledge of Baraitot and the oral traditions of the Bible, as well as its translation. His most important students were Abaye and Rava. An illness caused him to forget all his learning, but Abaye helped him to acquire it again. Rav Yosef also became blind. After Rav Yosef's death, Abaye succeeded him as head of the Pumbedita Yeshivah.

NOTES

וְאֵין מְשַׁלְּמִין מָמוֹן **But do not pay money.** The sum that the witnesses did not have to pay was the value of the woman's ketubah, which she would have forfeited had their testimony not been refuted. Even if the witnesses were not liable to the death penalty, they would not have had to pay the woman the full value of her ketubah, for it was never

HALAKHAH

הֵבִיא הַבַּעַל עֵדִים שֶׁזִּינְּתָה **If the husband brought witnesses that she committed adultery.** "If the husband brought witnesses who testified that his wife had committed adultery while betrothed, and the father brought a second set of witnesses who refuted the husband's witnesses, the husband's witnesses would be liable to execution. If the husband brought yet another set of witnesses who refuted the father's witnesses, the father's witnesses would then be

הַבַּעַל עֵדִים וְהֶזִימּוּם לְעֵדֵי הָאָב, [1]עֵדֵי הָאָב נֶהֱרָגִין [2]וּמְשַׁלְּמִין מָמוֹן — [3]מָמוֹן לָזֶה, [4]וּנְפָשׁוֹת לָזֶה.

[5]וְאָמַר רַב יוֹסֵף: ״פְּלוֹנִי רְבָעוֹ לְאוֹנְסוֹ״ — [6]הוּא וְאַחֵר מִצְטָרְפִין לְהָרְגוֹ. [7]״לִרְצוֹנוֹ״ — [8]רָשָׁע הוּא, [9]וְהַתּוֹרָה אָמְרָה: ״אַל תָּשֶׁת רָשָׁע עֵד״.

LITERAL TRANSLATION

witnesses again and they refuted the father's witnesses, [1]the father's witnesses are executed [2]and they pay money — [3]money for this one, [4]and execution for that one.

[5]And Rav Yosef said: "So-and-so sodomized him against his will" — [6]he and another join to execute him. [7]"With his consent" — [8]he is wicked, [9]and the Torah said: "Put not [your hand] with the wicked [to be] an [unrighteous] witness."

TRANSLATION AND COMMENTARY

witnesses who refuted the father's witnesses by testifying that the father's witnesses were with them at the time that they claimed they were elsewhere with the husband's first set of witnesses, the father's witnesses are now subject to the penalty imposed upon false, conspiring witnesses. Since the testimony of the father's witnesses would have led to the execution of the husband's witnesses, [1]**the father's witnesses are** now **liable to the death sentence.** [2]They must also **pay** the husband **money,** for had their testimony have gone unrefuted, the husband would have had to pay his wife's father a one-hundred-shekel fine for having falsely maintained that his daughter had committed adultery during their betrothal.

מָמוֹן לָזֶה וּנְפָשׁוֹת לָזֶה [3]Even though we generally say that two penalties are not imposed for the same offense, here the father's witnesses are liable to both the death penalty and monetary compensation. They must pay **money because of** the one-hundred-shekel fine that they had wanted to inflict on **one** party, the husband, [4]**and** they are liable to **execution because** of the death penalty that they had wanted to inflict on **the other party,** the husband's witnesses.

וְאָמַר רַב יוֹסֵף [5]The Gemara now cites another ruling by Rav Yosef about witnesses. **And Rav Yosef said:** If someone claims that **a certain man engaged in homosexual intercourse with him against his will, his** testimony against the rapist is valid. [6]Thus, **he can join together with another man** who witnessed the attack, and testify against the rapist, making him subject **to execution,** as prescribed by Torah law (Leviticus 20:13). [7]But if he says that the other man engaged in homosexual intercourse with him **with his consent,** his testimony against the other person is not valid, for by his own confession, [8]**he is a wicked person** who willingly committed a capital offense, [9]**and the Torah said** (Exodus 23:1): **"Put not your hand with the wicked to be an unrighteous witness,"** teaching that a criminal is disqualifed from giving testimony.

RASHI

והזימום לעדי האב — היאך אתם מזימים את אלו לומר שעמכם היו במקום פלוני, והלא אתם עמנו הייתם במקום פלוני. **עדי האב נהרגין** — שרצו להרוג עדי הבעל. **ומשלמין ממון** — מאה כסף לבעל שבאו לחייבו כשהזימו את עדיו. **ממון לזה** — לבעל. **ונפשות לזה** — ונהרגין בשביל העדים, דקסבר רב יוסף: כי פטר רחמנא מתחייב בנפשו מן התשלומין, היכא דמיתה וממון משום חד קאתו עליה. **פלוני רבעו** — במשכב זכור. **לאונסו** — על כרחו. **הוא ואחר** — הנרבע הזה כשר להעיד עליו, ואם יש אחר עמו נהרג הרובע על פיהם. **אל תשת רשע עד** — דכתיב (שמות כג) אל תשת ידך וגו׳.

BACKGROUND

רָשָׁע הוּא **He is wicked.** Since he has testified that he committed a transgression of his own free will, he has testified that he is an evildoer. Because he admits to his own evil, he is disqualified from testifying.

NOTES

certain that the woman would receive it, as she could have predeceased her husband. Rather, the witnesses would have had to pay the woman the amount for which she could have sold the rights to her ketubah to another person, a sum considerably less than the amount recorded in the ketubah.

HALAKHAH

liable to the death penalty, and they would also have to pay the husband the sum of the fine that he would have had to pay had their testimony been unrefuted." (*Rambam, Sefer Shofetim, Hilkhot Edut* 21:10.)

פְּלוֹנִי רְבָעוֹ לְאוֹנְסוֹ **So-and-so committed sodomy with him against his will.** "If someone claims that another man engaged in homosexual intercourse with him — whether against his will or even with his consent — his testimony is valid, and it can be combined with that of another witness so that the death penalty can be imposed on the offender, for a person cannot through his own evidence turn himself into a wicked man who is disqualified from serving as a witness," following Rava. *Rema* adds: "If a man confessed to a crime which would disqualify him from serving as a witness were the confession supported by the testimony of two valid witnesses, it is preferable that he not be called upon from the outset to serve as a witness." (*Rambam, Sefer Shofetim, Hilkhot Edut* 12:2; *Shulḥan Arukh, Ḥoshen Mishpat* 34:25.)

TRANSLATION AND COMMENTARY

רָבָא אָמַר [1]**Rava** disagreed with Rav Yosef and **said:** A man is not disqualified unless his guilt is established by two qualified witnesses. His own admission of guilt is not sufficient, for **a person is considerd a relative to himself,** and so cannot testify against himself, just as he cannot testify against any other person to whom he is related. [2]Since **a person is** unable to testify against himself, he **cannot** through his own confession **make himself out to be a wicked person** who is disqualified from serving as a witness. Thus, if a person says that he willingly engaged in homosexual intercourse with another man, he does not disqualify himself as a witness. We ignore those aspects of his testimony that concern his own crime, and accept the testimony insofar as it concerns the other man. If, therefore, a second witness can be found, the accused becomes subject to the death penalty.

אָמַר רָבָא [3]Similarly, **Rava said:** [10A] [4]"If someone appears in court and says that **So-and-so had sexual intercourse with my wife** with her consent," his testimony with respect to that person is valid. [5]Thus, **he and another** person who witnessed the adulterous act **can** testify **together** against the adulterer, so that the court may have power **to execute him.** [6]**But** the husband's testimony is **not** valid with respect to enabling the court **to execute her,** for a man is disqualified from testifying against his wife.

[1]רָבָא אָמַר: אָדָם קָרוֹב אֵצֶל עַצְמוֹ, [2]וְאֵין אָדָם מֵשִׂים עַצְמוֹ רָשָׁע.

[3]אָמַר רָבָא: [10A] [4]"פְּלוֹנִי בָּא עַל אִשְׁתִּי" — [5]הוּא וְאַחֵר מִצְטָרְפִין לְהוֹרְגוֹ, [6]אֲבָל לֹא לְהוֹרְגָהּ.

LITERAL TRANSLATION

[1]Rava said: A person is [considered] a relative to himself, [2]and a person cannot make himself out to be wicked.

[3]Rava said: [10A] [4]"So-and-so had sexual intercourse with my wife" — [5]he and another join to execute him, [6]but not to execute her.

RASHI

רבא אמר – אין אדם נפסל לעדות בהודאת פיו, דאדם קרוב אצל עצמו, הלכך אין אדם יכול לשום עצמו רשע, כלומר על עדות עצמו אינו נעשה רשע, שהרי תורה פסלה קרוב לעדות, ונהרג הרובע, דפלגינן דיבורא ומהימנינן ליה לגבי חבריה, ולא מהימנינן ליה לגבי דידיה לפסול לעדות. **פלוני בא על אשתי אבל לא להורגה** – לפי שקרוב הוא אצלה, ואף על גב דמהימנינן ליה בהאי סהדותא לגבי חבריה, לא מהימנינן ליה לגבי אשתו, והיינו פלגינן דיבורא, דהא חד דיבורא הוא ולגבי האי מהימן, ולא מהימן לגבי האי.

CONCEPTS

אָדָם קָרוֹב אֵצֶל עַצְמוֹ **A person is considered a relative to himself.** A principle in the laws of evidence. The relatives of the litigants or the accused in a lawsuit cannot testify as witnesses. Since a person has no closer relative than himself, an accused cannot give evidence in his own case — neither in his defense nor to incriminate himself. Thus no one can testify to his own guilt ("אֵין אָדָם מֵשִׂים עַצְמוֹ רָשָׁע"). Only in civil disputes is an admission by one of the litigants accepted, possibly because such an admission is comparable to a gift on the part of the litigant.

אֵין אָדָם מֵשִׂים עַצְמוֹ רָשָׁע **A person cannot make himself out to be wicked.** The formal aspect of this Halakhic ruling is based on the principle that we do not accept the testimony of relatives. Obviously, as we do not accept any testimony, either favorable or unfavorable, from relatives, and since אָדָם קָרוֹב אֵצֶל עַצְמוֹ ("a person is his own closest relative"), a person is certainly not permitted to testify about himself.

In a deeper sense, the principle behind this ruling is that testimony must be objective, and whenever there are grounds for suspecting that it is not objective, it is not juridically valid — for instance, when it is clear that a witness has an interest in the matter about which he is testifying. This is why the testimony of relatives is unacceptable — because of their relationship, they lose their objectivity (and in this respect there is no difference between testimony in favor of the relative or against him). It is clear that with respect to himself, a person cannot be objective. Therefore testimony regarding oneself — even self-incriminatory testimony — cannot be accepted in court.

Consequently, although in most juridical systems in the world an admission of guilt is regarded as the strongest testimony, it is entirely disregarded in Jewish law. *Rambam* speaks of the psychological problems that might lead a person to confess to a crime he has not

NOTES

רָבָא אָמַר: אָדָם קָרוֹב אֵצֶל עַצְמוֹ **Rava said: A person is considered a relative to himself.** The Rishonim comment: Rava's statement here seems to contradict what he says elsewhere. For it follows from his statement that here he says that a man who confesses to willingly engaging in homosexual intercourse does not disqualify himself as a witness, because he cannot testify against himself and turn himself into a wicked person. But if two other witnesses established the fact that he had engaged in homosexual intercourse, he would indeed be disqualified from serving as a witness on account of his transgression. Elsewhere (*Sanhedrin* 27a), however, Rava says that only a man who was found guilty of robbery or thievery is disqualified from serving as a witness. *Tosafot* and others argue that Rava agrees that any sinner who violates prohibitions in order to satisfy his appetite (as opposed to a sinner who violates prohibitions for the sake of defiance) is disqualified from serving as a witness, and a man who engages in homosexual intercourse falls into this category. *Remah* suggests that when Rava said that only a person who was found guilty of robbery or thievery is disqualified from serving as a witness, he was talking about people who violate prohibitions that do not carry the death penalty. But if a man committed a crime punishable by death, he is disqualified from serving as a witness, no matter what his crime was.

אֵין אָדָם מֵשִׂים עַצְמוֹ רָשָׁע **A person cannot make himself out to be a wicked person.** The rule that a person's self-incriminating testimony is not accepted in court as valid evidence is limited to testimony which, if accepted, would make him liable to a fine, or lashes, or the death penalty. But if a person admits owing money, his admission is accepted and is considered equal to the testimony of 100 witnesses — for a person can waive his rights to his money, but he cannot offer himself for lashes or execution.

If a person comes before a court, admits to his wrongdoing and wishes to repent for his sin, the court may impose punishment so that he can atone for the offense. However, he is not disqualified thereby from serving as a witness (*Geonim*).

פְּלוֹנִי בָּא עַל אִשְׁתִּי **So-and-so had sexual intercourse with my wife.** Even though it is clear that the husband must hate the man against whom he is testifying, for he committed adultery with his wife, his testimony is nevertheless accepted, as a person is not disqualified from testifying against a person he hates if his hatred stems from the subject of his testimony (*Margaliyot HaYam*).

HALAKHAH

פְּלוֹנִי בָּא עַל אִשְׁתִּי **So-and-so had sexual intercourse with my wife.** "If someone comes to court and testifies that a certain man had sexual intercourse with his wife, his testimony can be combined with that of another witness for the purpose of condemning the adulterer to death. However a husband's testimony cannot be used for the purpose of condemning his wife." (*Rambam, Sefer Shofetim, Hilkhot Edut* 12:2.)

LITERAL TRANSLATION

[1]What did he teach us? [2]That we divide the statement? [3]This is the same as that!

[4]You would have said: [5]A person is related to himself — we say, [6]to his wife — we do not say. [7][Hence,] it tells us.

[8]And Rava said: "So-and-so had sexual intercourse with a betrothed girl," [9]and they were refuted — [10]they are executed, [11]but do not pay money.

[1]מַאי קָא מַשְׁמַע לָן? [2]דִּמְפַלְּגִינַן בְּדִיבּוּרָא? [3]הַיְינוּ הַךְ!

[4]מַהוּ דְּתֵימָא: [5]אָדָם קָרוֹב אֵצֶל עַצְמוֹ — אָמְרִינַן, [6]אֵצֶל אִשְׁתּוֹ — לָא אָמְרִינַן. [7]קָא מַשְׁמַע לָן.

[8]וְאָמַר רָבָא: "פְּלוֹנִי בָּא עַל נַעֲרָה הַמְאוֹרָסָה" [9]וְהוּזְמוּ — [10]נֶהֱרָגִין, [11]וְאֵין מְשַׁלְּמִין מָמוֹן.

RASHI

אצל אשתו לא אמרינן — אדם קרוב לענין פלגינן דיבורא, והואיל ומהימן אההוא דיבורא למיקטליה לחבריה, ליקטלוה נמי לדידה — קא משמע לן. **נהרגין** — משום פלוני. **ואין משלמין ממון** — טובת הנאת כתובתה שרצו להפסידה, מאי טעמא שהרי לא הזכירו שם האשה ולמאן מפסדי.

committed, and legal scholars (as well as many police investigators) have been led by experience to the conclusion that confessions in general, and even more so those extorted under pressure (especially torture) are very unreliable indications of guilt.

TRANSLATION AND COMMENTARY

מַאי קָא מַשְׁמַע לָן [1]The Gemara asks: **What did** Rava mean to **teach us** with this ruling? [2]You might say that Rava meant to teach us **that** in certain cases the court **divides the** witness's **testimony,** accepting part (with respect to the man) and rejecting part (with respect to the woman). [3]But then **this** ruling **is** telling us essentially **the same** thing **as** the previous one, which informed us that if a person makes a statement that includes both self-incriminatory testimony and other information, the court divides his testimony and accepts as evidence only that which is not self-incriminating. What, then, did Rava mean to add with this second ruling?

מַהוּ דְּתֵימָא [4]The Gemara answers: Without the second ruling, **you would have said** [5]that **we say a person is** regarded as being **kin to himself** when it comes to disregarding testimony he offers against himself, [6]yet **we do not say** that a person is regarded as being kin **to his wife** for purposes of disregarding testimony he offers against her. Thus, one would think that if a husband testified about a certain man having had sexual intercourse with his wife, we would accept the testimony in its entirety and use it to condemn his wife as well. [7]**Hence, it** was necessary for Rava to **teach us** that this is not so, and that a man's wife is considered to be as kin to him as he is to himself. Thus, we disregard the portion of a husband's testimony which incriminates his wife, while preserving that portion which relates to another.

וְאָמַר רָבָא [8]The Gemara continues: **Rava said:** If two witnesses testified that **"So-and-so had sexual intercourse with a betrothed girl,"** but did not identify her by name, [9]**and** then **their evidence was refuted** by another set of witnesses who testified that they could not have seen what they claimed to have seen, as all of them were together elsewhere at the time — [10]the initial witnesses **are** subject to **execution** as punishment for their false and conspiring testimony, which would have resulted in the unwarranted death of the accused. [11]**But they do not** have to **pay** any **money** in compensation to the girl's father for the ketubah settlement she would have lost, since they did not identify her by name.

NOTES

אָדָם קָרוֹב אֵצֶל עַצְמוֹ אָמְרִינַן **A person is kin to himself — we say.** *Remah* explains the matter thus: It might have occurred to you to say that a person knows he is kin to himself and is thus disqualified from testifying against his own person. Consequently, when he makes self-incriminating remarks during his testimony, we must assume that he intends them not as formal testimony but merely as incidental talk. Therefore, we can divide his testimony, accepting the part offered against the other person while rejecting the part offered against himself. On the other hand, a person does not necessarily realize that he is considered kin to his wife and is thus disqualified from testifying against her, too. Thus, when he incriminates her during his testimony, he may indeed intend his remarks to be taken as part of the formal statement he is offering; perhaps, then, we do not divide his testimony at all, but rather reject or accept it in its entirety.

אָדָם קָרוֹב אֵצֶל אִשְׁתּוֹ **A person is kin to his wife.** *Ra'avad* points out that the kinship we identify between a man and his wife is not the same as that which disqualifies him from testifying against blood relations but, rather, is identical with the kinship he experiences toward himself, following the general principle that "a man's wife is as is his own body."

נֶהֱרָגִין וְאֵין מְשַׁלְּמִין מָמוֹן **They are executed but do not pay money.** *Remah* asks: Is it not obvious that the witnesses are exempt from paying any monetary compensation, since never having identified the girl, their testimony could not have resulted in any monetary loss?! He answers that in the case under discussion the witnesses did not mean to identify the girl when they came to testify; nevertheless, her identity became known in the course of examining their testimony. Rava teaches that in such a situation the witnesses are not liable to pay any monetary compensation, for they did not intend from the outset to testify against her or cause her any monetary loss.

[1]״בִּתּוֹ שֶׁל פְּלוֹנִי״ [2]וְהוּזְמוּ — [3]נֶהֱרָגִין, וּמְשַׁלְּמִין מָמוֹן. [4]מָמוֹן לָזֶה, [5]וּנְפָשׁוֹת לָזֶה.

[6]וְאָמַר רָבָא: ״פְּלוֹנִי רָבַע הַשּׁוֹר״ [7]וְהוּזְמוּ — [8]נֶהֱרָגִין, [9]וְאֵין מְשַׁלְּמִין מָמוֹן, [10]״שׁוֹרוֹ שֶׁל פְּלוֹנִי״ וְהוּזְמוּ — [11]נֶהֱרָגִין, [12]וּמְשַׁלְּמִין מָמוֹן, [13]מָמוֹן לָזֶה [14]וּנְפָשׁוֹת לָזֶה.

[15]הָא תּוּ לָמָּה לִי? [16]הַיְינוּ הַךְ!

[17]מִשּׁוּם דְּקָא בָּעֵי בַּעֲיָא עִילָּוֵיהּ, [18]דְּבָעֵי רָבָא: ״פְּלוֹנִי

LITERAL TRANSLATION

[1]"The daughter of So-and-so," [2]and they were refuted — [3]they are executed, and pay money. [4]Money to this, [5]and death to that one.

[6]And Rava said: "So-and-so sodomized an ox," [7]and they were refuted — [8]they are executed, [9]but do not pay money. [10]"So-and-so's ox," and they were refuted — [11]they are executed, [12]and pay money. [13]Money to this, [14]and death to that.

[15]This too why do I need? [16]This is the same as that!

[17]Because he asked a question on it, [18]for Rava asked: "So-and-so

TRANSLATION AND COMMENTARY

[1]If, however, the two witnesses testified that a certain man had sexual intercourse with **the daughter of So-and-so** who was betrothed to another man, [2]**and** then **their evidence was refuted** by another set of witnesses, [3]the initial witnesses **are** now subject to be **executed and** in addition must **pay money** in compensation to the girl's father for the ketubah she would have forfeited had their testimony been accepted. [4]They are liable to pay **money for** the financial loss that they wanted to inflict upon the girl's father, [5]while at the same time they are subject to **death for** the loss of life they wished to cause the girl herself and the man with whom she had supposedly engaged in sexual relations.

וְאָמַר רָבָא [6]**And** similarly **Rava said:** If two witnesses testified that **"So-and-so sodomized an ox,"** but did not mention to whom the ox belongs, [7]**and** then **their evidence was refuted** by a second set of witnesses, [8]the initial witnesses **are** now liable to be **executed,** for their testimony would have resulted in the death of the accused. [9]**But they do not** have to **pay** any **money** in compensation to the owner of the ox, who would not have incurred any financial loss. If, however, [10]the two witnesses testified that a certain man sodomized **So-and-so's ox, and** then **their evidence was refuted** by a another set of witnesses, [11]the initial witnesses **are** now liable to be **executed,** [12]**and** in addition must **pay money** in compensation to the ox's owner. [13]They are liable to pay **money for** the financial loss that they wanted to inflict on the ox's owner, since had their testimony been accepted, the ox would have been put to death; [14]while at the same time they are subject to **death for** the loss of life they wanted to cause the accused.

הָא תּוּ לָמָּה לִי [15]The Gemara asks: **Why do we need more** support for Rava's original ruling? [16]**This** case of the ox **is** essentially **the same as** that of the betrothed girl!

מִשּׁוּם [17]The Gemara answers: Indeed, Rava's ruling regarding witnesses who testified falsely about an ox was unnecessary after he had ruled about the witnesses who testified falsely against a betrothed girl. Nevertheless, Rava stated his ruling in that case **because he** wished to **ask a question** based **on it,** [18]**for Rava asked:** If someone came before a court and said that **"So-and-so sodomized my ox," what** is the law?

RASHI

בא על בתו של פלוני נהרגין — משום שניסת, שבאו להרוג אותו ואותה. **ומשלמין ממון** — שבאו להפסידה כתובתה מן האירוסין, ומשלמין טובת הנאת כתובה כדין כל זוממי כתובה, ולא פליגא דרבא אדרב יוסף דאמר לעיל עדי הבעל נהרגין ואין משלמין ממון, דהתם כיון דניסת הנך תשלומין דכתובה דידה בעו מיהוי, וכיון דעלה מקטלי, לא משלמי לה ממון, אבל היכא דלא ניסת, הנך תשלומין דהזמה דאב נינהו, דכל שבח נעוריה לאביה, והוה ליה ממון לזה — לאב, ונפשות — לזה, משום דבועל ונערה מיקטלי. **רבע השור** — ולא הזכירו שור של מי. **ואין משלמין** — דמי השור, דלא ידעינן מנו. **ממון לזה** — לבעל השור. **ונפשות** — בשביל פלוני הרובע. פלוני רבע שורי — הוא ואחר מצטרף עמו.

HALAKHAH

פְּלוֹנִי בָּא עַל נַעֲרָה הַמְאוֹרָסָה...רָבַע שׁוֹר **So-and-so had sexual intercourse with a betrothed girl...sodomized an ox.** "If two witnesses testify that a certain man had sexual intercourse with a girl who was betrothed to another man (without identifying the girl by name), and then are shown to be lying, the two witnesses are liable to be executed but need not provide any monetary compensation. If the two witnesses name the betrothed girl with whom the man had intercourse, and then are shown to be lying, they are not only liable to be executed but must also provide monetary compensation to the girl's father. Similarly, if two witnesses testify that a certain man sodomized an animal (without mentioning whom the animal belonged to), and then are shown to be lying, the witnesses are liable to be executed but need not provide any monetary compensation. If the two witnesses, however, identified the owner of the animal and then are shown to be lying, they are not only liable to be executed but must also provide monetary compensation to the animal's owner; this," in accordance with Rava. (*Rambam, Sefer Shofetim, Hilkhot Edut* 21:10.)

TRANSLATION AND COMMENTARY

If another witness corroborated his testimony, the person who engaged in bestiality would certainly be liable to the death penalty, but what is the law regarding the ox? [1]The Gemara clarifies the two sides of the question: **Do we say** that **a person is** considered to be **kin to himself,** and therefore cannot testify against himself any more than he can against any of his other relatives, [2]**but** that **he is not** considered to be **kin to his money** and possessions, and as such can offer valid testimony leading to the execution of his own ox? [3]**Or perhaps we say** that **a person is considered** to be **kin to his money** and possessions, too, and thus cannot testify against his ox?

בָּתַר [4]**After having raised the question,** Rava himself **resolved it:** [5]It stands to reason that **a person is** indeed considered to be **kin to himself, but a person is not considered** to be **kin to his money.** Thus, he can testify against his own ox.

מַכּוֹת בִּשְׁלֹשָׁה כו׳ [6]We learned in our Mishnah that any case involving the violation of a negative commandment that is punishable by **lashes** must be heard **by** a court of **three** judges. [7]**From where** in the Bible **is this law derived?** [8]**Rav Huna said: The verse** that mentions lashes (Deuteronomy 25:1-2) **states:** "If there be a controversy between men and they come unto judgment, and the judges judge them, by justifying the righteous and condemning the wicked, then it shall be, if the wicked man deserve to be beaten, that the judge shall cause him to lie down, and to be beaten before his face, according to the measure of his wickedness, by number." [9]The plural form in the expression **"and the judges judge them"** teaches that at least **two** judges are required to adjudicate the case. [10]**And** since **a court may not be** composed **of** an **even number** of judges, lest the opinions be evenly divided and the court be unable to arrive at a decision, [11]**we** must **add another** judge to the two. [12]**Hence here** we need **three** judges in all.

רָבַע שׁוֹרִי״, מַהוּ? [1]מִי אָמְרִינַן: אָדָם קָרוֹב אֵצֶל עַצְמוֹ, [2]וְאֵין אָדָם קָרוֹב אֵצֶל מָמוֹנוֹ. [3]אוֹ דִּילְמָא אָמְרִינַן: אָדָם קָרוֹב אֵצֶל מָמוֹנוֹ.

[4]בָּתַר דְּבָעֲיָא הֲדַר פְּשָׁטָהּ: [5]אָדָם קָרוֹב אֵצֶל עַצְמוֹ, וְאֵין אָדָם קָרוֹב אֵצֶל מָמוֹנוֹ.

[6]״מַכּוֹת בִּשְׁלֹשָׁה כו׳״. [7]מְנָהָנֵי מִילֵּי? [8]אָמַר רַב הוּנָא: אָמַר קְרָא: [9]״וּשְׁפָטוּם״ — שְׁנַיִם, [10]וְאֵין בֵּית דִּין שָׁקוּל, [11]מוֹסִיפִין עֲלֵיהֶם עוֹד אֶחָד. [12]הֲרֵי כָּאן שְׁלֹשָׁה.

LITERAL TRANSLATION

sodomized my ox," what [is the law]? [1]Do we say: A person is related to himself, [2]but a person is not related to his money? [3]Or perhaps we say: A person is related to his money!

[4]After having raised the question he resolved it: [5]A person is related to himself, but a person is not related to his money.

[6]"Lashes by three, etc." [7]From where [do we derive] these? [8]Rav Huna said: The verse states: [9]"And they [the judges] shall judge them" — two. [10]And a court may not be of even number, [11][so] we add to them another one. [12]Hence, here are three.

RASHI

מהו — פלוני ודאי מיקטיל, אלא שור מי מיקטיל. **מי אמרינן אדם קרוב אצל ממונו** — ופלגינן דבורא להימוני אחבריה ולא אשור, או דילמא לא אמרינן לענין פלגי דיבורא אדם קרוב אצל ממונו, אף על פי דפלגינן ליה לעיל אצל עצמו. **הדר פשטה** — לא אמרינן אדם קרוב אצל ממונו לענין פלגי דיבורא, והשור יסקל, וכי אמרינן בתמורה (כח,א) רובע או נרבע על פי הבעלים אסור לגבוה ומותר להדיוט דאינו נסקל, הני מילי היכא דלא העידו הבעלים על הרובע מי הוא, או העידו ולא היה עד שני עמהם, אבל הכא דגברא מיקטיל על פי בעל השור, לא פלגינן דיבורא משום ממון. **ושפטום** — גבי מלקות כתיב.

BACKGROUND

אָדָם קָרוֹב אֵצֶל מָמוֹנוֹ A man is related to his money. In a certain respect a person is undoubtedly close to his property, and in any testimony regarding property belonging to him, his words are not regarded as evidence but merely as a claim, for he is certainly personally involved in the matter. Here, however, we are discussing whether the fact that an ox belonged to someone constitutes the kind of closeness that invalidates the owner's testimony, or whether there is only suspicion of personal involvement (in this specific case, there is no such involvement, because the owner causes himself the loss of his property by that testimony).

NOTES

מַכּוֹת בִּשְׁלֹשָׁה Lashes by three. One might think that it is possible to deduce the need for three judges in a case involving lashes through the following *a fortiori* argument from civil cases: If a civil case, which merely involves financial restitution, requires a court of three, then surely a case which involves corporal punishment would also require a court of three! However, the argument does not work for the following reason: Three judges are required in a civil case for the purpose of ensuring that at least one of them is appropriately learned; a case involving lashes, however, can only be heard by expert judges, and thus one would think that even a single judge is sufficient. (*Margaliyot HaYam*).

HALAKHAH

פְּלוֹנִי רָבַע שׁוֹרִי So-and-so sodomized my ox. "If someone comes to court and testifies that a certain man sodomized his animal, his testimony can be combined with that of another witness so that both the offender and the animal are put to death, as a person is not disqualified from testifying against his personal property." (*Rambam, Sefer Shofetim, Hilkhot Edut* 12:2.)

מַכּוֹת בִּשְׁלֹשָׁה Lashes by three. "A case involving lashes may be adjudicated by a court of three judges, even though the offender might die as a result of the punishment," in accordance with the first Tanna of the Mishnah. (*Rambam, Sefer Shofetim, Hilkhot Sanhedrin* 5:4.)

[1]אֶלָּא מֵעַתָּה, "וְהִצְדִּיקוּ" שְׁנַיִם; [2]"וְהִרְשִׁיעוּ" — שְׁנַיִם, [3]הֲרֵי כָּאן שִׁבְעָה! [4]הַהוּא מִיבָּעֵי לֵיהּ כִּדְעוּלָּא, [5]דְּאָמַר עוּלָּא: רֶמֶז לְעֵדִים זוֹמְמִין מִן הַתּוֹרָה מִנַּיִן? [6]רֶמֶז לְעֵדִים זוֹמְמִין? [7]וְהָא כְּתִיב: "כַּאֲשֶׁר זָמַם"! [8]אֶלָּא, רֶמֶז לְעֵדִים זוֹמְמִין שֶׁלּוֹקִין מִנַּיִן? [9]דִּכְתִיב: "וְהִצְדִּיקוּ אֶת הַצַּדִּיק וְהִרְשִׁיעוּ אֶת הָרָשָׁע". [10]מִשּׁוּם דְּ"הִצְדִּיקוּ אֶת הַצַּדִּיק וְהִרְשִׁיעוּ אֶת הָרָשָׁע" — [11]"וְהָיָה אִם בִּן הַכּוֹת הָרָשָׁע"? [12]אֶלָּא: עֵדִים שֶׁהִרְשִׁיעוּ אֶת הַצַּדִּיק, [13]וְאָתוּ עֵדֵי אַחֲרִינֵי וְהִצְדִּיקוּ אֶת

LITERAL TRANSLATION

[1]But now, "And they shall exonerate" — two; [2]"And they shall condemn" — two, [3]hence here are seven! [4]That is needed for [the ruling of] Ulla, [5]because Ulla asked: From where is there a hint in the Torah regarding conspiring witnesses?

[6]A hint regarding conspiring witnesses? [7]But surely it is written: "As he had conspired"! [8]Rather, from where is there a hint that conspiring witnesses are flogged? [9]For it is written: "And they shall exonerate the righteous and condemn the wicked." [10]Because they "exonerated the righteous and condemned the wicked" — [11]"And it shall be, if the wicked man be worthy of flogging"? [12]Rather, [where] witnesses condemned the righteous, [13]and other witnesses came and exonerated

TRANSLATION AND COMMENTARY

אֶלָּא מֵעַתָּה [1]The Gemara challenges Rav Huna's derivation from the verse: **But now** that you say the plural form in the verse comes to teach us that we require at least two judges when hearing a case punishable by lashes, we should also consider the other plural forms found in that verse: **"And they shall exonerate** the righteous" should be understood as implying another **two** judges; [2]**"And they shall condemn** the wicked" should imply yet another **two** judges. This brings the total to six, and since a court may not be of even number, [3]we must add an additional judge — **hence here** we need **seven** judges in all!

הַהוּא מִיבָּעֵי לֵיהּ [4]The Gemara responds: **That** part of the verse containing the additional two plural verbs is unavailable to teach us anything about the number of judges required in a case involving lashes, since it **is needed** for another purpose altogether — **as** suggested **by Ulla.** [5]**For Ulla asked: Where in the Torah is there a hint regarding** the retaliatory measures taken against **conspiring witnesses?**

רֶמֶז לְעֵדִים זוֹמְמִין [6]The Gemara interrupts its presentation of Ulla's question with a question of its own: Did Ulla really ask where there is **a hint** in the Torah of the retaliatory measures taken against **conspiring witnesses?** [7]**But surely it is written** explicitly in the Torah (Deuteronomy 19:19): "Then you shall do to him **as he had conspired** to do to his brother; so shall you put the evil away from among you"!

אֶלָּא [8]**Rather,** Ulla's question must be understood as follows: **Where** in the Torah **is there a hint** of the law which dictates **that**, where the testimony of **conspiring witnesses** would have resulted in a penalty that could not be revisited upon them (for example, disqualification from the priesthood), they **are flogged** in any case for the sin of bearing false witness? [9]**For it is written** in the verse from Deuteronomy (25:1-2): "**And they shall exonerate the righteous and condemn the wicked.** And it shall be, if the wicked man be worthy of flogging." [10]It may be asked: Does it follow that just **because** the judges **"exonerated the righteous and condemned the wicked,"** [11]that **"and it shall be, if the wicked man be worthy of flogging"?!** Why, if we are dealing with a civil dispute between two litigants, would the wicked man (presumably the false accuser) be found worthy of flogging simply because the accused was exonerated? [12]**Rather,** it must be that the verse is alluding to a case **where** two **witnesses condemned the righteous person** through false testimony, [13]**and** then two **other witnesses came** and refuted the first set of witnesses by testifying that they were together with them somewhere else at the time they claimed to have seen the crime. Thus, the verse should be understood as follows: Where a second set of witnesses came "**and exonerated**

RASHI

רמז לעדים זוממין שלוקין — היכא דאין הזמה יכולה להתקיים בהם, כגון: מעידין אנו באיש פלוני שהוא בן גרושה, ונמצאו זוממין והרי הם כהנים אין אומרים יעשה זה בן גרושה תחתיו, אלא סופג את הארבעים, מנלן?

HALAKHAH

עֵדִים זוֹמְמִין שֶׁלּוֹקִין **That conspiring witnesses are flogged.** "If the testimony of the two witnesses was not aimed at condemning one to capital, corporal, or monetary punishment, as in the case of one who testified that a priest was not qualified for the priesthood or that a certain person had unintentionally killed someone (thereby consigning him to exile in a city of refuge), should the witnesses be refuted, they are liable to receive lashes for their false testimony since parallel retaliation cannot be executed." (*Rambam, Sefer Shofetim, Hilkhot Edut* 20:8-9.)

הַצַּדִּיק דְּמֵעִיקָּרָא, [1]וְשַׁוְּינְהוּ לְהָנָךְ רְשָׁעִים — [2]״וְהָיָה אִם בִּן הַכּוֹת הָרָשָׁע״.
[3]וְתֵיפּוֹק לֵיהּ מִ״לֹּא תַעֲנֶה״!
[4]מִשּׁוּם דַּהֲוָה לֵיהּ לָאו שֶׁאֵין בּוֹ מַעֲשֶׂה, [5]וְכָל לָאו שֶׁאֵין בּוֹ מַעֲשֶׂה — [6]אֵין לוֹקִין עָלָיו.
[7]״מִשּׁוּם רַבִּי יִשְׁמָעֵאל אָמְרוּ בְּעֶשְׂרִים וּשְׁלֹשָׁה״. [8]מַאי טַעֲמָא דְּרַבִּי יִשְׁמָעֵאל? [9]אֲמַר אַבַּיֵי: אָתְיָא, [10]״רָשָׁע״, ״רָשָׁע״ מֵחַיָּיבֵי מִיתוֹת. [11]כְּתִיב הָכָא: ״וְהָיָה אִם בִּן הַכּוֹת הָרָשָׁע״, [12]וּכְתִיב הָתָם: ״אֲשֶׁר הוּא רָשָׁע לָמוּת״, [13]מַה לְהַלָּן בְּעֶשְׂרִים וּשְׁלֹשָׁה, [14]אַף כָּאן בְּעֶשְׂרִים וּשְׁלֹשָׁה.

LITERAL TRANSLATION

the one who had been righteous from the beginning, [1]and rendered these wicked men — [2]"And it shall be, if the wicked man be worthy of flogging." [3]And let him derive it from: "You shall not bear [false witness]"! [4]Because that is a prohibition that does not involve an action, [5]and any prohibition that does not involve an action — [6][the court] does not flog one for [violating] it. [7]"In the name of Rabbi Yishmael they said: By twenty-three." [8]What is Rabbi Yishmael's reason? [9]Abaye said: It comes [from] [10]"wicked man," "wicked man" from those who are liable to die. [11]It is written here: "And it shall be, if the wicked man be worthy of flogging," [12]and it is written there: "Who is a wicked man liable to die." [13]Just as there by twenty-three, [14]so too here by twenty-three.

TRANSLATION AND COMMENTARY

the accused, **who had** actually **been righteous" from the beginning** by showing his accusers to have been conspiring witnesses, [1]**and** thereby **rendered these** first witnesses **wicked men** — [2]then **"and it shall be, if the wicked man be worthy of flogging,"** where for some reason the penalty he sought to impose upon the accused cannot be visited upon him, "that the judge shall cause him to lie down and he shall be flogged in his presence...."

וְתֵיפּוֹק לֵיהּ [3]The Gemara asks: Why is it necessary to search for a Scriptural hint regarding the lashes given to conspiring witnesses? **Let** Ulla **derive** this ruling **from** that which is written explicitly in the Torah as one of the Ten Commandments (Exodus 20:13): **"You shall not bear false witness** against your neighbor"! Surely conspiring witnesses are in violation of this prohibition, and as such are deserving of lashes, in accordance with the general rule that one who violates a negative commandment is punished by flogging.

מִשּׁוּם [4]The Gemara itself replies that Ulla's Scriptural derivation was indeed necessary, **seeing that** the prohibition forbidding false testimony **is** considered **a prohibition that does not involve a** physical **action,** but only speech. [5]**And** as a general rule, **any prohibition that does not involve a** physical **action,** [6]the court **does not flog one for** violating it. Thus the verse from Deuteronomy identified by Ulla serves as the only source for mandatory lashes in the case of one who bears false witness.

מִשּׁוּם [7]Our Mishnah continues: **"In the name of Rabbi Yishmael they said:** A case involving lashes must be adjudicated **by** a court of **twenty-three** judges." [8]**What is the reasoning of Rabbi Yishmael?** [9]**Abaye said:** Rabbi Yishmael's position **comes** as a result of a verbal analogy made between the above verse in Deuteronomy, [10]wherein the term **"wicked man"** appears, and a verse in Numbers (35:31) where the same term **"wicked man"** appears as well, but in the context of **those who are liable to die** by execution. [11]**It is written here,** in our verse from Deuteronomy: **"And it shall be, if the wicked man be worthy of flogging"**; [12]**and it is written there,** in Numbers: "And you shall not take ransom for the life of a murderer **who is a wicked man liable to die,** for he shall surely be put to death." [13]**Just as there,** in the case of the murderer, justice is administered **by** a court of **twenty-three** judges (as learned in our Mishnah), [14]**so too here,** in the case of one who is only liable to lashes, the case must be heard **by** a court of **twenty-three** judges.

RASHI

משום — דבית דין הצדיקו את הצדיק, והרשיעו את הרשע, והיה אם בן הכות את הרשע לצדקת צדיק למה הוזכרה כאן וכי משום לצדקת הצדיק מתחייב רשע מלקות אלא ודאי עדים (זוממין) רמיזי הכא, דאעדים קאי האי והיה אם בן הכות והכי קאמר: עדים שהרשיעו צדיק והוזמו, והצדיקו עדים אחרונים את הצדיק והרי נעשו רשעים אלו העדים הראשונים — וילקו, ואם אינו ענין לעדות ממון דהא אין לוקין ומשלמין תניהו ענין לבן גרושה וכיוצא בו. **לאו שאין בו מעשה אין לוקין עליו** — מאם לא תשמור לעשות וגו׳ והפלא ה׳ את מכותך וגו׳ באלו הן הלוקין (מכות יג,ב).

CONCEPTS

לָאו שֶׁאֵין בּוֹ מַעֲשֶׂה A prohibition that does not involve an action. Tractate *Makkot* contains long discussions on the details of this matter. Not only is this general principle not accepted by all the Tannaim, for some maintain that a person is also flogged for violating a negative commandment (in which no action is involved), but there is also the issue (which is discussed there, too) of the status of speech. Is it or is it not a physical action? For doubtless it does involve some physical action, such as moving the lips (עֲקִימַת שְׂפָתַיִם).

HALAKHAH

לָאו שֶׁאֵין בּוֹ מַעֲשֶׂה A prohibition that does not involve an action. "If a person violated a prohibition that does not involve a physical action, he is not liable to lashes except in the following cases: Where he swore falsely, or substituted another animal for one designated as a sacrifice, or cursed another person by using the name of God." (*Rambam, Sefer Shofetim, Hilkhot Sanhedrin* 18:2.)

BACKGROUND

בְּמְקוֹם מִיתָה עוֹמֶדֶת **Stands in place of execution.** *Rashi* explains the meaning of this statement: Anyone who intentionally violates a Torah commandment is a rebel against the Lord of the universe. For that reason, he merits execution. However, in practice he is not executed but punished in another way (just as there are four methods of execution, from severely painful to relatively mild); but that other punishment is to be regarded as a kind of death sentence.

אֲמָדוּהוּ לְקַבֵּל עֶשְׂרִים If they assessed him to receive twenty. Before being whipped the prisoner was examined by physicians to determine how many lashes he was capable of bearing, and he was lashed no more than that, for to exceed the prescribed number of lashes would be equivalent to executing him.

LITERAL TRANSLATION

[1] Rava said: Lashes stand in place of death.

[2] Rav Aḥa, the son of Rava, said to Rav Ashi: [3] If so, why do I need an assessment? [4] Let them strike him, [5] and if he dies, let him die!

[6] He said to him: The verse states: [7] "And your brother shall be degraded before your eyes." [8] When you strike, strike the back of one who is living.

[9] Rather, that which was taught: [10] "If they assessed him to receive twenty, [11] we flog him only [a number of] lashes that are divisible by three. [12] And how many would they be? [13] Eighteen."

[1] רָבָא אָמַר: מַלְקוּת בִּמְקוֹם מִיתָה עוֹמֶדֶת.

[2] אֲמַר רַב אַחָא בְּרֵיהּ דְּרָבָא לְרַב אַשִׁי: [3] אִי הָכִי אוּמְדָּנָא לָמָּה לִי? [4] לְמַחְיֵיהּ, [5] וְאִי מָאֵית, לֵימוּת!

[6] אֲמַר לֵיהּ: אֲמַר קְרָא: [7] "וְנִקְלָה אָחִיךָ לְעֵינֶיךָ". [8] כִּי מָחֵית, אַגַּבָּא דְּחַיֵּי מָחֵית.

[9] אֶלָּא, הָא דְּתַנְיָא: [10] "אֲמָדוּהוּ לְקַבֵּל עֶשְׂרִים, [11] אֵין מַכִּין אוֹתוֹ אֶלָּא מַכּוֹת הָרְאוּיוֹת לְהִשְׁתַּלֵּשׁ. [12] וְכַמָּה הֵן? [13] תְּמָנֵי סְרֵי".

TRANSLATION AND COMMENTARY

רָבָא אָמַר [1] **Rava said** that Rabbi Yishmael's position was based on a different consideration: Since the penalty of **lashes** actually **stands in place of death** by execution — the person violating a negative commandment deserving by right to die for his disobedience — it, too, can only be administered by a court of twenty-three judges.

אֲמַר [2] **Rav Aḥa, the son of Rava, said to Rav Ashi:** [3] **If** it is **so,** that lashes are a substitute for execution, then **why do I need an assessment** from a doctor as to how many of the thirty-nine Biblically mandated lashes can safely be administered without endangering the offender's life before commencing with his punishment? [4] **Let them strike him** with the maximum number of lashes, [5] **and if he dies** as a result, **let him die!** By right, he deserves to die anyway!

אֲמַר לֵיהּ [6] Rav Ashi **said to** Rav Aḥa, the son of Rava: An assessment of how many lashes the offender can withstand is required due to the fact that **the verse** (Deuteronomy 25:3) **states:** [7] "Forty lashes he may beat him but not exceed, lest if he exceed to beat him above these a great blow, **your brother shall be degraded before your eyes.**" [8] From here we learn that **when you strike** the offender, you must be careful to **strike the back of one who is living** and not one who is dead — as alluded to by the fact the verse refers to him as "your brother," meaning your brother in life.

אֶלָּא [9] **Rather** Rav Aḥa asked his question in regard to **what was taught** in the following Baraita: [10] **"If they assessed** the offender as strong enough **to receive twenty** lashes and no more, [11] **they flog him only** a number of **lashes that are divisible by three;** since lashes were administered in sets of three, two from behind and one in front. [12] **And how many** lashes **would they be** in this particular case, so as not to exceed twenty and still be divisible by three? [13] **Eighteen."**

RASHI

מלקות במקום מיתה עומדת — דכיון דעבר על אזהרת בורא ראוי הוא למות, ומיתה זו קנס עליו הכתוב, והרי הוא כאחת מן המיתות, וכי היכי דסקילה בפני עצמה, ושריפה בפני עצמה, והרג בפני עצמה, הוי נמי מלקות כאחת מן המיתות. **אי הכי** — דהוא גופיה מיתה הוא. אומדנא למה לי — דקתני באלו הן הלוקין (מכות כב,א) דאומדין אותו אם אינו יכול לקבל ארבעים מלקין אותו לפי מה שיכול לקבל. **ונקלה** — בשעת שלוקה יהא אחיך, שיכה את החי ולא את המת, וכיון דמית ליה בפלגא, כי מחי על אידך פלגא לאו על החי הוא. **אמדוהו לקבל עשרים** — וראו שאין יכול לקבל עשרים ואחת, ואם יכוהו עשרים ואחת ימות בה. **אין מכין אותו אלא** — שמונה עשרה, דמכות הראויות להשתלש לשלשה חלקים בעינן, שמכה שתי ידות מאחוריו ושליש מלפניו ומקרא נפקא לן באלו הן הלוקין (מכות כג,א).

NOTES

וְנִקְלָה אָחִיךָ לְעֵינֶיךָ And your brother shall be degraded before your eyes. Some authorities explain the need to assess the offender's physical endurance before giving him lashes as derived from the term, "he shall be degraded": Since a dead person cannot experience degradation, it must be determined that the offender is capable of surviving the infliction of pain and humiliation, which the Torah demanded he be subjected to. Alternatively, one can explain the need to ensure his survival as based upon the fact that the verse refers to him as "your brother," implying his status as one who still belongs to the fraternity of mitzvah obligation. Since a dead person cannot fulfill his Torah obligations, it must be ensured that the recipient of lashes can survive the punishment meted out to him (*Rashash*).

HALAKHAH

אֲמָדוּהוּ לְקַבֵּל עֶשְׂרִים If they assessed him to receive twenty. "Before lashes are administered, an assessment must be made as to how many the offender can safely withstand. Lashes can only be meted out in multiples of three. Thus, if the offender was assessed as strong enough to tolerate twenty lashes, he receives only eighteen." (*Rambam, Sefer Shofetim, Hilkhot Sanhedrin* 17:2.)

TRANSLATION AND COMMENTARY

[10B] [1]But if lashes are a substitute for execution, **let them strike him twenty-one** times, [2]**and should he die with** the delivery of **that** twenty-first lash, **let him die,** since he deserved to be executed in any case! And concerning the need for lashes to be administered while the offender is still living, there would be no problem, [3]**for when you strike** him the twenty-first time, [4]**it is the back of a living person you are striking** — given that he was assessed as strong enough to survive the first twenty lashes!

אֲמַר לֵיהּ [5]Rav Ashi **said to** Rav Aha, the son of Rava: Since the twenty-first lash might indeed kill the offender, delivering it could involve violating **the verse that states:** [6]**"And your brother shall be degraded before your eyes."** [7]Even **after** the offender **is flogged, it is necessary** that he still be in a condition that he can be called **"your brother"** who is fit to suffer degradation. [8]But if he dies as a result of this final lash, **he is no** longer considered "your brother."

עִיבּוּר הַחֹדֶשׁ בִּשְׁלֹשָׁה [9]We learned in the next clause of our Mishnah: **"The intercalation of the month** is performed **by** a court of **three** judges." In the time of the Temple, the New Moon was sanctified by proclamation of the High Court after the arrival of witnesses who testified to having seen the crescent of the moon. If this testimony was received on the thirtieth day of the concluding month, then that day was proclaimed to be the first of the new month. If, however, the testimony did not arrive by the thirtieth, then the next day would automatically be declared the first of the new month, regardless of whether witnesses came. A month of thirty days is called a "full month," whereas one which has only twenty-nine days, as a result of the New Moon having appeared on the thirtieth day, is called an "incomplete month." [10]The Gemara now considers the precise wording of the Mishnah: "**Calculation** of the month" (the consideration of certain extrinsic factors, which could affect the court's decision as to whether the present month should be intercalated), the Mishnah **does not teach** as requiring three judges; [11]**"sanctification** of the month" (the actual proclamation by the High Court sanctifying the New Moon), the Mishnah **does not teach** either as requiring three judges. [12]**But**

[10B] [1]לְמַחְיֵיהּ עֶשְׂרִים וַחֲדָא, [2]וְכִי מָיֵית בְּהַךְ חֲדָא, לֵימוּת, [3]דְּהָא כִּי מָחֵית [4]אַגַּבָּא דְּחַיָּיא קָא מָחֵית!

[5]אֲמַר לֵיהּ: אֲמַר קְרָא: [6]״וְנִקְלָה אָחִיךָ לְעֵינֶיךָ״ — [7]אַחַר שֶׁלָּקָה, אָחִיךָ בָּעֵינָא, [8]וְלֵיכָּא.

[9]״עִיבּוּר הַחֹדֶשׁ בִּשְׁלֹשָׁה״. [10]״חִישּׁוּב״ לָא קָתָנֵי, [11]״קִידּוּשׁ״ לָא קָתָנֵי. [12]אֶלָּא ״עִיבּוּר״.

LITERAL TRANSLATION

[10B] [1]Let them strike him twenty-one [times], [2]and should he die with that one, let him die, [3]for when you strike, [4]it is the back of a living person you are striking!

[5]He said to him: The verse states: [6]"And your brother shall be degraded before your eyes" — [7]after he is flogged, we need "your brother," [8]and there is not.

[9]"The intercalation of the month by three." [10]"Calculation," it does not teach; [11]"sanctification," it does not teach. [12]But rather "intercalation."

RASHI

למחייה עשרים וחדא — דהא אכתי חי הוא, ואגבא דחיי מחי. **עם חישוב לא קתני** — דנימא שצריך שלשה לחשב אם יעברו את החודש, דחושבנא תליא, אף על פי שצריך לעברו כגון משום ירקיא ומשום מתיא, אפילו הכי חושבנא בעי, כדתנן במסכת ערכין (ח,ב) אין פוחתין מארבעה חדשים המעוברין בשנה, ולא נראה לעבר יותר על שמונה, אבל תשעה מעוברין — לא עבדינן, דאם כן קדים ואתי סיהרא תלתא יומי ומחזי שיקרא, הלכך צריך לחשב תולדות הלבנה אם תקדים שלשה ימים או שנים לקביעות החדש — לא מעברינן ליה, דתמהי בה אינשי. **קידוש לא קתני** — דנימא דצריך שלשה לקבל עדות החדש מפי העדים, ולומר: מקודש החדש. **אלא עיבור החדש** — משמע שצריך שלשה לומר מעובר החדש — אמירה זו למה?

BACKGROUND

קִידּוּשׁ הַחֹדֶשׁ **Sanctifying a month.** Determining the first day of a month is important in itself, because Rosh Hodesh is a special day in several respects, and when the Temple stood a special Rosh Hodesh sacrifice was offered. Moreover, it is important because of the holidays that occur in that month, whose date is determined by Rosh Hodesh. For that reason, a court was needed to deliberate on the matter and determine the date of Rosh Hodesh for the entire Jewish people (this arrangement is discussed in detail in tractate *Rosh HaShanah*). On the other hand, the Jewish month is essentially a natural unit, and its length is determined by the lunar cycle. Hence there were grounds for arguing that it is not necessary to sanctify the New Moon at all, because its appearance becomes evident in reality ("Heaven sanctifies it"), or that the New Moon should be sanctified only when it is declared on a day when it is not clear whether it is truly Rosh Hodesh.

NOTES

חִישּׁוּב **Calculation.** Two types of calculation contribute to the decision whether a certain month should be full or incomplete. The first, which is identified by *Rashi* and *Ramah* as the subject of our Gemara, involves calculating the number of full months which have already occurred in that particular year. Since the Mishnah in *Arakhin* (2:2) teaches us that there may be no less than four and no more than eight full months in any single year, the court at times may have to ignore the status of the moon in deciding whether or not to intercalate the concluding month. For instance, if a particular year has already had eight full months, all the remaining months must be rendered incomplete by sanctifying the New Moon on the thirtieth, regardless of whether there was testimony as to the moon's appearance. Conversely, the last month of the year must be intercalated, even where witnesses testify to having seen the New Moon on the thirtieth, if it is determined that there have been less than four full months thus far.

The other calculation that affects the court's decision, which is the one *Meiri* suggests our Gemara is referring to, is that which is based upon astronomical laws and which seeks to pinpoint the exact time at which the moon can be expected to begin its new cycle. If this calculation determines that the New Moon will become visible on the night of the thirtieth, the court simply awaits the arrival of witnesses the next day and sanctifies the month accordingly. But if this calculation determines that the New Moon will not reappear on the night of the thirtieth, the court can ignore evidence to the contrary and decide to intercalate the month regardless.

[1]לָא לִיקַדְּשָׁא, [2]וּמִמֵּילָא לְעַבֵּר! [3]אֲמַר אַבַּיֵי: תְּנֵי "קִידּוּשׁ הַחֹדֶשׁ". [4]תַּנְיָא נַמִי הָכִי: "קִידּוּשׁ הַחֹדֶשׁ וְעִיבּוּר הַשָּׁנָה בִּשְׁלֹשָׁה, [5]דִּבְרֵי רַבִּי מֵאִיר". [6]אָמַר רָבָא: וְהָא עִיבּוּר קָתָנֵי! [7]אֶלָּא אָמַר רָבָא: [8]"קִידּוּשׁ בְּיוֹם עִיבּוּר בִּשְׁלֹשָׁה". [9]אַחַר עִיבּוּר — לֵיכָּא קִידּוּשׁ. [10]וּמַנִּי? [11]רַבִּי אֶלְעָזָר בֶּן צָדוֹק הִיא, דְּתַנְיָא: [12]"רַבִּי אֶלְעָזָר בֶּן צָדוֹק אוֹמֵר: אִם לֹא נִרְאָה בִּזְמַנּוֹ, [13]אֵין מְקַדְּשִׁין אוֹתוֹ, [14]שֶׁכְּבָר קִידְּשׁוּהוּ בַּשָּׁמַיִם".

LITERAL TRANSLATION

[1]Let them not sanctify, [2]and it will be intercalated automatically!

[3]Abaye said: Teach: "Sanctification of the month."

[4]It was also taught thus: "The sanctification of the month and the intercalation of the year by three; [5][these are] the words of Rabbi Meir."

[6]Rava said: But surely "intercalation" is taught!

[7]Rather, Rava said: [8]"Sanctification on a day of intercalation by three." [9]After intercalation — there is no sanctification. [10]And who is it? [11]It is Rabbi Elazar ben Tzadok, for it was taught: [12]"Rabbi Elazar ben Tzadok says: If it was not seen at its time, [13]they do not sanctify it, [14]for they already sanctified it in Heaven."

TRANSLATION AND COMMENTARY

rather it is **"intercalation** of the month" which the Mishnah teaches as requiring three judges, implying that if witnesses to the new moon did not arrive by the thirtieth, three judges must declare that month as officially "full." But why should such a declaration be necessary? [1]If testimony was not received on the thirtieth, **let them not sanctify** the new month on that day, [2]**and** the concluding month **will be intercalated automatically!**

אָמַר אַבַּיֵי [3]The Amoraim suggest several resolutions of this difficulty. **Abaye said:** In truth, intercalation does not require official proclamation by three judges. As for our Mishnah, it should be amended to **teach: "Sanctification of the month** is proclaimed by a court of three judges."

תַּנְיָא נַמִי הָכִי [4]The Gemara supports this suggestion by noting that **this was also taught** in the following Baraita: **"The sanctification of the month and the intercalation of the year** must be effected **by** a court composed of **three judges.** [5]These are **the words of Rabbi Meir."**

אָמַר רָבָא [6]**Rava said: But surely** the term "**intercalation" is taught** expressly in our Mishnah, and not "sanctification"!

אֶלָּא [7]**Rather, Rava said** the Mishnah retains the word "intercalation," but in the suggested context of sanctification: [8]**"Sanctification** of the new month **on a day** potentially subject to **intercalation** (the thirtieth of the concluding month) must be effected **by** a court of **three** judges." [9]It would then follow that **after** the day of **intercalation** has passed, **there is no** longer a need for **sanctification** of the new month by formal proclamation of the court, since in such a case the New Moon is sanctified automatically. [10]**And who is** the source of the ruling in our Mishnah according to this interpretation? [11]**It is Rabbi Elazar ben Tzadok, for it was taught** in the Mishnah (*Rosh HaShanah* 24a): [12]**"Rabbi Elazar ben Tzadok says: If** the New Moon **was not seen at its** anticipated **time** [on the thirtieth of the concluding month], [13]the court **does not sanctifiy it** on the following day, [14]**for** the celestial court **already sanctified it in Heaven,** precluding the need for any

RASHI

לא ליקדשיה ביום שלשים — וממילא כי מקדשינן ליה למחר, מיעבר החדש שעבר, דיום שלשים — בתריה שדית ליה. **תני קידוש — ועל** כל חדשי השנה קאי. **והא עבור קתני — דרך** תנא טועה בגירסא לחסר תיבה על ידי שכחה, אבל אין נחלף לתנא בין גירסת קידוש לגירסת עיבור. **ביום עיבור — יום** עיבור הוא יום שלשים, שממנו נעשה החדש מעובר כשרוצין לעברו. **קידוש ביום עיבור — כגון** בחדש חסר שעבר, צריך שלשה לקדש ראש חדש הבא, ביום שלשים לחדש שעבר. **לאחר עיבור — אם** עשו חודש שעבר מלא, וקבעו ראש חודש ביום שלשים ואחד, אין אומרין בו מקודש מקודש. **בזמנו — ביום** שלשים, דתולדתו ביום שלשים הוא, דאין חדש לבנה פחות מעשרים ותשעה יום ומחצה ושבע מאות תשעים ושלשה חלקים. **שבבר קידשוהו בשמים — בית** דין שלמעלה מאתמול.

NOTES

עִיבּוּר הַשָּׁנָה **Intercalation of the year.** Today's Jewish calendar is fixed in accordance with set astronomical calculations which guarantee a correlation between the lunar cycle governing the Jewish month and the solar cycle determining the appointed time for Jewish Festivals. This correlation is based on a nineteen-year cycle, of which seven are predetermined leap years. In ancient times, however, the calendar year was set by the High Court, which would decide annually on the basis of pertinent considerations as to whether a particular year should be intercalated.

שֶׁכְּבָר קִידְּשׁוּהוּ בַּשָּׁמַיִם **For they already sanctified it in Heaven.** Some interpret the heavenly sanctification referred to in Rabbi Elazar ben Tzadok's Baraita as a regular and automatic occurrence accompanying the monthly renewal of the lunar cycle. This appears to be the opinion of *Rashi* in our Gemara as well; he notes that the heavenly court always sanctifies the New Moon on the thirtieth of the concluding month, the day upon which the moon renews its cycle, though it is not always visible. *Tosafot* offers an alternative explanation, based upon *Rashi* in tractate *Rosh HaShanah* and supported by the Jerusalem Talmud, which interprets the heavenly sanctification referred to by Rabbi Elazar as a selective intervention by the celestial court that takes place on the morning of the thirty-first in the event that the earthly court has not managed to sanctify the New Moon until then.

CONCEPTS

עִיבּוּר הַשָּׁנָה **The intercalation of an extra month.** The months of the Hebrew calendar are reckoned according to the cycle of the moon, and years according to the cycle of the sun. The solar year (365.25 days) is slightly more than eleven days longer than a lunar year of twelve months (approximately 354 days). The Torah fixed the Festivals to specific dates, months and particular seasons. Passover must occur in the spring at the time of the barley harvest, and Sukkot at the time of the autumn equinox. In order that the Festivals fall at their appropriate times it is necessary to adjust the lunar calendar to the solar one. This is done by intercalating an additional month after the month of Adar. It is referred to as Adar Sheni ("Second Adar"). During the time when the calendar was still set every year by the Sanhedrin, the question of whether to add an extra month involved many complex considerations. For that reason the court had a special composition, for it was considered as having the highest authority, and only the Sanhedrin could appoint the judges who sat on it. Today, the Hebrew calendar operates on a fixed astronomical system using a nineteen-year cycle which correlates the lunar and the solar calendars. Months are added to seven years of the nineteen-year cycle.

SAGES

רַבִּי אֶלְעָזָר בְּרַבִּי צָדוֹק **Rabbi Elazar the son of Rabbi Tzadok.** He lived at the time of the destruction of the Temple, and was the son of a Sage of the previous generation who was famous for his piety and many fasts, and was one of the important priests in the Temple. The family of Rabbi Tzadok were extremely important to the Sages, and Rabban Yoḥanan ben Zakkai tried to save them from the destruction. Rabbi Elazar the son of Rabbi Tzadok was one of the friends of the Nasi, Rabban Gamliel of Yavneh, and was active in the Great Assembly of Sages that met in Yavneh. His teachings and personal memories are found in many passages in the

¹רַב נַחְמָן אָמַר: ²״קִידּוּשׁ אַחַר עִיבּוּר בִּשְׁלֹשָׁה״. ³בְּיוֹם עִיבּוּר — לֵיכָּא קִידּוּשׁ. ⁴וּמַנִּי? ⁵פְּלִימוֹ הִיא, דְּתַנְיָא: ⁶״פְּלִימוֹ אוֹמֵר: בִּזְמַנּוֹ, אֵין מְקַדְּשִׁין אוֹתוֹ. ⁷שֶׁלֹּא בִּזְמַנּוֹ, מְקַדְּשִׁין אוֹתוֹ״.

⁸רַב אַשִׁי אֲמַר: לְעוֹלָם ״חִישּׁוּב״ קָתָנֵי. ⁹וּמַאי עִיבּוּר? ¹⁰חִישּׁוּב דְּעִיבּוּר. ¹¹וְאַיְּידֵי דְּקָבָעֵי לְמִיתְנֵי ״עִיבּוּר שָׁנָה״, ¹²תָּנָא נַמִי ״עִיבּוּר חוֹדֶשׁ״.

¹³חִישּׁוּב חוֹדֶשׁ — אִין, ¹⁴קִידּוּשׁ חוֹדֶשׁ — לָא. ¹⁵מַנִּי? ¹⁶רַבִּי אֱלִיעֶזֶר הִיא. דְּתַנְיָא: ¹⁷״רַבִּי אֱלִיעֶזֶר אוֹמֵר: בֵּין בִּזְמַנּוֹ בֵּין שֶׁלֹּא בִּזְמַנּוֹ

LITERAL TRANSLATION

[1]Rav Naḥman said: [2]"Sanctification after intercalation by three." [3]On the day of intercalation — there is no sanctification. [4]And who is it? [5]It is Plimo, for it was taught: [6]"Plimo says: At its time, they do not sanctify it. [7]Not at its time, they sanctify it."

[8]Rav Ashi said: In fact, "calculation" is taught. [9]And what is "intercalation"? [10]The calculating of intercalation. [11]And since he wanted to teach "the intercalation of the year," [12]he also taught "the intercalation of the month."

[13]Calculating a month — yes; [14]sanctifying a month — not. [15]Who is it? [16]It is Rabbi Eliezer, for it was taught: [17]"Rabbi Eliezer says: Whether at its time or not at its time,

TRANSLATION AND COMMENTARY

additional sanctification here below.

רַב נַחְמָן אָמַר [1]**Rav Naḥman said** that the difficulty with the Mishnah can be resolved in just the opposite way: [2]**"Sanctification** of the new month on the day **after intercalation** [the thirty-first] must be effected **by** a court of **three** judges." [3]It would then follow that **on the day of intercalation** itself (the thirtieth) **there is no** need at all for official **sanctification,** as that is the day on which one would expect the New Moon to appear (judicial intervention being necessary only when the moon does not appear at its appointed time). [4]**And who is** the source of the ruling in our Mishnah, according to this interpretation? [5]**It is Plimo, for it was taught in** another Baraita: [6]**"Plimo says:** If the New Moon was seen **at its** anticipated **time** [on the thirtieth of the concluding month], the court **does not sanctify it,** for it appeared as expected. [7]But if the New Moon was **not** seen **at its** anticipated **time,** the court must intervene and **sanctify** the new month on the following day [the thirty-first]."

רַב אַשִׁי אָמַר [8]**Rav Ashi said** that the Mishnah may be understood in yet another manner: It is **in fact** the **calculation** of the month that **is taught** in the Mishnah as requiring three judges, as there is no need for a court to formally pronounce the intercalation of months which pass their thirtieth day without a sighting of the New Moon. [9]You may ask: **What,** then, **is** the meaning of the term **"intercalation"** that explicitly appears in the Mishnah? [10]The answer is that the Mishnah is referring specifically to **the calculating of intercalation** — a process whereby the court determines if it is appropriate, for other reasons, to render a particular month "full" or "incomplete." The reason the Tanna did not explicitly refer to the term "calculation" in the Mishnah was in order to maintain stylistic uniformity: [11]**Since he wanted to teach** us in the next clause about **"the intercalation of the year"** (the process of determining the need for a leap year and then formally proclaiming one), [12]**he also taught** the former rule using similar language: "**The intercalation of the month."**

חִישּׁוּב חוֹדֶשׁ [13]The Gemara notes: According to Rav Ashi's interpretation of the Mishnah, it appears that, although **calculating** the intercalation of **a** particular **month** would **indeed** require a court of three judges, [14]**sanctifying a** new **month** would **not.** [15]**Who,** then, **is** the source of this ruling in our Mishnah? [16]**It is Rabbi Eliezer, for it was taught** in another Baraita: [17]**"Rabbi Eliezer says: Whether** the crescent of the New Moon was seen **at its** anticipated **time or not** seen **at its** anticipated **time,**

RASHI

פלימו אומר בזמנו אין מקדשין אותו — שאין צריך לעשות חיזוק לדבר, שהרי זמנו בא. **חישוב דעבור** — לחשב אם יעברוהו, דאילו קידוש סבר תנא דידן דלא צריך לקדושי, לא מלא ולא חסר, וכרבי אלעזר ברבי שמעון לקמן, ואיידי דתני עיבור השנה דהוי נמי חישוב דעיבור השנה והתם לא סגי דלא תני עיבור, דאמירה בעי, שיקדשו אדר השני לשם אדר, דאי שתקי ממילא לשם ניסן מיקבע, תנא נמי גבי חדש עיבור החדש, וקרייה נמי לחישוב — עיבור, ואשמעינן דחישוב בעינן, אבל קידוש לא בעינן לא למלא ולא לחסר כרבי אליעזר.

Mishnah among the important testimonies of the Sages. He was apparently a merchant by profession, and his righteousness and piety are regarded in the Talmud as exemplary. He appears to have lived a long time and was active for many years. There were two Sages of this name, and the second of them was one of the last of the Tannaim, a member of the generation of Rabbi Yehudah HaNasi.

SAGES

פְּלִימוֹ Plimo. The Sage Plimo was a disciple of Rabbi Yehudah HaNasi, and we find him asking his teacher questions about the Halakhah. Some of his Halakhic teachings are reported in Baraitot, and we find him in disagreement with Rabbi's colleague, Rabbi Eliezer the son of Rabbi Shimon. Many stories are told about his great piety.

LANGUAGE

פְּלִימוֹ Plimo. The name Plimo is apparently derived from the Greek παλαιός, *palaios*, meaning "old." Similar names were used among Jewish communities, for the purpose of bringing good fortune.

HALAKHAH

עִיבּוּר הַחֹדֶשׁ The intercalation of the month. "The intercalation of the month requires a court of three judges. The sanctification of the month, as well as the calculations that go into determining whether the concluding month should be intercalated, also require a court of three judges. The new month is only sanctified if the crescent of the moon was seen at its anticipated time, on the thirtieth day of the concluding month," following Rabbi Elazar ben Tzadok. (*Rambam, Sefer Shofetim, Hilkhot Sanhedrin* 5:6; *Sefer Zemanin, Hilkhot Kiddush HaḤodesh* 2:8.)

TRANSLATION AND COMMENTARY

[1]the court **does not** have to **sanctify it** formally, [2]**for it is stated** in a verse from Leviticus [25:10]: **'And you shall sanctify the fiftieth year** and proclaim liberty throughout all the land to all of its inhabitants; it shall be a jubilee for you.' [3]We deduce from this verse that Jubilee **Years you** must formally **sanctify** in court, [4]**but you do not** have to formally **sanctify** ordinary **months** of the year as they are sanctified automatically by heavenly decree."

רַבָּן שִׁמְעוֹן בֶּן גַּמְלִיאֵל [5]The next clause of the Mishnah proceeds to explore further the rules governing intercalation of the year, a procedure whereby the court determines that an additional month be appended to the year immediately after the month of Adar, prior to Nisan (when the Festival of Pesaḥ occurs). This additional month, which is called Adar II, is inserted into the calendar year for very specific reasons that relate to the synchronization of the lunar and solar cycles, necessary for proper observance of the Jewish Festivals: **"Rabban Shimon ben Gamliel** disagrees with Rabbi Meir and **says:** As regards intercalation of the year, **with three** judges the court begins to consider the matter, **etc."** [6]**It was taught** in the following Baraita: **"What did Rabban Shimon ben Gamliel** say about the expanding composition of the court that oversees intercalation of the year? [7]**With three** judges the court **begin**s to consider the matter; [8]**and with five** judges **they deliberate** it; [9]**and they finalize** their decision **with seven** judges. The initial trio of judges, selected from the Sanhedrin, assemble to consider whether there is sufficient reason to open the entire issue of intercalation. [10]If **one** of the three judges **says** that there is sufficient reason **to sit** and deliberate the matter, [11]**and two say** that there is **not** sufficient reason **to sit** and do so, [12]**the single** judge's opinion advocating deliberation **is negated insofar as it is a minority** one, and so the matter ends there.

[1]אֵין מְקַדְּשִׁין אוֹתוֹ, [2]שֶׁנֶּאֱמַר: ׳וְקִדַּשְׁתֶּם אֵת שְׁנַת הַחֲמִשִּׁים שָׁנָה׳ — [3]שָׁנִים אַתָּה מְקַדֵּשׁ, [4]וְאִי אַתָּה מְקַדֵּשׁ חֳדָשִׁים״. [5]״רַבָּן שִׁמְעוֹן בֶּן גַּמְלִיאֵל אוֹמֵר: בִּשְׁלֹשָׁה כו׳״. [6]תַּנְיָא: ״כֵּיצַד אָמַר רַבָּן שִׁמְעוֹן בֶּן גַּמְלִיאֵל? [7]בִּשְׁלֹשָׁה מַתְחִילִין, [8]וּבַחֲמִשָּׁה נוֹשְׂאִין וְנוֹתְנִין, [9]וְגוֹמְרִין בְּשִׁבְעָה. [10]אֶחָד אוֹמֵר לֵישֵׁב, [11]וּשְׁנַיִם אוֹמְרִים שֶׁלֹּא לֵישֵׁב, [12]בָּטֵל יָחִיד בְּמִיעוּטוֹ.

LITERAL TRANSLATION

[1]they do not sanctify it, [2]for it is stated: 'And you shall sanctify the fiftieth year' — [3]years you sanctify, [4]but you do not sanctify months."

[5]"Rabban Shimon ben Gamliel says: With three, etc." [6]It was taught: "How did Rabban Shimon ben Gamliel say? [7]With three they begin, [8]and with five they deliberate, [9]and they finalize with seven. [10][If] one says to sit, [11]and two say not to sit, [12]the single one is negated in [so far as] it is a minority [opinion].

RASHI

שנים אתה מקדש — שנה של כל יובל ויובל מקדשין בית דין לשם יובל. **אחד אומר לישב** — אחד מן השלשה אומר צריך לישב ולעיין אם צריכה לעבר שנה זו מפני האביב, או התקופות או פירות האילנות, כדלקמן סנהדרין (יא,ב). **ושנים אומרים** — אינו צריך להושיב בית דין על כך, שאין כאן ספק, דודאי אינה צריכה לעבר. **בטל יחיד במיעוטו** — ולא ישבו החמשה עוד לעיין בדבר.

NOTES

הַשִּׁיטוֹת בְּקִידּוּשׁ הַחֹדֶשׁ Opinions about sanctifying the month.

The authority	Thirty days	Thirty-one days
The anonymous Tanna in *Rosh HaShanah*	They sanctify	They sanctify
Rabbi Elazar ben Tzadok	They sanctify	They do not sanctify
Plimo	They do not sanctify	They sanctify
Rabbi Eliezer	They do not sanctify	They do not sanctify

שָׁנִים אַתָּה מְקַדֵּשׁ Years you sanctify. *Ran* explains that Rabbi Eliezer's inference is based on the superfluous ה in the expression שְׁנַת הַחֲמִשִּׁים, "the fiftieth year." The emphasis created by that extraneous definite article implies that only years require sanctification, not months.

וְגוֹמְרִין בְּשִׁבְעָה And they finalize with seven. According to *Remah,* if the three judges with whom the deliberations began all agree that adding an extra month to the year is necessary, the court need not be augmented any further and they themselves can proceed to intercalate the year on their own. Expanding the court is only necessary when the initial tribunal is divided and at least two support further

HALAKHAH

בִּשְׁלֹשָׁה מַתְחִילִין With three, they begin. "The deliberations regarding the addition of an extra month to the year start with three judges selected from the Great Sanhedrin. If two of the three judges think that there are grounds to consider the matter further, two more judges are added and the deliberations continue. If three of the five judges conclude that adding an extra month is necessary, two more judges are added and the deliberations are reinitiated. Only when a majority of seven judges decide that it is necessary to intercalate the year is the additional — thirteenth — month added." This is all in accordance with Rabban Shimon ben Gamliel, whose views in the Mishnah are accepted as law, and whose opinion here seems to be accepted by the Gemara. (*Rambam, Sefer Zemanim, Hilkhot Kiddush HaḤodesh* 4:9-10.)

TRANSLATION AND COMMENTARY

[1]If, however, **two** of the three judges **say** that there is indeed reason **to sit** and deliberate the matter further, [2]**and one says** that there is **not** sufficient reason **to sit** and do so, the majority opinion of the two is accepted; [3]**and** so the Sanhedrin **adds to them another two judges, and** together the five judges **deliberate the matter.** [4]If **two** of these five judges then **say** that **it is necessary** to add an extra month to the year, **and three say** that **it is not necessary** to do so, [5]**the two** judges who advocate intercalation **are negated insofar as they are a minority** and the deliberations come to an end. [6]If, however, **three** of the five judges **say** that **it is** indeed **necessary** to add an extra month to the year, [7]**and two say** that **it is not necessary** to do so, [8]the Sanhedrin **adds to them another two** judges, [9]**for the quorum** needed to conclude the deliberations and officially proclaim a leap year **cannot be** composed of **fewer than seven** judges."

הָנֵי שְׁלֹשָׁה [10]The Gemara proceeds to ask with regard to Rabban Shimon ben Gamliel's three-staged judicial process: **These** varying formulae for constructing the court's composition — first **three,** then **five,** and finally **seven** judges — [11]**to whom** or to what were they intended **to correspond?**

פְּלִיגֵי בָּהּ [12]**Rabbi Yitzḥak bar Naḥmani and one** other scholar **who was with him disagreed about this** very issue. [13]**And who was** that other scholar? [14]**Rabbi Shimon ben Pazi.** [15]**And some say** that this was a

[1]שְׁנַיִם אוֹמְרִים לֵישֵׁב, [2]וְאֶחָד אוֹמֵר שֶׁלֹּא לֵישֵׁב [3]מוֹסִיפִין עֲלֵיהֶם עוֹד שְׁנַיִם, וְנוֹשְׂאִין וְנוֹתְנִין בַּדָּבָר. [4]שְׁנַיִם אוֹמְרִים צְרִיכָה, וּשְׁלֹשָׁה אוֹמְרִים אֵינָהּ צְרִיכָה, [5]בָּטְלוּ שְׁנַיִם בְּמִיעוּטָן. [6]שְׁלֹשָׁה אוֹמְרִים צְרִיכָה, [7]וּשְׁנַיִם אוֹמְרִים אֵינָהּ צְרִיכָה, [8]מוֹסִיפִין עֲלֵיהֶם עוֹד שְׁנַיִם, [9]שֶׁאֵין הַמִּנְיָן פָּחוֹת מִשִּׁבְעָה. [10]הָנֵי שְׁלֹשָׁה חֲמִשָּׁה וְשִׁבְעָה, [11]כְּנֶגֶד מִי? [12]פְּלִיגִי בָּהּ רַבִּי יִצְחָק בַּר נַחְמָנִי וְחַד דְּעִימֵּיהּ. [13]וּמַנּוּ? [14]רַבִּי שִׁמְעוֹן בֶּן פָּזִי. [15]וְאָמְרִי

LITERAL TRANSLATION

[1][If] two say to sit, [2]and one says not to sit, [3]they add to them another two and they deliberate the matter. [4][If] two say it is necessary, and three say it is not necessary, [5]the two are negated as a minority. [6][If] three say it is necessary, [7]and two say it is not necessary, [8]they add to them another two, [9]for the quorum cannot be fewer than seven."

[10]These three, five and seven, [11]corresponding to whom [are they]?

[12]Rabbi Yitzḥak bar Naḥmani and one who was with him disagreed about this. [13]And who was it? [14]Rabbi Shimon ben Pazi. [15]And some say:

RASHI

שנים אומרים לישב ואחד אומר שלא לישב – הולכין אחר השנים ויושבין לישא וליתן אם צריכה לעבר אם לאו, ומשא ומתן של עיבור צריך חמשה, לפיכך מוסיפין עוד שנים, ולקמן מפרש שלשה וחמשה ושבעה כנגד מי. **שנים אומרים צריכה** – לעבר, ושלשה אומרים: אין צריכה, בטלו שנים במיעוטן ועומדין והולכין להם. **שנים אומרים אינה צריכה ושלשה אומרים צריכה** – הולכין אחר הרוב, ומוסיפין עוד שנים להשלמת המנין, ומעברין.

NOTES

deliberation. *Rabbenu Yonah* and *Ran* disagree, maintaining that in any case the court's determination must be confirmed by panels of five and seven as well, as those numbers are derived from Scriptural sources.

Rambam maintains that the final panel of seven does not come to simply confirm the majority opinion arrived at by the panel of five, but rather reopens the entire issue to new deliberation so as to arrive at its own decision. The language of *Rashi* is somewhat ambiguous and may imply that when a majority of the five have determined that the year should be intercalated, the additional two judges are added only for the sake of formal proclamation and do not signal a new deliberation.

שְׁלֹשָׁה חֲמִשָּׁה וְשִׁבְעָה **Three, five and seven.** *Rashi* and others explain that, just as we find an earthly king ministered to and honored by an assemblage of three, five, and seven, so too is the Heavenly King honored by the assemblage of three, five, and seven judges here below who arrange the calendar year in accordance with the dictates of the Festival service. *Rashi* identifies the seven ministers referred to in the Gemara as those listed at the beginning of the Scroll of Esther as having served the Persian King Ahashverosh. *Tosafot* finds it hard to accept that the Gemara would have identified a pagan assembly as the model for a Jewish court, and so it adopts the opinion of *Rabbenu Tam* (supported by the Jerusalem Talmud) that identifies the seven ministers of our Gemara as those mentioned in Jeremiah (52:25) as having been carried away from Jerusalem into Babylonian exile.

The Jerusalem Talmud is also cited by various Rishonim as obliquely explaining the need for a combination of three, five and seven judges when intercalating the year in terms of coming to nullify the decree of the three, five, and seven. *Ran* identifies this decree as the one alluded to in the verse from Job (5:19): "He will deliver you in six troubles, and in seven no evil shall touch you." However, *Remah*, in seeking to reconcile this citation from the Jerusalem Talmud with our own Gemara, suggests that the decree referred to is that directed against Israel at the urging of the three, five, and seven ministers who counsel the non-Jewish kings as well.

לָהּ: רַבִּי שִׁמְעוֹן בֶּן פָּזִי וְחַד דְּעִימֵּיהּ. [1] וּמַנּוּ? [2] רַבִּי יִצְחָק בַּר נַחְמָנִי. [3] חַד אֲמַר: כְּנֶגֶד בִּרְכַּת כֹּהֲנִים. [4] וְחַד אֲמַר: שְׁלֹשָׁה — כְּנֶגֶד שׁוֹמְרֵי הַסַּף, [5] חֲמִשָּׁה מֵרוֹאֵי פְּנֵי הַמֶּלֶךְ, [6] שִׁבְעָה רוֹאֵי פְּנֵי הַמֶּלֶךְ.

[7] תָּנֵי רַב יוֹסֵף: [8] ״הָנֵי שְׁלֹשָׁה וַחֲמִשָּׁה וְשִׁבְעָה: [9] שְׁלֹשָׁה כְּנֶגֶד ׳שׁוֹמְרֵי הַסַּף׳, [10] חֲמִשָּׁה ׳מֵרוֹאֵי פְּנֵי הַמֶּלֶךְ׳, [11] שִׁבְעָה ׳רוֹאֵי פְּנֵי הַמֶּלֶךְ׳.

[12] אֲמַר לֵיהּ אַבָּיֵי לְרַב יוֹסֵף: [13] ׳עַד הָאִידָּנָא מַאי טַעֲמָא לָא פָּרֵישׁ לָן מָר הָכִי׳? [14] אֲמַר לְהוּ: ׳לָא הֲוָה יָדַעְנָא דִּצְרִיכִיתוּ. [15] מִי בְּעֵיתוּ מִנַּאי מִילְּתָא וְלָא אֲמַרִי לְכוּ׳״? [16] ״זִמֵּן, נָשִׂיא, צָרִיךְ, גְּדִי״ סִימָן.

LITERAL TRANSLATION

Rabbi Shimon ben Pazi and one who was with him. [1] And who was it? [2] Rabbi Yitzḥak bar Naḥmani. [3] One said: [It] corresponds to the Priestly Benediction. [4] And one said: Three — correspond to the "guards of the entrance"; [5] five — [correspond to] "from the king's ministers"; [6] seven — [correspond to] the king's ministers.

[7] Rav Yosef taught: [8] "These three, and five, and seven: [9] Three correspond to 'the guards of the entrance,' [10] five [correspond to] 'from the king's ministers,' [11] seven [correspond to] 'the king's ministers.'"

[12] Abaye said to Rav Yosef: [13] "What is the reason that until today Master did not explain it to us this way?" [14] He said to them: "I did not know that you needed [this]. [15] Have you asked me something and I did not tell you?"

[16] A mnemonic is "invited, chief, necessary, kid."

TRANSLATION AND COMMENTARY

matter of disagreement between **Rabbi Shimon ben Pazi and one** other scholar **who was with him.** [1] **And who was** that other scholar? [2] **Rabbi Yitzḥak bar Naḥmani.** [3] **One** of these two Amoraim **said:** The number of judges required for each of these three stages **corresponds to the** number of words found in the three verses (Numbers 6:24-26) that comprise the traditional **Priestly Benediction** recited before the congregation of Israel — they being three, five and seven words, respectively. [4] **And one** Amora **said:** The **three** judges required to begin the process **correspond to the** three **"guards of the** Temple **entrance"** carried away into exile by the Babylonian oppressor, Nevuzaradan (II Kings 25:18); [5] the **five** judges required in order to commence deliberations correspond to the five men **"from the king's ministers,"** who were also carried away in that exile (II Kings 25:19); [6] and the **seven** judges required for the final decision and proclamation correspond to another seven of **"the king's ministers."** Since these were all men of great rank and responsibility, their numbers were carried over in composing the court that was to be invested with the serious duty of intercalating the year.

תָּנֵי רַב יוֹסֵף [7] **Rav Yosef taught** the same thing in a Baraita which he transmitted: [8] **"These** varying formulae used in conceiving the court's composition — first **three,** then **five,** and finally **seven** judges — were derived as follows: [9] The **three** judges required at the beginning of the process **correspond to the** three **'guards of the entrance'** exiled by Nevuzaradan; [10] the **five** judges required in order to commence deliberations correspond to the five men **'from the king's ministers,'** who were also included in that exile; [11] and the **seven** judges required for the final decision correspond to another seven of **'the king's ministers.'"**

אֲמַר לֵיהּ אַבָּיֵי [12] **Abaye said to Rav Yosef:** [13] **"What is the reason that until now Master did not explain** the matter **to us in this way,** although you have taught us tractate *Sanhedrin* before? [14] Rav Yosef **said to them: "I did not know that you needed** this information, as I thought that you were already familiar with the Baraita. [15] **Have you** ever **asked me something and I did not tell you?"**

זִמֵּן [16] The Gemara now records several different regulations in regard to intercalating the year. **A mnemonic** that can be used to remember this string of regulations **is "invited, chief, necessary, kid,"** each word representing a different rule.

RASHI

כנגד ברכת כהנים — בפסוק ראשון שלש תיבות, והשני חמש, ושלישי שבע תיבות. **שלשה כנגד שומרי הסף כו׳** — כלומר אשכחנא דמלכותא דארעא שלשה ממונין, וחמשה ממונין, ושבעה ממונין, שלשה כנגד שומרי הסף בצדקיהו (מלכים ב׳ כה), גבי גלות נבוזראדן, והתם נמי משכחת חמשה מרואי פני המלך, ובאחשורוש (אסתר א) אשכחן שבעה שרי פרס ומדי, ועיבור שנה מטכסיסי מלכות שמים הוא ליישב סדר השנים על מכונן.

NOTES

כְּנֶגֶד בִּרְכַּת כֹּהֲנִים **Corresponding to the Priestly Benediction.** *Iyyun Ya'akov* explains the connection between the number of words in each verse of the Priestly Benediction and the number of judges who must participate in the intercalation of the year as follows: In the case of the Priestly Benediction, the priests utter it and then God Himself agrees to bestow His blessing upon the people, as stated in the verse (Numbers 6:27): "And they shall put My name upon the children of Israel, and I will bless them"; so, too, as regards the intercalation of the year, the judges decide that there is a need, and then God Himself agrees with their decision.

BACKGOUND

וְחַד דְּעִימֵּיהּ **One who was with him.** It was known that these two Sages, Rabbi Shimon ben Pazi and Rabbi Yitzḥak bar Naḥmani, who were colleagues and discussed various problems of Halakhah and Aggadah with each other, disagreed on the matter. When the tradition was examined closely, it was found that one of their names was stated explicitly, and the other name was to be deduced on the basis of knowledge of the relations between them.

SAGES

רַבִּי שִׁמְעוֹן בֶּן פָּזִי **Rabbi Shimon ben Pazi.** A Palestinian Amora of the third generation, Rabbi Shimon ben Pazi was the closest disciple of Rabbi Yehoshua ben Levi, and he presents many teachings in the latter's name. Most of Rabbi Shimon ben Pazi's teachings are Aggadic, though some Halakhic teachings are also presented in his name. Rabbi Shimon ben Pazi was a colleague of Rabbi Abbahu, of Rabbi Yitzḥak Nappaḥa, and of Rabbi Yitzḥak bar Naḥmani. Rabbi Shimon ben Pazi's son was Rabbi Yehudah the son of Rabbi Shimon ben Pazi, who was one of the Sages of the following generation.

רַבִּי יִצְחָק בַּר נַחְמָנִי **Rabbi Yitzḥak bar Naḥmani.** A Palestinian Amora of the third generation, Rabbi Yitzḥak bar Naḥmani, or bar Naḥman, as he is known in the Jerusalem Talmud, was apparently born in Babylonia, where he was a student of Shmuel's. However, he moved to Eretz Israel as a young man and had the privilege of studying Torah with the younger students of Rabbi Yehudah HaNasi. His principal teacher was Rabbi Yehoshua ben Levi, whose teachings he transmitted, in addition relating details about his conduct. Rabbi Yitzḥak bar Naḥmani lived to a great age and also related teachings in the name of his colleagues, the great students of Rabbi Yoḥanan.

TRANSLATION AND COMMENTARY

תָּנוּ רַבָּנַן [1] **Our Rabbis taught** the following Baraita: "The Sanhedrin does not **intercalate the year except** [11A] **with** judges **who were invited** in advance by the Nasi of the Sanhedrin **for** that specific purpose." [2] The Baraita illustrates this rule with the following story: **"It once happened that Rabban Gamliel,** the Nasi of the Sanhedrin, **said** to the Sages: [3] **'Awaken for me seven** members of the Sanhedrin **early** tomorrow morning and bring them **to the upper chamber** so that they may sit as a special court to decide whether to add an extra month to the year.' [4] Rabban Gamliel **awoke early** the next day, proceeded to the appointed place, **and found** there **eight** members of the Sanhedrin. [5] Rabban Gamliel **said** to them: **'Who came up here without permission? [6] Let him go down** at once.' [7] **Shmuel HaKatan rose and said: 'I am the one who came up here without permission. [8] But it was not** in order **to intercalate the year** that **I ascended,** [9] **but rather I found it necessary to learn** how **the law** is put **into practice.'** [10] Rabban Gamliel **said to** Shmuel HaKatan: **'Sit** down, **my son, sit** down. [11] Indeed, **all the years are fit to be intercalated by** a court which includes **you** as one of its members. [12] **But** what can I do? **The Sages said:** [13] The Sanhedrin **does not intercalate the year except with** judges **who were invited** by the Nasi of the Sanhedrin **for** that specific purpose.'" [14] The Gemara notes: **And** the eighth, uninvited judge **was not** really **Shmuel HaKatan, but another man** among them. [15] **And it was because of the shame** that other man would have experienced had it become known that he ascended without permission, **that** Shmuel HaKatan **did** what he did in taking the blame.

[1] תָּנוּ רַבָּנַן: ״אֵין מְעַבְּרִין אֶת הַשָּׁנָה אֶלָּא [11A] בִּמְזוּמָּנִין לָהּ. [2] מַעֲשֶׂה בְּרַבָּן גַּמְלִיאֵל שֶׁאָמַר: [3] ׳הַשְׁכִּימוּ לִי שִׁבְעָה לָעֲלִיָּיה׳. [4] הִשְׁכִּים וּמָצָא שְׁמוֹנָה. [5] אָמַר: ׳מִי הוּא שֶׁעָלָה שֶׁלֹּא בִּרְשׁוּת? [6] יֵרֵד׳! [7] עָמַד שְׁמוּאֵל הַקָּטָן וְאָמַר: ׳אֲנִי הוּא שֶׁעָלִיתִי שֶׁלֹּא בִּרְשׁוּת. [8] וְלֹא לְעַבֵּר הַשָּׁנָה עָלִיתִי, [9] אֶלָּא לִלְמוֹד הֲלָכָה לְמַעֲשֶׂה הוּצְרַכְתִּי׳. [10] אָמַר לוֹ: ׳שֵׁב בְּנִי, שֵׁב. [11] רְאוּיוֹת כָּל הַשָּׁנִים כּוּלָּן לְהִתְעַבֵּר עַל יָדְךָ. [12] אֶלָּא אָמְרוּ חֲכָמִים: [13] אֵין מְעַבְּרִין אֶת הַשָּׁנָה אֶלָּא בִּמְזוּמָּנִין לָהּ׳״. [14] וְלֹא שְׁמוּאֵל הַקָּטָן הֲוָה, אֶלָּא אִינִישׁ אַחֲרִינָא, [15] וּמֵחֲמַת כִּיסוּפָא הוּא דַּעֲבַד.

LITERAL TRANSLATION

[1] Our Rabbis taught: "They do not intercalate the year except [11A] with those who were invited for it. [2] It once happened that Rabban Gamliel said: [3] 'Awaken seven for me early to the upper chamber.' [4] He awoke early and found eight. [5] He said: 'Who is he that came up without permission? [6] Let him go down.' [7] Shmuel HaKatan rose and said: 'I am the one who came up without permission. [8] But it was not to intercalate the year that I came up, [9] but rather I found it necessary to learn the law in practice.' [10] He said to him: 'Sit, my son, sit. [11] All the years are fit to be intercalated by you. [12] But the Sages said: [13] They do not intercalate the year except with those who were invited for it.'" [14] And it was not Shmuel HaKatan, but rather another man, [15] and it was because of the shame that he did it.

RASHI

במזומנין לה — שהזמינן הנשיא מבערב. **השכימו לי** — מחר שבעה לעלייה המיוחדת, לישב בה בית דין. **ולא לעבר שנה עליתי** — להצטרף עמכם עכשיו. **אלא ללמוד** — תורה מכם, היאך תעשו. **מחמת כיסופא הוא דעבד** — שלא יכירו מי היה העולה שלא ברשות וילבינו פניו.

NOTES

הַשְׁכִּימוּ לִי שִׁבְעָה לָעֲלִיָּיה **Awaken seven for me early to the upper chamber.** The Rishonim ask: How is it that Rabban Gamliel did not know who arrived that morning uninvited? Surely, it was he who sent out the invitations! *Ran* suggests that Rabban Gamliel sent a deputy to invite seven members of the Sanhedrin to the special session discussing the intercalation of the year, but he did not specify which members to invite. *Remah* suggests that Rabban Gamliel approached a large group from the Sanhedrin and said that seven of them should come the next morning to a special session, but did not designate which ones. *Rabbenu Yonah* argues that, indeed, Rabban Gamliel did personally invite the seven by name, and thus knew who had arrived uninvited, but nevertheless refrained from singling him out so as not to embarrass him.

אֶלָּא בִּמְזוּמָּנִין לָהּ **With those who were invited for it.** *Remah* and others allude to the fact that if Shmuel HaKatan had really been invited, but left in order to save his colleague from embarrassment, then one of the remaining seven would not have been eligible to join in the deliberations, not having been invited to do so. For this reason, they cite the Jerusalem Talmud, where it is mentioned that the seven remaining judges indeed deliberated other matters that day, deferring deliberation on the calendar to another time.

HALAKHAH

בִּמְזוּמָּנִין לָהּ **With those who were invited for it.** "The year can only be intercalated by a court composed of judges who, as members of the Sanhedrin, were specifically invited by the Nasi to determine whether a month should be added to the calendar year," in accordance with Rabban Shimon ben Gamliel. (*Rambam, Sefer Zemanim, Hilkhot Kiddush HaḤodesh* 4:9.)

BACKGROUND

עֲלִיָּיה **Attic.** This term ordinarily refers to an attic, the upper story of a building, which was sometimes as large as the apartment beneath it and occupied by different tenants. Usually, however, the attic was a smaller structure, and access to it was by a ladder extending through the ceiling of the lower apartment.

The Talmud describes a number of meetings and assemblies of Sages held in attics. Usually they would meet there in rather limited groups, mainly concerning matters that they did not wish to be publicly known. Occasionally they met in attics to hide from the hostile authorities; and sometimes they did so when a protracted and detailed discussion was needed, and they did not wish to be disturbed. Any discussion about adding an intercalary month was of great importance for all the Jews, and many other matters depended upon it, both the celebration of the Festivals and monetary transactions. Hence it was carried out in a small, well-defined group, and sometimes it was termed "סוֹד הָעִיבּוּר", the intercalary secret.

SAGES

שְׁמוּאֵל הַקָּטָן **Shmuel HaKatan.** This Tanna lived during the Second Temple period. From various sources it appears that he was one of Hillel's younger students and lived to a great age, apparently until soon before the destruction of the Temple. Almost none of his Torah teachings are known to us, aside from a few Aggadic sayings. It seems that because of his great piety and modesty he was chosen to compose the blessing about heretics, actually a curse against heretics and informers, that is included in the *Shmoneh Esreh* prayer to this day.

Regarding his epithet, "the small," two opinions are found in the Jerusalem Talmud: (1) He made himself small because of his modesty; or (2) he was called "the small" in comparision to Samuel the Prophet ("for he was but little smaller than Samuel the Ramati").

He had no sons, and in

eulogizing him, Rabban Gamliel and Rabbi Eliezer said of him: "For him it is worthy to mourn....Kings die and leave their crowns to their sons. Shmuel HaKatan took all the treasures in the world and went away."

BACKGROUND

הֵרִיחַ רֵיחַ שׁוּם He smelled the odor of garlic. Rabbi Yehuda HaNasi was a refined man who could not stand the odor. Moreover, for a man to chew garlic in a public place, where many people might be inconvenienced by the smell, is a kind of impudence.

TRANSLATION AND COMMENTARY

כִּי הָא דְּיָתֵיב [1]This episode with Shmuel HaKatan is **similar to that** incident **where Rabbi** Yehudah HaNasi **was sitting** in the Academy **and expounding** the law, [2]**when** suddenly **he smelled the odor of garlic** on somebody's breath. Unable to tolerate the smell, [3]**he said** to his disciples: **"Whoever ate garlic, let him go out** of the room at once!" [4]Immediately, **Rabbi Ḥiyya rose and went out** of the room. [5]Out of respect for Rabbi Ḥiyya, **all** the others **rose and went out** as well. [6]**On the following morning, Rabbi Shimon, the son of Rabbi** Yehudah HaNasi, **found Rabbi Ḥiyya** [7]and **said to him: "Are you** really **the one who distressed Father** by arriving in the Academy yesterday with the smell of garlic on your breath?" [8]Rabbi Ḥiyya **said to him:** "Heaven forbid! **Let there never be** an act of disrespect **like that in Israel!"** Rather, Rabbi Ḥiyya accepted the responsibility for distressing Rabbi Yehudah HaNasi in order that the disciple who actually ate the garlic would avoid public humiliation.

וְרַבִּי חִיָּיא [9]**And Rabbi Ḥiyya, from where did he learn** that it is right to accept blame if it means sparing another humiliation? [10]**From Rabbi Meir, for it was taught** in a Baraita: [11]"There was once **an incident involving a** certain **woman who came to the Academy of Rabbi Meir,** [12]and **said to him: 'Master, one of you** in this academy **betrothed me** last night **through** the act of **intercourse,** and then disappeared. I ask that he who betrothed me either conclude the marriage or grant me a divorce so that I may marry another man.' Wishing not to embarrass anyone who may have engaged in the unseemly practice of betrothal through intercourse, [13]**Rabbi Meir rose and wrote out for** the woman **a bill of divorce, and gave it to her.** [14]Recognizing the signal, **all** the other members of the Academy **rose and wrote** out a bill of divorce for her as well, **and gave it to her.** As a result, the identity of the wrongdoer was never revealed."

וְרַבִּי מֵאִיר [15]**And Rabbi Meir, from where did he learn** to accept responsibility for somebody else's wrongdoing? [16]**From Shmuel HaKatan,** whose efforts to spare a wrongdoer public humiliation were related above. [17]**And Shmuel HaKatan, from where did he learn** to behave in this way? [18]**From Shekhanyah, the**

[1]כִּי הָא דְּיָתֵיב רַבִּי וְקָא דָּרֵישׁ,
[2]וְהֵרִיחַ רֵיחַ שׁוּם. [3]אָמַר: "מִי
שֶׁאָכַל שׁוּם יֵצֵא"! [4]עָמַד רַבִּי
חִיָּיא וְיָצָא. [5]עָמְדוּ כּוּלָּן וְיָצְאוּ.
[6]בַּשַּׁחַר מְצָאוֹ רַבִּי שִׁמְעוֹן
בְּרַבִּי לְרַבִּי חִיָּיא, [7]אָמַר לֵיהּ:
"אַתָּה הוּא שֶׁצִּיעַרְתָּ לְאַבָּא"?
[8]אָמַר לוֹ: "לֹא תְּהֵא כָּזֹאת
בְּיִשְׂרָאֵל"!
[9]וְרַבִּי חִיָּיא מֵהֵיכָא גְּמִיר לָהּ?
[10]מֵרַבִּי מֵאִיר, דְּתַנְיָא: [11]"מַעֲשֶׂה
בְּאִשָּׁה אַחַת שֶׁבָּאתָה לְבֵית
מִדְרָשׁוֹ שֶׁל רַבִּי מֵאִיר, [12]אָמְרָה
לוֹ: 'רַבִּי, אֶחָד מִכֶּם קִדְּשַׁנִי
בְּבִיאָה'. [13]עָמַד רַבִּי מֵאִיר וְכָתַב
לָהּ גֵּט כְּרִיתוּת, וְנָתַן לָהּ;
[14]עָמְדוּ כָּתְבוּ כּוּלָּם וְנָתְנוּ לָהּ.
[15]וְרַבִּי מֵאִיר מֵהֵיכָא גְּמִיר לָהּ?
[16]מִשְּׁמוּאֵל הַקָּטָן. [17]וּשְׁמוּאֵל
הַקָּטָן מֵהֵיכָא גְּמִיר לָהּ?
[18]מִשְּׁכַנְיָה בֶּן יְחִיאֵל, דִּכְתִיב:

LITERAL TRANSLATION

[1][It is] similar to that where Rabbi was sitting and expounding, [2]and he smelled the odor of garlic. [3]He said: "Whoever ate garlic, let him go out!" [4]Rabbi Ḥiyya rose and went out. [5]They all rose and went out. In the morning, [6]Rabbi Shimon, the son of Rabbi, found Rabbi Ḥiyya, [7][and] said to him: "Are you the one who distressed Father?" [8]He said to him: "Let there never be [an act] like that in Israel!"

[9]And Rabbi Ḥiyya, from where did he learn this? [10]From Rabbi Meir, for it was taught: [11]"[There was] an incident involving a woman who came to the academy of Rabbi Meir. [12]She said to him: 'Master, one of you betrothed me through intercourse.' [13]Rabbi Meir rose and wrote out for her a bill of divorce, and gave [it] to her; [14]they all rose and wrote and gave to her."

[15]And Rabbi Meir, from where did he learn this? [16]From Shmuel HaKatan. [17]And Shmuel HaKatan, from where did he learn this? [18]From Shekhanyah, the son of Yehiel, as it is written:

RASHI

שציערת לאבא – שאכלת השום ונדף הריח. **חס ושלום** – שאוכל השום בבואו לבית מדרשו, אלא כדי שלא להלבין פניו של אוכל השום יצאתי, כדי שיצאו כולם ולא ידעו מי הוא. **משמואל הקטן** – כדלקמן.

NOTES

עָמַד רַבִּי חִיָּיא וְיָצָא Rabbi Ḥiyya rose and left. It may be asked: What did Rabbi Ḥiyya hope to accomplish by leaving, since the Sage with the smell of garlic on his breath would continue to distress Rabbi Yehudah HaNasi by his presence? *Rabbi Yoshiyah Pinto* explains that Rabbi Ḥiyya had hoped that the Sage who had in fact eaten garlic would stand and leave together with him, not having to suffer public humiliation by doing so since no one would know which of them was the offender.

קִדְּשַׁנִי בְּבִיאָה Betrothed me through sexual intercourse. Even though betrothal is only valid when properly witnessed, Rabbi Meir did not investigate the matter to see whether there were indeed witnesses in this case, for he thought that such a step would expose the identity of the Sage who betrothed her and thus cause him public humiliation (*Geonim*).

son of Yehiel, for it is written in Ezra (10:2): [1]**"And Shekhanyah the son of Yehiel, one of the sons of Elam, answered and said to Ezra: We have dealt fraudulently with our God, and have dwelled with strange women from the peoples of the land; yet now there is hope for Israel concerning this."** In truth, Shekhanyah's name does not appear on the list of those who had actually taken non-Jewish wives (see Ezra 10:18-44); nevertheless, he implicated himself in order not to shame those who were truly guilty of the offense.

וּשְׁכַנְיָה בֶּן יְחִיאֵל [2]**And Shekhanyah the son of Yehiel, from where did he learn** that it is proper to accept responsibility for someone else's wrongdoing in order to avoid shaming him? [3]**From** what God said to **Joshua, for it is written** in Joshua (7:10-11): [4]**"And the Lord said to Joshua: 'Get you up; why have you fallen thus upon your face? Israel has sinned**...for they have taken of the consecrated property, and have also stolen, and have also denied, and they have also placed it in their own vessels.'" [5]In reply, Joshua **said before** God: **"Master of the Universe, who** in actuality are the ones who have **sinned?"** [6]God **said to him** in return: **"Am I an informer for you,** that you ask Me to reveal the identity of the wrongdoer! [7]**Cast lots** among yourselves, and the transgressor will incriminate himself!" Since God Himself sought to spare wrongdoers public humiliation, it is certainly proper for humans to act likewise.

וְאִיבָּעֵית אֵימָא [8]**And if you wish,** you can **say** that Shekhanyah learned to act in this manner **from** the rebuke that God addressed to Israel through **Moses,** [9]**for it is written** in Exodus (16:28): "And the Lord said to Moses: **Until when will you refuse** to keep my commandments and my laws?" Even though only a few individuals disregarded God's command and gathered manna on the Sabbath, God nevertheless castigated the entire people so as not to reveal the identity of the individual transgressors.

תָּנוּ רַבָּנַן [10]Shmuel HaKatan's virtuous character is the subject of yet another Baraita: **Our Rabbis taught: "When the last Prophets — Haggai, Zekharyah, and Malakhi — died,** [11]**the Holy Spirit** inspiring prophecy **was removed from Israel.** [12]**Yet even so** the Sages **would** often **make use of an echo from Heaven** to assist them

[1]״וַיַּעַן שְׁכַנְיָה בֶן יְחִיאֵל מִבְּנֵי עֵילָם וַיֹּאמֶר לְעֶזְרָא אֲנַחְנוּ מָעַלְנוּ בֵאלֹהֵינוּ וַנֹּשֶׁב נָשִׁים נָכְרִיּוֹת מֵעַמֵּי הָאָרֶץ וְעַתָּה יֵשׁ מִקְוֶה לְיִשְׂרָאֵל עַל זֹאת״.

[2]וּשְׁכַנְיָה בֶּן יְחִיאֵל מֵהֵיכָא גְּמַר לַהּ? [3]מִיהוֹשֻׁעַ, דִּכְתִיב: [4]״וַיֹּאמֶר ה׳ אֶל יְהוֹשֻׁעַ: קֻם לָךְ; לָמָּה זֶה אַתָּה נֹפֵל עַל פָּנֶיךָ? חָטָא יִשְׂרָאֵל״. [5]אָמַר לְפָנָיו: ״רִבּוֹנוֹ שֶׁל עוֹלָם, מִי חָטָא״? [6]אָמַר לוֹ: ״וְכִי דֵּילָטוֹר אֲנִי לְךָ? [7]הַטֵּל גּוֹרָלוֹת״.

[8]וְאִיבָּעֵית אֵימָא: מִמֹּשֶׁה, [9]דִּכְתִיב: ״עַד אָנָה מֵאַנְתֶּם״.

[10]תָּנוּ רַבָּנַן: ״מִשֶּׁמֵּתוּ נְבִיאִים הָאַחֲרוֹנִים — חַגַּי זְכַרְיָה וּמַלְאָכִי — [11]נִסְתַּלְּקָה רוּחַ הַקּוֹדֶשׁ מִיִּשְׂרָאֵל. [12]וְאַף עַל פִּי כֵן הָיוּ מִשְׁתַּמְּשִׁין בְּבַת קוֹל.

LITERAL TRANSLATION

[1]"And Shekhanyah the son of Yehiel, one of the sons of Elam, answered and said to Ezra: We have dealt fraudulently with our God, and have dwelled with strange women from the peoples of the land; yet now there is hope in Israel concerning this."

[2]And Shekhanyah, the son of Yehiel, from where did he learn this? [3]From Joshua, for it is written: [4]"And the Lord said to Joshua: Get you up; why have you fallen thus upon your face? Israel has sinned." [5]He said before Him: "Master of the Universe, who sinned?" [6]He said to him: "Am I an informer for you? [7]Cast lots!"

[8]And if you wish, say: From Moses, [9]for it is written: "Until when will you refuse?"

[10]Our Rabbis taught: "When the last Prophets — Haggai, Zekharyah, and Malakhi — died, [11]the Holy Spirit was removed from Israel. [12]Yet even so they would make use of an echo [from Heaven].

RASHI

אנחנו מעלנו — והוא לא נשא נכרית, והכניס עצמו בכלל, שלא להלבין פניהם.
מיהושע — ממעשה דיהושע שלא רצה הקדוש ברוך הוא לגלות לו מי הוא החוטא, והכניס את כולן בכלל, שנאמר חטא ישראל במעשה דעכן. **דילטור** — רכיל. **מאנתם** — כולן בכלל, והרי כולן לא יצאו ללקוט, אלא מקצת, דכתיב (שמות טז) יצאו מן העם ללקוט וגו׳.
משמתו נביאים כו׳ — משום שמואל הקטן נקט לה הכא.

LANGUAGE

דֵּילָטוֹר Informer. The word is derived from the Latin *delator,* meaning an informer.

NOTES

מִמֹּשֶׁה **From Moses.** *Meiri* brings another example of this type of behavior from Moses' statement wherein he included himself and all the other righteous of his generation among the wrongdoers of Israel: "You shall not do anything similar to that which we do here this day; every man, whatever is right in his eyes" (Deuteronomy 12:8).

מִשֶּׁמֵּתוּ נְבִיאִים אַחֲרוֹנִים **When the last Prophets died.** *Meiri* explains that there was no prophecy during the Second Temple period, because during most of that period the Jewish people was subject to foreign rule and oppression; and as is stated elsewhere (*Shabbat* 30b): "The Holy Spirit rests only on those who are joyous."

בַּת קוֹל **Echo.** The expression בַּת קוֹל, translated here as "echo," has been understood in various ways: Our translation accords with *Tosafot,* who understands the literal meaning of the expression, "daughter of a voice," as implying that,

LANGUAGE

הִי Alas. This is an interjection expressing grief and mourning, and it is found in the Bible (Ezekiel 2:10). Some authorities believe it is related to the word "נהי" which has the same meaning.

BACKGROUND

שִׁמְעוֹן וְיִשְׁמָעֵאל לְחַרְבָּא Shimon and Yishmael to the sword. This appears to be Rabban Shimon ben Gamliel the Elder, who was the head of the Sanhedrin and one of the moderate leaders of the Great Rebellion against Rome that ended with the destruction of the Second Temple. Yishmael was apparently Yishmael ben Elisha the High Priest, one of the last priests to serve in the Temple. He was famous for his physical beauty, and this brought about his cruel execution: His skin was stripped from his skull while he was still alive. Both men were executed together by the Romans, apparently because they were regarded as leaders of the rebellion.

SAGES

הִלֵּל הַזָּקֵן Hillel the Elder. The outstanding spiritual leader of the Jewish people in the century before the Tannaitic period (flourished c. 20 B.C.E.), Hillel founded the Rabbinic dynasty that presided over the Jewish community in Eretz Israel for a period of 450 years. He was the ancestor of all the heads of the Sanhedrin for fifteen generations. He was born in Babylonia, immigrated to Eretz Israel, studied under Shemayah and Avtalyon, and was the colleague of Shammai. He founded his own academy, which bore his name — Bet Hillel.

רַבִּי יְהוּדָה בֶּן בָּבָא Rabbi Yehudah ben Bava. He was one of the Tannaim who were active during the period between the destruction of the Temple and that of Betar. Rabbi Yehudah ben Bava began his studies when the Temple still stood, and he was mainly active during the time when the center of the Sanhedrin was in Yavneh. His teachings and testimonies are mentioned in various sources. Rabbi Yehudah ben Bava was

TRANSLATION AND COMMENTARY

in formulating their attitudes and actions. [1]It is related that **once** the Sages **were banqueting in the upper chamber of the house of Guryah in Jericho when an echo** of a voice **came to them from Heaven,** announcing: [2]**'There is one here who is worthy that the Divine Presence rest upon him like** it did upon **Moses our master,** [3]**but his generation does not deserve** to have prophecy revealed to its worthy ones.' [4]**The Sages** immediately **cast their eyes on Hillel the Elder,** understanding that the reference was to him. [5]**And when** Hillel **died,** his eulogizers **said about him: 'Alas the pious one, alas the humble one, the disciple of Ezra!'** [6]It **once again** happened that the Sages **were banqueting in an upper chamber in Yavneh when an echo** of a voice **came to them from Heaven,** announcing: [7]**'There is one here who is worthy that the Divine Presence rest upon him,** [8]**but his generation does not deserve** to have prophecy revealed to its worthy ones.' [9]**The Sages** immediately **cast their eyes on Shmuel HaKatan,** knowing that the heavenly voice was referring to him. [10]**And when** Shmuel HaKatan **died,** his eulogizers **said about him: 'Alas the pious one, alas the humble one, the disciple of Hillel** the Elder.' Shmuel HaKatan proved at the end of his life that the Divine Presence indeed did rest upon him, [11]as **even he at the time of his death stated** prophetically: [12]'Rabban **Shimon** ben Gamliel [the Nasi of the Sanhedrin] **and** Rabbi **Yishmael** ben Elisha [the High Priest] will fall **to the sword,** [13]**their colleagues** will be subject **to** other forms of **execution, the rest of the nation** will be open **to plunder,** [14]**and great troubles are destined to come upon the world.'** These predictions indeed came true, demonstrating that Shmuel HaKatan was truly worthy of having the Divine Spirit rest upon him. [15]**And about** Rabbi **Yehudah ben Bava,** the eulogizers **sought to say the same** — 'Alas the pious one, alas the humble one' — [16]**but** they were

[1]פַּעַם אַחַת הָיוּ מְסוּבִּין בַּעֲלִיַּית בֵּית גּוּרְיָה בִּירִיחוֹ וְנִתְּנָה עֲלֵיהֶם בַּת קוֹל מִן הַשָּׁמַיִם: [2]'יֵשׁ כָּאן אֶחָד שֶׁרָאוּי שֶׁתִּשְׁרֶה עָלָיו שְׁכִינָה כְּמֹשֶׁה רַבֵּינוּ, [3]אֶלָּא שֶׁאֵין דּוֹרוֹ זַכַּאי לְכָךְ'. [4]נָתְנוּ חֲכָמִים אֶת עֵינֵיהֶם בְּהִלֵּל הַזָּקֵן. [5]וּכְשֶׁמֵּת אָמְרוּ עָלָיו: 'הִי חָסִיד, הִי עָנָיו, תַּלְמִידוֹ שֶׁל עֶזְרָא'! [6]שׁוּב פַּעַם אַחַת הָיוּ מְסוּבִּין בָּעֲלִיָּה בְּיַבְנֶה, וְנִתְּנָה עֲלֵיהֶם בַּת קוֹל מִן הַשָּׁמַיִם: [7]'יֵשׁ כָּאן אֶחָד שֶׁרָאוּי שֶׁתִּשְׁרֶה עָלָיו שְׁכִינָה, [8]אֶלָּא שֶׁאֵין דּוֹרוֹ זַכַּאי לְכָךְ'. [9]נָתְנוּ חֲכָמִים אֶת עֵינֵיהֶם בִּשְׁמוּאֵל הַקָּטָן. [10]וּכְשֶׁמֵּת אָמְרוּ עָלָיו: 'הִי חָסִיד, הִי עָנָיו, תַּלְמִידוֹ שֶׁל הִלֵּל'. [11]אַף הוּא אָמַר בִּשְׁעַת מִיתָתוֹ: [12]שִׁמְעוֹן וְיִשְׁמָעֵאל לְחַרְבָּא, [13]וְחַבְרוֹהִי לִקְטָלָא, וּשְׁאָר עַמָּא לְבִיזָא, [14]וְעָקָן סַגִּיאָן עֲתִידָן לְמֵיתֵי עַל עָלְמָא. [15]וְעַל יְהוּדָה בֶּן בָּבָא בִּקְשׁוּ לוֹמַר כֵּן, [16]אֶלָּא

LITERAL TRANSLATION

[1]Once they were banqueting in the upper chamber of the house of Guryah in Jericho when an echo came to them from Heaven: [2]'There is one here who is worthy that the Divine Presence rest upon him like Moses our master, [3]but his generation is not deserving of it.' [4]The Sages cast their eyes on Hillel the Elder. [5]And when he died, they said about him: 'Alas the pious one, alas, the humble one, the disciple of Ezra!' [6]Once again they were banqueting in an upper chamber in Yavneh, and an echo came to them from Heaven. [7]'There is one here who is worthy that the Divine Presence rest upon him, [8]but his generation is not deserving of it.' [9]The Sages cast their eyes on Shmuel HaKatan. [10]And when he died, they said about him: 'Alas the pious one, alas the humble one, the disciple of Hillel.' [11]Even he at the time of his death said: [12]'Shimon and Yishmael to the sword, [13]and their colleagues to execution, and the rest of the nation to plunder, [14]and great troubles are destined to come upon the world.' [15]And about Yehudah ben Bava they sought to say the same, [16]but

RASHI

אף הוא — הוכיח סופו ששרתה עליו שכינה, שנתנבא בשעת מיתתו. **שמעון וישמעאל** — רבן שמעון בן גמליאל הנשיא, ורבי ישמעאל בן אלישע כהן גדול, יהרגו בחרב. **וחביריו** — כגון רבי עקיבא ורבי חנינא בן תרדיון. **לקטלא** — לשאר מיתות, רבי עקיבא במסרקות של ברזל, בפרק הרואה (ברכות סא,ב), רבי חנינא בשריפה, במסכת עבודה זרה (יח,א). **לומר כן** — אותו הספד.

NOTES

whereas direct communication from Heaven was no longer audible, a "daughter" — or echo — of such a communication could still be heard through some less direct form of divine inspiration. *Rabbi Tzvi Ḥayyot* notes that the expression is sometimes used in reference to a mysterious echo whose source cannot be identified, while at other times it refers to a meaningful divine communication conveyed to one unintentionally through random talk or conversation to which one is exposed. *Rosh* writes that a *bat kol* is a "measured voice" (a *bat* being a Biblical measure), thus implying a voice that can only be heard by those who are worthy of hearing it.

TRANSLATION AND COMMENTARY

unable to do so for **the time was** a **troubled** one, [1]**when they would not eulogize those executed by the** foreign **empire** out of fear of antagonizing it."

תָּנוּ רַבָּנַן [2]The Gemara returns once again to the issue of proclaiming a leap year: **Our Rabbis taught** the following Baraita: "The Sanhedrin **does not intercalate the year unless the Nasi wills it.** [3]**It once happened that Rabban Gamliel,** the Nasi of the Sanhedrin, **went to receive permission from a** Roman **governor in Syria** to carry out a certain policy affecting the Jews in Eretz Israel. [4]Rabban Gamliel **was delayed in returning home** untill after the deadline for deciding whether to institute a leap year, so the Sages **intercalated the year** on their own, but **on condition that Rabban Gamliel would want it** to be so upon his return. [5]**And when Rabban Gamliel came** back **and said: 'I will it,'** [6]**the year was considered intercalated** retroactively."

תָּנוּ רַבָּנַן [7]**Our Rabbis taught** the following Baraita with regard to the conditions that justify instituting a leap year: "The court **does not intercalate the year unless it is necessary because of the roads,** [8]**or because of the bridges** that often are washed away as a result of heavy winter rains, thereby making it difficult, without the added month, for even the local pilgrims to reach Jerusalem in time for Pesaḥ; [9]**or because of the Pesaḥ ovens,** used to roast the Paschal sacrifice,

שֶׁנִּטְרְפָה שָׁעָה, [1]שֶׁאֵין מַסְפִּידִין עַל הֲרוּגֵי מַלְכוּת".

[2]תָּנוּ רַבָּנַן: "אֵין מְעַבְּרִין אֶת הַשָּׁנָה אֶלָּא אִם כֵּן יִרְצֶה נָשִׂיא. [3]וּמַעֲשֶׂה בְּרַבָּן גַּמְלִיאֵל שֶׁהָלַךְ לִיטּוֹל רְשׁוּת אֵצֶל הֶגְמוֹן אֶחָד שֶׁבְּסוּרְיָא, [4]וְשָׁהָה לָבוֹא, וְעִיבְּרוּ אֶת הַשָּׁנָה עַל מְנָת שֶׁיִּרְצֶה רַבָּן גַּמְלִיאֵל. [5]וּכְשֶׁבָּא רַבָּן גַּמְלִיאֵל וְאָמַר 'רוֹצֶה אֲנִי', [6]נִמְצֵאת שָׁנָה מְעוּבֶּרֶת".

[7]תָּנוּ רַבָּנַן: "אֵין מְעַבְּרִין אֶת הַשָּׁנָה אֶלָּא אִם כֵּן הָיְתָה צְרִיכָה מִפְּנֵי הַדְּרָכִים, [8]וּמִפְּנֵי הַגְּשָׁרִים, [9]וּמִפְּנֵי תַנּוּרֵי פְסָחִים,

LITERAL TRANSLATION

the time was troubled, [1]when they would not eulogize those executed by the empire."

[2]Our Rabbis taught: "They do not intercalate the year unless the Nasi wills it. [3][There was] an incident where Rabban Gamliel went to receive permission from a governor who was in Syria, [4]and he was late in coming, and they intercalated the year on condition that Rabban Gamliel would want it. [5]And when Rabban Gamliel came and said: 'I will it,' [6]the year was considered intercalated."

[7]Our Rabbis taught: "They do not intercalate the year unless it was necessary because of the roads, [8]or because of the bridges, [9]or because of the Pesaḥ ovens,

RASHI

אלא שאין מספידין על הרוגי מלכות — מפני יראת המלך מיהרו לקוברן. **ליטול רשות** — לדבר על עסקי ציבור. **מפני הדרכים** — שנתקלקלו בימות החורף, ומפני הגשמים, ועדיין לא נתקנו ולא יוכלו עולי רגל לבא. **תנורי פסחים** — שצולין בהם פסחיהם, ונמוקו בגשמי החורף וצריכין חמה להתייבש.

NOTES

אֵין מַסְפִּידִין עַל הֲרוּגֵי מַלְכוּת We do not eulogize those executed by the empire. *Ramah* suggests several different reasons why eulogies should not be delivered for martyrs: First, so that martyrs can be brought to burial before the authorities decide not to allow them that honor. Second, so as not to antagonize the authorities by honoring those whom they saw fit to execute. And third, so that the authorities not view the eulogizers as sympathizers who should suffer the same fate as those they were burying.

אֶלָּא אִם כֵּן יִרְצֶה נָשִׂיא Unless the Nasi wills it. It has been stated by some that, while the Nasi is obligated to ratify whatever decision the court arrives at in regard to intercalating the year, his formal agreement with that decision must always be obtained (*Tzafnat Pa'ane'aḥ*).

שֶׁהָלַךְ לִיטּוֹל רְשׁוּת He went to receive permission. Our commentary follows *Rashi* and others who understand that Rabban Gamliel went to the Roman governor in order to discuss some communal business unrelated to the calendar issue. *Ramah*, however, suggests that Rabban Gamliel went specifically to ask permission to intercalate the year. Permission was needed because taxes and other levies were imposed on an annual basis, and extending the year involved a loss of income for the Roman authorities.

צְרִיכָה מִפְּנֵי הַדְּרָכִים It was necessary because of the roads. This Baraita is augmented by another which lists

HALAKHAH

אֵין מַסְפִּידִין עַל הֲרוּגֵי מַלְכוּת We do not eulogize those executed by the empire. "The mourning rites must be observed for a thief who was executed by a foreign regime, provided that this will not endanger the mourners." (*Shulḥan Arukh, Yoreh De'ah* 325:2 [*Rema*].)

אֶלָּא אִם כֵּן יִרְצֶה הַנָּשִׂיא Unless the Nasi wills it. "In the absence of the Nasi of the Sanhedrin, the year can only be intercalated on condition that he will consent to the decision upon his return. If, upon his return, the Nasi does not give his consent, the intercalation is not valid." (*Rambam, Sefer Zemanim, Hilkhot Kiddush HaḤodesh* 4:12.)

מִפְּנֵי הַדְּרָכִים וּמִפְּנֵי הַגְּשָׁרִים Because of the roads or the bridges. "A number of situations might make it necessary to declare a leap year: If the roads or bridges are in

famous for his righteousness and it was said that whenever "a pious man" was mentioned, the reference was either to Rabbi Yehudah ben Bava or to Rabbi Yehudah ben Il'ai. Judging by his chronology, at the time of his death he was probably over ninety years old.

BACKGROUND

אֵין מְעַבְּרִין אֶת הַשָּׁנָה They do not intercalate the year. The matter of adding an intercalary month is discussed in detail in the following pages. Today the intercalary month is added on the basis of astronomical calculations and according to a fixed cycle. However, this arrangement was made only because it was no longer possible to determine and proclaim the addition of an intercalary month in the proper manner. However, when the Sanhedrin still sat, an intercalary month was added when necessary, as will be explained below, and when it was desirable to extend the year for other reasons. Certain secondary considerations are taken into account in making this decision when the main factors are not sufficiently clear.

הֶגְמוֹן שֶׁבְּסוּרְיָא A ruler who was in Syria. Under Roman rule, Eretz Israel was subordinated administratively to Syria, which was a province in its own right. Therefore Rabban Gamliel, the head of the Sanhedrin, sometimes had to go to clarify matters with the central authorities in Syria.

LANGUAGE

הֶגְמוֹן Ruler. The word is derived from the Greek ἡγεμον, *hegemon,* which has the meaning of "leader," especially a military leader, and which in a later period was used with specific reference to the Roman proconsuls or their representatives, who were responsible for entire provinces.

[1]וּמִפְּנֵי גָּלֻיּוֹת יִשְׂרָאֵל שֶׁנֶּעֶקְרוּ מִמְּקוֹמָן וַעֲדַיִין לֹא הִגִּיעוּ. [2]אֲבָל לֹא מִפְּנֵי הַשֶּׁלֶג, וְלֹא מִפְּנֵי הַצִּינָּה, [3]וְלֹא מִפְּנֵי גָּלֻיּוֹת יִשְׂרָאֵל שֶׁלֹּא עָקְרוּ מִמְּקוֹמָן". [4]תָּנוּ רַבָּנַן: [5]"אֵין מְעַבְּרִין אֶת הַשָּׁנָה לֹא מִפְּנֵי הַגְּדָיִים, וְלֹא מִפְּנֵי הַטְּלָאִים, [6]וְלֹא מִפְּנֵי הַגּוֹזָלוֹת שֶׁלֹּא פֵּירְחוּ, [7]אֲבָל עוֹשִׂין אוֹתָן סַעַד לַשָּׁנָה. [8]כֵּיצַד? [9]רַבִּי יַנַּאי אוֹמֵר מִשּׁוּם רַבָּן שִׁמְעוֹן בֶּן גַּמְלִיאֵל: [10]'מְהוֹדְעִין אֲנַחְנָא לְכוֹן

LITERAL TRANSLATION

[1]or because of the exiled communities of Israel which uprooted themselves from their place but have not arrived. [2]But not because of snow nor because of cold, [3]nor because of the exiled communities of Israel which did not uproot themselves from their place."

[4]Our Rabbis taught: [5]"They do not intercalate the year, not because of the young goats nor because of the lambs, [6]nor because of the pigeons which cannot fly. [7]But we produce them as support for the year. [8]How so? [9]Rabbi Yannai said in the name of Rabban Shimon ben Gamliel: [10]'We inform you

TRANSLATION AND COMMENTARY

which are often damaged as well by rain and in need of drying out; [1]**or because of the** distant **exiled communities of Israel which have** already **uprooted themselves from their place** in the Diaspora in order to reach Jerusalem for Pesaḥ, **and which have not yet arrived** as the month of Nisan is approaching, due to hardships on the way. [2]**But** the year is not intercalated simply **because of snow or of cold,** as most people will not refrain from making the pilgrimage because of inclement weather; [3]**nor** is it intercalated **because of the exiled communities of Israel which have not** yet **uprooted themselves from their place** in the Diaspora by the time Nisan is approaching, even if as a result they will be prevented from reaching Jerusalem by Pesaḥ."

תָּנוּ רַבָּנַן [4]**Our Rabbis taught** another Baraita which deals with additional reasons that prove insufficient for instituting a leap year: [5]"The court **does not intercalate the year because of the** newly born **goats or the** newly born **lambs,** which can use some fattening up before they are brought as offerings on Pesaḥ, for they are nevertheless fit for sacrifice the way they are; [6]**nor** is the year intercalated **because of the** newly hatched **pigeons, which cannot fly** yet and which are used in various private sacrifices brought in the Temple during the Festival, for such birds can be used for that purpose regardless. [7]**But** even though we cannot proclaim a leap year on account of these considerations, **we** do **produce them as support for** intercalating **the year** when a more fundamental concern is already present, such as the fear that grain will not ripen by Pesaḥ or fruit by Shavuot, or the fear that either Pesaḥ or Sukkot will not fall in its appointed season [see below, 11b]. The Baraita now illustrates how this may work: [8]**How** is it that we combine considerations? [9]**Rabbi Yannai said in the name of Rabban Shimon ben Gamliel:** This is an example of just such a formula: [10]**'We** hereby **inform**

RASHI

ומפני גליות ישראל — בני הגולה הרחוקים, ונשמע לבית דין שנעקרו ממקומן, לעלות לרגל לעשות פסחיהם ועדיין לא הגיעו, שאם לא יעברוה — לא ירגילו לבא בפסח. **לא מפני השלג** — שלא יחדלו בכך מלבוא. **גדיים וטלאין** — שהן דקין, אין מעברין עליהן כדי שיגדלו ויעשו מהם פסחים, שהרי יכול להקריב קטנים. **גוזלות** — שצריכין לקיני יולדות שבכל ארץ ישראל, וכן זבין וזבות שכולן משהין קינייהם עד עלותן לרגל, אף על פי כן אין מעברין על כך, שיכולין להביא בני יונה שכשרים כשהם קטנים. **אבל עושין אותן סעד** — סייג וסמך לדבריהם לעבר את השנה, אם צריכה לעבר מפני אחד מן הדברים שמעברין עליהן, כגון על האביב ועל פירות האילן, ואמרינן לקמן: על שתים מהן — מעברין, ועל אחד מהן — אין מעברין, הללו — גדיים, וטלאים, וגוזלות, — נעשו סעד, ומצטרפין לאחד מהן ומעברין.

NOTES

additional reasons for intercalating the year, such as a delay in the ripening of grain or fruit or the arrival of a Festival prior to its appointed season. The Rishonim disagree in regard to the difference between these two Baraitot: *Tosafot* explains that, whereas any single factor mentioned in our Baraita provides sufficient reason to intercalate the year, the court would require two from those listed in the later Baraita. *Rabbenu Yonah* explains that, whereas the factors listed in our Baraita allow the Sages to intercalate the year, those listed in the later Baraita actually obligate them to do so.

HALAKHAH

disrepair, so that pilgrims on the way to Jerusalem will be unable to reach their destination by Pesaḥ, or will endanger themselves in the attempt; if the Pesaḥ ovens were damaged by the winter rains, so that the people arriving in Jerusalem will not have anywhere to roast their Paschal sacrifices; or if the Diaspora Jews have already departed from home, but will not arrive in Jerusalem in time for Pesaḥ." (*Rambam, Sefer Zemanim, Hilkhot Kiddush HaḤodesh* 4:5.)

עוֹשִׂין אוֹתָן סַעַד לַשָּׁנָה **We produce them as support for intercalating the year.** "A number of factors may be considered as auxiliary reasons for proclaiming a leap year if one of the principal reasons for intercalating the year is also applicable: If the newly born goats and lambs are

TRANSLATION AND COMMENTARY

you that the pigeons are tender, and the lambs are slender, [1]**and the time of spring** and the ripening of grain **has not** yet **arrived.** [2]Hence, **the matter appearing proper in my eyes,** [3]**I have added on to this year** an additional **thirty days.'"**

מֵיתִיבִי [4]Some Sages **raised an objection** against a certain detail in this Baraita: Does Rabban Shimon ben Gamliel indeed maintain that the intercalated month must have thirty days? But surely it was taught in another Baraita as follows: [5]**"How much is the intercalation of the year?** [6]The Sages say: **Thirty days.** [7]**Rabban Shimon ben Gamliel** disagrees and **says: A month,** meaning twenty-nine days."

אָמַר רַב פַּפָּא [8]**Rav Pappa said:** The Baraita poses no difficulty, for Rabban Shimon ben Gamliel's position can be understood as follows: The court was given the option of deciding how many days to add to the year. [9]**If they wanted,** they could add **a** typical **month** of twenty-nine days, [10]but **if they wanted,** they could alternatively have added a month of **thirty days.**

תָּא חֲזֵי [11]The Gemara now comments on the formula used by Rabban Shimon ben Gamliel in proclaiming the intercalation of the year: **Come and see what** difference **there is between** [11B] [12]**the early** Sages, who were **forceful** in character, yet deferential toward their peers, **and the later** Sages, who, although more **humble**, were less obliging toward each other. [13]**For it was taught** in a Baraita: **"It once happened that Rabban Gamliel was sitting on a step on the Temple Mount,** [14]**and Yoḥanan the scribe was standing before him,** ready to take dictation on **three cut scrolls** of parchment **which lay before him.** [15]Rabban Gamliel **said to** Yoḥanan: **Take one scroll** of parchment,

דְּגוֹזָלַיָּא רַכִּיכִין, וְאִימְרַיָּא דְּעָרְקִין, [1]וְזִימְנָא דַּאֲבִיבָא לָא מְטָא, [2]וּשְׁפַרַת מִילְּתָא בְּאַנְפַּאי [3]וְאוֹסִיפִית עַל שַׁתָּא דָּא תְּלָתִין יוֹמִין׳".

[4]מֵיתִיבִי: [5]"כַּמָּה עִיבּוּר הַשָּׁנָה? [6]שְׁלֹשִׁים יוֹם. [7]רַבָּן שִׁמְעוֹן בֶּן גַּמְלִיאֵל אוֹמֵר: חֹדֶשׁ"!

[8]אָמַר רַב פַּפָּא: [9]רָצוּ — חֹדֶשׁ, [10]רָצוּ — שְׁלֹשִׁים יוֹם.

[11]תָּא חֲזֵי מַאי אִיכָּא בֵּין [11B] [12]תַּקִּיפָאֵי קַדְמָאֵי לְעִינְוְותָנֵי בַּתְרָאֵי, [13]דְּתַנְיָא: "מַעֲשֶׂה בְּרַבָּן גַּמְלִיאֵל שֶׁהָיָה יוֹשֵׁב עַל גַּב מַעֲלָה בְּהַר הַבַּיִת, [14]וְהָיָה יוֹחָנָן סוֹפֵר הַלָּז עוֹמֵד לְפָנָיו, וְשָׁלֹשׁ אִיגְּרוֹת חֲתוּכוֹת לְפָנָיו מוּנָּחוֹת. [15]אָמַר לוֹ: טוֹל אִיגַּרְתָּא חֲדָא, וּכְתוֹב: 'לְאָחָנָא,

LITERAL TRANSLATION

that the pigeons are tender, and the lambs are slender, [1]and the time of spring has not arrived. [2]And the matter appearing proper in my eyes, [3]I have added on to this year thirty days.'"

[4]They raised an objection: [5]"How much is the intercalation of the year? [6]Thirty days. [7]Rabban Shimon ben Gamliel says: A month."

[8]Rav Pappa said: [9][If] they wanted, a month; [10][if] they wanted, thirty days.

[11]Come, see what [difference] there is between [11B] [12]the forceful early ones and the humble later ones, [13]for it was taught: "It once happened that Rabban Gamliel was sitting on a step on the Temple Mount, [14]and Yoḥanan the (lit., "that") scribe was standing before him, and three cut scrolls lay before him. [15]He said to him: Take one scroll, and write: 'To our brothers,

RASHI

וזימנא דאביבא לא מטא — הוא אחד מן הסימנים שמעברין עליהם כדלקמן. **חדש** — עשרים ותשעה ימים. **תקיפי קמאי** — רבן גמליאל שהיה נוהג שררה וזורק מורא בתלמידים, כדאשכחן בבכורות (לו,א) ובברכות (כז,ב) ובראש השנה (כה,א) דלעריה לרבי יהושע ואפילו הכי קתני ביה: ושפרא מילתא באנפאי ובאנפי חבראי, ורבן שמעון בריה דהוה מעינוותני בתראי, כדאמרינן ב"השוכר את הפועלים" (בבא מציעא פה,א) לא אמר: באנפי חבראי.

NOTES

עַל גַּב מַעֲלָה בְּהַר הַבַּיִת **On a step on the Temple Mount.** Even though Rabban Gamliel served as the Nasi of the Sanhedrin after the destruction of the Temple, he nevertheless dictated his proclamation of the leap year from a step on the Temple Mount so that it would issue forth from a place which was as close as possible to "the dwelling place of God." (*Rabbi Ya'akov Emden.*)

HALAKHAH

still small; or if the newly hatched pigeons are not yet able to fly." (*Rambam, Sefer Zemanim, Hilkhot Kiddush HaḤodesh* 4:7-8.)

רָצוּ חֹדֶשׁ רָצוּ שְׁלֹשִׁים יוֹם **If they wanted, a month; if they wanted, thirty days.** "When the court sends messengers to inform those who are far away that the year was intercalated, the message includes information with regard to whether the added month will be full or incomplete, as follows from Rav Pappa. However, the final determination by the Sanhedrin as to whether the month will in fact be full or incomplete is only made on the basis of available testimony at the time concerning the status of the New Moon, as is the case with all other months." (*Rambam, Sefer Zemanim, Hilkhot Kiddush HaḤodesh* 7:17.)

בְּנֵי גְלִילָאָה עִילָּאָה, וְלַאֲחָנָא, בְּנֵי גְלִילָאָה תַּתָּאָה, שְׁלוֹמְכוֹן יִסְגֵּא! [1] מְהוֹדְעִין אֲנַחְנָא לְכוֹן דִּזְמַן בִּיעוּרָא מְטָא, [2] לְאַפְרוּשֵׁי מַעְשְׂרָא מִמַּעְטָנָא דְּזֵיתָא׳. [3] וְטוֹל אִיגַּרְתָּא חֲדָא וּכְתוֹב: ׳לַאֲחָנָא, בְּנֵי דְרוֹמָא, שְׁלוֹמְכוֹן יִסְגֵּא! [4] מְהוֹדְעִין אֲנַחְנָא לְכוֹן דִּזְמַן בִּיעוּרָא מְטָא, [5] לְאַפְרוּשֵׁי מַעְשְׂרָא מֵעוֹמְרֵי שִׁיבְּלַיָּא׳. [6] וְטוֹל אִיגַּרְתָּא חֲדָא וּכְתוֹב: ׳לַאֲחָנָא, בְּנֵי גַלְוָותָא בְּבָבֶל, וְלַאֲחָנָא דִּבְמָדַי, וְלִשְׁאָר כָּל גַּלְוָותָא דְּיִשְׂרָאֵל, שְׁלוֹמְכוֹן יִסְגֵּא לְעָלַם! [7] מְהוֹדְעִין אֲנַחְנָא לְכוֹן דְּגוֹזְלַיָּא רַכִּיכִין, וְאִימְרַיָּא עָרְקִין, וְזִמְנָא דַּאֲבִיבָא לָא מְטָא; [8] וְשָׁפְרָא מִילְּתָא בְּאַנְפַּאי וּבְאַנְפֵּי חֲבֵירַיי, [9] וְאוֹסִיפִית עַל שַׁתָּא דָא יוֹמִין תְּלָתִין׳״.

TRANSLATION AND COMMENTARY

and write as follows: **'To our brothers, the Upper Galileans, and to our brothers, the Lower Galileans, may your peace increase!** [1] **We** hereby **inform you that the time for removal** of any tithes still in your possession **has arrived.** During the seven-year Sabbatical cycle, farmers are required to set aside various tithes for the priests, the Levites and the poor. After the completion of the third and sixth years in this cycle, one must see to it that any tithes which have accumulated in one's possession are removed and properly delivered to their respective beneficiaries by the eve of the coming Pesaḥ. Thus, now is the time, if you have not already done so, [2] **to separate the tithe from the vat of olives** [the major crop in the Galilee] in order that they may be properly distributed.' [3] Now **take one** other **scroll** of parchment, **and write** a second letter: **'To our brothers, the Southerners, may your peace increase!** [4] **We** hereby **inform you that the time for removal** of any tithes still in your possession **has arrived.** Now is the time, if you have not already done so, [5] **to separate the tithe from the sheaves of the ears** of grain [the major crop in the south] in order that they may be distributed by the coming Pesaḥ eve.' [6] **And take one** other **scroll** of parchment, **and write** a third letter: **'To our brothers, the exiled in Babylonia, and to our brothers who are** dwelling **in Medea, and to all the rest of the exiles of Israel, may your peace increase forever!** [7] **We** hereby **inform you that the pigeons are tender and the lambs are slender, and the time of the barley ripening has not** yet **arrived.** [8] Hence, **the matter appearing proper in my eyes and in the eyes of my colleagues,** [9] **I have added on to this year** an additional **thirty days.'"** Thus we see that Rabban Gamliel, who was of an earlier and more forceful generation of Sages, openly acknowledged his colleagues when announcing his decision to intercalate the year, whereas his son Rabban Shimon, who had a reputation for greater humility, made no mention whatsoever of his colleagues in the written proclamation that he dispatched to the Diaspora!

LITERAL TRANSLATION

the Upper Galileans, and to our brothers, the Lower Galileans, may your peace increase! [1] We inform you that the time for removal has arrived, [2] to separate the tithe from the vat of olives.' [3] And take one scroll, and write: 'To our brothers, the Southerners, may your peace increase! [4] We inform you that the time for removal has arrived, [5] to separate the tithes from the sheaves of ears.' [6] And take one scroll, and write: 'To our brothers, the exiled in Babylonia, and to our brothers who are in Medea, and to all the rest of the exiles of Israel, may your peace increase forever! [7] We inform you that the pigeons are tender and the lambs are slender, and the time of the first ripening has not arrived; and, [8] the matter appearing proper in my eyes and in the eyes of my colleagues, [9] I have added on to this year thirty days.'"

RASHI

דזמן ביעורא מטא — שנה שלישית או ששית לשמיטה, כל מי שהיה מעשרותיו של שנה ראשונה ושניה חייב לבערן עכשיו, תרומה — ניתן לכהן, ומעשר ראשון — ללוי, ומעשר עני — לעני, ומעשר שני — מתבער בכל מקום שהוא, שאם לא העלהו לירושלים קודם פסח היה מבערו ערב פסח ומתודה: "בערתי הקודש". **ממעטני זיתא** — מקום קיבוץ הזיתים להתחמם זה על זה. בגליל הוי זיתים מרובין, ובדרום חטים מרובין גליל ודרום מארץ ישראל הן, ואין צריך להודיען על העיבור שקרובים הן לבית דין, אבל לבני גולה שרחוקים מארץ ישראל צריך להודיעם על העיבור — שלא יאכלו חמץ בפסח.

BACKGROUND

גָּלִיל וְדָרוֹם Galilee and South. When the Jewish community of Eretz Israel was in place, it was divided into three regions: Judea, Galilee, and Transjordan, each of which was defined within separate geographical and climatic boundaries. Galilee was divided into two main areas: Lower Galilee, whose northern boundary roughly corresponded with a line drawn between the Sea of Galilee and the Mediterranean Sea; and Upper Galilee, to the north. The "South" ("Darom") was a term by which the scholars of Galilee referred to Judea, particularly after the destruction of Betar, when Lod was the main Torah center in Judea. This term was commonly used earlier as well, but then it was used to refer to Southern Judea.

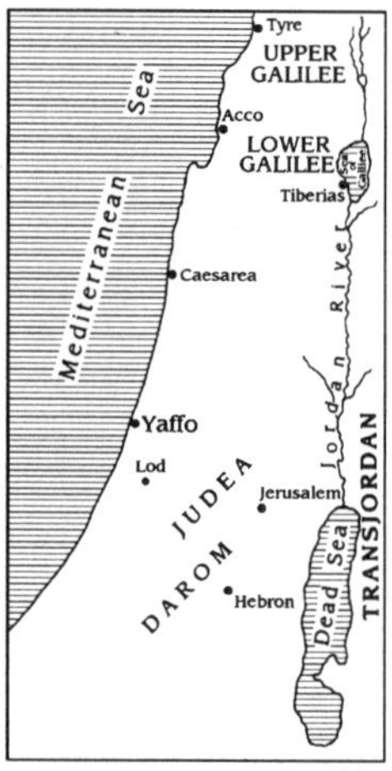

מַעְטָנָא Vat. A vessel or large bowl in which olives were placed before being pressed. The olives became softer in this vessel, so that the oil could be removed more easily when they were pressed.

NOTES

מְהוֹדְעִין אֲנַחְנָא לְכוֹן We inform you. According to *Rashi*, it was unnecessary to inform the residents of Eretz Israel of the leap year for, being close to the High Court, it was assumed they would hear by word of mouth. *Tosafot* (in tractate *Rosh HaShanah*) explains that the residents of Eretz Israel would naturally deduce that the year was intercalated when the messengers of the court, who normally reached them by the beginning of Nisan to inform them of the exact day on which to celebrate Pesaḥ, failed to arrive as expected. They would consequently assume that an additional month of Adar had been added to the year and that Pesaḥ would not be celebrated until the following month.

דְּגוֹזְלַיָּא רַכִּיכִין The pigeons are tender. The question has been raised: What difference did it make that the pigeons

[1]דִּילְמָא, בָּתַר דְּעַבְּרוּהוּ. [2]תָּנוּ רַבָּנַן: [3]"עַל שְׁלֹשָׁה דְּבָרִים מְעַבְּרִין אֶת הַשָּׁנָה: [4]עַל הָאָבִיב, [5]וְעַל פֵּירוֹת הָאִילָן, [6]וְעַל הַתְּקוּפָה. [7]עַל שְׁנַיִם מֵהֶן — מְעַבְּרִין, [8]וְעַל אֶחָד מֵהֶן — אֵין מְעַבְּרִין.

LITERAL TRANSLATION

[1]Perhaps, after they removed him.

[2]Our Rabbis taught: [3]"Because of three issues, they intercalate the year: [4]Because of the barley ripening, [5]and because of the fruit of the tree, [6]and because of the equinox. [7]Because of two of them — they intercalate, [8]but because of one of them — they cannot intercalate.

TRANSLATION AND COMMENTARY

דִּילְמָא [1]The Gemara, however, dismisses this conclusion: **Perhaps** this proclamation of Rabban Gamliel's was issued **after** his colleagues **removed him** from his position as reigning Nasi, first replacing him with Rabbi Eleazar ben Azaryah and then reinstating him as a co-Nasi over the Sanhedrin. This would account for the deferential tone of the communications issued by him in his new capacity, and would not necessarily reflect a general difference in character between earlier and later generations.

תָּנוּ רַבָּנַן [2]The Gemara continues its discussion of the consideratons that lead to the proclamation of a leap year: **Our Rabbis taught** the following Baraita: [3]**"Because of three issues** the judges of the High Court **intercalate the year:** [4]**Because of** the issue of Pesaḥ approaching before **the barley ripening** in spring, a Biblical condition for observing the holiday (see Deuteronmy 16:1); [5]**and because of** the issue of Shavuot approaching before **the fruit of the tree** has ripened, thus forcing the harvesters to delay bringing their ritual offering of the first-fruit, an offering associated with the observance of Shavuot (see Exodus 23:16), until their next trip to Jerusalem; [6]**and because of** the issue of **the equinox** not properly coinciding with its designated Festival observance, such as when the vernal equinox occurs after the 16th of Nisan, or the autumnal equinox occurs after the 21st of Tishrei. [7]**When two of** these conditions exist, **they** can **intercalate** the year, [8]**but** when only **one of them** exists, **they cannot intercalate** the year.

RASHI

דילמא בתר דעברוהו — לרבן גמליאל מנשיאותו נעשה עניו. **על האביב** — אם לא בישלה התבואה — מעברין, דקרא כתיב (שמות יג): "בחדש האביב", ואית דמפרשים: לפי שאין להם מהיכן להקריב העומר, וקשה לי: דאמרינן לקמן: על שלש ארצות מעברין את השנה, על שתים מהן מעברין, ואם בישלה תבואה ביהודה ולא בישלה בעבר הירדן ובגליל — מעברין השנה, ואי טעמא משום עומר הוא, הרי בישלה התבואה ביהודה! **ועל פירות האילן** — אם מתאחר בישולם יותר מזמן העצרת — מעברין, שעצרת זמן הבאת ביכורים דכתיב (במדבר כח): "וביום הביכורים", ואם לא יביאם בבואו לרגל צריך לטרוח ולעלות פעם אחרת. **ועל התקופה** — בין על תקופת תמוז שמתעכבת ונמשכת, שאין תקופת תשרי נופלת עד עבור החג — מעברין, דנפקא לן לקמן מקרא, בין על תקופת טבת שנמשך זמנה עד ששה עשר בניסן, שהבאת העומר דילה בתוך תקופת טבת — מעברין לדחות את המועדות כדלקמן סנהדרין (יג,ב).

NOTES

were tender and the lambs slender since Rabban Gamliel issued his proclamation subsequent to the destruction of the Temple, when sacrifices were no longer offered?! *Ran* explains that, even though the Temple was destroyed, the Sages in charge of intercalating the year took into account all those factors that would be relevant were it still standing, as a sign of their hope that the Temple would be imminently rebuilt, rendering these concerns once again pertinent. *Rabbi Ya'akov Emden* suggests that it may be possible to infer from this passage that sacrifices were offered on the altar even after the Temple itself was destroyed.

בָּתַר דְּעַבְּרוּהוּ **After they discharged him.** Some read these words as "after they intercalated it," in accordance with the other meaning of the root עבר. This alternative reading would suggest that the deference shown by Rabban Gamliel toward his colleagues in his written proclamation indicates that they had already intercalated the year in his absence, and that he was choosing now, upon his return, to ratify their decision (*Tosafot Rabbenu Peretz*).

עַל שְׁלֹשָׁה דְּבָרִים **Because of three issues.** *Riva* suggests that all three of these issues essentially point at the same concern: That the Festivals occur in their proper season. Furthermore, he suggests that each of the three issues relates to a different Festival: The concern with regard to the first ripening of grain relates to the importance of Pesaḥ being celebrated in its appropriate season; the concern with regard to the ripening of fruit relates to the practice of bringing the first-fruits during the Festival of Shavuot; finally, the concern with regard to the timing of the seasonal equinox relates to the importance of Sukkot commencing after autumn has officially begun.

פֵּירוֹת הָאִילָן **The fruit of the trees.** *Ri Migash* (cited by *Remah*) relates this issue to the observance of Sukkot,

HALAKHAH

עַל שְׁלֹשָׁה דְּבָרִים **Because of three issues.** "An extra month is added to the year: (1) If it appears that the vernal equinox will occur on or after the 16th of Nisan; (2) if it appears that the barley will not ripen sufficiently by Pesaḥ; or (3) if it appears that the fruit that ordinarily ripens around Pesaḥ time will not ripen by then. The lateness of the vernal equinox is by itself sufficient reason to add an extra month to the year, following Rabban Shimon ben Gamliel. But if it does not appear that the equinox will be late, the year is only intercalated if both of the other two factors are present." (*Rambam, Sefer Zemanim, Hilkhot Kiddush HaḤodesh* 4:2,3.)

[1]וּבִזְמַן שֶׁאָבִיב אֶחָד מֵהֶן, הַכֹּל שְׂמֵחִין, [2]רַבָּן שִׁמְעוֹן בֶּן גַּמְלִיאֵל אוֹמֵר: עַל הַתְּקוּפָה״. [3]אִיבַּעְיָא לְהוּ: ״עַל הַתְּקוּפָה״ שְׂמֵחִין, [4]אוֹ ״עַל הַתְּקוּפָה״ מְעַבְּרִין? [5]תֵּיקוּ. [6]תָּנוּ רַבָּנַן: ״עַל שְׁלֹשָׁה אֲרָצוֹת מְעַבְּרִין אֶת הַשָּׁנָה: [7]יְהוּדָה,

LITERAL TRANSLATION

[1]And at such time as the first ripening is one of them, all are happy. [2]Rabban Shimon ben Gamliel says: Because of the equinox."

[3]It was asked of them: "Because of the equinox" we are happy, [4]or "because of the equinox" they intercalate? [5]Let it stand.

[6]Our Rabbis taught: "Because of three regions, they intercalate the year: [7]Judea,

TRANSLATION AND COMMENTARY

[1]**And at such time as** the issue of a delay in **the barley ripening is one of** the two issues that lead to intercalation of the year, **all are happy**. Since the grain is not yet ready for harvest, adding one more month when one is prohibited to harvest and eat it (see Leviticus 23:14 for the source of this prohibition) is of no consequence. If, however, the grain did ripen by Pesaḥ, and nevertheless the year was intercalated on account of the other two issues, then people would indeed be unhappy since the harvestable grain would have to remain in the field for an additional month without any benefit to its grower. [2]**Rabban Shimon ben Gamliel says: Because of** the issue of **the equinox** not coinciding with the Festivals."

אִיבַּעְיָא לְהוּ [3]**It was asked of** those Sages discussing this Baraita: Does this last statement of Rabban Shimon ben Gamliel's imply that when the year is intercalated **because of** the issue of **the** autumn **equinox** commencing after the Festival of Sukkot has begun, **we are happy** as well; since otherwise, were autumn to begin before Sukkot and the year nevertheless be intercalated for other reasons, it would mean having the Festival pilgrims return to their homes in the midst of the rainy season? [4]**Or** perhaps Rabban Shimon ben Gamliel meant to argue with the first Tanna of the Baraita in maintaining that **over** the issue of **the equinox** alone, the High Court **can intercalate** the year without recourse to any of the other two reasons mentioned? [5]The Sages of the Gemara offer no solution to this query, and so it is concluded that we **let** the problem **stand** unresolved.

תָּנוּ רַבָּנַן [6]**Our Rabbis taught** the following Baraita: **"Because of** the issue of late ripening in **three regions** of the Land of Israel, the High Court **intercalates the year:** [7]The regions of **Judea, Transjordan,**

RASHI

ובזמן שאביב אחד — מן השנים שמתעברת שנה עליהן. הכל שמחין, שאין חוששין בדחיית הפסח לפי שאין התבואה ראויה, ואין איסור חדש נארך עליהם, אבל כשאביב ראוי ליקצר, והשנה מתעברת על הפירות והתקופות — עציבין, שזמן איסור חדש נארך עליהן. הכי גרסינן: רבן שמעון בן גמליאל אומר על התקופה ולא גרסינן: אף. **איבעיא להו על התקופה שמחין** — שאם התקופה נופלת כתיקונה בתחלת תשרי, והם מעברין השנה בשביל דברים אחרים, ודוחין את החג בתוך ימות החורף חודש, נמצאו עולי רגלים מצטערין בגשמים, לפי שהעיתים הולכין אחר תקופת החמה. לפיכך כשהיא צריכה לעבר על פירות האילן וזה מצטרף עמו — היו שמחין, או דילמא על התקופה לחודה מעברין, ומפני שעיבורה מן התורה אתא רבן שמעון בן גמליאל למיפלג. **על שלש ארצות** — שלא הגיע אביב שלהן, או שרואין בית דין שמתאחר בהן זמן בישול פירות האילן — מעברין, שלשתן מארץ ישראל הם.

BACKGROUND

שְׁלֹשָׁה אֲרָצוֹת **Three regions.** The Land of Israel was divided for various purposes into three regions that differed from each other in climate, vegetation, and the composition of the population. Judea and Galilee were separated by a "strip of Kutim," the area inhabited by the Samaritans. The Jordan was the border between the former regions and the Transjordan settlements. At various times these regions were set apart administratively as well, since they were ruled by different rulers. The division of the Land of Israel into three regions had significance in various areas of the Halakhah.

NOTES

rather than Shavuot, by suggesting that it refers not to the ripening of fruit but to its harvesting. Since Sukkot is referred to in the Bible as "the Festival of ingathering," the Rabbis were given the option of intercalating the year whenever it appeared to them that, if they did not do so, there would be insufficient time to "ingather" the fruits before the advent of Sukkot.

עַל הַתְּקוּפָה **Because of the equinox.** *Rashi* explains that Rabban Shimon ben Gamliel might have meant that an extra month can be added to the year if it appears that the equinox will be late, even if no other conditions are met, because this is a stipulation of Torah law. *Remah* rejects this explanation, arguing that the other factors are also matters of Torah law. Rather, the late occurrence of the equinox might be sufficient reason for adding an extra month to the year because the equinox occurs at a fixed time, and the times at which the grain and fruit ripen are usually related to the time of the equinox, although they also depend upon the year's rainfall and other climatic conditions. *Rabbenu Yonah* explains that the year might be intercalated because of the equinox, even if there is no other reason for adding another month to the year, because the time at which the equinox will occur can be calculated precisely, but the time at which the grain or the fruit will ripen can only be estimated. Hence an extra month can be added to the year only if it appears that neither the grain nor the fruit will ripen in time. *Tzafnat Pa'ane'aḥ* suggests another difference between

HALAKHAH

עַל שְׁלֹשָׁה אֲרָצוֹת מְעַבְּרִין **Because of three regions they intercalate.** "There are the three major areas of Eretz Israel that must be considered when assessing whether or not the grain or the fruit has ripened sufficiently: Judea, Transjordan, and Galilee. If it appears that the grain or the fruit will not ripen in time in two of these three areas, an extra month is added to the year. But if it appears that the grain or the fruit will not ripen in time in only one of these the equinox and

וְעֵבֶר הַיַּרְדֵּן, וְהַגָּלִיל. [1]עַל שְׁתַּיִם מֵהֶן — מְעַבְּרִין, [2]וְעַל אַחַת מֵהֶן — אֵין מְעַבְּרִין. [3]וּבִזְמַן שֶׁיְּהוּדָה אַחַת מֵהֶן — הַכֹּל שְׂמֵחִין, [4]שֶׁאֵין עוֹמֶר בָּא אֶלָּא מִיהוּדָה״.

[5]תָּנוּ רַבָּנַן: [6]״אֵין מְעַבְּרִין אֶת הַשָּׁנִים אֶלָּא בִּיהוּדָה. [7]וְאִם עִיבְּרוּהָ בַּגָּלִיל, מְעוּבֶּרֶת. [8]הֵעִיד חֲנַנְיָה אִישׁ אוֹנוֹ: אִם עִיבְּרוּהָ בַּגָּלִיל אֵינָהּ מְעוּבֶּרֶת״. [9]אָמַר רַבִּי יְהוּדָה בְּרֵיהּ דְּרַבִּי שִׁמְעוֹן בֶּן פָּזִי: [10]מַאי טַעֲמָא דַּחֲנַנְיָה אִישׁ אוֹנוֹ? [11]אָמַר קְרָא: ״לְשִׁכְנוֹ תִדְרְשׁוּ וּבָאתָ שָׁמָּה״. [12]כָּל דְּרִישָׁה שֶׁאַתָּה דּוֹרֵשׁ לֹא יִהְיוּ אֶלָּא בְּשִׁכְנוֹ שֶׁל מָקוֹם.

LITERAL TRANSLATION

Transjordan, and Galilee. [1]Because of two of them — they intercalate, [2]but because of one of them — they do not intercalate. [3]And at such time as Judea is one of them, all are happy, [4]for the omer should not come from [anywhere] other than from Judea."

[5]Our Rabbis taught: [6]"They do not intercalate the years except in Judea. [7]And if they intercalated in Galilee, it is intercalated. [8]Ḥananyah of Ono testified: If they intercalated in Galilee, it is not intercalated." [9]Rabbi Yehudah, the son of Rabbi Shimon ben Pazi, said: [10]What is the reason of Ḥananyah of Ono? [11]The verse states: "There you shall seek him, at his dwelling, and there you shall come." [12]Every seeking that you seek shall only be in the dwelling place of God (lit., "place").

TRANSLATION AND COMMENTARY

and Galilee. [1]**Because of** the late ripening in **two of** these three regions, **they intercalate** the year. [2]**But over** a delay in only **one of** these regions, even if that one is Judea (from where it is preferable that the first barley be harvested for the omer-offering in the Temple), **they do not intercalate the year** since crops will have ripened in the majority of the country. [3]**And when Judea is one of the** regions over which the year is intercalated, **all are happy,** [4]**for** optimally **the omer** barley-offering in the Temple **should not come** from any region **other than Judea.** Thus, when the year is intercalated in part because of the barley not yet having ripened in Judea, it is guaranteed that the first barley used for the omer-offering will indeed come from the freshly ripened crop in Judea. However, when the year is intercalated because of the crops not having yet ripened in the other two regions, the barley from Judea that did ripen on time will no longer be suitably moist and full for use in the omer offering a month later. In such a case, the priests will be forced to use the freshly ripened barley from one of the other regions, and all will be unhappy over not having been able to perform the rite in its optimal manner."

תָּנוּ רַבָּנַן [5]**Our Rabbis taught** another Baraita dealing with the intercalation of the year: [6]"The appointed court **does not intercalate the years except** when it is sitting **in Judea.** [7]**If,** however, **they intercalated** a year while sitting **in Galilee,** the year **is** still considered **intercalated.** [8]**Ḥananyah of Ono testified** otherwise: **If they intercalated** a year while sitting **in Galilee,** the year **is not intercalated."** [9]**Rabbi Yehudah, the son of Rabbi Shimon ben Pazi, said:** [10]**What is Ḥananyah of Ono's reason** for invalidating intercalation executed outside of Judea? [11]His reason is **the verse** in Deuteronomy (12:5) that **states**: "But to the place which the Lord your God shall choose out of all your tribes to put his name there, **there you shall seek him, at his dwelling, and there you shall come."** [12]The verse teaches that **every "seeking" that you seek** in relation to fulfilling God's will **shall only be** pursued **in** the region close to **the dwelling place of God** in Jerusalem.

RASHI

על שתים מהן — אפילו על עבר הירדן **והגליל** — מעברין, דהואיל וברובא דארץ ישראל לא מטא אביב לא קרינן ביה ״חדש האביב״. **ועל אחת מהן** — אין מעברין אפילו לא הגיע ביהודה והגיע בעבר הירדן והגליל — אין מעברין, דהואיל ומביאין עומר מעבר הירדן או מגליל, דתנן במנחות (סד,ב): ״כרמל״ — רך ומלא בעינן, מיכן אמרו: אין מביאין עומר אלא מן הקרוב לירושלים — דהיינו יהודה, לא ביכר הקרוב לירושלים — מביאין אותו ממקום רחוק, ומעשה שבא עומר מגגות צריפין כו׳, ושתי הלחם — מבקעת עין סוכר. **ובזמן שיהודה אחד** — מן המאוחרות, הכל שמחין, לפי שאין עומר בא להיות מצוה מן המובחר אלא מיהודה, הלכך, אם בישל ביהודה ועיברוה בשביל השתים, כשמגיע זמן העומר כבר יבשו תבואות שביהודה, ואנו רך ומלא בעינן — וצריך להביאו משאר ארצות. ועוד: שאם ביכר יהודה, ורואין ציבור שראוי להביא העומר, ובית דין מעברין בשביל השתים — מאריכין עליהם זמן איסור חדש, קשה להם הדבר. אבל בשלא ביכר יהודה ובאחת מהשתים — אין קשה להם, אף על פי שראוי להביא מהשלישית, לפי שמצותו להביא מיהודה. **שכנו של מקום** — ירושלים, והוא ביהודה.

BACKGROUND

וְאִם עִיבְּרוּהָ בַּגָּלִיל And if they intercalated in Galilee. This is what was attempted in most generations, even when the centers of Jewish settlement, including the Sanhedrin and the great yeshivot, were in Galilee, and even when Jerusalem was a non-Jewish city, and Jews were forbidden to live there. Nevertheless, the intercalation of the year, or at least the official decision to add an extra month, was made somewhere in the region of Judea.

SAGES

חֲנַנְיָא אִישׁ אוֹנוֹ Ḥananyah of Ono. Ḥananyah, who is also called Rabbi Ḥanina, the man of Ono, was a Tanna in the generation before the sealing of the Mishnah. He is seldom mentioned in the sources, but it is known that he was a student of Rabbi Akiva's and one of those sent to receive Torah teachings from him when Rabbi Akiva was imprisoned.

NOTES

the other two factors: The equinox occurs at the same time everywhere, but crops ripen at different times in different places.

HALAKHAH

areas, an extra month is not added to the year," following the Baraita. (*Rambam, Sefer Zemanim, Hilkhot Kiddush HaḤodesh* 4:4.)

אֶלָּא בִּיהוּדָה **Except in Judea.** "The year should only be

TRANSLATION AND COMMENTARY

תָּנוּ רַבָּנַן [1]**Our Rabbis taught** the following Baraita: "The appointed court **does not intercalate the year except by day.** [2]**And if they intercalated** the year **at night,** the year **is not intercalated.** [3]Similarly, the court **does not sanctify the new month except by day,** [4]**and if they sanctified it at night, it is not sanctified."** [5]**Rav Abba said: What verse** alludes to the importance of intercalating the year and sanctifying the month during the day? [6]It is the verse that states (Psalms 81:4): **"Blow the shofar at the new moon, when concealed, for the day of our festivity."** [7]**Which is the Festival that the New Moon conceals itself in,** hiding itself from view? [8]**Say it is Rosh HaShanah,** the New Year, which is the only Festival that falls on the first of the month, when the moon is barely visible. [9]**And it is written** in the very next verse (81:5): **"For this is a statute for Israel, a judgment unto the God of Jacob."** Thus an analogy can be drawn between the "statute" observed by Israel on Rosh HaShanah (the sanctification of the new month) and "judgment" in general: [10]**Just as judgment** in a court of law **is** carried out **by day,** as deduced later in our tractate (34b) from a Scriptural verse, [11]**so too sanctification of the** new **month is** carried out **by day.**

תָּנוּ רַבָּנַן [12]**Our Rabbis taught** another Baraita dealing with the intercalation of the year: "The court **does**

[1]תָּנוּ רַבָּנַן: ״אֵין מְעַבְּרִין אֶת הַשָּׁנָה אֶלָּא בַּיּוֹם, [2]וְאִם עִיבְּרוּהָ בַּלַּיְלָה, אֵינָהּ מְעוּבֶּרֶת. [3]וְאֵין מְקַדְּשִׁין אֶת הַחֹדֶשׁ אֶלָּא בַּיּוֹם, [4]וְאִם קִידְּשׁוּהוּ בַּלַּיְלָה, אֵינוֹ מְקוּדָּשׁ״. [5]אָמַר רַב אַבָּא: מַאי קְרָא? [6]״תִּקְעוּ בַחֹדֶשׁ שׁוֹפָר בַּכֶּסֶה לְיוֹם חַגֵּנוּ״. [7]אֵיזֶהוּ חַג שֶׁהַחֹדֶשׁ מִתְכַּסֶּה בּוֹ? [8]הֱוֵי אוֹמֵר זֶה רֹאשׁ הַשָּׁנָה. [9]וּכְתִיב: ״כִּי חֹק לְיִשְׂרָאֵל הוּא מִשְׁפָּט לֵאלֹהֵי יַעֲקֹב״. [10]מַה מִּשְׁפָּט בַּיּוֹם, [11]אַף קִידּוּשׁ הַחֹדֶשׁ בַּיּוֹם.

[12]תָּנוּ רַבָּנַן: ״אֵין מְעַבְּרִין אֶת

LITERAL TRANSLATION

[1]Our Rabbis taught: "They do not intercalate the year except by day, [2]and if they intercalated at night, it is not intercalated. [3]And they do not sanctify the month except by day, [4]and if they sanctified it at night, it is not sanctified." [5]Rav Abba said: What verse? [6]"Blow the shofar at the New Moon, when concealed, for the day of our festivity." [7]Which is the Festival that the New Moon conceals itself in? [8][You have to] say it is Rosh HaShanah. [9]And it is written: "For this is a statute for Israel, a judgment unto the God of Jacob." [10]Just as judgment is by day, [11]so too the sanctification of the month is by day.

[12]Our Rabbis taught: "They do not intercalate

RASHI

אין מעברין את השנה אלא — בבית דין הקבוע ביהודה. **שהחדש מתכסה בו** — שהלבנה אינה נראית בעליל לכל העולם, דכתיב "חדש...בכסה". **הוי אומר זה ראש השנה** — שחגה בראש חדש הוא, אבל שאר חגים באמצע החדש הם, וכתיב "כי חק" כלומר חג שישראל עושין באותו חג, דהיינו קידוש החדש, הרי הוא כ"משפט", ומשפט — ביום, דכתיב: "ביום הנחילו את בניו", כדדרשינן ב"אחד דיני ממונות" (סנהדרין לד,ב).

NOTES

שֶׁהַחֹדֶשׁ מִתְכַּסֶּה בּוֹ That the new moon conceals itself in. Our commentary follows *Rashi* and others who explain this expression in the Gemara as referring to the fact that Rosh HaShanah is the only Festival during which the moon is generally obscured from view. Others explain it as referring to the fact that on Rosh HaShanah the usual sin-offering associated with the New Moon is omitted from the service of the day (*Rabbenu Ḥananel; Tosafot, Rosh HaShanah* 8b). *Rabbenu Tam* suggests that the word מִתְכַּסֶּה be understood here as מְזֻמָּן, "appointed" (as in יוֹם הַכֶּסֶא, "the appointed day," from Proverbs 7:20), thereby implying that Rosh HaShanah is the only Festival on which the New Moon is "appointed," being the only one which occurs on the first of the month.

HALAKHAH

intercalated by a court sitting in Judea. If, however, the extra month was added by a court sitting in Galilee, the intercalation of the year is still valid," following the Baraita. (*Rambam, Sefer Zemanim, Hilkhot Kiddush HaḤodesh* 4:12.)

אֵין מְעַבְּרִין אֶת הַשָּׁנָה אֶלָּא בַּיּוֹם They only add an extra month to the year during the daytime. "The year should only be intercalated during the day. If the extra month was added at night, the intercalation is not valid," following the Baraita. (*Rambam, Sefer Zemanim, Hilkhot Kiddush HaḤodesh* 4:12.)

אֵין מְקַדְּשִׁין אֶת הַחֹדֶשׁ אֶלָּא בַּיּוֹם They only sanctify the month during the day. "The month should only be sanctified during the day. If the month was sanctified at night, the sanctification is not valid," following the Baraita. (*Rambam, Sefer Zemanim, Hilkhot Kiddush HaḤodesh* 4:2:8.)

"If on the New Moon someone forgot to insert *ya'aleh veyavo* into his evening prayer, he does not have to repeat the prayer, for the month can only be sanctified during the day." (*Shulḥan Arukh, Oraḥ Ḥayyim* 422:1.)

TRANSLATION AND COMMENTARY

not intercalate the year [12A] **in years of famine** when grain is in short supply, so as not to extend the period during which newly grown crops cannot be eaten. Such crops are only permitted after the 16th of Nisan, the day when the barley-offering of the omer was brought to the Temple. Intercalating the year would postpone the arrival of that day for an additional month."

תַּנְיָא [1]This ruling is confirmed by an incident reported in the Bible, for **it was taught** in a Baraita: [2]**"Rabbi** Yehudah HaNasi **says:** The verse states [II Kings 4:42]: **'And there came a man from Ba'al Shalishah, and brought the man of God bread of newly ripened grain, twenty loaves of barley,** and full ears of corn in his sack. And he said, Give to the people that they may eat.' Evidently the crops were late in ripening that year, [3]for **you have no** region **in all of Eretz Israel** where **the ripening of produce** is quicker **than** in **Ba'al Shalishah,** [4]**and even so only one species had ripened** by the time Pesaḥ had passed. [5]**Perhaps you will say** that the bread was made from newly ripened **wheat**, which normally ripens a good while after Pesaḥ? [6]This is not possible, though, for **the** Biblical **verse states** explicitly that the loaves were made from **"barley."** [7]**Perhaps you will say,** then, that this incident occurred **before the omer**-offering was brought on the 16th of Nisan, thereby explaining why only barley had ripened by then? [8]But this, too, is impossible, since **the** Biblical **verse states** as well: **'Give to the people, that they may eat'** — [9]proving that **it was after the omer**-offering was brought, and the new grain was permitted to be eaten, that this incident occurred. [10]Consequently, one must **say now that** the **year** in which this incident occurred **was** one which was **fit to be intercalated** due to a delay in ripening, and that is why only barley was available at such a late date.

הַשָּׁנָה [12A] בִּשְׁנֵי רְעָבוֹן״. [1]תַּנְיָא: ״רַבִּי אוֹמֵר: [2]׳וְאִישׁ בָּא מִבַּעַל שָׁלִישָׁה וַיָּבֵא לְאִישׁ הָאֱלֹהִים לֶחֶם בִּכּוּרִים עֶשְׂרִים לֶחֶם שְׂעֹרִים וגו׳״. [3]וְאֵין לְךָ קַלָּה בְּכָל אֶרֶץ יִשְׂרָאֵל לְבַשֵּׁל פֵּירוֹתֶיהָ יוֹתֵר מִבַּעַל שָׁלִישָׁה, [4]וְאַף עַל פִּי כֵן לֹא בִּכְּרָה אֶלָּא מִין אֶחָד. [5]שֶׁמָּא תֹּאמַר חִטִּים? [6]תַּלְמוּד לוֹמַר: ״שְׂעוֹרִים״ [7]שֶׁמָּא תֹּאמַר לִפְנֵי הָעוֹמֶר? [8]תַּלְמוּד לוֹמַר: ״תֵּן לָעָם וְיֹאכֵלוּ״ [9]אַחַר הָעוֹמֶר הָיָה. [10]אֱמוֹר מֵעַתָּה: רְאוּיָה הָיְתָה אוֹתָהּ שָׁנָה שֶׁתִּתְעַבֵּר.

LITERAL TRANSLATION

the year [12A] in years of famine." [1]It was taught: "Rabbi says: [2]'And there came a man from Ba'al Shalishah, and brought the man of God bread of newly ripened grain, twenty loaves of barley, etc.' [3]And you have no quicker [region] in all of Eretz Israel for the ripening of produce than Ba'al Shalishah, [4]and even so only one species had ripened. [5]Perhaps you will say wheat? [6]The verse states: 'Barley.' [7]Perhaps you will say before the omer? [8]The verse states: 'Give to the people, that they may eat' — [9]it was after the omer. [10]Say now: That year was fit to be intercalated.

RASHI

בשני רעבון — לפי שכלה התבואה וצריכין לאכול מן החדש. **לחם ביכורים** — לחם אביב, משמע שעכשיו היה מבכר. **ושמא תאמר חיטין היו** — שהן אפילות, לכך נתאחרו לבשל עד אחר הפסח — תלמוד לומר ״לחם שעורים״. **ושמא תאמר לפני העומר היה** — ובזמן ביכור — תלמוד לומר ״תן לעם ויאכלו״ מלמד שקרב העומר והותר החדש.

BACKGROUND

בַּעַל שָׁלִישָׁה Ba'al Shalishah. It is not clear where this is. Since it is described as a place where fruit ripens earlier than elsewhere in Eretz Israel, it was probably near Jericho, perhaps near Naḥal Uja. Some scholars identify it with a village named Thalath ("three") in Samaria.

NOTES

בִּשְׁנֵי רְעָבוֹן In years of famine. According to *Rambam,* the court would only refrain from intercalating a famine year when the factors arguing in its favor were of the kind that would not normally obligate intercalation, such as those factors which serve technically to impede the Festival pilgrimage (the disrepair of roads, bridges, Paschal ovens). However, if the factors arguing in favor of intercalation were of the more substantive variety that normally obligate such intervention (such as concern with a delay in ripening of produce or the timing of the equinox), then the court would have to intercalate the year even if it was one of famine. *Remah* and *Rash,* however, interpret the Baraita as making no distinction between the factors that argue in favor of intercalation when proscribing the practice during years of famine.

HALAKHAH

אֵין מְעַבְּרִין אֶת הַשָּׁנָה בִּשְׁנֵי רְעָבוֹן They do not intercalate the year in years of famine. "The court does not intercalate a year of famine, as everyone is running to the granaries in search of food upon which to subsist. Under such circumstances the court does not wish to prolong the period during which the new grain may not be eaten. However, if intercalation is being considered because of primary concerns, such as the timing of the equinox or a delay in the ripening of produce, then the court may intercalate the year even if it is one of famine." (*Rambam, Sefer Zemanim, Hilkhot Kiddush HaḤodesh* 4:15-16.)

[1] וּמִפְּנֵי מָה לֹא עִיבְּרָהּ אֱלִישָׁע? [2] שֶׁשְּׁנַת בַּצּוֹרֶת הָיְתָה, וְהָיוּ הַכֹּל רָצִין לְבֵית הַגְּרָנוֹת״.

[3] תָּנוּ רַבָּנַן: [4] ״אֵין מְעַבְּרִין אֶת הַשָּׁנָה לִפְנֵי רֹאשׁ הַשָּׁנָה. [5] וְאִם עִיבְּרוּהָ, אֵינָהּ מְעוּבֶּרֶת. [6] אֲבָל מִפְּנֵי הַדְּחָק, [7] מְעַבְּרִין אוֹתָהּ אַחַר רֹאשׁ הַשָּׁנָה מִיָּד. [8] וְאַף עַל פִּי כֵּן, אֵין מְעַבְּרִין אֶלָּא אֲדָר״.

LITERAL TRANSLATION

[1] And why did Elisha not intercalate? [2] Because it was a year of drought, and all were running to the granary."

[3] Our Rabbis taught: [4] "They do not intercalate the year before Rosh HaShanah. [5] And if they intercalated, it is not intercalated. [6] However, in case of emergency, [7] they may intercalate immediately after Rosh HaShanah. [8] And even then, they cannot intercalate [any month] other than Adar."

TRANSLATION AND COMMENTARY

[1] **And why,** then, **did Elisha not intercalate** the year? [2] **Because it was a year of drought, and all** the people **were running to the granary** for new grain, their supplies having run out. Had Elisha intercalated the year, and the new grain been forbidden for an additional month, it would have been even more difficult for them to survive the shortage of food."

תָּנוּ רַבָּנַן [3] **Our Rabbis taught** another Baraita dealing with the laws of intercalation: [4] "The appointed court **does not** convene for the purpose of considering whether to **intercalate the** coming **year before Rosh HaShanah** of that year. [5] **And if** the court goes ahead in any case and decides to **intercalate** the coming year before Rosh HaShanah has arrived, the year **is not intercalated.** [6] **However, in an emergency,** such as where there is concern that the court will not be able to convene the following Adar, [7] **they may** meet for the purpose of deciding whether to **intercalate** the year **immediately after Rosh HaShanah.** [8] **And even then they cannot intercalate,** through the adding of a month, any month **other than Adar.** Thus it is only the decision to intercalate that can be taken immediately following Rosh HaShanah; the actual intercalation itself must wait until the month of Adar half a year later, and only then is the additional month — Adar II — inserted into the year."

RASHI

אמור מעתה ראויה היתה אותה שנה להתעבר — על האביב, שכשהגיע ניסן עדיין לא היה רוב האביב, דהא לאחר ששה עשר בניסן לא ניכרו אלא שעורין, ולא קרינא ביה ״חדש האביב״. **ששנת בצורת היתה** — בקראי משכחת לה. **אין מעברין** — אין יושבין בית דין קודם ראש השנה לעיין ולומר: תתעבר שנה זו בשני אדרים, מפני שיש שכחה בדבר קודם שיגיע — ומזלזלי בחמץ. **אבל מפני הדחק** — שמא לא יהא שם בית דין מופלא סמוך לאדר, או שמא יצא המלך אדומי ויעכב על ידן — מעברין אותה, ומודיעין לגולה אחר ראש השנה מיד, שעיברנוה. **ואף על פי כן אין מעברין** — אותה בשני חדשים אחרים, אלא כשיגיע אדר — יעשו שני אדרים.

NOTES

לִפְנֵי רֹאשׁ הַשָּׁנָה **Before Rosh HaShanah.** According to *Rashi*, the reason for prohibiting the court to deliberate and decide the issue prior to Rosh HaShanah is the fear that people may forget by the time of the actual intercalation (prior to the month of Nisan) that an additional Adar was added to the year and, as a result, celebrate Pesaḥ at the wrong time. *Remah,* however, views the problem of early deliberation as related to the possibility of people mistakenly assuming that the month of Elul, immediately preceding Rosh HaShanah, is the month that actually gets repeated in the process of intercalation. Such a mistake would result in their neglecting to observe the Tishri Festivals of Rosh HaShanah, Yom Kippur and Sukkot in their proper time.

אֵין מְעַבְּרִין אֶלָּא אֲדָר **They cannot intercalate any month other than Adar.** The Rishonim explain this rule in various ways. *Tosafot* explains the reason for choosing Adar as the repeated month as aimed at preserving the ordinal number assigned to it in Scripture (Esther 3:7): "To the twelfth month, that is, the month of Adar." Were any other month chosen as the month to be repeated in a leap year, Adar would no longer be the twelfth month. By the same token, if the month of Elul were chosen to be intercalated, then Tishrei would no longer be the "seventh month," as it is referred to repeatedly in the Bible. *Remah* offers another reason: Since the important determining factors of whether the grain and the fruit could be expected to ripen on time were generally not known before Adar, the court was instructed

HALAKHAH

אֵין מְעַבְּרִין אֶת הַשָּׁנָה לִפְנֵי רֹאשׁ הַשָּׁנָה **They do not intercalate the year before Rosh HaShanah.** "Normally, the court does not publicize its decision to intercalate a particular year until the actual time of intercalation in the month of Adar, at which point a second Adar is declared in place of the month of Nisan, which would normally follow. However, in times of emergency, the decision can be publicized immediately after the Rosh HaShanah of that year. If it is publicized before Rosh HaShanah, the intercalation is invalid," in accordance with the Gemara. (*Rambam, Sefer Zemanim, Hilkhot Kiddush HaḤodesh* 4:13.)

אֵין מְעַבְּרִין אֶלָּא אֲדָר **They cannot intercalate any month other than Adar.** "The only month that can ever be repeated when instituting a leap year is the month of Adar, the last month of the Jewish calendar year as reckoned for the purpose of Festival observance." (*Rambam, Sefer Zemanim, Hilkhot Kiddush HaḤodesh* 4:1.)

LITERAL TRANSLATION

[1] Is this so? [2] But behold they sent to Rava: [3] "A couple came from Rakat, [4] and an eagle seized them, [5] and in their possession were things produced in Luz. [6] And what were they? [7] *Tekhelet*-dyed wool. [8] In the merit of [divine] mercy and in their own merit, they departed in peace. [9] And the burdened of the loins of Naḥshon sought to establish a certain post [*netziv*], [10] but that Edomite did not let him. [11] However, the masters of assembly assembled, [12] and they established a certain post in the month in which Aaron the priest died!"

[1] אִינִי? [2] וְהָא שָׁלְחוּ לֵיהּ לְרָבָא: [3] "זוּג בָּא מֵרַקַּת, [4] וּתְפָשׂוֹ נֶשֶׁר, [5] וּבְיָדָם דְּבָרִים הַנַּעֲשֶׂה בְּלוּז. [6] וּמַאי נִיהוּ? [7] תְּכֵלֶת. [8] בִּזְכוּת הָרַחֲמִים וּבִזְכוּתָם יָצְאוּ בְּשָׁלוֹם. [9] וַעֲמוּסֵי יְרֵיכֵי נַחְשׁוֹן בִּקְּשׁוּ לִקְבּוֹעַ נְצִיב אֶחָד, [10] וְלֹא הִנִּיחָן אֲדוֹמִי הַלָּז. [11] אֲבָל בַּעֲלֵי אֲסוּפוֹת נֶאֶסְפוּ, [12] וְקָבְעוּ לוֹ נְצִיב אֶחָד בַּיֶּרַח שֶׁמֵּת בּוֹ אַהֲרֹן הַכֹּהֵן"!

RASHI

זוג – שני תלמידי חכמים. בא מרקת – טבריא. ותפשו נשר – חיל רומיים. דברים הנעשים בלוז – תכלת – בלוז עושין אותה, כדאמרינן בסוטה (מו,ב): היא לוז שצובעין בה תכלת. עמוסי יריכי נחשון – נשיא שבארץ ישראל, שהוא מזרע נחשון בן עמינדב ראשון לנשיאים. בקשו לקבוע נציב אחד – בקשו להוסיף חדש אחד על השנה לעברה. ולא הניחן אדומי הלז – מלכות הרשעה גזרה גזירה עליהן. בירח שמת בו אהרן – באב, אלמא מפני הדחק מעיינין בעיבור שנה לפני ראש השנה.

TRANSLATION AND COMMENTARY

אִינִי [1] The Gemara questions the ruling in this Baraita: **Is it really so,** that the court cannot deliberate the issue of intercalation prior to Rosh HaShanah? [2] **But consider** the following coded message that the Sages in Eretz Israel **sent to Rava** in Babylonia during the time of the Roman occupation: [3] **"A couple came from Rakat** [a pair of Torah scholars set out for Babylonia from the Sanhedrin's temporary home in Tiberias, situated on the site of the Biblical city of Rakat]. [4] **And an eagle seized them** [the two Sages were captured by soldiers bearing the Roman Legion's emblem of the eagle]. [5] **And in** the couple's **possession were things produced in** the city of **Luz.** [6] **And what were** those things that they bore from Luz? [7] ***Tekhelet*-dyed wool** used in ritually fringed garments. [8] **Through** divine **mercy and because of their own merit, they departed in peace** and were not harmed by the Romans. Thus, they carried to Babylonia this message: [9] **The burdened of the loins of Naḥshon** [the Nasi of the Sanhedrin, a descendant of the tribe of Judah whose first prince was Naḥshon ben Aminadav] **sought to establish a certain post** [to decide on adding an additional month to the year], [10] **but the Edomite** [the Roman governor in charge] **did not let him.** [11] **However, the masters of assembly assembled** [the Sages of the generation, as they are called in Ecclesiastes 12:11], [12] **and they established** on their own **a certain post** [i.e., decided to add an additional month to the year] **in the month in which Aaron the priest died** [the month of Av, as indicated by Numbers 33:38]!" Thus we see that in times of emergency the Sages of the Sanhedrin would meet as early as the month of Av, two months before Rosh HaShanah, in order to deliberate the issue of intercalating the following year!

BACKGROUND

זוּג בָּא מֵרַקַּת A couple came from Rakat. The cryptic language in this letter, which was sent from Eretz Israel, was used for political reasons. For many years the Roman authorities persecuted the courts that added the intercalary month to the year and sought to announce its decisions to other countries. For as long as the intercalary month was added and the month was sanctified properly in Eretz Israel, the heads of the Sanhedrin maintained a degree of power over all the Jews everywhere in the world. The Roman authorities feared a Jewish revolt and wished to stifle political connections between the Jewish leaders in the Land of Israel and the leadership of other countries, especially Babylonia, which was under the rule of the Persian kingdom, a world power in competion with Rome. Hence they sought to stop the emissaries of the court in whichever way they could, until the head of the Sanhedrin at that time, Hillel the Younger, decided to depart from tradition and to determine the months and years for generations in advance. He transmitted the calculation of the intercalary year and the sanctification of the months to the Diaspora, inaugurating the system that we use to this day.

REALIA

נֶשֶׁר Eagle.

A standard-bearer of a Roman legion from the Talmudic period.

The eagle was one of the symbols of Roman rule, for it was found on the standard of

NOTES

specifically to intercalate that month in order to ensure that these factors were properly taken into consideration. The *Mekhilta* derives this rule from the verse (Deuteronomy 16:1): "Observe the month of ripening," which implies that any measure taken to ensure such observance must be taken in proximity to the month of ripening itself, i.e., during Adar (see also *Rashi, Rosh HaShanah* 7a). Others see this guideline for intercalating the year as deduced from the rule applied in intercalating the month: Just as the month is intercalated by adding an extra day upon its conclusion, so too is the year intercalated by adding an additional month upon *its* conclusion.

וּתְפָשׂוֹ נֶשֶׁר And an eagle seized them. Our commentary follows *Rashi* and others who interpret the eagle as a symbol for the Roman soldiers whose legionary emblem was an eagle. *Remah* cites a number of alternative interpretations, which view the eagle as a symbol either for the king himself (as in Ezekiel 17:3: "a great eagle") or for robbers in hiding who swoop upon their prey and then disappear. *Raḥ* suggests that the "eagle" (*nesher*) represents rain "falling" (*nosher*) from the sky, which delayed the scholars as they made their way to Babylonia.

דְּבָרִים הַנַּעֲשִׂים בְּלוּז Things produced in Luz. *Rabbi Tzvi Ḥayyot* suggests that this, too, is a reference to the intercalation of the year that was known to have been carried out for a time in the Judean city of Lod. By changing the name from Lod to Luz, and injecting the reference to *tekhelet*, the Rabbis were able to conceal the true meaning of their message from the Roman authorities who forbade the Jews from intercalating the year.

every legion. These "eagles" were more than flags, and actually served as virtual idols for each legion. Therefore, the eagle became a symbol of Rome and its army.

BACKGROUND

נְצִיב לִישָּׁנָא דְּיַרְחָא Naturally the word *natziv* does not mean "month," but the question was asked regarding the connection between *natziv* and the concept of "month," as it was used in this letter. The other cryptic expressions in the letter were common and well known.

TRANSLATION AND COMMENTARY

חֲשׁוּבֵי מְחַשְּׁבִי [1]The Gemara explains this discrepancy: The court **may indeed** at times convene before Rosh HaShanah and **make** its **calculations** as to whether the coming year should be intercalated. [2]However, as regards **publicizing** its decision, the Baraita quoted above comes to teach us that they may **not publicize** it until after Rosh HaShanah.

מַאי מַשְׁמַע [3]The Gemara now goes back to ponder the language of that message: **What is the reason for the** word ***netziv,*** literally a "post," **being** used as **a term** denoting **a month?** [4]The Gemara answers: **For it is written** (I Kings 4:7): **"And to Solomon were twelve commissioners** [*nitzavim*] appointed **over all of Israel, and they supplied the king and his household; one month a year,** it would be [incumbent] on each [commissioner] to supply the king." Since each *nitzav* maintained responsibility for one month a year, the term *nitzav* itself was used to symbolize a month in the coded message sent to Rava.

וְהָכְתִיב [5]The Gemara now raises a question about this verse in Kings: **But surely it is written** later in the same chapter (4:19): **"And one commissioner who was in the land,"** implying that there was an additional commissioner appointed by Solomon!

רַב יְהוּדָה וְרַב נַחְמָן [6]**Rav Yehudah and Rav Naḥman** disagreed about how to understand this verse. [7]**One** of them **said:** In addition to the twelve commissioners, each of whom supplied the king for a month, there was **one** who was **appointed over all of them.** [8]**And** the other **one said:** The additional commissioner only supplied the king in leap years, his month of duty **corresponding to the month of intercalation**.

תָּנוּ רַבָּנַן [9]**Our Rabbis taught** the following Baraita: "The appointed court **does not intercalate the year** in either of the following ways: [10]**Not from one year to its companion** year, i.e., they cannot intercalate the current year in anticipation of needing to do so in the following year; [11]**and not three years, one after the other**, so as to avoid having the month of Nisan in that third year falling well into the summer. [12]**Rabbi Shimon said: It once happened that Rabbi Akiva was incarcerated in a** Roman **prison**, awaiting execution, [13]**and**

[1]חֲשׁוּבֵי מְחַשְּׁבִי; [2]גַּלּוּיֵי — לָא מְגַלּוּ.
[3]מַאי מַשְׁמַע דְּהַאי נְצִיב לִישָּׁנָא דְּיַרְחָא הוּא? [4]דִּכְתִיב: "וְלִשְׁלֹמֹה שְׁנֵים עָשָׂר נִצָּבִים עַל כָּל יִשְׂרָאֵל וְכִלְכְּלוּ אֶת הַמֶּלֶךְ וְאֶת אַנְשֵׁיו חֹדֶשׁ בַּשָּׁנָה".
[5]וְהָכְתִיב: "וּנְצִיב אֶחָד [אֲשֶׁר] בָּאָרֶץ"!
[6]רַב יְהוּדָה וְרַב נַחְמָן. [7]חַד אָמַר: אֶחָד מְמוּנֶּה עַל כּוּלָּם. [8]וְחַד אָמַר: כְּנֶגֶד חֹדֶשׁ הָעִיבּוּר.
[9]תָּנוּ רַבָּנַן: "אֵין מְעַבְּרִין אֶת הַשָּׁנָה, [10]לֹא מִשָּׁנָה לַחֲבֶרְתָּהּ, [11]וְלֹא שָׁלֹשׁ שָׁנִים זוֹ אַחַר זוֹ. [12]אָמַר רַבִּי שִׁמְעוֹן: מַעֲשֶׂה בְּרַבִּי עֲקִיבָא שֶׁהָיָה חָבוּשׁ בְּבֵית הָאֲסוּרִים, [13]וְעִיבֵּר שָׁלֹשׁ

LITERAL TRANSLATION

[1]They may indeed make calculations; [2][however,] publicizing — they may not publicize.

[3]What is the meaning of that *netziv* being a term [denoting] a month? [4]For it is written: "And to Solomon were twelve commissioners over all of Israel and they supplied the king and his household; one month a year."

[5]But surely it is written: "And one commissioner who was in the land"!

[6]Rav Yehudah and Rav Naḥman [disagreed]. [7]One said: One appointed over all of them. [8]And [the other] one said: Corresponding to the month of intercalation.

[9]Our Rabbis taught: "They do not intercalate the year, [10]not from one year to the next [lit., 'its companion'], [11]and not three years, one after the other. [12]Rabbi Shimon said: It once happened that Rabbi Akiva was incarcerated in a prison, [13]and he intercalated three

RASHI

גלויי לא מגלו — עד לאחר ראש השנה, שלא ישכחו בני הגולה. **נציבים** — ממונים חדש בשנה — יהיה על כל אחד לכלכל. **כנגד חדש העיבור** — בשנה מעוברת היה אותו נציב מכלכל באדר השני. **משנה לחברתה** — אם שנה הבאה צריכה לעבר, אין מעברין שנה זו מפני צורכי שנה הבאה, אלא הצריכה תתעבר. **ולא שלש שנים זו אחר זו** — שאם כן משתנות השנים מתיקונם, ובא לו ניסן השלישי באמצע הקיץ.

NOTES

רַבִּי עֲקִיבָא עִיבֵּר שָׁלֹשׁ שָׁנִים Our commentary follows *Rashi,* who understands the Sages' interpretation of Rabbi Akiva's actions as indicating that he did not actually intercalate three consecutive years, but rather determined which three

HALAKHAH

חֲשׁוּבֵי מְחַשְּׁבִי They may indeed make calculations. "The court may make advance calculations with regard to intercalating any number of years to come in the future. However, it cannot publicize its decision until after Rosh HaShanah of the particular year being intercalated," this in accordance with the Gemara. (*Rambam, Sefer Zemanim, Hilkhot Kiddush HaḤodesh* 4:13.)

שָׁנִים, זוֹ אַחַר זוֹ. [1] אָמְרוּ לוֹ: מִשָּׁם רְאָיָה? [2] בֵּית דִּין יָשְׁבוּ וְקָבְעוּ אַחַת אַחַת בִּזְמַנָּהּ״.

[3] תָּנוּ רַבָּנַן: ״אֵין מְעַבְּרִין אֶת הַשָּׁנָה, [4] לֹא בַּשְּׁבִיעִית, וְלֹא בְּמוֹצָאֵי שְׁבִיעִית. [5] אֵימָתַי רְגִילִין לְעַבֵּר? [6] עֶרֶב שְׁבִיעִית. [7] שֶׁל בֵּית רַבָּן גַּמְלִיאֵל הָיוּ מְעַבְּרִין בְּמוֹצָאֵי שְׁבִיעִית״.

LITERAL TRANSLATION

years, one after the other! [1] They said to him: From there a proof? [2] A court sat and established one by one in its time."

[3] Our Rabbis taught: "They do not intercalate the year, [4] not in the Sabbatical Year, and not in the year following a Sabbatical Year. [5] When were they accustomed to intercalate? [6] [On] the eve of the Sabbatical Year. [7] [The scholars] of the academy of Rabban Gamliel would intercalate in the year following a Sabbatical Year."

TRANSLATION AND COMMENTARY

he intercalated three years, one after the other! Thus we see that three years in a row can indeed be intercalated! [1] The Sages **said to** Rabbi Shimon in reply to his challenge: **From there** you seek to bring **a proof** against our ruling?! Indeed, you misunderstood the circumstances. Rabbi Akiva, being an expert in this area, merely made the calculations necessary for determining when the next three occasions would arise that a year would need intercalating. [2] When eventually they had to intercalate these three nonconsecutive years, a special **court sat and established one by one** that each of these years be intercalated **in its time."**

תָּנוּ רַבָּנַן [3] **Our Rabbis taught** another Baraita dealing with the same subject: [4] "The appointed court **does not intercalate the year** at the following times: **Not in a Sabbatical Year,** as it would mean prolonging the period during which people would be prohibited from working their land; **and not in the year following a Sabbatical Year,** as that would mean extending for an additional month the prohibition against eating the eagerly anticipated new crop of grain, the first to be cultivated in well over a year. [5] **When,** indeed, **were they accustomed to intercalate** the year? [6] On **the eve of the Sabbatical Year,** during the year preceding it, when the additional month of working the land brought the most benefit. [7] It is related that the scholars **of the academy of Rabban Gamliel** disagreed, for they **would intercalate** even **in the year following a Sabbatical Year."**

RASHI

בית דין ישבו וקבעו כל אחת ואחת בזמנה — ולא עיברו שלש שנים רצופות ולא זו אחר זו היו, אלא מפני שר׳ עקיבא חכם גדול היה ובקי בעיבור השנה והוא עומד ליהרג באו בית דין וישבו עמו ועיינו בעיבור שלש שנים ולא רצופות, אלא כל אחת בזמנה, דהא אמרינן: מפני הדחק — חשובי מחשבינן, גלויי — לא מגלינן, לישנא אחרינא: ולא שלש שנים זו אחר זו — תנא קמא נמי בהא קאסר, שלא יעיינו בעיבור שלש שנים זו אחר זו בישיבה אחת, ואפילו לעברן בזמנן. **משם ראיה בית דין ישבו** — אחרי כן בכל שנת עיבור ועיבור וקבעוה, ולא סמכו על אותו מנין, אלא לפי שהיה רבי עקיבא חכם גדול, עיינו בשלשתם בימיו. **לא בשביעית** — לפי שמאריכין עליהן איסור עבודת קרקע. **ולא במוצאי שביעית** — בשמינית, לפי שכלה הישן מאריכין עליהן איסור החדש. **בערב שביעית** — להוסיף להם חדש לעבודת קרקע. **של בית רבן (שמעון) מעברין במוצאי שביעית** — ואין חוששין אם כילה הישן, דקסבר: מביאין ירק ותבואה מחוצה לארץ לארץ ישראל, מאותה שחרשו וזרעו בשביעית והתירם עומר של שביעית.

NOTES

of the coming years would require intercalation. Later, a special court acted upon his determination and intercalated each of those years in its own time. *Rabbenu Ḥananel* understands this differently: The Sages indeed concurred that Rabbi Akiva had decided upon the intercalation of three consecutive years; yet the actual intercalation itself was independently effected in each of those years by a court appointed for that purpose. The ruling that prohibits the intercalation of three consecutive years was circumvented in this instance due to special circumstances. In order to sufficiently synchronize the lunar and solar calendars, it is necessary to ensure that every nineteen years include at least seven which are intercalated. The particular cycle Rabbi Akiva was faced with (one which saw a famine year followed by a Sabbatical Year, followed by a Jubilee Year) was destined to fall short of these seven unless he intercalated three consecutive years at the end of the cycle.

אֵין מְעַבְּרִין אֶת הַשָּׁנָה לֹא בַּשְּׁבִיעִית **They do not intercalate the year during the Sabbatical Year.** *Rambam* (*Hilkhot Kiddush HaḤodesh* 4:15) understands the reason for prohibiting intercalation during the Sabbatical Year as the fear that people might consume in the course of an extended year all the available, uncultivated grain permissible for eating, leaving nothing for the omer and bread-offerings that must be brought during the Sabbatical Year as well.

HALAKHAH

אֵין מְעַבְּרִין אֶת הַשָּׁנָה לֹא בַּשְּׁבִיעִית **They do not intercalate the year in a Sabbatical Year.** "The court does not intercalate a Sabbatical Year, so as not to prolong the period during which the land cannot be cultivated or the new grain eaten. However, the year after a Sabbatical Year can be intercalated," in accordance with the opinion of Rabban Shimon ben Gamliel. *Rambam* maintains that in the case of a Sabbatical Year as well, should intercalation be deemed necessary as a result of the equinox not coinciding with its corresponding Festival, or a delay in the ripening of grain or fruit, then the court has the power to intercalate the year regardless. *Remah* and *Rash* once again disagree. (*Rambam, Sefer Zemanim, Hilkhot Kiddush HaḤodesh* 4:15-16.)

BACKGROUND

מִפְּנֵי הַטּוּמְאָה **Because of ritual impurity.** There is a legal principle known as טוּמְאָה דְּחוּיָה בְּצִיבּוּר— i.e., "ritual impurity is suspended in public" — which has the following effect: If an entire community, or the majority of a community, is impure, the normal course of Temple worship proceeds, despite the impurity. Here it appears that Hezekiah also wanted the people of Israel ("from Ephraim and Menasseh and Issachar and Zebulun"), who had been cut off from the Temple service in Jerusalem for many generations (as long as the Kingdom of Israel persisted), to be able to participate in eating the Paschal sacrifice.

TRANSLATION AND COMMENTARY

וּבִפְלוּגְתָּא דְּהָנֵי תַּנָּאֵי [1]**And it is in** line with **the dispute of these** other **Tannaim** that the academy of Rabban Gamliel came to disagree with the Sages of the Baraita, [2]**for it was taught** in an earlier Baraita: **"We do not bring vegetables** or grains **from outside the Land of Israel** into its boundaries. [3]**But** there are those among **our Rabbis** who disagreed and **permitted this** practice." The Sages in our Baraita, who maintain that the year following a Sabbatical Year should not be intercalated, agree with the first Tanna of this earlier Baraita, that produce may not be brought from outside Eretz Israel into the country. Their concern with regard to a possible food shortage in the year following a Sabbatical Year led them to prohibit the intercalation of that year so that the new crop of grain could be made available as soon as possible. The academy of Rabban Gamliel, on the other hand, accepted the opinion of the Rabbis who allowed the importation of foreign produce into Eretz Israel. Thus they had no qualms about permitting the intercalation of the year following a Sabbatical Year, since any possible shortage of domestic grain could be offset by the imported stock.

מַאי בֵּינַיְיהוּ [4]The Gemara asks: **What is** the point of disagreement **between** the Tannaim who dispute the permissibility of importing produce into Eretz Israel? [5]**Rabbi Yirmiyah said:** The issue of whether **we are concerned with the clods** of earth that cling to this produce **is** the point of disagreement that exists **between them.** The Tanna who forbade the importing of such produce was concerned that clods of earth from outside Eretz Israel, which are ritually impure, would confer impurity on those who use the produce. The dissenting Rabbis did not share that concern, and, as a result, allowed foreign produce to be imported into Eretz Israel.

תָּנוּ רַבָּנַן [6]**Our Rabbis taught** yet another Baraita dealing with the rules governing the intercalation of the year: "The appointed court **does not intercalate the year** simply **because of** its foreseeing a situation where **ritual impurity** threatens a majority of the community in such a way as purification would be impossible before the arrival of Pesaḥ, when purity is required for offering the Paschal sacrifice. [7]**Rabbi Yehudah** disagrees and **says: They do** in fact **intercalate** the year under such circumstances. [8]**Rabbi Yehudah** also **said: It once happened that Hezekiah, the King of Judea, intercalated the year**

[1]וּבִפְלוּגְתָּא דְּהָנֵי תַּנָּאֵי, [2]דְּתַנְיָא: ״אֵין מְבִיאִין יָרָק מֵחוּצָה לָאָרֶץ, [3]וְרַבּוֹתֵינוּ הִתִּירוּ״.
[4]מַאי בֵּינַיְיהוּ? [5]אָמַר רַבִּי יִרְמְיָה: חוֹשְׁשִׁין לְגוּשֵׁיהֶן אִיכָּא בֵּינַיְיהוּ.
[6]תָּנוּ רַבָּנַן: ״אֵין מְעַבְּרִין אֶת הַשָּׁנָה מִפְּנֵי הַטּוּמְאָה. [7]רַבִּי יְהוּדָה אוֹמֵר: מְעַבְּרִין. [8]אָמַר רַבִּי יְהוּדָה: מַעֲשֶׂה בְּחִזְקִיָּה מֶלֶךְ יְהוּדָה, שֶׁעִיבֵּר אֶת הַשָּׁנָה

LITERAL TRANSLATION

[1]And it is in the dispute of these Tannaim, [2]for it was taught: "We do not bring vegetables from outside the Land [of Israel], [3]but our Rabbis permitted [this]."

[4]What is [the difference] between them? [5]Rabbi Yirmiyah said: [Whether] we are concerned with their clods is [the difference] between them.

[6]Our Rabbis taught: "They do not intercalate the year because of ritual impurity. [7]Rabbi Yehudah said: They do intercalate. [8]Rabbi Yehudah said: [There was] an incident involving Hezekiah, the King of Judea, wherein he intercalated the year

RASHI

מאי בינייהו — במאי פליגי. **חוששין לגושייהו** — שמא יבא עמה מגוש ארץ העמים, שמטמא באהל, ויטמא טהרות של ארץ ישראל. **מפני הטומאה** — כגון שהיה נשיא חולה, ואמדוהו למות ערב הפסח או (שני) ימים קודם, ויהיו טמאים, או שהיה רובן טמאים בסוף אדר, וכלתה אפר הפרה ואין יכולין למצוא עכשיו פרה אדומה — אין מעברין בכך, אלא יעשו בטומאה.

NOTES

מִפְּנֵי הַטּוּמְאָה **Because of ritual impurity.** *Rashi* explains the ritual impurity that affected the people at the time of Hezekiah as having resulted from the contact they had with idols during the time that his father, Ahaz, ruled. Hezekiah brought about a revival of observance; yet he realized that if the year was not intercalated, many of the people would be unable to purify themselves before Pesaḥ. *Tosafot* cites the Jerusalem Talmud, which ascribes the ritual impurity at the time of Hezekiah to the discovery of Aravna the Jebusite's buried skull underneath the altar on the Temple Mount. *Ran* cites another opinion recorded in the Jerusalem Talmud, according to which Hezekiah intercalated the year so as to provide more time for removing the impure idolatrous engravings that were etched into the Temple walls.

HALAKHAH

חוֹשְׁשִׁין לְגוּשֵׁיהֶן **We are concerned with regard to the clods of earth.** "All earth that has its source outside Eretz Israel is considered by Rabbinic decree to be ritually impure and capable of imparting that impurity to things which come in contact with it." (*Rambam, Sefer Taharah, Hilkhot Tum'at Met* 2:16.)

מִפְּנֵי הַטּוּמְאָה, [1]וּבִקֵּשׁ רַחֲמִים עַל עַצְמוֹ, [2]דִּכְתִיב: ׳כִּי מַרְבִּית הָעָם רַבַּת מֵאֶפְרַיִם וּמְנַשֶּׁה יִשָּׂשכָר וּזְבֻלוּן, לֹא הִטֶּהָרוּ[12B] כִּי אָכְלוּ אֶת הַפֶּסַח בְּלֹא כַכָּתוּב. [3]כִּי הִתְפַּלֵּל חִזְקִיָּהוּ עֲלֵיהֶם, לֵאמֹר, ה׳ הַטּוֹב יְכַפֵּר בְּעַד׳. [4]רַבִּי שִׁמְעוֹן אוֹמֵר: אִם מִפְּנֵי הַטּוּמְאָה עִיבְּרוּהָ, מְעוּבֶּרֶת. [5]אֶלָּא מִפְּנֵי מָה בִּיקֵּשׁ רַחֲמִים עַל עַצְמוֹ? [6]שֶׁאֵין מְעַבְּרִין אֶלָּא אֲדָר, [7]וְהוּא עִיבֵּר נִיסָן בְּנִיסָן. [8]רַבִּי שִׁמְעוֹן בֶּן יְהוּדָה אוֹמֵר מִשּׁוּם רַבִּי שִׁמְעוֹן: [9]מִפְּנֵי שֶׁהִשִּׁיא אֶת יִשְׂרָאֵל לַעֲשׂוֹת פֶּסַח שֵׁנִי.״

[10]אָמַר מָר: [11]״רַבִּי יְהוּדָה אוֹמֵר: מְעַבְּרִין״. [12]אַלְמָא: אִית

LITERAL TRANSLATION

because of ritual impurity, [1]and he asked mercy upon himself, [2]for it is written: 'For a great part of the people, many of Ephraim and Menasseh, Issachar and Zebulun, had not purified themselves, [12B] so that they ate the Pesaḥ not as it was written. [3]But Hezekiah prayed for them, saying, The good Lord will pardon.' [4]Rabbi Shimon says: If they intercalated it because of ritual impurity, it is intercalated. [5]Rather, why did he ask mercy for himself? [6]For they cannot intercalate [any month] except for Adar, [7]and he intercalated Nisan in Nisan. [8]Rabbi Shimon ben Yehudah says in the name of Rabbi Shimon: [9]Because he advised Israel to make a second Pesaḥ."

[10]The master said: [11]"Rabbi Yehudah says: They do intercalate." [12]Hence,

TRANSLATION AND COMMENTARY

because of a situation where a majority of the community was in a state **of ritual impurity** and he wanted to give them time to purify themselves before Pesaḥ (see II Chronicles 30:2). [1]Later, however, **he asked** God to have **mercy upon him** and pardon his transgression, [2]**for it is written** (II Chronicles 30:18): **'For a great part of the people, many of Ephraim and Menasseh, Issachar and Zebulun, had not purified themselves,** [12B] **so that they ate the Pesaḥ not as it was written.** [3]**But Hezekiah prayed for them, saying, The good Lord will pardon.'** Rabbi Yehudah understands the verse as implying that Hezekiah begged pardon for having improperly intercalated the year because of ritual impurity, thus causing the community to eat the Paschal sacrifice a month later than they should have, as such intercalation is not valid. [4]**Rabbi Shimon says: If** the court **intercalated** the year **because** a majority of the people were in a state of **ritual impurity,** the year **is** indeed **intercalated.** [5]**Rather, why did** Hezekiah **ask mercy for himself?** He asked mercy and forgiveness for having intercalated the year at the wrong time, [6]**for the** court **cannot intercalate** any month **except Adar,** and only before the first Adar itself has passed. [7]Hezekiah, however, **intercalated** the month of **Nisan** by retroactively declaring a second Adar **in Nisan** itself and then resanctifying Nisan the following month. [8]**Rabbi Shimon ben Yehudah says in the name of Rabbi Shimon:** Hezekiah in fact never intercalated that particular year. [9]Thus, he asked mercy from God **because he** had wrongly **advised** the people of **Israel to make a second Pesaḥ,** i.e., to bring their Paschal sacrifice a month later than usual, on the 14h of Iyyar, as provided for in the Torah (Numbers 9:10) in regard to one who finds himself ritually impure on the eve of Pesaḥ proper. Hezekiah's ruling, however, was misguided, for the prohibition against offering a sacrifice while in a state of ritual impurity does not apply when a majority of the community is in that state, and so the people could have brought the Paschal sacrifice at its proper time on the 14th of Nisan."

אָמַר מָר [10]The Gemara now proceeds to analyze each of the positions recorded in the above Baraita: **The master** of the Baraita **said:** [11]**"Rabbi Yehudah says:** The court in fact **does intercalate** the year because of ritual impurity." [12]**Hence,** it follows that **Rabbi Yehudah maintains** that the prohibition against bringing

BACKGROUND

נִיסָן בְּנִיסָן Nisan in Nisan. From the context it seems that Hezekiah could only have known that so many people had come from the tribes of Israel just before Pesaḥ, and therefore he decided to add an intercalary month, a second Nisan, and postpone Pesaḥ.

RASHI

שיעבר את השנה מפני הטומאה — שנטמאו בימי אחז אביו מעבודה זרה, שלא חששו לתורה, והיה חזקיהו מחזירן למוטב, וידע שלא יספיקו כולן לבא וליטהר עד הפסח — ועיבר השנה. **ובקש רחמים על עצמו** — שימחל לו העון, ולקמן פריך: הואיל ואמר רבי יהודה: מעברין — למה ביקש רחמים על עצמו? **כי אכלו את הפסח בלא בכתוב** — שעיבר את השנה מפני הטומאה שלא כדת. **ניסן בניסן** — לאחר שקידשו לשם ניסן, חזר ונמלך ועשאו אדר השני. **רבי שמעון בן יהודה אומר** — לא עיברה, אלא השיאן לפסח שני שלא כדין, לפיכך ביקש רחמים על עצמו.

NOTES

לַעֲשׂוֹת פֶּסַח שֵׁנִי To make a second Pesaḥ. A question has been raised (see *Rabbenu Meshulam* and *Rashash*): The verse regarding this incident involving King Hezekiah states (II Chronicles 30:21): "And the children of Israel who were present at Jerusalem kept the feast of unleavened bread for seven days with great gladness." How, then, can Rabbi Shimon suggest that Hezekiah asked mercy for having advised the people to observe a second Pesaḥ? The second Pesaḥ is celebrated for only one day! It may perhaps be suggested that Hezekiah extended the second Pesaḥ for a full seven days as a temporary measure, so that the proper way of celebrating Pesaḥ not be forgotten.

CONCEPTS

צִיץ *Tzitz,* **The headplate worn by the High Priest across his forehead.** This was one of the eight vestments that the High Priest was required to wear. It was made of gold, and extended across the High Priest's forehead from one ear to the other. It was held in place by threads. On the plate was written 'קדש לה — "Holy to the Lord." The High Priest would lay it upon his forehead, close to the hairline. There is a difference of opinion among the Tannaim as to how these words were written on the *tzitz.* The *tzitz* atoned for any ritual impurity that was contracted by sacrifices in the Temple without the knowledge of those those who were offering them.

TRANSLATION AND COMMENTARY

sacrifices while in a state of **ritual impurity is** merely **suspended,** but not nullified, in the event that such a state affects the majority of **the community** and there is no way of circumventing it. [1]**But** this conclusion leads to a certain difficulty, for **surely it was taught** otherwise in the following Baraita: **"The** gold **plate** that the High Priest has to wear on his forehead serves to atone for unknown instances of a sacrifice becoming ritually defiled, [2]**whether it is** actually **on his forehead or not on his forehead,** it **atones** accordingly; [3]these are **the words of Rabbi Shimon.** [4]**Rabbi Yehudah** disagrees and **says: While** the plate **is still on** the High Priest's **forehead, it atones** for instances of ritual impurity, [5]but if **it is no longer on his forehead, it does not atone.** [6]**Rabbi Shimon said to** Rabbi Yehudah: The case of **the High Priest on Yom Kippur will prove** my position, [7]**for** the gold plate **is not on his forehead** during part of that day (when all he wears is white linen) **and** nevertheless **it atones** for any ritual defilement which may unwittingly occur in the course of his service! [8]**Rabbi Yehudah said** in reply **to** Rabbi Shimon: **Leave Yom Kippur** aside, **for** the sacrifices of that day are communal ones and serving while in a state of **ritual impurity is permitted in the community** context. Thus there is no need to effect atonement for having defiled sacrifices on Yom Kippur. From here we see that, according to Rabbi Yehudah, bringing a sacrifice while in a state of ritual impurity is permitted when it is the community that is affected. Why, then, in our case does he allow the intercalation of the year simply to avoid having the members of community bring their Paschal offerings while in a state of ritually impurity? Let it be permitted for them to bring those offerings in any case!

לֵיהּ לְרַבִּי יְהוּדָה טוּמְאָה דְּחוּיָה הִיא בַּצִּיבּוּר. [1]וְהָא תַּנְיָא: ״צִיץ, [2]בֵּין שֶׁיֶּשְׁנוֹ עַל מִצְחוֹ וּבֵין שֶׁאֵינוֹ עַל מִצְחוֹ, מְרַצֶּה, [3]דִּבְרֵי רַבִּי שִׁמְעוֹן. [4]רַבִּי יְהוּדָה אוֹמֵר: עוֹדוֹ עַל מִצְחוֹ, מְרַצֶּה. [5]אֵין עוֹדוֹ עַל מִצְחוֹ, אֵינוֹ מְרַצֶּה. [6]אָמַר לוֹ רַבִּי שִׁמְעוֹן: כֹּהֵן גָּדוֹל בְּיוֹם הַכִּיפּוּרִים יוֹכִיחַ, [7]שֶׁאֵינוֹ עַל מִצְחוֹ וּמְרַצֶּה! [8]אָמַר לוֹ רַבִּי יְהוּדָה: הַנַּח לְיוֹם הַכִּיפּוּרִים שֶׁטּוּמְאָה הוּתְּרָה בַּצִּיבּוּר!

LITERAL TRANSLATION

Rabbi Yehudah maintains: Ritual impurity is suspended for (lit., "in") the community. [1]But surely it was taught: "The headplate, [2]whether it is on his forehead or not on his forehead, atones; [3][these are] the words of Rabbi Shimon. [4]Rabbi Yehudah says: [While] it is still on his forehead, it atones. [5][If] it is no longer on his forehead, it does not atone. [6]Rabbi Shimon said to him: The High Priest on Yom Kippur will prove [it], [7]for it is not on his forehead, and it atones! [8]Rabbi Yehudah said to him: Leave Yom Kippur, for ritual impurity is permitted for the community."

RASHI

דחויה בציבור — כלומר בקושי הותרה טומאה בציבור, וכל כמה דאפשר להדורי לעשותו בטהרה — מהדרין, ולכך מעברין כדי שיעשו בטהרה. **ציץ מרצה** — על טומאת זבחים לעלות לרצון. **בין שישנו על מצח** — כהן גדול בשעת טומאה, בין שאינו על מצחו — מרצה. **כהן גדול** — בבואו לפני לפנים ביום הכיפורים יוכיח, שאינו לובש בגדי זהב ואם אירעה טומאה בקדשים מרצה הציץ. **אמר לו** — הנח ליום הכיפורים שכולו עבודת ציבור הוא, וטומאה הותרה בקרבן ציבור כטהרה גמורה, ואין צריך ציץ לרצות, אלמא היתר גמור הוא.

NOTES

טוּמְאָה דְּחוּיָה וְטוּמְאָה הוּתְּרָה Ritual impurity is suspended or permitted. Ordinarily, one may not offer a sacrifice when in a state of ritual impurity. We derive from the Torah, however, that in the case of the Paschal sacrifice, one may bring the offering even in a state of ritual impurity if a majority of the community are similarly impure. By use of Biblical hermeneutics, this dispensation is extended to all communal sacrifices that are brought on a fixed date where a majority of the priests are ritually impure. The nature of this dispensation is the subject of a dispute which is recorded in several places in the Talmud. According to one opinion, the prohibition against bringing sacrifices while in a state of ritual impurity remains in effect at all times; however, when a majority of the community are in a state of impurity, the Torah temporarily suspends the prohibition so that the sacrifice can be brought at its appointed time. Since the sacrifice is still regarded as being somewhat tainted, all possible efforts should be made to offer it while

HALAKHAH

טוּמְאָה דְּחוּיָה הִיא בַּצִּיבּוּר Ritual impurity is suspended for a community. "The prohibition against bringing sacrifices while in a state of ritual impurity is not rescinded when a majority of the community are ritually impure. Rather, the prohibition remains in force, but is temporarily suspended because of the great need," following the Gemara's conclusion in *Pesaḥim* and *Yoma.* (*Rambam, Sefer Avodah, Hilkhot Bi'at Mikdash* 4:15.)

צִיץ The plate worn by the High Priest across his forehead. "The golden plate worn by the High Priest atones for the ritual impurity contracted by sacrifices only when it is on the High Priest's forehead," following Rabbi Yehudah against Rabbi Shimon. (*Rambam, Sefer Avodah, Hilkhot Bi'at Mikdash* 4:8.)

TRANSLATION AND COMMENTARY

וְלִיטַעֲמִיךְ [1]The Gemara now addresses this argument: **According to your reasoning,** that Rabbi Yehudah should forbid intercalation if it is simply to avoid problems of ritual impurity within the community, [2]the Baraita **itself should be** just as **difficult for you,** since as it stands we find an internal contradiction between Rabbi Yehudah's two statements. [3]On the one hand, the Baraita teaches: **"Rabbi Yehudah says: They do intercalate** the year if a majority of the people are in a state of ritual impurity." [4]On the other hand, "**Rabbi Yehudah** also **said: It once happened that Hezekiah, the King of Judea, intercalated the year because of** a majority of the people being in a state of **ritual impurity,** [5]**and** later **he asked** that God have **mercy upon him** for his transgression." Now, if Rabbi Yehudah is of the opinion that the year may indeed be intercalated because of ritual impurity, how can he deduce from the verse that King Hezekiah asked forgiveness for having done just that, intercalating the year due to the people's impurity?

אֶלָּא [6]**Rather,** it must be concluded that the text of the Baraita, as we have it, **is incomplete,** [7]**and this is how it should be taught:** "The appointed court **does not intercalate the year** simply **because** it foresees a situation where **ritual impurity** threatens a majority of the community in such a way that purification would be impossible before the arrival of Pesaḥ. [8]**But if they intercalated** the year in this situation the year **is** nevertheless considered legitimately **intercalated.** [9]**Rabbi Yehudah** disagrees and **says:** If the court went ahead and intercalated the year because of ritual impurity, **it is** indeed **not** considered legitimately **intercalated,** for, as Rabbi Yehudah said above, bringing sacrifices while the community is in a state of impurity, is permitted; thus, the intercalation of the year in this case was totally unnecessary. [10]**And Rabbi Yehudah** also **said** that there was an incident involving Hezekiah, King of Judea, where he intercalated the year because of ritual impurity, but later asked mercy for having acted wrongly." This emendation of the Baraita resolves the internal contradiction between the two statements of Rabbi Yehudah, as well as the contradiction between Rabbi Yehudah's positions here, in this Baraita, and in the Baraita relating to the High Priest's headplate.

אִי הָכִי [11]The Gemara now raises an objection to this emendation of the Baraita: **If** the Baraita is to be read this way, then a difficulty arises in relation to its next clause, which states: [12]**"Rabbi Shimon says: If** the court **intercalated** the year **because** a majority of the people were in a statc of **ritual impurity,** the year **is** indeed **intercalated."** [13]According to the amended form of the Baraita, **this is** exactly what was said by **the first Tanna** of the Baraita!

[1]וְלִיטַעֲמִיךְ, [2]תִּיקְשֵׁי לָךְ הִיא גּוּפָהּ: [3]"רַבִּי יְהוּדָה אוֹמֵר: מְעַבְּרִין. [4]וְאָמַר רַבִּי יְהוּדָה: מַעֲשֶׂה בְּחִזְקִיָּה מֶלֶךְ יְהוּדָה שֶׁעִיבֵּר אֶת הַשָּׁנָה מִפְּנֵי הַטּוּמְאָה, [5]וּבִיקֵּשׁ רַחֲמִים עַל עַצְמוֹ"!

[6]אֶלָּא, חַסּוּרֵי מִחַסְּרָא, [7]וְהָכִי קָתָנֵי: "אֵין מְעַבְּרִין אֶת הַשָּׁנָה מִפְּנֵי הַטּוּמְאָה. [8]וְאִם עִיבְּרוּהָ, מְעוּבֶּרֶת. [9]רַבִּי יְהוּדָה אוֹמֵר: אֵינָהּ מְעוּבֶּרֶת. [10]וְאָמַר רַבִּי יְהוּדָה, וכו׳."

[11]אִי הָכִי, [12]"רַבִּי שִׁמְעוֹן אוֹמֵר: אִם מִפְּנֵי הַטּוּמְאָה עִיבְּרוּהָ" — [13]מְעוּבֶּרֶת הַיְינוּ תַּנָּא קַמָּא!

LITERAL TRANSLATION

[1]And according to your reasoning, [2]this itself should be difficult for you: [3]"Rabbi Yehudah says: They do intercalate. [4]And Rabbi Yehudah said: It once happened that Hezekiah, the King of Judea, intercalated the year because of ritual impurity, [5]and he asked mercy upon himself!"

[6]Rather, [the Baraita] is incomplete, [7]and this is how it should be taught: "They do not intercalate the year because of ritual impurity. [8][But] if they intercalated it, it is intercalated. [9]Rabbi Yehudah says: It is not intercalated. [10]And Rabbi Yehudah said, etc."

[11]If so, [12]"Rabbi Shimon says: If they intercalated it because of ritual impurity, it is intercalated" — [13]this is the first Tanna!

RASHI

רבי יהודה אומר אינה מעוברת — לפי שטומאה היתר היא בציבור, ושלא לצורך עיברוה.

NOTES

in a state of ritual purity. According to the dissenting opinion, the Torah determined that when a majority of the community are in a state of ritual impurity, the prohibition against offering sacrifices in such a state is disregarded altogether in order that the sacrifice can be brought at its proper time. Hence, there is no need to make special efforts to offer the sacrifice in a state of ritual purity.

HALAKHAH

אֵין מְעַבְּרִין אֶת הַשָּׁנָה מִפְּנֵי הַטּוּמְאָה **They do not intercalate the year because of ritual impurity.** "An extra month should not be added to the year because a majority of the people or a majority of the priests are ritually impure. But

[1]אָמַר רָבָא: לְכַתְּחִלָּה אִיכָּא בֵּינַיְיהוּ.

[2]תַּנְיָא נַמִּי הָכִי: [3]"אֵין מְעַבְּרִין אֶת הַשָּׁנָה מִפְּנֵי הַטּוּמְאָה לְכַתְּחִילָּה. [4]רַבִּי שִׁמְעוֹן אוֹמֵר: מְעַבְּרִין. [5]אֶלָּא, מִפְּנֵי מָה בִּקֵּשׁ רַחֲמִים עַל עַצְמוֹ? [6]שֶׁאֵין מְעַבְּרִין אֶלָּא אֲדָר, [7]וְהוּא עִיבֵּר נִיסָן בְּנִיסָן".

[8]אָמַר מָר: [9]"שֶׁאֵין מְעַבְּרִין אֶלָּא אֲדָר, [10]וְהוּא עִיבֵּר נִיסָן בְּנִיסָן". [11]וְלֵית לֵיהּ לְחִזְקִיָּה: [12]"הַחֹדֶשׁ הַזֶּה לָכֶם", [13]זֶה — נִיסָן, [14]וְאֵין אַחֵר נִיסָן? [15]טָעָה בִּדְשְׁמוּאֵל. [16]דְּאָמַר שְׁמוּאֵל: אֵין מְעַבְּרִין אֶת הַשָּׁנָה בְּיוֹם שְׁלֹשִׁים שֶׁל אֲדָר, [17]הוֹאִיל וְרָאוּי לִקְבוֹעוֹ נִיסָן.

LITERAL TRANSLATION

[1]Rava said: From the outset, there is between them. [2]It was also taught thus: [3]"They do not intercalate the year from the outset because of ritual impurity. [4]Rabbi Shimon says: They do intercalate. [5]Rather, why did he ask mercy on himself? [6]For they do not intercalate [any month] except Adar, [7]and he intercalated Nisan in Nisan."

[8]The master said: [9]"For they do not intercalate [any month] except Adar, [10]and he intercalated Nisan in Nisan." [11]Did Hezekiah not accept (lit., "have"): [12]"This month shall be for you" — [13]this is Nisan, [14]and no other is Nisan?

[15]He erred in that of Shmuel, [16]for Shmuel said: They do not intercalate the year on the thirtieth day of Adar, [17]since it is possible (lit., "suitable") to establish it as Nisan.

TRANSLATION AND COMMENTARY

אָמַר רָבָא [1]**Rava said:** In regard to how the court is allowed to act **from the outset, there is** a difference of opinion **between** these two Tannaim: The first Tanna of the Baraita maintains that the year may not be intercalated from the outset for reasons of ritual impurity, but if it was, the interclation is valid. Rabbi Shimon disagrees and says that even from the outset the year may be intercalated on account of ritual impurity. Nevertheless, his statement was worded as if it related to an *ex post facto* situation so as to maintain stylistic uniformity with the preceding statement of Rabbi Yehudah's.

תַּנְיָא נַמִּי הָכִי [2]The Gemara notes: This difference between the first Tanna and Rabbi Shimon **was also taught** in another Baraita: [3]"The court **does not intercalate the year from the outset** only **because** the majority of the community were in a state **of ritual impurity.** If, however, the year was intercalated for that reason, the intercalation is valid. [4]**Rabbi Shimon** disagrees and **says: They** indeed **do intercalate** the year in such an event, even from the outset. [5]**Rather, why did** Hezekiah **ask mercy on himself** for having intercalated the year due to ritual impurity? [6]He asked forgiveness because the court, as a rule, **does not intercalate** any month **except Adar** during that month, [7]**and he intercalated Nisan** during **Nisan."**

אָמַר מָר [8]The Gemara questions Rabbi Shimon's interpretation of Hezekiah's transgression: **The master** of the above Baraita **said:** [9]"Hezekiah sought forgiveness **because** the court as a rule **does not intercalate** any month **except Adar** during the month of Adar [10]**and he intercalated** the month of **Nisan** during **Nisan."** [11]**Did Hezekiah not accept** the following tradition derived from Exodus (12:2): [12]**"This month shall be for you** the beginning of months; it shall be the first month of the year for you" — [13]teaching us that **"this"** month, the one first sanctified as Nisan, **is** the definitive **Nisan,** the "first month of the year," [14]**and no other** month which you may sanctify later can qualify as **Nisan?**

טָעָה בִּדְשְׁמוּאֵל [15]The Gemara explains that Hezekiah **did not understand** properly the point that was formulated centuries later by **Shmuel,** [16]**for Shmuel said:** The court **does not intercalate the year on the 30th of Adar,** even though it has been taught that the month of Adar is the appropriate time for intercalation. [17]Nevertheless, **since it is suitable** on occasion **to establish** the 30th of Adar **as** the 1st of **Nisan,** such as when witnesses testify that they saw the New Moon the night before, the court relates to the entire day as if it were already declared such; thus, the year can no longer be intercalated.

RASHI

לכתחילה איכא בינייהו — דתנא קמא קאמר אין מעברין לכתחילה, ולרבי שמעון מעברין לכתחילה, ואיידי דקאמר רבי יהודה: אינה מעוברת, אמר איהו: מעוברת, והוא הדין לכתחילה. **ואין אחר ניסן** — משקבעתו זה ניסן, אין אתה יכול לעשות זה אדר והאחר ניסן. **ביום שלשים של אדר** — אם לא ישבו עד הנה בעיבור שנה, לא יעברוה עוד, הואיל והיום ראוי לקבוע ניסן אם היה אדר חסר.

HALAKHAH

if the year was intercalated for that reason, the intercalation is valid," following the anonymous first Tanna of the Baraita. (*Rambam, Sefer Zemanin, Hilkhot Kiddush HaḤodesh* 4:6.)

אֵין מְעַבְּרִין אֶת הַשָּׁנָה בְּיוֹם שְׁלֹשִׁים שֶׁל אֲדָר **They do not intercalate the year on the 30th of Adar.** "If the

TRANSLATION AND COMMENTARY

וְאִיהוּ סָבַר [1]In the incident involving King Hezekiah, the year was intercalated on the 30th of Adar as **he** then **maintained** that **we do not say** that **since it is suitable** on occasion to declare the 30th of Adar as the 1st of Nisan, we relate to it as such, precluding intercalation of the year on that day. Later, Hezekiah modified his understanding of this issue, anticipating the way it was understood by Shmuel centuries later. Consequently, he begged forgiveness for having improperly intercalated the year on the 30th of Adar.

תַּנְיָא נַמִי הָכִי [2]**It was also taught thus** in another Baraita: **"They do not intercalate the year on the 30th day of Adar** [3]**since it is possible to establish** that day **as** the 1st of **Nisan."**

רַבִּי שִׁמְעוֹן בֶּן יְהוּדָה [4]The Gemara returns to the Baraita cited at the outset of this discussion and examines the next opinion recorded in it: **"Rabbi Shimon ben Yehudah says in the name of Rabbi Shimon:** Hezekiah in fact never intercalated that particular year. [5]Rather, he asked mercy from God **because he** had wrongly **advised** the people of **Israel to make a second Pesaḥ,** i.e., to bring their Paschal sacrifice a month later than usual, on the 14th of Iyyar, as called for in the Torah [see Numbers 9:10] in the event one finds oneself ritually impure on the eve of Pesaḥ proper." [6]**How** exactly **is** this mistake of Hezekiah's **to be considered?** Surely he was familiar with the law allowing the Paschal sacrifice to be brought in its proper time so long as the majority of the community were ritually impure!

אָמַר רַב אַשִׁי [7]**Rav Ashi said:** Consider the case **as one where** the community of **Israel was half impure and half pure,** with the impure outnumbering the pure amongst the men while amongst the women the pure were the majority. [8]In fact, **the** number of pure **women** in the community was so great that they succeeded not only in **completing the** number of the **pure** but even in **outnumbering** the men who were impure, which had the effect of granting the pure sector an overall majority. [9]**Originally,** Hezekiah **maintained** that bringing the Paschal sacrifice **on the first** occasion of Pesaḥ **was** as much **an obligation** for **women** as for men. [10]Thus he advised the impure to postpone their offering, **for** according to this assumption **it was a minority of** the

[1]וְאִיהוּ סָבַר: "הוֹאִיל וְרָאוּי" לָא אָמְרִינַן.

[2]תַּנְיָא נַמִי הָכִי: "אֵין מְעַבְּרִין אֶת הַשָּׁנָה בְּיוֹם שְׁלֹשִׁים שֶׁל אֲדָר, [3]הוֹאִיל וְרָאוּי לְקוֹבְעוֹ נִיסָן".

[4]"רַבִּי שִׁמְעוֹן בֶּן יְהוּדָה אוֹמֵר מִשּׁוּם רַבִּי שִׁמְעוֹן: [5]מִפְּנֵי שֶׁהִשִּׁיא אֶת יִשְׂרָאֵל לַעֲשׂוֹת פֶּסַח שֵׁנִי". [6]הֵיכִי דָּמֵי? [7]אָמַר רַב אַשִׁי: כְּגוֹן שֶׁהָיוּ יִשְׂרָאֵל מֶחֱצָה טְמֵאִים מֶחֱצָה טְהוֹרִים, [8]וְנָשִׁים מַשְׁלִימוֹת לַטְּהוֹרִים, וְעוֹדְפוֹת עֲלֵיהֶם. [9]מֵעִיקָּרָא סָבַר: נָשִׁים בָּרִאשׁוֹן חוֹבָה, [10]דְּהָווּ מִיעוּטָן טְמֵאִים

LITERAL TRANSLATION

[1]And he maintained: We do not say "since it is suitable."

[2]It was also taught thus: "They do not intercalate the year on the thirtieth day of Adar, [3]since it is possible to establish it as Nisan."

[4]"Rabbi Shimon ben Yehudah says in the name of Rabbi Shimon: [5]Because he advised Israel to make a second Pesaḥ." [6]How is it to be considered (lit., "how is it like")?

[7]Rav Ashi said: Such as where Israel was half impure and half pure, [8]the women completing the [number of the] pure and outnumbering [the impure]. [9]Originally he maintained: Women on the first [Pesaḥ are under] obligation, [10]so that it was a minority of them who were ritually impure,

RASHI

ואיהו — מעיקרא סבר: הואיל וראוי לא אמרינן — ועיברה, ולבסוף הודה לשמואל וביקש רחמים על עצמו. **היכי דמי** — דמעיקרא הכי ולבסוף חזר בו. **מחצה** — לאו דווקא, אלא כדמפרש ואזיל שהזכרים היו טמאים יותר מן הטהורים, ונשים היו רובן טהורות עד שהנשים טהורות משלימות את מחצה טהורים ועודפות עליהן, שכשאתה מונה אנשים ונשים כאחת בטמאים ובטהורים, נמצאו טהורים יתירים, ופלוגתא בפרק האשה (פסחים צא,ב), דאיכא למאן דאמר נשים חובה בהבאת הפסח ראשון, ואיכא למאן דאמר נשים רשות, וחזקיה מעיקרא סבר: נשים בפסח ראשון חובה — ומיצטרפו, הלכך הוו טמאים מיעוטא — ומידחו, ולבסוף סבר: נשים בפסח ראשון רשות — ולא מיצטרפי, והוו להו טמאים רובא, ואיש נדחה לפסח שני, ואין ציבור נידחין.

HALAKHAH

year has not yet been intercalated by the 30th of Adar, an extra month may no longer be added to the year. But if the court nevertheless intercalated the year on the 30th of Adar, the intercalation is valid." (*Rambam, Sefer Zemanim, Hilkhot Kiddush HaḤodesh* 4:14.)

נָשִׁים בָּרִאשׁוֹן חוֹבָה Women are obligated in the first Pesaḥ. "Both men and women are obligated to bring the first Paschal sacrifice," following Rabbi Yose and Rabbi Yehudah against Rabbi Shimon. (*Rambam, Sefer Avodah, Hilkhot Korban Pesaḥ* 1:1.)

TRANSLATION AND COMMENTARY

people obligated to bring the Paschal sacrifice **who were ritually impure;** [1]**and** the law is that where **a minority** are ritually impure, they **postpone** their offering **until the "second Pesaḥ"** on the 14th of Iyyar, one month later. [2]However, **in the end** Hezekiah altered his position and **maintained** that bringing the Paschal sacrifice **on the first** occasion of Pesaḥ **was** not an obligation for **women** at all but rather **an option.** [3]Thus he never should have advised anyone to postpone his offering, **for the ritually impure were** actually the ones who were in **the majority,** since the women didn't count; [4]**and** the law is that where **the majority** of people are ritually impure, they **do not postpone** their Paschal offering **until the "second Pesaḥ,"** but rather bring it as usual on the 14th of Nisan. Consequently, Hezekiah needed to ask forgiveness for having wrongly advised the ritually impure to postpone their Paschal sacrifices until the "second Pesaḥ."

[1]וּמִיעוּטָן מִידְחוּ לְפֶסַח שֵׁנִי. [2]וּלְבַסּוֹף סָבַר: נָשִׁים בָּרִאשׁוֹן רְשׁוּת, [3]דַּהֲווֹ לְהוּ טְמֵאִים רוּבָּא, [4]וְרוּבָּא לָא מִדְחוּ לְפֶסַח שֵׁנִי.

[5]גּוּפָא: אָמַר שְׁמוּאֵל: [6]אֵין מְעַבְּרִין אֶת הַשָּׁנָה בְּיוֹם שְׁלֹשִׁים שֶׁל אֲדָר, הוֹאִיל וְרָאוּי לְקוֹבְעוֹ נִיסָן. [7]עִיבְּרוּהָ, מַאי? [8]אָמַר עוּלָּא: [9]אֵין מְקַדְּשִׁין אֶת הַחֹדֶשׁ.

[10]קִידְּשׁוּ מַאי? [11]אָמַר רָבָא: בָּטֵל הָעִיבּוּר. [12]רַב נַחְמָן אָמַר: מְעוּבָּר וּמְקוּדָּשׁ.

LITERAL TRANSLATION

[1]and a minority postpone themselves until the second Pesaḥ. [2]And in the end he maintained: Women on the first [Pesaḥ] [have] an option, [3]so that the ritually impure were the majority, [4]and the majority do not postpone themselves until the second Pesaḥ.

[5][In] the text itself: Shmuel said: [6]They do not intercalate the year on the thirtieth day of Adar, since it is possible to establish it as Nisan. [7]If they added an extra month, what [is the law]?

[8]Ulla said: [9]They do not sanctify the month.

[10][If] they sanctified [the month], what [is the law]?

[11]Rava said: The intercalation is void. [12]Rav Naḥman said: It is intercalated and sanctified.

RASHI

אין מקדשין את החדש — לומר "מקודש הוא" לאדר השני, דכיון דראוי לקבוע ניסן, קרינא ביה זה ניסן, ואין אחר ניסן, אלא שתקי, וכי מטי ריש ירחא אחרינא, מקדשי ליה לניסן.

גּוּפָא [5]The Gemara now considers the ruling of Shmuel that was incidentally cited in the previous discussion: In **the text itself Shmuel said:** [6]The court **does not intercalate the year on the 30th of Adar, since it is possible** on occasion **to establish** that day **as** the 1st of **Nisan.** [7]The question arises: **If** the court **intercalated** the year regardless on the 30th of Adar, **what is** the law? Is the intercalation valid or not?

אָמַר עוּלָּא [8]**Ulla said:** If the year was intercalated on the 30th of Adar, the intercalation is valid. However, in order to ensure that the day of intercalation remains identified with the concluding month of Adar, [9]the court **does not sanctify** that day as the first of **the new month,** even if witnesses come and testify to having seen the moon the night before.

קִידְּשׁוּ מַאי [10]The Gemara asks: And if the court nevertheless **sanctified** that day as the first of the new month after having just intercalated the year, **what is the law?**

אָמַר רָבָא [11]**Rava said:** In such a case, **the intercalation** of the year **is** retroactively rendered null and **void,** since it now becomes clear that the day upon which the year was intercalated was eligible to be the 1st of Nisan, when all agree the year cannot be intercalated. [12]**Rav Naḥman said:** In such a case, the year remains **intercalated and** the month remains **sanctified,** with the intercalation itself determining that the new month be declared Adar II rather than Nisan.

NOTES

אֵין מְקַדְּשִׁין אֶת הַחֹדֶשׁ **They do not sanctify the month.** *Rashi* interprets this to mean that if the court intercalated the year on the 30th of Adar, it cannot subsequently sanctify that day as the 1st of Adar II should witnesses come and testify that they saw the New Moon the night before. The reason for this is that, by doing so, the court would be rendering the day as one which could just as easily have been the 1st of Nisan, in which case the intercalation would have been invalid. Consequently the court refrains from sanctifying Adar II altogether and simply waits another month for the next New Moon in order to sanctify the month of Nisan. *Rosh* differs with *Rashi* on this point and contends that the court should sanctify the next day, the 31st, as the 1st of Adar II in the event that they intercalated the year on the 30th. *Remah* rejects the positions of *Rashi* and *Rosh*

HALAKHAH

מְעוּבָּר וּמְקוּדָּשׁ **It is intercalated and sanctified.** "If the year was intercalated on the 30th day of Adar, and then witnesses came and testified that on the previous night they had sighted the crescent of the New Moon, the new

LITERAL TRANSLATION

[1]Rava said to Rav Naḥman: [2]Since from Purim to Pesaḥ there are thirty days, [3]and from Purim we expound the laws of Pesaḥ, [4]for it was taught: "We inquire about the laws of Pesaḥ thirty days before Pesaḥ. [5]Rabban Shimon ben Gamliel says: Two weeks." [6]And [if] when the New Moon arrives they postpone it, [7]they will come to disregard [the prohibition against eating] leavened bread!

[8]He said to him: They surely know that the matter of an intercalated year depends on calculations. [9]They will say: The Rabbis did not complete the calculation until now.

[1]אֲמַר לֵיהּ רָבָא לְרַב נַחְמָן: [2]מִכְּדִי, מִפּוּרְיָא לְפִיסְחָא תְּלָתִין יוֹמִין הָווּ, [3]וּמִפּוּרְיָא דָּרְשִׁינַן בְּהִלְכוֹת הַפֶּסַח, [4]דְּתַנְיָא: "שׁוֹאֲלִין בְּהִלְכוֹת הַפֶּסַח קוֹדֶם לַפֶּסַח שְׁלֹשִׁים יוֹם. [5]רַבָּן שִׁמְעוֹן בֶּן גַּמְלִיאֵל אוֹמֵר: שְׁתֵּי שַׁבָּתוֹת". [6]וְכִי מָטֵי רֵישׁ יַרְחָא מְרַחֲקִין לֵיהּ, [7]אָתֵי לְזַלְזוּלֵי בֶּחָמֵץ!

[8]אֲמַר לֵיהּ: מֵידַע יְדִיעֵי דְּשַׁתָּא מַעֲבַּרְתָּא בְּחוּשְׁבְּנָא תַּלְיָא מִילְּתָא. [9]אָמְרִי: חוּשְׁבְּנָא הוּא דְּלָא סְלֵיק לְהוּ לְרַבָּנַן עַד הָשְׁתָּא.

RASHI

ומפוריא דרשינן בהלכות הפסח – וכיון דלא עיברוה קודם הפורים, ושמעו דרשה של הלכות הפסח כי הדר מעברי בית דין לשתא ומודעי לעלמא, לא מהימני להו לשלוחי בית דין, ומזלזלי בחמץ. **בחושבנא תליא מילתא** – שהקין והחורף לפי חשבון תקופת החמה הם מתגלגלין, וכשרבין ימי שנות החמה על שנות הלבנה יותר מדאי מתאחר האביב אחר הפסח, שהמועדות אנו קובעין אחר תולדות הלבנה.

TRANSLATION AND COMMENTARY

אֲמַר לֵיהּ רָבָא [1]**Rava said to Rav Naḥman:** There is a certain difficulty with your position. [2]**Since** it is well established that **from Purim,** on the 14th of Adar, **to Pesaḥ there are thirty days,** [3]**and** for that reason it is **from Purim** that **we** begin publicly to **expound upon the laws of Pesaḥ** if the year was not intercalated up till then ([4]**for it was taught** in a Baraita: **"We** begin publicly to **inquire into the laws of Pesaḥ thirty days before Pesaḥ.** [5]**Rabban Shimon ben Gamliel** disagrees and **says:** We begin inquiring into the laws of Pesaḥ **two weeks** before Pesaḥ"), it follows accordingly that the public will expect Pesaḥ to occur at the end of this thirty-day period. [6]Now, if **when the** anticipated **New Moon** of Nisan **arrives,** the court **postpones** declaring **it** as such for another month in order to intercalate the year and allow for a second Adar, [7]there is a danger that the people **will come to disregard** the prohibition against eating **leavened bread** on the newly designated date for observing Pesaḥ! It is feared that even though messengers of the court will arrive to notify them of the intercalation, many will not believe them because they have already prepared themselves to observe the Pesaḥ holiday. Consequently, these people will insist upon celebrating Pesaḥ in the middle of Adar II and end up eating leaven when it is really Pesaḥ one month later!

אֲמַר לֵיהּ [8]Rav Naḥman **said to** Rava: There is no such danger, for the people **surely know that the matter of** determining **an intercalated year depends on** complicated astronomical **calculations.** Even if the year was only intercalated on the 30th of Adar after the Pesaḥ lectures had already begun, there is no concern that people will make light of the prohibition against eating leavened bread on Pesaḥ, [9]for they **will say** that the year was not intercalated until the very end of Adar because **the Rabbis had not completed their calculations before that time.**

BACKGROUND

שׁוֹאֲלִין בְּהִלְכוֹת הַפֶּסַח We inquire about the laws of Pesaḥ. Lectures used to be given in public on matters pertaining to Pesaḥ. Thus, not only would everyone know the Halakhot nececessary for the holiday, but they would also know its importance and date. Similarly, four special Torah portions are read before and after Purim. The latter two, of "the Red Heifer" and of "the Month," were also direct preparations for Pesaḥ. Thus the postponement of Pesaḥ from its ordinary date would have been known to everyone.

בְּחוּשְׁבְּנָא תַּלְיָא מִילְּתָא The matter of an intercalated year depends on calculations. In addition to calculation of the equinox, it was known that the court took a number of factors into account with respect to determining the years (as noted above, it tried not to intercalate the seventh or the first year of the Sabbatical cycle), not only for the current year, but also for the coming, intercalary year. Other considerations depended on the weather, on the crops of that year, and so on. Hence people would assume that the court that had convened to study the matter needed a long time in order to clarify and coordinate the various factors until they reached a decision.

NOTES

on the basis of Rabbi Elazar bar Tzadok, who stated that in the event the court does not sanctify the month on the 30th, the 31st is automatically sanctified in Heaven as the 1st of the new month. Thus there is no need, as *Rosh* contends, for the court below to sanctify any month on the 31st. Neither is *Rashi* correct in assuming that without sanctification of Adar II we avoid the problem, for were Adar II not sanctified in Heaven, the day upon which the intercalation took place would still have been potentially connected to Nisan.

מִפּוּרְיָא לְפִיסְחָא From Purim to Pesaḥ. The Rishonim ask: Why does Rava ask this question only according to Rav Naḥman? As *Tosafot* and others point out, Rava's question can be asked of anyone who maintains that the year can be intercalated between Purim and the end of Adar, including himself! *Remah* answers that, according to Rava, who validates intercalation during this period only if the court refrains from sanctifying the 30th as the new

HALAKHAH

month is sanctified on that day, and that day becomes the 1st of Adar II," following Rav Naḥman. (*Rambam, Sefer Zemanim, Hilkhot Kiddush HaḤodesh* 4:14.)

שׁוֹאֲלִין בְּהִלְכוֹת הַפֶּסַח They ask about the laws of Pesaḥ. "We begin to discuss and publicly expound the laws of Pesaḥ thirty days before the holiday arrives. According to some authorities, a similar regulation applies to the other Festivals as well (*Mishnah Berurah*)." (*Shulḥan Arukh, Oraḥ Ḥayyim* 429:1.)

CONCEPTS

תְּקוּפָה **Exquinox.** This term refers to one of the four days that mark the beginning of a season and upon which there is a significant change in the length of the day. The four seasons are: תְּקוּפַת תִּשְׁרֵי, autumn, which begins on September 23, the autumnal equinox; תְּקוּפַת טֵבֵת, winter, which begins on December 22, the winter solstice; תְּקוּפַת נִיסָן, spring, which begins on March 21, the vernal equinox; תְּקוּפַת תַּמּוּז, summer, which begins on June 22, the summer solstice.
Since the seasons begin on dates determined by the solar calendar, it is clear that, according to the Jewish calendar, which is based on lunar months, the seasons do not begin on the same date every year. Sometimes the summer ends in the month of Elul and sometimes in Tishri. When it is calculated that the autumn will begin too long after Rosh HaShanah, the year is extended to have Rosh HaShanah fall later in the solar calendar.

BACKGROUND

חֹדֶשׁ תִּשְׁרֵי **The month of Tishri.**

1 Rosh HaShanah
2
3
4
6
7
8
9
10 Yom Kippur
11
12
13
14
15 Sukkot
16
17
18
19
20
21
(16–21: the intermediate days of the holiday of Sukkot)
22 Shemini Atzeret

This calendar shows that if the autumnal equinox falls on the 16th of Tishri (lacking sixteen days), most of the intermediate days of the holiday will occur during the autumn season. According to Rabbi Yose, if the autumnal equinox falls on the 21st of Tishri, some of the holiday still falls in the new season.

¹אָמַר רַב יְהוּדָה אָמַר שְׁמוּאֵל: ²אֵין מְעַבְּרִין אֶת הַשָּׁנָה אֶלָּא אִם כֵּן הָיְתָה תְּקוּפָה חֲסֵירָה רוּבָּהּ שֶׁל חוֹדֶשׁ. ³וְכַמָּה "רוּבָּהּ שֶׁל חוֹדֶשׁ"? ⁴שִׁשָּׁה עָשָׂר יוֹם. ⁵דִּבְרֵי רַבִּי יְהוּדָה. [13A] ⁶רַבִּי יוֹסֵי אוֹמֵר: אֶחָד וְעֶשְׂרִים יוֹם. ⁷וּשְׁנֵיהֶם מִקְרָא אֶחָד דָּרְשׁוּ: ⁸"חַג הָאָסִיף תְּקוּפַת הַשָּׁנָה".

LITERAL TRANSLATION

[1] Rav Yehudah said in the name of Shmuel: [2] They do not intercalate the year unless the season would be incomplete for most of the month. [3] And how much is "most of the month"? [4] Sixteen days. [5] [These are] the words of Rabbi Yehudah. [13A] [6] Rabbi Yose says: Twenty-one days. [7] And both of them interpreted the same verse: [8] "[And] the Festival of the Ingathering at the turn of the year."

TRANSLATION AND COMMENTARY

אָמַר רַב יְהוּדָה [1] The Gemara now discusses the issue of intercalating the year because of a problem with the equinox: **Rav Yehudah said in the name of Shmuel:** [2] The appointed court **does not intercalate the year** because of a delay in the autumnal equinox, **unless** according to the Sages' calculations **the summer season would be incomplete** (not amount to its full ninety-one-and-a-quarter days) **for most of the month** of Tishri. In such a case, the year may be intercalated so as to ensure that the autumnal equinox begins before most of Tishri has already passed. [3] **How much is "most of the month"** in this regard? [4] **Sixteen days.** If the summer season extends sixteen or more days into Tishri, the previous year must be intercalated; however, should it only extend up to the fifteenth, the year need not be adjusted. [5] These are **the words of Rabbi Yehudah.** [13A] [6] **Rabbi Yose says:** Here "most of the month" means **twenty-one days.** If the equinox will occur on the 22nd of Tishri or later, the previous year must be intercalated, but if it will occur on the 21st of Tishri or earlier, the previous year is not intercalated. [7] **And both of them** — Rabbi Yehudah and Rabbi Yose — **interpreted the same verse** (Exodus 34:22): [8] **"And the Festival of the Ingathering at the turn of the year."** Both Sages understood the term, "the turn of the year," as referring to the new season inaugurated by the autumnal equinox. Thus, the verse teaches that the time of the Festival of the Ingathering, which is the Festival of Sukkot, the intermediate days of the Festival on

RASHI

אין מעברין את השנה — על התקופה, אלא אם כן חישבו ומצאו שתקופת תמוז חסירה מהשלמת תשעים ואחד יום שלה רובו של חדש תשרי. **ששה עשר יום** — ותקופת תשרי נופלת בשבעה עשר, אבל אם היתה תקופת תשרי נופלת בששה עשר, אין מעברין, ולקמיה יליף טעמא. **רבי יוסי אומר אחד ועשרים יום** — אם צריך להשלים עשרים ואחד יום מחודש תשרי על תקופת תמוז, שתקופת תשרי נופלת בעשרים ושנים — מעברין ומוסיפין חודש אחד, ודוחין את המועדות כדי שתקדים תקופת תשרי לחג, אבל אם היתה תקופת תשרי נופלת בעשרים ואחד, דהיינו יום אחד בתוך חולו של מועד — אין מעברין. **חג האסיף** — זמן האסיף שבחג, דהיינו חולו של חג, שיכול לאסוף בו דבר האבד — השמר שיהא בתקופת שנה הנכנסת, ולא בתוך תקופת תמוז שהיא משנה שעברה, רבי יהודה סבר: כולו חג בעינן, כלומר כל חולו של מועד בעינן בתקופה חדשה, הלכך כשתקופת תמוז חסירה ששה עשר, הרי יום אחד מחולו של מועד נמשך לתוכה, דחמשה עשר — יום טוב, ויום ששה עשר — חולו של מועד. אבל אם היתה תקופת תשרי נופלת ביום ששה עשר, הרי כל חולו של מועד בתקופה חדשה — ואין מעברין, רבי יוסי אומר: מקצת חולו של מועד בעינן בתקופה חדשה, הלכך כשתקופת תשרי נופלת ביום עשרים ושנים שהוא יום טוב האחרון — מעברין את השנה ודוחין את המועדות כדי להקדים תקופה לחג. אבל אם רואין בית דין באדר, שתפול תקופת תשרי ביום עשרים ואחד שהוא שביעי של ערבה, דאיכא מקצת חולו של מועד בתקופה חדשה — אין מעברין, ולמיעבריה לאלול ולידחייה למועד חד יומא, ואיכא לרבי יהודה כוליה חג ולרבי יוסי מקצת חג, כדפרכינן לקמן גבי תקופת ניסן: ליעברוה לאדר — לא אפשר, משום דלא מיקלע לן תשרי ביומא דחזיא אי מיעברינן לאלול, דהא מעיקרא מסדרינן לירחא דסיתוא כי היכי דלא ליקלע תשרי באד"ו, משום דאתו תרי שבי בהדדי, ומשום שביעי של ערבה דלא ליקלע בשבת, וכדאמרינן התם (ראש השנה יט,ב): מימות עזרא ואילך לא מצינו אלול מעובר, דלא איצטריך, דמעיקרא סדרינן לירחי דלא ליקלע באד"ו, ואי ניצטריך לעבורי — מקלקלא ראש השנה, כדאמרינן בראש השנה (שם י"ט ע"ב), ובמסכת סוכה (מג,ב) נמי גבי שביעית של ערבה אמרינן לא מיקלע אלול בשבת. אלמא אנן הוא דמעיינינן במילתא מעיקרא, ומסדרינן לירחי כי היכי דלא מיקלע באד"ו, הלכך כיון דיום שלשים של אלול מיקלע בשלשה או בחמשה או בשבעה, אי דחית ליה חד יומא, בין על ידי עיבור אלול, בין על ידי עיבור חדש אחר — מיקלע ראש השנה באד"ו, ואי מיקלע בשני בשבת דאפשר למידחייה למחר, הואיל וברוב השנים לא שכיח לא פרכינן ליה. ולעבורי תרי ירחי ולדחייה תרי יומי לא אפשר, דקיימא לן במסכת ערכין (ח,ב) דלא נראה לחכמים לעבר שמנה חדשים בשנה, אלא אם כן היתה שנה שלפניה מעוברת, וכיון דבסדר החדשים אחד מלא ואחד חסר, מיקלע לן תקופה ביום שבעה עשר לרבי יהודה, או בעשרים ושנים לרבי יוסי, אי מעברין עוד תרי ירחי — הוו להו שמנה מעוברין, הלכך מעברין את השנה.

NOTES

month, the people will realize that the calendar year has changed by virtue of the fact that Nisan was not sanctified as anticipated. However, according to Rav Naḥman, who allows the court to go ahead and sanctify the new month as usual on the 30th, even though the year was just intercalated, there will be nothing unusual to intimate that perhaps a change was made in the length of the year.

אֶלָּא אִם כֵּן הָיְתָה תְּקוּפָה חֲסֵירָה **Unless the season would be incomplete.** Our commentary follows *Rashi,* who understands the subject of this clause to be the summer season that extends into the major part of Tishri, thus rendering it "incomplete" for the first sixteen days of the month.

TRANSLATION AND COMMENTARY

which the harvest of perishable crops is permitted, must occur in the new season, after the autumnal equinox. Yet they disagreed about the following matter: [1]One **master** — Rabbi Yehudah — **maintained** that **we need all** of the intermediate days **of the** Sukkot **Festival,** beginning with the 16th of Tishri, to be **in the new season.** [2]**And** the other **master** — Rabbi Yose — **maintained** that **we need** only **part** of the intermediate period **of the Festival** to be **in the new season.** Thus, even if only the 21st of Tishri, the last intermediate day of Sukkot, was to occur in the new season, there would be no need for intercalation.

מַאי קָא סָבְרִי [3]**What** in essence **do** these two Tannaim **maintain?** [4]**If they** both **maintain that the** very **day** on which the **equinox** falls **completes** the old season, then why did Rabbi Yehudah speak about at least sixteen days of Tishri before the autumnal equinox, and Rabbi Yose about at least twenty-one? [5]Even **without that** many days passing before the equinox, it should **also** be necessary to intercalate the year! [6]For **neither according to** Rabbi Yehudah **nor according to** Rabbi Yose **is there** such a situation. Rabbi Yehudah **says** we need **all** the intermediate days **of the** Sukkot **Festival** to be in the new season, and **there is** no such situation (since if the equinox occurs on the 16th of Tishri, the first intermediate day of the Festival will belong to the old season); [7]**and according to** Rabbi Yose, **who says** that we need only **part** of the intermediate period **of the Festival** to be in the new season, **there is** no such situation either (since if the equinox should occur on the 21st of Tishri, all the intermediate days of Sukkot will belong to the old season). [8]**Rather,** it must be concluded that **they** both **maintain that the** very **day** on which the **equinox** falls **begins** the new season. Thus, according to Rabbi Yehudah, if the equinox occurs on the 16th of Tishri, all the intermediate days of Sukkot will be in the new season; and according to Rabbi Yose, if the equinox occurs on the 21st of Tishri, one of the intermediate days of the Festival will be in the new season.

מֵיתִיבִי [9]The Sages **raised an objection** against Shmuel's interpretation from a Baraita: **"The** very **day** on which the **equinox** falls **completes** the old season; [10]these are **the words of Rabbi Yehudah.** [11]**Rabbi Yose** disagrees and **says: The** very **day** on which the **equinox** falls **begins** the new season." If Rabbi Yehudah maintains that the day of the equinox completes the old season, how can Shmuel claim that he takes a

[1]מָר סָבַר: כּוּלֵּיהּ חַג בָּעֵינַן בִּתְקוּפָה חֲדָשָׁה. [2]וּמָר סָבַר: מִקְצָת חַג בָּעֵינַן בִּתְקוּפָה חֲדָשָׁה.

[3]מַאי קָא סָבְרִי? [4]אִי קָסָבְרִי יוֹם תְּקוּפָה גּוֹמֵר, [5]בְּלָאו הָכִי נַמִי — [6]לָא לְמַאן דַּאֲמַר כּוּלֵּיהּ חַג, אִיכָּא, [7]וְלָא לְמַאן דַּאֲמַר מִקְצָת חַג, אִיכָּא! [8]אֶלָּא קָסָבְרִי יוֹם תְּקוּפָה מַתְחִיל.

[9]מֵיתִיבִי: יוֹם תְּקוּפָה גּוֹמֵר; [10]דִּבְרֵי רַבִּי יְהוּדָה. [11]רַבִּי יוֹסֵי אוֹמֵר: יוֹם תְּקוּפָה מַתְחִיל.

LITERAL TRANSLATION

[1]One master maintained: We need all of the Festival in the new season. [2]And one master maintained: We need part of the Festival in the new season.

[3]What do they maintain? [4]If they maintain that the day of the equinox completes, [5]without this also — [6]neither according to the one who says all of the Festival, is there, [7]and neither according to the one who says part of the Festival, is there! [8]Rather, they maintain that the day of the equinox begins.

[9]They raised an objection: "The day of the equinox completes; [10][these are] the words of Rabbi Yehudah. [11]Rabbi Yose says: The day of the equinox begins."

RASHI

אי קסברי יום תקופה גומר — יום שהתקופה נופלת בו הוא גמר תקופה שעברה — ואינה מתקופה חדשה, למה לי לרבי יהודה ששה עשר חסירה ולרבי יוסי עשרים ואחד בלאו הכי אפילו לא חסרה אלא חמשה עשר לרבי יהודה ותפול חדשה בששה עשר, או עשרים לרבי יוסי ותפול באחד ועשרים, לא לרבי יהודה איכא כוליה חג, ולא לרבי יוסי איכא מקצת חג, דהא יום שביעי של ערבה שנופלת בו תקופה מאותה שעברה הוא, ולרבי יהודה נמי יום ששה עשר מתקופה שעברה, וליכא כוליה חג. **מתחיל** — הוא ראשון לימי תקופה הבאה, הלכך לרבי יהודה אם תפול בששה עשר שהוא ראשון לחולו של מועד — איכא כוליה חג, ולרבי יוסי אם תפול בשביעי של ערבה — איכא מקצת. **מיתיבי יום תקופה גומר דברי רבי יהודה** — וכיון דיום תקופה גומר, למה לי חסירה ששה עשר.

BACKGROUND

יוֹם תְּקוּפָה The day of the equinox. The phrase חג האיסף ותקופת השנה— "the Festival of harvest and the season of the year" — is not entirely clear. We understand from it that the harvest Festival is connected to a certain date related to the solar calendar (the season). It must be remembered that the expression תקופה — "season" — can have two meanings. It can refer to the period (one-quarter of a year) in which the lengths of the night and the day change in relation to each other, and it can also refer to one of the days when it is possible to point out that a change has taken place in that relation (the autumnal and vernal equinox, the winter and summer solstice). One of the questions raised here is whether "the day of the season" belongs to the past or the coming season.

NOTES

Remah suggests an alternative way of explaining the clause: The subject of the clause is the autumnal equinox which, by first occurring on the 17th of Tishri, is in effect "lacking" for most of the month. The two approaches, of course, do not differ in their basic interpretation of the ruling.

יוֹם תְּקוּפָה גּוֹמֵר וּמַתְחִיל **The day of the equinox completes or begins.** The Tannaitic dispute over whether the day of the equinox completes the old season or begins the new one reflects the fact that the equinox does not fall precisely at the beginning of the day or night, neither according to Shmuel nor according to Rav Adda, who disagree elsewhere about the precise length of the seasons (*Remah*).

BACKGROUND

שִׁשָּׁה עָשָׂר יוֹם לִפְנֵי הַפֶּסַח Sixteen days before Pesaḥ. In the Torah, Pesaḥ is not connected to the vernal equinox but rather to the crops. Known as מוֹעֵד חֹדֶשׁ הָאָבִיב — "the holiday of the spring month" — Pesaḥ is itself the holiday of spring crops (the first fruits of the barley, as explained in Exodus 9:31), and their appearance determines its date. However, if Pesaḥ is celebrated too late, Sukkot cannot fall at the time of the autumnal equinox.

תְּקוּפַת נִיסָן וְתִשְׁרֵי The vernal and the autumnal equinox. Shmuel's method assumes that each season lasts precisely ninety-one days and six hours. Hence the difference in time between the vernal and the autumnal equinox is 180½. If, as noted, the vernal equinox occurred on the 16th of Nisan, the following results:

15 Nisan to

1 Iyyar:	14 days.
1 Sivan:	29 days.
1 Tammuz:	30 days.
1 Av:	29 days.
1 Elul:	30 days.
1 Tishri:	29 days.
Total:	161 days.

Hence the autumnal equinox will occur in the middle of the 22nd of Tishri, after the entire harvest holiday is over.

TRANSLATION AND COMMENTARY

position which is based on the opposite contention, that it begins the new season? [1]**And furthermore, it was taught** in another Baraita: "The appointed court **does not intercalate the year unless** according to the Sages' calculations **the** summer **season will be incomplete** (not amount to its full ninety-one-and-a-quarter days) **for most of the month** of Tishri. [2]**How much is "most of the month"** in this regard? [3]**Sixteen days.** If the autumnal equinox will occur on the 17th of Tishri or later, the previous year must be intercalated, but if it will occur on the 16th of Tishri or earlier, the previous year is not intercalated. This is the position of the first Tanna, who maintains that all the intermediate days of Sukkot must be in the new season, and the day upon which the equinox falls begins the new season.

רַבִּי יְהוּדָה [4]**Rabbi Yehudah says:** Here "most of the month" means **two parts** (i.e. two-thirds) **of the month.** [5]**And how much is "two parts of the month"?** [6]**Twenty days.** If the equinox will occur on the 21st of Tishri or later, the previous year must be intercalated, for according to Rabbi Yehudah at least one of the intermediate days of Sukkot must be in the new season, and the day on which the equinox falls is considered the last day of the old season. [7]**Rabbi Yose says:** The Rabbis must **calculate** as follows: [8]If the first **sixteen** days of Nisan will be in the season **before Pesaḥ**, so that the vernal equinox will fall only on the seventeenth day of the month, the court **intercalates** the year, for if the vernal equinox occurs on the 17th of Nisan, the autumnal equinox will fall on the 22nd of Tishri (see note), and none of the intermediate days of Sukkot will be in the new season. [9]But if the first **sixteen** days of Tishri will be in the season that is **before the Festival** of Sukkot, so that the autumnal equinox will fall on the seventeenth day of the month, **they do not intercalate** the year, for some of the intermediate days of Sukkot will still be in the new season. [10]**Rabbi Shimon says: Even** when the first **sixteen** days of Tishri will be in the season **before the Festival** of Sukkot, so that the autumnal equinox will fall

[1]וְעוֹד, תַּנְיָא: ״אֵין מְעַבְּרִין אֶת הַשָּׁנָה אֶלָּא אִם כֵּן הָיְתָה תְּקוּפָה חֲסֵירָה רוּבּוֹ שֶׁל חוֹדֶשׁ. [2]וְכַמָּה רוּבּוֹ שֶׁל חֹדֶשׁ? [3]שִׁשָּׁה עָשָׂר יוֹם.

[4]רַבִּי יְהוּדָה אוֹמֵר: שְׁתֵּי יָדוֹת בַּחוֹדֶשׁ. [5]וְכַמָּה שְׁתֵּי יָדוֹת בַּחֹדֶשׁ? [6]עֶשְׂרִים יוֹם. [7]רַבִּי יוֹסֵי אוֹמֵר: מְחַשְּׁבִין. [8]שִׁשָּׁה עָשָׂר לִפְנֵי הַפֶּסַח, מְעַבְּרִין. [9]שִׁשָּׁה עָשָׂר לִפְנֵי הֶחָג, אֵין מְעַבְּרִין. [10]רַבִּי שִׁמְעוֹן אוֹמֵר: אַף שִׁשָּׁה עָשָׂר לִפְנֵי הֶחָג

LITERAL TRANSLATION

[1]And furthermore, it was taught: "They do not intercalate the year unless the season will be incomplete for most of a month. [2]And how much is most of a month? [3]Sixteen days.

[4]Rabbi Yehudah says: Two parts of the month. [5]And how much is two parts of the month? [6]Twenty days. [7]Rabbi Yose says: [8]They calculate. [If] sixteen [days will be] before Pesaḥ, they intercalate [the year]. [9][If] sixteen [days will be] before the Festival [of Sukkot], they do not intercalate [the year]. [10]Rabbi Shimon says: Even [when] sixteen [days will be] before the Festival [of Sukkot],

RASHI

ועוד תניא — לרבי יהודה עשרים, דשמעינן מינה דרבי יהודה מקצת חג הוא דבעי, וקשיא לשמואל בתרתי. **ששה עשר** — ונופלת בשבעה עשר. **עשרים** — ונופלת בעשרים ואחד, ואף על גב דהוא יום אחרון לחולו של מועד ליכא מקצת חג, דלרבי יהודה יום תקופה גומר, ואינו מן החדשה. **ששה עשר לפני הפסח מעברין** — אם תקופה שלפני הפסח דהיינו תקופת טבת חסירה ששה עשר בניסן, ותקופה נופלת בשבעה עשר — מעברין את השנה. שכשאתה מונה משבעה עשר בניסן תשעים ואחד יום לתקופת ניסן, ותשעים ואחד יום לשל תמוז, הרי הם כלים בעשרים ואחד בתשרי, ותקופה נופלת בעשרים ושנים. ואף על גב דלרבי יוסי מיום תקופה מתחיל, ליכא מקצת חג בתקופה חדשה — כיצד טול ארבעה עשר דניסן שהוא מלא, ואייר וסיון חמישים ותשעה, ותמוז ואב חמישים ותשעה, הרי מאה שלשים ושנים, ואלול עשרים ותשעה שהוא חסר, הרי מאה ששים ואחד, ועשרים ואחד דתשרי הרי מאה שמנים ושנים ימי שתי תקופות, ושל תשרי נופלת בעשרים ושנים — משום הכי מעברין. אבל נפלה תקופת תשרי ביום עשרים ואחד — אין מעברין, דיום תקופה מתחיל, ואיכא יום אחד מחולו של מועד בתקופה חדשה. **ששה עשר לפני החג** — אם חסרה תקופת תמוז שהוא לפני החג ששה עשר מימי תשרי, ונפלה של תשרי בשבעה עשר — אין מעברין, דאיכא מחולו של מועד בתקופה חדשה טובא, ולקמן פריך: אמאי אמר שיתסר, אפילו חסרה שיבסר, ותמניסר, ותשעה עשר, ועשרים קאמר נמי רבי יוסי דאין מעברין, דהא ששה עשר לפני הפסח הוא דמעברין, דהיינו משום דמטית תקופת תשרי בעשרים ושנים. **אף ששה עשר לפני החג מעברין** — דקסבר כוליה חג בעינן, ולקמן פריך: היינו תנא קמא!

NOTES

שְׁתֵּי יָדוֹת Two-thirds. Rabbi Yehudah accepts the first Tanna's position that the year is only intercalated if it is clear that the summer season will not achieve completion until most of the month of Tishri has passed. But instead of interpreting this as referring to a majority of the days of the month, he understands that this refers to a majority of the parts of the month — two-thirds or twenty days (*Remah*).

TRANSLATION AND COMMENTARY

on the 17th of Tishri, the court **intercalates** the year, for all the intermediate days of Sukkot must belong to the new season, and in this case the first intermediate day is in the old season. [1]**Others say:** The year is intercalated because of a late equinox, even if it only involves **a minority** of the month. [2]**And how much is a "minority** of the month" in this regard? [3]**Fourteen days.** If the equinox will occur on the fifteenth of the month or later, the previous year must be intercalated, but if it will occur on the fourteenth of the month or earlier, the previous year is not intercalated." Now, this Baraita contradicts Shmuel, for, according to Shmuel, Rabbi Yehudah maintains that the year is intercalated if the autumnal equinox will occur on or after the 17th of Tishri, whereas the Baraita teaches that, according to Rabbi Yehudah, the year is only intercalated if the autumnal equinox will not occur before the 21st of Tishri!

מְעַבְּרִין. [1]אֲחֵרִים אוֹמְרִים: מִיעוּטוֹ. [2]וְכַמָּה מִיעוּטוֹ? [3]אַרְבָּעָה עָשָׂר יוֹם! [4]קַשְׁיָא.

[5]אָמַר מָר: [6]״רַבִּי יְהוּדָה אוֹמֵר: שְׁתֵּי יָדוֹת בַּחוֹדֶשׁ. [7]עֶשְׂרִים יוֹם. [8]רַבִּי יוֹסֵי אוֹמֵר: מְחַשְּׁבִין. [9]שִׁשָּׁה עָשָׂר יוֹם לִפְנֵי הַפֶּסַח, מְעַבְּרִין״. [10]הַיְינוּ רַבִּי יְהוּדָה!

[11]יוֹם תְּקוּפָה גּוֹמֵר וְיוֹם תְּקוּפָה מַתְחִיל אִיכָּא בֵּינַיְיהוּ.

LITERAL TRANSLATION

they intercalate [the year]. [1]Others say: A minority [of the month]. [2]And how much is a minority? [3]Fourteen days."

[4]It is difficult.

[5]The master said: [6]"Rabbi Yehudah says: Two parts of the month. [7]Twenty days. [8]Rabbi Yose says: They calculate. [9][If] sixteen [days will be] before Pesah, they intercalate [the year]." [10]This is [the same as] Rabbi Yehudah!

[11]There exists between them [a dispute whether] the day of the equinox completes or the day of the equinox begins.

RASHI

אחרים — מפרש טעמייהו לקמן. **היינו רבי יהודה** — דתרוייהו מקלת חג בעי.

קַשְׁיָא [4]Indeed, the Baraita **is problematic** according to Shmuel, and that difficulty remains unresolved.

אָמַר מָר [5]The Gemara now proceeds to discuss at greater length the various positions recorded in the Baraita just cited: **The master** of the above Baraita **said:** [6]**"Rabbi Yehudah says:** Here 'most of the month' means **two parts** [two-thirds] **of the month.** And how much is 'two parts of the month'? [7]**Twenty days.** If the equinox will occur on the 21st of Tishri or later, the previous year must be intercalated, for at least one of the intermediate days of Sukkot must be in the new season. [8]**Rabbi Yose says:** The Rabbis must **calculate** as follows: [9]If the first **sixteen** days of Nisan will be in the season **before Pesaḥ,** so that the vernal equinox will occur only on the seventeenth of the month, the court **intercalates** the year, for if the vernal equinox falls on the 17th of Nisan, the autumnal equinox will fall on the 22nd of Tishri, and none of the intermediate days of Sukkot will be in the new season." [10]Now, **this** position of Rabbi Yose **is** essentially the same as that of **Rabbi Yehudah,** for both are based on the premise that at least one of the intermediate days of Sukkot must be in the new season. Why, then, does Rabbi Yehudah say that the year is intercalated if the autumnal equinox will otherwise occur on the 21st of Tishri, while Rabbi Yose says that the year is only intercalated if that equinox will otherwise occur on the 22nd of Tishri?

יוֹם תְּקוּפָה [11]The difference that **exists between them** relates to the issue of whether **the day** itself on which the **equinox** falls **completes** the old season **or begins** the new season. Rabbi Yehudah maintains that the day on which the equinox falls is considered the last day of the old season. Thus, the year must be intercalated if the autumnal equinox will otherwise occur on the 21st of Tishri, for in such a case none of the intermediate days of Sukkot will be in the new season. And Rabbi Yose maintains that the day on which the equinox falls is considered the first day of the new season. Thus, there is no need to intercalate the year if the autumnal equinox will otherwise occur on the 21st of Tishri, for in such a case one of the intermediate days of Sukkot will be in the new season.

NOTES

קַשְׁיָא It is difficult. The Rishonim note that the Gemara concludes this passage with the term *kashya* — which means that no solution to the objection raised against the Amoraic statement was found, but not necessarily that the problematic Amoraic statement must be rejected. Had the passage ended with the term *teyuvta*, this would have implied that the refutation of Shmuel's statement was conclusive. Since *Remah* explains the matter by arguing that Shmuel was not the source of the statement, but Rav. Since Rav has the status of a Tanna, he is authorized to disagree with other Tannaim. Thus, his position cannot be conclusively refuted by a Baraita.

[1]אָמַר מָר: [2]"שִׁשָּׁה עָשָׂר לִפְנֵי הֶחָג אֵין מְעַבְּרִין". [3]אֶלָּא לְרַבִּי יוֹסֵי, שִׁשָּׁה עָשָׂר לִפְנֵי הֶחָג הוּא דְּלָא. [4]הָא שִׁיבְסַר וּתְמָנֵיסַר, [5]מְעַבְּרִין? [6]וְהָאָמַר: שִׁשָּׁה עָשָׂר לִפְנֵי הַפֶּסַח, אִין; [7]בְּצִיר, לָא!

[8]לָא. [9]אִידִי וְאִידִי, [10]אֵין מְעַבְּרִין, [11]וְאַיְּידֵי דִּתְנָא רֵישָׁא "שִׁשָּׁה עָשָׂר לִפְנֵי הַפֶּסַח", [12]תְּנָא נַמִּי "שִׁשָּׁה עָשָׂר לִפְנֵי הֶחָג".

[13]"רַבִּי שִׁמְעוֹן אוֹמֵר: אַף שִׁשָּׁה עָשָׂר לִפְנֵי הֶחָג, [14]מְעַבְּרִין". [15]הַיְינוּ תַּנָּא קַמָּא!

LITERAL TRANSLATION

[1]The master said: [2]"[If] sixteen [days will be] before the Festival [of Sukkot], they do not intercalate [the year]." [3]Rather according to Rabbi Yose, it is [if] sixteen [days will be] before the Festival [of Sukkot] that they do not [intercalate]. [4]But [if] seventeen or eighteen [days will be], [5]they do intercalate! [6]But surely he said: [If] sixteen [days will be] before Pesaḥ, yes; [7][but] less, no!

[8]No. [9][In the case of both] this and that, [10]they do not intercalate [the year]. [11]And since he taught the first [clause] "sixteen [days] before Pesaḥ", [12]he taught also "sixteen [days] before the Festival [of Sukkot]."

[13]"Rabbi Shimon says: Even [when] sixteen [days will be] before the Festival [of Sukkot], [14]they intercalate [the year]." [15]This is [the same as] the first Tanna!

TRANSLATION AND COMMENTARY

אָמַר מָר [1]There is an internal contradiction between the two clauses of Rabbi Yose's ruling, as the Gemara now demonstrates: The **master** in the Baraita above **said:** [2]"Rabbi Yose says:...If the first **sixteen** days of Tishri will be in the season that is **before the Festival** of Sukkot, so that the autumnal equinox will fall on the seventeenth of the month, the court **does not intercalate** the year, for some of the intermediate days of Sukkot will be in the new season." [3]**Rather,** would one say, **according to Rabbi Yose,** that **it is** only if **sixteen** days of Tishrei will be in the season that is **before the Festival** of Sukkot, so that the autumnal equinox will occur on the seventeenth of the month, **that** the year is **not** intercalated; [4]**but** if **seventeen or eighteen** days of Tishri will otherwise be in the season **before the Festival** of Sukkot, so that the autumnal equinox will occur on the eighteenth or nineteenth of the month, [5]**they do intercalate** the year! [6]**But** this is problematic, for **surely** Rabbi Yose **said** in the previous clause: If the first **sixteen** days of Nisan will be in the season **before Pesaḥ,** so that the vernal equinox will fall on the seventeenth of the month, they **indeed** do intercalate the year, for if the vernal equinox falls on the 17th of Nisan, the autumnal equinox will occur on the 22nd of Tishri, and none of the intermediate days of Sukkot will be in the new season. [7]But if **less** than sixteen days of Nisan will be in the season before Pesaḥ, the year is **not** intercalated, because the autumnal equinox will occur on the 21st of Tishri or earlier, and some of the intermediate days of Sukkot will be in the new season!

לָא [8]The Gemara continues: **No,** the inference that was drawn from the second half of Rabbi Yose's statement is incorrect, [9]for both in **this** case — where the autumnal equinox will otherwise occur on the 17th of Tishri — **and** in **that** case — where the autumnal equinox will otherwise occur on the 18th, 19th, 20th or 21st of Tishri — [10]the court **does not intercalate** the year, for in all these cases at least one of the intermediate days of Sukkot will be in the new season. When Rabbi Yose said, in the second clause of his statement, that if the first sixteen days of Tishri will be in the season that is before the Festival of Sukkot, the year is not intercalated, he did not mean to imply that if seventeen to twenty days of Tishri will be in that season, the year is intercalated. He only mentioned sixteen days in order to maintain stylistic uniformity. [11]**Since he taught** in **the first clause** the law that applies if the first **sixteen** days of Nisan will be in the season **before Pesaḥ,** [12]**he also taught** in the second clause the law that applies if the first **sixteen days** of Tishri will be in the season **before the Festival** of Sukkot. But the same law applies if seventeen, eighteen, nineteen, or twenty days will be in the season before the Festival of Sukkot — the year is not intercalated, for at least one of the intermediate days of Sukkot will be in the new season.

רַבִּי שִׁמְעוֹן אוֹמֵר [13]It was taught in the next clause of the Baraita: **"Rabbi Shimon says: Even** when the first **sixteen** days of Tishri will be in the season **before the Festival** of Sukkot, so that the autumnal equinox will fall on the 17th of Tishri, [14]the court **intercalates** the year, for all the intermediate days of Sukkot must belong to the new season, and in this case the first intermediate day is in the old season." [15]The Gemara objects: **This** position, attributed to Rabbi Shimon, **is** the same as that of **the first Tanna** of the Baraita, who says that the year is intercalated if most of the month of Tishri, sixteen days, will have passed before the autumnal equinox!

[13B] [1]אִיכָּא בֵּינַיְיהוּ יוֹם תְּקוּפָה מַתְחִיל, [2]וְיוֹם תְּקוּפָה גּוֹמֵר. [3]וְלֹא מְסַיְּימִי.
[4]אֲחֵרִים אוֹמְרִים: מִיעוּטוֹ. [5]וְכַמָּה מִיעוּטוֹ? [6]אַרְבָּעָה עָשָׂר יוֹם. [7]מַאי קָסָבְרִי? [8]אִי קָסָבְרִי יוֹם תְּקוּפָה גּוֹמֵר, [9]וְכוּלֵּיהּ חַג בָּעֵינַן, [10]הָאִיכָּא!
[11]אָמַר רַב שְׁמוּאֵל בַּר רַב יִצְחָק: [12]אֲחֵרִים בִּתְקוּפַת נִיסָן קַיְימִי, [13]דִּכְתִיב: ״שָׁמוֹר אֶת חֹדֶשׁ הָאָבִיב״ — [14]שְׁמוֹר אָבִיב

LITERAL TRANSLATION

[13B] [1]There is between them [a dispute whether] the day of the equinox begins, [2]or the day of the equinox completes. [3]And they are not defined.

[4]"Others say: A minority [of the month]. [5]And how much is a minority? [6]Fourteen days." [7]What do they maintain? [8]If they maintain [that] the day of the equinox completes, [9]and we need all of the Festival [of Sukkot], [10]surely there is!

[11]Rav Shmuel bar Rav Yitzḥak said: [12]The others are dealing with the equinox of Nisan, [13]for it is written: "Observe the month of the first ripening" — [14]observe the vernal

TRANSLATION AND COMMENTARY

אִיכָּא בֵּינַיְיהוּ [13B] [1]In truth their positions are not the same, for **there is** a difference **between them** with regard to whether **the day** on which **the equinox** falls **begins** the new season, [2]**or the day** on which **the equinox** falls **completes** the old season. According to the one who takes the former position, the court intercalates the year only if the "sixteen days" will completely pass before the autumnal equinox (occurring on the seventeenth), whereas according to the one who takes the latter position, they intercalate the year even if the "sixteen days" are expected to culminate with the equinox itself occurring on the sixteenth. [3]Nevertheless, their respective statements **are not defined** enough for us to determine which position is that of the first Tanna and which is that of Rabbi Shimon.

אֲחֵרִים אוֹמְרִים [4]The Baraita cited above concludes: **"Others say:** The year is intercalated because of a late equinox, even if it only involves **a minority** of the month. [5]**And how much is a 'minority** of the month' in this regard? [6]**Fourteen days.** If the equinox will occur on the fifteenth of the month or later, the previous year must be intercalated, but if it will occur on the fourteenth of the month or earlier, the previous year is not intercalated." [7]**What do** these other Sages **maintain** as the basis of their position? [8]Even **if they maintain that the day** on which **the equinox** falls **completes** the old season, [9]**and** that **we need all of the** intermediate days of the **Festival** of Sukkot to fall in the new season, [10]**surely there is** complete fulfillment of these conditions even when the equinox occurs on the 15th of Tishri! Conversely, if they maintain that the day on which the equinox falls begins the new season, or that only one of the intermediate days of Sukkot must be in the new season, then all the more so should it be unnecessary to intercalate the year when the equinox will otherwise fall on the 15th of Tishri!

אָמַר רַב שְׁמוּאֵל בַּר רַב יִצְחָק [11]**Rav Shmuel bar Rav Yitzḥak said:** [12]**The other** Sages cited in the Baraita are not addressing the issue of the autumnal equinox at all, but rather **are dealing with the** vernal **equinox,** which falls in the month **of Nisan,** [13]**for it is written** (Deuteronomy 16:1): **"Observe the month of the first ripening,"** and these other Sages interpret it as follows: [14]**Observe the vernal equinox** — which ushers in

RASHI

איכא ביניידו — דלרבי יהודה יום תקופה גומר, ואפילו לא חסרה אלא עשרים ונפלה בעשרים ואחד, ליכא מקלת חג, ולרבי יוסי יום תקופה מתחיל, ואם נפלה בעשרים ואחד איכא מקלת חג, עד שתחסר עשרים ואחד, ותפול חדשה בעשרים ושנים, והוה ששה עשר לפני הפסח דהוי ההיא לפני החג חסירה עשרים ואחד, הוא דמעברין, אבל חסירה בציר מהכי — לא. **ולא מסיימי** — אין סימן איזה מהן קאמר ששה עשר חסירה, ובשבעה עשר תפול — מעברין, אבל נפלה בששה עשר — אין מעברין, דיום תקופה מתחיל, ואיכא כוליה חג. וחד מינייהו קאמר: אפילו נפלה בששה עשר — מעברין, דיום תקופה גומר, וליכא כוליה חג. ואף על גב דתרווייהו אמרי כחדא ששה עשר, חד — קאי אחיסרון, וחד — קאי אנפילה, ולא ידעינן הי מינייהו. **שמור את חודש האביב שמור אביב של תקופה שיהא בחודש ניסן** — שמור תקופת חדש ניסן של חמה שיהא בתוך חידושה של לבנה. אביב הוא ניסן של חמה, שאין ניסן קרוי אביב אלא על פי בישול התבואה שמתבכרת בו. וכל ביכור התבואה ועתי הקיץ והחורף לחשבון החמה הם, ואמר רחמנא שמור שיהא חדש ניסן של חמה

TERMINOLOGY

אֲחֵרִים אוֹמְרִים Others say. Although the Sages in every generation endeavored to transmit every Halakhic teaching in its author's name, and they were very scrupulous in this matter (even when it was of no Halakhic significance), some teachings are reported anonymously with the phrase, "others say." The Talmud explains that when Rabban Shimon ben Gamliel II was serving as Nasi of the Sanhedrin, the greatest of the Sages, Rabbi Natan and Rabbi Meir, tried to rebel against his authority. After their effort failed, Rabbi Shimon ben Gamliel punished them, declaring that their teachings would not be transmitted in their names but with an epithet. The words of Rabbi Natan were introduced by the expression וְיֵשׁ אוֹמְרִים — "And some say"; and those of Rabbi Meir, with the expression אֲחֵרִים אוֹמְרִים — "Others say." After many years Rabban Shimon ben Gamliel, in consultation with his son, Rabbi Yehudah HaNasi, agreed to rescind this ruling. However, it was not done completely, and therefore in many cases Rabbi Meir's name does not appear, but instead we find the expression, "others."

NOTES

שָׁמוֹר אֶת חֹדֶשׁ הָאָבִיב Observe the month of the first ripening. Our commentary follows *Rashi*, who explains the verse as implying that the vernal equinox — alluded to by the word אָבִיב, which also means "spring" — must occur

HALAKHAH

שָׁמוֹר אֶת חֹדֶשׁ הָאָבִיב Observe the month of spring. "An extra month is added to the year so that Pesaḥ will occur in the spring, as the verse states: 'Observe the month of spring' — see that this month falls in spring. Were a month not occasionally added to the year, Pesaḥ would sometimes occur in the wrong season." (*Rambam, Sefer Zemanim, Hilkhot Kiddush HaḤodesh* 4:1.)

שֶׁל תְּקוּפָה שֶׁיְּהֵא בְּחֹדֶשׁ נִיסָן. [1]וְלִיעַבְּרֵיהּ לַאֲדָר! [2]אָמַר רַב אַחָא בַּר יַעֲקֹב: תַּנָּא מִלְמַעְלָה לְמַטָּה קָחָשֵׁיב, [3]וְהָכִי קָאָמַר: עַד מִיעוּטוֹ מְעַבְּרִין. [4]וְכַמָּה מִיעוּטוֹ? [5]אַרְבָּעָה עָשָׂר יוֹם.

LITERAL TRANSLATION

equinox that it should be during the [waxing of the moon] of Nisan.

[1]But let them intercalate [a day] into Adar!

[2]Rav Aḥa bar Ya'akov said: The Tanna is counting from top to bottom, [3]and this is what he is saying: Up to a minority [of the month] they intercalate [the year]. [4]And how much is a minority? [5]Fourteen days.

TRANSLATION AND COMMENTARY

the spring (אָבִיב) when the earliest grain ripens — **that it should be during the waxing of the moon during Nisan** — so that it should occur during the first half of the month when the moon is still new and before it achieves fullness. Hence, if the vernal equinox is expected to occur on the fifteenth of the month or later, the previous year must be intercalated so that at least part of the first half of Nisan will be in the spring season.

וְלִיעַבְּרֵיהּ לַאֲדָר [1]The Gemara asks: If the vernal equinox is expected to occur on the 15th of Nisan, why should it be necessary to intercalate an entire month into the year, thereby causing the equinox to occur a month earlier on the 15th of Adar? **Let them intercalate** just one additional day **into** the preceding month of **Adar,** making it a full month, and in that way the equinox will fall on the 14th of Nisan!

אָמַר רַב אַחָא בַּר יַעֲקֹב [2]**Rav Aḥa bar Ya'akov said: The Tanna is counting from top to bottom,** from a higher number to a lower number, [3]**and this is what he is** really **saying:** The Sages of the court **intercalate** the year if, according to their calculations, the vernal equinox is expected to occur either on the nineteenth or the eighteenth or any day earlier than that **up to** and not including that day which is preceded by **a minority** of the month, at which point the year is no longer intercalated. [4]**And how much is a minority** of the month in this regard? [5]**Fourteen days.** Consequently, if the vernal equinox is expected to occur on the fifteenth of the month, the year is not intercalated; rather, an additional day is added to the month of Adar, so that the equinox will fall on the 14th of Nisan instead of the 15th. In this way, the same purpose is achieved without having to intercalate an entire month into the year.

RASHI

נמשך לתוך ימי חידושה של לבנה, דכתיב "חדש", ואין לשון חידוש נופל אלא על לבנה המתחדשת, ואשמועינן שיהא ניסן של חמה נמשך בתוך ימי חידוש הלבנה במקצת, וכמה הן ימי חידושה — ארבעה עשר ימים, מכאן ואילך היא ישנה. **וליעברה לאדר** — ולידחייה לפסח חד יומא, ואי נמי מיקלע פסח בבד"ו לא איכפת לן, דהא דלא עבדינן פסח בבד"ו טעמא משום תשרי הוא, והיכא דלא אפשר — מוטב דלעבריה לאדר וליקלע בבד"ו, וניעבר בקייטא חד ירחא חסר טפי מכסדרן, וניהדר לתשרי בדוכתא ביום הגון, ולא ניעברוה לשתא למידחינהו לכולהו מועדות חדש שלם. **תנא** — דאחרים מלמעלה למטה קחשיב, והכי קאמר: מעברין עד מיעוטה, ולא מיעוטה בכלל, כלומר, אם תחסר תקופת טבת שמונה עשר ימים, או שבעה עשר, או ששה עשר או חמשה עשר, ותפול תקופת ניסן ביום ששה עשר — מעברין. אבל אם חסרה ארבעה עשר ותפול תקופת ניסן בחמשה עשר — אין מעברין, דמעברין לאדר, ותפול תקופת ניסן בארבעה עשר, ויום תקופה מתחיל, ויעשה פסח בתקופה חדשה.

NOTES

during the first half of the month of Nisan — alluded to by the word חֹדֶשׁ, whose root literally means "renewal," thereby suggesting that period of the month when the moon is in the process of renewing itself. *Rabbenu Ḥananel* understands the matter differently: The verse, by stating "observe the month of the first ripening and make Pesaḥ," implies that the court should see to it, by intercalating the year if necessary, that the vernal equinox occurs by the time the Paschal sacrifice is to be offered, on the 14th of Nisan. An additional explanation cited by *Rah* interprets the verse thus: See to it that all the work connected with the first ripening of grain (preparing the barley-offering to be brought on the 16th of Nisan) is performed during the new season.

וְלִיעַבְּרֵיהּ לַאֲדָר **But let them intercalate an additional day into Adar.** The Rishonim ask: Why does the Gemara only ask this question according to Rav Shmuel bar Yitzḥak's interpretation of the "others" cited in the Baraita? The same question could just as well be raised in regard to the other Tannaim there, who maintain that a delay of one day in the arrival of the autumnal equinox is sufficient reason to intercalate the year! According to them, let an extra day be added to Elul (the month before Tishri and Sukkot), and in that way the autumnal equinox will occur one day earlier! There are indeed some commentators who explain that the question as well as the answer are pertinent to all the opinions (*Rabbenu Tam*). But some Rishonim maintain that there is a difference. *Rashi* explains that an additional day cannot be added to Elul, because that would lead to a violation of the rule that Rosh HaShanah may not occur on Sunday, Wednesday, or Friday. *Ramban* suggests that the Gemara raised its question only in regard to Rav Shmuel bar Yitzḥak since, according to his interpretation of the "others" in the Baraita, the year may be intercalated on account of a single factor — the arrival of the vernal equinox after the 14th of Nisan. Thus, the Gemara argues that if the equinox can be pushed up to the 14th of Nisan by adding an extra day to Adar, there should be no reason to intercalate the year. However, according to those Sages who interpret the "others" in the Baraita as referring to a delay in the autumnal equinox, there is no question, for they maintain

TRANSLATION AND COMMENTARY

רָבִינָא אָמַר [1]Ravina disagreed with Rav Shmuel bar Rav Yitzḥak and **said:** [2]**In fact,** we need not alter our original assumption about the Baraita. **The other** Sages cited there **are** also **dealing with** the autumnal equinox, which occurs in the month of **Tishri.** The reason the year must be intercalated even if the autumnal equinox is expected to occur on the fifteenth of the month, is because these [3]**other** Sages **maintain** that **we need all of the Festival** of Sukkot, [4]**and** this includes not only the intermediate days but **the first Festival day** as well, to fall within the new season. Since they maintain that the day on which the equinox falls completes the old season, if that day coincides with the 15th of Tishri, the first Festival day of Sukkot will belong to the old season unless the year is intercalated.

יוֹם טוֹב רִאשׁוֹן [5]But how can these other Sages say that even **the first Festival day** of Sukkot must fall within the new season? If we look at the verse from where we learned above (13a) that all or some of the intermediate days of Sukkot must fall within the new season, [6]we find **written** there (Exodus 34:22): **"And the festival of ingathering** at the turn of the year," which implies that it is the time of harvesting (the intermediate days of the Festival when harvesting perishable crops is permitted). How, then, can the verse be understood as implying that the first day of the Festival must also be in the new season, since harvesting crops on that day is forbidden?

חַג הַבָּא בִּזְמַן אֲסִיפָה [7]The Gemara answers: The "others" in our Baraita understand the expression "the festival of ingathering" as referring not only to those specific days of the Festival when the crops can actually be harvested, but to **the Festival** as a whole **which comes during the time of** year when **ingathering** the crops is customary, the autumn season. Thus, the previous year must be intercalated, even if only the first Festival day of Sukkot is expected to occur in the old season.

סְמִיכַת זְקֵנִים [8]The next clause of our Mishnah stated: "**The laying of hands by the elders** of the Sanhedrin requires three elders according to Rabbi Shimon and five according to Rabbi Yehudah." If the Sanhedrin issued an erroneous Halakhic ruling, mistakenly permitting the commission of an act punishable by *karet* ("excision") if committed intentionally and necessitating a sin-offering when committed unintentionally, and a majority of the community acted in accordance with that ruling — when the error is realized, the Sanhedrin must bring a bull to be sacrificed in the Temple as a communal sin-offering (see Leviticus 4:13-21). [9]**Our Rabbis taught** a Baraita which deals with the Scriptural source of the dispute between Rabbi Yehudah and

[1]רָבִינָא אָמַר: [2]לְעוֹלָם אֲחֵרִים בְּתִשְׁרֵי קַיְימֵי, [3]וְקָסָבְרִי אֲחֵרִים: כּוּלֵּיהּ חַג בָּעֵינַן [4]וְיוֹם טוֹב רִאשׁוֹן.

[5]יוֹם טוֹב רִאשׁוֹן? [6]״חַג הָאָסִיף״ כְּתִיב!

[7]חַג הַבָּא בִּזְמַן אֲסִיפָה.

[8]״סְמִיכַת זְקֵנִים״. [9]תָּנוּ רַבָּנַן:

LITERAL TRANSLATION

[1]Ravina said: [2]In fact, the others are dealing with Tishri, [3]and the others maintain: We need all of the Festival [4]and the first Festival day.

[5]The first Festival day? [6]It is written: "The festival of ingathering."

[7]The Festival which comes during the time of ingathering.

[8]"Laying of hands by the elders." [9]Our Rabbis taught:

RASHI

לעולם בתשרי קיימי — ומשום הכי ליכא לתקוני מילתא בעבורי ירחי, ומדחייא חד יומא למועד, כדמפרש לעיל דתשרי לא מידחי חד יומא הוא, ודאמרינן: הא איכא כולה חול המועד בתקופה חדשה, קסברי אחרים כוליה חג בעינן, ואפילו יום טוב ראשון בתקופה חדשה, ויום תקופה גומר, הלכך כי נפלה תקופה בחמשה עשר — מעברינן. **חג האסיף כתיב** — חולו של מועד משמע, ומשנינן: אחרים הכי משמע להו קרא: "חג האסיף" — חג הבא בזמן אסיפה, דהיינו סוכות יהא בתקופה חדשה.

NOTES

that the year can only be intercalated if two out of three factors are present: The barley not ripening sufficiently by Pesaḥ, or the fruit not ripening by Shavuot, or the equinox occurring too late (see above, 11b). Thus, even if it were possible to rectify the problem of a late equinox by adding an extra day to the preceding month, there would still be an additional factor arguing for intercalation. In such a case, there is no reason to avoid intercalating the year by extending the previous month and thereby causing the vernal equinox to occur a day earlier.

HALAKHAH

סְמִיכַת זְקֵנִים **The laying of hands by elders of the Sanhedrin.** "If the Sanhedrin issued an erroneous ruling, which led most of the community to commit a transgression punishable by *karet,* a bull must be sacrificed as a communal sin-offering and three members of the Sanhedrin must press their hands down on the head of the animal." This accords Rabbi Shimon's view, which is supported by an anonymous Baraita as well as by a decision in the Jerusalem Talmud. (*Rambam, Sefer Avodah, Hilkhot Ma'aseh HaKorbanot* 3:10.)

״[]׳וְסָמְכוּ זִקְנֵי׳. [1]יָכוֹל זִקְנֵי הַשּׁוּק. [2]תַּלְמוּד לוֹמַר: ׳עֵדָה׳, [3]אִי ׳עֵדָה׳ [4]יָכוֹל קְטַנֵּי עֵדָה. [5]תַּלְמוּד לוֹמַר: ׳הָעֵדָה׳ [6]מְיוּחָדִין שֶׁבָּעֵדָה. [7]וְכַמָּה הֵן? [8]׳וְסָמְכוּ׳ שְׁנַיִם [9]׳זִקְנֵי׳ — שְׁנַיִם. [10]וְאֵין בֵּית דִּין שָׁקוּל, מוֹסִיפִין עֲלֵיהֶם עוֹד אֶחָד. [11]הֲרֵי כָּאן חֲמִשָּׁה; [12]דִּבְרֵי רַבִּי יְהוּדָה. [13]רַבִּי שִׁמְעוֹן אוֹמֵר: ׳זִקְנֵי׳ — שְׁנַיִם. [14]וְאֵין בֵּית דִּין שָׁקוּל, מוֹסִיפִין עֲלֵיהֶן עוֹד אֶחָד. [15]הֲרֵי כָּאן שְׁלֹשָׁה״.

[16]וְרַבִּי שִׁמְעוֹן? [17]הָכְתִיב: ״וְסָמְכוּ״!

[18]הַהוּא מִיבָּעֵי לֵיהּ לְגוּפֵיהּ.

[19]וְרַבִּי יְהוּדָה?

LITERAL TRANSLATION

"'And the elders [of the congregation] shall lay their hands.' [1]It is possible [even] elders of the market. [2]Therefore the Torah states: 'Congregation.' [3]If [it had stated:] 'Congregation,' [4]it is possible [even] minor [representatives] of the congregation. [5]Therefore the Torah states: 'The congregation' — [6]the distinguished of the congregation. [7]And how many are they? [8]'And they shall lay [their hands]' — two. [9]'The elders' — two. [10]And a court may not be even, [so] we add to them another one. [11]So [there are] here five; [12][these are] the words of Rabbi Yehudah. [13]Rabbi Shimon says: 'The elders' — two. [14]And a court may not be even, [so] we add to them another one. [15]So [there are] three."

[16]And Rabbi Shimon? [17]Surely it is written: "And they shall lay [their hands]"!

[18]It is needed for itself.

[19]And Rabbi Yehudah?

TRANSLATION AND COMMENTARY

Rabbi Shimon: "The verse states [Leviticus 4:15]: **'And the elders of the congregation shall lay their hands** on the head of the bullock before the Lord.' Now, had the verse stated simply that elders shall lay their hands on the head of the animal, [1]**it is possible** you would have said that the rite could be performed by any elders, even **elders of the market**. [2]Therefore **the Torah** explicitly **states:** 'The elders of the **congregation,'** implying that the ceremony must be performed by communal representatives, meaning members of the Sanhedrin. [3]And if the Torah had stated **'congregration'** alone, instead of 'the congregation,' [4]**it is possible** you would have said that the rite could be performed even by **minor** representatives **of the congregation,** those who presided over the smaller, local, Sanhedrins. [5]Therefore **the Torah** explicitly **states: 'The congregation'** — [6]implying **the** most **distinguished** elders **of the congregation,** the members of the Great Sanhedrin. [7]**And how many** members of the Great Sanhedrin **are they** who must participate in this rite? [8]The verse states: **'And they shall lay their hands'** — the plural form of the verb implying that **two** members of the Sanhedrin are needed. [9]And the verse states: **'The elders'** — the plural form of the noun implying that another **two** members of the Sanhedrin are necessary, bringing the total to four. [10]**And** since **a court may comprise an even** number of its judges, **we** must **add to** these four **another** judge, [11]**so** that we have **here five** judges altogether participating in the rite of laying hands on the head of the sacrificial animal. [12]These are **the words of Rabbi Yehudah.** [13]However, **Rabbi Shimon** disagrees and **says:** The verse states: **'The elders'** — the plural form of the noun implying that **two** members of the Sanhedrin are needed. [14]**And** since **a court may not comprise an even** number of its judges, **we** must **add to** these two **another** judge, [15]so that **behold** we have **here three** judges in all laying their hands on the head of the animal."

וְרַבִּי שִׁמְעוֹן [16]The Gemara asks: What does **Rabbi Shimon** do with the proof text cited by Rabbi Yehudah? [17]**Surely** he agrees that **it is written** in the verse: **"And they shall lay** their hands," the plural form of the verb implying an additional two judges beyond the three that he requires!

הַהוּא [18]According to Rabbi Shimon, an exegetical inference may not be drawn from the verb "lay" in "And they shall lay their hands," for that phrase **is needed for** the matter of the verse **itself,** to teach us that the elders must lay their hands on the head of the animal.

וְרַבִּי יְהוּדָה [19]**And Rabbi Yehudah**, how does he manage to include this verb in his exposition of the verse?

BACKGROUND

הָעֵדָה מְיוּחָדִין שֶׁבָּעֵדָה **The congregation is a particular congregation.** The Sages interpret every passage where the definite article (*heh hayedi'a*) appears before a noun that has not previously been mentioned and is not, in itself, something known, as having significance as a reference to something particularly important. Thus הָעֵדָה — "the congregation" — means a special court of the most important kind, i.e., the Great Sanhedrin.

RASHI

זקני השוק — שאינן מסנהדרין. **קטני עדה** — מסנהדרי קטנה. **מיוחדין שבעדה** — סנהדרי גדולה.

NOTES

וְאֵין בֵּית דִּין שָׁקוּל **And a court may not comprise an even number.** As was explained earlier in the chapter, we forbid courts from convening with an even number of judges so as to avoid split decisions. Here, however, the court is not adjudicating a case but rather performing a rite (laying hands on the head of a sacrificial animal). Nevertheless, since ordinarily a court may not be made up of an even number, we make no distinction and require the same wherever it functions as a court. (*Imrei Zevi.*)

[1]לְגוּפֵיהּ לֹא צָרִיךְ. [2]דְּאִם כֵּן, דְּלָא אָתֵי "וְסָמְכוּ" לִדְרָשָׁה, [3]לִיכְתּוֹב: "זִקְנֵי הָעֵדִים יְדֵיהֶם עַל רֹאשׁ הַפָּר".

[4]וְרַבִּי שִׁמְעוֹן? [5]אִי כְּתִיב הָכִי, [6]הֲוָה אָמִינָא: מַאי "עַל"? [7]בְּסָמוּךְ.

[8]וְרַבִּי יְהוּדָה? [9]גְּמַר "רֹאשׁ" "רֹאשׁ" מֵעוֹלָה.

[10]וְרַבִּי שִׁמְעוֹן? [11]לָא גְּמַר "רֹאשׁ" "רֹאשׁ" מֵעוֹלָה.

[12]תָּנָא: "סְמִיכָה וּסְמִיכַת זְקֵנִים בִּשְׁלֹשָׁה". [13]מַאי "סְמִיכָה" וּמַאי "סְמִיכַת זְקֵנִים"? [14]אָמַר רַבִּי יוֹחָנָן: מִיסְמַךְ סָבֵי.

LITERAL TRANSLATION

[1]It is not needed for itself. [2]For if so, that "and they shall lay [their hands]" does not come for the exposition, [3]let it be written: "The elders of the congregation, their hands on the head of the bullock."

[4]And Rabbi Shimon? [5]If it had been written thus, [6]I might have said: What is *"al"*? [7]Next to.

[8]And Rabbi Yehudah? [9]He deduced "head" "head" from a burnt-offering.

[10]And Rabbi Shimon? [11]He did not deduce "head" "head" from a burnt-offering.

[12][A Tanna] taught: "Laying of hands and laying of hands of the elders, by three." [13]What is "laying of hands" and what is "laying of hands of the elders"? [14]Said Rabbi Yoḥanan: Ordaining elders.

RASHI

על בסמוך — ולא צריך למיסמך ממש, כתב רחמנא "וסמכו" ממש. ולר' יהודה משום סמיכה ממש לא איצטריך "וסמכו", אלא ליכתוב "את ידיהם על ראש", ואנא גמיר "ראש" "ראש" מ"וסמך ידו על ראש העולה" (ויקרא א). **מיסמיך סבי** — לקרות להם רבי.

TRANSLATION AND COMMENTARY

לְגוּפֵיהּ [1]According to Rabbi Yehudah, the verb **is not needed for** the matter of the verse **itself,** [2]**for if** it were **so, that** the expression **"and they shall lay** their hands" **does not come for the** purpose of exegetical **exposition,** [3]then **it should have been** simply **stated: "The elders of the congregation, their hands on the head of the bullock," and** we would have understood that the elders must place their hands on the head of the animal!

וְרַבִּי שִׁמְעוֹן [4]**And Rabbi Shimon,** how does he respond to this contention? [5]**If it had** indeed **been written thus,** without explicit mention of the verb "lay," [6]**I might have asked: What is the** meaning of the word *al* ("on," in "on the head of the bullock")? [7]**"Next to,"** as it is occasionally understood in other Scriptural contexts. Thus I would have concluded that the elders may lay their hands on any part adjoining the head. Therefore the Torah stated explicitly that the elders must lay their hands down on the animal's head. Consequently, these words are not available for purposes of exegetical inference.

וְרַבִּי יְהוּדָה [8]**And Rabbi Yehudah,** how does he avoid the potential confusion created by disassociating the verb, "lay," from its immediate context in the verse? [9]**He deduced** that the elders must place their hands directly on the head of the animal by employing the hermeneutical principle of *gezerah shavah* (verbal analogy): Since the word **"head** [of the bullock]" appears in our verse as well as in an earlier verse (Leviticus 1:4) referring to laying one's hands "on the **head** of the burnt-offering," the analogy can be made that, just as in the case of **a burnt-offering,** the one bringing the sacrifice must lay his hands directly on the animal's head, so too in the case of the elders. Thus, the verb "lay" is there for the purpose of teaching that an additional two elders are required for the rite of laying hands on the sacrifice.

וְרַבִּי שִׁמְעוֹן [10]The Gemara concludes its discussion of the respective positions of the Tannaim: A *gezerah shavah* may not be advanced independently, but only by someone who received it as a tradition from his teachers. And **Rabbi Shimon** [11]**did not** have a tradition allowing him to **deduce from** the case of **a burnt-offering** an analogy between the word **"head"** mentioned there and the word **"head"** mentioned in our verse.

תָּנָא [12]In a related Baraita **a Tanna taught:** "The **laying of hands and** the **laying of hands of the elders** must be executed **by three** members of the Sanhedrin." The Gemara asks about the apparent redundancy: [13]**What** is meant in the Baraita by the nonspecific **"laying of hands," and what** is meant by the **"laying of hands of the elders"?** Surely one of these terms refers to the laying of hands by the Sanhedrin on the head of the communal sin-offering brought by them for having issued an erroneous ruling. But what does the second term refer to?

אָמַר רַבִּי יוֹחָנָן [14]**Rabbi Yoḥanan said:** The second term refers to the **ordaining** of **elders** with Rabbinic appointment and title, qualifying them to decide Halakhic questions.

TRANSLATION AND COMMENTARY

אָמַר לֵיהּ אַבַּיֵי [2] **Abaye said to Rav Yosef: From where do we have it** that **ordaining elders** requires **three** judges? [3] **If you say** that we derive this **from that which is written** in regard to the ordination of Joshua (Numbers 27:23): **"And he** [Moses] **laid his hands upon him** [Joshua]" — there is a difficulty, [4] for **if** it is **so** that this is the source of the law, **it should suffice** to grant ordination **with** only **one** judge, just as Moses ordained Joshua all by himself! [5] **And if you say that Moses** was different, for he **stood in place of** the **seventy-one** members of the Sanhedrin — [6] **if so, let them require seventy-one** judges for every ordination!

קַשְׁיָא [7] The Gemara concludes: Indeed **it is problematic.**

אֲמַר לֵיהּ [8] The Gemara now raises another question about ordination: **Rav Aḥa, the son of Rava, said to Rav Ashi:** [9] When a scholar is ordained, **do** the Sages who **ordain him** do so **with their hands, literally?**

[10] Rav Ashi **said to** Rav Aḥa: The Sages **ordain** the scholar verbally **with a title, calling him "Rabbi,"** [11] **and granting him the authority to adjudicate** cases which involve the **laws of fines.**

וְחַד לָא סָמֵיךְ [12] **And is it indeed so, that one** Sage **cannot ordain** a scholar by himself? [13] **But surely Rav Yehudah said in the name of Rav: Indeed, let that man be remembered favorably,** [14] **and Rabbi Yehudah**

[2] אֲמַר לֵיהּ אַבַּיֵי לְרַב יוֹסֵף: מִיסְמַךְ סָבֵי בִּשְׁלֹשָׁה, מְנָלַן? [3] אִילֵימָא מִדִּכְתִיב: ״וַיִּסְמֹךְ אֶת יָדָיו עָלָיו״ — [4] אִי הָכִי, תִּסְגֵּי בְּחַד. [5] וְכִי תֵּימָא מֹשֶׁה בִּמְקוֹם שִׁבְעִים וְחַד קָאֵי — [6] אִי הָכִי, לִיבָּעֵי שִׁבְעִים וְחַד! [7] קַשְׁיָא.

[8] אֲמַר לֵיהּ רַב אַחָא בְּרֵיהּ דְּרָבָא לְרַב אַשִׁי: [9] בִּידָא מַמָּשׁ סָמְכִין לֵיהּ? [10] אֲמַר לֵיהּ: סָמְכִין לֵיהּ בִּשְׁמָא, קָרֵי לֵיהּ ״רַבִּי״, [11] וְיָהֲבֵי לֵיהּ רְשׁוּתָא לְמֵידַן דִּינֵי קְנָסוֹת.

[12] וְחַד לָא סָמֵיךְ? [13] וְהָא אָמַר רַב יְהוּדָה אָמַר רַב: בְּרַם, זָכוּר אוֹתוֹ הָאִישׁ לַטּוֹב, [14] וְרַבִּי

LITERAL TRANSLATION

[2] Abaye said to Rav Yosef: The ordination of elders by three, from where do we have it? [3] If you say from that which is written: "And he laid his hands upon him" — [4] if so, it should suffice with one! [5] And if you say [that] Moses stood in place of seventy-one — [6] if so, let them require seventy-one!

[7] It is difficult!

[8] Rav Aḥa, the son of Rava, said to Rav Ashi: [9] Do they ordain him with their hands, literally?

[10] He said to him: They ordain him with a title, call him "Rabbi," [11] and grant him the authority to adjudicate laws of fines.

[12] And one cannot ordain? [13] But surely Rav Yehudah said in the name of Rav: Indeed, let that man be remembered favorably, [14] and Rabbi

RASHI

במקום שבעים וחד קאי — לפי שהיה משה ראש להם ושקול ככולם. **בידא ממש סמכי ליה** — בלשון בעיא גרסינן ליה, כלומר מי בעו לאתנוחי ידייהו על רישיה דסבא. **למידן דיני קנסות** — ד״אלהים״ כתיב (שמות כב), דמשמע דייני מומחין, והיינו סמוכין. ובשאר דיני ממונות לא בעינן מומחין, כדאוקימנא בריש פירקין סנהדרין (ב,ב) משום נעילת דלת, והיכא דליכא נעילת דלת כגון בארבעה שומרין, וגזילות, דיינינן בבבל אף על גב דליכא סמוכין, דשליחותייהו קא עבדינן, כדמפרש ב״החובל״ (בבא קמא פד,ב), אבל בקנסא — לא עבדינן שליחותייהו, משום דלא שכיחא, ולית בה חסרון כיס.

BACKGROUND

בִּמְקוֹם שִׁבְעִים וְחַד קָאֵי **He stands in the place of seventy-one.** The seventy elders in the tribunal receive their power and authority from the inspiration of Moses' spirit upon them, as described in Numbers 11. This tribunal stands in the place of Moses and as the highest authority in the Jewish people.

לְמֵידַן דִּינֵי קְנָסוֹת **We learn the laws of fines.** The imposition of fines is the most common example of the special function of ordained judges, and also the example that existed for the longest time. In ordinary judgments of monetary matters, as well as in ritual prohibitions and permissions, the judge must know the laws of the Torah, but his ruling is merely instruction to others (informing them what the Torah law is). However, the laws of fines require the expenditure of money that is not connected to the immediate damage that was caused, and they are levied only on the basis of the special authority of the court, which represents the Torah itself and Moses. However, the authority of ordained judges is not limited to the laws of fines but also includes the corporal punishments mentioned in the Torah (flogging and execution), and these, too, may be imposed only by ordained judges.

LANGUAGE

בְּרַם **Indeed.** The word is found as early as the Book of Daniel, and it is Aramaic. Though it does not have the same meaning everywhere it appears, the main sense is "but," "however," "nevertheless." Some authorities believe that the source of the word is ברר — "to select," while others maintain that it is a contraction of בַּר מִן — "outside of."

NOTES

סְמִיכָה בִּשְׁלֹשָׁה **Ordination is conferred by three Sages.** Only ordained Rabbis could serve as members of the Sanhedrin, and only they had the authority to adjudicate capital cases as well as cases involving fines or penalties. The ordination procedure is also referred to as *semikhah*, in line with the verse cited in the Gemara, even though it does not require the actual laying of hands upon the ordainee. Ordination, in order to be valid, has to be conferred by three Sages, of whom at least one must himself have been properly ordained, and with the express permission of the president of the Sanhedrin.

לִיבָּעֵי שִׁבְעִים וְחַד **Let them require seventy-one**. The Gemara does not resolve the problem it raised, but the Aḥaronim suggest several resolutions: Some say that two others indeed joined Moses to ordain Joshua, but Scripture does not mention them out of respect for Moses (*Ḥamra Vehaye*). Others suggest that Moses acting alone was considered to be the equivalent of three judges since we find him referred to in the Bible as *elohim* (Exodus 7:1), a term which normally, when applied to judges, refers to a tribunal of three. (*Rabbi David Pardo.*)

HALAKHAH

סְמִיכָה בִּשְׁלֹשָׁה **The ordination of scholars by three.** "Ordination can only be conferred upon a Rabbinic scholar by three Sages," following the Baraita. One of the ordaining Sages must himself be ordained (as may be learned from the Gemara which derives the rules regarding ordination from the ordination conferred upon Joshua by Moses; *Kesef Mishneh*). (*Rambam, Sefer Shofetim, Hilkhot Sanhedrin* 4:3.)

סָמְכִין לֵיהּ בִּשְׁמָא **They ordain him with a title.** "What is the ordination procedure? It is not necessary for the ordaining Sages to lay their hands on the head of the ordainee. Rather, they call him Rabbi and notify him that he is ordained and authorized to adjudicate even cases involving fines or penalties." (*Rambam, Sefer Shofetim, Hilkhot Sanhedrin* 4:2.)

TRANSLATION AND COMMENTARY

ben Bava was his name, for had it not been for him, [1]the laws of fines would have been forgotten in Israel.

נִשְׁתַּכְּחוּ [2]The Gemara interrupts this story with a question: Would the laws of fines really have been **forgotten** forever? If it should so happen that they are forgotten, [3]**let them** simply **learn them** over again!

אֶלָּא [4]**Rather,** [14A] [5]Rabbi Yehudah ben Bava should be remembered favorably, for had it not been for him, **the laws of fines would have been canceled in Israel.** Cases involving fines can only be adjudicated by ordained Rabbis, and it was Rabbi Yehudah ben Bava who dared to transgress the Roman decree forbidding the ordination of Rabbis and thus maintained the chain of ordination. [6]**For** it **once** happened that **the wicked kingdom** of Rome **enacted a persecutory decree against** the people of **Israel,** forbidding the ordination of Rabbinic scholars, [7]and threatening **that whoever ordained** a Rabbinic scholar **would be killed,** [8]**and whoever received ordination would be killed,** [9]**and the city in which the ordination was conferred would be destroyed,** [10]**and the district** surrounding the city **where ordination was conferred would be uprooted.** (This was the area of 2,000 cubits around the city where the inhabitants could freely walk on Shabbat). [11]**What did** Rabbi **Yehudah ben Bava do** in order to confer ordination without unnecessarily endangering the nearby community? [12]**He went and sat down** in a remote place **between two high mountains, and between two big cities,** [13]**and between two Shabbat districts, between** the Galilean cities of **Usha and Shefar'am,** so that if the matter of his ordaining Rabbis became known, a collective punishment would not be imposed on the inhabitants of any city. [14]While he was **there he ordained five Torah scholars,** [15]**and they are: Rabbi Meir, Rabbi Yehudah, Rabbi Shimon, Rabbi Yose, and Rabbi Elazar ben Shamu'a.** [16]**Rav Avyah adds:** Rabbi Yehudah ben Bava **also** ordained **Rabbi Neḥemyah.** [17]**When their** Roman **enemies discovered** that an ordination ceremony was taking place, Rabbi Yehudah ben Bava

יְהוּדָה בֶּן בָּבָא שְׁמוֹ, שֶׁאִילְמָלֵא הוּא, [1]נִשְׁתַּכְּחוּ דִּינֵי קְנָסוֹת מִיִּשְׂרָאֵל.

[2]נִשְׁתַּכְּחוּ? [3]נִגְרוֹסִינְהוּ!

[4]אֶלָּא, [14A] [5]בָּטְלוּ דִּינֵי קְנָסוֹת מִיִּשְׂרָאֵל. [6]שֶׁפַּעַם אַחַת גָּזְרָה מַלְכוּת הָרְשָׁעָה שְׁמָד עַל יִשְׂרָאֵל, [7]שֶׁכָּל הַסּוֹמֵךְ יֵהָרֵג, [8]וְכָל הַנִּסְמָךְ יֵהָרֵג, [9]וְעִיר שֶׁסּוֹמְכִין בָּהּ תֵּיחָרֵב, [10]וּתְחוּמִין שֶׁסּוֹמְכִין בָּהֶן — יֵעָקְרוּ. [11]מֶה עָשָׂה יְהוּדָה בֶּן בָּבָא? [12]הָלַךְ וְיָשַׁב לוֹ בֵּין שְׁנֵי הָרִים גְּדוֹלִים, וּבֵין שְׁתֵּי עֲיָירוֹת גְּדוֹלוֹת, [13]וּבֵין שְׁנֵי תְחוּמֵי שַׁבָּת, בֵּין אוּשָׁא לִשְׁפַרְעָם, [14]וְסָמַךְ שָׁם חֲמִשָּׁה זְקֵנִים. [15]וְאֵלּוּ הֵן: רַבִּי מֵאִיר, וְרַבִּי יְהוּדָה, וְרַבִּי שִׁמְעוֹן, וְרַבִּי יוֹסֵי, וְרַבִּי אֶלְעָזָר בֶּן שַׁמּוּעַ. [16]רַב אַוְיָא מוֹסִיף: אַף רַבִּי נְחֶמְיָה. [17]כֵּיוָן שֶׁהִכִּירוּ אוֹיְבֵיהֶם בָּהֶן אָמַר לָהֶן:

LITERAL TRANSLATION

Yehudah ben Bava was his name, for had it not been for him, [1]the laws of fines would have been forgotten in Israel.

[2]Forgotten? [3]Let them learn them!

[4]Rather, [14A] [5]the laws of fines would have been canceled in Israel, [6]for once the wicked kingdom decreed apostasy upon Israel, [7]that whoever ordains will be killed, [8]and whoever is ordained will be killed, [9]and the city where they ordain will be destroyed, [10]and the district in which they ordain will be uprooted. [11]What did Yehudah ben Bava do? [12]He went and sat between two high mountains, and between two big cities, [13]and between two Shabbat districts, between Usha and Shefar'am, [14]and he ordained there five elders. [15]And they are the following: Rabbi Meir, and Rabbi Yehudah, and Rabbi Shimon, and Rabbi Yose, and Rabbi Elazar ben Shamu'a. [16]Rav Avyah adds: Also Rabbi Neḥemyah. [17]When their enemies discovered them, he said to them:

RASHI

בטלו דיני קנסות — דכיון דליכא סמיכה, בטלו. **בין שתי עיירות גדולות** — ולא בתוך העיר, שאם יוודע — שלא יחריבו את העיר.

BACKGROUND

שֶׁכָּל הַסּוֹמֵךְ יֵהָרֵג **For anyone who ordains shall be killed.** It is explained that ordination is not merely a matter of imposing fines. Rather, the presence of ordained Sages is the basis for the creation of the major Jewish courts, the tribunal of twenty-three and that of seventy-one. As long as the Great Sanhedrin exists, the Jewish people has a single spiritual and Torah center, for that High Court has the authority to determine matters that obligated the entire Jewish people. The Romans' attempts to abolish ordination were part of their political effort to weaken the Jews of Palestine by abolishing the centrality of the Land of Israel and its Sages for the entire Jewish people. For the same reason Rabbi Yehuda ben Bava sacrificed his life, and other Sages risked theirs in order to maintain the chain of ordination. However, with the passage of time and the thinning out of the Jewish population in the Land of Israel, and also as a result of the decrees of the authorities, ordination was discontinued, and no center such as the Sanhedrin has ever arisen for the Jewish people again. Efforts to reestablish the system of ordination have not succeeded.

אוּשָׁא וּשְׁפַרְעָם **Usha and Shefar'am.** Usha was a city in Lower Galilee, and for a time it was also the seat of the Sanhedrin. To this day there is an Arab village named Husha. She-far'am is another city in the Lower Galilee (the Valley of Zevulon) to which the Sanhedrin moved from Usha. There was a Jewish community there until 1920. Today it is a Druze and Christian town named Shefa-Amar. The distance between these places was about three kilometers in a mountainous area. A cave at the point midway between them is traditionally identified as that of Rabbi Yehudah ben Bava. Near it is a Greek inscription marking the Shabbat boundary of Usha.

NOTES

בֵּין שְׁנֵי הָרִים **Between two mountains.** *Remah* explains that Rabbi Yehudah ben Bava chose to conduct the ordination ceremony between these two mountains because they themselves served as local boundary markers for the Shabbat and thus could not be uprooted in the event that his actions were discovered. *Rabbi Ya'akov Emden* suggests that he chose that site because he thought it would shield him from the view of the Roman authorities.

HALAKHAH

וְסָמַךְ שָׁם חֲמִשָּׁה זְקֵנִים **And he ordained there five elders.** "Ordination may be conferred upon many scholars at the same time (as is proven by the incident involving Rabbi Yehudah ben Bava; *Radbaz*)." (*Rambam, Sefer Shofetim, Hilkhot Sanhedrin* 4:7.)

SAGES

רַבִּי יְהוּדָה בֶּן בָּבָא **Rabbi Yehudah ben Bava.** He was one of the Tannaim who was

[1]"בָּנַיי, רוּצוּ"! [2]אָמְרוּ לוֹ: "רַבִּי, מַה תְּהֵא עָלֶיךָ?" [3]אָמַר לָהֶן: "הֲרֵינִי מוּטָּל לִפְנֵיהֶם כְּאֶבֶן שֶׁאֵין לָהּ הוֹפְכִים. [4]אָמְרוּ: לֹא זָזוּ מִשָּׁם עַד שֶׁנָּעֲצוּ בּוֹ שְׁלֹשׁ מֵאוֹת לוּנְבִיאוֹת שֶׁל בַּרְזֶל, [5]וַעֲשָׂאוּהוּ כִּכְבָרָה.

[6]רַבִּי יְהוּדָה בֶּן בָּבָא אַחֲרִינֵי הָווּ בַּהֲדֵיהּ. [7]וְהַאי דְּלָא חָשֵׁיב לְהוּ מִשּׁוּם כְּבוֹדוֹ דְּרַבִּי יְהוּדָה בֶּן בָּבָא.

[8]וְרַבִּי מֵאִיר רַבִּי יְהוּדָה בֶּן בָּבָא סְמַכֵיהּ? [9]וְהָא אָמַר רַבָּה בַּר בַּר חָנָה אָמַר רַבִּי יוֹחָנָן: [10]כָּל הָאוֹמֵר רַבִּי מֵאִיר לֹא סְמָכוֹ רַבִּי עֲקִיבָא אֵינוֹ אֶלָּא טוֹעֶה! [11]סְמַכֵיהּ רַבִּי עֲקִיבָא, וְלָא קִיבְּלוּ. [12]סְמַכֵיהּ רַבִּי יְהוּדָה בֶּן בָּבָא, וְקִיבְּלוּ.

[13]אָמַר רַבִּי יְהוֹשֻׁעַ בֶּן לֵוִי: אֵין סְמִיכָה בְּחוּצָה לָאָרֶץ.

LITERAL TRANSLATION

[1]"My sons, run!" [2]They said to him: "Master, what will be with you?" [3]He said to them: "I lie before them as a stone which cannot be overturned." [4]They said: They did not move from there until they stuck into him three hundred iron spearheads, [5]and made him like a sieve.

[6]Others were with Rabbi Yehudah ben Bava. [7]And he did not list them because of the honor of Rabbi Yehudah ben Bava.

[8]But did Rabbi Yehudah ben Bava ordain Rabbi Meir? [9]But surely Rabbah bar Bar Ḥanah said in the name of Rabbi Yoḥanan: [10]Whoever says that Rabbi Akiva did not ordain Rabbi Meir is mistaken! [11]Rabbi Akiva ordained him, but they did not accept it. [12]Rabbi Yehudah ben Bava ordained him, and they accepted it.

[13]Rabbi Yehoshua ben Levi said: There is no ordination outside Eretz Israel.

RASHI

לונביאות – חניתות. ולא קבלו – לפי שעדיין היה בחור.

TRANSLATION AND COMMENTARY

said to the new ordainees: [1]**"My sons, run** for your lives." [2]**They said to him: "Master, what will be with you,** for you are too old to run?" [3]Rabbi Yehudah ben Bava **said to them: "I lie before them like a stone which cannot be overturned.** I will not succeed in escaping even if you try to help me." The five newly ordained Rabbis fled, the chain of ordination was saved, but Rabbi Yehudah ben Bava was put to death by the Romans. [4]**It was related that when** the Romans found Rabbi Yehudah ben Bava, **they did not move from** the site **until they stuck into** his body **three hundred iron spearheads,** [5]which **made him** look **like a sieve.** This story of Rabbi Yehudah ben Bava's heroic rescue of the chain of ordination contradicts the ruling that ordination can only be conferred by three Sages, for Rabbi Yehudah ben Bava ordained the five scholars by himself!

רַבִּי יְהוּדָה בֶּן בָּבָא [6]The Gemara answers: There **were** in fact two **other** Sages **with Rabbi Yehudah ben Bava** when he ordained the five scholars. [7]Those other Sages **were not mentioned** in the story **out of respect for Rabbi Yehudah ben Bava.**

וְרַבִּי מֵאִיר [8]The Gemara asks another question about this incident: **But did Rabbi Yehudah ben Bava** really **ordain Rabbi Meir?** [9]**But surely Rabbah bar Bar Ḥanah said in the name of Rabbi Yoḥanan:** [10]**Whoever says that Rabbi Akiva did not ordain Rabbi Meir is mistaken!** If Rabbi Akiva already ordained Rabbi Meir, why then was it necessary for Rabbi Yehudah ben Bava to ordain hi m a second time?

[11]The Gemara answers: Indeed, **Rabbi Akiva did ordain** Rabbi Meir, **but the people did not accept** the ordination, for Rabbi Meir was still very young at the time. [12]**Rabbi Yehudah ben Bava** later **ordained** Rabbi Meir again, **and** then **the people accepted it,** for by that time Rabbi Meir had reached the appropriate age.

אָמַר רַבִּי יְהוֹשֻׁעַ בֶּן לֵוִי [13]The Gemara continues its discussion of ordination: **Rabbi Yehoshua ben Levi said: There is no ordination outside Eretz Israel.**

active during the period between the destruction of the Temple and that of Betar. Rabbi Yehudah ben Bava's studies began when the Temple was still standing. He was mainly active during the period when the seat of the Sanhedrin was in Yavneh. His Torah teachings and testimony are mentioned in various sources. Rabbi Yehudah ben Bava was famous for his piety, and it is said that wherever the Talmud speaks of "the story of a certain pious man," this is a reference to Rabbi Yehudah ben Bava or to Rabbi Yehudah ben Il'ai. On the basis of chronological indications it seems that he lived to be ninety or older.

LANGUAGE

לוּנְבִיאוֹת This word is derived from the Greek λόγχη (*lonkhi*), meaning a spear or lance.

A Roman soldier holding a spear from the Talmudic period.

NOTES

מִשּׁוּם כְּבוֹדוֹ Out of respect for Rabbi Yehudah ben Bava. According to many Rishonim (*Rambam, Ran, Meiri*), only one of the three Sages required for ordaining a Rabbinic scholar need be ordained himself. Thus, it is understandable why only Rabbi Yehudah ben Bava was mentioned, for it is very possible that the other two who participated in the ordination ceremony may not have been ordained Rabbis. Rabbi Yehudah ben Bava might even have formed his court of three by recruiting two of the five scholars who themselves were there to be ordained. However, according to *Remah* (and perhaps *Rashi*), all three members of the court conducting the ordination rite must themselves be ordained.

אֵין סְמִיכָה בְּחוּצָה לָאָרֶץ There is no ordination outside Eretz Israel. The Jerusalem Talmud (*Bikkurim* 3:3) derives this from a combination of verses: One verse describes the courts as situated "in all your dwelling places." At the same time, there is a verse in Ezekiel (36:17) which implies that the term "dwelling" (יְשִׁיבָה) is only applied to Israel as long as they reside in their own land: "Son of man, when the house of Israel dwelt in their own land." It has also been suggested that when a Torah scholar receives ordination, he becomes invested with a measure of the Holy Spirit that initially resided in Moses himself. Thus, the ordination ceremony must take place in Eretz Israel, for according to tradition the Holy Spirit does not rest upon one who lives outside its borders (*Ḥiddushei Geonim*).

TRANSLATION AND COMMENTARY

מַאי אֵין סְמִיכָה [1]The Gemara asks: **What is meant by** the statement that **there is no ordination** outside Eretz Israel? [2]**You might say that this** means that the courts **do not adjudicate cases involving fines outside Eretz Israel.** And Rabbi Yehoshua ben Levi's statement can be understood as follows: Ordination has no validity outside Eretz Israel, and so fines can only be imposed in Eretz Israel. [3]**But** this is not true, for **surely we have learned** elsewhere in the Mishnah (*Makkot* 7a): [4]**"A Sanhedrin** of twenty- three judges **is** authorized to judge capital cases, and all the more so cases involving fines, **both in Eretz Israel and outside Eretz Israel,** if its members were ordained in Eretz Israel"!

אֶלָּא [5]**Rather,** suggests the Gemara, Rabbi Yehoshua ben Levi meant **that ordination cannot be conferred outside Eretz Israel.**

פְּשִׁיטָא [6]The Gemara clarifies certain details relating to this ruling: **It is obvious that if the ordaining** Sages **are outside Eretz Israel, and** the scholars **being ordained are in Eretz Israel,** [7]**surely we have** just **said that** the ordination is **not** valid, for it cannot be conferred outside Eretz Israel. [8]**But what is the law if the ordaining** Sages **are in Eretz Israel and** the scholars **being ordained are outside Eretz Israel?**

תָּא שְׁמַע [9]The Gemara suggests a solution: **Come and hear** an answer to this question from the following anecdote, [10]**for Rabbi Yoḥanan was distressed that Rav Shemen bar Abba was not with him** in Eretz Israel **so that he could ordain him.** This shows that ordination is valid only if the ordaining Sages and the scholar being ordained are all in Eretz Israel.

רַבִּי שִׁמְעוֹן בֶּן זֵירוּד [11]A similar story is told about **Rabbi Shimon ben Zerud and a colleague of his.** [12]**And who is that?** [13]**Rabbi Yonatan ben Akhmai.** [14]**And some relate** the story about **Rabbi Yonatan ben Akhmai and a colleague of his.** [15]**And who is that?** [16]**Rabbi Shimon ben Zerud.** Even though the two were equal in standing, [17]**only one of them was with** the Sages in Eretz Israel when they were prepared to confer ordination, and

[1]מַאי ״אֵין סְמִיכָה״? [2]אִילֵימָא דְּלָא דָּיְינִי דִּינֵי קְנָסוֹת כְּלָל בְּחוּצָה לָאָרֶץ, [3]וְהָא תְּנַן: [4]״סַנְהֶדְרִין נוֹהֶגֶת בֵּין בָּאָרֶץ וּבֵין בְּחוּצָה לָאָרֶץ״! [5]אֶלָּא, דְּלָא סָמְכִינַן בְּחוּצָה לָאָרֶץ. [6]פְּשִׁיטָא, סוֹמְכִין בְּחוּצָה לָאָרֶץ וְנִסְמָכִין בָּאָרֶץ, [7]הָא אָמְרִינַן דְּלָא. [8]אֶלָּא סוֹמְכִין בָּאָרֶץ וְנִסְמָכִין בְּחוּצָה לָאָרֶץ מַאי? [9]תָּא שְׁמַע: [10]דְּרַבִּי יוֹחָנָן הֲוָה מִצְטַעֵר עֲלֵיהּ דְּרַב שֶׁמֶן בַּר אַבָּא דְּלָא הֲוָה גַּבַּיְיהוּ דְּלִיסְמְכֵיהּ. [11]רַבִּי שִׁמְעוֹן בֶּן זֵירוּד וְחַד דְּעִימֵּיהּ. [12]וּמַנּוּ? [13]רַבִּי יוֹנָתָן בֶּן עַכְמַאי. [14]וְאָמְרִי לַהּ: רַבִּי יוֹנָתָן בֶּן עַכְמַאי וְחַד דְּעִימֵּיהּ, [15]וּמַנּוּ? [16]רַבִּי שִׁמְעוֹן בֶּן זֵירוּד. [17]חַד דַּהֲוָה גַּבַּיְיהוּ סָמְכוּהוּ.

LITERAL TRANSLATION

[1]What is [meant by] "there is no ordination"? [2]If you say that they do not judge laws of fines at all outside Eretz Israel, [3]but surely we have learned: [4]"A Sanhedrin functions both in Eretz Israel and outside Eretz Israel"!

[5]Rather, that they do not ordain outside Eretz Israel.

[6]It is obvious [that if] the ordainers are outside Eretz Israel and the ordainees are in Eretz Israel, [7]surely we have said no. [8]But what [is the law if] the ordainers are in Eretz Israel and the ordainees are outside Eretz Israel?

[9]Come [and] hear: [10]For Rabbi Yoḥanan was distressed that Rav Shemen bar Abba was not with them so that he could ordain him.

[11]Rabbi Shimon ben Zerud and one who was with him. [12]And who is it? [13]Rabbi Yonatan ben Akhmai. [14]And some say: Rabbi Yonatan ben Akhmai and one who was with him. [15]And who is it? [16]Rabbi Shimon ben Zerud. [17]The one who was with them they ordained.

RASHI

אילימא דלא דיינינן דיני קנסות בחוצה לארץ — והכי קאמר: אין סמיכה מועלת בחוצה לארץ ואפילו סמכוהו בארץ. **פשיטא, סומכין בחוצה לארץ ונסמכין בארץ** — אם בני בבל נותנין רשות לאחד שבארץ ישראל לדון קנסות. **הא אמרן דלא** — דאין סמיכה בחוצה לארץ, וכיון דאי הוה גבן הכא לא מצינו למסמכיה, כל שכן היכא דליתיה גבן. **סומכין בארץ ונסמכין בחוצה לארץ מאי** — אם הסומך עומד בארץ והנסמך עומד בבבל, וליתיה גבי סומך, מי מהני כאילו איתיה גביה בשעת סמיכה ומאי למידן בחוצה לארץ, כדתנן: סנהדרין נוהגין בחוצה לארץ, או דילמא, כיון דליתיה גבייהו בשעת סמיכה — לא מהניא ליה.

HALAKHAH

סַנְהֶדְרִין נוֹהֶגֶת בֵּין בָּאָרֶץ וּבֵין בְּחוּצָה לָאָרֶץ **The Sanhedrin applies both in Eretz Israel and outside Eretz Israel.** "A court whose members were ordained in Eretz Israel and then left the country is authorized to adjudicate cases involving fines even outside Eretz Israel, for a Sanhedrin's authority applies both in Eretz Israel and outside it, provided that the court's members were properly ordained." (*Rambam, Sefer Shofetim, Hilkhot Sanhedrin* 4:12.)

דְּלָא סָמְכִינַן בְּחוּצָה לָאָרֶץ **That they do not ordain outside Eretz Israel.** "Ordination cannot be conferred outside

[1]וְחַד דְּלָא הֲוָה גַּבַּיְיהוּ לָא סְמָכוּהוּ.

[2]רַבִּי חֲנִינָא וְרַבִּי הוֹשַׁעְיָא הֲוָה קָא מִשְׁתַּקֵּיד רַבִּי יוֹחָנָן לְמִיסְמְכִינְהוּ, [3]לָא הֲוָה מִסְתַּיְּיעָא מִילְּתָא, [4]הֲוָה קָא מִצְטַעֵר טוּבָא. [5]אָמְרוּ לֵיהּ: לָא נִצְטַעַר מָר, [6]דַּאֲנַן מִדְּבֵית עֵלִי קָאָתֵינַן. [7]דְּאָמַר רַבִּי שְׁמוּאֵל בַּר נַחְמָן אָמַר רַבִּי יוֹנָתָן: [8]מִנַּיִין שֶׁאֵין נִסְמָכִין לְבֵית עֵלִי? [9]שֶׁנֶּאֱמַר "לֹא יִהְיֶה זָקֵן בְּבֵיתְךָ כָּל הַיָּמִים". [10]מַאי "זָקֵן"? [11]אִילֵימָא זָקֵן, מַמָּשׁ — [12]וְהָכְתִיב: "כָּל מַרְבִּית בֵּיתְךָ יָמוּתוּ אֲנָשִׁים"! [13]אֶלָּא, סְמִיכָה.

LITERAL TRANSLATION

[1]And the one who was not with them, they did not ordain.

[2]Rabbi Yoḥanan was anxious to ordain Rabbi Ḥanina and Rabbi Hoshaya, [3]but the matter was not feasible. [4]He was very distressed. [5]They said to him: Do not be distressed, Sir, [6]for we come from the House of Eli, [7][about whom] Rabbi Shmuel bar Naḥman said in the name of Rabbi Yonatan: [8]From where [do we know] that no one is ordained of the House of Eli? [9]For it is written: "And there shall not be an old man in your house forever." [10]What is "an old man"? [11]If you say an old man, literally — [12]but surely it is written: "And all the greater folk of your house shall die in the flower of their age"! [13]Rather, ordination.

TRANSLATION AND COMMENTARY

he was **ordained.** [1]**But the one who was not with** the Sages in Eretz Israel at the time was **not ordained.**

רַבִּי חֲנִינָא [2]The Gemara continues with another anecdote relating to ordination: It was said that **Rabbi Yoḥanan was anxious to ordain Rabbi Ḥanina and Rabbi Hoshaya,** and thus give formal recognition to their Torah scholarship, [3]**but the matter was never accomplished.** [4]Rabbi Yoḥanan **was very distressed,** [5]but Rabbi Ḥanina and Rabbi Hoshaya **said to him: Do not be distressed, Sir,** that we have not received our ordination. We have long known that we would never be ordained, [6]**for we come from the House of Eli,** the priest in the sanctuary at Shiloh in the days of Samuel. [7]And **Rabbi Shmuel bar Naḥman said in the name of Rabbi Yonatan:** [8]**How do we know that no ordained** scholars will come **from the House of Eli?** [9]**For the verse states** (I Samuel 2:32): **"And there shall not be an old man [זָקֵן] in your house forever."** [10]**What is** meant here by the word *zaken,* tanslated here in its usual sense as **"an old man"?** [11]**If you say** that here, too, the word should be understood as **"an old man," literally,** there is a difficulty, [12]**for surely the** next **verse states** (2:33): **"And all the greater folk of your house shall die in the flower of their age"!** Now if the second verse teaches that Eli's descendants will die while they are still young, why should the first verse have to say that there will not be any old men among them? [13]**Rather,** the word *zaken* used here refers to a Torah scholar upon whom **ordination** was conferred. As is explained elsewhere (*Rosh HaShanah* 18a), Torah study and good deeds can eliminate the curse of the descendants of Eli and his sons, and so it is possible for his descendants to reach old age, but Rabbinic ordination will never be conferred upon them.

RASHI

לא הוה מסתייע מילתא — כשהיו אצלו לא היה מוצא שנים שיצטרפו עמו לסומכו, ואנן תלתא בעינן. **משתקיד** — מחזר ומצפה לסומכו כמו (ירמיה א): "כי שוקד אני". **מנין שאין נסמכין לבית עלי** — שאינן זוכין להיות נסמכין. **זקן ממש** — בא בימים. **הכתיב כל מרבית ביתך ימותו אנשים** — כשבאין לכלל אנשים בן שמנה עשרה שנה, למה לי למיהדר ומכתביה. **אלא סמיכה** — שאפילו חכמים הבאים לכלל זקנה כגון על ידי תורה וגמילות חסדים, כדאמרינן בראש השנה (יח,א): בזבח ומנחה אינו מתכפר, אבל מתכפר הוא בתורה ובגמילות חסדים, מכל מקום לא תהא תורת זקנה עליהם להיות ראויים לסנהדרין.

NOTES

לָא הֲוָה מִסְתַּיְּיעָא מִילְּתָא **The matter was not successful.** *Remah* explains that Rabbi Yoḥanan was unsuccessful in ordaining Rabbi Ḥanina and Rabbi Hoshaya due to his being unable to find another two ordained Sages who could join him in the process. According to *Rambam,* it might be that Rabbi Yoḥanan was unable to ordain Rabbi Ḥanina and Rabbi Hoshaya for some other technical reason, such as the two ordainees being outside Eretz Israel when ordination was being conferred.

אֲנַן מִדְּבֵית עֵלִי קָאָתֵינַן **We come from the House of Eli.** It is explained elsewhere (*Rosh HaShanah* 18a) that there were descendants of Eli who reached old age in spite of the curse against his line by seriously dedicating themselves to Torah study and good deeds, though even then Rabbinic ordination remained outside their grasp.

HALAKHAH

Eretz Israel, even if the ordaining Rabbis were themselves ordained in Eretz Israel. Ordination cannot be conferred outside Eretz Israel, even if the ordaining Rabbis are in Eretz Israel, and only the scholars being ordained are abroad, and all the more so if the ordaining Rabbis are abroad, and only the scholars being ordained are in Eretz Israel. If not only the ordaining Rabbis but also the scholars being ordained are in Eretz Israel, even if they are not together in the same place, ordination may be conferred, either in writing or by way of a deputy." (*Rambam, Sefer Shofetim, Hilkhot Sanhedrin* 4:6.)

SAGES

רַבִּי חֲנִינָא וְרַבִּי הוֹשַׁעְיָא **Rabbi Ḥanina and Rabbi Hoshaya.** These two Sages were brothers, students of Rabbi Yoḥanan (some say they were originally from Babylonia and brothers of the great Amora Rabba). They learned Torah from Rabbi Yoḥanan and his great disciples, and many Sages of the following generation presented teachings in their name. The Talmud tells of their great righteousness. They did not enjoy the honor given to the Torah but worked for their living as cobblers in the prostitutes' market. Nevertheless, everyone accorded them great honor. It is told that even the prostitutes swore "on the lives of the holy Rabbis of the Land of Israel." The Talmud also notes that they used to study the Torah in secret.

BACKGROUND

לָא הֲוָה מִסְתַּיְּיעָא מִילְּתָא **The thing did not succeed.** Apparently, ordination was ordinarily conferred at a large celebration, with special permission granted by the Nasi of the Sanhedrin. Therefore on occasion there was no appropriate opportunity to ordain Sages who were worthy of it in every respect.

[1]רַבִּי זֵירָא הֲוָה מִיטַּמַּר לְמִיסְמְכֵיהּ. [2]דְּאָמַר רַבִּי אֶלְעָזָר: לְעוֹלָם הֱוֵה קָבֵל [3]וְקַיָּים! [4]כֵּיוָן דִּשְׁמָעָהּ לְהָא דְּאָמַר רַבִּי אֶלְעָזָר: [5]אֵין אָדָם עוֹלֶה לִגְדוּלָּה אֶלָּא אִם כֵּן מוֹחֲלִין לוֹ עַל כָּל עֲוֹנוֹתָיו — [6]אִמְצִי לֵיהּ אַנַּפְשֵׁיהּ.

[7]כִּי סְמָכוּהּ לְרַבִּי זֵירָא שָׁרוּ לֵיהּ הָכִי: לֹא כָּחָל וְלֹא שָׂרָק וְלֹא פִּירְכּוּס — [8]וְיַעֲלַת חֵן.

[9]כִּי סְמָכוּהּ לְרַבִּי אַמִי וּלְרַבִּי אַסִי, שָׁרוּ לְהוּ הָכִי: [10]כָּל מִן דֵּין כָּל מִן דֵּין סְמוֹכוּ לָנָא. [11]לָא תִּסְמְכוּ לָנָא לָא מִסַּרְמִיטִין, וְלָא מִסַּרְמִיסִין.

TRANSLATION AND COMMENTARY

רַבִּי זֵירָא [1]It was further related that **Rabbi Zera would hide to avoid being ordained,** [2]in accordance with what **Rabbi Elazar said: Forever be in the dark** — out of the limelight — [3]**and** you will **live** a long life! [4]However, **once he heard what Rabbi Elazar said,** [5]that **a person does not rise to** a position of **greatness unless all his sins are forgiven** — [6]**he strove** to have **himself** ordained.

כִּי סְמָכוּהּ [7]It was also related that **when** the Rabbis in Eretz Israel **ordained Rabbi Zera,** the Sages present at the time **sang** a popular bridal lyric **to him as follows:** "She uses **no mascara, no rouge, and no hair-dye,** [8]**and** yet she is as beautiful as **a graceful gazelle,"** thereby implying that just as a beautiful woman need not adorn herself in order to find favor, so too Rabbi Zera need not be formally ordained for people to recognize his merits.

כִּי סְמָכוּהּ [9]**When** the Rabbis in Eretz Israel **ordained Rabbi Ammi and Rabbi Assi,** the Sages present at the time **sang to them as follows:** [10]**"Anyone like these, anyone like these, ordain for us** [for they are outstanding examples of men fit to be ordained], [11]but **do not ordain for us, not** from ***sarmitin*** **and not** from ***sarmisin*,"** rhyming terms for incompetent or worthless scholars. *Sarmitin* are those who present their ideas in sloppy or rough fashion, whereas *sarmisin* are those who pervert the

LITERAL TRANSLATION

[1]Rabbi Zera would hide from being ordained. [2]For Rabbi Elazar said: Forever be in the dark [3]and live! [4]When he heard that which Rabbi Elazar said: [5]A person does not rise to greatness unless they pardon him for all his sins — [6]he strove [to have] himself [ordained].

[7]When they ordained Rabbi Zera, they sang for him as follows: No mascara, and no rouge, and no dyeing [of the hair] — [8]and [yet] a graceful gazelle.

[9]When they ordained Rabbi Ammi and Rabbi Assi, they sang to them as follows: [10]Anyone like this one [and] anyone like this one ordain for us. [11]Do not ordain for us, not *sarmitin* and not *sarmisin*.

BACKGROUND

כָּחָל ***Kohl.*** This bluish-black pigment was produced in antiquity from the mineral stibnite, a native trisulfate of antimony (SB_2S_3). The stibnite was ground and applied around the eyes to make them stand out and appear larger.

RASHI

הוי קבל — אפל. **וקיים** — ותחיה, כלומר הרחק מן הרבנות שמקברת את בעליה, "אפילה" מתרגם: קבלה (שמות י). **כחל** — לעינים. **שרק** — לפנים. **פירכוס** — לשיער, שיר הוא לכלה נאה שמעלת חן בלא קישוט. **כל מן דין** — כל כמו אלו וכיוצא בהן היו סומכין לנו, שראויים הם לסמיכה. **סרמיטין** — לשון הפכנים, כמו: סרס את המקרא מסופו לראשו (בבא בתרא קיט,ב), שמהפכין את טעמי תורה. **סרמיטין** — לשון סמרטוט, כלומר שאין נותנים טעם הגון לדבריהם.

NOTES

לְעוֹלָם הֱוֵה קָבֵל וְקַיָּים! **Forever be in the dark and live!** *Rashi* understands this as a recommendation not to accept any high position of communal responsibility because of the ongoing pressure and strain that it entails. *Rabbi Tzvi Ḥayyot* understands the underlying rationale a bit differently. Taking a high position generally means having one's behavior subjected to excessive public scrutiny. The negative outcome of such scrutiny can impede one's effectiveness as an arbiter of moral standards in the community. However, after hearing Rabbi Elazar's other statement — that meriting a prominent position implies that one's sins have been pardoned — Rabbi Zera decided to accept ordination nonetheless. For even if his personal failings were brought to light, he could now be assured that this would not diminish his moral authority within the community.

עוֹלֶה לִגְדוּלָּה **Rise to greatness.** The Jerusalem Talmud (*Bikkurim* 3:3) teaches that, on the day that a Sage or a Nasi attains office, all his sins are pardoned; likewise as regards a bridegroom on the day of his marriage. Scriptural support is adduced with respect to each of these three types of persons. Regarding a Sage, we are taught that the juxtaposition of the verse regarding an elder Sage (Leviticus 19:32: "You shall honor the face of an elder") with the verse regarding a proselyte (19:33): "And if a proselyte sojourn with you") comes to inform us that, just as the proselyte's sins are pardoned on the day he converts to Judaism, so too are the Sage's sins pardoned on the day he attains office. *Maharsha* explains that a person does not rise to a high position unless God wills it, and surely God would not bestow such an honor upon a person without first pardoning all his sins.

סַרְמִיטִין, סַרְמִיסִין, חֲמִיסִין, טוּרְמִיסִין ***Sarmitin, sarmisin, ḥamisin, turmisin.*** It is clear that all these terms are

HALAKHAH

הֲוָה מִיטַּמַּר לְמִיסְמְכֵיהּ **He would hide from being ordained.** "The early Sages would make great efforts not to be appointed as judges, unless they were convinced that nobody was as qualified for the position as they were, and even then they would only accept the responsibility after being pressed into it by the community and its leaders," as is proven by the story relating to Rabbi Zera. (*Shulḥan Arukh, Ḥoshen Mishpat* 8:3.)

SAGES

רַבִּי אַבָּהוּ Rabbi Abbahu. He was a resident of the city of Caesarea and was highly respected by the Roman authorities. Although he had no official position, he in fact served as the representative of the Jewish people. "The house of the emperor" here is apparently the palace of the Roman governor in the city of Caesarea itself, where Rabbi Abbahu also had an independent yeshivah.

TRANSLATION AND COMMENTARY

reading or meaning of Biblical texts and the law. [1]**Some say** that the Sages used these epithets: **"Not from *ḥamisin* and not from *turmisin*."** *Ḥamisin* are those who refuse to explain their positions, whereas *turmisin* are simply base and vulgar people.

רַבִּי אַבָּהוּ [2]Having touched on the topic of songs sung in honor of various scholars, the Gemara relates that **when Rabbi Abbahu would come from the Academy to the house of the** Roman **emperor** to discuss communal matters, [3]**the matrons of the house of the emperor would come out and sing to him** as follows: [4]**"Master of his people, leader of his nation, lamp of light,** [5]**blessed is your coming in peace."**

עֲרִיפַת עֶגְלָה בִּשְׁלֹשָׁה [6]The next clause of our Mishnah addresses an additional responsibility of the Sanhedrin mandated as part of the procedure prescribed by the Bible (Deuteronomy 21:1-9) in the event a slain body is found in an open field with no indication of who perpetrated the murder. In such a case, members of the Sanhedrin must come to the site and measure the distances to surrounding towns in order to determine which lies closest to the corpse. Elders of that town must then bring a heifer that has never been worked and break its neck in an uncultivated ravine, after which they wash their hands and make a statement absolving themselves of any indirect guilt in the murder. Our Mishnah comes to inform us that the measurements carried out by the Sanhedrin prior to the **breaking** of **the neck of the heifer** have to be made **by three** judges. [7]**Our Rabbis taught** a related Baraita: "The verse states [Deuteronomy 21:2]: **'And your elders and your judges shall go out,** and they shall measure to the cities that are round about the slain corpse.' [8]The plural term **'your elders'** implies that **two** judges are needed. [9]The plural term **'your judges'** implies that another **two** judges are required, bringing the total to four. [10]And since **a court may not comprise an even number** of judges, **we** must **add to** these four **one other**

[1]וְאָמְרִי לָהּ: לָא מֵחֲמִיסִין, וְלָא מִטּוּרְמִיסִין.
[2]רַבִּי אַבָּהוּ כִּי הֲוָה אָתֵי מִמְּתִיבְתָּא לְבֵי קֵיסָר, [3]נָפְקִי מַטְרוֹנִיתָא דְּבֵי קֵיסָר וּמְשַׁרְיָין לֵיהּ: [4]"רַבָּה דְּעַמֵּיהּ, מַדְבְּרָנָא דְּאוּמָּתֵיהּ, בּוּצִינָא דִּנְהוֹרָא, [5]בְּרִיךְ מְתָיָיךְ לִשְׁלָם".
[6]"עֲרִיפַת עֶגְלָה בִּשְׁלֹשָׁה". [7]תָּנוּ רַבָּנַן: "'וְיָצְאוּ זְקֵנֶיךָ וְשֹׁפְטֶיךָ'. [8]'זְקֵנֶיךָ' — שְׁנַיִם. [9]'שֹׁפְטֶיךָ' שְׁנַיִם. [10]וְאֵין בֵּית דִּין שָׁקוּל, מוֹסִיפִין עֲלֵיהֶן עוֹד אֶחָד.

LITERAL TRANSLATION

[1]And some say: Not *ḥamisin* and not *turmisin*.

[2]When Rabbi Abbahu would come from the Academy to the house of the emperor, [3]the matrons of the house of the emperor would come out and sing to him: [4]"Master of his nation, leader of his people, bright light, [5]may your coming be blessed in peace."

[6]"Breaking the neck of the heifer by three." [7]Our Rabbis taught: "'And your elders and your judges shall go out.' [8]'Your elders' — two. [9]'Your judges' — two. [10]And a court may not be an even number, [so] we add to them another one.

RASHI

חמיסין — חמסין, שמונעין מלומר טעמי תורה. **טורמיסין** — לא איתפרש. **רבה דעמיה** — נשיא בעמיו. **מדברנא** — מנהיג, על שם שהיה פרנס וקרוב למלכות. **בוצינא דנהורא** — על שם שהיה גדול בנוי, כדאמרינן ב"השוכר את הפועלים" (בבא מציעא פד,ב) שופריה דרבי אבהו מעין שופריה דיעקב אבינו. **בריך מתייך** — ברוך בואך.

NOTES

unflattering epithets, but it is not clear exactly what they mean. Our commentary follows Rashi, who interprets *sarmisin* as a derivation of the root סרס, which means "to pervert"; *sarmitin,* which is related to סְמַרְטוּט — "a rag," refers to people who have nothing worthwhile to say; *hamisin* comes from חָמָס, "extortion," and refers to people who refuse to explain their positions. In a parallel Talmudic discussion (*Ketubot* 17a), *Rashi* explains *ḥamisin* as related to חָמֵשׁ, meaning "five," referring to people who know only one-fifth of the reasoning. *Rashi* does not elucidate *turmisin,* but a marginal note inserted in his commentary explains that it is a variant of the word *tulmisin,* which appears in the Jerusalem Talmud (chapter 7 of *Ketubot*) as synonymous with base, vulgar people.

Arukh cites a Geonic tradition according to which *sarmisin* derives from the root סכסך, "to entangle"; *sarmitin* comes from סרטט, "to underscore," referring to people who do not express themselves clearly; *ḥamisin* comes from the root חמס, "to seize," referring to people who are impatient; and *turmisin* comes from תּוּרְמוּס, a very bitter legume that required special preparation before it could be eaten.

HALAKHAH

עֲרִיפַת עֶגְלָה Breaking the neck of the heifer. "Measurement of the distance between the corpse and the closest town, which precedes the breaking of the neck of the heifer, must be done by three judges selected from the Sanhedrin, following Rabbi Yehudah, (either because in general the law is in accordance with Rabbi Yehudah against Rabbi Shimon [*Kesef Mishneh*], or because the Jerusalem Talmud rules here in accordance with his view [*Leḥem Mishneh*]. The neck of the heifer must be broken in the presence of the judges of the city closest to the corpse.

[1]הֲרֵי כָּאן חֲמִשָּׁה; [2]דִּבְרֵי רַבִּי יְהוּדָה. [3]רַבִּי שִׁמְעוֹן אוֹמֵר: 'זְקֵנֶיךָ' — שְׁנַיִם, [4]וְאֵין בֵּית דִּין שָׁקוּל — מוֹסִיפִין עֲלֵיהֶם עוֹד אֶחָד. [5]הֲרֵי כָּאן שְׁלֹשָׁה".

[6]וְרַבִּי שִׁמְעוֹן, הַאי "שֹׁפְטֶיךָ" מַאי עָבֵיד לֵיהּ? [7]הַהוּא מִיבָּעֵי לֵיהּ לִמְיוּחָדִין שֶׁבְּשׁוֹפְטֶיךָ.

[8]וְרַבִּי יְהוּדָה? [9]מִ"זְּקֵנֵי" "זְקֵנֶיךָ" נָפְקָא.

[10]וְרַבִּי שִׁמְעוֹן? [11]אִי מִ"זִּקְנֵי", [12]הֲוָה אָמִינָא: זִקְנֵי הַשּׁוּק, [13]כָּתַב רַחֲמָנָא "זְקֵנֶיךָ". [14]וְאִי כְּתִיב, "זְקֵנֶיךָ" [15]הֲוָה אָמִינָא: סַנְהֶדְרִי קְטַנָּה. [16]כָּתַב רַחֲמָנָא, "וְשֹׁפְטֶיךָ" — [17]מִמְּיוּחָדִין שֶׁבְּשׁוֹפְטֶיךָ.

[18]וְרַבִּי יְהוּדָה? [19]גָּמַר "זִקְנֵי" "זִקְנֵי" [20]מִ"וְסָמְכוּ זִקְנֵי הָעֵדָה אֶת יְדֵיהֶם". [21]מַה לְהַלָּן

LITERAL TRANSLATION

[1]Here are five; [2][these are] the words of Rabbi Yehudah. [3]Rabbi Shimon says: 'Your elders' — two. [4]And a court may not be [composed] of an even number, [so] we add to them another one. [5]Here are three."

[6]And Rabbi Shimon, what does he do with "your judges"? [7]That he needs for the distinguished among your judges.

[8]And Rabbi Yehudah? [9][This] emerges from "elders" "your elders."

[10]And Rabbi Shimon? [11]If from "elders," [12]I might have said: The elders of the market, [13][therefore] the Torah (lit., "the Merciful") wrote, "your elders." [14]And if it was written, "your elders," [15]I might have said: A Lesser Sanhedrin. [16][Therefore] the Torah wrote, "and your judges" — [17]from the distinguished among your judges.

[18]And Rabbi Yehudah? [19]He learned "elders" "elders" [20]from "and the elders of the congregation shall place their hands." [21]Just as there

TRANSLATION AND COMMENTARY

judge, [1]so that **behold** we have **here five** judges in all. [2]These are **the words of Rabbi Yehudah.** [3]But **Rabbi Shimon** disagrees and **says: 'Your elders'** — implies that **two** judges are needed. [4]**And** since **a court may not comprise** an **even** number of judges, **we** must **add to** these two **one other** judge, [5]so that **behold** we have **here three** judges in all."

וְרַבִּי שִׁמְעוֹן [6]The Gemara asks: **And Rabbi Shimon, what does he do with that** additional plural term in the verse, **"your judges"?** [7]According to Rabbi Shimon, the term "your judges" **is needed** to teach us that those chosen to carry out these measurements must be from **the** most **distinguished among your judges,** members of the Great Sanhedrin.

וְרַבִּי יְהוּדָה [8]**And** from where does **Rabbi Yehudah** learn that the participating judges must be members of the Great Sanhedrin? [9]**From** the fact that the verse could have read **"elders,"** but instead reads **"your elders,"** **it emerges** that not just any elders are qualified for this responsibility; rather, they must be "your elders," chosen among the members of the Great Sanhedrin who are judges over all of you.

וְרַבִּי שִׁמְעוֹן [10]**And** why does **Rabbi Shimon** not accept Rabbi Yehudah's argument? [11]**If** the verse had read **"elders"** instead of "your elders," [12]**I might have said** that it refers to any group of elders, even those **elders of the market** who are not judges at all. [13]Therefore, **the Torah wrote: "your elders"** — implying that they must be recognized by the community as elders, having been appointed as judges. [14]**And if it had** simply been **written "your elders,"** [15]**I might have said** that even elders sitting on **a Lesser Sanhedrin** could carry out these measurements. [16]Therefore, **the Torah wrote: "And your judges,"** implying that the participating elders must come [17]**from the** most **distinguished among your judges,** those numbered among the Great Sanhedrin.

וְרַבִּי יְהוּדָה [18]**And** how does **Rabbi Yehudah** counter this argument? [19]According to Rabbi Yehudah, the need to employ members of the Great Sanhedrin in this task is **deduced** from a *gezerah shavah* (verbal analogy) between the word **"elders"** as it appears in our verse and the word **"elders"** [20]**from** the verse in Leviticus (4:15): **"And the elders of the congregation shall lay their hands** on the head of the animal." [21]**Just**

BACKGROUND

כָּתַב רַחֲמָנָא וְשֹׁפְטֶיךָ **The Torah wrote "and your judges."** Rabbi Shimon understands that "your elders" and "your judges" refer to the same people, who are both elders and judges, or, in other words, the chief Sages of the generation, the members of the Great Sanhedrin. According to this approach, the conjunction in "and your judges" is not meant to include other people but rather to ascribe two different titles to the Sages.

RASHI

מיוחדים שבשופטיך — שיהו מזקני סנהדרי גדולה. **מה להלן מיוחדין שבעדה** — כדפרישית לעיל סנהדרין (יג,ב).

NOTES

זִקְנֵי הַשּׁוּק **Elders of the market.** *Ran* understands this term as referring to ordained Sages who are not members of a Sanhedrin.

HALAKHAH

מְיוּחָדִין שֶׁבְּשׁוֹפְטֶיךָ **The distinguished among your judges.** "The five judges who measure the distance between the corpse and the closest city must be members of the Great Sanhedrin." (*Rambam, Sefer Nezikin, Hilkhot Rotze'aḥ* 9:1.)

According to *Radbaz, Rambam* maintains that the breaking of the neck of the heifer itself needs five judges from the Sanhedrin, and the measurements must be made by the entire Sanhedrin," following Rabbi Eliezer ben Ya'akov. (*Rambam, Sefer Shofetim, Hilkhot Sanhedrin* 5:5.)

TRANSLATION AND COMMENTARY

as there, in Leviticus, the reference is specifically to those elders who are counted among **the** most **distinguished of the congregation,** i.e., the Great Sanhedrin (see above, 13b), [1]**so too here**, only those who qualify as **the** most **distinguished among your elders,** members of the Great Sanhedrin, may carry out the measurements attendant to breaking the neck of the heifer.

אִי יָלֵיף [2]The Gemara raises a question: **If** Rabbi Yehudah **learns** this one detail from a verbal analogy between our passage and the passage in Leviticus, [3]then **let him learn all** the details pertaining to this measurement, including the number of judges needed to carry it out, **from** the passage in Leviticus! Just as five judges are needed for that laying of hands, so too should five judges be required to measure the distance to the closest town. [4]**Why,** then, according to Rabbi Yehudah, **do I have** to derive this detail from the words **"your elders and your judges"**?

אֶלָּא [5]**Rather**, it must be concluded that Rabbi Yehudah did not in fact deduce anything through verbal analogy between these two passages. Insofar as requiring members of the Sanhedrin to carry out the necessary measurements, Rabbi Yehudah agrees with Rabbi Shimon that this requirement is derived from the term "your judges" in the verse itself. Although originally Rabbi Yehudah was said to have derived from this term the need to add an additional two judges to the delegation, [6]it is now evident that according to him **the** extraneous letter **"vav,"** which appears as a prefix in the word וְשֹׁפְטֶיךָ, **"and your judges," is** the source **for** increasing **the number** of judges.

וְרַבִּי שִׁמְעוֹן [7]**And** what does **Rabbi Shimon** do with this extraneous vav? [8]Rabbi Shimon **does not interpret the vav** as having any exegetical significance.

אֶלָּא מֵעַתָּה [9]The Gemara now raises a question against both Rabbi Yehudah and Rabbi Shimon: **Now, however,** that you both have identified the plural terms "your elders" and "your judges" as bases for deriving the requisite number of judges needed to carry out the measurements, the additional appearance in the same verse of two plural verbs should serve to inflate the number even further: [10]The plural form of **"and they** [the elders and judges] **shall go out"** should be understood as implying an additional **two** judges, [11]as should the plural form of **"and they shall measure"** imply another **two** judges. [12]Thus, **according to Rabbi Yehudah,** who until now has maintained that we require five judges, **nine** judges should actually be needed; [13]and **according to Rabbi Shimon,** who only required three until now, **seven** should be needed!

הַהוּא מִיבָּעֵי לֵיהּ [14]The Gemara answers: **Those** two verbs **are** actually **needed for** the purpose of teaching us other details regarding the necessary measurement, for instance **what was taught** in the following Baraita: [15]"The verse states: **'And they shall go out'** — thereby implying that the judges themselves, **and not their agents,** must go out to make the measurements. [16]The verse continues: **'And they shall measure** the distances to the cities that are in the area of the slain corpse' — implying that the measurement is mandatory under all circumstances, **even if** the corpse **was found** [14B] **close to a** particular **city,** [17]**it is** still

מְיוּחָדִין שֶׁבָּעֵדָה — [1]אַף כָּאן מְיוּחָדִין שֶׁבִּזְקֵנֶיךָ.
[2]אִי יָלֵיף, [3]לֵילַף כּוּלָּהּ מֵהָתָם.
[4]"זְקֵנֶיךָ" "וְשֹׁפְטֶיךָ" לָמָּה לִי?
[5]אֶלָּא, [6]וי"ו "וְשֹׁפְטֶיךָ" לְמִנְיָינָא.
[7]וְרַבִּי שִׁמְעוֹן? [8]וי"ו לָא דָּרֵישׁ.
[9]אֶלָּא מֵעַתָּה, [10]"וְיָצְאוּ" — שְׁנַיִם; [11]"וּמָדְדוּ" — שְׁנַיִם.
[12]לְרַבִּי יְהוּדָה — הֲרֵי תִּשְׁעָה;
[13]לְרַבִּי שִׁמְעוֹן — שִׁבְעָה!
[14]הַהוּא מִיבָּעֵי לֵיהּ לְכִדְתַנְיָא:
[15]"'וְיָצְאוּ' — הֵן וְלֹא שְׁלוּחָן.
[16]'וּמָדְדוּ' — שֶׁאֲפִילּוּ נִמְצָא [14B] בַּעֲלִיל לָעִיר, [17]צָרִיךְ

LITERAL TRANSLATION

the distinguished among the congregation, [1]so too here the distinguished among your elders.

[2]If he learns, [3]let him learn it all from there. [4]Why do I need "your elders and your judges"?

[5]Rather, [6]the vav of "and your judges [וְשׁוֹפְטֶיךָ]" is for the number.

[7]And Rabbi Shimon? [8]He does not expound the vav.

[9]Now, however, [10]"and they shall go out" — two; [11]"and they shall measure" — two. [12]According to Rabbi Yehudah — nine; [13]according to Rabbi Shimon — seven!

[14]That he needs for that which was taught: [15]"'And they shall go out' — they and not their agents. [16]'And they shall measure' — even if he was found [14B] in clear [proximity] to a city, [17]it is necessary

BACKGROUND

אֶלָּא מֵעַתָּה וְיָצְאוּ שְׁנַיִם **But from now and two went out.** According to the approach explained in the beginning of the chapter (page 4a), the repetition of a noun or a verb has significance for the number of people involved, and every time such a word is added, it is a hint that another one or two people are added.

RASHI

ליגמריה לכולה מילתא — ואפילו מניינא דחמשה מהתם תיפוק, דהא תניא לעיל (סנהדרין יג): "וסמכו" — שנים, "זקני" — שנים. **אלא** — לעולם לא גמר גזירה שוה, "ושופטיך" למיוחדין איצטריך, ומניינא — מרבויא דוי"ו, הכי גרסינן: אלא וי"ו ד"ושופטיך" למניינא, ורבי שמעון וי"ו לא דריש. **בעליל לעיר** — במפורסם לכל שקרוב הוא לעיר זו מכל עיירות.

NOTES

אֲפִילּוּ נִמְצָא בַּעֲלִיל **Even if he was found in clear proximity.** Even if it is clear to all which city the corpse is closest to,

TRANSLATION AND COMMENTARY

necessary for the judges **to engage in measuring** the distances between them."

מַתְנִיתִין [1]**Our Mishnah is not in accordance with** the following **Tanna,** [2]**for it was taught** in a Baraita: **"Rabbi Eliezer ben Ya'akov says:** The verse states: [3]**'And your elders and your judges shall go out.'** [4]**'Your elders' — this is** a reference to members of **the Sanhedrin,** who must go out and measure the distance between the corpse and the closest town. [5]**'And your judges' — this is** a reference to **the king and the High Priest,** who must also participate in the measuring. [6]We know that **a king** is called a judge, **for it is written** [Proverbs 29:4]: [7]**'The king by justice establishes the land.'** [8]We also know that the **High Priest** is considered a judge, **for it is written** [Deuteronomy 17:9]: [9]**'And you shall come to the Levite priests and to the judge** who shall be in those days' — the judge in this verse alluding to the High Priest." Our Mishnah does not mention the participation of the king and the High Priest, apparently in disagreement with the view of Rabbi Eliezer ben Ya'akov.

אִיבַּעֲיָא לְהוּ [10]The following question **was asked of the** Sages discussing this matter: [11]**Does Rabbi Eliezer ben Ya'akov disagree** with our Mishnah **about** only **one** issue, [12]**or does he disagree about two** issues? [13]That is, should we say that **he disagrees** with our Mishnah only **about the king and the High Priest** participating in the measuring, [14]**but regarding the** number of **Sanhedrin** members who are required to participate in this measuring as well, [15]he maintains **either like Rabbi Yehudah** that five are needed, **or like Rabbi Shimon** that only three are needed? [16]**Or perhaps** we should say that Rabbi Eliezer ben Ya'akov **disagrees** with our Mishnah **also about the** number of **Sanhedrin** members who must participate in the measuring, [17]and we should understand him **as** if **he said** that **we need the entire Sanhedrin** to go out and make the necessary measurements?

אָמַר רַב יוֹסֵף [18]**Rav Yosef said: Come and hear** an answer to this question from the following Baraita that deals with the laws pertaining to a "rebellious elder" — the title applied to any ordained Rabbi who instructs others to comport themselves in a way that contradicts an earlier decision rendered by a majority of the Sanhedrin (see Deuteronomy 17:8-13): [19]**"If a** Sage **found** members of the Sanhedrin **at Bet Pagei** [a Jerusalem suburb], rather than in the Temple Chamber that served as their permanent seat in Jerusalem,

לַעֲסוֹק בִּמְדִידָה״.
[1]מַתְנִיתִין דְּלָא כִּי הַאי תַּנָּא,
[2]דְּתַנְיָא: ״רַבִּי אֱלִיעֶזֶר בֶּן יַעֲקֹב
אוֹמֵר: [3]׳וְיָצְאוּ זְקֵנֶיךָ וְשֹׁפְטֶיךָ׳.
[4]׳זְקֵנֶיךָ׳ — זוֹ סַנְהֶדְרִין.
[5]׳וְשֹׁפְטֶיךָ׳ — זֶה מֶלֶךְ וְכֹהֵן
גָּדוֹל. [6]מֶלֶךְ, דִּכְתִיב: [7]׳מֶלֶךְ
בְּמִשְׁפָּט יַעֲמִיד אָרֶץ׳. [8]כֹּהֵן
גָּדוֹל, דִּכְתִיב: [9]׳וּבָאתָ אֶל
הַכֹּהֲנִים הַלְוִיִּם וְאֶל הַשֹּׁפֵט׳״.
[10]אִיבַּעֲיָא לְהוּ: [11]רַבִּי אֱלִיעֶזֶר
בֶּן יַעֲקֹב בַּחֲדָא פָּלֵיג, [12]אוֹ
בְּתַרְתֵּי פָּלֵיג? [13]בְּמֶלֶךְ וְכֹהֵן
גָּדוֹל פָּלֵיג, [14]אֲבָל בְּסַנְהֶדְרִי
[15]אִי כְּרַבִּי יְהוּדָה אִי כְּרַבִּי
שִׁמְעוֹן. [16]אוֹ דִילְמָא, בְּסַנְהֶדְרִי
נַמִי פָּלֵיג, [17]דְּאָמַר: כּוּלָּהּ
סַנְהֶדְרִי בָּעֵינַן!
[18]אָמַר רַב יוֹסֵף: תָּא שְׁמַע:
[19]״מְצָאָן אַבֵּית פָּגֵי וְהִמְרָה

LITERAL TRANSLATION

to engage in measuring."

[1]Our Mishnah is not in accordance with this Tanna, [2]for it was taught: "Rabbi Eliezer ben Ya'akov says: [3]'And your elders and your judges shall go out.' [4]'Your elders' — this is the Sanhedrin. [5]'And your judges' — this is the king and the High Priest. [6]A king, for it is written: [7]'The king by justice establishes the land.' [8]The High Priest, for it is written: [9]'And you shall come to the Levite priests and to the judge.'"

[10]It was asked of them: [11]Does Rabbi Eliezer ben Ya'akov disagree about one, [12]or does he disagree about two? [13]He disagrees about the king and the High Priest, [14]but regarding the Sanhedrin, [15][he maintains] either like Rabbi Yehudah or like Rabbi Shimon. [16]Or perhaps, he disagrees as well about the Sanhedrin, [17]for he said: We need the entire Sanhedrin!

[18]Rav Yosef said: Come [and] hear: [19]"If he found them at Bet Pagei and rebelled

RASHI

בית פגי — מקום לפנים מן חומת העיר, ונדון כירושלים לכל דבריו. **מצאן** — זקן ממרא לסנהדרין חוץ ללשכת הגזית שהיתה בהר הבית.

BACKGROUND

בֵּית פָּגֵי Bet Pagei. There are various opinions regarding the identity and location of Bet Pagei. Moreover, the name does not always refer to the same place, for there were apparently two places with the same name. Some authorities believe that the Bet Pagei mentioned here and in other sources derived its name from the Greek word φαγω, *phago*, meaning to eat. Thus Bet Pagei would be the place where it was permitted to eat the sacrifices, i.e., within the walls of Jerusalem (*Ravam*). In other sources it seems that it was the name of a neighborhood of Jerusalem, which might have been called Bet Pagei because of the figs (פגים) growing there, and that it was outside the walls of Jerusalem.

NOTES

formal measurements of the distance between the corpse and the closest city must still be taken, for that will give the matter a certain notoriety which might lead to the discovery of witnesses and a solution to the crime (*Meiri*).

HALAKHAH

צָרִיךְ לַעֲסוֹק בִּמְדִידָה **It is necessary to engage in measuring.** "Even if a particular city is clearly the closest to the corpse, we are still commanded to measure the distance between the corpse and all other surrounding settlements." (*Rambam, Sefer Nezikin, Hilkhot Rotze'aḥ* 9:1.)

TRANSLATION AND COMMENTARY

and rebelled against them by promoting a practice that ran contrary to their teachings, [1]**it is possible** to think that **his rebellion should be** considered **a** formal **rebellion** to the extent that he is liable to the death penalty for his actions. [2]Therefore **the Torah states** [Deuteronomy 17:8]: **'And you shall arise and go up to the place** which the Lord your God shall choose' in order to seek there justice and guidance, [3]thereby **teaching that the place** itself that was divinely chosen as the seat of the Sanhedrin, the Chamber of Hewn Stone in the Temple precinct, **determines** the liability of any elder who contradicts a decision issued there. Hence, if the Sanhedrin reached a decision while sitting outside its appointed headquarters, any Sage who subsequently rebels against that decision is exempt from punishment." [4]In the case addressed by the above Baraita, **how many** members of the Sanhedrin were there **that went out** and convened in Bet Pagei? [5]**If you should say** that only **a few of them** convened there, leaving a majority of the Sanhedrin in their official chamber, why should the rebellious Sage be held accountable for contradicting their decision? [6]**Perhaps those** members of the Sanhedrin **who are** still **inside** the Temple precinct, and who constitute a majority, **think as he does!** [7]**Rather, it is obvious that all** the members **of** the Sanhedrin **went out** and convened in Bet Pagei.[8]Now, **for what** reason would the members of the Sanhedrin leave their Temple Chamber? [9]**If you should say** that they left **for** the sake of attending to **an optional matter** unrelated to their ritual duty, [10]**may** the entire Sanhedrin indeed **go out** of their chamber for such a reason? [11]**But surely it is written** (Song of Songs 7:3): **"Your navel is like a rounded goblet, that never lacks blended wine"!** Elsewhere (*Sanhedrin* 37a), the Gemara interprets this to mean that the seventy-one member Sanhedrin, which sits in a semi-circular formation resembling a rounded goblet, must never be reduced to less than one-third of its membership (twenty-three members), one-third being the percentage of pure wine found in the

עֲלֵיהֶן, [1]יָכוֹל תְּהֵא הַמְרָאָתוֹ הַמְרָאָה. [2]תַּלְמוּד לוֹמַר: ׳וְקַמְתָּ וְעָלִיתָ אֶל הַמָּקוֹם׳, [3]מְלַמֵּד שֶׁהַמָּקוֹם גּוֹרֵם. [4]דְּנַפוּק כַּמָּה? [5]אִילֵימָא מִקְצָתָן, [6]דִּילְמָא הָנָךְ דְּאִיכָּא גַּוָּאֵי קַיְימִי כְּוָותֵיהּ, [7]אֶלָּא, פְּשִׁיטָא דְּנַפּוּק כּוּלְּהוּ. [8]לְמַאי? [9]אִילֵימָא לִדְבַר הָרְשׁוּת — [10]מִי מָצוּ נָפְקִי? [11]וְהָכְתִיב: ״שָׁרְרֵךְ אַגַּן הַסַּהַר אַל יֶחְסַר

LITERAL TRANSLATION

against them, [1]it is possible his rebellion is a rebellion. [2][Therefore] the Torah states: 'And you shall arise and go up to the place,' [3]teaching that the place determines." [4]How many [were there] that went out? [5]If you should say a few of them, [6]perhaps those who are inside maintain like him. [7]Rather, it is obvious that all of them went out. [8]For what? [9]If you should say for an optional matter — [10]may they go out? [11]But surely it is written: "Your navel is like a rounded goblet, that never lacks

RASHI

יכול תהא המראתו המראה — לידון בחנק. **אילימא** — דנפוק מקצתן והורו אותן שבחוץ והמרה על דבריהם, מאי איריא מקום גורם תיפוק ליה דפטור משום דילמא הנך דבלשכה, כוותיה סבירא להו. **שררך אגן הסהר** — כתיב, ודרשינן ב״אחד דיני ממונות״ סנהדרין (לז,א): ״אל יחסר המזג״, אם נצרך אחד מהן לצאת, אם יש שם עשרים ושלשה כנגד סנהדרי קטנה — יוצא, ואם לאו — אינו יוצא.

BACKGROUND

שָׁרְרֵךְ אַגַּן הַסַּהַר "Your navel is like a round goblet." All of the Song of Songs has been interpreted, from early times, as an allegory of the Jewish people, with references to various events and individuals. This verse, then, is interpreted as referring to the Great Sanhedrin. The word שָׁרְרֵךְ is taken as שרים, or rulers, and אַגַּן הַסַּהַר means "sitting in a half-circle," like the crescent moon (סַהַר). The verse continues, אַל יֶחְסַר הַמָּזֶג — "let mixed wine not be lacking," here read to mean, "let no more of them be missing from their seats than the proportion of wine with water," normally two parts water to one part wine. Hence, when the Sanhedrin was in session (but not actually deliberating a case), at least a third of the members had to be present, i.e., approximately twenty-three, who themselves could constitute a Lesser Sanhedrin.

NOTES

דִּילְמָא הָנָךְ דְּאִיכָּא גַּוָּאֵי **Perhaps those who are inside.** Granted that the rebellious elder is not held culpable if he contradicted a decision reached by only a minority of the Sanhedrin, but why should we presume that it was the entire Sanhedrin that convened in Bet Pagei and whose decision he contradicted? It would seem to be sufficient for even a majority of the Sanhedrin to have convened there and issued a ruling in order for his act of dissent to be considered rebellious! *Remah* explains that, so long as a significant minority of the Sanhedrin were not present, any decision reached by the majority could not be considered authoritative, since the minority may have persuaded them to decide otherwise in the course of deliberations. Thus, the rebellious elder would not have been liable for his actions at Bet Pagei unless it was the entire Sanhedrin that had convened there and issued a ruling.

HALAKHAH

מְלַמֵּד שֶׁהַמָּקוֹם גּוֹרֵם **Teaching that the place determines.** "If a Sage found the members of the Sanhedrin outside the Chamber of Hewn Stone, and rebelled against them, he is exempt from the death penalty, for the verse states: 'And you shall arise and go up to the place,' which teaches that the place where the Sanhedrin sits determines the rebellious elder's liability." (*Rambam, Sefer Shofetim, Hilkhot Mamrim* 3:7.)

לִדְבַר הָרְשׁוּת **For an optional matter.** "It is not necessary for all seventy-one members of the Great Sanhedrin to remain in their place in the Temple at all times. When it is necessary for them all to be there, they must all assemble. But at other times, any member who has personal business to attend to may leave, but only after he is certain that at least twenty-three members remain. If twenty-three are not present, he must wait for others to return before taking leave." (*Rambam, Sefer Shofetim, Hilkhot Sanhedrin* 3:2.)

הַמָּזֶג״. [1]אֶלָּא פְּשִׁיטָא לִדְבַר מִצְוָה. [2]הֵיכִי דָּמֵי? [3]לָאו לִמְדִידַת עֶגְלָה, [4]וְרַבִּי אֱלִיעֶזֶר בֶּן יַעֲקֹב הִיא, [5]דְּאָמַר: כּוּלֵּי סַנְהֶדְרִי בָּעֵינַן!

[6]אָמַר לֵיהּ אַבַּיֵי: לֹא. [7]כְּגוֹן שֶׁיָּצְאוּ לְהוֹסִיף עַל הָעִיר וְעַל הָעֲזָרוֹת. [8]כִּדְתְנַן: ״אֵין מוֹסִיפִין עַל הָעִיר וְעַל הָעֲזָרוֹת אֶלָּא בְּבֵית דִּין שֶׁל שִׁבְעִים וְאֶחָד״.

[9]תַּנְיָא כְּוָותֵיהּ דְּרַב יוֹסֵף: [10]״מְצָאָן אַבֵּית פָּאגֵי וְהִמְרָה עֲלֵיהֶן, [11]כְּגוֹן שֶׁיָּצְאוּ לִמְדִידַת עֶגְלָה, [12]וּלְהוֹסִיף עַל הָעִיר וְעַל הָעֲזָרוֹת, [13]יָכוֹל שֶׁתְּהֵא הַמְרָאָתוֹ הַמְרָאָה. [14]תַּלְמוּד לוֹמַר: ׳וְקַמְתָּ וְעָלִיתָ אֶל הַמָּקוֹם׳, [15]מְלַמֵּד שֶׁהַמָּקוֹם גּוֹרֵם״.

[16]״נֶטַע רְבָעִי וּמַעֲשֵׂר שֵׁנִי

LITERAL TRANSLATION

blended wine." [1]Rather, it is obvious [that they left] for a matter of mitzvah. [2]How is it to be considered? [3]Is it not for measuring a heifer, [4]and it is [in accordance with] Rabbi Eliezer ben Ya'akov [5]who said: We need the entire Sanhedrin!

[6]Abaye said to him: No, [7]when they went out to add to the city or to the [Temple] Courtyards, [8]as we have learned: "We do not add to the city or to the [Temple] Courtyards except by a [High] Court of seventy-one."

[9]It was taught in accordance with Rav Yosef: [10]"If he found them at Bet Pagei and rebelled against them, [11]such as when they went out for [the sake of] measuring a heifer, [12]or to add onto the city or to the [Temple] Courtyards, [13]it is possible that his rebellion is a rebellion. [14][Therefore] the Torah states: 'And you shall arise and go up to the place,' [15]teaching that the place determines."

[16]"Fourth-year fruit and second tithe

TRANSLATION AND COMMENTARY

customary blend of wine and water. [1]**Rather, it is obvious** that the Baraita must be referring to a case where the judges left their chamber **for a mitzvah**-related **matter.** [2]Now, **how is** such a case **to be considered?** What circumstances would require the entire Sanhedrin to leave the Temple Chambers? [3]**Is it not** that they left **for** the purpose of **measuring** distances prior to breaking the neck of **a heifer,** [4]**which is** in accordance with **Rabbi Eliezer ben Ya'akov,** [5]**who said** that **we need the entire Sanhedrin** to perform the measurement?

אָמַר לֵיהּ אַבַּיֵי [6]**Abaye said to** Rav Yosef: There is **no** proof from this Baraita that the Sanhedrin in its entirety must participate in the required measurement, for the Baraita could just as well have been referring to a different situation altogether, [7]**such as when** the Sanhedrin **left** its quarters in order **to add** new territory **to the city** of Jerusalem **or to the** Temple **Courtyards,** [8]**as we have learned** in our Mishnah: "**We do not add** new territory **to the city** of Jerusalem **or to the Temple Courtyards except by** act of **a** High **Court of seventy-one** members, the Great Sanhedrin."

תַּנְיָא כְּוָותֵיהּ [9]Moreover, a Baraita **was taught in accordance with** the view of **Rav Yosef:** [10]"**If** a Sage **found** the members of the Sanhedrin **at Bet Pagei and rebelled against them** by promoting a practice that ran contrary to their teachings — and the reason they were outside their chamber was related to a mitzvah, [11]**such as when they left for** the sake of **measuring** distances, which is part of the process that must precede the breaking of the neck of **a heifer,** [12]**or** in order **to add** new territory **to the city** of Jerusalem **or to the Temple Courtyards** — [13]**it is possible** to consider **his rebellion a** formal **one** to the extent that he be liable to the death penalty for his actions. [14]Therefore **the Torah states** [Deuteronomy 17:8]: **'And you shall arise and go up to the place** which the Lord your God shall choose' in order to seek there justice and guidance, [15]thereby **teaching that the place** itself which was divinely chosen as the seat of the Sanhedrin, the Temple precinct, **determines** the liability of any elder who contradicts a decision rendered there."

נֶטַע רְבָעִי [16]We learned in the next clause of our Mishnah that "**fourth-year fruit,** as well as produce

RASHI

על העיר — על ירושלים, וצריך לקדש התוספת בשתי תודות ובשיר, כדאמרינן בשבועות (יד,א).

NOTES

נֶטַע רְבָעִי וּמַעֲשֵׂר שֵׁנִי **Fourth-year fruit and second tithe.** It has been asked: From where do we know that the redemption of fourth-year fruit and second-tithe produce, the precise value of which is not known, requires the assessment of three experts? *Ran* explains that the laws pertaining to the redemption of the second tithe are found in the same Biblical passage as the laws pertaining to the redemption of consecrated property (Leviticus 27), and so an analogy may be drawn between the two: Just as consecrated property must be assessed by three expert

HALAKHAH

מַעֲשֵׂר שֵׁנִי **Second tithe.** "A person who wishes to redeem second-tithe produce may not approximate its quantity, but rather must measure it precisely. If the precise value of the produce is not known, such as in the case of wine which

BACKGROUND

שֶׁאֵין דָּמָיו יְדוּעִין Whose value is not known. Fruit and other produce when intact have a set market price, and a court is not required to determine it. Rather, the normal price is accepted.

יַיִן שֶׁהִקְרִים Wine that soured. When wine is attacked by bacteria, it turns sour, and its surface is covered by a a gray film, which differs in appearance depending on what kind of bacteria have attacked the wine. For that reason, wine that has soured is called wine that has formed a film.

לָקוֹחוֹת Here the word appears in an unusual meaning. Normally a לָקוֹחַ is a client, but in this context the Talmud is clearly referring to professional buyers, people who constantly engage in commerce and can estimate the price of merchandise according to its quality, whether it is choice produce or damaged.

LANGUAGE (RASHI)

דרויי״לא* Its apparent source is the Old French *"de rouil,"* meaning rusty.

שֶׁאֵין דָּמָיו יְדוּעִין בִּשְׁלֹשָׁה״. [1] תָּנוּ רַבָּנַן: אֵיזֶהוּ מַעֲשֵׂר שֵׁנִי שֶׁאֵין דָּמָיו יְדוּעִין? [2] פֵּירוֹת שֶׁהִרְקִיבוּ, וְיַיִן שֶׁהִקְרִים, וּמָעוֹת שֶׁהֶחֱלִידוּ״.

[3] תָּנוּ רַבָּנַן: ״מַעֲשֵׂר שֵׁנִי שֶׁאֵין דָּמָיו יְדוּעִין פּוֹדִין אוֹתוֹ בִּשְׁלֹשָׁה לָקוֹחוֹת, [4] אֲבָל לֹא בִּשְׁלֹשָׁה שֶׁאֵין לָקוֹחוֹת, [5] אֲפִילּוּ נָכְרִי אֶחָד מֵהֶן, אֲפִילּוּ אֶחָד מֵהֶם בְּעָלִים״.

LITERAL TRANSLATION

whose value is not known, by three." [1] Our Rabbis taught: "Which is second tithe whose value is not known? [2] Fruit that rotted, and wine that soured, and coins that rusted."

[3] Our Rabbis taught: "Second tithe whose value is not known — we redeem it through three purchasers, [4] but not through three who are not purchasers, [5] even if one of them is a non-Jew, even if one of them is the owner."

RASHI

הקרים — החמיץ. **החלידו** — *דרויי״לא בלעז. **לקוחות** — סוחרים בקיאים בשומא.

TRANSLATION AND COMMENTARY

of the **second tithe whose value is not known,** must be assessed **by three** experts before the owner can redeem them." As taught in the Bible, one is not allowed to derive any benefit from the fruit produced during a tree's first three years of growth. The harvest of the fourth year can be eaten, but only within the sanctified confines of Jerusalem. If it is technically unfeasible to transport all the fourth-year fruit to Jerusalem, one can "redeem" the fruit by transferring its sanctity onto coins which are equivalent in their value to the worth of the fruit. The fruit, losing its sanctity, becomes permissible to be eaten anywhere, while the redemption money must be taken to Jerusalem and used there to purchase provisions for one's stay, which are then consumed in the holy city. The same applies to the produce set aside as the "second tithe" during the first, second, fourth, and fifth years of the Sabbatical cycle. Like fourth-year fruit, second-tithe produce must either be taken to Jerusalem and eaten there, or "redeemed" in the fashion just mentioned so that the redemption money can be taken to Jerusalem and converted there into edibles. Our Mishnah comes to teach that the redemption value, either of fourth-year fruit or of second-tithe produce whose precise value is not known, must be determined by three who have expertise in the market value of such merchandise. [1] **Our Rabbis taught** a Baraita which clarifies the Mishnah's ruling: **"What is** an example of **second-tithe** produce **whose** precise **value is not known?** [2] **Fruit that has rotted, wine that has become sour, and coins that have rusted** to the point where they perhaps can no longer be circulated. All of these lack a fixed value, and as such must be redeemed in accordance with the assessment of three expert appraisers."

תָּנוּ רַבָּנַן [3] **Our Rabbis taught** a related Baraita: **"Second-tithe produce whose** precise **value is not known — we redeem it through** the assessment of **three** knowledgeable **purchasers** of merchandise, [4] **but not through** the assessment of **three who are not** knowledgeable **purchasers.** The assessment may be made by any three merchants, [5] **even if one of them is a non-Jew,** and **even if one of them is** himself **the owner** of the produce being redeemed."

NOTES

appraisers before it is redeemed, so too must second tithe. This law is then extended to fourth-year fruit by way of an analogy drawn between it and second tithe.

Meiri nevertheless suggests a difference between the appraisal of consecrated property on the one hand and the appraisal of second-tithe produce and fourth-year fruit on the other: Consecrated property must be assessed by three, even if its value is known, while second-tithe produce and fourth-year fruit must only be assessed by three when their value is unknown. In the case of consecrated property, three expert appraisers are always needed, because the property belongs to the Temple treasury, and there is concern that the consecrator might undervalue the property so that he can redeem it at a lower cost to himself. Second-tithe produce and fourth-year fruit, on the other hand, remain the owner's to eat in Jerusalem, and so he does not gain anything by assessing it at less than its actual value.

לָקוֹחוֹת Purchasers of merchandise. *Rashi* explains that the purchasers who appraise second-tithe produce of unknown value are professional merchants expert at determining the market value of produce. *Remah* and *Ran* (see also *Tosafot*) understand them as being ordinary purchasers interested in buying the produce in question. It is assumed that each will try to assess the produce at premium value so as to obtain the option to buy after the produce has been redeemed. Rabbi Yirmiyah's question regarding appraisal by three financial partners supports this interpretation, since, as partners, they might agree among

HALAKHAH

has begun to turn sour or fruit which has begun to rot, he must redeem it in accordance with the assessment of three merchants who are expert at appraising such produce. The assessment may be made by any three merchants, even if one of them is a non-Jew or is himself the owner of the second tithe. The assessment may even be made by a man and his two wives," following the Baraita. (*Rambam, Sefer Zeraim, Hilkhot Ma'aser Sheni* 4:20.)

LITERAL TRANSLATION

[1]בָּעֵי רַבִּי יִרְמְיָה: שְׁלֹשָׁה וּמַטִּילִין לְתוֹךְ כִּיס אֶחָד, מַהוּ? [2]תָּא שְׁמַע: [3]״אִישׁ וּשְׁתֵּי נָשָׁיו פּוֹדִין מַעֲשֵׂר שֵׁנִי שֶׁאֵין דָּמָיו יְדוּעִין״.

[4]דִּילְמָא כְּגוֹן רַב פַּפָּא וּבַת אַבָּא סוּרָאָה.

[5]״הַהֶקְדֵּשׁוֹת בִּשְׁלֹשָׁה״. [6]מַתְנִיתִין דְּלָא כִּי הַאי תַּנָּא, דְּתַנְיָא: [7]״רַבִּי אֱלִיעֶזֶר בֶּן יַעֲקֹב אוֹמֵר: אֲפִילּוּ צִינּוֹרָא שֶׁל הֶקְדֵּשׁ צְרִיכָה עֲשָׂרָה בְּנֵי אָדָם לִפְדּוֹתָהּ״.

[8]אֲמַר לֵיהּ רַב פַּפָּא לְאַבַּיֵי: [9]בִּשְׁלָמָא לְרַבִּי אֱלִיעֶזֶר בֶּן יַעֲקֹב דְּאָמַר כִּשְׁמוּאֵל. [10]דְּאָמַר שְׁמוּאֵל: עֲשָׂרָה כֹּהֲנִים כְּתוּבִין

LITERAL TRANSLATION

[1]Rabbi Yirmiyah asked: Three who cast into one purse, what [is the law]?

[2]Come [and] hear: [3]"A man and his two wives may redeem second tithe whose value is not known."

[4]Perhaps such as Rav Pappa and the daughter of Abba of Sura.

[5]"Consecrated objects by three." [6]Our Mishnah is not in accordance with this Tanna, for it was taught: [7]"Rabbi Eliezer ben Ya'akov says: Even a hook of consecrated property needs ten people to redeem it."

[8]Rav Pappa said to Abaye: [9]Granted that Rabbi Eliezer ben Ya'akov [agrees with Shmuel] for he stated in accordance with Shmuel, [10]for Shmuel said: Ten priests are written

TRANSLATION AND COMMENTARY

בָּעֵי רַבִּי יִרְמְיָה [1]**Rabbi Yirmiyah asked: What is the law** with respect to **three** financial partners **who cast** their money **into one purse,** sharing equally their expenses and the profits? Are they three independent people with respect to assessing the redemption value of second-tithe produce, or are they counted as one?

תָּא שְׁמַע [2]**Come and hear** an answer to this question from the following Baraita: [3]**"A man and his two wives may** make the assessment that is necessary in order to **redeem second-tithe** produce **whose** precise **value is not known."** Now, spouses must surely be considered financial partners as well, since the husband provides for his wife in return for any income she may generate. Hence, financial partners are considered as independent of each other with respect to assessing the redemption value of second-tithe produce.

דִּילְמָא [4]**Perhaps** the Baraita is referring to spouses **such as Rav Pappa and the daughter of Abba of Sura.** She supported herself and as a result the two kept separate accounts. Hence it is not surprising that they were regarded as independent entities with respect to assessing the redemption value of second-tithe produce. True financial partners, however, might perhaps not be considered as independent of each other in this regard. Consequently Rabbi Yirmiyah's question is not resolved.

הַהֶקְדֵּשׁוֹת בִּשְׁלֹשָׁה [5]Our Mishnah continues: **"Consecrated objects** designated for use in the Temple can be redeemed by their original owners, but only after having first been assessed **by three** expert appraisers." [6]The Gemara notes that **our Mishnah is not in accordance with** the following **Tanna, for it was taught** in a Baraita: **"Rabbi Eliezer ben Ya'akov says:** [7]**Even a hook of consecrated property needs ten people** to assess its value if one is **to redeem it."**

אֲמַר לֵיהּ [8]**Rav Pappa said to Abaye:** [9]Granted that **Rabbi Eliezer ben Ya'akov agrees with Shmuel, for** the position **he stated** is **in accordance with Shmuel,** [10]**who said: Ten** times the word **"priest"** is found **written in the** Biblical **section** dealing with the redemption of consecrated property (Leviticus 27): Three times in regard to personal valuation (vv. 1-8), three times in regard to the consecration of animals (vv. 9-13), and four times in regard to the consecration of land (vv. 14-25). Corresponding to the ten times that the

RASHI

בת אבא סוראה — אשת רב פפא כדאמר בכתובות פרק ״אלו נערות״ (לט,א): אמר רב פפא: אמרה לי בת אבא סוראה כו׳, והיתה עושה לעצמה. **צינורא** — מזלג קטן שטוין בו זהב. **כשמואל** — לקמן בשמעתין. **עשרה כהנים כתובין** — בפדיון הקדישות: שלשה בפרשת ערכין שהיא ראשונה, ושלשה בפדיון בהמה, וארבעה בקרקעות.

SAGES

רַב פַּפָּא Rav Pappa. A member of the fifth generation of Amoraim in Babylonia, Rav Pappa was the disciple of Rava, but also studied with Abaye and other Sages. His Halakhic and Aggadic teachings are found throughout the Babylonian Talmud, both his dicta and his discussions with his teachers. Very often he debated the Halakhah with his close friend, Rav Huna the son of Rav Yehoshua; he also debated with many other Sages of his generation. Rav Pappa lived in the city of Narash, and after his death Rava established a great yeshivah there. Rav Pappa's teachings are transmitted by many Amoraim of the following generation. According to tradition he died in the year 372 and was over seventy years old. In his youth he owned a small farm and also engaged in commerce, but later turned to the manufacture of alcoholic beverages and became a wealthy man. His first wife was the daughter of Abba Sura'a, and from that marriage was born his son, Mar bar Rav Pappa, who was one of the Sages of the following generation.

BACKGROUND

צִינּוֹרָא Hook. This refers to a kind of fork or metal rod bent in a hook at the end. A big one was used in the Temple to push large pieces of sacrificial meat into the fire on the altar. Smaller ones are used for knitting and crocheting.

NOTES

themselves not to outbid each other. According to *Rashi,* however, Rabbi Yirmiyah's question appears somewhat irrelevant: What difference does it make whether or not the merchants are partners, as long as they are expert appraisers? Some suggest that *Rashi* agrees with *Remah* and *Ran* that the three must actually want to buy the produce, but nevertheless maintains that they must be expert appraisers as well (*Rabbenu Yonah*).

HALAKHAH

הֶקְדֵּשׁוֹת בִּשְׁלֹשָׁה Consecrated objects must be assessed by three. "If a person wishes to redeem objects which have been consecrated to the Temple, an assessment of the objects must be made by three expert appraisers." (*Rambam, Sefer Hafla'ah, Hilkhot Arkhin* 8:2.)

בַּפָּרָשָׁה. [1]אֶלָּא לְרַבָּנַן, שְׁלֹשָׁה מְנָא לְהוּ? [2]וְכִי תֵּימָא דִּכְתִיב בְּהוּ שְׁלֹשָׁה — [3]קַרְקָעוֹת, דִּכְתִיב בְּהוּ אַרְבָּעָה, תִּיסְגֵּי בְּאַרְבָּעָה! [4]וְכִי תֵּימָא הָכִי נַמִי, [5]אַלְמָה תְּנַן: ״הַקַּרְקָעוֹת תִּשְׁעָה וְכֹהֵן! [6]אֶלָּא מַאי? [7]דְּמַשְׁלְמִי בְּהוּ עֲשָׂרָה. [8]הֶקְדֵּשׁוֹת דְּמַשְׁלְמִי בְּהוּ שִׁיתָּא — [9]לִיבָּעוּ שִׁיתָּא? [10]קַשְׁיָא.

[11]״הָעֲרָכִין כו׳״. [12]מַאי ״עֲרָכִין הַמִּטַּלְטְלִין״? [13]אָמַר רַב גִּידֵּל אָמַר רַב: בְּאוֹמֵר: [14]״עֵרֶךְ כְּלִי זֶה עָלַי״. [15]דְּאָמַר רַב גִּידֵּל אָמַר רַב: [15A] [16]הָאוֹמֵר: ״עֵרֶךְ כְּלִי זֶה עָלַי״, [17]נוֹתֵן דָּמָיו. [18]מַאי טַעֲמָא? [19]אָדָם יוֹדֵעַ שֶׁאֵין עֵרֶךְ

LITERAL TRANSLATION

in the section. [1]However, according to the Rabbis, from where do they [derive] three? [2]And if you say that it is written three [times] in regard to them — [3]land, in regard to which it is written four [times], should be sufficient by four! [4]And if you say so too [it is], [5]why have we learned: "Land — nine and a priest"? [6]Rather what? [7]Because the ten come to completion in them. [8]Consecrated objects in which six come to completion — [9]let them require six!

[10]It is difficult.

[11]"Valuations, etc." [12]What is "movable valuations"? [13]Rav Gidel said in the name of Rav: In regard to one who says: [14]"The value of this utensil is upon me." [15]For Rav Gidel said in the name of Rav: [15A] [16]One who says: "The valuation of this utensil is upon me," [17]contributes its value. [18]What is the reason? [19]A person knows that there is no valuation

TRANSLATION AND COMMENTARY

word "priest" is mentioned in this section, ten experts are required to assess the value of consecrated property. [1]**However,** a question arises **according to the Rabbis** of our Mishnah: **From where do they** derive the idea that only **three** people are needed to assess the value of consecrated objects? [2]**And if you** should wish to **say that** the reason three are needed to assess consecrated objects is because the word "priest" **is written three** times **in regard to** such objects (consecrated animals), there is a difficulty. [3]For if this is the basis for determining how many appraisers are needed, consecrated **land — in regard to which** the word "priest" **is written four** times — **should be considered sufficiently** redeemable only after having been assessed **by four** experts! [4]**And if you** should wish to **say** that indeed, it is **also** the case that only four are needed to assess land, [5]then **why have we learned** otherwise in our Mishnah: "Consecrated **land** is only redeemed by its original owner after having been assessed by ten experts — **nine** ordinary Israelites **and a priest**"? [6]**Rather, what** is the reason, according to the Rabbis, that ten are needed in order to assess land? [7]Perhaps it is **because** the section dealing with the consecration of land is the last section dealing with consecrated property, and **in** that section **the** count of **ten** times that the word "priest" is mentioned **is completed.** But this leads to a difficulty, for the same reasoning can be applied to movable property. Since in the section dealing with movable **property** which had been **consecrated** to the Temple, the section dealing with consecrated animals, the count of **six** times that the word "priest" is mentioned **is completed,** the assessment of movable property which had been consecrated **should require six** people, and not three!

קַשְׁיָא [10]Indeed, **it is difficult** and not at all clear why the Rabbis of our Mishnah maintain that three people are needed to assess the value of consecrated objects.

הָעֲרָכִין [11]We have learned in our Mishnah: "Movable **valuations** must be assessed by three." [12]**What is** meant by **"movable valuations"?** The laws of valuation discussed in the Torah (Leviticus 27:1-8) deal specifically with the valuation of people and not of goods, setting fixed values relative to one's sex and age which a person can pledge to the Temple. How, then, do valuations relate to movable objects or goods? [13]**Rav Gidel said in the name of Rav:** The Mishnah is **referring to one who says:** [14]**"The value of this utensil is** incumbent **upon me** as a contribution to the Temple." In such a case, one must pass on to the Temple treasury the market value of the utensil, [15]**for Rav Gidel said in the name of Rav:** [15A] [16]**One who says: "The** fixed **valuation of this utensil,** I hereby take **upon myself** to contribute to the Temple," [17]**must contribute its** relative market **value** to the Temple treasury. [18]**What is the reason** for this ruling? [19]**A person knows** very well **that there is no** such thing as a fixed **valuation for a utensil,** for valuations were only fixed in the Torah

RASHI

אילימא משום דכתיב בהו — שלשה כהנים בפדיון בהמה, דהיינו פדיון הקדש, והוא הדין לשאר הקדשות. **תסגי בארבע אלמה תנן הקרקעות תשעה וכהן** — אלא משום הכי בעי קרקעות עשרה, משום דפרשה אחרונה היא, וכדשלים פרשת הקרקעות כבר נשלמו עשרה כהנים — ותלמד תחתונה מעליונה. ״לכהן תהיה אחוזתו״ לא ממניינן דלאו בשומא כתב, אלא ״והעריכו הכהן״, ״כערכך הכהן״, ״וחשב לו הכהן״ וכיוצא בהן. **הקדשות** — דהיינו פדיון בהמה טמאה שהיא אמצעית, ומשלמי בה שיתא כהנים, דהא איכתיבא לה פרשת ערכין גבה, ניבעי שיתא. **ערך** — לא שייך גבי כלים אלא באדם, ונותן לפי שניו, כמו שכתוב בפרשה. **האומר ערך כלי זה עלי נותן דמיו** — כמו שהוא שוה, דיודע הוא שאין לומר לשון ערך לכלי, ואין ערכו קצוב, וגמר ואמר לשם דמים, דאין אדם מוציא דבריו לבטלה.

LITERAL TRANSLATION

of a utensil, [1]so he decided and said for whatever value; [2]therefore he contributes its value.
[3]Is this "movable valuations"? [4]He should have [said] "valuations of movable goods"!
[5]Teach: "Valuations of movable goods."
[6]Rav Ḥisda said in the name of Avimi: [7][The Mishnah is speaking] about one who consecrates movable goods for the valuation.
[8]Is this "movable valuations"? [9]He should have [said] "movable goods of valuations"!
[10]Teach: "Movable goods of valuations."
[11]Rabbi Abbahu said: [The Mishnah is speaking] about one who says: "My valuation is upon me." [12][If] a priest came to collect

[1] לִכְלִי, וְגָמַר וְאָמַר לְשׁוּם דָּמִים; [2] מִשּׁוּם הָכִי נוֹתֵן דָּמָיו.
[3] הַאי "עֲרָכִין הַמִּטַּלְטְלִין"? [4] "עֲרָכִין שֶׁל מִטַּלְטְלִין" מִבָּעֲיָא לֵיהּ!
[5] תְּנֵי: "עֲרָכִין שֶׁל מִטַּלְטְלִין".
[6] רַב חִסְדָּא אָמַר אֲבִימִי: [7] בְּמַתְפִּיס מִטַּלְטְלִין לַעֲרָכִין.
[8] הַאי "עֲרָכִין הַמִּטַּלְטְלִין"? [9] "מִטַּלְטְלִין שֶׁל עֲרָכִין" מִיבָּעֵי לֵיהּ!
[10] תְּנֵי: "מִטַּלְטְלִין שֶׁל עֲרָכִין".
[11] רַבִּי אֲבָהוּ אָמַר: בְּאוֹמֵר: "עֶרְכִּי עָלַי". [12] בָּא כֹּהֵן לִגְבּוֹת

RASHI

ערכין המטלטלין – משמע שהערכין מיטלטלין. **במתפיס מטלטלין לערכו** – שאומר: ערכי עלי, ונתחייב ערך הקצוב לפי שניו, והיה לו מטלטלין ואמר: הרי אלו לערכי, וחלה עליהן קדושה ובא לפדותן – צריך שלשה להוציאן מיד הקדש. **רבי אבהו אומר באומר ערכי עלי** – ואינו פורע, ובא כהן למשכנו ומצא לו מטלטלין. והכי קאמר: הערכין – דהיינו ערך אדם, ובא ליתן מטלטלין – נגבין בשלשה שמאין.

TRANSLATION AND COMMENTARY

in regard to human beings. [1]But as people do not utter vows in vain, it must be assumed that the person who made the vow was not careful in his use of language; he **decided** to donate to the Temple, and when **he said** that he wanted to dedicate the utensil's fixed value, he must have been referring **to whatever value** the utensil might possess in the market. [2]**Therefore, he contributed the** utensil's market **value** to the Temple. Our Mishnah teaches that the worth of a utensil whose market value has been pledged to the Temple treasury must be assessed by three experts before it can be redeemed by its original owner and returned to nonsacred use.

הַאי [3]The Gemara notes that explanation does not fit in well with the language of the Mishnah and asks: **Is this** a proper interpretation of the expression **"movable valuations"**? If the Mishnah were indeed referring to such a case, [4]the Tanna **should have** said: **"Valuations of movable goods"!**

תְּנֵי [5]The Gemara answers: Indeed, **teach** the text of the Mishnah with the reading just suggested: **"Valuations of movable goods** [must be assessed] by three."

רַב חִסְדָּא אָמַר [6]The Gemara now proposes an alternative explanation of the language in the Mishnah: **Rav Hisda said in the name of Avimi:** [7]The Mishnah is speaking **about one who** pledges to the Temple a fixed valuation as defined in the Torah with regard to people, but **consecrates** certain **movable goods** in his possession so that they may be given to the Temple in lieu of money **for the valuation** that he pledged.

הַאי [8]The Gemara points out that the language of the Mishnah is problematic according to this explanation as well: **Is this** a proper interpretation of the expression **"movable valuations"?** If the Mishnah were indeed referring to such a case, [9]the Tanna **should have** said: **"Movable goods of valuations"!**

תְּנֵי [10]The Gemara again suggests that the text of the Mishnah be amended so that it **teach: "Movable goods of valuations** [must be assessed] by three."

רַבִּי אֲבָהוּ אָמַר [11]The Gemara offers a third way of understanding the Mishnah: **Rabbi Abbahu said:** The Mishnah is speaking **about one who says: "My** own **valuation,** as defined by the Torah, I hereby take **upon myself** to contribute to the Temple," but does not have available funds to pay his pledge. [12]The Mishnah informs us that **if a priest comes to collect movable goods from him** as payment for his pledge, the

NOTES

בָּא כֹּהֵן לִגְבּוֹת מִמֶּנּוּ מִטַּלְטְלִין **If a priest came to collect movable goods from him.** *Rashash* comments: Rabbi Abbahu's explanation of the Mishnah is problematic, for it suggests that the Mishnah is teaching us a law in regard to vows of valuation which we know to be applicable in all cases of consecration: If a person pledged a sum to the Temple that he was then unable to pay, and a priest came to collect the debt from his movable goods, the goods must be

HALAKHAH

עֲרָכִין הַמִּטַּלְטְלִין **Movable valuations.** "If a person has taken a vow of valuation, and a priest comes to collect the debt from his movable goods, the goods must be assessed by three people," following Rabbi Abbahu. (*Rambam, Sefer Hafla'ah, Hilkhot Arkhin* 8:2.)

מִמֶּנּוּ מִטַּלְטְלִין — בִּשְׁלֹשָׁה,
[1]קַרְקָעוֹת — בַּעֲשָׂרָה.
[2]אָמַר לֵיהּ רַב אַחָא מִדִּיפְתִּי לְרָבִינָא: [3]בִּשְׁלָמָא לְאַפּוּקֵי מֵהֶקְדֵּשׁ [4]בָּעֵינַן שְׁלֹשָׁה, [5]אֶלָּא לְעַיּוּלֵי לְהֶקְדֵּשׁ, [6]שְׁלֹשָׁה לָמָּה לִי?
[7]אָמַר לֵיהּ: סְבָרָא הוּא. [8]מַה לִּי עַיּוּלֵי, מַה לִּי אַפּוּקֵי? [9]אַפּוּקֵי — מַאי טַעֲמָא? [10]דִּילְמָא, טָעֵי. [11]עַיּוּלֵי נַמִי — [12]דִּילְמָא, טָעֵי.
[13]״רַבִּי יְהוּדָה אוֹמֵר כו׳.״ [14]אָמַר לֵיהּ רַב פַּפָּא לְאַבַּיֵּי: בִּשְׁלָמָא לְרַבִּי יְהוּדָה, [15]הַיְינוּ דִּכְתִיב כֹּהֵן. [16]אֶלָּא לְרַבָּנַן, כֹּהֵן לָמָּה לְהוּ?

LITERAL TRANSLATION

from him movable goods — by three. [1]Land — by ten.

[2]Rav Aḥa of Difti said to Ravina: [3]Granted that to remove it from sacred property [4]we need three. [5]But to introduce it into sacred property, [6]why do I need three?

[7]He said to him: It is a commonsense argument. [8]What is it to me removing, what is it to me introducing? [9]Removing — what is the reason? [10]Perhaps, he will err. Introducing too — [11]perhaps, he will err.

[12]"Rabbi Yehudah says, etc." [13]Rav Pappa said to Abaye: [14]It is well according to Rabbi Yehudah, [15]this is [why] "priest" is written. [16]But according to the Rabbis, why according to them [is] "priest" [written]?

TRANSLATION AND COMMENTARY

property must first be assessed **by three** people. [1]And if he comes to collect the debt from **land**, the land must be assessed **by ten** people.

אָמַר לֵיהּ רַב אַחָא [2]**Rav Aḥa of Difti said to Ravina:** [3]**Granted** according to Rav Gidel and Rav Ḥisda, who understand the Mishnah as teaching us that, **to remove** a consecrated object **from** the realm of **sacred property** dedicated to the Temple, [4]**we need three** experts to assess its value — for if the object were not redeemed in accordance with its full value, use of the object would be forbidden. [5]**But** according to Rabbi Abbahu, who understands the Mishnah as teaching us that in order **to introduce** an object **into** the realm of **sacred property,** one needs to first have its value assessed by three experts, [6]**why do I need three** people for this purpose at all?

אָמַר לֵיהּ [7]Ravina **said to** Rav Aḥa: Rabbi Abbahu's interpretation is based on **a commonsense argument:** [8]**What** difference **does it** make **it to me** whether we are **removing** an object from sacred use **or introducing** it into such use? When **removing** an object from sacred use, [9]**what is the reason** that three people are needed to assess its value? [10]**Perhaps** the person redeeming the object **will err** and pay the Temple less than its full value. [11]Similarly, when **introducing** an object into sacred use, three experts are needed to determine the object's true value — for if left to the one consecrating the object, [12]**perhaps he will err** and assess it at more than its value, thereby causing the Temple to receive less than it would have if the pledge had been paid in hard currency.

רַבִּי יְהוּדָה אוֹמֵר [13]We learned in the next clause of the Mishnah: **"Rabbi Yehudah says:** One of the three appraisers must be a priest." [14]**Rav Pappa said to Abaye:** Granted **that according, to Rabbi Yehudah,** who requires a priest to participate in the appraisal, [15]**this is** why the word **"priest" is written** in the Biblical section dealing with the redemption of consecrated property. [16]**But according to the Rabbis** who disagree with Rabbi Yehudah and maintain that we do not require a priest as one of the appraisers, **why** is the word **"priest"** written in the passage?

RASHI

בשלמא לאפוקי מהקדש — כגון דרב גידל ורב חסדא, הוא דבעי שלשה, דכיון דחל עליו הקדש, לא ניפוק עד שיפדנו בשויו. **אלא לעיולי** — כגון דרבי אבהו. **עיולי נמי דילמא טעו** — ויקחנו להקדש ביותר משויו.

NOTES

assessed by three experts, but if the priest came to collect from land, the appraisal requires ten experts. *Rashash* suggests that Rabbi Abbahu's intention was to ascribe two laws to the Mishnah, the first of which is specific to vows of valuation. That law states that, in the event a person cannot pay the full sum fixed by the Torah with regard to pledges of valuation, we appoint three people to assess whether he can at least make partial payment — in accordance with the verse (Leviticus 27:8): "And if he be too poor for the valuation, then he shall present himself before the priest, and the priest shall evaluate him; according to the ability of he that vowed shall the priest evaluate him." In addition to this law, specific to valuations, the Mishnah informs us that the general law of appraisal applied in other cases of consecration (movable goods by three, land by ten) applies here as well.

כֹּהֵן לָמָּה לְהוּ? Why according to the Rabbis is "priest" written? *Remah* notes that this is indeed a problem, but

HALAKHAH

קַרְקָעוֹת — בַּעֲשָׂרָה Land — by ten. "If a person consecrated land and now wishes to redeem it, or if a priest comes to collect a pledge of valuation from a person's land, the land must be assessed by ten people — nine ordinary Israelites and a priest." (*Rambam, Sefer Hafla'ah, Hilkhot Arkhin* 8:2.)

TRANSLATION AND COMMENTARY

קַשְׁיָא [1]Indeed, **it is difficult,** for it is not at all clear why the word "priest" is mentioned in the passage according to the Rabbis who disagree with Rabbi Yehudah.

הַקַּרְקָעוֹת תִּשְׁעָה וְכֹהֵן [2]The next clause of our Mishnah states: "Consecrated **land** must be assessed by ten people — **nine** ordinary Israelites **and a priest.**" [3]From where in Scripture **are these words** derived?

אָמַר שְׁמוּאֵל [4]**Shmuel said: Ten** times we find the word **"priest" written in the** Biblical **section** dealing with the redemption of consecrated property (Leviticus 27:1-25), implying that ten people are required to assess the value of such property. [5]**One** of the appearances of the word "priest" is needed **for** the sake of teaching us the law **itself,** which requires a priest to participate in the appraisal. [6]Each of **the other** nine appearances of the word, however, **comprises** an instance of one **restrictive expression following** another **restrictive expression.** The appearance of the word "priest" is considered to be restrictive insofar as it implies that only a priest — and no other member of the community — may conduct the appraisal. [7]Nevertheless, there is a general rule which states that **one restrictive expression does not follow another restrictive expression** in Scripture **other than for** the sake of **expanding** the implication of the text. Thus, every time the word "priest" repeats itself in the section dealing with consecrated property, it serves to extend the criteria applied to appraisers so as to allow non-priests to participate in the assessment as well. Hence, using the above hermeneutics, [8]we may conclude **that** the assessment of consecrated land can **even** be made **by nine** ordinary **Israelites and one priest.**

מַתְקִיף לָה [9]Rav Huna, the son of Rav Natan, strongly objected to this line of reasoning: [10]Using such principles, **say that five priests and five** ordinary **Israelites** are implied in the verse! For the first time that the word "priest" is mentioned, it serves as a restrictive expression, teaching that the assessor must be a priest. The second time the word appears, it is considered a restrictive expression following another restrictive expression, which according to our rule implies the inclusion of an ordinary Israelite. However, once interpreted as inclusive, we can no longer say that the next appearance of the word qualifies as "following a restrictive expression." Thus, the third appearance of the word "priest" reverts to implying a restriction, so that only a priest can serve as the third assessor. And so it continues, with each new appearance of the word alternating between restrictive and inclusive in its connotation, until eventually all ten references are interpreted in such a way as to imply that half of the assessors must be priests while the other half may be ordinary Israelites.

קַשְׁיָא [11]Once again, the Gemara leaves the question of Scriptural derivation unresolved, concluding that Shmuel's attempt **to explain** it **is** indeed **difficult.**

LITERAL TRANSLATION

[1]It is difficult.

[2]"Land — nine and a priest." [3]From where are these words [derived]?

[4]Shmuel said: Ten "priests" are written in the section. [5]One for itself. [6]The others comprise [one] restrictive expression following [another] restrictive expression, [7]and [one] restrictive expression does not follow [another] restrictive expression other than for expanding, [8]that even nine Israelites and one priest. [9]Rav Huna the son of Rav Natan strongly objected to it: [10]Say five priests and five Israelites.

[11]It is difficult.

קַשְׁיָא.[1]

[2]"הַקַּרְקָעוֹת תִּשְׁעָה וְכֹהֵן". [3]מְנָהֲנֵי מִילֵי? [4]אָמַר שְׁמוּאֵל: "עֲשָׂרָה" כֹּהֲנִים כְּתוּבִין בַּפָּרְשָׁה. [5]חַד לְגוּפֵיהּ. [6]הָנָךְ הָוֵי מִיעוּט אַחַר מִיעוּט, [7]וְאֵין מִיעוּט אַחַר מִיעוּט אֶלָּא לְרַבּוֹת, [8]דַּאֲפִילוּ תִּשְׁעָה יִשְׂרָאֵל וְאֶחָד כֹּהֵן. [9]מַתְקִיף לָהּ רַב הוּנָא בְּרֵיהּ דְּרַב נָתָן: [10]אֵימָא חֲמִשָּׁה כֹּהֲנִים וַחֲמִשָּׁה יִשְׂרְאֵלִים? קַשְׁיָא.[11]

RASHI

חד לגופיה — דניבעי כהן. מיעוט אחר מיעוט — דכולהו ממעטי ישראל. דמשמע כהן ולא ישראל. ואימא חמשה כהנים וחמשה ישראל — בעינן, דקמא לגופיה, ושני לו הוי מיעוט אחר מיעוט ושלישי הדר איצטריך לגופיה דניהוי כהן, דכיון דאיתרבי ליה ממיעוט אחר מיעוט, דאפילו ישראל כי הדר כתב "כהן" — דוקא כתביה — דלאו מיעוט אחר מיעוט הוא, דהא שני לאו מיעוט הוא אלא ריבוי, וכן כולם, חד — דווקא, וחד — הוי מיעוט אחר מיעוט.

NOTES

not a conclusive refutation, for it could be argued that while the appraisal is indeed valid if performed by three ordinary Israelites, the word "priest" teaches that it is still preferable that one of the appraisers be a priest.

מִיעוּט אַחַר מִיעוּט **One restrictive expression following another.** The rationale for this rule of exegesis, as well as its companion rule, that "one inclusive expression following another comes only to restrict," is the subject of some

TRANSLATION AND COMMENTARY

וְאָדָם כַּיּוֹצֵא בָּהֶן [1]We learned in the next clause of our Mishnah: **"And** assessing the value of **a person is similar to** assessing land, insofar as it also requires nine ordinary Israelites and a priest." [2]The Gemara asks: **Is a person**'s body subject to **consecration** like a plot of land?

אָמַר רַבִּי אַבָּהוּ [3]**Rabbi Abbahu said:** The Mishnah is speaking **about one who says:** [4]"The equivalent of **my worth,** I hereby take **upon myself** to contribute to the Temple treasury." [5]**For it was taught** in a Baraita: **"One who says:** [6]'The equivalent of **my worth,** I hereby take **upon myself** to contribute to the Temple treasury,' [7]**they assess him as** if he were **a slave who is sold in the market** in order to determine the amount he is obligated to pay the Temple treasury." [8]**And** our Mishnah comes to teach that this assessment must be made by ten people — nine ordinary Israelites and a priest — for **a slave is likened to land** by virtue of the Biblical verse (Leviticus 25:46). Hence, we apply the same criteria for assessing consecrated land to the appraisal of one who has pledged his worth as a slave.

בָּעֵי רַבִּי אָבִין [9]**Rabbi Avin asked** the following question: If a person's **hair** was **ready to be clipped** and he consecrated it for Temple use, [10]**how many** people must assess the hair in order to determine its value should he now wish to redeem it? The Gemara explains the two sides of the question: [11]**Is** the hair **considered as** if it were already **clipped, and** therefore require assessment **by three,** like any other movable property? [12]**Or is** the hair still **considered as attached** to his person, **and** in need of assessment **by ten,** just like the rest of his body?

תָּא שְׁמַע [13]**Come and hear** a dispute between Tannaim which relates to this question: "If **one consecrates his** non-Jewish **slave** for the benefit of the Temple, [14]**we do not** transgress the laws of *me'ilah* by **using** the slave for our own purposes. The laws of *me'ilah*, which forbid one to derive any benefit from consecrated property, do not apply to land (see *Me'ilah* 18b); and since, as we saw above, a slave is likened to land, it follows that *me'ilah* is inapplicable to slaves as well. [15]**Rabban Shimon ben Gamliel** disagrees and **says: We**

[1]"וְאָדָם כַּיּוֹצֵא בָּהֶן". [2]אָדָם מִי קָדוֹשׁ?

[3]אָמַר רַבִּי אַבָּהוּ: בְּאוֹמֵר: [4]"דָּמַי עָלַי", [5]דְּתַנְיָא: "הָאוֹמֵר: [6]'דָּמַי עָלַי', [7]שָׁמִין אוֹתוֹ כְּעֶבֶד הַנִּמְכָּר בַּשּׁוּק". [8]וְעֶבֶד אִתַּקַּשׁ לְקַרְקָעוֹת.

[9]בָּעֵי רַבִּי אָבִין: שֵׂעָר הָעוֹמֵד לִיגְּזוֹז — [10]בְּכַמָּה? [11]כְּגָזוּז דָּמֵי, וּבִשְׁלֹשָׁה. [12]אוֹ כִּמְחוּבָּר דָּמֵי — וּבַעֲשָׂרָה?

[13]תָּא שְׁמַע: "הַמַּקְדִּישׁ אֶת עַבְדּוֹ, [14]אֵין מוֹעֲלִין בּוֹ. [15]רַבָּן

LITERAL TRANSLATION

[1]"And a person is similar to them." [2]Is a person consecrated?

[3]Rabbi Abbahu said: [The Mishnah is speaking] about one who says: [4]"My worth is upon me," [5]for it was taught: "One who says: [6]'My worth is upon me,' [7]they assess him as a slave who is sold in the market." [8]And a slave is likened to land.

[9]Rabbi Avin asked: Hair ready to be clipped — [10]with how many? [11]Is it considered as clipped, and by three, [12]or is it considered as attached — and by ten?

[13]Come [and] hear: "[If] one consecrates his slave, [14]there is no *me'ilah* in him. [15]Rabban

RASHI

ואדם כיוצא בהן — כקרקעות דבעי נמי תשע, וכהן לשומו. **ועבד איתקש לקרקעות** — "והתנחלתם אותם" (ויקרא כה). **שער העומד ליגזוז** — והקדישו ובא לפדותו בשויו, שעושין משער אדם יפה וקילקלי ושבק. **בגזוז דמי** — והוו להו מטלטלין, ובשלשה. **אין מועלין בו** — דעבד הרי הוא כקרקע, ואין מעילה בקרקע, ובמסכת מעילה (יח,ב) גמר "חטא" "חטא" מתרומה, בפרק "הנהנה".

CONCEPTS

מְעִילָה ***Me'ilah.*** The laws of *me'ilah* deal with the unlawful use of consecrated property. Anyone who derives benefit from consecrated property, or damages it through use, is guilty of *me'ilah*. Intentional *me'ilah* is punishable by death at the hands of Heaven, according to some authorities, and by lashes, according to others. One who commits *me'ilah* unintentionally, or even under duress, must repay the Temple treasury the equivalent of either the loss it sustained through damage to the property or the benefit he gained, in addition to a penalty amounting to one-fifth the value of such loss or benefit. The unintentional offender must also bring a special guilt-offering for having committed his trespass. The laws of *me'ilah* apply to movable goods, but not to land or anything else which is equated to land.

NOTES

discussion. There are those who say that the two rules are nothing more than fiats, possessing no identifiable rationale. Others do identify a rationale: Had the initial expression (be it restrictive or inclusive) not been repeated, its implication would have been taken as binding within the context in which it appears; the fact that it was repeated, however, indicates that its appearance in the text was only routine and not meant to be particularly instructive.

אָדָם מִי קָדוֹשׁ? **Is a person consecrated?** *Tosafot* and others asked: Why did the Gemara not suggest that the Mishnah is referring to one who consecrated his slave, for a slave does qualify as a person who can be consecrated for the

HALAKHAH

הָאוֹמֵר: "דָּמַי עָלַי" **One who says: "My worth upon me."** "If a person pledges his own worth to the Temple treasury, he must pay according to his presumed worth were he to be sold in the market as a slave, as assessed by ten people — nine ordinary Israelites and a priest." (*Rambam, Sefer Hafla'ah, Hilkhot Arkhin* 8:2;1:9.)

הַמַּקְדִּישׁ אֶת עַבְדּוֹ **One who consecrates his slave.** "If someone consecrated his slave for the benefit of the Temple, the slave is not subject to the laws of *me'ilah*. And as long as it remains attached to his body, the slave's hair is also not subject to the laws of *me'ilah*, even if it is ready to be clipped, for it continues to improve in value

LITERAL TRANSLATION

Shimon ben Gamliel says: There is *me'ilah* in his hair." [1]And we have established that it is in regard to hair that is ready to be clipped that they argue. [2]Conclude from this.

[3]Shall we say that these Tannaim are like those Tannaim? [4]For we have learned: "Rabbi Meir says: [5]There are things which are like land, and are not like land. [6]But the Sages do not agree with him. [7]How so? [8][If one says:] 'I handed over to you ten laden vines,' [9]and the other says: 'There are only five,' [10]Rabbi Meir obligates him [to take an oath]. [11]But the Sages say: All that is attached to the ground

שִׁמְעוֹן בֶּן גַּמְלִיאֵל אוֹמֵר: מוֹעֲלִין בִּשְׂעָרוֹ. [1]וְקַיְימָא לָן דְּבִשְׂעָרוֹ הָעוֹמֵד לִיגְזוֹז פְּלִיגִי. [2]שְׁמַע מִינָּהּ.

[3]נֵימָא הָנֵי תַּנָּאֵי כְּהָנֵי תַּנָּאֵי. [4]דִּתְנַן: "רַבִּי מֵאִיר אוֹמֵר: [5]יֵשׁ דְּבָרִים שֶׁהֵן כַּקַּרְקַע וְאֵינָן כַּקַּרְקַע. [6]וְאֵין חֲכָמִים מוֹדִים לוֹ. [7]כֵּיצַד? [8]'עֶשֶׂר גְּפָנִים טְעוּנוֹת מָסַרְתִּי לְךָ', [9]וְהַלָּה אוֹמֵר: 'אֵינָן אֶלָּא חָמֵשׁ', [10]רַבִּי מֵאִיר מְחַיֵּיב. [11]וַחֲכָמִים אוֹמְרִים: כָּל הַמְחוּבָּר לְקַרְקַע

RASHI

מועלים בשערו – דשערו לאו כגופו, והוה ליה כשאר מטלטלין. **העומד ליגזוז** – שכבר שילא פרע וראוי להסתפר. **שמע מינה** – פלוגתא דתנאי הוא, לתנא קמא דאמר: לית בהו מעילה – סבר כמחובר דמי, ולענין פדייה נמי בעי עשרה, ולרבן שמעון – כגזוז דמיא. **דברים שהן בקרקע** – מחוברין לקרקע. **ואינן בקרקע** – אלא כמטלטלין. **רבי מאיר מחייב** – לישבע על השאר שהודה מקצת הטענה, אף על גב דאין נשבעין על הקרקעות כדילפינן ב"שבועת הדיינים" (שבועות מב,א) הכא – כיון דאין צריכין לקרקע דעומדות ליבצר הן, כדמוקי רבי יוסי בר חנינא לפלוגתיה כבצורות דמיין – ונשבעין.

TRANSLATION AND COMMENTARY

do transgress the laws of *me'ilah* when we **use** the slave's **hair."** [1]**And we have established that it is in regard to** a slave's **hair which is ready to be clipped that** the Tannaim **disagree.** According to the Sages, hair which is ready to be clipped is still considered as attached to the slave's body, so it is not subject to the laws of *me'ilah.* Rabban Shimon ben Gamliel maintains that such hair is considered as if it were already clipped, and so it is subject to the laws of *me'ilah,* like any other movable property. [2]We can thus **conclude from** this that the question raised by Rabbi Avin in regard to the status of hair ready to be clipped is the subject of a Tannaitic dispute.

נֵימָא הָנֵי [3]**Shall we say that these Tannaim** who disagree about hair ready to be clipped **are** arguing about the same principle **as** the following **Tannaim?** [4]**For we have learned** elsewhere in the Mishnah (*Shevuot* 42b): **"Rabbi Meir says:** [5]**There are things which are like land, and** yet **are not** legally treated **like land.** [6]**But the Sages do not agree with** Rabbi Meir. [7]**How so? If one person says to another:** [8]**'I handed over to you ten laden vines** to look after. Please return them to me now,' [9]**and the other one says: 'There are only five** such vines,' [10]**Rabbi Meir obligates** the bailee **to take an** oath that he never received the other five vines in question, as is the case whenever one admits to part of a claim brought against him with respect to movable goods. Hence, even though the vines are like land, being attached to the ground, they are not legally treated like land. [11]**But the Sages say: All that is**

NOTES

benefit of the Temple? They answer that had the Mishnah been referring to the case of a consecrated slave, it would have stated so explicitly. Furthermore, the Mishnah states that ten are needed for this assessment, and if the subject of the assessment was a consecrated slave, only three should have been required — for we are taught in the Jerusalem Talmud that the Rabbis were concerned lest a consecrated slave flee before the ten appraisers congregate and thus only required three.

HALAKHAH

(following the first Tanna of the Baraita). Nevertheless, one should refrain from deriving any benefit from a consecrated slave." (*Rambam, Sefer Avodah, Hilkhot Me'ilah* 5:10; *Bet Yosef* in the name of the *Rashbah*; *Meiri.*)

עֶשֶׂר גְּפָנִים טְעוּנוֹת **Ten laden vines.** "If the plaintiff claims grapes or wheat plants that are ready to be harvested, and the defendant admits to part of the claim, and the grapes or wheat plants no longer need to be attached to the soil, the defendant is required to take an oath, just as he would with regard to any other claim involving movable property. But if the grapes or wheat plants still need to be attached to the soil, they are treated like land, and a Torah oath is not administered." (*Rambam, Sefer Mishpatim, Hilkhot To'en VeNit'an* 5:4.)

כָּל הַמְחוּבָּר לְקַרְקַע **All that is attached to the ground.** "Whatever is attached to the ground is considered like land with respect to the laws of acquisition. However, produce which no longer needs to be attached to the ground, such as grapes which are ready to be harvested, should be treated like movable property. *Rema* notes that, according to some authorities, whatever is attached to the ground, even if it no longer needs to be attached, is considered like land with respect to the laws of acquisition." (*Rambam, Sefer Kinyan, Hilkhot Mekhirah* 1:17; *Shulḥan Arukh, Ḥoshen Mishpat* 193:1.)

TRANSLATION AND COMMENTARY

attached to the ground is treated **like land,** and for this reason no oath is necessary." [1]**And Rabbi Yose bar Hanina said**, explaining this dispute: [2]**We are dealing** here **with grapes that are ready to be harvested.** [3]One **master,** Rabbi Meir, **maintained** that once the grapes are ready to be harvested, **they are considered as** if they have **already** been **harvested,** and thus, as is the case with all movable goods, require an oath. [4]**But** the other **master,** the Sages, **maintained** that fully ripened grapes **are not considered as** if they have **already** been **harvested,** since they are still attached to the ground; therefore, they are legally treated like land and do not require an oath."

It would appear that the dispute between the Sages and Rabban Shimon ben Gamliel in regard to the status of hair that is ready to be clipped parallels this dispute between the Sages and Rabbi Meir in regard to the status of grapes ready to be harvested.

לא [5]The Gemara, however, rejects this assumption: **No,** the two disputes do not necessarily parallel each other, for **you can even say** that **Rabbi Meir,** who maintains that grapes ready to be harvested are treated as if they were already harvested, would agree with the Sages that hair ready to be clipped is treated in all respects as still attached to the body. [6]For **until now Rabbi Meir has only stated** his opinion, that we are to treat things ready to be detached as if they already were, in the case **there** regarding fully ripened grapes. [7]This is **because the longer one leaves them** on the vine, **the** more **they** ripen and **deteriorate.** [8]**But** as regards a slave's **hair** which is ready to be cut, [9]**the longer one leaves it** uncut, the more **it appreciates** in value as it continues to grow without degenerating. Thus, even Rabbi Meir might agree with the Sages that hair which is ready to be cut is treated in all respects as still attached to the body, and therefore not subject to the laws of *me'ilah.*

דִּינֵי נְפָשׁוֹת [10]The Gemara now proceeds to the next clause of the Mishnah which states: **Capital cases** are adjudicated by a court of twenty-three judges. Similarly, an animal which sodomizes a person as well as an animal that is sodomized by a person are sentenced to stoning by a court of twenty-three judges." [11]The Gemara notes that the author of the Mishnah **decided and taught** categorically that such is the rule with regard to any animal which sodomizes a person, implying that [12]**there is no difference between an**

הֲרֵי הוּא כַּקַּרְקַע". [1]וְאָמַר רַבִּי יוֹסֵי בַּר חֲנִינָא: [2]בַּעֲנָבִים הָעוֹמְדוֹת לִיבָּצֵר עָסְקִינַן, [3]מָר סָבַר: כִּבְצוּרוֹת דָּמְיָין. [4]וּמָר סָבַר: לָאו כִּבְצוּרוֹת דָּמְיָין.

[5]לָא. אֲפִילּוּ תֵּימָא רַבִּי מֵאִיר. [6]עַד כָּאן לֹא קָאָמַר רַבִּי מֵאִיר הָתָם. [7]כָּל כַּמָּה דְּשָׁבְקָה לְהוּ, מִיכְחַשׁ כָּחֲשֵׁי. [8]אֲבָל שְׂעָרוֹ, [9]כָּל כַּמָּה דְּשָׁבְקָה לְהוּ, אַשְׁבּוּחֵי מַשְׁבַּח.

[10]"דִּינֵי נְפָשׁוֹת כו׳". [11]קָא פָּסֵיק וְתָנֵי: [12]לָא שְׁנָא רוֹבֵעַ זָכָר

LITERAL TRANSLATION

is like land." [1]And Rabbi Yose bar Ḥanina said: [2]We are dealing with grapes that are ready to be harvested. [3][One] master maintained: They are considered as harvested. [4]But [another] master maintained: They are not considered as harvested.

[5]No. You can even say Rabbi Meir. [6]Until now Rabbi Meir has only stated [his opinion] there. [7]The longer that one leaves them, they deteriorate. [8]But his hair, [9]the longer one leaves it, it appreciates.

[10]"Capital cases etc." [11]He decided and taught: [12]There is no difference between an animal which sodomizes a male

RASHI

לא – התם בענבים כל כמה דשבקת להו – מיכחש כחשי, אבל שערו – אשבוחי משבח, הלכך אפילו רבי מאיר בשער כרבנן סבירא ליה. קא פסיק ותני – מתניתין רובע סתמא בעשרים ושלשה. לא שנא – שור שרבע אדם זכר, ולא שנא שור שרבע אשה נקבה, דנפקא לן תרווייהו מקראי בפרק "ארבע מיתות" (סנהדרין נד,ב) שהן בסקילה, ותנא דמתניתין מרבי להו לעשרים ושלשה.

NOTES

עֲנָבִים הָעוֹמְדוֹת לִיבָּצֵר Grapes that are ready to be harvested. The status of produce which is still attached to the ground but ready for harvest varies, depending on the Halachic context. Regarding Sabbath law, such produce is not considered to have already been harvested, so that picking such produce on the Sabbath qualifies as a violation of the prohibition forbidding the picking or the harvesting of produce on the day of rest. However, with regard to debt recovery, we do consider such produce as already harvested, and therefore a creditor cannot exercise a lien over this produce in the same way as he can over a debtor's land (*Rosh*).

HALAKHAH

רוֹבֵעַ An animal which sodomized someone. "If an animal sodomized someone, or was sodomized by someone, both the animal and the person are sentenced to stoning by a court of twenty-three judges." (*Rambam, Sefer Shofetim, Hilkhot Sanhedrin* 5:2.)

TRANSLATION AND COMMENTARY

animal which sodomizes a male and an animal which sodomizes a female. [1]**It is well** that a court of twenty-three is required when sentencing **an animal which sodomized a female,** [2]**for it is written** (Leviticus 20:16): **"And** if a woman approach any beast in order that it should sodomize her, **you shall kill the woman and the beast;** they shall surely be put to death; their blood shall be upon them." The verse itself makes clear the analogy between the woman's execution and the beast's — just as a court of twenty-three is required for sentencing the woman, so too with respect to the beast. [3]**But** as for **an animal which sodomized a male, from where do we** know that it too can only be sentenced by a court of twenty-three? [4]**For it is written** (Exodus 22:18): **"Whoever lies with a beast shall surely be put to death."** [5]**If** this verse **has no relevance to the** case of a **man who** actively **lies** with (sodomizes) a beast — for the law in that case is clear from another verse (Leviticus 20:15): "And if a man lie with a beast, he shall surely be put to death; and you shall slay the beast" — [6]**teach it as having relevance to the** case of a **man who** allows himself to be **laid** (sodomized) by a beast, so that it may be understood as mandating death in that case as well. [7]**And the** reason the **Torah brought** this verse **forth with language** implying **a man who** actively **lies** with a beast was [8]**in order to equate** the case of **a man laid** by a beast **to** the case of **a man who lies** with a beast: [9]**Just as** in the case of **a man who lies** with a beast, both **he and the beast** are sentenced **by** a court of **twenty-three** judges, [10]**so too** in the case of **a man who** allows himself to be **laid** by a beast, [11]both **he and the beast** are sentenced **by** a court of **twenty-three** judges.

וְלָא שְׁנָא רוֹבֵעַ נְקֵבָה. 1 בִּשְׁלָמָא רוֹבֵעַ נְקֵבָה, 2 דִּכְתִיב: ״וְהָרַגְתָּ אֶת הָאִשָּׁה וְאֶת הַבְּהֵמָה״. 3 אֶלָּא רוֹבֵעַ זָכָר מְנָא לָן? 4 דִּכְתִיב: ״כָּל שֹׁכֵב עִם בְּהֵמָה מוֹת יוּמָת״. 5 אִם אֵינוֹ עִנְיָן לַשּׁוֹכֵב, 6 תְּנֵיהוּ עִנְיָן לַנִּשְׁכָּב. 7 וְאַפְּקֵיהּ רַחֲמָנָא בִּלְשׁוֹן שׁוֹכֵב, 8 לְאַקּוּשֵׁי נִשְׁכָּב לְשׁוֹכֵב. 9 מַה שׁוֹכֵב — הוּא וּבְהֶמְתּוֹ בְּעֶשְׂרִים וּשְׁלֹשָׁה, 10 אַף נִשְׁכָּב — 11 הוּא וּבְהֶמְתּוֹ בְּעֶשְׂרִים וּשְׁלֹשָׁה.

12 ״שׁוֹר הַנִּסְקָל בְּעֶשְׂרִים וּשְׁלֹשָׁה, 13 שֶׁנֶּאֱמַר: ׳הַשּׁוֹר יִסָּקֵל וְגַם בְּעָלָיו יוּמָת׳. 14 כְּמִיתַת הַבְּעָלִים, 15 כָּךְ מִיתַת

LITERAL TRANSLATION

and an animal which sodomizes a female. [1]It is well [regarding] an animal which sodomized a female, [2]for it is written: "And you shall kill the woman and the beast." [3]But an animal which sodomized a male, from where do we [know it]? [4]For it is written: "Whoever lies with a beast shall surely be put to death." [5]If it has no relevance to the man who lies [with a beast], [6]teach it as having relevance to the man who was laid [by a beast]. [7]And [the reason] the Torah (lit., "the Merciful") brought it forth with language of one who lies [8][was] in order to equate a man laid [by a beast] to a man who lies [with a beast]. [9]Just as a man who lies [with a beast] — he and his beast by twenty-three, [10]so too a man who was laid [by a beast] — [11]he and his beast by twenty-three.

[12]"The ox that is stoned by twenty-three, [13]as it is stated: 'The ox shall be stoned, and also its owner shall be put to death.' [14]As the owner's death, [15]so

RASHI

בשלמא רובע נקבה — כתיב ב״ד עשרים ושלשה, דכתיב ״והרגת את האשה ואת הבהמה״ — איתקש בהמה לאשה, ודיני נפשות נפקינן לקמן בעשרים ושלשה. **אלא רובע זכר** — מנלן דבעי עשרים ושלשה דכתיב כל שוכב וגו׳, ומהאי קרא נפקא לן ב״ארבע מיתות״ לרובע זכר. **דאם אינו ענין** — לאדם הבא על הבהמה, דהא קרא אחרינא כתיב (ויקרא כ): ״איש אשר יתן שכבתו וגו׳״. **תניהו ענין לנשכב** — למביא בהמה עליו, ומדאפקיה בלשון שוכב — לידון כשוכב, מה בא על הבהמה הוא והיא בעשרים ושלשה, כדילפינן מ״ואת הבהמה תהרוגו״ (שם), דאיתקש בהמה לאדם, אף מביא בהמה עליו — שניהם בעשרים ושלשה.

שׁוֹר הַנִּסְקָל בְּעֶשְׂרִים וּשְׁלֹשָׁה [12]Our Mishnah continues: **"The ox that is stoned** to death for having gored and killed a person is sentenced **by** a court of **twenty-three** judges, [13]**for it is stated** in the verse [Exodus 21:29]: 'But if the ox was of the goring kind from days gone by, and its owner had been warned, yet he did not guard it, and it killed a man or a woman, **the ox shall be stoned, and also its owner shall be put to death.'** [14]The analogy drawn at the end of this verse teaches us that, just **as the owner's death,** in the event he himself committed a capital offense, is called for by a court of twenty three judges, [15]**so** too is **the ox's**

NOTES

שׁוֹר הַנִּסְקָל בְּעֶשְׂרִים וּשְׁלֹשָׁה **The ox that is to be stoned by twenty-three.** According to the Jerusalem Talmud, it is only due to Scriptural decree that the animal is sentenced by a court of twenty-three judges, for in essence this is a civil case involving damages attributable to one's property and not a capital one that would require twenty three judges. Since the execution of the animal is essentially a civil penalty imposed upon its owner, we can well

TRANSLATION AND COMMENTARY

death in this case." [1] **Abaye said to Rava: From where** do we know **that this** clause, **"And its owner also shall be put to death,"** [2] **comes to** teach us that just **as the owner's death** is determined elsewhere by a court of twenty three, **so** too is **the ox's death** here? [15B] [3] **Say that it comes** to teach us the need **for execution** to be meted out against the ox's owner in this case itself, due to his negligence in guarding his animal!

אִם כֵּן [4] Rava answered: **If** that were **so, let** the Torah **write:** [5] "The ox shall be stoned, **and also its owner,"** [6] **and** then **let it be silent.** The unnecessary addition of יוּמָת — "he shall be put to death" — implies that the verse is referring to the owner's execution under different circumstances, thus enabling us to interpet the verse as we have.

אִי כָּתַב [7] Abaye countered: **If the Torah had written** the verse **thus,** as you have suggested, [8] **I might have said** that the owner is to be executed **by stoning,** just like his animal. Therefore the Torah adds the additional word יוּמָת so as to inform us that the ox's owner is executed by strangulation, the form of capital punishment administered when no other form is specifically indicated in the verse.

בִּסְקִילָה [9] This argument is rejected: **Would you** possibly **have thought,** had the verse been written without this additional word, that the ox's owner should be executed **by stoning?** [10] **If he** himself **had killed** someone with his own hands, he would have been liable to decapitation **by the sword** (see *Sanhedrin* 52b), a lesser form of capital punishment. [11] How, then, could it be that if **his** ox, a mere **asset** of his, had killed another person, he would be liable for death **by stoning** — the most severe form of capital punishment?

הַשּׁוֹר". [1] אָמַר לֵיהּ אַבַּיֵי לְרָבָא: מִמַּאי דְּהַאי "וְגַם בְּעָלָיו יוּמָת" [2] לְכְמִיתַת בְּעָלִים, כָּךְ מִיתַת הַשּׁוֹר הוּא דַּאֲתָא, [15B] [3] אֵימָא לִקְטָלָא הוּא דַּאֲתָא? [4] אִם כֵּן, לִיכְתּוֹב: [5] "וְגַם בְּעָלָיו", [6] וְלִישְׁתּוֹק. [7] אִי כָּתַב רַחֲמָנָא הָכִי, [8] הֲוָה אָמִינָא: בִּסְקִילָה. [9] בִּסְקִילָה סָלְקָא דַּעְתָּךְ? [10] קָטַל אִיהוּ בְּסַיִיף; [11] מָמוֹנוֹ, בִּסְקִילָה!

LITERAL TRANSLATION

the ox's death." [1] Abaye said to Rava: From where [do we know] that this "And its owner also shall be put to death" [2] comes [to teach] that as the owner's death, so the ox's death? [15B] [3] Say that it comes for execution!

[4] If so, let it write: [5] "And its owner also," [6] and let it be silent.

[7] If the Torah (lit., "the Merciful") had written thus, [8] I might have said by stoning.

[9] Would you have thought by stoning? [10] [If] he had killed, by the sword; [11] [if] his asset [had killed], by stoning!

RASHI

אימא לקטלא — לחייב מיתה לבעליו וניחייביה מיתה, והיכי מפקינן לה מפשטיה לגמרי. **אי כתב הכי** — קושיא היא, כלומר איצטריך "יומת" לדונו במיתה האמורה בתורה סתם, דאינו אלא חנק, דלא תימא גם בעליו יסקל. **קטל איהו בסייף** — דקיימא לן לקמן סנהדרין (נב) רוצח בסייף. **קטל שורו נימא בסקילה** — דחמירה מכולן, בתמיה.

NOTES

understand the position put forth by some Sages that an ownerless animal is not put to death in the event that it kills someone.

Others see in this law the extension of a principle identified with a previous verse (Genesis 9:5-6): "But for your own life-blood I will demand a reckoning; from every beast will I require it, and from man too; from one's fellow man will I demand reckoning for another man's life. Whosoever sheds a man's blood, by man shall his blood be shed: for in the image of God made He man." Out of respect for the image of God in which man was created, any man or beast who takes a human life forfeits his own (*Ramban*).

מִמַּאי דְּהַאי "וְגַם בְּעָלָיו יוּמָת" From where do we know that this clause, "And its owner also shall be put to death." The Gemara implies that were we to understand the verse as teaching that the owner of the ox is himself liable to execution if his animal killed someone, then we would not be able to derive from it an analogy between the execution of the owner and the execution of the ox insofar as requiring twenty-three judges in the latter instance. The Rishonim ask: Why not? *Tosafot* explains the implication of the Gemara in terms of the accepted principle that when applying an analogy between two references in a verse, we always learn from the first reference to the second, and not the other way around. In our verse, the execution of the animal is referred to before that of its owner. Nevertheless, if the second reference is found to be altogether superfluous to the verse — as in our case should the owner of the ox be assumed not to deserve punishment when his animal kills someone — then the analogy can be drawn in the opposite direction as well, thereby allowing us to apply the requirement of twenty-three judges to the execution of the ox. *Rabbenu Ya'akov* suggests that the reason the Gemara assumes at this point that an analogy cannot be drawn between the execution of the owner and that of his animal is because it maintains, in accordance with a later contention, that the owner is liable to death by strangulation, whereas the animal dies by stoning. Since their forms of execution are dissimilar, the Gemara assumes we cannot draw an analogy between them.

[1]וְדִילְמָא הַאי דְּכָתַב רַחֲמָנָא "יוּמָת" [2]לְאַקּוּלֵי עִילָּוֵיהּ, לְאַפּוּקֵי מִסַּיִיף לְחֶנֶק?
[3]הָנִיחָא לְמַאן דַּאֲמַר חֶנֶק חָמוּר. [4]אֶלָּא לְמַאן דַּאֲמַר חֶנֶק קִיל, [5]מַאי אִיכָּא לְמֵימַר?
[6]לָא סָלְקָא דַּעֲתָךְ, [7]דִּכְתִיב: "אִם כֹּפֶר יוּשַׁת עָלָיו". [8]וְאִי סָלְקָא דַּעֲתָךְ בַּר קְטָלָא הוּא, [9]וְהָכְתִיב: "לֹא תִקְחוּ כֹפֶר לְנֶפֶשׁ רֹצֵחַ".
[10]אַדְּרַבָּה, מִשּׁוּם הִיא גּוּפָהּ: [11]קָטַל אִיהוּ לָא תִּיסְגֵּי לֵיהּ בְּמָמוֹנָא, [12]אֶלָּא בִּקְטָלָא, [13]קָטַל שׁוֹרוֹ, [14]לִיפְרוֹק נַפְשֵׁיהּ בְּמָמוֹנָא!
[15]אֶלָּא, אָמַר חִזְקִיָּה, וְכֵן תָּנָא דְּבֵי חִזְקִיָּה: [16]"אָמַר קְרָא 'מוֹת יוּמַת הַמַּכֶּה רֹצֵחַ הוּא' [17]עַל רְצִיחָתוֹ אַתָּה הוֹרְגוֹ, [18]וְאִי

LITERAL TRANSLATION

[1]But perhaps that which the Torah wrote, "He shall be put to death," [2]was to be lenient with him, to commute it from the sword to strangulation!

[3]Granted [that] according to the one who said [that] strangulation is [more] severe [this argument would not hold]. [4]But according to the one who said [that] strangulation is [more] lenient, [5]what is there to say?

[6]You cannot have thought [thus], [7]for it is written: "If a ransom be placed upon him." [8]And if you thought that he is subject to execution, [9]surely it is written: "You shall take no ransom for the life of a murderer"!

[10]On the contrary, because of it itself: [11][If] he killed, it would not suffice for him with money, [12]but rather through execution. [13][If] his ox killed, [14]let him redeem himself by money!

[15]Rather, Ḥizkiyah said, and so it is taught by the School of Ḥizkiyah: [16]"The verse states: 'He that smote shall surely be put to death; he is a murderer.' [17]For his murdering, you execute him, [18]but

TRANSLATION AND COMMENTARY

וְדִילְמָא [1]Abaye restated his argument: **Perhaps** if the Torah had not added this word, I might have thought that the owner is executed in the same manner as he would have been had he personally committed murder himself — by decapitation. The reason **that the Torah wrote** the word יוּמָת, **"he shall be put to death,"** [2]**was** in order **to be lenient with him by commuting** his sentence **from** decapitation by **the sword to strangulation,** the form administered when no other is specifically indicated!

הָנִיחָא לְמַאן דַּאֲמַר [3]The Gemara does not accept this idea either: **Granted** that, **according to the one who said** that death by **strangulation is** a more **severe** form of execution than death by the sword, this argument would not hold, for the punishment imposed upon the owner when his animal killed someone cannot be more severe than that imposed upon him for killing someone with his own hands. [4]**But according to the one who said that strangulation is** a more **lenient** form of execution than death by the sword, [5]**what is there to say?**

לָא סָלְקָא דַּעֲתָךְ [6]This argument is also rejected: **You cannot** possibly **have thought** that the verse comes to teach that the owner of an ox that kills someone is liable to capital punishment, [7]**for it is written** in the next verse (Exodus 21:30): **"If a ransom be placed upon him,** then he shall give as ransom for his life whatever is placed upon him." [8]**And if you thought that** the owner of the ox **is subject to execution,** how can he exempt himself from such punishment by paying a ransom? [9]**Surely it is written** elsewhere (Numbers 35:31): **"You shall take no ransom for the life of a murderer** who was convicted to die; for he shall surely be put to death"!

אַדְּרַבָּה [10]However, the Gemara rebuts this: **On the contrary, because of** the claim **itself,** that one who killed someone should not be allowed to exempt himself from punishment by paying a ransom, it was necessary for the Torah to tell us that this is not so in our case. [11]If **he** himself had **killed** someone, **it would not suffice for him** to atone for his sin **with money,** [12]**but rather** he would have to achieve his atonement **through execution.** [13]However, if it was **his ox** that **killed,** [14]**let him redeem himself by** offering ransom **money.** Hence it cannot be proven from this verse that the ox's owner is exempt from death should his animal gore and kill someone!

אֶלָּא, אָמַר חִזְקִיָּה [15]**Rather, Ḥizkiyah said, and so it is** stated in a Baraita **taught by a Sage of the School of Ḥizkiyah:** [16]**"The verse states** [Numbers 35:21]: **'He that smote shall surely be put to death; he is a murderer.'** [17]The emphasis placed here on the fact that '*he* is a murderer' teaches that it is **for his murdering** someone **that you execute him,** [18]**but you do not execute him for his ox murdering** someone." Thus, our verse cannot

RASHI

הניחא – הא דעקרת ליה לקרא מפשטיה, ולא מוקמינן ליה למיתת חנק ממש. **למאן דאמר חנק חמור** – מסייף, בפרק "ארבע מיתות" (סנהדרין נ,ב) הלכך איכא למיפרך: קטל איהו בסייף, קטל שורו בחנק? **אלא למאן דאמר חנק קל** – אימא למיתת חנק אתא. **משום היא גופה** – משום הך קשיא גופא, דלא תימא "לא תקחו כופר" כתב רחמנא וליקטול – כתב רחמנא "ונתן פדיון נפשו" למימר דהיכא דקטל איהו – לא תסגי ליה בממונא כו׳, אבל קטל שורו – סגי ליה בממונא, ואי לא יהיב כופר – חייב חנק.

אַתָּה הוֹרְגוֹ עַל רְצִיחַת שׁוֹרוֹ". [1]אִיבַּעְיָא לְהוּ: [2]שׁוֹר סִינַי בְּכַמָּה? [3]מִי גָּמַר שָׁעָה מִדּוֹרוֹת, [4]אוֹ לָא? [5]תָּא שְׁמַע, דְּתָנֵי רָמִי בַּר יְחֶזְקֵאל: [6]"'אִם בְּהֵמָה אִם אִישׁ לֹא יִחְיֶה'. [7]מָה אִישׁ בְּעֶשְׂרִים וּשְׁלֹשָׁה — [8]אַף בְּהֵמָה בְּעֶשְׂרִים וּשְׁלֹשָׁה". [9]"הָאֲרִי וְהַזְּאֵב כו'". [10]אָמַר רֵישׁ לָקִישׁ: וְהוּא שֶׁהֵמִיתוּ, [11]אֲבָל לֹא הֵמִיתוּ, לֹא. [12]אַלְמָא קָסָבַר: יֵשׁ לָהֶן תַּרְבּוּת, וְיֵשׁ לָהֶן בְּעָלִים. [13]רַבִּי יוֹחָנָן אָמַר: אַף עַל פִּי שֶׁלֹּא הֵמִיתוּ,

LITERAL TRANSLATION

you do not execute him for his ox murdering." [1]It was asked of them: [2]An ox [at] Sinai, by how many? [3]Do we learn the temporary from the permanent, [4]or not?

[5]Come [and] hear, for Rami bar Yeḥezkel taught: [6]"'Whether beast or man, it shall not live.' [7]Just as a man by twenty-three, [8]so too a beast by twenty-three."

[9]"The lion, or the wolf, etc." [10]Resh Lakish said: And that is where they had killed, [11]but if they had not killed, not. [12]Hence he maintains: They have domestication and they have owners. [13]Rabbi Yoḥanan said: Even though they have not killed.

TRANSLATION AND COMMENTARY

possibly be interpreted to imply that the owner of the ox is subject to the death penalty. Instead we derive from it the principle stated in our Mishnah — that a goring ox is sentenced to die by a court of twenty-three judges, just as its owner would be had he committed a capital offense of his own.

אִיבַּעְיָא לְהוּ [1]The following question **was asked of** the Sages as they discussed these issues: [2]**An ox** that was present at Mount **Sinai** when God gave the Torah, and that strayed beyond the permissible boundary thus incurring the death penalty (see Exodus 19:13: "He shall surely be stoned, or cast off; whether beast or man, it shall not live"), **how many** judges were required to deliver its sentence? [3]The Gemara clarifies the issue in question: **Do we learn** the details relevant to **a temporary** edict (that which mandated death for an animal that trespassed at Sinai) **from** those which pertain to **a permanent** one (that which mandates death for an ox that killed someone), in which case the trespassing ox would also require a court of twenty-three; [4]**or** do we **not** learn one from the other?

תָּא שְׁמַע [5]**Come and hear** a solution to the problem, **for Rami bar Yeḥezkel taught** the following Baraita: "The verse regarding Sinai states: [6]**'Whether beast or man, it shall not live'** — implying that an analogy may be drawn between a man who trespassed and a beast. [7]**Just as a man** could only have been sentenced at the time **by** a court of **twenty-three**, [8]**so too a beast** could only have been sentenced to death **by** a court of **twenty-three** judges."

הָאֲרִי וְהַזְּאֵב [9]We learned in the next clause of the Mishnah: **"The lion, or the wolf,** or the bear, or the leopard, or the hyena, or the snake that killed someone — their slaughter is carried out by a court of twenty-three judges. Rabbi Eliezer says: Whoever is first to kill them, merits a reward." [10]**Resh Lakish said:** Rabbi Eliezer's dictum **is** applicable only **where** these creatures **had killed** someone, implying that they need not be slaughtered exclusively by the court; [11]**but** if **they had not killed** anyone, one may **not** kill them. [12]**Hence** it follows that Resh Lakish **maintains** that these creatures **have** the potential for **domestication and** therefore may **have owners**. For this reason, one may not kill them unless they have caused mortal injury. [13]**Rabbi Yoḥanan** disagreed and **said:** According to Rabbi Eliezer, one merits a reward for destroying

RASHI

שור סיני — בהמה שקרבה להר בעוד שהשכינה שם, דכתיב "אם בהמה אם איש לא יחיה". **בבמה** — דיינים נידון.
מה איש בעשרים ושלשה — דאיש פשיטא לן, דכבר הוקבעו לישראל סנהדראות מיתרו ואילך. **ברדלס** — חיה היא, ובלעז קורין אותה פוטויו"ש. **אמר ריש לקיש** — הא דאמר רבי אליעזר: כל הקודם להורגן — זכה, והוא שהמיתו נפש, ואמילתא דתנא קמא דאיירי כשהמיתו קאי רבי אליעזר. **יש להם תרבות** — מותר לגדלן, לפי שאדם יכול ללמדן שלא יזיקו, הלכך שם בעלים נקרא עליהן ולא הוי כהפקר, ואסור להורגן אם לא המיתו, אבל אם המיתו סופן מוכיח על תחילתן שלא אלו בני תרבות, ואין צריכין לדונן. **רבי יוחנן אמר אף על גב שלא המיתו** — אמר רבי אליעזר: כל הקודם להרגן זכה. והכי קאמר ליה לתנא קמא: דקאמרת כשהמיתו צריכי עשרים ושלשה דיינין, אני אומר אפילו לא המיתו מותר להורגן כל הקודם, וכל שכן אם המיתו.

NOTES

שׁוֹר סִינַי בְּכַמָּה? **An ox at Sinai, by how many?** The Rishonim ask: Why does the Gemara discuss this matter at all? Whatever may have been the law then should be of no concern to us now! *Remah* maintains that any legal issue raised in Scripture comprises a legitimate subject for Talmudic analysis, regardless of its practical relevance. Some Rishonim see in the resolution of this question the possibility of practical ramifications. For example, if one decided to take a vow of Naziritism on condition that twenty-three judges were required to sentence an animal that trespassed the boundary line at Mount Sinai, resolving this issue would determine whether or not he is a

TRANSLATION AND COMMENTARY

these creatures **even though they have not killed** anyone. [1]**Hence** it follows that Rabbi Yoḥanan **maintains** that such creatures **do not have** the potential for **domestication and** therefore **do not have owners.** For this reason, one is permitted to kill them in order to prevent future harm from taking place.

תְּנַן [2]The Gemara now considers these two opinions in light of what **we have learned** in our Mishnah: [3]**"Rabbi Eliezer says: Whoever is first to kill them, merits** a reward." [4]**This is acceptable according to Rabbi Yoḥanan,** who interpreted Rabbi Eliezer as permitting one to kill such creatures even though they had not killed anyone: [5]**and what did** the killer **merit?** [6]**He merited** the creatures' **hides,** for one is permitted to derive benefit from the carcass of an animal unless the animal had been executed by a court. [7]**But according to Resh Lakish,** who interpreted Rabbi Eliezer as permitting the destruction of such creatures only if they had killed someone, [8]**what did** the one who killed the animal **merit?** [9]**Since** these creatures **had killed** someone, [10]**the Rabbis considered them as those whose sentences had** already **been concluded** in a proper court, [11]and therefore seeing that **they are** now in the category of **things from which benefit is forbidden,** there is nothing their killer could merit in reward.

מַאי זָכָה [12]The Gemara answers: **What does** the one who kills the animal **merit** according to Resh Lakish? [13]**He merits** a reward in **Heaven** for having performed a virtuous deed.

תַּנְיָא כְּוָותֵיהּ [14]The following Baraita **was taught in accordance with** the view of **Resh Lakish:** [15]**"Be it an ox that killed** someone **or** some other domesticated **animal or** wild **beast that killed** someone, the sentence must be delivered **by** a court of **twenty-three** judges. [16]**Rabbi Eliezer says:** If it was **an ox that killed** someone, its judgement is rendered **by** a court of **twenty-three**. [17]But if it were **other animals or beasts that killed** someone, [18]**whoever is first to kill them, merits through** killing **them** a reward in **Heaven."**

[1]אַלְמָא קָסָבַר: אֵין לָהֶם תַּרְבּוּת, וְאֵין לָהֶם בְּעָלִים. [2]תְּנַן: [3]״רַבִּי אֱלִיעֶזֶר אוֹמֵר: כָּל הַקּוֹדֵם לְהוֹרְגָן זָכָה״. [4]בִּשְׁלָמָא לְרַבִּי יוֹחָנָן, [5]לְמַאי זָכָה? [6]זָכָה לְעוֹרָן. [7]אֶלָּא לְרֵישׁ לָקִישׁ, [8]לְמַאי זָכָה? [9]כֵּיוָן שֶׁהֱמִיתוּ, [10]שָׁוִינְהוּ רַבָּנַן כְּמַאן דְּגָמַר דִּינַיְיהוּ, [11]וְאִיסּוּרֵי הֲנָאָה נִינְהוּ! [12]מַאי זָכָה? [13]זָכָה לַשָּׁמַיִם. [14]תַּנְיָא כְּוָותֵיהּ דְּרֵישׁ לָקִישׁ: [15]״אֶחָד שׁוֹר שֶׁהֵמִית וְאֶחָד בְּהֵמָה וְחַיָּה שֶׁהֱמִיתוּ בְּעֶשְׂרִים וּשְׁלֹשָׁה. [16]רַבִּי אֱלִיעֶזֶר אוֹמֵר: שׁוֹר שֶׁהֵמִית בְּעֶשְׂרִים וּשְׁלֹשָׁה. [17]וּשְׁאָר בְּהֵמָה וְחַיָּה שֶׁהֱמִיתוּ — [18]כָּל הַקּוֹדֵם לְהוֹרְגָן זָכָה בָּהֶן לַשָּׁמַיִם.

LITERAL TRANSLATION

[1]Hence he maintains: They do not have domestication, and they do not have owners.

[2]We have learned: [3]"Rabbi Eliezer says: Whoever is first to kill them, merits."

[4]Granted according to Rabbi Yoḥanan, [5]what did he merit? [6]He merited their hides. [7]But according to Resh Lakish, [8]what did he merit? [9]Since they had killed, [10]the Rabbis considered them as those whose sentences had been concluded, [11]and they are things from which benefit is forbidden!

[12]What does he merit? [13]He merits Heaven.

[14]It was taught in accordance with Resh Lakish: [15]"Be it an ox that killed or an animal or beast that killed, by twenty-three. [16]Rabbi Eliezer says: An ox that killed, by twenty-three. [17]And other animals or beasts that killed — [18]whoever is first to kill them, merits through them Heaven."

RASHI

ואין להם בעלים – כלומר אין שם הבעלים חל עליהם, ולא הוו אלא כהפקר, לפי שלא היה לו לגדלן. **זכה** – משמע נשתכר. **זכה בעורן** – העור שלו, כיון דאין להם בעלים. **כיון דהמיתו** – ואמור רבנן דאין צריך לדונן בבית דין – הוו להו כמאן דגמר דינייהו, ואסירי בהנאה, כדקיימא לן שאם שחטו לאחר שנגמר דינו – אסור, בפרק ״שור שנגח״ (בבא קמא מא,א). **זכה לשמים** – צדקה עשה.

BACKGROUND

אֵין לָהֶם תַּרְבּוּת They do not have domestication. Rav Yoḥanan maintained that, in the opinion of Rabbi Eliezer, beasts of prey cannot be domesticated, and therefore those who keep them are not considered their owners, but rather as people who keep something that causes damage at all times. Therefore anyone is permitted to kill creatures at any time.

זָכָה לְעוֹרָן He merited their hides. Since, in the opinion of Rabbi Yoḥanan, beasts of prey have no owners, whoever kills them first gains possession of the carcass, like any unowned property. Because such animals are not kosher, the reward of the person who kills them is their pelt and other parts which have monetary value.

שָׁוִינְהוּ רַבָּנַן כְּמַאן דְּגָמַר דִּינַיְיהוּ The Rabbis considered them as those whose sentences had been concluded. In Rabbi Eliezer's opinion, these animals are not tried by a court; but he, too, admits that they should be killed like anything else that causes damage. The Gemara believes that Rabbi Eliezer would also maintain that they have been condemned to death like a domesticated animal which has killed someone, though there is no need to convene a tribunal for that purpose. Hence, like domestic animals which have killed someone, it is forbidden to derive profit from them.

NOTES

Nazirite (*Ran*). Similarly, if one pledged to clothe as many poor as there were judges required to sentence an animal at Sinai, answering the Gemara's question would have practical consequences as well (*Meiri*).

וּשְׁאָר בְּהֵמָה וְחַיָּה And other domesticated animals or wild beasts. *Remah* explains the position of Rabbi Eliezer,

HALAKHAH

אֶחָד שׁוֹר שֶׁהֵמִית וְאֶחָד בְּהֵמָה וְחַיָּה שֶׁהֱמִיתוּ Both an ox that killed and a domesticated animal or wild beast that killed. "An ox that killed someone can only be sentenced to death by a court of twenty-three judges. Even if the animal was a lion or a bear — animals which can be tamed and occasionally have owners — it can also only be sentenced to death by a court of twenty-three judges (following Resh Lakish; *Kesef Mishneh*). But if a snake killed

BACKGROUND

איכא בינייהו נחש There is between them a snake. As *Rashi* explains, this is in accordance with the principle that a snake is always regarded as though a legal warning had been issued that it is dangerous (נָחָשׁ מוּעָד לְעוֹלָם); thus it is always meritorious to kill a venomous snake, even before it has done any harm.

TRANSLATION AND COMMENTARY

רַבִּי עֲקִיבָא אוֹמֵר [1]We learned in the next clause of our Mishnah: **"Rabbi Akiva says:** The destruction of these creatures is carried out by a court of twenty-three judges." [2]The view of **Rabbi Akiva is** exactly **the same as** that of **the first Tanna**, for they both state that we need a court of twenty-three judges in order to destroy these animals!

אִיכָּא בֵּינַיְיהוּ [3]The Gemara answers: **There is** a difference **between** Rabbi Akiva and the first Tanna with regard to **a snake,** for Rabbi Akiva maintains that anyone can kill a snake if the snake has killed somebody.

אֵין דָּנִין [4]Our Mishnah continues: **"We do not judge** a tribe of Israel that has sinned other than by a court of seventy-one judges." [5]**This tribe which has sinned, in what** way did it sin? [6]**If you should say** that the Mishnah is referring to **a tribe that** intentionally **desecrated the Sabbath,** there is a problem. [7]One can **say that the Torah distinguished between** the law regarding **individuals and** that regarding **multitudes** when it pertains **to a matter of idolatry,** for we find in the Torah that a city whose entire population (or the majority thereof) committed idolatry must be judged by a court of seventy-one, whereas an individual who committed idolatry is only judged by a court of twenty-three. [8]However, insofar as **the remaining commandments** are concerned, **did** the Torah ever **distinguish** between the law regarding individuals and that regarding multitudes? [9]**Rather,** the Mishnah must be speaking **about a tribe which was led astray** into idol worship and which is judged in accordance with the laws of an idolatrous city.

לְמֵימְרָא [10]The Gemara raises an objection: Are we indeed **to say that we judge** a tribe that committed idolatry **in accordance with the** same **law** that we apply in the case of **public** violation by an entire city, which was led astray into idol worship? [11]If so, in accordance **with whose** views is our Mishnah? [12]It is **not like** the view of **Rabbi Yoshiyah, and not like** the view of **Rabbi Yoḥanan!** [13]**For it was taught** in a Baraita: **"Up to how many people** must there be in an idolatrous locale in order that **we apply** the laws of **a city led astray** into idol

[1]"רַבִּי עֲקִיבָא אוֹמֵר וכו׳". [2]רַבִּי עֲקִיבָא הַיְינוּ תַּנָּא קַמָּא!
[3]אִיכָּא בֵּינַיְיהוּ נָחָשׁ.
[4]"אֵין דָּנִין כו׳". [5]הַאי שֵׁבֶט דְּחָטָא — בְּמַאי? [6]אִילֵימָא שֵׁבֶט שֶׁחִלֵּל אֶת הַשַּׁבָּת — [7]אֵימַר דִּפְלֵיג רַחֲמָנָא בֵּין יְחִידִים לִמְרוּבִּין לְעִנְיַן עֲבוֹדַת כּוֹכָבִים. [8]בִּשְׁאָר מִצְוֹת, מִי פָּלֵיג? [9]אֶלָּא, בְּשֵׁבֶט שֶׁהוּדַּח.
[10]לְמֵימְרָא דִּבְדִינָא דְּרַבִּים דָּיְינִינַן לֵיהּ? [11]כְּמַאן? [12]לֹא כְּרַבִּי יֹאשִׁיָּה וְלֹא כְּרַבִּי יוֹנָתָן!
[13]דְּתַנְיָא: "עַד כַּמָּה עוֹשִׂין עִיר

LITERAL TRANSLATION

[1]"Rabbi Akiva says, etc." [2]Rabbi Akiva is the same as the first Tanna!

[3]There is between them a snake.

[4]"We do not judge etc." [5]This tribe that sinned — in what? [6]If you should say a tribe that desecrated the Sabbath — [7]say that the Torah (lit., "the Merciful") distinguished between individuals and multitudes in regard to a matter of idolatry. [8]In the remaining commandments, did it distinguish? [9]Rather, [the Mishnah is speaking] about a tribe which was led astray [into idolatry].

[10][Are we] to say that we judge it in accordance with the law of a [sinning] public? [11]Like whom? [12]Not like Rabbi Yoshiyah and not like Rabbi Yoḥanan! [13]For it was taught: "Up to how many [people] do we apply [the law of] a city

RASHI

איכא בינייהו נחש — דתנא קמא חשיב ליה בהדי הנך, ובעי עשרים ושלשה, ורבי עקיבא באינך סבירא ליה כוותיה, בר מנחש כדאמרינן ב"ארבעה אבות נזיקין" (בבא קמא טו,ב): נחש מועד לעולם דברי הכל. **לענין עבודה זרה** — חלק בין יחידים למרובים, דעיר הנדחת בעי סנהדרי גדולה, כדיליף לקמן סנהדרין (טז,א), ויחיד נידון בעשרים ושלשה, דכתיב (דברים יז): "והוצאת את האיש ההוא וגו׳ אל שעריך" — בית דין שבשעריך. **למימרא** — דשבט שלם שהודח בדינא דרבים דיינינן ליה, כדינא דעיר הנדחת, דמיקרי מרובין, דיינינן ליה בסייף ובסנהדרי גדולה?

NOTES

according to Resh Lakish, as follows: The law calling for the stoning of a killer ox by a court of twenty-three is derived from Scriptural decree, and as such should not be extended to other animals which may have also been responsible for taking human life. However, one may take the initiative and destroy any animal that has killed someone, in line with the verse that states: "And you shall wipe out the evil from within your midst."

HALAKHAH

someone, anybody can destroy it," following Rabbi Akiva (for even Rabbi Eliezer agrees with him on that matter, in opposition to the first Tanna; *Kesef Mishneh*). (*Rambam, Sefer Shofetim, Hilkhot Sanhedrin* 5:2.)

בְּשֵׁבֶט שֶׁהוּדַּח A tribe that was led astray into idolatry. "If an entire tribe was led astray into idolatry, it can only be judged by a court of seventy-one," following the Gemara's conclusion below. (*Rambam, Sefer Shofetim, Hilkhot Sanhedrin* 5:1.)

עַד כַּמָּה עוֹשִׂין עִיר הַנִּדַּחַת? Up to how many people can we apply the law of an idolatrous city? "A city can only be condemned as idolatrous if at least a majority of its

TRANSLATION AND COMMENTARY

worship?[1] **From ten to a hundred.** Fewer than ten people do not constitute a city, whereas more than a hundred are considered a 'community.' In either case, the offenders would not be judged as a 'city,' but rather as individuals. [2]These are **the words of Rabbi Yoshiyah.** [3]**Rabbi Yonatan** disagrees and **says:** A city for these purposes can be defined as any population whose number ranges **from a hundred to a majority of a tribe.**" [4]**Now even Rabbi Yonatan only said** that we can treat a city according to these laws if it numbers no more than **a majority** of a tribe [5]**but** if it houses **an entire** tribe he would also agree that the laws of an idolatrous city do **not** apply! How, then, are we to understand the Mishnah, which addresses the issue of an entire tribe that has sinned?

אָמַר רַב מַתָּנָה [6]**Rabbi Matenah said: Here** in the Mishnah [16A] [7]**we are** not **dealing** with a tribe that sinned, but rather **with the chief of a tribe who sinned,** committing a capital offense. [8]**Did not Rav Adda bar Ahavah say**: "When it was suggested to Moses in the verse [Exodus 18:22] that: **'Every great matter they shall bring to you'** for judgment, the phrase 'every great matter' should be understood as referring to [9]**the matter of a great man** who has committed a capital offense"? Since Moses' judgment was tantamount to that of a seventy-one-member Sanhedrin, it would follow that the chief of a tribe who committed a capital offense must be tried by a court of seventy-one, [10]for **he too is** considered **a great man.**

עוּלָּא אָמַר [11]The Gemara now suggests an alternative explanation of the Mishnah: **Ulla said in the name of Rabbi Elazar:** [12]The Mishnah is dealing **with** tribes that **come** to settle their differences in court **over matters** relating to their tribal **inheritance** in the Land of Israel, [13]**and** its intention is to teach us that any such dispute must be treated just **like** it would have been at **the beginning of the** process when the **Land of Israel** was divided into tribal territories, in the days of Joshua. [14]**Just as** at the **beginning** the tribal territories were established by a court of **seventy-one,** [15]**so too here** in later times the disagreement that arises between the tribes about these matters must be settled by a court of **seventy-one.**

הַנִּדַּחַת? [1]מֵעֲשָׂרָה וְעַד מֵאָה; [2]דִּבְרֵי רַבִּי יֹאשִׁיָּה. [3]רַבִּי יוֹנָתָן אוֹמֵר: מִמֵּאָה וְעַד רוּבּוֹ שֶׁל שֵׁבֶט". [4]וַאֲפִילּוּ רַבִּי יוֹנָתָן לָא קָאָמַר אֶלָּא רוּבּוֹ, [5]אֲבָל כּוּלּוֹ — לֹא!

[6]אָמַר רַב מַתָּנָה: הָכָא [16A] [7]בִּנְשִׂיא שֵׁבֶט שֶׁחָטָא עָסְקִינַן. [8]מִי לֹא אָמַר רַב אַדָּא בַּר אַהֲבָה: "כָּל הַדָּבָר הַגָּדֹל יָבִיאוּ אֵלֶיךָ" — [9]דְּבָרָיו שֶׁל גָּדוֹל. [10]הַאי נַמִי גָּדוֹל הוּא.

[11]עוּלָּא אָמַר רַבִּי אֶלְעָזָר: [12]בְּבָאִין עַל עִסְקֵי נְחָלוֹת, [13]וְכִתְחִילָּתָהּ שֶׁל אֶרֶץ יִשְׂרָאֵל. [14]מַה תְּחִילָּתָהּ שִׁבְעִים וְאֶחָד, [15]אַף כָּאן שִׁבְעִים וְאֶחָד.

LITERAL TRANSLATION

led astray? [1]From ten to a hundred; [2][these are] the words of Rabbi Yoshiyah. [3]Rabbi Yonatan says: From a hundred to a majority of a tribe." [4]And even Rabbi Yonatan only said a majority, [5]but an entire [tribe] — not!

[6]Rabbi Matenah said: Here [16A] [7]we are dealing with the chief of a tribe who sinned. [8]Did not Rav Adda bar Ahavah say: "Every great matter they shall bring to you" — [9]the matter of a great man. [10]He too is a great man.

[11]Ulla said in the name of Rabbi Elazar: [12][The Mishnah is dealing] with those that come about matters of inheritance, [13]and like the beginning of [inheriting] the Land of Israel. [14]Just as its beginning [required] seventy-one, [15]so too here seventy-one.

RASHI

מעשרה ועד מאה — בציר מעשרה לא מקרי עיר, וטפי ממאה נפקא מתורת עיר, והוו להו ציבור, ובציבור לא כתיב סייף, הלכך, כל אחד נידון בפני עצמו, ובסקילה. **בנשיא שבט שחטא** — ובאחת מכל מיתות בית דין. **דרב אדא בר אהבה** — לקמן. **וכתחילתה של ארץ ישראל** — כך דינה לעולם, אם נפלה מחלוקת נחלה בשבט.

BACKGROUND

!אֲבָל כּוּלּוֹ — לֹא But an entire tribe — not! Though it would seem logical that an entire tribe would be judged by a Great Sanhedrin, nevertheless it appears that the law concerning a city that has been led astray applies only to a single small city of sinners, whose citizens are tried by the Great Sanhedrin for their grave transgressions. Not only are they condemned to death if found guilty, but their property is also confiscated. However, when an entire tribe has sinned, it is impossible to judge it as a warning to the many, but rather every individual is tried individually.

NOTES

בְּבָאִין עַל עִסְקֵי נְחָלוֹת When they come to argue about matters of inheritances. The Jerusalem Talmud formulates this in a slightly different manner: The Mishnah is dealing with a situation where two tribes disagree over the division of grazing rights Rabbinically mandated in the forested area between their two territories. Even though the dispute is not over the actual boundaries of inheritance set by the Torah, nevertheless it involves a matter of concern to the tribes as a whole and therefore is deemed by our Mishnah as worthy of adjudication by a court of seventy-one judges.

HALAKHAH

residents, numbering anywhere between a hundred and a majority of the tribe, were led astray into idol worship. If a majority of the tribe or more were led astray, they are judged as individuals," following Rabbi Yonatan (for in the Jerusalem Talmud, the matter is the subject of a Tannaitic dispute, and Rabbi Yonatan's view is supported by Rabbi Yehudah; *Kesef Mishneh*). (*Rambam, Sefer Mada, Hilkhot Avodah Zarah* 4:2.)

LANGUAGE

קַלְפֵּי Lottery. This word derives from the Greek χάλπις, *kalpis* or χάλπη, *kalpi,* meaning an urn or box, and, in the narrower sense, an urn used for casting ballots or drawing lots.

TRANSLATION AND COMMENTARY

אִי מָה [1]The Gemara asks: If so, **should it** also **be that just as** the **beginning** of the process required **a lottery,** [2]the consulting of **the** oracular **Urim and Tumim, and** the presence of **all of Israel,** [3]so **too here,** when resolving a later disagreement, we should also require **a lottery, the Urim and Tumim, and** the presence of **all of Israel?** Since we do not need any of these, a court of seventy-one would be unnecessary as well!

אֶלָּא [4]**Rather, it is clear** that Ulla's explanation cannot be accepted, and that the Mishnah must be understood **in accordance with** the explanation **of Rav Matenah,** who proposed that it is referring to a Nasi who sinned.

רָבִינָא אָמַר [5]The Gemara now returns to its initial suggestion as to how to understand the Mishnah. **Ravina said:** [6]The Mishnah can, **in fact,** be understood as speaking about **a tribe that was led astray** into idol worship. [7]**And** as for **that which was difficult for you** in accepting this proposal — how **can we judge** an entire tribe that committed idolatry **in accordance with the** same **law** that we apply in the case of **public** violation by a "city led astray," when neither Rabbi Yoshiyah nor Rabbi Yoḥanan recognizes an entire tribe as constituting a "city" in this regard? [8]It can be resolved as follows: **Indeed, even though** the special laws applying to a "city led astray" (the decapitation of its inhabitants and the destruction of its property) do not apply in the case of an entire tribe that committed idolatry, for **we execute** the tribe's members **as** we would **an individual** who worshiped idols, [9]nevertheless **we do judge them in** the same **court** that is designated for **public** cases of idol worship, a court of seventy-one. [10]The Gemara now explains why this is so: **Did not Rabbi Ḥama, the son of Rabbi Yose, say in the name of Rabbi Oshaya:** The verse regarding an individual who committed idolatry states (Deuteronomy 17:5): [11]**"And you shall take out that man or that woman,** who did that wicked thing, unto your gates, and you shall stone them, the man or the woman, until they die"? [12]We learn from this verse that **you take out an** individual **man or woman** who committed idolatry **to** appear before the court that sits within **your** city **gates,** the Lesser Sanhedrin of twenty-three members. [13]However, **you do not take out an entire city** which committed

[1]אִי מָה תְּחִילָּתָהּ קַלְפֵּי,
[2]אוּרִים וְתוּמִּים, וְכָל יִשְׂרָאֵל,
[3]אַף כָּאן קַלְפֵּי, אוּרִים וְתוּמִּים,
וְכָל יִשְׂרָאֵל!
[4]אֶלָּא, מְחַוַּורְתָּא כִּדְרַב מַתָּנָה.
[5]רָבִינָא אָמַר: [6]לְעוֹלָם, בְּשֵׁבֶט
שֶׁהוּדַּח. [7]וּדְקָא קַשְׁיָא לָךְ —
בְּדִינָא דְּרַבִּים דָּיְינִינַן לֵיהּ?
[8]אִין, אַף עַל גַּב דְּקָטְלִינַן בְּיָחִיד
[9]בֵּי דִינָא דְּרַבִּים דָּיְינִינַן לֵיהּ.
[10]מִי לָא אָמַר רַבִּי חָמָא בְּרַבִּי
יוֹסֵי אָמַר רַבִּי אוֹשַׁעְיָא:
[11]"וְהוֹצֵאתָ אֶת הָאִישׁ הַהוּא אוֹ
אֶת הָאִשָּׁה הַהִוא וגו׳"?
[12]אִישׁ וְאִשָּׁה אַתָּה מוֹצִיא
לִשְׁעָרֶיךָ, [13]וְאִי אַתָּה מוֹצִיא

LITERAL TRANSLATION

[1]Should it be that just as its beginning [required] a lottery, [2]the Urim and Tumim, and all of Israel, [3]here too a lottery, the Urim and Tumim, and all of Israel?

[4]Rather, it is clear in accordance with that of Rav Matenah. [5]Ravina said: [6]In fact, a tribe that was led astray. [7]And that which was difficult for you — can we judge in acccordance with the law of public [violation]? [8]Indeed, even though we execute them as individuals, [9]we judge them in a court of the public. [10]Did not Rabbi Ḥama, the son of Rabbi Yose, say in the name of Rabbi Oshaya: [11]"And you shall take out that man or that woman, etc."? [12]A man or a woman you take out to your gates, [13]but you do not take out

RASHI

קלפי אורים ותומים — ב״ש נוטלין (בבא בתרא קכב,א) מפורש. **אף על גב דקטלינן ביחיד** — דדינא של שבט בסקילה — אפילו הכי בדינא **דרבים דיינינן ליה** — דבעי שבעים ואחד, ולא בדינא דיחיד — בעשרים ושלשה. **לשעריך** — לבית דין שבשעריך, דהיינו סנהדרי קטנה, ואי אתה מוציא כולה אלא בסנהדרי גדולה. **דרבי חמא בר׳ יוסי** — לקמן.

NOTES

אוּרִים וְתוּמִּים Urim and Tumim. Among the special garments worn by the High Priest in the Temple was a woven breastplate, or *Ḥoshen,* upon which were set twelve precious stones, each engraved with one of the names of the twelve tribes of Israel. In between the folds of the *Ḥoshen* were placed the *Urim* and *Tumim* (which some say was a parchment upon which was inscribed God's Ineffable Name). When the High Priest wished to receive prophetic

HALAKHAH

בֵּי דִינָא דְּרַבִּים דָּיְינִינַן לֵיהּ We judge them in a public court. "Individuals accused of practicing idolatry are judged by a Lesser Sanhedrin. If all the inhabitants of a city or the majority thereof, or all the members of a tribe or the majority thereof, were led astray into idolatry, they are judged by the Great Sanhedrin." (*Rambam, Sefer Mada, Hilkhot Avodah Zarah* 4:3.)

כָּל הָעִיר כּוּלָּהּ לִשְׁעָרֶיךָ. [1]הָכָא נַמִי, אִישׁ וְאִשָּׁה אַתָּה מוֹצִיא לִשְׁעָרֶיךָ, [2]וְאִי אַתָּה מוֹצִיא כָּל הַשֵּׁבֶט כּוּלּוֹ לִשְׁעָרֶיךָ.

[3]״לֹא אֶת נְבִיא הַשֶּׁקֶר״. [4]מְנָהָנֵי מִילֵּי? [5]אָמַר רַבִּי יוֹסֵי בְּרַבִּי חֲנִינָא: אָתְיָא ״הֲזָדָה״, [6]״הֲזָדָה״ מִזָּקֵן מַמְרֵא. [7]מַה לְהַלָּן בְּשִׁבְעִים וְאֶחָד, [8]אַף כָּאן בְּשִׁבְעִים וְאֶחָד.

[9]וְהָא הֲזָדָה כִּי כְּתִיבָא, [10]בִּקְטָלָא הוּא דִּכְתִיבָא, [11]וּקְטָלָא בְּעֶשְׂרִין וּתְלָתָא הוּא! [12]אֶלָּא, אָמַר רֵישׁ לָקִישׁ: גָּמַר

LITERAL TRANSLATION

an entire city to your gates. [1]Here as well, a man or a woman you take out to your gates, [2]but you do not take out an entire tribe to your gates.

[3]"Not the false prophet." [4]From where are these words [derived]? [5]Rabbi Yose the son of Rabbi Ḥanina said: It is derived by "willfulness" [6]"willfulness" from a rebellious elder. [7]Just as there by seventy-one, [8]so too here by seventy-one.

[9]But surely when "willfulness" is written, [10]it is in [the context of] execution that it is written, [11]and execution is by twenty-three!

[12]Rather, Resh Lakish said: [The Mishnah] learned

RASHI

אתיא הזדה הזדה — בנביא השקר כתיב (דברים יח): "אך הנביא אשר יזיד" ובזקן ממרא כתיב (שם יז): "והאיש אשר יעשה בזדון", מה זקן אינו נהרג אלא אם כן המרה על פי בית דין הגדול, דכתיב (שם יז) "וקמת ועלית", אף נביא אינו נידון אלא בבית דין הגדול. **והא הזדה** — דזקן ממרא. **כי כתיבא בקטלא כתיבא** — וקטלא דידיה בעשרים ושלשה, דכי כתיב "וקמת ועלית" בהוראה כתיב, שבאין לשואלו מה יורו וחוזר לעירו, ואם הורה לעשות כבתחילה נידון כשאר המומתין בעשרים ושלשה, דהא לא תני במתניתין (ב,א): "ולא את זקן ממרא".

TRANSLATION AND COMMENTARY

idolatry **to** appear before the court that sits within **your gates,** but rather they must appear before the Great Sanhedrin. [1]The same can be said **here as well: You take out an** individual **man or woman to** appear before the court that sits within **your** city **gates,** [2]but **you do not take out an entire tribe to** appear before the court within **your gates.** Rather they appear before the Great Sanhedrin.

לֹא אֶת נְבִיא הַשֶּׁקֶר [3]We learned in our Mishnah: "We do **not** judge **the false prophet** other than by a court of seventy-one." [4]The Gemara asks: **From where** in Scripture are **these words** derived? [5]**Rabbi Yose the son of Rabbi Ḥanina said:** The law pertaining to the false prophet **is derived from** a *gezerah shavah* (verbal analogy) between two verses which contain a common reference to **"willfulness"**: The verse dealing with a false prophet (Deuteronomy 18:20): [6]"But the prophet who shall **willfully** speak a word in My name, which I have not commanded him to speak, or who shall speak in the name of other gods, that prophet shall die," and that dealing with the execution of **a rebellious elder** (Deuteronomy 17:12): "And the man who will act with *willfulness,* by not hearkening to the priest who stands to minister there before the Lord your God, or to the judge, that man shall die, and you shall eliminate the evil from Israel." [7]**Just as there,** in the case of the rebellious elder, the verse is referring to one who sinned **by** willfully rebelling against a court of **seventy-one,** [8]**so too here,** in the case of the false prophet, the verse implies that he can only be tried **by** a court of **seventy-one.**

וְהָא הֲזָדָה [9]The Gemara asks: **But surely when "willfulness" is written** in the verse referring to the rebellious elder, [10]**it is in** the context of his **execution that it is written.** [11]**And** while it is true that his rebellion must be directed against a court of seventy-one, the verdict regarding his **execution is** arrived at **by** a court of **twenty-three!** Thus, if anything is to be learned from a *gezerah shavah* between these two verses, it should be that a false prophet is tried by a court of twenty-three!

אֶלָּא [12]**Rather, Resh Lakish said:** The Mishnah **deduced** that a false prophet must be tried by a court of seventy-one from a *gezerah shavah* between two verses in which the term **"word"** appeared: The verse dealing with a false prophet (Deuteronomy 18:20): "But the prophet who shall willfully speak a

NOTES

guidance from the Lord in respect to a crucial matter affecting the nation, he would address the *Urim* and *Tumim,* which in turn would selectively illuminate the letters etched upon the stones of the *Ḥoshen* so that they could be combined by the High Priest into the divinely intended response.

HALAKHAH

נְבִיא שֶׁקֶר **A false prophet.** "A false prophet is tried by a court of seventy-one judges," following the Mishnah. (*Rambam, Sefer Shofetim, Hilkhot Sanhedrin* 5:1.)

TRANSLATION AND COMMENTARY

word in My name, which I have not commanded him to speak," [1]and the verse **from** which we derive the actual prohibition involved in an elder's **rebelling** against the Sanhedrin (Deuteronomy 17:10): "And you shall do according to the *word* which they shall tell you, from that place which the Lord shall choose." Just as in the case of the rebellious elder, the verse is referring to one who rose up against a court of seventy-one, so too in the case of the false prophet, the verse is implying that he can only be tried by a court of seventy-one.

וְלֶהְדַּר זָקֵן מַמְרֵא [2]The Gemara asks: If so, **let** the case of **a rebellious elder** now **return** for further consideration, [3]and **learn** through the previous *gezerah shavah,* based on the common Scriptural reference to **"willfulness,"** that the rebellious elder should be tried by the same number of judges as **the false prophet** — seventy-one!

דָּבָר [4]The Gemara answers: The reason Resh Lakish applied one *gezerah shavah* and not the other is because **he learned** of the analogy between **"word"** and **"word"** through a tradition that he received from his teachers, [5]whereas **he did not learn** of any analogy between **"willfulness"** and **"willfulness"** through a similar tradition. And it is well established that one may use a *gezerah shavah* only when it has been handed down by one's teachers.

וְלֹא אֶת כֹּהֵן גָּדוֹל [6]Our Mishnah continues: "**And** we do **not** judge **a High Priest** who committed a capital offense other than by a court of seventy-one judges." [7]**From where** in Scripture is the position evident in **these words** derived? [8]**Rav Adda bar Ahavah said:** It is clear that this must be the law, **for the verse states** in regard to Moses' judicial responsibilities (Exodus 18:22): [9]**"Every great matter they shall bring to you,"** [10]and the phrase "every great matter" is understood as referring to **the matter of a great man** who has committed a capital offense. Since Moses served in the same capacity as a court of seventy-one judges, we can learn from here that a High Priest who committed a capital offense must be tried by a court of seventy-one.

מֵיתִיבֵי [11]Some Sages **raised an objection** against this derivation of the law on the basis of the following Baraita: The verse states: [12]"'**Every great matter** they shall bring to you' — meaning that, whereas a normal matter could be brought to the lower courts for adjudication, [13]a more **difficult matter** would have to be brought to Moses who stood in place of the Sanhedrin. [14]Now, **do you** really mean to **say** that the Torah refers here to **a difficult matter,** [15]**or** perhaps **it is only** referring to **the matter of a great man** who committed

"דָּבָר" [1]"דָּבָר" מֵהַמְרָאָתוֹ.
[2]וְלֶהְדַּר זָקֵן מַמְרֵא [3]וְלִגְמַר הֲזָדָה הֲזָדָה מִנְּבִיא הַשֶּׁקֶר!
[4]"דָּבָר" "דָּבָר" — גְּמִיר.
[5]"הֲזָדָה" "הֲזָדָה" — לָא גְּמִיר.
[6]"וְלֹא אֶת כֹּהֵן גָּדוֹל". [7]מְנָהָנֵי מִילֵּי? [8]אָמַר רַב אַדָּא בַּר אַהֲבָה: דְּאָמַר קְרָא: [9]"כָּל הַדָּבָר הַגָּדֹל יָבִיאוּ אֵלֶיךָ" — [10]דְּבָרָיו שֶׁל גָּדוֹל.
[11]מֵיתִיבֵי: [12]"דָּבָר גָּדֹל" — [13]דָּבָר קָשֶׁה. [14]אַתָּה אוֹמֵר דָּבָר קָשֶׁה, [15]אוֹ אֵינוֹ אֶלָּא דְּבָרָיו

LITERAL TRANSLATION

"word" [1]"word" from his rebelling.
[2]Let [the case of] a rebellious elder return [3]and learn "willfulness" "willfulness" from the false prophet!
[4]He learned "word" "word."
[5]"Wilfulness" "willfulness" he did not learn.
[6]"And not a High Priest." [7]From where are these words [derived]? [8]Rav Ada bar Ahavah said: For the verse states: [9]"Every great matter they shall bring to you" — [10]the matter of a great man.
[11]They raised an objection: [12]"'[Every] great matter' — [13]a difficult matter. [14]Do you say a difficult matter, [15]or [perhaps] it is only the matter

RASHI

דבר דבר מהמראתו — בנביא בקטליה כתיב (דברים יח): "אשר יזיד לדבר דבר וגו׳" ובהמראת זקן כתיב (שם יז): "ועשית על פי הדבר". **וליהדר זקן ממרא וניגמר** — קטליה בסנהדרי גדולה "הזדה" "הזדה" מנביא, דהא בקטלא דתרווייהו כתיב הזדה, ונימא: מה נביא בסנהדרי גדולה דהא גמרינן מהמראת זקן — אף מיתת זקן בסנהדרי גדולה, וניתני במתניתין (ב,א): "ולא את הזקן ממרא אלא בבית דין של שבעים ואחד". **דבר דבר** — הך גזירה שוה ד"דבר" "דבר" גמיר ליה האי תנא מרביה, אבל הך ד"הזדה" "הזדה" לא גמיר ליה מרביה, וקל וחומר אדם דן מעצמו, ואין אדם דן גזירה שוה מעצמו אלא אם כן קיבל מרבו הלכה למשה מסיני, דאיכא למימר — קרא למילתא אחריתא אתא, וכן הלכה רווחת בישראל. **יביאו אליך** — ומשה במקום שבעים ואחד קאי. **דבריו של גדול** — דינו של בעל שררה, כגון נשיא וכהן גדול.

NOTES

דָּבָר גָּדֹל — דָּבָר קָשֶׁה Every great matter — a difficult matter. It has been suggested that this interpretation is based on the spelling of the word גדל, which appears in this verse without a vav. Thus it indicates that the verse is

HALAKHAH

כֹּהֵן גָּדוֹל A High Priest. "A High Priest is tried for capital offenses by a court of seventy-one judges, but civil cases involving the High Priest are adjudicated by a court of three." (*Rambam, Sefer Shofetim, Hilkhot Sanhedrin* 5:1.)

LITERAL TRANSLATION

of a great man? [1]When it states: 'The difficult matter they brought to Moses' — [2]behold the difficult matter is stated."

[3]He stated in accordance with that Tanna, [4]who taught: "'[Every] great matter' — [5]the matter of a great man. [6]Do you say the matter of a great man, [7]or [perhaps] it is only a difficult matter? [8]When it states: 'The difficult matter' — [9]a difficult matter is stated. [10]How then do I establish '[Every] great matter'? [11]The matter of a great man."

[12]And [according to] that Tanna, [13]why do I need two verses?

[14]One just for a directive, [15]and one for execution.

[16]And the other?

[17]If so, [18]let it write either "great" "great" or "difficult" "difficult." [19]What is "great" and what is "difficult"? [20]Understand from this two.

[21]Rabbi Elazar asked: [22]The ox of

שֶׁל גָּדוֹל? [1]כְּשֶׁהוּא אוֹמֵר "אֶת הַדָּבָר הַקָּשֶׁה יְבִיאוּן אֶל מֹשֶׁה" — [2]הֲרֵי דָּבָר קָשֶׁה אָמוּר.

[3]הוּא דַּאֲמַר כִּי הַאי תַּנָּא, [4]דְּתַנְיָא: "דָּבָר גָּדֹל" — [5]דְּבָרָיו שֶׁל גָּדוֹל. [6]אַתָּה אוֹמֵר דְּבָרָיו שֶׁל גָּדוֹל, [7]אוֹ אֵינוֹ אֶלָּא דָּבָר הַקָּשֶׁה? [8]כְּשֶׁהוּא אוֹמֵר: 'הַדָּבָר הַקָּשֶׁה' — [9]הֲרֵי דָּבָר קָשֶׁה אָמוּר, [10]הָא מָה אֲנִי מְקַיֵּים "דָּבָר גָּדֹל"? [11]דְּבָרָיו שֶׁל גָּדוֹל.

[12]וְהַאי תַּנָּא, [13]תְּרֵי קְרָאֵי לָמָּה לִי?

[14]חַד לְצַוָּאָה בְּעָלְמָא, [15]וְחַד לַעֲשִׂיָּיה.

[16]וְאִידָּךְ?

[17]אִם כֵּן, [18]לִכְתּוֹב אוֹ "גָּדוֹל" "גָּדוֹל" אוֹ "קָשֶׁה" "קָשֶׁה". [19]מַאי "גָּדוֹל וּמַאי "קָשֶׁה" — [20]שְׁמַע מִינָּהּ תַּרְתֵּי.

[21]בָּעֵי רַבִּי אֶלְעָזָר: [22]שׁוֹרוֹ שֶׁל

RASHI

והאי תנא — דדרש: "דבר גדול" — דבר קשה, למה לי תרי קראי? **שורו של כהן גדול** — אם המית איש.

TRANSLATION AND COMMENTARY

a capital offense? [1]**When** the Torah subsequently **states** (Exodus 18:26): **'The difficult matter they brought to Moses,'** [2]it becomes clear that **the difficult matter** that **is stated** in this verse as well as the phrase 'every great matter' stated in the earlier verse have the same meaning. And so we see that the Baraita rejects Rav Adah bar Ahavah's interpretation of the phrase as referring to 'the matter of a great man'"!

הוּא דַּאֲמַר [3]The Gemara answers that Rav Adda bar Ahavah's position has Tannaitic support as well, for **he stated** his view **in accordance with that Tanna** [4]**who taught** in another Baraita: "The verse states: **'Every great matter** they shall bring to you' — [5]meaning that **the matter of a great man** who committed a capital offense was to be brought before Moses for adjudication. [6]Now, **do you** mean to **say** that the Torah refers here to **the matter of a great man** who committed a capital offense, [7]**or** perhaps **it is only** referring to **a difficult matter** which cannot be resolved by a lesser court? [8]**When** the Torah subsequently **states: 'The difficult matter** they brought to Moses,' [9]the case of **a difficult matter is stated** outright. [10]**How then do I establish** the meaning of the verse **'Every great matter** they shall bring to you'? [11]It must be referring to **the matter of a great man** who committed a capital offense."

וְהַאי תַּנָּא [12]The Gemara tries to understand the first Baraita: According to **that Tanna** who maintained that the two expressions, "great matter" and "difficult matter," refer to the same thing, [13]**why do I need two** different **verses** to teach me the same thing?

חַד לְצַוָּאָה בְּעָלְמָא [14]The Gemara answers: **One** verse teaches us **merely** that Jethro **instructed** Moses to appoint judges to deal with the lesser matters and to limit his involvement to the more difficult cases. [15]**And one** verse teaches us that **Moses executed** the plan that was suggested by Jethro.

וְאִידָּךְ [16]The Gemara asks: **And** why does **the other** Tanna not accept this argument?

אִם כֵּן [17]The answer is: **If** it were **so,** that the terms "great matter" and "difficult matter" refer to the same thing, [18]the Torah would have **said either "great"** in both cases **or "difficult"** in both cases! [19]**What is** the significance of referring to a **"great** matter" in the earlier verse **and** a **"difficult** matter" in the latter one? [20]This Tanna concludes that we must **understand from this** that **two** separate issues are being addressed.

בָּעֵי רַבִּי אֶלְעָזָר [21]**Rabbi Elazar asked** the following question: [22]If **the ox of a High Priest** killed somebody,

NOTES

referring to a matter which is not necessarily of great significance, but is nevertheless difficult to understand.

שׁוֹרוֹ שֶׁל כֹּהֵן גָּדוֹל The High Priest's ox. *Rabbi Akiva Eiger* asks: Why was Rabbi Elazar in doubt about this matter?

HALAKHAH

שׁוֹרוֹ שֶׁל כֹּהֵן גָּדוֹל The High Priest's ox. "*Rambam* does not issue an explicit ruling regarding an animal that belongs to the High Priest and that killed someone. According to *Radbaz,* the case is tried by a court of

TRANSLATION AND COMMENTARY

by how many judges must it be sentenced? [1]**Do we compare** the legal process employed in destroying this animal **to** that which determines **the death of its owner,** the High Priest, when convicted of a capital offense, in which case the ox should be sentenced by a court of seventy-one? [2]**Or do we perhaps we compare it to** the legal process that determines **the death of** animal-**owners in general,** who in capital cases are tried and convicted by a court of twenty-three?

אָמַר אַבַּיֵי [3]**Abaye said: Since** Rabbi Elazar only **asked** about a High Priest's **ox,** [4]this proves **by implication that it was obvious to him** that in other cases involving the High Priest's **money,** justice was to be rendered by a regular civil court of three judges.

פְּשִׁיטָא [5]The Gemara concedes: Such a conclusion **is** indeed **obvious!** Why would anyone have thought otherwise?

מַהוּ דְּתֵימָא [6]The Gemara answers: **You might have said** erroneously that, **since** the Torah **wrote:** [7]**"Every great matter** they shall bring to you," [8]**all matters** involving **a great man,** including monetary disputes, must be brought before a court of seventy-one. [9]Therefore, Abaye **teaches us** that this is not so.

אֵין מוֹצִיאִין [10]We learned in the Mishnah: "The leaders of the nation **do not take** the people **out** to fight a discretionary war unless they receive permission to do so from the High Court of seventy-one judges, the Great Sanhedrin." [11]**From where** in Scripture is the rule expressed by **these words** derived? [12]**Rabbi Abbahu said:** It is derived from **the verse stated** at the time of Joshua's appointment as the leader of Israel, where the guidelines were set for his leading the people in the campaign to conquer the land of Canaan (Numbers 27:21): [13]**"And before Elazar the priest shall he stand,** and he shall ask counsel of the Urim before the Lord; by

כֹּהֵן גָּדוֹל בְּכַמָּה? [1]לְמִיתַת בְּעָלִים דִּידֵיהּ מְדַמִּינַן לֵיהּ, [2]אוֹ דִּילְמָא לְמִיתַת בְּעָלִים דְּעָלְמָא מְדַמִּינַן לֵיהּ?

[3]אֲמַר אַבַּיֵי: מִדְּקָא מִבָּעֲיָא לֵיהּ שׁוֹרוֹ, [4]מִכְּלָל דְּמָמוֹנוֹ פְּשִׁיטָא לֵיהּ.

[5]פְּשִׁיטָא!

[6]מַהוּ דְּתֵימָא? הוֹאִיל וְכָתַב: [7]"כָּל הַדָּבָר הַגָּדֹל" — [8]כָּל דְּבָרָיו שֶׁל גָּדוֹל, [9]קָא מַשְׁמַע לָן.

[10]"אֵין מוֹצִיאִין וכו׳". [11]מְנָהָנֵי מִילֵּי? [12]אָמַר רַבִּי אַבָּהוּ: דְּאָמַר קְרָא [13]"וְלִפְנֵי אֶלְעָזָר הַכֹּהֵן

LITERAL TRANSLATION

a High Priest by how many? [1]Do we compare it to the death of its owner, [2]or perhaps we compare it to the death of owners in general?

[3]Abaye said: Since he asked [about] his ox, [4][this proves] by implication that his money was obvious to him.

[5]It is obvious!

[6]What would you have said? Since it wrote: [7]"Every great matter" — [8]all matters of a great man. [9][Therefore] it teaches us.

[10]"We do not take out, etc." [11]From where are these words [derived]? [12]Rabbi Abbahu said: For the verse states: [13]"And before Elazar the priest

RASHI

מדקא מיבעיא ליה שורו — שמע מינה שורו הוא דמספקא ליה, משום דכתיב (שמות כא): "וגם בעליו יומת" — כמיתת בעלים, אבל שאר ממונו פשיטא לן דבשלשה, ככל דיני ממונות. **כל דבריו** — ואפילו ממונו ליבעי סנהדרי גדולה.

NOTES

Surely we learn in the next chapter (18b) that if the High Priest is accused of a lesser transgression, one that is not a capital offense, he is treated like any other person and tried by a court of three! *Tzafnat Pa'ane'aḥ* bases an answer upon the Jerusalem Talmud, where it is suggested that respect for the High Priest is what determines that he not have to appear before the Great Sanhedrin every time a minor charge is brought against him. This rationale would appear relevant when it is the High Priest himself who is charged with the offense and thus stands to be demeaned. However, when it is his animal that is being brought before a court, the stature of the High Priest might actually dictate that a court of seventy-one be convened in order to determine the fate of his property. An alternative explanation of the reason why the High Priest himself is treated like any other person and judged by a court of three when accused of a noncapital offense suggests that it is due to the diminution in his stature brought about by the suspicion of wrongdoing. However, when it is his animal that has done damage, the High Priest's stature remains intact, thereby requiring that a court of seventy-one judges be convened in order to decide the case (*Imrei Tzvi*.)

מִלְחֶמֶת רְשׁוּת A discretionary war. A mandatory war is one which is waged for the sake of conquering the Land of Israel from the Canaanites, or destroying the nation of Amalek, or defending Israel from attack by its other enemies. Mandatory war may be waged without prior permission from the Sanhedrin, and all Jews are required to participate. A discretionary war is one waged in order to enlarge the territorial boundaries of Israel or to resolve a conflict between neighboring nations, and it may only be waged with prior permission of the Great Sanhedrin.

וְלִפְנֵי אֶלְעָזָר הַכֹּהֵן יַעֲמֹד And he shall stand before Elazar the priest. The Rishonim ask: How can the Gemara derive

HALAKHAH

twenty-three, whereas according to *Leḥem Mishneh,* it is tried by a court of seventy-one." (*Rambam, Sefer Shofetim, Hilkhot Sanhedrin* 5:1.)

TRANSLATION AND COMMENTARY

his word they shall go out, and by his word they shall come in, both he and all the children of Israel with him, and all the congregation." [1]**"He" — this** refers to **the King** of Israel, or any leader who has the status of a king — such as Joshua. [2]**"And all the children of Israel with him"** — [3]**this** refers to **the** priest who was specially **anointed for war** so as to accompany soldiers into battle (see Deuteronomy 20:2). [4]**"And all the congregation" — this** refers to **the Sanhedrin,** who elsewhere in the Torah are called a "congregation." Mention of the Sanhedrin here in the verse that authorizes the king to mobilize his people for battle indicates that their permission is necessary before he can do so.

וְדִילְמָא לְסַנְהֶדְרִי הוּא [5]The Gemara argues that this verse can be understood differently: **Perhaps it is to the** members of the **Sanhedrin that the Torah** is speaking when the verse **states that they should ask** counsel **of the Urim and Tumim**, thus indicating that any of three communal authorities referred to in the verse were allowed to make use of the Urim and Tumim. However, insofar as mobilizing the people for war, the king could act on his own without permission from the Sanhedrin.

אֶלָּא [6]**Rather,** the rule stated in our Mishnah is derived from the way King David behaved, **in accordance with what Rav Aḥa bar Bizna said in the name of Rabbi Shimon Ḥasida:** [7]**A lyre was suspended over** King **David's bed,** [8]and **when** it was **midnight, a northern wind would blow through** the instrument, **and it would play by itself.** [9]**Immediately David would arise** from his sleep **and engage in Torah** study **until dawn appeared.** [10]**Once dawn appeared, the Sages of Israel would come to him,** [11]and **say to him: "Our lord, the king,** [12]many of **your people, Israel, are in need of** material **support,** but they do not know where to seek it." [13]David **would say to them: "Go** out then and **support yourselves,**

LITERAL TRANSLATION

shall he stand." [1]"He" — this is the king. [2]"And all the children of Israel with him" — [3]this is the priest anointed for war. [4]"And all the congregation" — this is the Sanhedrin.

[5]But perhaps it is to the Sanhedrin that the Torah (lit., "the Merciful") states that they should ask of the Urim and Tumim!

[6]Rather, it is in accordance with that which Rav Aḥa bar Bizna said in the name of Rabbi Shimon Ḥasida: [7]A lyre was suspended over David's bed. [8]When midnight would arrive, a northern wind would blow through it, and it would play by itself. [9]Immediately David would arise and engage in Torah until the first ray of dawn appeared. [10]Once dawn appeared, the Sages of Israel would come in by him, [11][and] say to him: "Our lord, the king, [12]your people, Israel, are in need of support!" [13]He said to them: "Go,

יַעֲמֹד", [1]"הוּא" — זֶה מֶלֶךְ, [2]"וְכָל בְּנֵי יִשְׂרָאֵל אִתּוֹ" — [3]זֶה מְשׁוּחַ מִלְחָמָה. [4]"וְכָל הָעֵדָה" — זֶה סַנְהֶדְרִי.

[5]וְדִילְמָא לְסַנְהֶדְרִי הוּא דְּקָאָמַר לְהוּ רַחֲמָנָא דְּלִישַׁיְּילוּ בְּאוּרִים וְתוּמִּים?

[6]אֶלָּא, כִּי הָא דַּאֲמַר רַב אַחָא בַּר בִּיזְנָא אָמַר רַבִּי שִׁמְעוֹן חֲסִידָא: [7]כִּנּוֹר הָיָה תָּלוּי לְמַעְלָה מִמִּטָּתוֹ שֶׁל דָּוִד. [8]כֵּיוָן שֶׁהִגִּיעַ חֲצוֹת לַיְלָה רוּחַ צְפוֹנִית מְנַשֶּׁבֶת בּוֹ, וְהָיָה מְנַגֵּן מֵאֵלָיו. [9]מִיָּד הָיָה דָּוִד עוֹמֵד וְעוֹסֵק בַּתּוֹרָה עַד שֶׁעָלָה עַמּוּד הַשַּׁחַר. [10]כֵּיוָן שֶׁעָלָה עַמּוּד הַשַּׁחַר, נִכְנְסוּ חַכְמֵי יִשְׂרָאֵל אֶצְלוֹ, [11]אָמְרוּ לוֹ: אֲדוֹנֵינוּ הַמֶּלֶךְ, [12]עַמְּךָ יִשְׂרָאֵל צְרִיכִין לְפַרְנָסָה"! [13]אָמַר לָהֶן: "לְכוּ,

RASHI

ודילמא — הא דקא מדכר קרא בסנהדרי גדולה משום שאילת אורים ותומים הוא אתא, לאשמעינן דנשאלין לסנהדרין באורים ותומים, וכן למלך, וכן למשוח מלחמה, אבל לא להדיוט, ולעולם לענין לצאת למלחמה — יוצאין בלא רשות סנהדרי. **כנור** — נקב שלו כלפי צפון היה, ובלילה רוח צפונית מנשבת, דקיימא לן (בבבא בתרא כה,א): ארבע רוחות מנשבות בכל יום, מזרחית בבקר, ורוח דרומית בחצי היום, ומערבית בתחילת לילה, וצפונית בחצי לילה, כמהלך חמה, שמהלכת ממזרח לדרום, ומדרום למערב, וממערב לצפון. ותניא ביבמות (עב,א): כל אותן ארבעים שנה שהיו ישראל במדבר, אף על פי שנזופים היו ולא נשבה להם רוח צפונית ביום, לא היה יום שלא נשבה להם רוח צפונית בחצי הלילה, אלמא חצות לילה עת נשיבתה לעולם, ופעמים שהיא מנשבת אף ביום, והיא רוח נוחה ויפה לבריות והיום מאיר בה. **והיה דוד עומד ועוסק בתורה** — כדכתיב חצות לילה אקום (תהלים קיט).

REALIA

כִּנּוֹרוֹ שֶׁל דָּוִד The lyre of David.

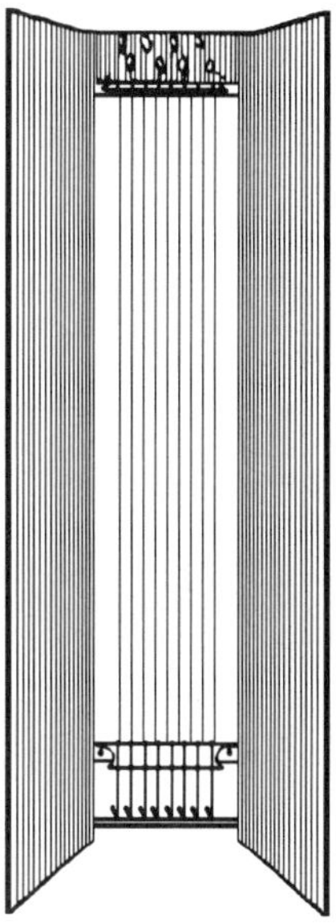

A modern Aeolian Harp.

The Geonim explain that David's lyre was a special instrument upon which the wind played. In European languages such an instrument is known as an Aeolian Harp, and it is constructed of a resonator with strings stretched over it in such a way that the wind will make them sound.

BACKGROUND

רוּחַ צְפוֹנִית A northern wind. A true north wind is rare in Jerusalem, but this expression apparently refers to the wind that passes through the City of David in the Kidron Valley. Because of the topography, it blows from north to south, and indeed the wind does grow appreciably stronger after midnight.

NOTES

a regulation concerning the waging of an optional war from this reference to Joshua? Surely Joshua's war for the conquest of the Land of Israel was a mandatory one! *Rabbenu Yonah* answers that, indeed, the Gemara could have raised this question, but it chose to ask a different one instead.. *Remah* suggests that the verse is alluding to an optional war since its references to permission from the Sanhedrin and the appointment of a specially anointed priest to accompany them in battle are not relevant in the case of a mandatory war.

LANGUAGE

הַקּוֹמֶץ וְהָאֲרִי Some authorities have interpreted the word "קוֹמֶץ" here to mean "grasshopper," for in the Aramaic translations of the Torah, the Hebrew "חֲגָבִים" — "grasshoppers" is translated as קַמְצִין. That is to say, a single grasshopper will not satisfy a lion's hunger.

REALIA

חוּלְיַית הַבּוֹר A cistern and its frame.

This expression refers to a slightly raised stone frame that was placed around the mouths of cisterns. Clearly, the rain falling directly into the mouth of the cistern and even on the stone frame could not fill the cistern, and a system of pipes and gutters was needed to bring water into it from many places.

BACKGROUND

בְּנָיָהוּ בֶּן יְהוֹיָדָע Benaiah son of Jehoiada. The Talmud understands that David's heroes were not only warriors but also "heroes in the Torah," great men who constituted the king's supreme council, and that Benaiah son of Jehoiada was the leader of the Cherethites and the Pelethites, among the most important followers of King David; and later he was King Solomon's military commander. Therefore the terms "*Kereti and Peleti*" are not interpreted in their ordinary sense as auxiliary brigades of foreign troops, but as an allusion to the Great Sanhedrin.

וְהִתְפַּרְנְסוּ זֶה מִזֶּה״. [1]אָמְרוּ לוֹ: ״אֵין הַקּוֹמֶץ מַשְׂבִּיעַ אֶת הָאֲרִי, [2]וְאֵין הַבּוֹר מִתְמַלֵּא מֵחוּלְיָיתוֹ״. [3]אָמַר לָהֶם: ״לְכוּ פִּשְׁטוּ יְדֵיכֶם בִּגְדוּד״. [4]מִיָּד יוֹעֲצִין בַּאֲחִיתוֹפֶל, [5]וְנִמְלָכִין בְּסַנְהֶדְרִין, [6]וְשׁוֹאֲלִין בְּאוּרִים וְתוּמִּים.

[7]אָמַר רַב יוֹסֵף: מַאי קְרָא? [16B] [8]״וְאַחֲרֵי אֲחִיתֹפֶל בְּנָיָהוּ בֶּן יְהוֹיָדָע וְאֶבְיָתָר וְשַׂר צָבָא לַמֶּלֶךְ יוֹאָב. [9]״אֲחִיתוֹפֶל״ — זֶה יוֹעֵץ. [10]וְכֵן הוּא אוֹמֵר: ״וַעֲצַת אֲחִיתֹפֶל אֲשֶׁר יָעַץ וגו׳״, [11]״וּבְנָיָהוּ בֶּן יְהוֹיָדָע״ — זוֹ סַנְהֶדְרִין. [12]״אֶבְיָתָר״ — אֵלּוּ אוּרִים וְתוּמִּים, [13]וְכֵן הוּא אוֹמֵר: ״וּבְנָיָהוּ בֶּן יְהוֹיָדָע עַל הַכְּרֵתִי וְעַל הַפְּלֵתִי״. [14]וְלָמָּה נִקְרָא שְׁמָן כְּרֵתִי וּפְלֵתִי? [15]כְּרֵתִי — שֶׁכּוֹרְתִין דִּבְרֵיהֶן,

LITERAL TRANSLATION

support yourselves, one from the other!" [1]They said to him: "A handful does not satisfy a lion, [2]and a pit cannot fill itself from its own water." [3]He said to them: "Go [and] stretch your hands out into bands." [4]Immediately they were consulting with Ahitophel, [5]asking permission of the Sanhedrin, [6]and inquiring of the Urim and Tumim.

[7]Rav Yosef said: What [is the] verse? [16B] [8]"And after Ahitophel [came] Benaiah the son of Jehoiada, and Abiathar; and the general of the king's army was Joab." [9]"Ahitophel" — this is the counselor. [10]And so it states: "And the counsel of Ahitophel which he counseled, etc." [11]"And Benaiah the son of Jehoiada" — this is the Sanhedrin. [12]"Abiathar" — this is the Urim and Tumim. [13]And so it states: "And Benaiah the son of Jehoiada was above the Kereti and the Peleti." [14]And why was their name called Kereti and Peleti? [15]Kereti — because they cut their words.

TRANSLATION AND COMMENTARY

one from the other, i.e., the community should take care of those in need!" [1]The Sages **said to** David in reply: "As the saying goes: **A handful** of feed **does not satisfy a lion.** [2]**And** in the words of another adage: **A cistern cannot fill itself up from its own waters.** So, too, the community must find outside sources to support itself." [3]David **said to** the Sages: **"Go** then **and stretch your hands out** in order to retake the booty pillaged from us by **bands** of neighboring oppressors." [4]**Immediately** we find the Sages going out and **consulting with Ahitophel** as to where and when they should wage battle, [5]**asking permission of the Sanhedrin** to enter into conflict, [6]**and inquiring of the Urim and Tumim** as to whether they should embark on the adventure.

אָמַר רַב יוֹסֵף [7]**Rav Yosef said: What verse** alludes to this event? [16B] [8]The verse that states (I Chronicles 27:34): **"And after Ahitophel [came] Benaiah the son of Jehoiada, and Abiathar; and the general of the king's army was Joab."** The order in which the people are mentioned in the verse can be explained as follows: [9]**"Ahitophel" — this** refers to **the counselor** who offered advice about when and where the fighting should begin. [10]**And so** the verse **states** (II Samuel 27:23): **"And the counsel of Ahitophel, which he counseled** in those days, was as if a man would inquire of the word of God." [11]**"And Benaiah the son of Jehoiada" — this** refers to the head of **the Sanhedrin,** which granted the king permission to wage war. [12]**"Abiathar" — this** refers to the High Priest, who wore **the Urim and Tumim** that had to be consulted before the people went out to battle. And how do we know that Benaiah the son of Jehoiada was head of the Sanhedrin? [13]For **so** the verse **states** (I Chronicles 18:17): **"And Benaiah the son of Jehoiada was above the Kereti and the Peleti."** [14]**And why were** the members of the Sanhedrin **called by the name Kereti and Peleti?** [15]They were called **Kereti**

RASHI

קומץ — פרנסה מועטת. **ואין הבור מתמלא מחולייתו** — עוקר חוליא מבור עמוק וחוזר והשליכה לתוכו, אינו מתמלא בכך, כלומר אין סיפק בידינו לפרנס עניים שבתוכנו. **ונמלכין בסנהדרין** — נוטלין רשות מהן, והיינו מתניתין. **בניהו בן יהוידע זה סנהדרין** — שהיה מופלא שבבית דין. **ואביתר אלו אורים ותומים וכן הוא אומר ובניהו בן יהוידע על הכרתי ועל הפלתי** — הוא למעלה מהם וקודם היה להם, ומדסמך בקרא קמא אביתר בתר בניהו — שמע מינה אביתר היינו כרתי ופלתי. וספרים דכתיב בהו ״ואביתר על הכרתי״, שיבוש הוא, שאין מקרא זה בכל הנביאים. **שכורתין** — חותכין דברים באמונתן.

NOTES

וְאַחֲרֵי אֲחִיתֹפֶל בְּנָיָהוּ And after Ahitophel came Benaiah. The Rishonim (see *Tosafot* and others) point out that the verse (I Chronicles 27:34) does not read: "And after Ahitophel came Benaiah the son of Jehoiada," but rather: "And after Ahitophel came Jehoiada the son of Benaiah." The Geonim argue that our passage should be corrected in accordance with the Scriptural text. According to the corrected reading, the verse from which the Gemara proves that the head of the Sanhedrin is consulted before the Urim and Tumim (I Chronicles 18:17: "And Benaiah the son of Jehoiada was over the Kereti and the Peleti") actually refers to the father of the Jehoiada mentioned in the later verse together with Ahitophel. Jehoiada took over the position as head of the Sanhedrin from his father, in accordance with the rule that a son is given precedence over all others, provided that he has the proper qualifications.

[1]וּפְלֵתִי — שֶׁמּוּפְלָאִין מַעֲשֵׂיהֶן. [2]וְאַחַר כָּךְ — ״שַׂר הַצָּבָא לַמֶּלֶךְ יוֹאָב״.
[3]אָמַר רַבִּי יִצְחָק בְּרֵיהּ דְּרַב אַדָּא [4]וְאָמְרִי לָהּ אָמַר רַבִּי יִצְחָק בַּר אֲבוּדִימִי: [5]מַאי קְרָא? [6]״עוּרָה כְבוֹדִי עוּרָה הַנֵּבֶל וְכִנּוֹר אָעִירָה שָּׁחַר״.
[7]״וְאֵין מוֹסִיפִין עַל הָעִיר״. [8]מְנָהָנֵי מִילֵּי? [9]אָמַר רַב שִׁימִי בַּר חִיָּיא: אָמַר קְרָא: [10]״כְּכֹל אֲשֶׁר אֲנִי מַרְאֶה אוֹתְךָ אֵת תַּבְנִית הַמִּשְׁכָּן...וְכֵן תַּעֲשׂוּ״ — [11]לַדּוֹרוֹת הַבָּאִין.

LITERAL TRANSLATION

[1]And Peleti — because their actions are wondrous. [2]And afterwards — "And the general of the king's army was Joab."

[3]Rabbi Yitzḥak, the son of Rav Adda, said [4]and some say Rabbi Yitzḥak bar Avudimi said: [5]What is the verse? [6]"Awake, my glory; awake, the harp and the lyre; I will awaken the dawn."

[7]"We do not add to the city." [8]From where are these words [derived]? [9]Rav Shimi bar Ḥiyya said: The verse states: [10]"According to all that I show you, the pattern of the tabernacle... and so shall you make it" — [11]for the coming generations.

TRANSLATION AND COMMENTARY

(כְּרֵתִי) because they **"cut** [כרת] **their words,"** i.e., delivered incisive decisions. [1]**And they** were called **Peleti** (פְּלֵתִי) **because their actions were wondrous** (מוּפְלָאִין). [2]Only **after** Aḥitophel gave his advice, and the Sanhedrin granted its permission, and the Urim and Tumim were consulted, did the people go out to war, and thus the verse concludes: **"And the general of the king's army was Joab"** — who actually led the people into battle.

אָמַר [3]**Rabbi Yitzḥak, the son of Rav Ada, said** [4]**(and some say** that it was **Rabbi Yitzḥak bar Avudimi** who **said):** [5]**What verse** alludes to the lyre that would wake David up in the middle of the night? As the verse states (Psalms 57:9): [6]**"Awake, my glory; awake, the harp and the lyre; I will awaken the dawn."**

וְאֵין מוֹסִיפִין עַל הָעִיר [7]The Mishnah continues: **"We do not add** new territory **to the city** of Jerusalem or to the Temple precincts except by permission of a High Court of seventy-one." [8]**From where** in Scripture **are these words** derived? [9]**Rav Shimi bar Ḥiyya said:** From **the verse** that **states** (Exodus 25:8-9): "Let them make me a sanctuary that I might dwell among them. [10]**According to all that I show you, the pattern of the tabernacle**, and the pattern of all its vessels, **and so shall you make it."** The clause "and so shall you make it" implies that, just as you established the Tabernacle in the desert, [11]so too shall you establish the Temple **in coming generations.** Since the area of the Tabernacle was sanctified by Moses, it would follow that the area of the Temple and its Courtyards, as well as the area of Jerusalem in which they were situated, could only be sanctified by the Sanhedrin, whose mandate was the same as that exercised by Moses in the desert.

RASHI

מאי קרא — דכנור תלוי על מטתו של דוד ומקילו לדוד משנתו, דכתיב ״אעירה השחר״, אני מעורר השחר, ולא כשאר מלכים שהשחר קודם ומעוררן. **כן תעשו לדורות** — מה משכן על פי משה והוא במקום סנהדרי גדולה, אף לדורות על פי סנהדרי גדולה.

NOTES

אֵין מוֹסִיפִין עַל הָעִיר We do not add onto the city. We learn elsewhere in the Mishnah (*Shevuot* 14a) that the territory of Jerusalem and of the Temple Courtyards could only be augmented by express permission of the king, a Prophet, the Urim and Tumim, and the Great Sanhedrin. In addition, the ceremony itself required the accompaniment of two thank-offerings and songs sung by the Levites. The Jerusalem Talmud derives these conditions from verses in the Torah as well as in the Prophets: In the Torah we learn from Moses' participation in the dedication of the Tabernacle that the dedication of sanctified ground requires a king and a Prophet. From Aaron the High Priest's participation we derive that the Urim and Tumim are necessary. Finally, we derive the need for a Sanhedrin from the verse (Numbers 11:16): "And the Lord said to Moses: Gather to me seventy men of the elders of Israel." Just as these conditions were met in the desert, so too were they to be met in future generations whenever the Temple area was to be sanctified. An additional number of verses in the Prophets reflect the same set of conditions: From II Samuel (24:19): "And David, according to the saying of Gad, went up as the Lord commanded," we learn that a king and a Prophet are necessary when determining the area of a Sanctuary. The verse from II Chronicles (3:1): "Then Solomon began to build the house of the Lord in Jerusalem on Mount Moriah, where the Lord appeared to David his father," teaches us that we need "the Lord's appearance" as well, in the form of the Urim and Tumim; whereas the expression "to David his father" alludes to the Sanhedrin (following Deuteronomy 32:7: "Ask your father, and he will

HALAKHAH

אֵין מוֹסִיפִין עַל הָעִיר We do not add to the city. "The boundaries of Jerusalem and of the Temple Courtyards can only be expanded with the permission of the Sanhedrin," following the Mishnah. As explained elsewhere, the king, a Prophet and the *Urim* and *Tumim* must also be consulted. (*Rambam, Sefer Shofetim, Hilkhot Sanhedrin* 5:1; *Sefer Avodah, Hilkhot Bet HaBekhirah* 6:11.)

LITERAL TRANSLATION

[1]Rava objected: [2]"All the utensils which Moses manufactured, [3]their anointment sanctifies them. [4]From then onwards, [5]their service initiates them." [6]But why? [7]Let us say: "Even so shall you make it" — [8]for the coming generations! [9]It is different there, for the verse states: [10]"And he anointed them and sanctified them" — [11]those by anointing, [12]but for generations [to come] — not by anointing. [13]But say: Those by anointing, [14]but for generations [to come] — either by anointing or by service! [15]Rav Pappa said: [16]The verse states: "With which they shall serve in the sanctuary" — [17]Scripture makes them dependent upon service.

[1]מְתִיב רָבָא: [2]"כָּל הַכֵּלִים שֶׁעָשָׂה מֹשֶׁה, [3]מְשִׁיחָתָן מְקַדְּשָׁן. [4]מִיכָּן וְאֵילָךְ — [5]עֲבוֹדָתָן מְחַנַּכְתָּן". [6]וְאַמַּאי? [7]נֵימָא: "וְכֵן תַּעֲשׂוּ" — [8]לַדּוֹרוֹת הַבָּאִין! [9]שָׁאנֵי הָתָם, דַּאֲמַר קְרָא: [10]"וַיִּמְשָׁחֵם וַיְקַדֵּשׁ אֹתָם" — [11]אוֹתָם בִּמְשִׁיחָה, וְלֹא [12]לְדוֹרוֹת — בִּמְשִׁיחָה. [13]וְאֵימָא: אוֹתָם בִּמְשִׁיחָה, [14]וּלְדוֹרוֹת — אִי בִּמְשִׁיחָה אִי בַּעֲבוֹדָה! [15]אָמַר רַב פַּפָּא: [16]אָמַר קְרָא: "אֲשֶׁר יְשָׁרְתוּ בָם בַּקֹּדֶשׁ" — [17]הַכָּתוּב תְּלָאָן בְּשֵׁירוּת.

RASHI

מיכן ואילך — כלים שעשו אחרי כן עבודתן מחנכתן, משעה שמתחנכים בעבודה — מתקדשין. **אותם** — מיעוטא הוא. **אשר ישרתו** — להבא, משמע לדורות הבאים נתנו בשירות, מדכתיב (במדבר ד): "כל כלי השרת אשר ישרתו". הכי גרסינן: אי לאו "אותם" הוה אמינא לדורות במשיחה ובעבודה, דהא כתיב "וכן תעשו".

TRANSLATION AND COMMENTARY

מְתִיב רָבָא [1]**Rava objected** to Rav Shimi bar Ḥiyya's interpretation of the verse from a Baraita which stated: [2]**"All of the utensils which Moses manufactured** for use in the Tabernacle — [3]**their anointment** with the holy oil served to **sanctify them** so that they could be employed in the Temple service. [4]**From then onwards,** when utensils were manufactured for the Temple, they did not require special anointing in order to become endowed with sanctity. [5]Rather, **their** first actual use in the Temple **service** itself served to **initiate them** directly into the realm of the sacred." [6]**But why** should this be so according to Rav Shimi bar Ḥiyya? [7]**Let us say** that his interpretation of the words **"and so shall you make it"** indicates that, just as the utensils made by Moses for the Tabernacle became sanctified through anointment, [8]so too should all utensils made **in coming generations** for the Temple require anointment in order to become sanctified!

שָׁאנֵי הָתָם [9]Rather, the situation **is different there** in respect to the utensils manufactured by Moses for the Tabernacle, **for the verse** explicitly **states** (Numbers 7:1): "And it came to pass on the day that Moses completed erecting the Tabernacle, that he anointed it, and sanctified it and all its vessels, and the altar and all its vessels, [10]**and he anointed them and sanctified them."** From the emphasis in the verse on the word "them," [11]we learn that only **those** utensils manufactured by Moses were to be specifically sanctified **by anointing.** [12]However, those manufactured **for generations** to come were **not** to be sanctified **by anointing**, but rather by their initial use in the Temple service.

וְאֵימָא [13]The Gemara asks: Perhaps we may **say** that the emphasis on "them" was intended to communicate that **those** utensils made by Moses be sanctified **by anointing,** [14]while those made **for generations** to come be sanctified **either by anointing or by** employing them in the actual Temple **service!**

אָמַר רַב פַּפָּא [15]**Rav Pappa said:** Rav Shimi bar Ḥiyya's teaching is indeed valid; nevertheless, future utensils cannot be sanctified through anointing, [16]for **the verse states** (Numbers 4:12): "And they shall take all the vessels of ministry **with which they shall serve** [יְשָׁרְתוּ] **in the sanctuary."** The future form of the verb, "they shall serve," implies that the verse is alluding to vessels that will be made in future generations. [17]Thus **Scripture makes** the sanctification of the utensils to be made in later generations **dependent upon** their actual use in the Temple **service.**

NOTES

recount it to you; your elders, and they will tell you"). The need for thank-offerings and Levitical songs are learned from verses in Neḥemiah (12:27-32): "And at the dedication of the wall of Jerusalem they sought out the Levites from all their places, to bring them to Jerusalem, to observe the dedication with gladness, and with thank-offerings, and with singing.... And I brought up the princes of Judea upon the wall, and appointed two great companies that gave thanks and went in procession."

HALAKHAH

כָּל הַכֵּלִים שֶׁעָשָׂה מֹשֶׁה All the utensils that Moses manufactured. "All the sacred utensils whose manufacture Moses supervised in the desert became sanctified when they were anointed. But from then on sacred utensils

TRANSLATION AND COMMENTARY

אֶלָּא [1]**But**, asks the Gemara, if this verse teaches us that utensils made in later generations become sanctified when used for the first time in the Temple service, then **why do I** also **need** the word **"them"** in the earlier verse to teach me the same law?

אִי לָאו אֹתָם [2]The Gemara answers: That teaching was also necessary, for **were it not** for the emphasis on the word **"them"** in that verse, [3]**I might have said** that in later **generations** utensils could only be sanctified **by** a combination of **anointing and** actual use in the Temple **service,** [4]**for it is written** in that earlier verse: **"And so shall you make it,"** implying that anointment is required in later generations, just as it was in the days of Moses. [5]Therefore, **the Torah wrote** the word **"them,"** [6]from which we learn that **those** utensils made by Moses were sanctified **by anointing,** [7]whereas the utensils fashioned in later **generations** are **not** sanctified **by anointing** but rather by their first use in the Temple service.

וְאֵין עוֹשִׂין סַנְהֶדְרָאוֹת [8]**We learned in the Mishnah: "And we do not appoint courts** of twenty-three judges to exercise jurisdiction over the tribes of Israel other than by permission of the High Court of seventy-one judges." [9]**From where** in Scripture **do we** derive this regulation? [10]It is in fact the same principle **as that which we find in** the case of **Moses, who established** a local network of minor **courts** to share in the responsibility of judging the community of Israel (see Exodus 18:25). [11]Since **Moses stood in place of the seventy-one** members of the Sanhedrin, it follows that in later generations permission from the High Court was necessary in order to appoint local courts of twenty-three.

תָּנוּ רַבָּנָן [12]In a related Baraita, **our Rabbis taught: "From where** is it learned **that we must establish judges over** all of **Israel?** [13]This is learned from the **verse** that **states** [Deuteronomy 16:18]: **'You shall place judges…**over yourselves.' [14]And **from where** do we know that **officers** must be appointed **over** all of **Israel** to execute the rulings issued by the judges? [15]This is learned from part of **the same verse** that **states: 'You shall place…officers** over yourselves.' [16]And **from where** do we know that not only must judges be appointed over all of Israel, but separate **judges** must also be appointed **for each and every tribe?** [17]This is learned

LITERAL TRANSLATION

[1]But why do I need "them"?
[2]Were it not for "them," [3]I might have said: For generations [to come] — by anointing and service, [4]as it is written: "And so shall you make it."
[5][Therefore] the Torah (lit., "the Merciful") wrote "them" — [6]those by anointing, [7]but for generations [to come] — not by anointing.
[8]"And we do not appoint courts, etc." [9]From where do we [derive this]? [10]As that which we find in connection Moses, who established courts, [11]and Moses stood in place of seventy-one.
[12]Our Rabbis taught: "From where [is it learned] that we must establish judges over Israel? [13]The Torah states: 'You shall place judges.' [14]Officers over Israel, from where? [15]The Torah states: 'You shall place officers.' [16]Judges for each and every tribe, from where? [17]The Torah states: 'Judges…

אֶלָּא, "אֹתָם" לָמָּה לִי?
[2]אִי לָאו "אֹתָם", [3]הֲוָה אָמִינָא: לְדוֹרוֹת — בִּמְשִׁיחָה וּבַעֲבוֹדָה, [4]דְּהָא כְּתִיב: "וְכֵן תַּעֲשׂוּ". [5]כָּתַב רַחֲמָנָא "אֹתָם" — [6]אוֹתָם בִּמְשִׁיחָה, [7]וְלֹא לְדוֹרוֹת — בִּמְשִׁיחָה.
[8]"וְאֵין עוֹשִׂין סַנְהֶדְרָאוֹת כו'". [9]מְנָא לָן? [10]כִּדְאַשְׁכְּחַן בְּמֹשֶׁה, דְּאוֹקֵי סַנְהֶדְרָאוֹת, [11]וּמֹשֶׁה בִּמְקוֹם שִׁבְעִים וְחַד קָאֵי.
[12]תָּנוּ רַבָּנָן: "מִנַּיִן שֶׁמַּעֲמִידִין שׁוֹפְטִים לְיִשְׂרָאֵל? [13]תַּלְמוּד לוֹמַר: 'שֹׁפְטִים תִּתֶּן'. [14]שׁוֹטְרִים לְיִשְׂרָאֵל מִנַּיִן? [15]תַּלְמוּד לוֹמַר: 'שֹׁטְרִים תִּתֶּן'. [16]שׁוֹפְטִים לְכָל שֵׁבֶט וָשֵׁבֶט מִנַּיִן? [17]תַּלְמוּד לוֹמַר: 'שֹׁפְטִים…

RASHI

דאוקי סנהדראות — בעצת יתרו, ומשה היה שופט ודיין על פי הדבור, ושקול כסנהדרי גדולה שבירושלים. שוטרים — גולייריש חובטין במקלות על פי השופטים לכל מי שאינו שומע.

BACKGROUND

מֹשֶׁה בִּמְקוֹם שִׁבְעִים וְחַד **Moses stood in place of seventy-one.** The Torah (Numbers 11) explains that Moses appointed the tribunal of seventy elders, and all of them derived their authority from him, as the verse (11:17) states: "And I shall draw upon the spirit that is upon you and place it upon them." Therefore, even after the first judges had been appointed, Moses alone had the authority of the Great Sanhedrin.

NOTES

שׁוֹפְטִים לְכָל שֵׁבֶט **Judges for each and every tribe.** The tribal courts adjudicated disputes arising between residents of different cities within the same tribal territory, including disputes which arose between the cities themselves, such as in the case of disagreement over borders (*Rabbi Ya'akov Emden*).

HALAKHAH

became sanctified upon their initial use in the Temple," following the Gemara. (*Rambam, Sefer Avodah, Hilkhot Kelei HaMikdash* 1:12.)

וְאֵין עוֹשִׂין סַנְהֶדְרָאוֹת **We do not appoint courts.** "Courts of twenty-three judges can only be appointed for each tribe

and city by the High Court of seventy-one judges," following the Mishnah. (*Rambam, Sefer Shofetim, Hilkhot Sanhedrin* 5:1.)

מִנַּיִן שֶׁמַּעֲמִידִין שׁוֹפְטִים? **From where do we know that we establish judges over Israel?** "There is a positive Biblical

[1]לִשְׁבָטֶיךָ׳. שׁוֹטְרִים לְכָל שֵׁבֶט וָשֵׁבֶט מִנַּיִין? [2]תַּלְמוּד לוֹמַר: ׳שֹׁטְרִים...לִשְׁבָטֶיךָ׳. [3]שׁוֹפְטִים לְכָל עִיר וְעִיר מִנַּיִין? [4]תַּלְמוּד לוֹמַר: ׳שֹׁפְטִים...לִשְׁעָרֶיךָ׳. [5]שׁוֹטְרִים לְכָל עִיר וְעִיר מִנַּיִין? [6]תַּלְמוּד לוֹמַר: ׳שֹׁטְרִים... לִשְׁעָרֶיךָ׳. [7]רַבִּי יְהוּדָה אוֹמֵר: אֶחָד מְמוּנֶּה עַל כּוּלָּן, [8]שֶׁנֶּאֱמַר: ׳תִּתֵּן לְךָ׳. [9]רַבָּן שִׁמְעוֹן בֶּן גַּמְלִיאֵל אוֹמֵר: [10]׳לִשְׁבָטֶיךָ וְשָׁפְטוּ׳ — [11]מִצְוָה בַּשֵּׁבֶט לָדוּן אֶת שִׁבְטוֹ״.

[12]״וְאֵין עוֹשִׂין עִיר הַנִּדַּחַת״. [13]מְנָא הָנֵי מִילֵּי? [14]אָמַר רַבִּי חִיָּיא בַּר יוֹסֵף אָמַר רַבִּי אוֹשַׁעְיָא: [15]דְּאָמַר קְרָא: ״וְהוֹצֵאתָ אֶת הָאִישׁ הַהוּא אוֹ אֶת הָאִשָּׁה הַהִיא״ — [16]אִישׁ וְאִשָּׁה אַתָּה מוֹצִיא לִשְׁעָרֶיךָ, [17]וְאִי אַתָּה מוֹצִיא כָּל הָעִיר כּוּלָּהּ לִשְׁעָרֶיךָ.

LITERAL TRANSLATION

for your tribes.' [1]Officers for each and every tribe, from where? [2]The Torah states: 'Officers…for your tribes.' [3]Judges for each and every city, from where? [4]The Torah states: 'Judges…for your gates.' [5]Officers for each and every city, from where? [6]The Torah states: 'Officers…for your gates.' [7]Rabbi Yehudah says: One is appointed over all of them, [8]for it is stated: 'You shall place over yourselves.' [9]Rabban Shimon ben Gamliel says: [10]'For your tribes, and they shall judge' — [11]there is a mitzvah for each tribe to judge its own tribe."

[12]"We do not apply the status of a city led astray." [13]From where are these words [derived]? [14]Rabbi Ḥiyya bar Yosef said in the name of Rabbi Oshaya: [15]"For the verse states: "And you shall take out that man or that woman" — [16]a man or a woman you take out to your gates, [17]but you do not take out an entire city to your gates.

TRANSLATION AND COMMENTARY

from the part of **the verse** that **states**: 'You shall place **judges**…**for your tribes.'** [1]And **from where** do we know that separate **officers** must also be appointed **for each and every tribe?** [2]This is learned from the part of **the verse** that **states:** 'You shall place **officers**…**for your tribes.'** [3]And **from where** do we know that, in addition, **judges** must be appointed **for each and every city?** [4]This is learned from the part of **the verse** that **states:** 'You shall place **judges**…**in all your gates,"** meaning the gates of each of your cities. [5]And **from where** do we know that **officers** must also be appointed **for each and every city?** [6]This is learned from the part of **the verse** that **states:** 'You shall place **officers**…**in all your gates.'** [7]**Rabbi Yehudah says: One** court — the Great Sanhedrin in Jerusalem — **is appointed over all the** other courts, [8]**for it is stated** in the verse we have been discussing: **'You shall place** judges…**over yourselves,'** and they will oversee the appointment of those judges and officers alluded to in the remainder of the verse. [9]**Rabban Shimon ben Gamliel says:** The same verse leads to an additional conclusion, for when it states: [10]'You shall place judges…**over your tribes, and they shall judge,'** [11]it means to teach that **there is a mitzvah for each tribe to judge** the members **of its own tribe,** and not those of another."

וְאֵין עוֹשִׂין עִיר הַנִּדַּחַת [12]We learned in our Mishnah: **"We do not apply the status of a city led astray** into idolatry except by order of the High Court." [13]**From where** in Scripture **are these words derived?** [14]**Rabbi Ḥiyya bar Yosef said in the name of Rabbi Oshaya:** [15]From **the verse** that **states** in regard to an individual who commits idolatry (Deuteronomy 17:5): **"And you shall take out that man or that woman,** who has done this wicked thing, unto your gates." [16]This verse teaches that **an** individual **man or woman** who is suspected of committing idolatry, **you take out to** the local court that sits by **your** city **gates**, and consists of twenty-three members; however, [17]**you do not take out** the population of **an entire city** which committed idolatry **to the** court that sits by **your gates.** Rather, they must be tried by the Great Sanhedrin of seventy-one judges sitting in Jerusalem.

RASHI

אחד ממונה על כולן — זו סנהדרי גדולה. **מצוה בשבט לדון את שבטו** — ולא ילכו בני שבט זה לבית דין של שבט אחר. **לשעריך** — לבית דין שבכל עיר ועיר.

NOTES

מִצְוָה בַּשֵּׁבֶט לָדוּן אֶת שִׁבְטוֹ There is a mitzvah for each tribe to judge its own. *Rabbi Ya'akov Emden* suggests that this rule provides the background for understanding the war that was waged by the rest of the tribes against the tribe of Benjamin following the crime committed against the Levite's concubine (see Judges 19-20). The Benjaminites rejected the interference of other tribes in adjudicating the case since the offenders were of their own tribe and thus

HALAKHAH

commandment to appoint judges and officers of the court for each district and for each city," following the Gemara. (*Rambam, Sefer Shofetim, Hilkhot Sanhedrin* 1:1.)

TRANSLATION AND COMMENTARY

אֵין עוֹשִׂין עִיר הַנִּדַּחַת בַּסְּפָר [1]Our Mishnah continues: **"We do not apply the status of a city led astray** into idol worship to a city which is located **on the border** of Israel." [2]**What is the reason** for this rule? [3]**The Torah stated** in its description of a city led astray (Deuteronomy 13:14): "Certain men, persons without conscience, have gone out **from your midst,** and have led astray the inhabitants of their city" — the emphasis of the verse being on those who are "from your midst" [4]**and not from** settlements on the **border**.

וְלֹא שָׁלֹשׁ עָרֵי הַנִּדַּחַת [5]The next clause of the Mishnah teaches: "We do **not** apply the status of a city led astray **to three** such **cities."** [6]The reason **for** this is because **it is written** (Deuteronomy 13:13): "If you shall hear about **one** of your cities which the Lord your God has given you to dwell there...." The emphasis on *"one* of your cities" implies that only a single city can be declared idolatrous. [7]**"But we do apply this status to one or** even **two** cities," [8]**for it is written** in that very same verse, **"your cities,"** implying that more than one may be condemned.

תָּנוּ רַבָּנַן [9]**Our Rabbis taught** a related Baraita: "The verse states: 'If you shall hear about **one** of your cities' — [10]implying that **one** city can be condemned as idolatrous, **but not three.** [11]Now, **do you** really mean to **say** that the verse implies that **one** city may be condemned **but not three,** [12]**or** perhaps **it is** even implying that **one** city may be condemned **but not two?** This second possibility must be rejected, [13]for **when** the verse **states 'your cities,'** [14]the applicability of these laws to **two** cities **is** explicitly **stated.** [15]**How, then, do I establish** the meaning of the word **'one'** cited earlier in the verse? [16]It is there to imply that **one** city may be condemned, **but not three."**

זִימְנִין אָמַר רַב [17]**At times Rav said** as follows: **It is** only **in** the context of **a single** High **Court that we cannot apply the status** of a "city led astray" to more than two cities. [18]**But in two or three** different High **Courts,** as occurs whenever new judges are appointed to replace those who have died, **we do apply this status** to

[1]"אֵין עוֹשִׂין עִיר הַנִּדַּחַת בַּסְּפָר". [2]מַאי טַעְמָא? [3]"מִקִּרְבֶּךָ", אָמַר רַחֲמָנָא, [4]וְלֹא מִן הַסְּפָר.

[5]"וְלֹא שָׁלֹשׁ עָרֵי הַנִּדַּחַת". [6]דִּכְתִיב: "אַחַת". [7]"אֲבָל עוֹשִׂין אַחַת אוֹ שְׁתַּיִם". [8]דִּכְתִיב: "עָרֶיךָ".

[9]תָּנוּ רַבָּנַן: "'אַחַת' — [10]אַחַת וְלֹא שָׁלֹשׁ. [11]אַתָּה אוֹמֵר אַחַת וְלֹא שָׁלֹשׁ, [12]אוֹ אֵינוֹ אֶלָּא אַחַת וְלֹא שְׁתַּיִם? [13]כְּשֶׁהוּא אוֹמֵר: 'עָרֶיךָ' — [14]הֲרֵי שְׁתַּיִם אָמוּר. [15]הָא מָה אֲנִי מְקַיֵּים 'אַחַת' — [16]אַחַת וְלֹא שָׁלֹשׁ".

[17]זִימְנִין אָמַר רַב: בְּבֵית דִּין אֶחָד הוּא דְּאֵין עוֹשִׂין; [18]הָא בִּשְׁנַיִם וּשְׁלֹשָׁה בָּתֵּי דִינִין

LITERAL TRANSLATION

[1]"We do not apply the status of a city led astray on the border." [2]What is the reason? [3]"From your midst," stated the Torah (lit., "the Merciful"), [4]and not from the border.

[5]"And not to three cities." [6]For it is written: "One." [7]"But we do apply this status to one or two." [8]For it is written: "Your cities."

[9]Our Rabbis taught: "'One' — [10]one, and not three. [11]Do you say one and not three, [12]or [perhaps] it is one and not two? [13]When it states: 'Your cities' — [14]so two is stated. [15]How then do I establish 'one'? [16]One and not three."

[17]At times Rav said: It is in a single court that we cannot apply this status [more than twice]; [18]but in two or three courts

RASHI

בבית דין אחד – כל זמן סנהדרי זו קיימא, אבל מתו אלו ונתמנו אחרים, עושין.

NOTES

the mitzvah was theirs. The other tribes argued that the crime fell under the jurisdiction of the Great Sanhedrin since the victim was not of the tribe of Benjamin.

HALAKHAH

וְלֹא שָׁלֹשׁ עָרֵי הַנִּדַּחַת Nor three idolatrous cities. According to *Rambam,* the same court cannot condemn as idolatrous three cities that are situated one next to the other. But if the three cities are far from each other, the same court can indeed condemn them as idolatrous. (*Rambam* apparently rules in accordance with Resh Lakish and the first version of Rav's position. Perhaps he maintains that Rabbi Yoḥanan only disagrees with Resh Lakish in regard to three cities found in the same region. But if they are in different regions, for example, two in Judea and the third in Galilee, and also not near each other, Rabbi Yoḥanan agrees that the same court can condemn them all as idolatrous cities.) *Ra'avad* disagrees and says that three cities can never be condemned together as idolatrous, even if they are situated far from each other, and even if more than one court is involved." This follows the opinion of Rabbi Yoḥanan and the second version of Rav's position. (*Rambam, Sefer Mada, Hilkhot Avodah Zarah* 4:4.)

LITERAL TRANSLATION

we do apply this status [more than twice]. [1]And at times Rav said: Even in two or three courts, [2]we never apply this status [more than twice]. [3]What is the reason? [4]On account of a depopulation (lit., "baldness").

[5]Resh Lakish said: They did not teach [this] except in one region, [6]but in two or three regions, we can apply this status. [7]Rabbi Yoḥanan said: We do not apply this status, [8]on account of a depopulation.

[9]It was taught in accordance with Rabbi Yoḥanan: [10]"We never declare three cities in the Land of Israel as led astray, but we do declare two. [11]For example, one in Judea, and one in Galilee. [12]But two in Judea or two in Galilee [13]we do not declare. [14]And adjacent to the border, [15]even one we do not condemn." [16]What is the reason? [17]Perhaps the non-Jews will hear, and destroy the Land of Israel.

[18]But derive it from that [which] the Torah stated: "From your midst," [19]and not from the border!

עוֹשִׂין. [1]וְזִימְנִין אָמַר רַב: אֲפִילּוּ בִּשְׁנַיִם וּשְׁלֹשָׁה בָּתֵּי דִינִין, [2]לְעוֹלָם אֵין עוֹשִׂין. [3]מַאי טַעְמָא דְּרַב? [4]מִשּׁוּם קָרְחָה.

[5]אָמַר רֵישׁ לָקִישׁ: לֹא שָׁנוּ אֶלָּא בְּמָקוֹם אֶחָד, [6]אֲבָל בִּשְׁנַיִם וּשְׁלֹשָׁה מְקוֹמוֹת, עוֹשִׂין. [7]רַבִּי יוֹחָנָן אָמַר: אֵין עוֹשִׂין, [8]מִשּׁוּם קָרְחָה.

[9]תַּנְיָא כְּוָותֵיהּ דְּרַבִּי יוֹחָנָן: [10]״אֵין עוֹשִׂין שָׁלֹשׁ עֲיָירוֹת מְנוּדָּחוֹת בְּאֶרֶץ יִשְׂרָאֵל אֲבָל עוֹשִׂין אוֹתָם שְׁתַּיִם. [11]כְּגוֹן, אַחַת בִּיהוּדָה וְאַחַת בַּגָּלִיל. [12]אֲבָל שְׁתַּיִם בִּיהוּדָה וּשְׁתַּיִם בַּגָּלִיל [13]אֵין עוֹשִׂין. [14]וּסְמוּכָה לַסְּפָר, [15]אֲפִילּוּ אַחַת אֵין עוֹשִׂין״. [16]מַאי טַעְמָא? [17]שֶׁמָּא יִשְׁמְעוּ נׇכְרִים וְיַחֲרִיבוּ אֶת אֶרֶץ יִשְׂרָאֵל.

[18]וְתִיפּוֹק לִי דְּ״מִקִּרְבֶּךָ״ אָמַר רַחֲמָנָא, [19]וְלֹא מִן הַסְּפָר!

RASHI

במקום אחד — כגון בגליל או ביהודה.

TRANSLATION AND COMMENTARY

more than two cities. [1]**And at times Rav said** otherwise: **Even in two or three** High **Courts,** [2]**we never apply this status** more than twice. [3]**What is Rav's reason** for saying that three cities can never be declared idolatrous, even by more than one High Court? [4]He made his statement **on account of** the fear that if there was no limit to the number of cities that could be condemned as idolatrous, **a depopulation** of the country might occur.

אָמַר רֵישׁ לָקִישׁ [5]**Resh Lakish said:** The Mishnah **did not teach** this rule, that three cities cannot be condemned as idolatrous, **except** where all three cities are located **in one region,** such as in Judea or Galilee. [6]**But** if the three cities are found **in two or three** different **regions, we can apply this status** to all of them. [7]**Rabbi Yoḥanan** disagreed and **said: We do not apply this status** to more than two cities, even if they are found in two or three different regions, [8]because we fear **a depopulation** of Jewish settlement in the Land of Israel.

תַּנְיָא כְּוָותֵיהּ [9]A Baraita **was taught in accordance with** the view of **Rabbi Yoḥanan** that we never apply the category of a "city led astray" to more than two cities: [10]**"We never declare three** or more **cities in the Land of Israel as "led astray," but we do declare two** cities as such if, [11]**for example, one** is found **in Judea and one in Galilee.** [12]**But** if the **two** cities are both found **in Judea or** the **two** cities are both found **in Galilee,** [13]**we do not declare** them both idolatrous and worthy of destruction. [On this last point, the Baraita is more stringent than Rabbi Yoḥanan.] [14]**And** if the city happens to be **adjacent to the border,** [15]**we do not declare even** that **one** city idolatrous.[16]**What is the reason** that a border town cannot be condemned as idolatrous? [17]It is based on the fear that **perhaps the non-Jews** living in the neighboring land **will hear** that the town has been destroyed, **and** will take advantage of the breach in security to attempt to **destroy the Land of Israel."**

וְתִיפּוֹק לִי [18]The Gemara asks: **But** why resort to this reason? **Derive** the law as we did above, **from** the fact **that the Torah stated** (Deuteronomy 13:14): "Certain men, wicked persons, have gone out **from your midst,** and have drawn away the inhabitants of their city." [19]This verse teaches that a city that is among you, in the center of the country, can be condemned as an idolatrous city, **but** a city that is situated **on the border** of israel can**not** be condemned in that way!

NOTES

מִשּׁוּם קָרְחָה **On account of depopulation.** Some suggest that this be understood in light of the verses (Exodus 23:29-30): "I will not drive [your enemies] out from before you in one year; lest the land become desolate, and the wild beasts multiply against you. Little by little I will drive them out from before you, until you be increased, and inherit the land." The destruction of three idolatrous cities would create an imbalance between settled areas and desolate ones, which could eventually endanger the survival of the country (*Ḥokhmat Manoaḥ*). Others understand the danger of depopulation as related to the fear that it might encourage Israel's enemies to come and add to the devastation (*Imrei Tzvi*).

TRANSLATION AND COMMENTARY

רַבִּי שִׁמְעוֹן הִיא [1]The Gemara answers: The Baraita that offers a rationale for exempting border towns is according to **Rabbi Shimon,** [2]**who** believes that one is allowed to **interpret the reason** underlying **a** derivation from a Biblical **verse** as a basis for drawing Halakhic conclusions. The Baraita therefore interprets the exemption of a border town as being based on the desire not to impair the country's defenses.

סַנְהֶדְרִי גְּדוֹלָה הָיְתָה [3]We learned in the next section of our Mishnah: **"The Great Sanhedrin was** composed of seventy-one men.... From where do we know this? For the verse states [Numbers 11:16]: 'Gather unto me seventy men from the elders of Israel,' and Moses was over them. Rabbi Yehudah says: The Great Sanhedrin was composed of only seventy men." [4]The Gemara asks: **What is the reason of the Rabbis for saying 'and Moses was over them,'** thereby implying that for all generations the Great Sanhedrin would require seventy-one members? [5]They understood this from the fact that **the** above **verse states** in its continuation: "And take them to the Tent of Meeting, **and they shall stand there** [17A] **with you."** [6]The seventy elders will stand there **with you, and you with them** — as the seventy-first member of the Sanhedrin.

וְרַבִּי יְהוּדָה [7]**And Rabbi Yehudah,** who maintains that the Great Sanhedrin had only seventy members — how does he interpret this verse? [8]He understands the stipulation in the verse that the elders stand **"with you,"** [9]Moses, as necessary **on account of the** need to bestow upon them a measure of the **Divine Presence** that rested upon him, as in the verse (Numbers 11:17) wherein God states to Moses: "And I will come down and talk with you there, and I will take a portion of the spirit which is upon you, and place it upon them."

וְרַבָּנַן [10]**And** how do **the Rabbis** counter this argument? [11]On the basis of **the verse** that **states** (Numbers 11:17): **"And they shall bear with you the burden of the people,"** [12]the Rabbis reassert their contention that the elders were meant to bear the burden of the people **with you,** Moses **and you with them** as the seventy-first member of the Sanhedrin.

וְרַבִּי יְהוּדָה [13]**And** how does **Rabbi Yehudah** answer this in turn? According to him, [14]the emphasis on **"with you"** in this verse implies that the members of the Sanhedrin must be people **who are similar to you,** Moses, in pedigree and character.

וְרַבָּנַן [15]**And** how then do **the Rabbis** derive this need to ensure that the members of the Sanhedrin should be like Moses? [16]According to them, **it is derived from** the verse regarding the appointment of local courts to assist Moses in judging the people (Exodus 18:22): **"And it** [the burden] **shall be lightened from upon you, and they shall bear with you,"** the words "with you" implying that the judges must possess traits similar to those of Moses. [17]**And** the quality of the members of **the Great Sanhedrin is learned from** this

LITERAL TRANSLATION

[1]It is Rabbi Shimon, [2]who interprets the reason of a verse.

[3]"The Great Sanhedrin was." [4]What is the reason of the Rabbis for saying that Moses was over them?

[5]The verse states: "And they shall stand there [17A] with you" — [6]with you, and you with them.

[7]And Rabbi Yehudah? [8]"With you" — [9]on account of the Divine Presence.

[10]And the Rabbis? [11]The verse states: "And they shall bear the burden of the people with you" — [12]with you, and you with them.

[13]And Rabbi Yehudah? [14]"With you" — with those who are similar to you.

[15]And the Rabbis? [16]It is derived from "And it shall be lightened from upon you, and they shall bear with you." [17]And the

[1]רַבִּי שִׁמְעוֹן הִיא, דְּדָרֵישׁ [2]טַעֲמָא דִּקְרָא.

[3]״סַנְהֶדְרִי גְּדוֹלָה הָיְתָה״. [4]מַאי טַעֲמַיְיהוּ דְּרַבָּנַן דְּאָמְרִי וּמֹשֶׁה עַל גַּבֵּיהֶן? [5]אָמַר קְרָא: ״וְהִתְיַצְּבוּ שָׁם [17A] עִמָּךְ״ — [6]עִמָּךְ, וְאַתְּ בַּהֲדַיְיהוּ.

[7]וְרַבִּי יְהוּדָה? [8]״עִמָּךְ״ — [9]מִשּׁוּם שְׁכִינָה.

[10]וְרַבָּנַן? [11]אָמַר קְרָא: ״וְנָשְׂאוּ אִתְּךָ בְּמַשָּׂא הָעָם״, [12]אִתְּךָ — וְאַתְּ בַּהֲדַיְיהוּ.

[13]וְרַבִּי יְהוּדָה? [14]״אִתְּךָ״ — בְּדוֹמִין לְךָ.

[15]וְרַבָּנַן? [16]מִ״וְהָקֵל מֵעָלֶיךָ וְנָשְׂאוּ אִתָּךְ״ נָפְקָא, [17]וְיָלְפָא

BACKGROUND

דְּדָרֵישׁ טַעֲמָא דִּקְרָא **Who interprets the reason of a verse.** Rabbi Shimon's approach here is mentioned in many other places in the Talmud (see below, 21a). Other Sages also interpreted and explained the meanings of verses, but they viewed them as explanations of the commandments in the Torah, whereas Rabbi Shimon interpreted the meanings of verses and derived Halakhic conclusions from them.

״עִמָּךְ״ — מִשּׁוּם שְׁכִינָה **"With you" — on account of the Divine Presence.** That is to say, Moses did not participate with the seventy elders in the court by virtue of his position as the head of the tribunal. Rather, his participation depended upon his being a Prophet, from whose mouth the Divine Presence spoke. Hence, in following generations the court numbered only seventy members.

RASHI

רבי שמעון דריש טעמא דקרא — ב״המקבל״ (בבא מציעא קטו,א). **עמך משום שכינה** — עמך יעמדו מחוץ לאהל ולא יבאו לאהל — משום שכינה, לשון אחר: משום שכינה שתשרה שכינה עליהם הוצרכו להיות משה עמהן, כדכתיב (במדבר יא): ואצלתי מן הרוח אשר עליך וגו׳. **בדומין לך** — מיוחסין ומנוקין ממום. **ורבנן** — נפקא להו בדומין לך מונשאו אתך דסנהדראות קטנות שנאמרו ביתרו, וילפא גדולה מקטנה.

HALAKHAH

אִתְּךָ בְּדוֹמִין לְךָ **"With you" — with those who are similar to you.** "In order to be appointed to the Great Sanhedrin

TRANSLATION AND COMMENTARY

stipulation regarding **the Lesser Sanhedrin.**

תָּנוּ רַבָּנַן [1]**Our Rabbis taught** the following Baraita about the selection of the judges who formed the first Sanhedrin: "After God invested the seventy elders with Divine Spirit, we are told in the verse [Numbers 11:26]: [2]**'And two of the men remained in the camp,** the name of the one was Eldad, and the name of the other Medad; and the spirit rested upon them; and they were among those who were written, but who did not go out to the tent; and they prophesied in the camp.' [3]**Some say** that their ballots **remained in the lottery box.** How so? [4]**For at the time that the Holy One, blessed be He, said to Moses** [Numbers 11:16]: [5]**'Gather to me seventy men from the elders of Israel,'** [6]**Moses said** to himself: **What shall I do?** [7]**If I select six** judges **from each tribe,** [8]**two extra will be found,** for twelve times six amounts to seventy-two. [9]And **if I select five** judges **from each tribe,** [10]**ten will be found lacking,** since twelve times five amounts to only sixty. [11]And **should I select six from this tribe and five from another tribe,** [12]**I will cause envy among the tribes.'** [13]**What** did Moses **do?** [14]**He selected six** judges **each** from every tribe, **and brought** out **seventy-two ballots.** [15]**On seventy** of those ballots **he wrote** the word **'elder,'** and the remaining **two he left blank.** [16]**He** then **mixed them** all up, **and placed them in the lottery box**. Turning to the seventy-two elders whom he had assembled, [17]**he said to them: 'Come and draw your ballots!'** [18]**Whoever's hand drew up** a ballot saying **'elder,'** [19]Moses **said** to him: **'Heaven has already sanctified you.'** [20]And **whoever's hand drew up a blank** ballot, [21]Moses **said** to him: 'If **God does not desire you** on the Sanhedrin, **what** more **can I do**

סַנְהֶדְרִי גְּדוֹלָה מִסַּנְהֶדְרִי קְטַנָּה.
[1]תָּנוּ רַבָּנַן: [2]"'וַיִּשָּׁאֲרוּ שְׁנֵי אֲנָשִׁים בַּמַּחֲנֶה'. [3]יֵשׁ אוֹמְרִים בַּקַּלְפֵּי נִשְׁתַּיְּירוּ. [4]שֶׁבְּשָׁעָה שֶׁאָמַר לוֹ הַקָּדוֹשׁ בָּרוּךְ הוּא לְמֹשֶׁה: [5]'אֶסְפָה לִּי שִׁבְעִים אִישׁ מִזִּקְנֵי יִשְׂרָאֵל', [6]אָמַר מֹשֶׁה: 'כֵּיצַד אֶעֱשֶׂה? [7]אֶבְרוֹר שִׁשָּׁה מִכָּל שֵׁבֶט וָשֵׁבֶט, [8]נִמְצְאוּ שְׁנַיִם יְתֵירִים. [9]אֶבְרוֹר חֲמִשָּׁה חֲמִשָּׁה מִכָּל שֵׁבֶט וָשֵׁבֶט, [10]נִמְצְאוּ עֲשָׂרָה חֲסֵרִים. [11]אֶבְרוֹר שִׁשָּׁה מִשֵּׁבֶט זֶה וַחֲמִשָּׁה מִשֵּׁבֶט זֶה, [12]הֲרֵינִי מַטִּיל קִנְאָה בֵּין הַשְּׁבָטִים'. [13]מֶה עָשָׂה? [14]בֵּירֵר שִׁשָּׁה שִׁשָּׁה, וְהֵבִיא שִׁבְעִים וּשְׁנַיִם פִּיתָּקִין. [15]עַל שִׁבְעִים כָּתַב 'זָקֵן' וּשְׁנַיִם הִנִּיחַ חָלָק, [16]בְּלָלָן וּנְתָנָן בַּקַּלְפֵּי. [17]אָמַר לָהֶם: 'בּוֹאוּ וּטְלוּ פִּיתָּקֵיכֶם'! [18]כָּל מִי שֶׁעָלָה בְּיָדוֹ 'זָקֵן'; [19]אָמַר: 'כְּבָר קִידֶּשְׁךָ שָׁמַיִם'. [20]מִי שֶׁעָלָה בְּיָדוֹ חָלָק, [21]אָמַר: 'הַמָּקוֹם לֹא

LITERAL TRANSLATION

Great Sanhedrin is learned from the Lesser Sanhedrin.

[1]Our Rabbis taught: [2]"'And two of the men remained in the camp.' [3]Some say they remained in the lottery box. [4]For at the time that the Holy One, blessed be He, said to Moses: [5]'Gather to me seventy men from the elders of Israel,' [6]Moses said: 'What shall I do? [7][If] I select six from each tribe, [8]two extra will be found. [9][If] I select five from each tribe, [10]ten will be found lacking. [11][If] I select six from this tribe and five from that tribe, [12]I will cause envy among the tribes.' [13]What did he do? [14]He selected six each, and brought seventy-two ballots. [15]On seventy he wrote 'elder,' [16]and two he left blank. He mixed them, and placed them in the lottery box. [17]He said to them: 'Come and draw your ballots!' [18]Whoever's hand drew up [a ballot saying] 'elder,' [19]he said [to him]: 'Heaven has already sanctified you.' [20]Whoever's hand drew up a blank [ballot], [21]he said [to him]: 'God does not

RASHI

ושנים חלק – לא נכתב עליהן "זקן". **מי שעלה ביד חלק כו'** – ושניים מאותן שבעים שהלכו ליטול עלה בידו חלק, ונשתיירו שני פתקין שהיו כתובין בקלפי שהיו של אלדד ומידד שלא הלכו ליטול, שנתייראו שלא יעלה בידן חלק.

LANGUAGE

פִּתָּק Ballots. This word derives from the Greek πιττάκιον, *pitakhion,* meaning a small tablet, a piece or paper on parchment that people write on.

NOTES

בֵּירֵר שִׁשָּׁה שִׁשָּׁה He selected six from each tribe. The Rishonim ask: Why did Moses prepare seventy-two ballots to be drawn by each of the seventy-two candidates for the Sanhedrin? He could just as well have prepared twelve ballots, ten reading "six," and the remaining two reading "five." Each tribe could then have drawn one ballot and selected five or six members to sit on the Sanhedrin accordingly. *Ran* answers that if two of the tribes had to select which five of its six candidates would sit on the Sanhedrin, intratribal quarrels might have arisen.

HALAKHAH

or even to a Lesser Sanhedrin, a person had to be wise and understanding, with a mastery of Torah law, and familiarity with other fields of knowledge, such as medicine, mathematics and astronomy. In addition, he had to be of sufficiently unblemished lineage that he could marry his daughter to one of the priestly class." (*Rambam, Sefer Shofetim, Hilkhot Sanhedrin* 2:1.)

חָפֵץ בְּךָ. אֲנִי מָה אֶעֱשֶׂה לְךָ׳? [1]כַּיּוֹצֵא בַּדָּבָר אַתָּה אוֹמֵר: [2]׳וְלָקַחְתָּ חֲמֵשֶׁת חֲמֵשֶׁת שְׁקָלִים לַגֻּלְגֹּלֶת׳. [3]אָמַר מֹשֶׁה: ׳כֵּיצַד אֶעֱשֶׂה לָהֶן לְיִשְׂרָאֵל? [4]אִם אוֹמַר לוֹ: תֵּן לִי פִּדְיוֹנְךָ וָצֵא, [5]יֹאמַר לִי: כְּבָר פְּדָאַנִי בֶּן לֵוִי׳. [6]מֶה עָשָׂה? [7]הֵבִיא עֶשְׂרִים וּשְׁנַיִם אֲלָפִים פִּיתָקִין, וְכָתַב עֲלֵיהֶן ׳בֶּן לֵוִי׳, [8]וְעַל שְׁלֹשָׁה וְשִׁבְעִים וּמָאתַיִם כָּתַב עֲלֵיהֶן ׳חֲמִשָּׁה שְׁקָלִים׳. [9]בְּלָלָן וּנְתָנָן בַּקַּלְפֵּי. [10]אָמַר לָהֶן: ׳טְלוּ פִּיתָקֵיכֶם׳! [11]מִי שֶׁעָלָה בְּיָדוֹ ׳בֶּן לֵוִי׳ [12]אָמַר לוֹ: ׳כְּבָר פְּדָאֲךָ בֶּן לֵוִי׳. [13]מִי שֶׁעָלָה בְּיָדוֹ ׳חֲמֵשֶׁת שְׁקָלִים׳, [14]אָמַר לוֹ: ׳תֵּן פִּדְיוֹנְךָ וָצֵא׳״.

[15]״רַבִּי שִׁמְעוֹן אוֹמֵר: [16]בַּמַּחֲנֶה נִשְׁתַּיְּירוּ. [17]בְּשָׁעָה שֶׁאָמַר לוֹ הַקָּדוֹשׁ בָּרוּךְ הוּא לְמֹשֶׁה: [18]׳אֶסְפָה לִי שִׁבְעִים אִישׁ׳, [19]אָמְרוּ אֶלְדָּד וּמֵידָד: ׳אֵין אָנוּ רְאוּיִין לְאוֹתָהּ גְּדוּלָּה׳.

LITERAL TRANSLATION

desire you. What can I do for you?' [1]You may say in a similar manner: [2]'You shall take five shekels per head.' [3]Moses said: 'How shall I execute [this] for them, for Israel? [4]If I say to him: Give me your redemption [money] and go out, [5]he will say to me: A Levite already redeemed me.' [6]What did he do? [7]He brought twenty-two-thousand ballots, and wrote on them 'Levite,' [8]and on two-hundred-and-seventy-three [ballots] he wrote 'five shekels.' [9]He mixed them, and placed them into the lottery box. [10]He said to them: 'Draw your ballots!' [11]Whoever's hand drew up [a ballot saying] 'Levite,' [12]he said [to him]: 'A Levite has already redeemed you.' [13]Whoever's hand drew up [a ballot saying] 'five shekels,' [14]he said [to him]: 'Give your redemption [money], and go out.'"

[15]"Rabbi Shimon said: [16]They remained in the camp. [17]At the hour when the Holy One, blessed be He, said to Moses: [18]'Gather to me seventy men,' [19]Eldad and Medad said: 'We are not worthy of that greatness.'

RASHI

ולקחת חמשת חמשת — בבכורות העודפים על מנין הלוים. **אמר להן** — לכל הבכורות: באו טלו פיתקיכן.

TRANSLATION AND COMMENTARY

for you?' After seventy of the lots had been drawn, including the two blank ones, two remained in the box with the word "elder" written upon them. These belonged to Eldad and Medad, who refused to draw their ballots out of fear that they might be rejected. [1]**You may say** that **in a similar manner** Moses oversaw the Levites' redemption of the firstborn of Israel. As described in Numbers (chapter 3), God decreed that the tribe of Levi replace the firstborn of Israel as those designated for a life of exclusive dedication to divine service. At the time, however, there were two-hundred-and-seventy-three more firstborn than there were Levites. Consequently, God decided that these additional firstborn should redeem themselves by paying a sum of money to Aaron and his sons, heads of the priestly class. And so He commanded Moses in the verse [Numbers 3:47]: [2]**'You shall take five shekels per head**...and give the money to Aaron and his sons as a redemption for the remaining among them.' After receiving God's instructions on the matter, [3]**Moses said** to himself: **'How shall I execute** this redemption **for them, for** the firstborn of **Israel?** [4]**If I say to** any one of them: **Give me** five shekels as **your redemption** money **and go out,** for you are one of the two-hundred-and-seventy-three firstborn in need of monetary redemption, [5]**he will** deny it and **say to me: A Levite** from among the twenty-two-thousand that were able personally to replace the firstborn **already redeemed me.'** [6]**What did** Moses **do?** [7]**He brought** out **twenty-two-thousand ballots and wrote on** each of **them 'Levite,'** [8]**and on two-hundred-and-seventy-three** additional ballots **he wrote 'five shekels.'** [9]**He** then **mixed them** all up, **and placed them into the lottery box.** [10]**He said to** the firstborn: 'Come and **draw your ballots!'** [11]**Whoever's hand drew up** a ballot saying **'Levite,'** [12]Moses **said to him: 'A Levite has already redeemed you.'** [13]And **whoever's hand drew up** a ballot saying **'five shekels,'** [14]**he said to him: 'Give** me five shekels as **your redemption** money **and go out.'"**

רַבִּי שִׁמְעוֹן אוֹמֵר [15]The Baraita continues with an alternative interpretation of the verse, "And there remained two men in the camp": **"Rabbi Shimon said:** [16]Eldad and Medad **remained in the camp** rather than participate in the lottery, because they were afraid to be chosen as elders. [17]**At the hour when the Holy One, blessed be He, said to Moses:** [18]**'Gather to me seventy men** from the elders of Israel,' [19]**Eldad and Medad said:**

NOTES

Meiri suggests that had the ballots been drawn by tribe, all those in the tribes that had drawn the ballots marked "five" might have felt stigmatized. The way Moses organized the lottery limited the possibility of such feelings to the two candidates who drew the blank ballots.

[1] אָמַר הַקָּדוֹשׁ בָּרוּךְ הוּא: 'הוֹאִיל וּמִיעַטְתֶּם עַצְמְכֶם, הֲרֵינִי מוֹסִיף גְּדוּלָּה עַל גְּדוּלַּתְכֶם'. [2] וּמַה גְּדוּלָּה הוֹסִיף לָהֶם? [3] שֶׁהַנְּבִיאִים כּוּלָּן נִתְנַבְּאוּ וּפָסְקוּ, [4] וְהֵם נִתְנַבְּאוּ וְלֹא פָּסְקוּ". [5] וּמַה נְּבוּאָה נִתְנַבְּאוּ? [6] אָמְרוּ: 'מֹשֶׁה מֵת, יְהוֹשֻׁעַ מַכְנִיס אֶת יִשְׂרָאֵל לָאָרֶץ'". [7] "אַבָּא חָנִין אוֹמֵר מִשּׁוּם רַבִּי אֱלִיעֶזֶר: [8] עַל עִסְקֵי שְׂלָיו הֵן מִתְנַבְּאִים. [9] 'עֲלִי שְׂלָיו, עֲלִי שְׂלָיו'"! [10] רַב נַחְמָן אָמַר: עַל עִסְקֵי גּוֹג וּמָגוֹג הָיוּ מִתְנַבְּאִין, [11] שֶׁנֶּאֱמַר: "כֹּה אָמַר ה' אֱלֹהִים הַאַתָּה הוּא אֲשֶׁר דִּבַּרְתִּי בְּיָמִים קַדְמוֹנִים בְּיַד עֲבָדַי נְבִיאֵי יִשְׂרָאֵל הַנִּבְּאִים בַּיָּמִים הָהֵם שָׁנִים לְהָבִיא אֹתְךָ עֲלֵיהֶם וגו'". [12] אַל תִּיקְרֵי "שָׁנִים" אֶלָּא "שְׁנַיִם". [13] וְאֵיזוֹ הֵן שְׁנַיִם נְבִיאִים שֶׁנִּתְנַבְּאוּ בְּפֶרֶק אֶחָד נְבוּאָה אַחַת? [14] הֱוֵי אוֹמֵר אֶלְדָּד וּמֵידָד. [15] אָמַר מָר: "כָּל הַנְּבִיאִים כּוּלָּן נִתְנַבְּאוּ וּפָסְקוּ, וְהֵן נִתְנַבְּאוּ וְלֹא פָּסְקוּ". [16] מְנָא לָן דְּפָסְקוּ?

LITERAL TRANSLATION

[1] The Holy One, blessed be He, said: 'Since you made yourselves small, I shall add greatness to the greatness that is yours.' [2] And what greatness did He add to them? [3] That all the Prophets prophesied and ceased, [4] and they prophesied and did not cease." [5] "And what prophesy did they prophesy? [6] They said: 'Moses will die, [and] Joshua will bring Israel into the land.'" [7] "Abba Ḥanin said in the name of Rabbi Eliezer: [8] They prophesied about the matter of the quail. [9] 'Rise, quail, rise, quail.'" [10] Rav Naḥman said: They were prophesying about the matter of Gog and Magog, [11] for it is stated: "Thus says the Lord God: Are you the one of whom I spoke in ancient days, through my servants the Prophets of Israel, who prophesied in those days for many years that I would bring you against them?" [12] Do not read "years" (שָׁנִים), but rather "two" (שְׁנַיִם). [13] And who are the two Prophets who prophesied one prophecy at the same time? [14] Say Eldad and Medad. [15] The master said: "All the Prophets prophesied and ceased, and they prophesied and did not cease." [16] From where do we [know] that they ceased?

TRANSLATION AND COMMENTARY

'We are not worthy of that greatness.' [1] **The Holy One, blessed be He, said** to them: **'Since you made yourselves small, behold I shall add greatness to the greatness that is** already **yours** as chosen elders.' [2] **And what greatness did** God **add to them?** [3] **That** when **all the** other elders became **Prophets** at the hour of their investiture, they **prophesied** a single time **and** then **ceased** to prophesy, [4] whereas Eldad and Medad **prophesied** at that hour **and did not cease."**

וּמַה נְּבוּאָה [5] **"And what prophecy did** Eldad and Medad **prophesy?** [6] **They said: 'Moses will die, and Joshua will bring** the people of **Israel into the** Promised **Land.'"**

אַבָּא חָנִין [7] **"Abba Ḥanin said in the name of Rabbi Eliezer:** [8] Eldad and Medad **prophesied about the matter of the quail** that God would send in response to the people's demand for meat. Their prophecy consisted of the declaration: [9] **'Rise, quail, rise, quail.'"**

רַב נַחְמָן אָמַר [10] **Rav Naḥman said:** Eldad and Medad **were prophesying about the matter of Gog and Magog** and the war that they are destined to wage against Israel at the end of days, [11] **for it is stated** in regard to Gog and Magog (Ezekiel 38:17-18): **"Thus says the Lord God: Are you the one of whom I spoke in ancient days, through my servants the Prophets of Israel, who prophesied in those days for many years** [שָׁנִים] **that I would bring you against them?"** [12] **Do not read** the word שָׁנִים in the verse as *shanim*, **"years," but rather** as *shenayim*, **"two."** [13] **And who are the two Prophets who prophesied** this **one prophecy at the same time?** [14] **Say** that they were **Eldad and Medad.**

אָמַר מָר [15] **The master** (Rabbi Shimon) **said** in the above Baraita: "When **all the** other elders became **Prophets** at the hour of their investiture, they **prophesied** a single time **and** then **ceased** to prophesy, whereas Eldad and Medad **prophesied** at that hour **and did not cease**." [16] The Gemara asks: **From where do we know**

RASHI

שכל הנביאים כולן — אותן שבעים זקנים נתנבאו אותה שעה ראשונה לבדה, כנוח עליהם הרוח סביבות האהל — ופסקו. **על עסקי שליו** — לצורך שעה היתה. **אל תקרי שנים** — אלא שנים.

NOTES

מַה נְּבוּאָה נִתְנַבְּאוּ What prophecy did they prophesy? *Maharsha* explains that all three opinions regarding the subject of the prophecy of Eldad and Medad are based on an allusion in the verse (Numbers 11:26): "And they prophesied in the camp," implying that their prophecy was somehow related to the subject of a camp. Hence, the suggestion that they prophesied about the future leadership of the camp, or about the quail that were to fall in the

[1]אִילֵימָא מִדִּכְתִיב: [2]"וַיִּתְנַבְּאוּ וְלֹא יָסָפוּ", [3]אֶלָּא מֵעַתָּה "קוֹל גָּדוֹל וְלֹא יָסָף", [4]הָכִי נַמִי דְּלָא אוֹסִיף הוּא? [5]אֶלָּא, דְּלָא פָּסַק הוּא!

[6]אֶלָּא, הָכָא כְּתִיב: [7]"וַיִּתְנַבְּאוּ", [8]הָתָם כְּתִיב: [9]"מִתְנַבְּאִים" — [10]עֲדַיִין מִתְנַבְּאִים וְהוֹלְכִים.

[11]בִּשְׁלָמָא לְמַאן דַּאֲמַר "מֹשֶׁה מֵת" — [12]הַיְינוּ דִּכְתִיב: "אֲדֹנִי מֹשֶׁה כְּלָאֵם". [13]אֶלָּא לְמַאן דַּאֲמַר הָנָךְ תַּרְתֵּי, [14]מַאי "אֲדֹנִי מֹשֶׁה כְּלָאֵם"?

[15]דְּלָאו אוֹרַח אַרְעָא, [16]דַּהֲוָה לֵיהּ כְּתַלְמִיד הַמּוֹרֶה הֲלָכָה לִפְנֵי רַבּוֹ.

[17]בִּשְׁלָמָא לְמַאן דַּאֲמַר הָנָךְ תַּרְתֵּי — [18]הַיְינוּ דִּכְתִיב: "מִי יִתֵּן". [19]אֶלָּא לְמַאן דַּאֲמַר: "מֹשֶׁה מֵת", [20]מֵינָח הֲוָה נִיחָא לֵיהּ?

LITERAL TRANSLATION

[1]If you should say from that which is written: [2]"And they prophesied and did not continue [*velo yasafu*]," [3]but now "A great voice [and he added no more — *velo yasaf*]," [4]here too [does it mean] that it did not continue? [5]Rather, it [means] that it did not cease!

[6]Rather, here it is written: [7]"And they prophesied," [8][and] there it is written: [9]"They are prophesying" — [10]they are still proceeding to prophesize.

[11]It is well according to the one who said [that they prophesied] "Moses will die" — [12]that is [why] it is written: "My lord, Moses, restrain them." [13]But according to the ones who said those two, [14]what is "My lord, Moses, restrain them"?

[15]That it is not proper behavior, [16]for it is similar to a disciple who teaches a law before his master.

[17]It is well according to the ones who said those two — [18]that is [why] it is written: "Were it that [lit., 'who will give']. [19]But according to the one who said: "Moses will die," [20]would it have been agreeable to him?

TRANSLATION AND COMMENTARY

that the other elders **ceased** to prophesy? [1]**If you should say** that we know this **from that which is written** (Numbers 11:25): [2]**"And they** [the other elders] **prophesied and did not continue** [וְלֹא יָסָפוּ — *velo yasafu*]," it is difficult, [3]for then how are we **now** to understand the following description of the revelation at Mount Sinai (Deuteronomy 5:19): "These words God spoke to all your assembly...with **a great voice** and he added no more [וְלֹא יָסָף — *velo yasaf*]"? [4]Are we to say that **here, too,** the verb יסף is to be understood as meaning **that** God's voice **did not continue** to be heard? [5]**Rather, it** surely means **that** God's voice **did not cease**, so the verb *yasaf,* describing the prophecy of the elders, has the same meaning, and we should say that their prophecy did not cease as well!

אֶלָּא [6]**Rather,** the proof that the other elders ceased to prophesy after their first experience is as follows: **Here,** in the verse regarding the elders (Numbers 11:25), **it is written:** [7]**"And they prophesied,"** employing the past tense to indicate that they only prophesied once. [8]**There,** in the verse regarding Eldad and Medad, **it is written** (v. 27): [9]"Eldad and Medad **are prophesying** in the camp," [10]using the present tense to imply that **they are still proceeding to prophesy.**

בִּשְׁלָמָא לְמַאן דַּאֲמַר [11]The Gemara now returns to the disagreement concerning the prophecy of Eldad and Medad: Granted **it is well according to the one who said that** their prophecy consisted of the declaration: **"Moses will die** and Joshua will bring the people of Israel into the Promised Land"; [12]**that is** the reason **that** we find **written** in the next verse (v. 28) that Joshua said to Moses: "**My lord, Moses, restrain them"** for calling your authority into question. [13]**But according to the ones who said** that Eldad and Medad uttered one of **those two** other prophecies, about the quail or Gog and Magog, [14]**what is** the meaning of Joshua's plea: **"My lord, Moses, restrain them"?**

דְּלָאו אוֹרַח אַרְעָא [15]The Gemara answers that Joshua thought **that it was not proper behavior** (lit. "the way of the land") for Eldad and Medad to publicly prophesy in Moses' presence, [16]**for it was similar to a disciple who teaches a law before his master.**

בִּשְׁלָמָא לְמַאן דַּאֲמַר [17]Granted **it is well according to the ones who said** that Eldad and Medad uttered one of **those** other **two** prophecies; [18]**that is** the reason **that** we find **written** in the next verse (v. 29) Moses' response to Joshua: "Do you envy for my sake? **Were it that** all the Lord's people were prophets!" [19]**But according to the one who said** that Eldad and Medad prophesied: **"Moses will die,** and Joshua will bring the people of Israel into the Promised Land," [20]**would it** really **have been agreeable to** Moses to proclaim such a prophecy!

RASHI

אילימא דכתיב בהו — בשאר זקנים "ולא יספו" ומפרשת ליה: ולא יוסיפו. **אלא מעתה קול גדול ולא יסף** — דשכינה, הכי נמי דלא אוסיף, אלא על כרחיך דלא פסק הוא, קול שכינה אינו פוסק.

NOTES

camp, or about the war to be waged against Israel by the camp of Gog and Magog.

לָאו אוֹרַח אַרְעָא **It is not proper behavior.** It has been asked: What choice did Eldad and Medad have in regard

[1]לָא סִיְּימוּהָ קַמֵּיהּ.
[2]מַאי ״כְּלָאֵם״?
[3]אָמַר לֵיהּ: ״הַטֵּל עֲלֵיהֶן צָרְכֵי צִיבּוּר, [4]וְהֵן כָּלִין מֵאֵילֵיהֶן״.
[5]״מִנַּיִין לְהָבִיא עוֹד שְׁלֹשָׁה״.
[6]סוֹף סוֹף, לְרָעָה עַל פִּי שְׁנַיִם לֹא מַשְׁכַּחַתְּ לַהּ. [7]אִי אַחַד עָשָׂר מְזַכִּין וּשְׁנֵים עָשָׂר מְחַיְּיבִין, [8]אַכַּתִּי חַד הוּא, [9]אִי עֲשָׂרָה מְזַכִּין וּשְׁלֹשָׁה עָשָׂר מְחַיְּיבִין, [10]תְּלָתָא הָווּ!
[11]אָמַר רַבִּי אַבָּהוּ: אִי אַתָּה מוֹצֵא אֶלָּא בְּמוֹסִיפִין, [12]וְדִבְרֵי הַכֹּל, [13]וּבְסַנְהֶדְרִי גְּדוֹלָה, וְאַלִּיבָּא דְּרַבִּי יְהוּדָה דְּאָמַר שִׁבְעִים.

LITERAL TRANSLATION

[1]They did not specify before him.
[2]What is "restrain them"?
[3]He said to him: "Place upon them communal needs, [4]and they will cease by themselves."
[5]"And from where [do we know] to bring another three?"
[6]Ultimately, you will not find [a decision] for evil on the basis of two. [7]If eleven acquit and twelve convict, [8]there is still one. [9]If ten acquit and thirteen convict, [10]there are three!
[11]Rabbi Abbahu said: You do not find [it] except when we add, [12]and it is the opinion of all, [13]and in the Great Sanhedrin, and according to Rabbi Yehudah who said seventy.

TRANSLATION AND COMMENTARY

לָא סִיְּימוּהָ קַמֵּיהּ [1]The Gemara answers that when the people informed Moses of the prophesying of Eldad and Medad, **they did not specify** the content of their prophecy.

מַאי כְּלָאֵם [2]Returning to the verse mentioned above, the Gemara asks: **What is** the meaning of Joshua's wish that Moses **"restrain them"?**

אָמַר לֵיהּ [3]Joshua **said to** Moses as follows: **"Place upon them** responsibility for seeing to **communal needs,** just like the other elders, [4]**and they will** soon be so burdened with their work that they will **cease** prophesying **by themselves."** The verb כלה (to cease) is similar to the verb in the verse, כלא (to restrain).

מִנַּיִין [5]The next clause of our Mishnah explained how we know that a Lesser Sanhedrin has twenty-three members: The relevant verses (Numbers 35:24-25: "And the congregation shall judge... and the congregation shall rescue") teach that, in order to try capital cases, we need a court large enough to contain two "congregations" (two assemblies of ten), one to argue that the defendant be found guilty and the other to see to it that he not be wrongly convicted. The Mishnah then asks: **"From where** is it learned that we are **to bring another three** judges in order to augment the initial twenty?" The Mishnah explains, on the basis of the verse (Exodus 23:2): "You shall not follow the many to do evil," that we are not to follow an ordinary majority of one for purposes of convicting someone and thereby inflicting harm, but rather must convict by a majority of two. Thus the court must add another two judges to its initial quorum. However, since a court may not be composed of an even number of judges, we add another, bringing the total to twenty-three. [6]The Gemara asks: If, **ultimately,** we have to add another judge so that the court not comprise an even number, **you will not find** an instance where the court decides **for evil on the basis of** a majority of **two,** [7]because **if eleven** judges wish to **acquit** the defendant **and twelve** wish to **convict** him, [8]**there is still** only a majority of **one.** [9]And **if ten** wish to **acquit while thirteen** wish to **convict,** [10]**there** is a majority of **three** in favor of conviction and not two.

אָמַר רַבִּי אַבָּהוּ [11]**Rabbi Abbahu said: You do not find** a case of conviction being delivered by a majority of two **except when we add** two additional judges to a court split in its decision due to one of the original twenty-three abstaining (see *Sanhedrin* 40a). If the two additional judges both decide in favor of a conviction, [12]then **it is the opinion of all** that the defendant be sentenced accordingly on the basis of a majority of two. [13]Such an instance can also occur **in the Great Sanhedrin,** but only **according to Rabbi Yehudah, who said** in our Mishnah that the Great Sanhedrin is composed of **seventy** judges: If thirty-six convict and thirty-four acquit, the defendant will have been convicted by a majority of two.

RASHI

אלא במוסיפין ודברי הכל — דתנן ב״היו בודקין״ (סנהדרין מ,א): אחד עשר מזכין, ואחד עשר מחייבין, ואחד אומר ״איני יודע״ — יוסיפו הדיינין שנים, דהשתא הוה ליה בית דין שקול, דאינו יודע — כמאן דליתיה הוא, ופשו להו עשרים וארבעה, משכחת ליה על פי שנים, אחד עשר מזכין ושלשה עשר מחייבין. **ובסנהדרי גדולה** — לרבי יהודה זוגות נינהו.

NOTES

to communicating their prophecy? Surely we have learned that one who suppresses his prophecy is liable to the death sentence! *Rabbi Ḥayyim Vital* explains that the objection against them was that they didn't approach Moses first with their prophecy before announcing it to the rest of the community. Thus, Joshua suggested that they be restrained, for their unbecoming behavior demonstrated that they were unfit to continue prophesying.

TRANSLATION AND COMMENTARY

וְאָמַר רַבִּי אַבָּהוּ [1]**And Rabbi Abbahu said:** In the case **where we add** two judges to a court of twenty-three which has become split due to an abstention, **we make it into an even-numbered court.** Even so, we need not hesitate and may do so **from the outset.**

פְּשִׁיטָא [2]**This is obvious!** As mentioned above, in accordance with a later Mishnah, when one of the judges cannot decide, two additional judges are added. And since the judge who abstained is no longer counted, it is obvious that the resulting quorum will be even in number!

מַהוּ דְּתֵימָא [3]Nevertheless, it was necessary for Rabbi Abbahu to state that an even-numbered court can be established from the outset under these circumstances, for otherwise **what would you have said?** [4]That the judge **who said "I do not know** how to decide" **is** still **considered as one who is present,** [5]so that **if he** later wishes to **say something** relevant, **we listen to him** and admit his opinion as part of the deliberation. [6]Therefore Rabbi Abbahu **teaches us that** in such an instance the court is considered to be even in number, since the judge **who said "I do not know** how to rule" **is considered as one who is not present;** [7]**and** so, **if he** later wishes to **state a reason** for convicting or acquitting, **we do not listen to him.**

אָמַר רַב כָּהֲנָא [8]**Rav Kahana said:** In the event of **a** Lesser **Sanhedrin** judging a capital case, [9]**where all** the judges without exception **see** the defendant as deserving **condemnation, we acquit him.** [10]**What is the reason** that he is acquitted in such a case? [11]**Since we have learned** that it is necessary, when the

[1]וְאָמַר רַבִּי אַבָּהוּ: בְּמוֹסִיפִין עוֹשִׂין בֵּית דִּין שָׁקוּל לְכַתְּחִילָּה.
[2]פְּשִׁיטָא!
[3]מַהוּ דְּתֵימָא? [4]הַאי דְּקָאָמַר "אֵינִי יוֹדֵעַ" כְּמַאן דְּאִיתֵיהּ דָּמֵי, [5]וְאִי אָמַר מִילְּתָא, שָׁמְעִינַן לֵיהּ, [6]קָא מַשְׁמַע לָן דְּהַאי דְּקָאָמַר "אֵינִי יוֹדֵעַ" כְּמַאן דְּלֵיתֵיהּ דָּמֵי, [7]וְאִי אָמַר טַעֲמָא, לָא שָׁמְעִינַן לֵיהּ.
[8]אָמַר רַב כָּהֲנָא: סַנְהֶדְרִי שֶׁרָאוּ כּוּלָּן לְחוֹבָה, [9]פּוֹטְרִין אוֹתוֹ. [10]מַאי טַעֲמָא? [11]כֵּיוָן

LITERAL TRANSLATION

[1]And Rabbi Abbahu said: When we add, we make [it into] an even-numbered court from the outset.
[2]This is obvious!
[3]What would you have said? [4]He who said "I do not know" is considered as one who is present, [5]and if he says something, we listen to him. [6][Therefore] he teaches us that he who said "I do not know" is considered as one who is not present, [7]and if he states a reason, we do not listen to him.
[8]Rav Kahana said: [In the case of] a Sanhedrin where all of them saw for condemnation, [9]we acquit him. [10]What is the reason? [11]Since

RASHI

במוסיפין — עושין בית דין שקול כדפרישית. **פשיטא** — דהכי בהדיא תנן (שם מ'): וכמה מוסיפין — שנים שנים, וכיון דחד אמר אינו יודע, הוו להו בית דין שקול. **ואי אמר טעמא** — מראה פנים לחובה ומראה פנים לזכות, ומשום הכי מספקא ליה.

BACKGROUND

שֶׁרָאוּ כּוּלָּן לְחוֹבָה **Where all of them saw for condemnation.** Here and elsewhere in the Talmud we see that the Sages feared that whenever there was unanimous agreement, with no abstentions or objections, it was likely that ulterior motives (emotional or public) had led the judges to a unanimous decision, and it was impossible to discover the truth of the matter (a situation similar to elections in which nearly 100% of the electorate vote for a certain candidate).

NOTES

אִי אָמַר טַעֲמָא לָא שָׁמְעִינַן לֵיהּ **If he states a reason, we do not listen to him.** *Tosafot* and others understand this to mean that the arguments of an abstaining judge are to be ignored only when they support a conviction; but if they support an acquittal, we admit them before the court no less than we would the words of any Rabbinical student who wishes to put forward an argument in the defendant's favor (see *Sanhedrin* 40a).

כּוּלָּן לְחוֹבָה **Where they were all for condemnation.** *Rosh* explains Rav Kahana's ruling in a novel way: If, in a capital

HALAKHAH

בְּמוֹסִיפִין עוֹשִׂין בֵּית דִּין שָׁקוּל **When we add, we make it into an even-numbered court.** "If the members of a Lesser Sanhedrin disagree about a capital case, with twelve in favor of acquittal and eleven in favor of conviction, the defendant is acquitted. If twelve are in favor of conviction and eleven in favor of acquittal, or if eleven are in favor of conviction and the same number in favor of acquittal and one is in doubt about how to rule (or even if twenty-two are in favor of either conviction or acquittal and one is in doubt about how to rule), two judges are added to the court, and the judge with doubts is considered as if he were absent. If twelve judges are then in favor of acquittal and twelve in favor of conviction, the accused is acquitted. This reading was accepted by *Maharam Padua*, but rejected by *Tosafot Yom Tov,* who suggested that this last ruling refers to a case where thirteen were in favor of acquittal and twelve in favor of conviction. But if the court remains evenly divided even after adding two judges, the court continues to be expanded by two judges at a time until there is a majority of one in favor of acquittal or a majority of two in favor of conviction, or until the court reaches its maximum size of seventy-one members." (*Rambam, Sefer Shofetim, Hilkhot Sanhedrin* 9:2.)

סַנְהֶדְרִי שֶׁרָאוּ כּוּלָּן לְחוֹבָה **A Sanhedrin whose members all saw him fit for condemnation.** "If all the judges in a capital case rule in favor of conviction, the defendant is acquitted, for the defendant can only be convicted if there is a minority opinion in favor of acquittal," following Rav Kahana. (*Rambam, Sefer Shofetim, Hilkhot Sanhedrin* 9:1.)

BACKGROUND

בַּעֲלֵי קוֹמָה, בַּעֲלֵי מַרְאֶה **Possessed of stature, possessed of appearance.** Although the Sanhedrin enjoyed considerable coercive power, the judges wished that power to derive not only from their rank, but also from their powers of personal persuasion. Therefore, the judges were required not only to be wise and learned in Torah, but also to be endowed with other traits that would induce the public to accept their decisions. Hence, whenever possible, men of impressive appearance were chosen.

שִׁבְעִים לָשׁוֹן **Seventy languages.** The expressions "seventy languages" and "seventy nations" are connected to the list of Noah's descendants in Genesis 10. According to this list, it appears that the seventy languages are not all foreign and different from each other; some of them are related dialects spoken by neighboring peoples, and many of these languages belong to the same linguistic family.

לְטַהֵר אֶת הַשֶּׁרֶץ **Render a creeping creature ritually pure.** The expression, "to purify the creeping thing" has become proverbial for describing a person with a very sharp mind who can prove anything, even something preposterous. In the context of the debate here, it must be recalled that since the litigants and the defendants in Jewish courts were not represented by attorneys, it was one of the functions of the judges themselves to represent the accused, and for that reason they had to be capable of marshaling all the claims that an attorney would make in order to present his client's case favorably. Indeed, there were Sages who wondered why it was necessary to seek out men who could make use of "vain cleverness" to prove something that was false. Thus they argued that what was meant here was to prove that the blood of a crawling thing was ritually pure, because it was not explicitly declared impure by the Torah. Nevertheless, the main point made here concerns the judge's intellectual ability and his capacity to see both sides of every

TRANSLATION AND COMMENTARY

majority of a court have decided on conviction, to **suspend** issuing **the verdict overnight in order** that the court might **produce** further arguments in the defendant's **favor;** and since these judges, unanimous in their determination to convict, [1]can **no longer** be expected to **see** any points in his favor — it was decided that the defendant be acquitted rather than deprived of a final chance to have his innocence established.

אָמַר רַבִּי יוֹחָנָן [2]**Rabbi Yoḥanan said: We do not seat** judges **in the Sanhedrin unless they are possessed of** imposing **stature, and possessed of wisdom, and possessed of** a distinguished **appearance, and possessed of maturity in years** so that they may command the public's respect. [3]The candidates must also be **possessed of** knowledge of **sorcery,** so that they may know how to judge someone charged with practicing it. [4]They must also be **knowledgeable in** the **seventy languages** of the nations, [5]**so that** if witnesses come forward who do not speak Hebrew, **the Sanhedrin will not** have to **hear** their testimony **from the mouth of an interpreter,** which would be considered invalid hearsay.

אָמַר רַב יְהוּדָה [6]**Rav Yehudah said in the name of Rav: We do not seat** a judge **on the Sanhedrin unless he is** clever enough to **know how to render** an impure **creeping creature** (see Leviticus 11:29-37) **ritually pure** by bringing proof **from the Torah.**

דִּגְמִירִי הֲלָנַת דִּין לְמֶעְבַּד לֵיהּ זְכוּתָא, [1]וְהָנֵי תּוּ לָא חֲזוּ לֵיהּ.
[2]אָמַר רַבִּי יוֹחָנָן: אֵין מוֹשִׁיבִין בְּסַנְהֶדְרִי אֶלָּא בַּעֲלֵי קוֹמָה, וּבַעֲלֵי חָכְמָה, וּבַעֲלֵי מַרְאֶה, וּבַעֲלֵי זִקְנָה, [3]וּבַעֲלֵי כְשָׁפִים, [4]וְיוֹדְעִים בְּשִׁבְעִים לָשׁוֹן, [5]שֶׁלֹּא תְּהֵא סַנְהֶדְרִי שׁוֹמַעַת מִפִּי הַמְּתוּרְגְּמָן.
[6]אָמַר רַב יְהוּדָה אָמַר רַב: אֵין מוֹשִׁיבִין בְּסַנְהֶדְרִין אֶלָּא מִי שֶׁיּוֹדֵעַ לְטַהֵר אֶת הַשֶּׁרֶץ מִן הַתּוֹרָה.

LITERAL TRANSLATION

we have learned that we suspend the verdict overnight in order to produce for him a merit, [1]and these no longer see [any merit].

[2]Rabbi Yoḥanan said: We do not seat [judges] in the Sanhedrin unless they are possessed of stature, and possessed of wisdom, and possessed of appearance, and possessed of maturity in years, [3]and possessed of sorcery, [4]and knowledgeable in seventy languages, [5]so that the Sanhedrin will not hear from the mouth of an interpreter.

[6]Rav Yehudah said in the name of Rav: We do not seat [a judge] in the Sanhedrin unless he is one who knows how to render a creeping creature ritually pure from the Torah.

RASHI

כיון דגמירי — דבעי הלנת דין, בפרק "היו בודקין" (שם) שאם לא מצאו לו זכות יום ראשון, מלינין אותו למחרת, שמא ימצאו להם טעמי זכות. **בעלי קומה ומראה** — שתהא אימתן מוטלת על הבריות. **ובעלי כשפים** — להמית מכשפים הבוטחים בכשפיהם להנצל מידי בית דין, ולגלות על המכשפין המסיתין ומדיחין בכשפיהן, כגון המצרים (השמטת הצנזורה: כגון ישו הנוצרי). **מפי המתורגמן** — כשבאין עדי לועזים להעיד בפניהם לא יצטרכו להעמיד מליצים ביניהם, דהוה ליה עד מפי עד.

NOTES

case, all the judges found the defendant guilty, we absolve the court of having to deliberate further so that it may deliver the verdict immediately and implement punishment.

בַּעֲלֵי זִקְנָה **Possessed of maturity in years.** Rabbi Yoḥanan does not mean to say that a judge should be elderly, for one too advanced in years is in fact disqualified from sitting on the Sanhedrin. Rather, he means that a judge should be old enough to have sufficient life experience of the hardship entailed in raising children.

לְטַהֵר אֶת הַשֶּׁרֶץ **To render a creeping creature ritually pure.** The Torah (Leviticus 11:29-37) enumerates eight species of creeping creatures whose carcasses impart ritual impurity to those who come into contact with them. *Talmidei Rabbenu Peretz* note that the purpose of presenting a logical argument in favor of rendering such a creature ritually pure is to show that ultimately the laws of ritual impurity derive from the authority of Scripture and not from logic or reason. *Meiri* suggests that the need for a judge to show a Biblical basis for modifying the laws of ritual impurity stems from his having to prove his ability to provide adequate Scriptural support in future for Rabbinic decrees or enactments that he might deem necessary. *Maharsha* explains this passage in the context of the previous one regarding a defendant who is perceived as guilty by the entire Sanhedrin: Just as the judges of the Sanhedrin must be capable of arguing for the purity of a patently unclean, creeping creature, so too must they be capable of arguing for the acquittal of an obviously guilty criminal.

HALAKHAH

אֵין מוֹשִׁיבִין בְּסַנְהֶדְרִי אֶלָּא **We do not seat a judge in the Sanhedrin unless.** "Judges sitting in a Sanhedrin must be free of physical blemishes. They should be mature men, of imposing stature and distinguished appearance. They should be familiar with the magical arts so as to know when someone has committed the crime of sorcery, and they should be fluent in many languages so as not to rely on testimony conveyed through an interpreter." (*Rambam, Sefer Shofetim, Hilkhot Sanhedrin* 2:1,6.)

TRANSLATION AND COMMENTARY

אָמַר רַב [1]**Rav said: I will** now **argue** accordingly **and render** a creeping animal **ritually pure** on the basis of a Torah verse [17B] [2]**If a snake, which kills and** thus **increases ritual impurity** in the world (for corpses and carcasses impart ritual impurity), **is** nevertheless **ritually pure** (as it does not appear on the Biblical list of creeping animals whose carcasses defile), [3]**is it not logical that a creeping animal**, which **does not kill and** does not **increase ritual impurity** in the world, **should** all the more so **be ritually pure** when it dies?! [4]The Gemara rejects this argument: **It is not** a valid argument that Rav offers, **for** the fact that something kills and thus increases ritual impurity in the world is not connected with the issue of whether it imparts ritual impurity. In this respect, a snake **is something like an ordinary thorn** which occasionally causes injury and can even lead to death, though no one would argue that a thorn should be declared ritually impure.

אָמַר רַב יְהוּדָה [5]**Rav Yehudah said in the name of Rav: Any city which does not have in it** at least **two** judges who know how **to speak** seventy languages, **and** at least **one** other judge who **understands** that number of tongues, even though he does not speak them — [6]**we do not seat a** Lesser **Sanhedrin in** that city, for there must always be at least three judges capable of receiving testimony offered in a foreign tongue. [7]**In** the city of **Betar there were three** who spoke seventy languages, **and in Yavneh** there were **four:** [8]**Rabbi Eliezer, Rabbi Yehoshua, Rabbi Akiva,** [9]**and** also **Shimon HaTimni,** who, though not ordained, **argued before** the court while sitting **on the ground** in the area set aside for astute disciples.

[1]אָמַר רַב: אֲנִי אָדוּן וַאֲטַהֲרֶנּוּ: [17B] [2]וּמַה נָּחָשׁ שֶׁמֵּמִית וּמַרְבֶּה טוּמְאָה טָהוֹר, [3]שֶׁרֶץ שֶׁאֵינוֹ מֵמִית וּמַרְבֶּה טוּמְאָה אֵינוֹ דִּין שֶׁיְּהֵא טָהוֹר!? [4]וְלָא הִיא, מִידֵּי דַּהֲוָה אַקּוֹץ בְּעָלְמָא.

[5]אָמַר רַב יְהוּדָה אָמַר רַב: כָּל עִיר שֶׁאֵין בָּהּ שְׁנַיִם לְדַבֵּר וְאֶחָד לִשְׁמוֹעַ, [6]אֵין מוֹשִׁיבִין בָּהּ סַנְהֶדְרִי. [7]וּבְבֵיתָר הָווּ שְׁלֹשָׁה, וּבְיַבְנֶה אַרְבָּעָה: [8]רַבִּי אֱלִיעֶזֶר, וְרַבִּי יְהוֹשֻׁעַ, וְרַבִּי עֲקִיבָא, [9]וְשִׁמְעוֹן הַתִּימְנִי דָּן לִפְנֵיהֶם בַּקַּרְקַע.

LITERAL TRANSLATION

[1]Rav said: I will argue and render it ritually pure: [17B] [2]If a snake which kills and increases ritual impurity is ritually pure, [3]is it not logical that a creeping animal which does not kill or increase ritual impurity should be ritually pure?! [4]But it is not so, for it is something like an ordinary thorn.

[5]Rav Yehudah said in the name of Rav: Any city which does not have in it two to speak and one to understand, [6]we do not seat a Sanhedrin in it. [7]And in Betar there were three, and in Yavneh four: [8]Rabbi Eliezer, and Rabbi Yehoshua, and Rabbi Akiva, [9]and Shimon HaTimni who argued before them on the ground.

RASHI

ומה נחש שממית – אדם ובהמה, ומרבה טומאת נבילות וטומאת מת בעולם, הרי הוא טהור כשהוא מת, שאינו בכלל שמנה שרצים. **ולא היא** – לאו קל וחומר הוא, דאין זה חומר אם הוא ממית ומרבה טומאה, שהרי כמו כן יש קוצים שהן ממיתין ומרבין טומאה – והן טהורין. **שנים לדבר** – בשבעים לשון, ואחד לשמוע, שיהא מבין בשבעים לשון אף על פי שאינו יודע להשיב. **שמעון התימני** – תלמיד היה, ולא נסמך, שלא בא לכלל זקנה.

matter, even against common opinion. This ability is necessary for Sages and communal leaders who must make decisions that will be valid for generations.

BACKGROUND

דָּן לִפְנֵיהֶם בַּקַּרְקַע Argued before them on the ground. This expression describes the seating arrangement at certain times, when important Sages would sit on a raised place, or at least on cushions, facing the audience, and the important students would sit before them on the ground.

NOTES

לְדַבֵּר וּלִשְׁמוֹעַ Who speak and who understand. Our commentary follows *Rashi* and others who explain that Rav means judges who speak and understand foreign languages. At least two members of the Lesser Sanhedrin must speak seventy languages, while a third must at least understand them. Thus, there will always be a court of three judges to accept the testimony of witnesses who do not speak Hebrew. It follows, according to this position, that while capital cases can only be judged by a court of twenty-three judges, testimony in such a case can be received by an adjunct court of three. *Ramban* and *Ran* reject this position, arguing that if capital cases can only be judged by a court of twenty-three, then all twenty-three judges must also be capable of receiving witnesses' testimony. Thus, the entire Sanhedrin must be familiar with seventy languages.

Rabbenu Sherira Gaon, Rambam and others understand Rav as referring to the judges' mastery of Torah. At least two members of the Lesser Sanhedrin (according to *Rambam*'s reading, only one; see Halakhah) must have mastered Torah so thoroughly that they can expound and rule upon any aspect of Torah law, and at least one other member must be able to follow the Halakhic discussions of the first two and raise questions about their positions.

HALAKHAH

שְׁנַיִם לְדַבֵּר וְאֶחָד לִשְׁמוֹעַ Two who speak and one who understands. "A Lesser Sanhedrin may only be established in a city which has two great scholars, one who is fit to teach and rule upon all aspects of the Torah, and a second who understands and can raise and answer questions. *Rambam* apparently had the reading: 'Two, one who speaks and one who understands,' and followed the Geonim who interpret 'speaking' as referring to a total mastery of the Torah." (*Rambam, Sefer Shofetim, Hilkhot Sanhedrin* 1:5.)

TRANSLATION AND COMMENTARY

מֵיתִיבֵי [1]Some Sages **objected** to Rav Yehudah's ruling on the basis of the following Baraita: "If the court has **a third** judge who is conversant in seventy languages, **it is** regarded as a **wise** court. [2]If it has **a fourth, there is no** court **loftier than it."** This Baraita implies that a court wise enough to hear capital cases must have no fewer than three judges who can speak foreign tongues, whereas Rav Yehudah states that two are enough as long as a third understands!

הוּא דְּאָמַר [3]Rav Yehudah **stated** his position **in accordance with that Tanna** [4]**who taught** in a Baraita: "If the court has **a second** judge who is conversant in seventy languages, **it is** regarded as a **wise** court. [5]If it has **a third, there is no** court **loftier than it."**

לְמֵידִין לִפְנֵי חֲכָמִים [6]Since Shimon HaTimni was described above as one who "argued before the court while sitting on the ground," the Gemara proceeds to identify other phrases used to describe particular Sages: Whenever the Gemara uses the expression, **"they learn before the Sages,"** [7]it is referring to **Levi,** who learned Torah **from Rabbi** Yehudah HaNasi. [8]And whenever it speaks of those who would **"argue before the Sages,"** [9]it is referring to **Shimon ben Azai, Shimon ben Zoma, Ḥanan the Egyptian, and Ḥananyah ben Ḥakhinai.** [10]**Rav Naḥman bar Yitzḥak taught** that this expression refers to **five** Sages: **Shimon** ben Azzai, **Shimon** ben Zoma, **Shimon** HaTimni, **Ḥanan** the Egyptian, **and Ḥananyah** ben Ḥakhinai. These five Sages were not ordained, and so they "argued before the Sages." [11]The term, **"our Rabbis in Babylonia,"** [12]always refers to **Rav and Shmuel.** [13]The expression, **"our Rabbis in Eretz Israel,"** [14]always refers to **Rabbi Abba.** [15]Whenever the Gemara uses the expression, **"the judges of the Diaspora,"** [16]it is referring to the court headed by **Karna.** [17]Whenever it speaks of **"the judges of Eretz Israel,"** [18]it is referring to **Rabbi Ammi and Rabbi Assi.** [19]The expression, **"the judges of Pumbedita,"** [20]is always used in connection with the court headed by **Rav Pappa bar Shmuel.** [21]The expression, **"the judges of Neharde'a,"** [22]refers to the court of **Rav Adda bar Manyomi.** [23]Whenever the Gemara speaks of **"the elders of Sura,"** [24]it is referring to **Rav Huna and Rav Ḥisda.** [25]Whenever it mentions **"the elders of Pumbedita,"** [26]it has in mind **Rav Yehudah and Rav Eina.** [27]The expression, **"the sharp ones of Pumbedita,"** [28]always refers to **Eifa and Avimi the sons of Reḥavah.** [29]The expression, **"the Amoraim of Pumbedita,"** [30]is always used in connection with **Rabbah and Rav Yosef.**

[1]מֵיתִיבֵי: "שְׁלִישִׁית — חֲכָמָה; [2]רְבִיעִית — אֵין לְמַעְלָה הֵימֶנָּה"! [3]הוּא דְּאָמַר כִּי הַאי תַּנָּא, [4]דְּתַנְיָא: "שְׁנִיָּה — חֲכָמָה; [5]שְׁלִישִׁית — אֵין לְמַעְלָה הֵימֶנָּה". [6]"לְמֵידִין לִפְנֵי חֲכָמִים" — [7]לֵוִי מֵרַבִּי. [8]"דָּנִין לִפְנֵי חֲכָמִים" — [9]שִׁמְעוֹן בֶּן עַזַּאי, וְשִׁמְעוֹן בֶּן זוֹמָא, וְחָנָן הַמִּצְרִי, וַחֲנַנְיָא בֶּן חֲכִינַאי. [10]רַב נַחְמָן בַּר יִצְחָק מַתְנֵי חֲמִשָּׁה: שִׁמְעוֹן, שִׁמְעוֹן, וְשִׁמְעוֹן, חָנָן, וַחֲנַנְיָה. [11]"רַבּוֹתֵינוּ שֶׁבְּבָבֶל" — [12]רַב וּשְׁמוּאֵל. [13]"רַבּוֹתֵינוּ שֶׁבְּאֶרֶץ יִשְׂרָאֵל" — [14]רַבִּי אַבָּא. [15]"דַּיָּינֵי גוֹלָה" — [16]קַרְנָא. [17]"דַּיָּינֵי דְּאֶרֶץ יִשְׂרָאֵל" — [18]רַבִּי אַמִי וְרַבִּי אַסִי. [19]"דַּיָּינֵי דְפוּמְבְּדִיתָא" — [20]רַב פַּפָּא בַּר שְׁמוּאֵל, [21]"דַּיָּינֵי דִּנְהַרְדְּעָא" — [22]רַב אַדָּא בַּר מַנְיוֹמִי, [23]"סָבֵי דְסוּרָא" — [24]רַב הוּנָא וְרַב חִסְדָּא. [25]"סָבֵי דְּפוּמְבְּדִיתָא" — [26]רַב יְהוּדָה וְרַב עֵינָא, [27]"חֲרִיפֵי דְפוּמְבְּדִיתָא" — [28]עֵיפָה וַאֲבִימִי בְּנֵי רַחֲבָה. [29]"אָמוֹרָאֵי דְפוּמְבְּדִיתָא" — [30]רַבָּה וְרַב

LITERAL TRANSLATION

[1]They objected: "A third — [it is] wise; [2]a fourth — there is none loftier than it!"

[3]He stated in accordance with that Tanna [4]who taught: "A second — [it is] wise; [5]a third — there is none loftier than it."

[6]"They learn before the Sages" — [7]Levi from Rabbi. [8]"They argue before the Sages" — [9]Shimon ben Azzai and Shimon ben Zoma, and Ḥanan the Egyptian, and Ḥananyah ben Ḥakhinai. [10]Rav Naḥman bar Yitzḥak taught five: Shimon, Shimon, Shimon, Ḥanan, and Ḥananyah. [11]"Our Rabbis in Babylonia" — [12]Rav and Shmuel. [13]"Our Rabbis in Eretz Israel" — [14]Rabbi Abba. [15]"The judges of the Diaspora" — [16]Karna. [17]"The judges of Eretz Israel" — [18]Rabbi Ammi and Rabbi Assi. [19]"The judges of Pumbedita" — [20]Rav Pappa bar Shmuel. [21]"The judges of Neharde'a" — [22]Rav Adda bar Manyomi. [23]"The elders of Sura" — [24]Rav Huna and Rav Ḥisda. [25]"The elders of Pumbedita" — [26]Rav Yehudah and Rav Eina. [27]"The sharp ones of Pumbedita" — [28]Eifa and Avimi the sons of Reḥavah. [29]"The Amoraim of Pumbedita" — [30]Rabbah and Rav

RASHI

שלישית חכמה — סנהדרין שיש בה שלשה מדברים בשבעים לשון חכמה היא וכשירה, אלמא שלשה בעינן לדבר. **למידין לפני חכמים** — כל היכא דאיתמר "למידין לפני חכמים" היינו לוי, שהיה למד לפני רבי. **רב נחמן** — מוסיף שמעון התימני, וחמשתן לא באו לזקנה ויושבין בקרקע, ומשיבין תשובות קושיות לזקנים, והיינו דנין בהלכה.

BACKGROUND

לְמֵידִין לִפְנֵי חֲכָמִים They learn before the Sages. Although in general the Sages of the Talmud sought to report every teaching in the name of its author, occasionally they did not wish to give prominence to a certain Sage, but rather expressed his opinion in a more general way: לְמֵידִין לִפְנֵי חֲכָמִים — "we learn before the Sages"; בֵּי רַב — "in the house of Rav"; אָמְרֵי בְּמַעַרְבָא — "they say in the West." Sometimes this was done because the opinion was not that of a single man but rather of someone who stood at the head of a group of Sages (large or small). Even though a certain Sage (or Sages) would be among the leading speakers, other men were involved. *Rambam* explains that even when a teaching is transmitted in the name of a particular Jewish Sage, it usually expresses the opinion of a group of Sages who share that opinion. Later generations, especially the Meiri, used epithets for certain Sages, not mentioning them by name but calling them "the greatest Rabbis," or "the greatest authors."

יוֹסֵף. [1]״אֲמוֹרָאֵי דִּנְהַרְדְּעֵי״ — [2]רַב חָמָא. [3]״נְהַרְבְּלָאֵי מַתְנוּ״ — [4]רָמִי בַּר בְּרַבִּי. [5]״אָמְרִי בֵּי רַב״ — [6]רַב הוּנָא.

[7]וְהָאָמַר רַב הוּנָא: אָמְרִי בֵּי רַב!

[8]אֶלָּא: רַב הַמְנוּנָא.

[9]״אָמְרִי בְּמַעַרְבָא״ — [10]רַבִּי יִרְמְיָה. [11]״שָׁלְחוּ מִתָּם״ — [12]רַבִּי יוֹסֵי בַּר חֲנִינָא. [13]״מְחַכוּ עֲלָהּ בְּמַעַרְבָא״ — [14]רַבִּי אֶלְעָזָר.

[15]וְהָא ״שָׁלְחוּ מִתָּם״ לְדִבְרֵי רַבִּי יוֹסֵי בַּר חֲנִינָא!

[16]אֶלָּא אֵיפּוֹךְ: [17]״שָׁלְחוּ מִתָּם״ — רַבִּי אֶלְעָזָר, [18]״מְחַכוּ עֲלָהּ בְּמַעַרְבָא״ — רַבִּי יוֹסֵי בַּר חֲנִינָא.

[19]״וְכַמָּה יְהֵא בָּעִיר וִיהֵא רְאוּיָה לְסַנְהֶדְרִין? [20]מֵאָה וְעֶשְׂרִים וכו׳״. [21]מֵאָה וְעֶשְׂרִים מַאי עֲבִידְתַּיְיהוּ?

LITERAL TRANSLATION

Yosef. [1]"The Amoraim of Neharde'a" — [2]Rav Ḥama. [3]"[The scholars of] Neharbel taught" — [4]Rami bar Berabi. [5]"They said in the School of Rav" — [6]Rav Huna.

[7]But Rav Huna said: They said in the School of Rav!

[8]Rather, Rav Hamnuna.

[9]"They said in the Land of Israel [lit., 'the West']" — [10]Rabbi Yirmeyah. [11]"They sent from there" — [12]Rabbi Yose bar Ḥanina. [13]"They laughed at this in Eretz Israel" — [14]Rabbi Elazar.

[15]But "they sent from there according to the words of Rabbi Yose bar Ḥanina"!

[16]Rather, reverse it: [17]"They sent from there" — Rabbi Elazar. [18]"They laughed at this in Eretz Israel" — Rabbi Yose bar Ḥanina.

[19]"And how many must there be in the town that it be fit for a Sanhedrin? [20]One-hundred-and-twenty, etc." [21]One-hundred-and-twenty, what is their business?

TRANSLATION AND COMMENTARY

[1]When referring to **"the Amoraim of Neharde'a,"** [2]the Gemara means **Rav Ḥama.** [3]Whenever the Gemara says that **"the scholars of Neharbel taught,"** [4]it is referring to **Rami bar Berabi.** [5]And whenever it states that **"they said in the School of Rav,"** [6]it is referring to **Rav Huna.**

וְהָאָמַר רַב הוּנָא [7]The Gemara interrupts the discussion to ask: **But Rav Huna** is reported to have himself **said: "They said in the School of Rav,"** implying that the source alluded to is someone other than himself!

אֶלָּא [8]**Rather,** the expression, "they said in the name of Rav," always refers to **Rav Hamnuna.**

אָמְרִי בְּמַעַרְבָא [9]On the same theme, whenever the Gemara uses the expression, **"they said in Eretz Israel** [lit., 'the West')," [10]it refers to **Rabbi Yirmeyah.** [11]The expression, **"they sent from there** [from Eretz Israel]," [12]always refers to **Rabbi Yose bar Ḥanina.** [13]And whenever the Gemara uses the expression, **"they laughed at this in Eretz Israel,"** [14]it refers to **Rabbi Elazar**'s response to opinions he found unacceptable.

וְהָא שָׁלְחוּ מִתָּם [15]**But** it was reported elsewhere that **"they sent from there** that such is the law **according to the words of Rabbi Yose bar Ḥanina,"** implying that those who "sent from there" are not to be identified with Rabbi Yose bar Ḥanina himself!

אֶלָּא אֵיפּוֹךְ [16]**Rather, reverse** these last two attributions and say that whenever the Gemara uses the expression, [17]**"they sent from there,"** it is referring to **Rabbi Elazar,** and whenever it uses the expression, [18]**"they laughed at this in Eretz Israel,"** it has in mind **Rabbi Yose bar Ḥanina.**

וְכַמָּה יְהֵא בָּעִיר [19]It is learned at the end of our Mishnah: **"And how many** inhabitants **must there be in the town,** in order **that it be fit** to house **a** Lesser **Sanhedrin**? [20]The city must have a population of at least **one-hundred-and-twenty."** [21]**What business** do **one-hundred-and-twenty** inhabitants have being mentioned in our Mishnah as justification for establishing a Lesser Sanhedrin in their midst?

RASHI

והא שלחו מתם לדברי רבי יוסי בר חנינא — מוליא [אני] מכלל רבנן בפרק "אחד דיני ממונות" (סנהדרין לד,א) אלמא שלחו מתם לאו רבי יוסי בר חנינא היא.

BACKGROUND

כַּמָּה יְהֵא בָּעִיר And how many must there be in the town. Naturally not every town with one-hundred-and-twenty men housed a Lesser Sanhedrin, but sometimes there was a concentration of Sages in a place who were worthy of sitting on a Lesser Sanhedrin. Thus it was ruled that there must be at least one-hundred-and-twenty men in such a place, so that there would be an audience and a public, and not only judges.

NOTES

מֵאָה וְעֶשְׂרִים One-hundred-and-twenty. The Rishonim suggest different ways of reaching the final count of one-hundred-and-twenty. Our commentary follows the opinion of *Yad Ramah*. According to *Rashi,* the six people alluded to in the Baraita are the two charity collectors, the three charity distributors (a separate function), and a sixth person who can theoretically serve as the doctor, the bloodletter, the scribe and the teacher all in one. *Rambam* counts the six as follows: Three to administer both the collecting and the distributing of the charity fund, a doctor who is also a

HALAKHAH

וְכַמָּה יְהֵא בָּעִיר וִיהֵא רְאוּיָה לְסַנְהֶדְרִין? And how many must there be in the town that it should be fit for a Sanhedrin? A Lesser Sanhedrin is not established in a city with a population of less than one-hundred-and-twenty men," following the Sages. (*Rambam, Sefer Shofetim, Hilkhot Sanhedrin* 1:3,10.)

TRANSLATION AND COMMENTARY

עֶשְׂרִים וּשְׁלֹשָׁה [1]The Gemara explains: There must be **twenty-three** inhabitants in the city **corresponding to** the number of judges appointed to **the Lesser Sanhedrin.** [2]Sixty-nine additional people are needed to fill the **three rows of twenty-three** Rabbinical students who sit before the court, ready to be added to its ranks should that become necessary (see *Sanhedrin* 37a). [3]**So,** this brings the number of inhabitants to **ninety-two.** [4]There must also be another **ten** men, **unemployed** and with no overriding obligations, who are available to constitute the morning and evening quorums for public prayer and tend to other communal needs **of the synagogue.** [5]**So,** this brings the total to **one-hundred-and-two** people. [6]Add to this **two scribes** to record the arguments of the court (see *Sanhedrin* 40a), **two sheriffs** to summon the litigants and administer lashes, the **two litigants** themselves, **two witnesses** brought by one of those litigants, **two** other witnesses **who can refute** the first two by testifying that they had been elsewhere when the alleged incident took place, **and** finally **two** additional witnesses **who can refute the** two who **refute** the original witnesses (see Deuteronomy 19:15-21), [7]and, the total is brought to **one-hundred-and-fourteen.** [8]The need for an additional six people in the town is derived from the Baraita in which **the following was taught:** [9]**"A Torah scholar is not permitted to dwell in any town which does not have in it these ten things:** [10]**A court which flogs and** otherwise **punishes** when necessary, [11]**a charity fund which is collected by two** people **and distributed** to the poor

[1]עֶשְׂרִים וּשְׁלֹשָׁה כְּנֶגֶד סַנְהֶדְרִי קְטַנָּה, [2]וְשָׁלֹשׁ שׁוּרוֹת שֶׁל עֶשְׂרִים וּשְׁלֹשָׁה — [3]הֲרֵי תִּשְׁעִים וְתַרְתֵּי. [4]וַעֲשָׂרָה בַּטְלָנִין שֶׁל בֵּית הַכְּנֶסֶת — [5]הֲרֵי מֵאָה וּתְרֵי. [6]וּשְׁנֵי סוֹפְרִים, וּשְׁנֵי חַזָּנִין, וּשְׁנֵי בַעֲלֵי דִינִין וּשְׁנֵי עֵדִים, וּשְׁנֵי זוֹמְמִין, וּשְׁנֵי זוֹמְמֵי זוֹמְמִין — [7]הֲרֵי מֵאָה וְאַרְבֵּיסַר. [8]וְתַנְיָא: [9]״כָּל עִיר שֶׁאֵין בָּהּ עֲשָׂרָה דְּבָרִים הַלָּלוּ — אֵין תַּלְמִיד חָכָם רַשַּׁאי לָדוּר בְּתוֹכָהּ: [10]בֵּית דִּין מַכִּין וְעוֹנְשִׁין, [11]וְקוּפָּה שֶׁל צְדָקָה נִגְבֵּית בִּשְׁנַיִם וּמִתְחַלֶּקֶת

LITERAL TRANSLATION

[1]Twenty-three corresponding to the Lesser Sanhedrin, [2]and three rows of twenty-three — [3]are ninety-two. [4]And ten idle men of the synagogue — [5]are one-hundred-and-two. [6]And two scribes, and two sheriffs, and two litigants, and two witnesses, and two who can refute them, and two who can refute the refuters — [7]are one-hundred-and-fourteen. [8]And it was taught: [9]"Any town which does not have in it these ten things — a Torah scholar is not permitted to dwell in its midst: [10]A court which flogs and punishes, [11]and a charity fund [lit., 'chest'] which is collected by two and distributed

RASHI

שלש שורות — לקמן תנינן להו ב״אחד דיני ממונות״ (לז,א), שאם הוצרכו לסמוך ולהוסיף על הדיינין — סומכין מהן. **ועשרה בטלנין** — עשרה בני אדם בטלין מכל מלאכה, להיות מזומנין לבית הכנסת שחרית וערבית. דאמרינן בברכות (ו,ב): כיון שבא הקדוש ברוך הוא לבית הכנסת ולא מצא שם עשרה, מיד כועס, דקיימא לן (מגילה ג,ב): כל כרך שאין בו עשרה בטלנין נידון ככפר. הלכך אי ליתנהו — לא חזיא לסנהדרי. **שני סופרים** — ליכתוב דברי המזכין ודברי המחייבין, וכל שעה יושבין לפני הדיינין, לקמן בפרק ״היו בודקין״ (מ,א). **ושני חזנין** — שמשי בית דין להלקות החייב, ולהזמין בעלי דינים לדין. **ושני בעלי דינין** — שאם לא כן את מי הם דנין. **ושני זוממין** — שיתייראו העדים להעיד שקר שלא יוזמו. **ושני זוממי זוממין** — שמא יתחייב בעל דין על פי עדים וישכיר שנים להזימן, לפיכך צריך שנים אחרים בעיר שיתייראו אלו מהם — אם נבוא להזים העדים יבאו אלו השנים ויזימו אותנו. **עשרה דברים** — בית דין והגבאין מחלקין להם, והוי להו תלת מילי.

BACKGROUND

אֵין תַּלְמִיד חָכָם רַשַּׁאי לָדוּר A Torah scholar is not permitted to dwell in its midst. This ruling does not apply solely to Torah scholars, for we have here a definition of the things considered essential for every Jewish person living in a town, so as to satisfy the needs of his soul and his body. This ruling was probably applied to a Torah scholar because, if he lives in a place lacking the things necessary for normal Jewish life, he must make a great effort and go elsewhere from time to time to find what he is missing; and it is a shame to have him interrupt his studies for that purpose.

בֵּית דִּין מַכִּין וְכוּ׳ A court which flogs, etc. This apparently refers to a tribunal of three, but one with authority and not simply a panel of three citizens of a city convening to discuss the city's disputes.

NOTES

bloodletter, a scribe and a teacher. Still others (see *Talmidei Rabbenu Peretz*) argue that if a bathhouse is necessary, then so too must there be a bathhouse attendant, and so one of the six must assume this occupation as well.

עֲשָׂרָה בַּטְלָנִין Ten idle men. It has been suggested that these ten men divide up the responsibilities as follows: Three sit as a permanent court to adjudicate civil cases, and a fourth serves as their enforcer; three administer the community charity fund; one serves as the town scribe; one acts as the sexton of the synagogue; and one serves as the town's teacher of young children. (*Rav Aḥa of Shabha, Halakhot Gedolot.*)

שְׁנֵי בַעֲלֵי דִינִין Two litigants. *Remah* explains that this does not necessarily refer to the litigants themselves, since the actual litigants could have been any of the people already mentioned. Rather, it refers to an additional two people who are always available to take over the litigants' duties or jobs should they be unable to perform them as a result of the litigation.

נִגְבֵּית בִּשְׁנַיִם וּמִתְחַלֶּקֶת בִּשְׁלֹשָׁה Which is collected by two and distributed by three. It is unnecessary for an official committee of three to collect the communal dues, as the

HALAKHAH

כָּל עִיר שֶׁאֵין בָּהּ עֲשָׂרָה דְּבָרִים הַלָּלוּ Any city that does not have the following ten things. "A Torah scholar is not permitted to live in a city that does not have a doctor, a bloodletter, a bathhouse, an outhouse, a water source, a synagogue, a teacher of young children, a scribe, charity collectors, and a court which administers punishments," in accordance with the Baraita. (*Rambam, Sefer Mada, Hilkhot De'ot* 4:23.)

TRANSLATION AND COMMENTARY

by three, [1]**a synagogue** for public prayer, **a bathhouse** for maintaining proper hygiene, **an outhouse** in close proximity, [2]**a doctor**, **a bloodletter**, **a scribe** to copy sacred texts and legal documents, **a** competent **slaughterer** to supply him with meat, **and a teacher of young children**. [3]**In the name of Rabbi Akiva they said:** [4]**So, too,** must the city have many **varieties of fruit,** [5]**for varieties of fruit illuminate the eyes."** From this Baraita, we derive the need for at least an additional six people: three to administer the charity fund, one to serve as a doctor and bloodletter, one to serve as a slaughterer, and one to serve as a scribe. (Judging and teaching are functions that can be filled by those counted earlier.) Hence the need for at least one-hundred-and-twenty male inhabitants in a city before it can be a suitable venue for a Lesser Sanhedrin.

רַבִּי נְחֶמְיָה אוֹמֵר [6]We learned in the Mishnah: **"Rabbi Neḥemyah** disagrees with the first Tanna and **says** that a city is not fit to have a Lesser Sanhedrin established there unless it has a population of at least two-hundred-and-thirty people." [7]A third opinion is cited in a Baraita in which **it was taught: "Rabbi** Yehudah HaNasi **says:** [18A] [8]To serve as a venue for a Lesser Sanhedrin, a city must have at least **two-hundred-and-seventy-seven** inhabitants." Rabbi Yehudah HaNasi agrees with Rabbi Neḥemyah's opinion as cited in the Mishnah, that in order that each of the twenty-three members of the Lesser Sanhedrin assume the minimal degree of personal jurisdiction prescribed in the Bible — jurisdiction over ten inhabitants (see Exodus 18:25-6) — a city must have at least two-hundred-and-thirty such inhabitants. However, in accordance with the position referred to above regarding the need to increase the ranks of the Lesser Sanhedrin in the event of a stalemate, Rabbi Yehudah HaNasi asserts further that an additional reserve of forty-seven individuals must dwell in the city so that, if need be, the twenty-three-member court could be expanded up to but not beyond seventy members, the number of judges comprising the Great Sanhedrin.

וְהָתַנְיָא [9]**But surely it was taught** otherwise in the following Baraita: **"Rabbi** Yehudah HaNasi **says:** A city must have at least **two-hundred-and-seventy-eight** inhabitants in order to serve as a venue for a Lesser Sanhedrin"!

בִּשְׁלֹשָׁה, [1]וּבֵית הַכְּנֶסֶת, וּבֵית הַמֶּרְחָץ, וּבֵית הַכִּסֵּא, [2]רוֹפֵא, וְאוּמָּן, וְלַבְלָר, וְטַבָּח, וּמְלַמֵּד תִּינוֹקוֹת. [3]מִשּׁוּם רַבִּי עֲקִיבָא אָמְרוּ: [4]אַף מִינֵי פֵּירָא, [5]מִפְּנֵי שֶׁמִּינֵי פֵּירָא מְאִירִין אֶת הָעֵינַיִם".

[6]"רַבִּי נְחֶמְיָה אוֹמֵר וכו'".

[7]תַּנְיָא: "רַבִּי אוֹמֵר: [18A] [8]מָאתַיִם וְשִׁבְעִים וְשִׁבְעָה".

[9]וְהָתַנְיָא: "רַבִּי אוֹמֵר: מָאתַיִם שִׁבְעִים וּשְׁמֹנָה"!

LITERAL TRANSLATION

by three, [1]and a synagogue, and a bathhouse, and an outhouse, [2]a doctor, a bloodletter, a scribe, a slaughterer, and a teacher of young children. [3]In the name of Rabbi Akiva they said: [4]Also varieties of fruit, [5]for varieties of fruit illuminate the eyes."

[6]"Rabbi Neḥemyah says, etc."

[7]It was taught: "Rabbi says: [18A] [8]Two-hundred-and-seventy-seven."

[9]But surely it was taught: "Rabbi says: Two-hundred-and-seventy-eight!"

RASHI

רופא — למול תינוקות. **אומן** — מקיז דם. **לבלר** — לכתוב ספרים. **קופה נגבית בשנים ומתחלקת בשלשה** — טעמא מפרש ב"השותפין" (בבא בתרא ח,ב). **בית דין מכין וחובשין** — הא חשבינן להו לעיל דאיכא סנהדרי גובין ומחלקין הוי להו חמשה משיתא דבעי לעיל, רופא ואומן ולבלר ומלמד חד גברא הוי לכל הני. **מאתים ושבעים ושבעה** — מאתים ושלשים כר' נחמיה, ועוד ארבעים ושבעה שאם יתחלקו בית דין — אחד עשר מזכין, ואחד עשר מחייבין, ואחד אומר "איני יודע" — יוסיפו מאלו ארבעים ושבעה עד שבעים, כדאמרינן ב"היו בודקין" (מ,א) שמוסיפין שנים על העשרים ושלשה, אם יזכוהו שניהם הרי שלשה עשר מזכין ואחד עשר מחייבין — זכאי, ואם יחייבוהו — חייב, דאיכא הטייה לרעה על פי שנים, ואם יחלקו צריך עוד להוסיף שנים, וכן לעולם עד שיהיו שבעים לר' יהודה, ושבעים ואחד לרבנן.

LANGUAGE

לַבְלָר **Scribe.** This word is derived from *libellarius,* the Latin word for a scribe, a person whose profession it was to copy books and to write official documents.

NOTES

committee of three to collect the communal dues, as the amount that each person contributes to the charity fund is not determined by the collectors themselves but by the town's lay leaders. The reason the money is not collected by a single person is to avoid any suspicion of embezzlement. Three people are needed to distribute the money to the poor, for it cannot be distributed without first assessing who is in need and how needy he is, and such an assessment requires an official committee of three.

בֵּית הַכִּסֵּא **An outhouse.** There were apparently places where a single outhouse served the needs of an entire community. The Baraita teaches that in such a case the outhouse should not be built too far away from the residential areas. Even in towns where facilities are attached to people's houses, a public toilet should be placed near the town center (*Rabbi Ya'akov Emden*).

מָאתַיִם וְשִׁבְעִים וְשִׁבְעָה **Two-hundred-and-seventy-seven.** The Jerusalem Talmud explains that, according to Rabbi Yehudah HaNasi, the two-hundred-and-seventy-seven inhabitants necessary in order to establish a Lesser Sanhedrin in a town correspond to the aggregate number of judges sitting on the twelve tribal courts (12 times 23 = 276) with Moses at their head.

[1]לָא קַשְׁיָא. [2]הָא — רַבִּי יְהוּדָה; [3]הָא — רַבָּנַן.
[4]תָּנוּ רַבָּנַן: [5]״׳וְשַׂמְתָּ עֲלֵיהֶם שָׂרֵי אֲלָפִים שָׂרֵי מֵאוֹת שָׂרֵי חֲמִשִּׁים וְשָׂרֵי עֲשָׂרֹת׳. [6]שָׂרֵי אֲלָפִים — שֵׁשׁ מֵאוֹת; [7]שָׂרֵי מֵאוֹת — שֵׁשֶׁת אֲלָפִים; [8]שָׂרֵי חֲמִשִּׁים — שְׁנֵים עָשָׂר אֶלֶף; [9]שָׂרֵי עֲשָׂרוֹת — שֵׁשֶׁת רִיבּוֹא. [10]נִמְצְאוּ דַּיָּינֵי יִשְׂרָאֵל שִׁבְעַת רִיבּוֹא וּשְׁמוֹנַת אֲלָפִים וְשֵׁשׁ מֵאוֹת״.

הדרן עלך דיני ממונות

LITERAL TRANSLATION

[1]It is not difficult. [2]This — Rabbi Yehudah; [3]this — the Rabbis.

[4]Our Rabbis taught: [5]"'And place over them officers of thousands, officers of hundreds, officers of fifties, and officers of tens.' [6]Officers of thousands — six hundred; [7]officers of hundreds — six thousand; [8]officers of fifties — twelve thousand; [9]officers of tens — sixty thousand. [10]The judges of Israel were found to be seventy-eight-thousand-and-six-hundred [judges of Israel]."

TRANSLATION AND COMMENTARY

לָא קַשְׁיָא [1]**It is** really **not difficult.** [2]In the first Baraita, Rabbi Yehudah HaNasi taught in accordance with the view of **Rabbi Yehudah,** who maintains that the Great Sanhedrin had seventy members, or forty-seven more than a Lesser Sanhedrin. Hence, the need for two-hundred-and-seventy-seven inhabitants (230 plus 47). [3]In the second Baraita, however, Rabbi Yehudah HaNasi taught in accordance with the view of **the Rabbis,** who maintain that the Great Sanhedrin had seventy-one members, forty-eight more than a Lesser Sanhedrin. Hence, the prescription in that Baraita, that a city must have at least two-hundred-and-seventy-eight inhabitants (230 plus 48).

תָּנוּ רַבָּנַן [4]The chapter concludes with a Baraita in which **our Rabbis taught:** [5]"The verse states [Exodus 18:21]: **'And place over them officers of thousands, officers of hundreds, officers of fifties, and officers of tens.'** As Scripture tells us [Exodus 12:37], six hundred thousand Israelites, besides the women and children, left Egypt. [6]Thus the **officers of thousands** appointed by Moses numbered **six hundred;** [7]the **officers of hundreds** numbered **six thousand;** [8]the **officers of fifties** numbered **twelve thousand;** [9]and the **officers of tens** numbered **sixty thousand.** [10]Thus, in all, **there were found** to be **seventy-eight-thousand-and-six-hundred judges of Israel** serving in the desert."

RASHI

שרי אלפים שש מאות — היו, שהרי שש מאות אלף רגלי.

הדרן עלך דיני ממונות בשלשה

Conclusion to Chapter One

This chapter deals with many topics, for it mentions most of the matters which fall under the jurisdiction of the Jewish judicial system, but it does not discuss all of them comprehensively. Most of the topics mentioned here are treated more fully elsewhere in the tractate or in other tractates, and here the discussion is limited to place of each area of the law within the system as a whole.

The Gemara is primarily interested in locating the source for each of the Mishnah's statements regarding the composition of the court which is competent to judge each different matter. For the most part, the Gemara expands upon and clarifies what is already stated in the Mishnah.

This chapter summarizes the jurisdiction of each element of the judicial system. Courts composed of three judges are competent to adjudicate monetary matters, civil cases as well as criminal. A court of twenty-three judges is required for capital cases. The Great Sanhedrin deals with matters that affect the entire nation: War and peace, criminal cases involving national leaders, and fundamental rulings on matters of faith and law. Special courts with five, seven, or ten members are also mentioned. These courts do not have a regular judicial function, but are required for certain ritual matters.

This chapter also contains lengthy discussions of some of the basic issues raised in the Mishnah. The authority granted to a court of three is analyzed comprehensively, and the authority of a single judge who is recognized as an expert in the law (of whom no mention is made in the Mishnah) is also explained. This leads to a full discussion of *semikhah* — a Torah scholar's ordination which allows him to sit as a judge — its source, authority and limitations in time, place and scope.

The question of judicial authority is connected to another problem which has both a legal component and an ethical one — effecting a compromise between litigants. Compromise is often the easy solution, but is it also ethical? Does it not entail a deviation from the absolute truth? What is the binding force of a compromise? The

Gemara tends to favor compromise (a tendency which became even stronger in later generations) and give it legal force, but it does not require the parties to submit to a compromise if they are not willing to do so.

Two topics outside the central theme of the chapter are also discussed. The Gemara deals at length with an issue falling under the category of Talmudic hermeneutics — whether or not a word in Scripture can be interpreted in accordance with its consonantal spelling, or in accordance with its traditional Masoretic vocalization.

Another topic discussed is the intercalation of the year. Since there is no special tractate devoted to this fundamental issue, the matter is treated here in a most comprehensive manner. The Gemara discusses when a year is intercalated, what the Biblical sources are for intercalation, and under what circumstances a year is intercalated. It considers the relationship between the two Biblical sources for intercalation, the one requiring Pesah to be celebrated in the Spring, and the other requiring Sukkot to fall after the autumnal equinox. The Gemara also discusses the climactic and agricultural conditions which indicate that intercalation is necessary.

Today, intercalation of the year follows the fixed calendar established by Hillel II, which does not take into consideration all of the factors mentioned in our chapter. But the principles regarding intercalation remain as they were, and will once again be put into practice when the Great Sanhedrin is reestablished.

List of Sources

Aḥaronim, lit., "the last," meaning Rabbinic authorities from the time of the publication of Rabbi Yosef Caro's code of Halakhah, *Shulḥan Arukh* (1555).

Arba'ah Turim, code of Halakhah by Rabbi Ya'akov ben Asher, b. Germany, active in Spain (c. 1270-1343).

Arukh, Talmudic dictionary, by Rabbi Natan of Rome, 11th century.

Baḥ (Bayit Ḥadash), commentary on *Arba'ah Turim*, by Rabbi Yoel Sirkes, Poland (1561-1640).

Bet Yosef, Halakhic commentary on *Arba'ah Turim* by Rabbi Yosef Caro (1488-1575), which is the basis of his authoritative Halakhic code, *Shulḥan Arukh.*

Even HaEzer, section of *Shulḥan Arukh* dealing with marriage, divorce, and related topics.

Geonim, heads of the academies of Sura and Pumbedita in Babylonia from the late 6th century to the mid-11th century.

Halakhot Gedolot, a code of Halakhic decisions written in the Geonic period. This work has been ascribed to Sherira Gaon, Rav Hai Gaon, Rav Yehudah Gaon and Rabbi Shimon Kayyara.

Ḥamra Veḥaye, novellae on tractate *Sanhedrin,* by Rabbi Ḥayyim Benevisti, Turkey, 17th century.

Ḥokhmat Manoaḥ, commentary on the Talmud by Rabbi Manoaḥ ben Shemaryah, Poland, 16th century.

Ḥoshen Mishpat, section of *Shulḥan Arukh* dealing with civil and criminal law.

Imrei Tzvi, novellae of the Talmud by Rabbi Tzvi Kohen, Vilna, 19th century.

Iyyun Ya'akov, commentary on *Ein Ya'akov,* by Rabbi Ya'akov bar Yosef Riesher, Prague, Poland, and France (d. 1733).

Kesef Mishneh, commentary on *Mishneh Torah,* by Rabbi Yosef Caro, author of *Shulḥan Arukh.*

Leḥem Mishneh, commentary on the Mishneh Torah by Rabbi Avraham di Boton, Salonica (1560-1609).

Maharam Schiff, novellae on the Talmud by Rabbi Meir ben Ya'akov HaKohen Schiff (1605-1641), Frankfurt, Germany.

Maharik, Rabbi Yosef Kolon, France and Italy (c. 1420-1480). Responsa literature.

Maharsha, Rabbi Shmuel Eliezer ben Yehudah HaLevi Edels, Poland (1555-1631). Novellae on the Talmud.

Maharshal, Rabbi Shlomo ben Yeḥiel Luria, Poland (1510-1573). Novellae on the Talmud.

Margoliyot HaYam, novellae on tractate *Sanhedrin* by Rabbi Reuben Margoliyot, Poland, 20th century.

Meiri, commentary on the Talmud (called *Bet HaBeḥirah*), by Rabbi Menaḥem ben Shlomo, Provence (1249-1316).

Mekhilta, Halakhic Midrash on the Book of Exodus.

Mishnah Berurah, commentary on *Shulḥan Arukh, Oraḥ Ḥayyim,* by Rabbi Yisrael Meir HaKohen, Poland (1837-1933).

Oraḥ Ḥayyim, section of *Shulḥan Arukh* dealing with daily religious observances, prayers, and the laws of the Sabbath and Festivals.

Pitḥei Teshuvah, compilation of responsa literature on the *Shulḥan Arukh* by Rabbi Avraham Tzvi Eisenstadt, Russia (1812-1868).

Ra'avad, Rabbi Avraham ben David, commentator and Halakhic authority. Wrote comments on *Mishneh Torah.* Provence (c. 1125-1198?).

Rabbenu Ḥananel (ben Ḥushiel), commentator on the Talmud, North Africa (990-1055).

Rabbenu Meshulam, French Tosafist, 12th century.

Rabbenu Tam, commentator on the Talmud, Tosafist, France (1100-1171).

Rabbenu Yonah, see *Talmidei Rabbenu Yonah.*

Rabbi David Bonfil (Bonfied), commentary on tractate *Sanhedrin* by Rabbi David Bonfil (Bonfied), France, 11th century.

Rabbi David Pardo, novellae on the Talmud, Italy, 18th century.

Rabbi Issac Ḥaver, novellae on the Talmud by Rabbi Issac Ḥaver, Poland, 18th century.

Rabbi Ya'akov Emden, Talmudist and Halakhic authority, Germany (1697-1776).

Rabbi Yehudah Almandri, author of commentary on *Rif,* tractate *Sanhedrin,* Syria, 13th century.

Rabbi Yitzḥak Ibn Giyyat, Halakhist, Bible commentator and liturgical poet, Spain (1038-1089).

Rabbi Yosef of Jerusalem, French Tosafist of the twelfth and thirteenth centuries, France and Eretz Israel.

Rabbi Yoshiyah Pinto, Eretz Israel and Syria (1565-1648). Commentary on *Ein Ya'akov.*

Rabbi Zeraḥyah ben Yitzḥak HaLevi, Spain, 12th century. Author of *HaMa'or*, Halakhic commentary on *Hilkhot HaRif.*

Radbaz, Rabbi David ben Shlomo Avi Zimra, Spain, Egypt, Eretz Israel, and North Africa (1479-1574). Commentary on *Mishneh Torah.*

Raḥ, Rabbenu Ḥananel (ben Ḥushiel), commentator on the Talmud, North Africa (990-1055).

Rambam, Rabbi Moshe ben Maimon, Rabbi and philosopher, known also as Maimonides. Author of *Mishneh Torah,* Spain and Egypt (1135-1204).

Ramban, Rabbi Moshe ben Naḥman, commentator on Bible and Talmud, known also as Naḥmanides, Spain and Eretz Israel (1194-1270).

Ran, Rabbi Nissim ben Reuven Gerondi, Spanish Talmudist (1310?-1375?).

Rash, Rabbi Shimshon ben Avraham, Tosafist, commentator on the Mishnah, Sens (late 12th- early 13th century).

Rashash, Rabbi Shmuel ben Yosef Shtrashun, Lithuanian Talmud scholar (1794-1872).

Rashi, Rabbi Shlomo ben Yitzḥak, the paramount commentator on the Bible and the Talmud, France (1040-1105).

Rav Aha of Sabha, author of *She'iltot,* Babylonia, 8th century.

Rav Natronai Gaon, of the Sura Yeshivah, 9th century.

Rav Sherira Gaon, of the Pumbedita Yeshivah, 10th century.

Rema, Rabbi Moshe ben Yisrael Isserles, Halakhic authority, Poland (1525-1572).

Remah, novellae on the Talmud by Rabbi Meir ben Todros HaLevi Abulafiya, Spain (c. 1170-1244). See *Yad Ramah.*

Ri Almandri, Rabbi Yehudah Almandri. Author of commentary on *Rif,* tractate *Sanhedrin,* Syria, 13th century.

Ri Migash, Rabbi Yosef Ibn Migash, commentator on the Talmud, Spain (1077-1141).

Rif, Rabbi Yitzḥak Alfasi, Halakhist, author of *Hilkhot HaRif,* North Africa (1013-1103).

Rishonim, lit., "the first," meaning Rabbinic authorities active between the end of the Geonic period (mid-11th century) and the publication of *Shulḥan Arukh* (1555).

Ritva, novellae and commentary on the Talmud by Rabbi Yom Tov ben Avraham Ishbili, Spain (c. 1250-1330).

Riva, Rabbenu Yitzḥak ben Asher, Tosafist, novellae on tractate *Sanhedrin.*

Rosh, Rabbi Asher ben Yeḥiel, also known as Asheri, commentator and Halakhist, German and Spain (c. 1250-1327).

Sanhedrei Ketanah, novellae on tractate *Sanhedrin* by Rabbi Avraham Yehoshua Bornstein, Russia, 19th century.

Shakh (Siftei Kohen), commentary on the *Shulḥan Arukh* by Rabbi Shabbetai ben Meir HaKohen, Lithuania (1621-1662).

Shelah (Shenei Luḥot HaBrit), an extensive work on Halakhah, ethics and Kabbalah by Rabbi Yeshyahu ben Avraham HaLevi Horowitz. Prague, Poland and Eretz Israel (c. 1565-1630).

Shulḥan Arukh, code of Halakhah by Rabbi Yosef Caro, b. Spain, active in Eretz Israel (1488-1575).

Sifrei, Halakhic Midrash on the Books of Numbers and Deuteronomy.

Talmidei Rabbenu Yonah, commentary on *Hilkhot HaRif* by the school of Rabbi Yonah of Gerondi, Spain (1190-1263).

Tosafot, collection of commentaries and novellae on the Talmud, expanding on Rashi's commentary, by the French-German Tosafists (12th and 13th centuries).

Tosefot Rabbenu Peretz, Tosefot of the school of Rabbi Peretz ben Eliyahu of Corbeil (d. 1295).

Tosefot Rosh, an edition based on *Tosefot Sens* by the *Rosh*, Rabbi Asher ben Yeḥiel, Germany and Spain (c. 1250-1327).

Tosefot Yom Tov, commentary on the Mishnah by Rabbi Yom Tov Lipman HaLevi Heller, Prague and Poland (1579-1654).

Tur, abbreviation of *Arba'ah Turim,* Halakhic code by Rabbi Ya'akov ben Asher, b. Germany, active in Spain (c. 1270-1343).

Tzafnat Pa'ane'ah, novellae and commentaries by Rabbi Yosef Rozin, Lithuania (1858-1936).

Yafeh Mar'eh, commentary on the Midrash by Rabbi Shmuel Yaffe, Turkey, 16th century.

Yoreh De'ah, section of *Shulḥan Arukh* dealing mainly with dietary laws, interest, ritual purity, and mourning.

About the Type

This book was set in Leawood, a contemporary typeface designed by Leslie Usherwood. His staff completed the design upon Usherwood's death in 1984. It is a friendly, inviting face that goes particularly well with sans serif type.